Spatial Plan and Climate

C000255696

Spatial planning has a vital role to play in the move to a low carbon energy future and in adapting to climate change. To do this, spatial planning must develop and implement new approaches.

Wilson and Piper explore a wide range of issues in this comprehensive book on the relationship between our changing climate and spatial planning, and suggest ways of addressing the challenges by taking a longer-sighted approach to our preparation for the future.

This text includes:

- an overview of what we know already about future climate change and its impacts, as we attempt to both adapt to these changes and to reduce the emissions which cause them
- the role of spatial planning in relation to climate change, offering some theoretical and political explanations for the challenges that planning faces in the coming decades
- a review of policy and legislation and at international, EU and UK levels in regard to climate change, and the support this gives to the planning system
- case studies detailing what responses the UK and the Netherlands have made so far in light of the evidence
- ways to help new and existing urban developments to reduce energy use and to adapt to climate change, through strengthening the relationships between urban and rural areas to avoid water shortage, floods or loss of biodiversity.

The authors take an evidence-based look at this hugely important topic, providing a well-illustrated text for spatial planning professionals, politicians and the interested public, as well as a useful reference for postgraduate planning, geography, urban studies, urban design and environmental studies students.

Elizabeth Wilson is Reader in Enviornmental Planning in the School of the Built Environment at Oxford Brookes University.

Jake Piper is a Senior Research Fellow in the School of the Built Environment at Oxford Brookes University.

The Natural and Built Environment Series
Editor: Professor John Glasson, Oxford Brookes University

Water and the City
Iain White

Urban Planning and Real Estate Development
John Ratcliffe and Michael Stubbs

Transport Policy and Planning in Great Britain
Peter Headicar

Introduction to Rural Planning
Nick Gallent, Meri Juntti, Sue Kidd and Dave Shaw

Regional Planning
John Glasson and Tim Marshall

Strategic Planning for Regional Development
Harry T. Dimitriou and Robin Thompson

Introduction to Environmental Impact Assessment
John Glasson, Riki Therivel and Andrew Chadwick

Methods of Environmental Impact Assessment
Peter Morris and Riki Therivel

Public Transport
Peter White

Landscape Planning and Environmental Impact Design
Tom Turner

Controlling Development
Philip Booth

Partnership Agencies in British Urban Policy
Nicholas Bailey, Alison Barker and Kelvin MacDonald

Development Control
Keith Thomas

Expert Systems and Geographic Information Systems for Impact Assessment
Agustin Rodriguez-Bachiller and John Glasson

Spatial Planning and Climate Change

Elizabeth Wilson and Jake Piper

Routledge

Taylor & Francis Group

LONDON AND NEW YORK

First published 2010
by Routledge
2 Park Square, Milton Park, Abingdon, Oxon, OX14 4RN

Simultaneously published in the USA and Canada
by Routledge
270 Madison Avenue, New York, NY 10016

Routledge is an imprint of the Taylor & Francis Group, an informa business

© 2010 Elizabeth Wilson and Jake Piper

Typeset in Stone Serif and Akzidenz Grotesk by
Pindar NZ, Auckland, New Zealand
Printed and bound in Great Britain by
CPI Antony Rowe, Chippenham, Wiltshire

British Library Cataloguing in Publication Data
A catalogue record for this book is available from the British Library

Library of Congress Cataloging-in-Publication Data
Wilson, Elizabeth.
Spatial planning and climate change / Elizabeth Wilson and Jake Piper.
    p. cm. – (The natural and built environment)
  Includes bibliographical references and index.
  1. Regional planning. 2. Spatial behavior. 3. Climatic changes.
I. Piper, Jake. II. Title.
  HT391.W54 2011
  307.1'2—dc22   2010004282

ISBN13: 978-0-415-49590-5 (hbk)
ISBN13: 978-0-415-49591-2 (pbk)
ISBN13: 978-0-203-84653-7 (ebk)

For our families

Contents

Illustrations

· ·

Figures

Tables

Boxes

Abbreviations

· ·

ABI	Association of British Insurers
ACCELERATES	Assessing climate change effects on land use and ecosystems: from regional analysis to the European scale (UK research programme)
ADAM	Adaptation and mitigation strategies: supporting European climate policy (EU Research programme)
ALARM	Assessing large scale risks for biodiversity with tested methods (EU research programme)
AR4	Fourth Assessment Report (IPCC)
ARCADIA	Adaptation and Resilience in Cities: Analysis and Decision making using Integrated Assessment (UK research project)
ARCC	Adaptation and Resilience in a Changing Climate (UK research programme)
ASCCUE	Adaptation Strategies for Climate Change in the Urban Environment (UK research project)
ATEAM	Advanced Terrestrial Ecosystem Analysis and Modelling (EU research programme)
AWP	Aviation White Paper
BAP	Biodiversity Action Plan
BERR	Department for Business, Enterprise and Regulatory Reform (superseded)
BESEECH	Building Economic and Social information for Examining the Effects of Climate cHange
BETWIXT	Built Environment: Weather Scenarios for Investigation of Impacts and Extremes (UK research project)
BIS	Department for Business, Innovation and Skills
BKCC	Building Knowledge for a Changing Climate (UK research programme)
BRANCH	Biodiversity Requires Adaptation in NW Europe under a changing climate (EU research programme)
BRE	Building Research Establishment
BREEAM	BRE Environmental Assessment Method

BWEA	British Wind Energy Association
CABE	Commission for Architecture and the Built Environment
CAMS	Catchment Abstraction Management Strategy
CBD	Convention on Biological Diversity
CC	Climate change
CCC	Committee on Climate Change
CcSP	Climate *changes* Spatial Planning (Netherlands Research programme)
CDM	Clean Development Mechanism
CEAA	Canadian Environmental Assessment Agency
CEC	Commission of the European Communities
CFC	Chlorofluorocarbon
CfIT	Commission for Integrated Transport
CFMP	Catchment Flood Management Plan
CHP	Combined Heat and Power
CIBSE	Chartered Institution of Building Services Engineers
CIRIA	Construction Industry Research and Information Association
CO_2	Carbon dioxide
COP	Conference of Parties
CRRESCENDO	Combined rational and renewable energy strategies in cities, for existing and new dwellings and optimal quality of life
CSH	Code for Sustainable Homes (EU research programme)
CZM	Coastal Zone Management
DC	District Council
DCLG	Department for Communities and Local Government
DCMS	Department for Culture Media and Sport
DECC	Department of Energy and Climate Change
DECORUM	Domestic Energy, Carbon Counting and Carbon Reduction Model
Defra	Department for Environment, Food and Rural Affairs
DETR	Department of the Environment, Transport and the Regions (superseded)
DfT	Department for Transport
DG Env	Directorate-General Environment (EC)
DG-Regio	Directorate-General for the Regions (EC)
DG TREN	Directorate-General Energy and Transport (until February 2010) (EC)
DTI	Department of Trade and Industry (superseded)
EA	Environment Agency (England and Wales)
EC	European Commission
ECCP	European Climate Change Programme
EEA	European Environment Agency
EEC	European Economic Community (now referred to as EU)
EH	English Heritage
EIA	Environmental impact assessment

EIT	Economies in Transition
EPL	Energy Performance of Location
ERA	Environmental risk assessment
ESC	Environmentally sustainable construction
ESCo	Energy Service Company
ESDP	European Spatial Development Perspective
ESPACE	European Spatial Planning: Adapting to Climate Events
ESPON	European Observation Network, Territorial Development and Cohesion
ETS (UK)	Emissions Trading Scheme
ETS (EU)	Emissions Trading System
EU	European Union
EZ	Ministry of Economic Affairs (Ministerie van Economische Zaken) (Netherlands)
FAR	First Assessment Report
FoE	Friends of the Earth
GCM	Global Climate Model
GDP	Gross Domestic product
GHG	Greenhouse gas
GI	Green infrastructure
GIS	Geographical Information System
GLA	Greater London Authority
GNP	Gross National Product
GONW	Government Office for the North West
GOSE	Government Office for the South East
GOYH	Government Office for Yorkshire and the Humber
GRaBS	Green and blue space adaptation for urban areas and eco-towns (EU research programme)
GVA	Gross value added
GW	Gigawatt
HCA	Homes and Communities Academy
HESS	Heat and Energy Saving Strategy
HGV	Heavy goods vehicle
HMG/HM Govt	Her Majesty's Government
ICLEI	Local Governments for Sustainability (formerly International Council for Local Environmental Initiatives)
ICZM	Integrated Coastal Zone Management
IEMA	Institute of Environmental Management and Assessment
IME	Institution of Mechanical Engineers
INTERREG	Innovation and Environment – Regions of Europe Sharing Solutions (Series of EU-funded programmes to enable Europe's regions to form partnerships and work together on common projects)
IPC	Infrastructure Planning Commission
IPCC	Intergovernmental Panel on Climate Change

IPO	Association of Provinces (Interprovinciaal Overleg) (Netherlands)
IT	Information technology
IWRS	Integrated Water Resources Study
JI	Joint implementation
JNCC	Joint Nature Conservation Committee
LCCP	London Climate Change Partnership
LCLIP	Local Climate Impacts Profile
LCWO	Low Carbon West Oxford
LDF	Local Development Framework
LGA	Local Government Association
LGV	Light goods vehicle
LNV	Ministry of Agriculture, Nature and Food Quality (Ministerie van Landbouw, Natuurbeheer en Voedselkwaliteit) (Netherlands)
LPA	Local Planning Authority
LSP	Local Strategic Partnership
LTP	Local Transport Plan
LULUCF	Land use, land-use change and forestry
M/m	Million
M&A	Mitigation and Adaptation
MACIS	Minimization of and adaptation to climate impacts on biodiversity (EU research programme)
MATISSE	Methods and tools for integrated sustainability assessment (EU research programme)
MBI	Market-based Instrument
MCA	Multi-criteria Analysis
MCCIP	Marine Climate Change Impacts Partnership
MEA	Millennium Ecosystem Assessment
MMO	Marine Management Organization
MONARCH	Modelling natural resources response to climate change (UK research programme)
MS, MSs	Member State/s
$MtCO_2$	million tonnes of CO_2
MuSCo	Municipal Service Company
MV&W/MVenW	Ministry of Transport, Public Works and Water Management (Ministerie van Verkeer en Waterstaat) (Netherlands)
MW	Megawatt
NAPA	National Adaptation Programme of Action
NCEA	Netherlands Commission for Environmental Assessment
NE	Natural England
NEN	National Ecological Network (Netherlands)
NENW	Natural Economy Office for the North West
NEPP	National Environmental Policy Plan (Netherlands)
NESTA	National Endowment for Science Technology and the Arts

NGO	Non-governmental organization
NI	National Indicator
NPS	National Policy Statement
NRM	Natural Resources Management
OC–W/OCenW	Ministry of Education, Culture and Science (Ministerie van Onderwijs, Cultuur en Wetenschap) (Netherlands)
ODPM	Office of the Deputy Prime Minister
OECD	Organization for Economic Co-operation and Development
OECD/DAC	OECD Development Assistance Committee
OSPAR	Cooperation mechanism under which European governments and the EC protect the marine environment of the North East Atlantic
PA	Planning authority
PES	Payments for Ecosystem Services
PoM	Programme of Measures (under RBMPs)
POST	Parliamentary Office of Science and Technology
PPA	Planning Performance Agreement
PPG	Planning Policy Guidance Note
ppm	Parts per million
PPP	Policies, plans and programmes
PPS	Planning Policy Statement
PV	Photovoltaic
PUSH	Partnership for Urban South Hampshire
R&D	Research and Development
RBD	River Basin District
RBMP	River Basin Management Plan
RCEP	Royal Commission on Environmental Pollution
RDA	Regional Development Agency
REAP	Rotterdam Energy Approach and Planning
REDD	Reducing emissions from deforestation and forest degradation
RFC	Reasons for concern
RFRA	Regional Flood Risk Assessment
RIGS	Regionally Important Geological and Geomorphological Sites
RMU	Removal unit (under Kyoto Protocol)
RS	Regional Strategy
RSL	Registered Social Landlord
RSPB	Royal Society for the Protection of Birds
RSS	Regional Spatial Strategy
RTCCP	Round Table on Climate Change and Poverty
RTPI	Royal Town Planning Institute
SA	Sustainability Appraisal
SAC	Special Area of Conservation (designated under EC Habitats Directive)

SAP	Standard Assessment Procedure
SAR	Second Assessment Report (IPCC)
SCORCHIO	Sustainable cities: options for responding to climate change impacts and outcomes (UK research programme)
SDC	Sustainable Development Commission
SEA	Strategic Environmental Assessment
SECCP	South East Climate Change Partnership
SECTORS	South East climate threats and opportunities (Research project for South East Climate Change Partnership)
SEDD	Scottish Executive Development Department
SEEPB	South East England Partnership Board
SEERA	South East England Regional Assembly
SEMBE	Sustainable Energy Management and the Built Environment (UK research programme)
SEPA	Scottish Environment Protection Agency
SES	Socio-economic Scenarios
SFRA	Strategic Flood Risk Assessment
SKCC	Sustaining knowledge for a changing climate (UK research programme)
SLR	Sea-level Rise
SMP	Shoreline Management Plan
SNACC	Suburban Neighbourhood Adaptation for a Changing Climate (UK research project)
SNCI	Site of Nature Conservation Interest
SNIFFER	Scotland and Northern Ireland Forum for Environmental Research
SPA	Special Protection Area (under EC Birds Directive)
SPKD	Spatial Planning Key Decision (Netherlands)
SRES	Special Report on Emissions Scenarios (IPCC report)
SSSI	Site of Special Scientific Interest
SuDS/SUDS	Sustainable (urban) drainage system/s
SWRDA	South West Regional Development Agency
TAR	Third Assessment Report (IPCC)
tCO_2	Tonnes of CO_2
TCPA	Town and Country Planning Association
TE2100	Thames Estuary 2100
TEEB	The Economics of Ecosystems and Biodiversity (EU research project)
TEN-T	Trans-European Network – Transport
UHI	Urban heat island
UKBAP	UK Biodiversity Action Plan
UKBP	UK Biodiversity Partnership
UKCIP	UK Climate Impacts Programme
UKCP09	UK Climate Projections 2009
UK-GBC	UK Green Building Council

UNCED	UN Conference on Environment and Development
UNDP	UN Development Programme
UNEP	UN Environment Programme
UNFCCC	UN Framework Convention on Climate Change
UvW	Union of Netherlands Water Authorities (Unie van Waterschappen)
VIBAT	Visioning and Backcasting for Transport Policy (UK research programme)
VINEX	Part 4 of 1993 Netherlands Spatial Planning Key Decision (Vierde Nota over de Ruimtelijke Ordening Extra) VROM policy document
VMT	vehicle miles travelled
VNG	Association of Netherlands Municipalities (Vereniging van Nederlandse Gemeenten)
VROM	Ministry of Housing, Spatial Planning and the Environment (Ministerie van Volkshuisvesting, Ruimtelijke Ordening en Milieu) (Netherlands)
WA/WAG	Welsh Assembly/Government
WCED	World Conference on Environment and Development
WCS	Water Cycle Study
WFD	Water Framework Directive
WG	Working Group
WLMP	Water Level Management Plan
WMO	World Meteorological Organization
WRI	World Resources Institute
WRMP	Water Resources Management Plan
WWF	World Wide Fund for Nature

Preface

Climate change as a phenomenon and as an idea represents an extraordinary challenge to us all as societies and individuals. This book explores the important role of spatial and environmental planning in addressing both the causes of climate change and the impacts of unavoidable climate change. This new role involves a reframing of spatial planning interventions, with a renewed but different interpretation of sustainable development, giving greater regard to longer time horizons, more attention to the relationship between new and existing built form, and increased emphasis on environmental planning.

Yet there is evidence that – whether it be promoting wind-farms, avoiding areas at risk of flooding, designing energy-conserving settlements and transport, or taking account of climate change in assessment processes – this reframing of spatial planning is contentious and difficult. This book explores some of the reasons for this. It examines the different discourses of the climate change and spatial planning policy communities, the implications of the changing scale of planning concerns, and the challenge to conventional planning processes and skills.

The speed of change in this new field of enquiry and action around climate change and spatial planning means that any book published on the subject is at risk of being overtaken by events. While we have been able to reflect on the outcomes of COP15 at Copenhagen in December 2009, the UK government's revised policy on planning for climate change is still awaited, and there will be many further developments in the science of climate change and the scope and direction of policy responses over the next few years. However, we wanted in this book to bring out the significant progress made in areas on which we have been working for the last ten years.

We draw on a range of sources, in particular from our involvement in research projects such as the Planning Response to Climate Change (with CAG Consultants), the SECTORS project (with Atkins), the Adaptation in the Growth Areas project (with Land Use Consultants), the ASCCUE project (with the Universities of Manchester, Cardiff and Southampton), the BRANCH project with the University of Oxford, and the MACIS project (with the Helmholtz Institute and other European Universities). We have also drawn on the wider research literature and on reports and evidence from governments, planning practitioners, consultancies and professional institutes seeking to address the challenges in innovative ways.

We hope that this range of sources will provide the planning students, post-graduates and practitioners at whom the book is aimed a vantage point from which to see the breadth of the field and routes into some of the detail of work that has been already carried out. The onrush of legislation and policy alone makes it difficult for academics and for practitioners to keep up. But we have also wanted to draw attention to some of the activity taking place outside the statutory policymaking processes: national campaigns such as the 'Big Ask' (which led to the Climate Change Act) and the 'Great British Refurb', and many local actions and initiatives such as low carbon community groups. Spatial planning needs to respond to all these.

The book ranges from the international (UN and European policymaking) to the very local (community and individual activism and actions to address climate change). But, in order to provide a coherent account of the field, we have focused on two countries: the UK (specifically, England) and the Netherlands. There are evident drawbacks in this approach – practice in Scotland and Wales is in some ways ahead of that in England (for instance, in having national planning frameworks, and, in the case of Scotland, already having a National Climate Change Adaptation Framework). However, we believe that focusing on England and the Netherlands enables us to contrast and compare their experiences (for instance, in national attitudes to the project of spatial planning) and to point to ways in which they are sharing certain responses (such as in new modes of water management).

2010 is the UN Year of Biodiversity, and we have given particular space in this book to the relationship between the built environment and the natural environment, especially the complex and dynamic web of ecosystems and the vital part played by water. Biodiversity (species, genes and habitats) is increasingly described as 'our own species' life assurance policy' – a phrase coined by Klaus Toepfer at UNEP in 2000 – and increasingly recognized for the valuable services and functions natural systems provide. Water is crucial in these systems, and we look at the ways in which planning in the Netherlands and in the UK is changing in its approach to water (albeit in two countries where cultural and institutional attitudes to water have formerly been very different).

Climate change is in many areas bringing about a remarkable policy innovation which has already produced outcomes: the legally binding carbon budgets under the Climate Change Act 2008, for instance, will be cascaded down to regional and local tiers, and the Marine and Coastal Access Act 2009 has already led to the designation of the first Marine Conservation Zone around Lundy Island. Whilst there has not been sufficient time for considered reflection on all the new developments (such as how far the new Flood and Water Management Act in England and Wales will resolve some of the perceived and actual problems over implementing sustainable urban drainage systems, and in what ways the new Infrastructure Planning Commission will interpret the concept of the national interest), we think it is important to show how much is coming forward.

There are other topics that we would have wished to address – such as food security, local sourcing, living off the land, eco-footprinting, waste management and landscape planning. However, we consider that the scope of this book is already at risk of becoming too wide.

This book is not a how-to manual – there is plenty of guidance around on the themes of planning and urban design for climate change (and indeed, there is some evidence as we show in Chapter 13 that there is advice-fatigue). Rather, we have tried to show the importance of appreciating the wider context within which the spatial planning project is understood and negotiated; and the different discourses adopted by different groups (sometimes in surprising coalitions or networks) to achieve their aims and objectives. What we have tried to convey also is the need for interdisciplinary understanding and awareness. To some extent, this reflects our own interests and professional development: one of us as a former planning practitioner from a background in politics and philosophy, and one of us a natural resources manager with practical experience in environmental assessment.

The argument of the book is set out in four parts. Part I provides the context for the planning response to climate change: it gives a brief account of the science of climate change and of spatial planning in the context of sustainable development, and shows how planning can help to integrate climate change mitigation and adaptation. The principal policy and legislative framework for this planning response at international, European and national levels is outlined.

Part II explores some of the wider issues governing the relationship of planning and climate change: the discourses used by the different policy communities and networks, and the way in which those planning communities appeal to the issue of climate change at and across different scales. We review the arguments for futures-thinking in planning for climate change, and the importance of equity within and between generations. Anticipatory assessment of both climate change and risk is discussed as an essential tool in decision-making. Throughout Part II real-world examples are used to illustrate and highlight the dilemmas in planning, for example in energy generation and aviation.

Part III then addresses five substantive issues: first, at the regional level, we examine planning for the location of development which both mitigates and adapts to climate change. We then discuss the wide array of initiatives at urban level to mitigate and respond to climate change in the built environment. Features of the new regimes in planning for water and in flood risk, coastal and marine planning are explored to see how far measures have already been introduced that address climate change and might be appropriately applied in other sectors. Finally, we explore the increasing recognition of a role for biodiversity as an integrative force in human and natural systems, through an ecosystems approach to planning and the evaluation of ecosystem services.

In Part IV we step outside the spatial planning framework to look at wider issues of attitudes, behaviour and social learning, before concluding with some reflections on future prospects for the spatial planning response to climate change.

Acknowledgements

· ·

Our especial thanks for their stimulus, support and repartee go to our colleagues attached to the Impact Assessment Unit at Oxford Brookes University: Riki Therivel, John Glasson, Joe Weston, Graham Wood, Bridget Durning, Tim Marshall and Stewart Thompson. We would like to acknowledge our debt for understanding and enlightenment to Pam Berry at the University of Oxford and to John Handley and colleagues at the University of Manchester. We would also like to thank our students for their insights and challenges.

We also wish to acknowledge the contribution of the following people and institutions in the preparation of this book: Joel Smith of the IPCC for kind permission to use the 'burning embers' illustration (Figure 1.2); Chris West of UKCIP for kind permission to use the UKCIP risk, uncertainty and decision-making framework (Figure 2.5) and the socio-economic scenarios matrix (Figure 6.2); Sanne Vammen Larsen of Aalborg University for kind permission to use the diagram of SEA and climate change (Figure 7.1); Sustainability East for kind permission to use the map of East of England climate subregions (Figure 8.9); Esther Rijken of the Dutch Delta Commission for kind permission to use the map of the Dutch Delta programme (Figure 9.8); Nico Tillie of Rotterdam City Council for kind permission to use the map of Rotterdam Watercity (Figure 9.9); Roger Nowell at Sheffield City Council and Robert Bray Associates for kind permission to use the map of the Manor Park SUDS (Figure 11.2); RCEP for permission to use their figure showing the extent of marine planning controls (Figure 11.3); to RIBA-Building Futures and the ICE for permission to use the sketches of urban coastal options (Figure 11.5); Sebastian Kopf of Massachusetts Institute of Technology for kind permission to use the climate analogues map of European capitals (Figure 13.1); John Isaacs at the Urban Water Technology Centre at the University of Abertay for provision of the coastal visualization example (Figure 13.2).

And finally we are tremendously grateful for all the assistance from Nick, Ben and our families and friends during the preparation of this book, a period which will have been as demanding for them as for us. Their patience and support have made it possible.

All errors are our own – and of course all our opinions are open to challenge.

Part I

Introduction

·····································

1 Introduction

Spatial planning, climate change and sustainable development

1.1 Introduction

Spatial planning has an important role to play in responding to the urgent need to address both the causes of climate change and the impacts of unavoidable climate change. To do so requires a reframing of spatial planning interventions, with a renewed and revised interpretation of sustainable development, which has more regard to longer time horizons, pays more attention to the relationship between new and existing built form, and has a closer focus on integrating the built environment with natural processes such as the carbon and water cycles, and ecosystems.

Yet there is evidence that – whether it be promoting wind farms, controlling development of areas at risk of flooding, designing energy-conserving settlements and transport, or taking account of climate change in assessment processes – this reframing of spatial planning is contentious and difficult. This book explores some of the reasons for this. It examines the different discourses of the climate change and spatial planning policy communities, the implications of the changing scale of planning concerns, and the challenge to conventional planning processes and skills. These concepts are more fully explored in Parts II and III.

In this chapter we set out our conception of spatial planning, and indicate how its scope is extending in response to the issue of climate change. But first we draw on the work of the global climate science community to outline briefly the causes and impacts of climate change, and hence the need for urgent action to address it.

1.2 Urgency of response to climate change

1.2.1 Observed changes

Evidence of climate change has been observed across the globe. These changes are seen in physical systems such as the transport of heat across the globe in oceanic circulation, in storm systems, and in polar ice seasonal accumulation and thinning. They are also seen in biological processes: such changes as earlier onset of spring events, including bud-break, bird migration and egg-laying, as well as shifts in the ranges of plants and animals both towards the poles and to higher altitudes. Both physical and biological systems have fundamental importance for the stability of life on this planet, and, through the UN Framework Convention on Climate Change, international institutions and national governments are working towards introducing measures and policies aimed at limiting the changes. Vital components of the global environment that underpin the natural systems have already been changed significantly (in particular, the composition of the atmosphere and the temperature of the oceans), so some ongoing changes are now unavoidable and must be managed – insofar as is possible.

Figure 1.1 reproduces the well-known 'hockey stick' graph published in the Third Assessment Report of the Intergovernmental Panel on Climate Change (IPCC), which shows the extent to which the observed average annual surface temperature of the northern hemisphere has tended to vary over the past millennium (based on many data sources, as shown) in comparison with a baseline period between 1961 and 1990 (IPCC, 2001, figure 2.3). The figure points to a warming trend quite out of proportion with previous variation over ten centuries. These changes and their implications are discussed in Chapter 2.

Across the globe different impacts will predominate. Within Europe, the regions considered to be most at risk are the mountain areas and Scandinavia, the Mediterranean region and coastal areas and densely populated flood plains

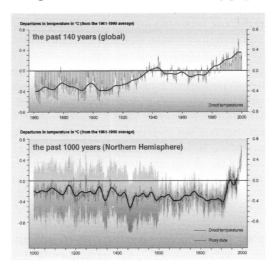

Figure 1.1

Variations in the Earth's surface temperature for the past 1,000 years
Source: IPCC, 2001

Box 1.1 Observed climate change in the UK

Average UK temperature has risen since the mid-twentieth century, as have average sea level and sea surface temperature around the UK coast. Over the same time period, trends in precipitation and storminess are harder to identify.

- Central England temperature has risen by about a degree Celsius since the 1970s, with 2006 being the warmest on record.* Temperatures in Scotland and Northern Ireland have risen by about 0.8°C since about 1980, but this rise has not been attributed to specific causes.
- Annual mean precipitation over England and Wales has not changed significantly since records began in 1766. Seasonal rainfall is highly variable, but appears to have decreased in summer and increased in winter, although with little change in the latter over the last fifty years.
- All regions of the UK have experienced an increase over the past forty-five years in the contribution to winter rainfall from heavy precipitation events; in summer all regions except NE England and N Scotland show decreases.
- Severe windstorms around the UK have become more frequent in the past few decades, though not above the level seen in the 1920s.
- Sea surface temperatures around the UK coast have risen over the past three decades by about 0.7 °C. Sea level around the UK rose by about 1 mm/yr in the twentieth century, corrected for land movement. The rate for the 1990s and 2000s has been higher than this.

Source: UK Climate Projections UKCP09 *Key findings* (adapted from Defra, 2009a)

* 'Most of the observed increase in global average temperatures since the mid-20th century is *very likely* due to the observed increase in anthropogenic GHG concentrations.' (IPCC, 2007a, p. 39)

(CEC, 2009a). In north-west Europe predicted trends include warmer, wetter winters and warmer, drier summers, with increased risk from river and coastal flooding. There is accumulating evidence of these changes already occurring (see Box 1.1 for UK observations of climate change).

1.2.2 Essentials of the science of climate change

Awareness of the consequences of changing the composition of the Earth's atmosphere has been growing in line with the measured increase in the proportion of greenhouse gases. This was demonstrated by observations by Keeling (1960, 1998), for the period from 1957, and subsequently shown to have been increasing since the beginning of the industrial period (IPCC, 2007b). Our understanding of the greenhouse effect, under which the atmosphere warms when heat is cumulatively gained and stored at an increasing rate, has its roots in the work of physical scientists including Fourier, Saussure and Tyndall. By

1996, the rise in CO_2 had been shown to be 'uniquely' linked to the burning of fossil fuels, as reported in the historical overview of climate change science for the IPCC Fourth Assessment Report (IPCC, 2007a, p. 100). In addition, whilst early work associated the greenhouse effect principally with carbon dioxide (CO_2) and water, evidence had accumulated by the 1970s that other gases – some newly synthesized by industry – were also implicated in atmospheric warming, notably methane, nitrous oxide and chlorofluorocarbons (CH_4, N_2O and CFCs). The role of certain other atmospheric constituents – such as sulphate aerosols – in reflecting sunlight and so, to a degree, offsetting global warming, was also identified (Reader and Boer, 1998), further developing scientific understanding of the complex reactions affecting atmospheric temperatures and contributing to climate change. Other work has attempted to identify similarities between the variations and instabilities accompanying abrupt climatic changes in the past and the current changes. So far, these comparisons have not shown up any similar episodes in the past (IPCC, 2007b, ch. 1).

Further detail on the climate system and 'climate forcing' can be found in Working Group I's report for the IPCC's Fourth Assessment Report (IPCC, 2007a). This report identifies the key physical and biogeochemical processes in the Earth system connected with changing climate as being atmospheric composition, chemistry, the carbon cycle and feedbacks between the carbon cycle, ecosystems and atmospheric greenhouse gases (these feedbacks will affect CO_2 abundance in a warmer world, see Box 1.2). The feedback processes identified include, amongst others, interaction between ice pack melt and sunlight reflection, surface warming and the release of methane from permafrost.

Box 1.2 Change in atmospheric carbon dioxide (CO_2)

Atmospheric CO_2 presently contributes 63% of the gaseous radiative forcing responsible for anthropogenic climate change (radiative forcing is a measure of how the energy balance of the Earth–atmosphere system is influenced when factors that affect climate are altered). The mean global atmospheric CO_2 concentration has increased from 280 ppm in the 1700s to 380 ppm in 2005, at a progressively faster rate each decade. This growth is governed by the global budget of atmospheric CO_2, which includes two major forcing fluxes induced by human activities:

(i) CO_2 emissions from fossil-fuel combustion and industrial processes and
(ii) the CO_2 flux from land-use change, mainly land clearing.

Source: Raupach *et al.*, 2007, p. 10288

1.2.3 Rate of change

Long-term assessments of the atmosphere in the past – based for example on evidence from ice-cores and marine sediments – show a gradual increase in greenhouse gases until the mid-twentieth century. Raupach *et al.* (2007) have pointed to the increasing rate of CO_2 emissions from fossil fuel burning and industrial processes; they note that since 2000 the emissions growth rate has been greater than for the highest forecast scenario of greenhouse gas emissions as published in the *Special Report on Emissions Scenarios* (IPCC, 2000). Earlier declining trends in energy intensity of national GDP (energy/GDP) have been reversed and population rates and GDP per capita rates have continued to rise – contributing to higher emissions. These researchers note that no geographical region is decarbonizing its energy supply, so progress towards the necessary abatement of emissions is negligible. Rapidly developing economies, especially China, lead the growth rate in emissions. In 2004, 73 per cent of global emissions growth came from developing and least-developed countries, though this group accounts for 'only 23% of global cumulative emissions since the industrial revolution' (Raupach *et al.*, 2007, p. 10292).

The more rapid increase of emissions has led to fears amongst scientists and policymakers of rapidly deteriorating conditions, including the 'runaway greenhouse', with very significant impacts foreseen upon natural systems and for life on Earth. These conditions were set out in the Al Gore film *An Inconvenient Truth*, as well as by Lynas (2007) and Lovelock (2006).

1.2.4 Dangerous climate change

There have been attempts to identify what the 'acceptable' level of change is, either in terms of greenhouse gases in the atmosphere (expressed as 'equivalent concentration of CO_2') or expressed as temperature increase. In terms of temperature change, the 2007 UN Bali Climate Change Conference heard that a 'tipping point' would be reached if average global temperature increases by 2°C. In other words, change beyond that level might lead to self-perpetuating feedback loops and ever-greater uncontrolled change. Controversy remains as to what level of reduction of emissions is needed to avoid a 2°C increase. A peak concentration of 500 ppm in the atmosphere, falling back to 450 ppm, has been judged as the 'stabilization level' to prevent dangerous climate change (CCC, 2008, p. xiv). The IPCC Third Assessment Report (2001) identified five 'reasons for concern' (RFCs) resulting from climate change: risks to unique and threatened systems, risk of extreme weather events, inequalities in the distribution of impacts, aggregate impacts and risks of large-scale discontinuities (such as deglaciation of the West Antarctic or Greenland ice sheets). The relationships between the impacts of each RFC and increases in global mean temperatures were depicted in a diagram showing increases in level of risk associated with each RFC. In 2009 a group of IPCC member scientists, Smith *et al.*, updated and republished this graph – known as the 'burning embers graph' – to show how risks change as global mean temperature increases (the graph does not show how risks change at different rates of warming). Smith *et al.* (2009) explain the motives for their assessment as being increased reasons for concern across all five RFCs. The original 2001 (Panel A) and subsequent 2009 (Panel B) assessments are shown in Figure 1.2.

Smith *et al.* (2009) stress that the updated graph 'should not be interpreted as representing "dangerous" anthropogenic interference'. Nevertheless, they explain that their conclusion that the risk associated with specified expected levels of warming should now be assessed as more serious than was indicated in 2001 (they term this the shifting of risk transitions to lower global mean temperatures) results from further research and advancement of understanding since the first risk assessment. Their updated view thus rests on (i) observations of impacts already occurring, (ii) better understanding of and confidence in assessments of likelihoods for climatic events and magnitude of impacts, and (iii) more precise identification of impacts upon particular groups.

Risks associated with water availability and flooding are widespread. Whereas at the Bali conference in 2007 it was generally claimed that a 50 per cent reduction of global emissions below 1990 levels by 2050 would be the 'most stringent achievable target', Parry (2008) later pointed out that this would not be sufficient to avoid major global impacts. The co-chair of IPCC Working Group II (Impacts, Adaptation and Vulnerability) has stated (in Parry *et al.*, 2008) that, at this level of emissions, there would be 'an even chance of around 1 billion extra people being short of water by 2050, a number that rises as high as 2 billion by 2100' (p. 69). In order to limit impacts to acceptable levels by 2050 and beyond, what would be needed would be an 80 per cent cut in global emissions by 2050. Such a policy, Parry *et al.* argued, would lead to a stabilization

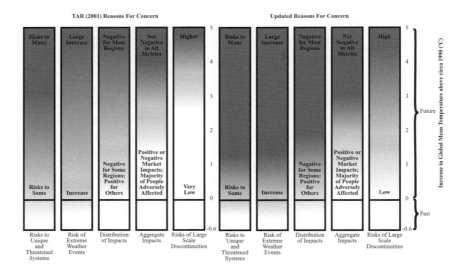

Figure 1.2

Burning embers: updating 'reasons for concern' associated with climate change
Source: Smith, Schneider *et al.*, 2009

of greenhouse gases at 400–470 ppm CO_2 equivalents and would 'halve the population put at risk of water stress and flooding by climate change' (p. 69). This target has been adopted within the EU (see Chapter 2). Risks associated with water (flood and drought) are not the only dangerous impacts of climate change – others include health impacts of heatwaves and impacts upon food supply across the globe, as well as impacts upon ecosystems leading to other indirect impacts, e.g. degradation and loss of soils.

International progress on keeping within or below the level of greenhouse gas emissions hypothesized in the IPCC scenarios has not been good. Raupach *et al.* (2007) point out that global emissions for the period to 2007 were as high as or higher than the highest IPCC scenarios (A1F1), and that growth in atmospheric CO_2 concentrations is a third faster since 2000 than in the previous two decades.

For these reasons – the current and possible future rate of change, the risks of dangerous climate change, the need to stabilize carbon levels through mitigation of anthropogenic climate change and the need to adapt to expected changes at least over the next fifty years – major societal and individual responses are required. These responses are usually classified by the climate change science community into two types: mitigation, that is reducing emissions to avoid unmanageable climate change, and adaptation, which entails making changes to activities and lifestyles to manage unavoidable climate change.

1.3 Role of Spatial Planning

1.3.1 Identifying the role of spatial planning

Spatial planning has been identified by many authors and reports as being essential, though not sufficient, both in achieving sustainable development and in addressing the causes and the consequences of climate change. For instance, the IPCC argues that policies and measures to address climate change mitigation include influencing mobility through land-use regulations and infrastructure planning, and demand-side management programmes for buildings. To address adaptation, land-use policies and regulations that integrate climate change considerations into settlement and infrastructure planning are necessary (IPCC, 2007a). Similarly, the highly influential Stern Review argues that, to reduce the causes of climate change, a range of policy responses is required. Stern's preference is for taxation and trading, carbon pricing and technological innovation. But he also argues for regulatory measures to 'promote efficiency through strategic coordination of key markets, for example by reducing long-run transport demand through integrated land-use planning and infrastructure development' (Stern, 2007, p. 432). For adaptation, Stern suggests that 'the planning system will be a key tool for encouraging both private and public investments towards locations that are less vulnerable to climate risks today and in the future' (2007, p. 477). In his later, more personally committed book, he argues that 'buildings, transport, infrastructure and urban design must all be simultaneously climate-resistant, energy-efficient and low-carbon' (Stern, 2009, p. 72).

At the European level, the EU's White Paper on adapting to climate change also points to the vital role of planning, but takes a wider view of spatial planning, more in tune with the interpretation in this book: 'A more strategic and long-term approach to spatial planning will be necessary, both on land and on marine areas, including in transport, regional development, industry, tourism and energy policies' (CEC, 2009a, p. 4). The potential scope for spatial planning is therefore immense. In a series of articles (Campbell, 2006), the question was raised as to whether 'the issue of climate change is too big for spatial planning'. We hope to show in this book it is not, but that a different and more positive, while nevertheless realistic, conception of spatial planning is needed in order to take a role in addressing climate change.

1.3.2 Scope of spatial planning

Spatial planning, like sustainable development, is a concept that has been contested and debated over the late twentieth and early twenty-first centuries. We interpret it as meaning the ability to plan, in a democratically accountable way, the activities of economic and service sectors (such as housing, energy, economic development, transport, water, waste, social welfare and health) that have spatial or land-use consequences in their wider social and environmental context. In this sense, it is wider than the more tightly defined emphasis of land-use planning (such as that in the UK following the innovative planning legislation of 1947). It is also wider than merely coordinating the spatial development of different economic and social sectors. In this book, we take the view that spatial planning requires a holistic understanding of the natural and environmental resources that underpin human societies. Climate change is not wholly or perhaps even largely an environmental issue, but it does raise issues of the distribution of and access to shared natural resources such as the atmosphere, water and energy sources, as well as to land. All these fall within the remit of spatial planning; moreover, planning requires the integration and coordination of both the drivers and the outcomes of these policy sectors, and the integration of demand management in influencing societal choices.

This interpretation reflects the dynamism and interrelationship of socio-economic and environmental factors with physical forms, which, as Healey (2007) argues, requires collective objective-setting and strategy-making.

More prosaically, in a European context, spatial planning has been defined as

> the methods used largely by the public sector to influence the future distribution of activities in space. It is undertaken with the aims of creating a more rational territorial organisation of land uses and the links between them, to balance demand for development with the need to protect the

environment, and to achieve social and economic objectives. Spatial planning embraces measures to co-ordinate the spatial impacts of other sectoral policies, to achieve a more even distribution of economic development between regions than would otherwise be created by market forces, and to regulate the conversion of land and property uses.

(CEC, 1997, p. 24)

Glasson and Marshall (2007) argue that the new Labour government of 1997 was keen on promoting European conceptions of spatial change and hence the terminology of spatial planning. The government now affirms this integrative role: 'spatial planning goes beyond traditional land use planning to bring together and integrate policies for the development and use of land with other policies and programmes which influence the nature of places and how they can function' (ODPM, 2005, para. 30). Haughton *et al.* (2010) refer to the widening scope of the 'new spatial plannings' within the British Isles (that is, Ireland and the UK), with some planning taking place in wider governance structures outside the formal processes of planning. They suggest that, while the term is still contested and changing, it has four principal dimensions: an emphasis on long-term strategic thinking; a mechanism for joined up policy-making; a central role in moving towards sustainable development; and an emphasis on inclusivity (p. 5).

Spatial planning in this sense can be seen as a predominantly European conception. However, it has some equivalences in the urban growth and 'smart growth' movements of the US (Ruth, 2006; Donaghy, 2007), and in the municipal, regional and provincial/territorial and federal state-led planning of Canada and Australia. It also has some similarities with the district plans prepared under New Zealand's much contested Resource Management Act of 1991, and the strategic community plans under the Local Government Act 2002 (Jackson and Dixon, 2007). While this book focuses primarily on the UK within the European context, it is hoped it also has relevance for other such contexts.

This conception of spatial planning presupposes institutional structures with the ability to make decisions on land use and activities, and to adopt and implement policies, plans and processes to integrate and coordinate these activities. It requires governance systems with mature and relatively stable institutions equipped with sets of legislation, regulation and policies which are generally observed and implemented. These tend to be found in industrialized countries which now have lower rates of urbanization (the migration of rural populations to urban areas) – although, of course, the form in which urban areas are growing in a planned way might be spatially extensive or concentrated (EEA, 2006). Moreover, these countries, while having distinctive planning systems, have experienced a sharing of planning concepts through the diffusion of ideas such as Garden Cities, growth management, green belts and the compact city (Ward, 2002; Amati, 2008). Planning can, of course, take various institutional forms. Within Europe, as we shall see in Chapter 5, there are countries with prescriptive national spatial plans (such as formerly in the Netherlands), countries with indicative spatial plans (such as Scotland and Wales), and countries such as England without national spatial plans. Within Europe, the EU itself has no spatial planning competence, although it adopted a European Spatial Development Perspective (ESDP) in 1999 (CEC, 1999), which gives spatial expression to its objectives for territorial cohesion and development, and, as indicated above, has been influential in widening the British conception of planning (see also Chapter 3.3.4).

There are also quirks of inclusion and exclusion in the scope of spatial planning. For instance, in the UK, decisions on some of the major land-users in terms of area (namely agriculture, forestry and horticulture) are outside the scope of the statutory planning system. By contrast, in Germany the long-standing tradition of *raumplanung* includes landscape planning, incorporating both urban and rural land uses. In the Netherlands, the practice of landscape and physical planning (such as the experience described by Cobbold and Santema, 2001) provides a wider and more coherent scope for spatial planning. These exclusions are important in the context of addressing climate change, and one of the themes of this book (developed in Part III) is the need to integrate rural and urban planning (Selman, 2006) with the ecosystem, catchment and productive functions of 'non-developed' land. Moreover, we interpret spatial planning to include coastal and marine or maritime planning within its scope. This is supported by the EU White Paper on adaptation, by initiatives at the EU level (CEC, 2008a; 2008b) and by individual member states, for maritime spatial planning. (The EU's policy consultation favours the term 'maritime' over 'marine' spatial planning in order 'to underline the holistic cross-sectoral approach of the process' [CEC, 2008a, p. 2].) In the UK, for instance, the Labour Party in its manifesto for the 1997 election made a commitment to a Marine Bill, responding to a strong campaign by both environmental and conservation non-governmental organizations (NGOs) for a spatial framework to plan for pressures from the growth of offshore oil and gas, aggregates dredging, and offshore wind developments. This became the Marine and Coastal Access Bill and received Royal Assent on 12 November 2009 (it is discussed further in Chapter 11).

1.3.3 The state and planning for the future

David Hume, the eighteenth-century Scottish philosopher of the Enlightenment, argued in his *Treatise of Human Nature* that 'There is no quality in human nature, which causes more fatal errors in our conduct, than that which leads us to prefer whatever is present to the distant and remote' (Hume, 1739–40, p. 345). His inference was that we therefore need good government to assist in correcting this distortion of disregard for the future. While the task of futures thinking is by no means the sole prerogative of the state, our conception of collective and statutory spatial planning does involve forward planning through futures thinking and the appraisal of possible options. A major theme of this book is that the issue of climate change requires us to reorient our spatial planning to pay more explicit and systematic attention to future possible pathways. It is also important not to use that foresighting as a reason for inaction now. Instead, such foresight can demonstrate (as in the Stern Review) that the costs of inaction hugely outweigh the costs of timely action. We discuss futures thinking and planning time horizons more fully in Chapter 6.

From a rather different perspective, Giddens, in his book *The Politics of Climate Change* (2009), argues that the crisis of climate change requires a 'return to planning', and that the state must 'help us to think ahead [...] governments should encourage a shift towards long-term thinking among companies, third sector organizations and individual citizens' (2009, p. 92). He concludes (somewhat reluctantly) that, in any attempt to think systematically about the future, 'planning of some sort is inevitable' (p. 95). His reluctance comes from what he regards as the negative associations of the word planning, 'since it conjures up images of authoritarianism on the one hand and ineptness on the other' (p. 7). He argues that post-war planning fell out of favour, being associated with Soviet-era centralized economic planning or, in the West, with 'faceless bureaucrats who could intervene in communities without much thought for local concerns or sensitivities' (p. 95). It is the contention of our book that planning has a much more positive story to tell, and that, rather than this reluctance, we should celebrate the power of planning as enabling us to 'influence the future for the better and to illuminate the choices available as to what that future might be' (Headicar, 2009, p. 448).

While we base much of the analysis in the book on an assumption about the essential role of the state, we also observe that the issue of climate change is prompting many communities to generate their own plans and strategies – similar to the Local Agenda 21 initiatives of the 1990s following the Rio Summit (Owens and Cowell, 2001; Baker and Eckerberg, 2008), the Slow Towns and Cities movement, local food networks, the Transition Towns and many other initiatives for low-carbon communities (While, 2008). We argue therefore that statutory spatial plan-making is not the only way in which different forms of governance are addressing climate change, and, indeed, that such formal processes need to be alert to and engage with community-led processes. Otherwise, the necessarily procedural and formal processes of statutory plan-making might become increasingly disconnected from (and possibly be seen as a constraint on) community-led visions and initiatives. We address the relationship between these in Chapters 5, 9 and 13.

1.3.4 Planning and scale

The unprecedented nature of the climate change crisis – requiring global as well as national and individual action – raises profound questions for the scale of planning. The UN Framework Convention on Climate Change, and its subsequent protocols, and the EU's Emissions Trading Scheme set binding targets on developed nations for carbon reduction. In the UK, as a result of a powerfully argued campaign by civil society, led by third-sector organizations as well as parliamentarians (under the banners of Friends of the Earth's Big Ask campaign and the Stop Climate Chaos coalition), a Climate Change Act was passed in 2008 (claimed by the government as the world's first long-term legally binding framework to tackle climate change), which sets a legally binding target of at least an 80 per cent cut in greenhouse gas emissions by 2050, against a 1990 baseline, as well as a reduction in CO_2 emissions of 26 per cent by 2026. Budgets set to deliver these will require the cascading of targets to all levels of governance (and possibly at some stage to individuals in the form of carbon budgets). We argue in this book that the global experience of climate change, especially the likelihood that its impacts will fall most heavily on the poor and vulnerable in countries under development (as outlined in IPCC, 2007c), and the obligations on different countries, raise a new and unprecedented set of imperatives on spatial planning systems in industrialized countries. The integration of international, national and local scales of decision-making, and the new relations of state and civil society, make for a potentially volatile and unpredictable set of outcomes, with the ability of both the nation state and the local state or civil society to appeal to other tiers. This may be a particularly new phenomenon for the UK, which, as an island state, has had less need to pay attention to transboundary issues. The implications of this multi-scalar nature of planning for climate change are discussed in Chapter 5.

1.3.5 Planning, implementation and management

While the principal scope of this book lies in policies and planning, it also addresses the role of management of activities, land uses and the demands for them. This is for three reasons. First, there is an implementation gap, through which plans and strategies may fail to be implemented at all, or not be implemented as intended. This may be the result of factors such as different perspectives on the nature or significance of the problem or its solutions, misunderstanding of the causal relationship between action and problem, ineffective action, lack of powers or resources for those tasked with implementation, or time-lags between intention and action during which the initial conditions will have changed (Trudgill, 1990; Hill, 2005). Healey expresses this nicely: the linear conception of policy formulation and implementation 'has been replaced with notions of strategy-formation and use in the public domain as some form of collaboration among diverse actors, through a mixture of formal and informal interactive processes, drawing on diverse forms of knowledge' (2007, p. 31). While professional planners may have a realistic rather than idealized view of the linear implementation of plans, there is nevertheless a tendency for commentators (such as Giddens) to express surprise that not all plans are implemented straightforwardly. This book therefore pays attention (in

Chapters 4 and 13) to some of these issues of knowledge and learning amongst planning professionals, the public and elected representatives.

A second reason for this book's focus on how plans work out on the ground is that there is a revived interest in the delivery of spatial planning, through other measures as well as through formal land-use decisions. This arises partly in response to changes in energy generation (for instance, with more distributed networks changing the way in which households interact with the energy sector (Walker and Cass, 2007)). It also arises because of interest in demand management and behaviour, such as in travel and transport modes, and the energy-conservation practices of occupants and users of land and buildings. There are also prompts from the valuation of ecosystem services, such as mitigation banking or similar measures for the enhancement of ecosystem services, or compensation for their replacement as a result of the environmental impact procedures (see Chapters 2, 7 and 12). In our interpretation of spatial planning, therefore, we include some of these elements which traditionally might have been seen as unrelated to plan-making.

A third reason for addressing plan implementation lies in the need for spatial planning to address both existing and planned new development (an issue also linked to the need for longer-term planning horizons). In the UK, this represents a radical departure from past practice, but one which is being prompted by the climate change crisis. The physical elements of the UK's urban areas and infrastructure tend to have long lives – up to fifty years for major infrastructure and longer for many domestic dwellings – as this is a country with a long history of urbanization and industrialization. It is argued, for instance, that even in times of high economic growth and associated construction activity, annual new build only represents 1 per cent of building stock – and that, for instance, by 2050 (at which time the UK should have achieved at least an 80 per cent reduction in greenhouse gases) 80 per cent of homes then being occupied already exist today (Foresight, 2008). This is illustrated in Figure 9.6 in Chapter 9. Not only do we need to address the energy consumption of the building stock, but, as the climate changes, we also need to adapt by addressing issues such as water consumption and flood risk. Developments therefore have to pay attention to the consequences of climate change, both for new development and also for existing development. We will argue in Part III that this reinforces the need for holistic spatial planning to encompass the networks such as energy and water systems which can support development into the future.

1.4 Implications for sustainable development

Sustainability, as with spatial planning, is a normative and contested concept. The understanding we give it in this book draws on two key definitions of sustainability. That from the conservation movement is 'Improving the quality of life while living within the carrying capacity of supporting eco-systems' (Munro and Holdgate, 1991). The Brundtland Report's definition is as follows:

sustainable development is development that meets the needs of the present without compromising the ability of future generations to meet their own needs. It contains within it two concepts: the concept of needs, in particular the essential needs of the world's poor, to which over-riding priority should be given; and the idea of limitations posed by the state of technology and social organization on the environment's ability to meet present and future needs.

(WCED, 1987, section 2.1)

Drawing on both these definitions, we emphasize the principles embedded within the concept: the principle of futurity (long-term thinking and owing a duty to future generations); the principle of equity for current generations; community engagement in these processes; and the concept of quality of life within environmental carrying capacities.

All these issues are discussed in greater depth within the book. We also consider that, rather as the concept of sustainable development in the 1990s was argued to provide a justification and a new lease of life for planning (such as Owens and Cowell, 2002), climate change provides a further justification. But planning remains a contested concept, as we saw in Chapter 1.3.3. Even if spatial planning takes a deliberative and collaborative turn as advocated by Healey (1997), there will be debate, disagreement and conflict (Rydin, 2003). Spatial planning for climate change and sustainable development might promote no- or low-regrets actions to meet sustainability principles such as equity. For instance, reducing fuel poverty through a programme of insulation can also reduce carbon emissions. And certainly responses to climate change do, as we shall see, offer some opportunities for synergies and mutual benefits. But these are not guaranteed – indeed, there are plenty of examples where actions for mitigation may challenge and undermine the ability of systems to adapt to climate change (see, for instance, examples in Part III). Spatial planning is nevertheless relatively well-suited to the role of reducing these conflicts and maximizing positive synergies. It has experience with futures and plans, with community engagement and public participation, with option appraisal and negotiating trade-offs and critical thresholds. It therefore offers considerable scope, as Swart and Raes (2007) argue, for a more integrated approach to mitigation and adaptation which can be mainstreamed into sustainable development. (They conclude that: 'generally the global, regional and, in most countries, national potential of synergetic options to mitigate and adapt to climate change is relatively low, and both strategies should be considered as complementary' (p. 288), and they identify opportunities in the areas of land and water management and urban planning.) But, as with sustainability, we need to acknowledge that spatial planning is but one part of the process of sharing responsibility, and that its scope needs to be integrated with the range of other powers and measures available to society, such as collective action by individuals, communities and companies.

1.5 Conclusions

This introduction has demonstrated the urgency of the need to respond to changing climates, through both the reduction of emissions causing the change and by accommodating to the coming changes. Spatial planning has a central role in meeting this need as it is holistic, concerned with the interface between governance and implementation and looks forward to relatively distant futures. The spatial planning system also engages the public and other stakeholders in order to find consensual approaches to change. Moreover, many of the mitigation and adaptation actions that will need to be investigated and implemented require the involvement of the spatial planning system (for example the siting of new energy-generating facilities or designs for the regeneration of cities), so there is a significant opportunity both to promote the reduction of emissions and to enable climate change adaptation to take place.

Public policy for spatial planning in both the UK and the Netherlands is moving in this direction. The UK government is revising its guidance on planning and climate change: the consultation (DCLG, 2010a) stresses the need to plan for mitigation and adaptation together, for instance through the provision of green infrastructure. The guidance supports the role of planning in promoting a low carbon economy, while also requiring consideration of community resilience to future climate change, especially amongst vulnerable communities in areas of existing development. In the Netherlands, the Delta Act 2010 has been drafted for parliamentary approval, as part of the implementation of the Delta Programme of making the Netherlands more resilient to future climate change. However, the tentative outcomes of Copenhagen 2009, and reports of the continuing loss of global and European biodiversity, with the uncertainties of the economic recession, present serious challenges for spatial planning.

2 Climate change mitigation and adaptation

Impacts and opportunities

2.1 Introduction and definitions

2.1.1 Impacts of climate and climate change

Local and regional climates over time have shaped and determined landform and natural environments, such as slope angles, soils and natural habitats. Climate has also helped determine our built environments (though the strength of this influence is changing): for instance, the angles of roofs, and the ratio of window to wall, have been influenced in the past by local climatic norms for rainfall intensity and temperature. We experience the climate of a location every day as weather, which includes temperature, rainfall and snow, frost, sunshine hours, cloud cover and wind speed. Climate change leads to changes in all of these in terms of absolute levels experienced and their frequency, intensity or length (e.g. of storms, droughts or heatwaves). Climate change is also resulting in rises in sea level. The process of warming of the low-level atmosphere – which evidence suggests has been particularly marked since about 1950 (IPCC 2007b) – gives rise to impacts across the range of economic sectors, environments and systems (physical, human and biological). The extent of change and impacts experienced will depend upon other factors including geographical location (e.g. altitude, latitude, distance from coasts), the nature of the local environment and the extent to which it is already under pressure from human populations.

The impacts of the weather upon people, our environments and the resources we use are, under a stable climatic regime, predictable and manageable. As climates change, the man-made elements within the environment, which have been specifically designed for the pre-existing climate, may no longer be suitable. For example, the size of drainage pipes needed to carry away surface water run-off after heavy rain and the foundations of buildings located on permafrost may both need to be redesigned. Similarly, natural elements may no longer be well suited to the location: the range of natural species at a site (from the smallest animals to the largest trees) may find their new conditions unsuitable and may either become extinct or need to find a way to move to more suitable environments.

Projections have been made of future climates, based on likely future presence of greenhouse gases in the atmosphere and observed trends both globally and for the UK (IPCC, 2001; UKCIP, 2009). Although in some parts of the world climate change may lead to opportunities and benefits, there is no doubt that the projected changes also endanger human life, threaten natural habitats and urban areas as now built, and threaten resources and assets. The first response is therefore to reduce the rate of climate change by reducing emissions of greenhouse gases to the atmosphere: this is referred to as climate change *mitigation*. However, to the extent that climates are already committed to change because of past emissions, it is also necessary *to adapt* to the changes that will take place.

2.1.2 Definitions

The IPCC uses the definitions of responses to climate change given in Box 2.1 to help ensure a common understanding.

Succinctly expressed, mitigation is about avoiding the unmanageable, whilst adaptation is about managing the unavoidable. Unfortunately, not all of the unmanageable impacts of climate change can be avoided, and we must do our best to manage the unavoidable. Identifying the source of emissions is a starting point.

2.1.3 Sources of emissions

Climate change is now acknowledged (IPCC, 2007a, p. 72) to be the result of the accumulation of greenhouse gases in the atmosphere as a result of human activities. The greenhouse gases accumulate as flows of gases produced (and especially CO_2) exceed the capacity of those elements of the system which 'lock up' carbon as vegetation (including wood), soils and dissolved CO_2 in the oceans (Figure 2.1).

Estimates of the major sources of greenhouse gas emissions exist at global and national levels, as well as for biogeographical regions such as the Atlantic, Continental, pre-Alpine, Boreal and Mediterranean regions within Europe. Both absolute levels and distribution amongst sources depend largely on the level of economic growth. Figure 2.2 shows the global trend in increasing emissions from 1970 to 2004 (from 28.7 $GtCO_2$-eq/year to 49.0 $GtCO_2$-eq/year), as well as emissions by sector for years between 1970 and 2004. Between 2000 and 2008, fossil fuel emissions increased by 29 per cent (le Quéré *et al.*,

Box 2.1 Definitions: Climate change impacts and responses

Climate change impacts: the effects of climate change on natural and human systems

- **Potential impacts**: all impacts that may occur given a projected change in climate, without considering adaptation.
- **Residual impacts**: the impacts of climate change that remain after adaptation measures have been taken.

Mitigation ~~emissions~~ _m + Em_
Intervention (by governments, institutions, companies, etc.) to reduce emissions of greenhouse gases to the atmosphere; it includes strategies to reduce greenhouse gas sources and emissions and enhancing greenhouse gas sinks. (It is also referred to as reducing the anthropogenic forcing of the climate system).

Adaptation _ADAPT_
The adjustment in natural or human systems in response to actual or expected climates and weather, or their effects, in order to moderate harm or exploit beneficial opportunities. Distinct types of adaptation: anticipatory, autonomous and planned adaptation.

- **Anticipatory adaptation** – Adaptation that takes place before impacts of climate change are observed. Also referred to as proactive adaptation.
- **Autonomous adaptation** – Adaptation that does not constitute a conscious response to climatic stimuli but is triggered by ecological changes in natural systems and by market or welfare changes in human systems. Also referred to as spontaneous adaptation.
- **Planned adaptation** – Adaptation that is the result of a deliberate policy decision, based on an awareness that conditions have changed or are about to change and that action is required to return to, maintain, or achieve a desired state.

Source: IPCC, 2007c: Appendix I – Glossary (pp. 869–83).

2009) mainly as a result of three factors: increased emissions from emerging economies, from the production and international trade of goods and services, and from the use of coal as a fuel source. Emissions from another major source, land-use changes, were nearly constant (le Quéré et al., 2009). 'Average atmospheric CO_2 in 2008 reached a concentration of 385 ppm, which is 38% above pre-industrial levels' (le Quéré et al., 2009, p. 834). Figure 2.2 shows that worldwide energy supply is responsible for 25.9 per cent of emissions, and industry for 19.4 per cent. Figure 2.3 presents estimated greenhouse gas emissions by sector for the European Union (EU-27, in 2007). Assumptions behind such statistical accounting are not always identical, so a direct comparison between Figures 2.2 and 2.3 is not possible. National reports to the UNFCCC

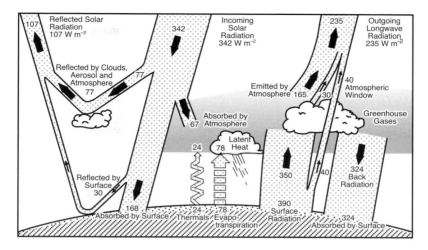

Figure 2.1

The Earth's energy balance
Source: Kiehl and Trenberth, 1997

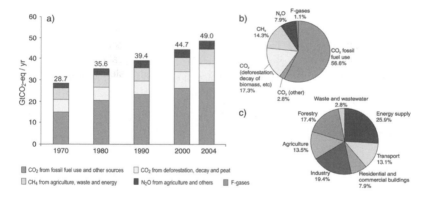

Figure 2.2

(a) Global annual emissions of anthropogenic greenhouse gases from 1970 to 2004
(b) Share of different anthropogenic greenhouse gases in total emissions in 2004 in terms
of CO_2-eq. (c) Share of different sectors in total anthropogenic greenhouse gas emissions
in 2004 in terms of CO_2-eq
Source: IPCC, 2007a

(UN Framework Convention on Climate Change) present data on greenhouse
gas emissions on a country basis.

The pie charts in Figure 2.2 show that there are sectors that are major emitters of greenhouse gases which are also sectors in which spatial planning has

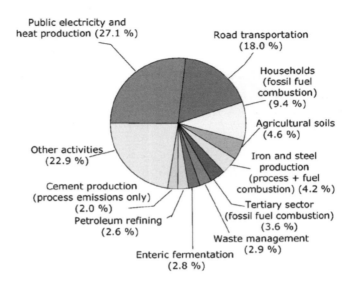

Public electricity and heat production (27.1 %)

Road transportation (18.0 %)

Households (fossil fuel combustion) (9.4 %)

Agricultural soils (4.6 %)

Other activities (22.9 %)

Iron and steel production (process + fuel combustion) (4.2 %)

Cement production (process emissions only) (2.0 %)

Tertiary sector (fossil fuel combustion) (3.6 %)

Petroleum refining (2.6 %)

Waste management (2.9 %)

Enteric fermentation (2.8 %)

Figure 2.3

Greenhouse gas emissions in the EU-27 by main source of activity, 2007
Source: EEA, 2008c Fig 2.2

a major role, notably transport, buildings and the management of waste. In addition, spatial planning has a contribution to make with regard to energy supply through influencing energy sources and power plant locations. This role – the political context, the opportunities and constraints – is explored in more detail in the following chapters, and in Chapter 2, Section 2.4 with respect to adaptation. Six routes to mitigation exist:

- Carbon conservation (conservation *in situ* of natural stocks of carbon, in forests, peat soils or wild areas as vegetation)
- Carbon capture (promote capture of carbon in either timber/wood or from energy generation from fossil fuels)
- Energy conservation (use less, reduce the need to use energy)
- Energy efficiency (use less to achieve the same or more output/work)
- Renewable, carbon free and carbon neutral energy sources
- New technologies, e.g. for direct reduction of emissions.

IPCC (Intergovernmental Panel on Climate Change) Working Group III on Mitigation (2007e) has assessed emissions and mitigation options. The working group concludes that greenhouse gas emissions have grown since pre-industrial times, and between 1970 and 2004 increased by 70 per cent – this trend is expected to continue for 'the next few decades' (p. 4). Nevertheless, there are opportunities for mitigation, though these may be associated with costs – WG III has attempted to identify these costs, which will depend on how taxing the target is for stabilization of greenhouse gases (i.e., the level of emissions to be attained) – and are also country- or region-dependent. As an example, however, WG III calculated that a stabilization target of 445–710 ppm CO_2 equivalents would be associated with a cost level in a range between a 3 per cent *decrease* in global GDP and a small *increase*, compared with the baseline (p. 11). However, health benefits would also accrue from reducing air pollution, which would offset 'a substantial fraction' of the costs of moving towards a reduction of emissions (p. 12). *The Stern Review* of 2006 calculated that

> the overall costs and risks of climate change will be equivalent to losing at least 5% of global GDP each year, now and forever. If a wider range of risks and impacts is taken into account, the estimates of damage could rise to 20% of GDP or more. In contrast, the costs of action – reducing greenhouse gas emissions to avoid the worst impacts of climate change – can be limited to around 1% of global GDP each year.
>
> (Stern, 2007, p. xv)

Stern remarks, moreover, that 'The investment that takes place in the next 10–20 years will have a profound effect on the climate in the second half of this century and in the next' (Stern, 2007, p. xv).

IPCC's WG III has stated that mitigation efforts over the next twenty to thirty years will strongly affect the achievement of stabilization of atmospheric greenhouse gases at lower concentrations (IPCC, 2007e). WG III recognizes that the process of making decisions about what this level might be would need to examine both mitigation and adaptation options, assessing risks, co-benefits and avoided damages as well as sustainability issues including equity. Whilst many policy approaches and instruments to help with mitigation already exist, what is applicable in one country may not be appropriate elsewhere: disadvantages and advantages need to be explored.

Moreover, as significant climate change is already 'locked in' to future climates (as a result of the increased emissions load in the atmosphere and the warming of the atmosphere and oceans), it is also essential that we find routes to adapt to climate change. This book therefore focuses on the ways in which the spatial planning system can promote both mitigation and adaptation, and can assess the impacts and risks associated with proposed options for planned development and responses to climate change.

2.2 Impacts and opportunities of climate change

2.2.1 Identifying impacts

Studies of the likely impacts of climate change have been in progress since the 1980s and have focused on a range of levels and topics; there have been impact studies to cover different spatial scales (countries, regions, cities), different environments (e.g. rural and urban areas), particular economic sectors (such as tourism or transport), and topics such as health, biodiversity and air quality. Impact studies follow a format that generally covers the environmental, sectoral and policy framework, and then identifies areas of special vulnerability or risk, expected levels and impacts of climate change (frequency and extent), predicted responses by receptors (i.e., a sector or environment) and the consequences of those responses. Possible measures needed to mitigate adverse effects or enhance beneficial effects are suggested, leading to identification of residual effects. Climate impact studies, typically, have used scenarios of future climate change (based on GCMs – global climate models) to indicate the likely extent of change to be accommodated (Box 2.2 summarizes projections for the UK). Other pressures such as population and lifestyle change, as well as economic growth, are also included in the studies to attempt a realistic representation of future circumstances under different conditions. Chapter 6, Section 6.6 provides further discussion of future scenarios.

Box 2.2 UKCP09 climate projections 2020s, 2050s and 2080s

UKCIP has published the UKCP09 projections for average annual precipitation across the UK for three emissions scenarios (low, medium and high) and for three time slices (2020s, 2050s and 2080s). Probabilities are shown, indicating 10%, 33%, 50%, 67% and 90% probability levels. The scenarios thus provide a complex set of projections of a range of parameters by emissions scenario and location (administrative region or lower scale) expressed in terms of probabilities. To take the central estimate (50% probability) of two parameters (mean winter and mean summer temperatures) for a single region, the medium emissions scenario and two time slices, projections for South East England show:

Mean winter temperature: increase of 2.0°C in 2050s and 3.0°C in 2080s
Mean summer temperature: increase of 2.8°C in 2050s and 3.9°C in 2080s

The scenarios indicate winter precipitation increasing over time, and faster in the high emissions scenario. For example, across all the UK and under the medium emissions scenario, the 'central estimate' for 2050 for winter precipitation is an increase of between 10% and 20%. The central estimate of summer precipitation, on the other hand, is a fall of between −10% and −20%. Note that the central estimate is the 50% probability value.

The mapped projections can be viewed in full at the UKCP09 website.

Source: Project website: http://ukclimateprojections.defra.gov.uk/ (adapted from Defra, 2009a)

A strategic (international, national or sectoral) climate change impact assessment typically includes a response strategy comprising both mitigation (emissions reduction) and adaptation measures. But it is also recognized that there are cases where there are synergies between mitigation and adaptation

options, and where opportunities can be maximized – or there may be contradictions, so both need to be taken together to avoid pitfalls (Paterson *et al.*,
2008; Berry, 2009). We discuss the role of spatial planning in this respect in
Section 2.4. Other developments in climate change impact assessment have
included the use of indicators (for example, EEA, 2008a). Since the mid-2000s
economic studies have been prepared, exploring the costs of mitigation and
adaptation responses, and comparing these with the costs of no response (such
as Stern, 2007; IPCC, 2007d; EEA, 2007a).

2.2.2 Opportunities arising from climate change

Opportunities are expected to arise not only from the processes of climate
change, but also from our responses to it (Pfeifer and Sullivan, 2008). The
opportunities may relate to business, to the environment, to society, health
and culture, or to governance. Opportunities may arise:

- directly from climate change, such as new economic opportunities in
  agriculture or tourism;
- from climate change mitigation, such as the development of new technologies
  of energy generation;
- from adaptation (autonomous or planned), for example via the recognition
  of vulnerabilities and enhanced resilience;
- or they may address other sustainable development issues, e.g. choosing
  management or investment options that improve equity or quality of
  life.

Opportunities will arise from both adverse and beneficial impacts of climate
change, and it must be a role of government at all levels to ensure that appropriate beneficial opportunities are pursued. Whilst it is probably true that impact
studies tend to highlight adverse impacts, beneficial impacts may also be identified, and exploring these is important. New opportunities may arise which, with
appropriate planning and management, can help offset adverse impacts.

Business-related opportunities in the UK have been identified – for example,
greater tourism potential for South East England (GOSE, 2009), and expansion
of vineyards. An adverse impact – such as an increase in an invasive species –
might provide a new resource for business. Developing opportunities may lead
to improved social and environmental conditions, perhaps producing 'snow-
ball' effects in local areas via regulation, taxation or market-based instruments
which can improve local environmental quality and quality of life or skills
development. Social and cultural opportunities may be concerned with society and health, such as better opportunities for outdoor recreation, or lower
health risks in milder winters. Increased opportunities may arise for cultural
exchange with other locations, or for sports events. Within the built environment, new opportunities are arising – through increased awareness of climate

change – to encourage collective action to address not only climate change but also other local issues, including urban areas of declining quality (Saavedra and Budd, 2009, p. 251). Adger (2003) has discussed social factors in increasing vulnerability to risk, and quotes research into heatwave survival in Chicago in 1995 – individuals in certain housing types, without social networks and who were unlikely or unable to leave their homes, were at far greater risk of death (pp. 29–49). Adger sees social capital as the 'glue' that builds both communities and social resilience. Climate change adaptation which promotes social capital might thus be seen as an opportunity for promoting better quality of life for vulnerable individuals throughout the year, not only at times of risk.

A changing climate and environment presents opportunities not only for people but also for wildlife. Some existing species currently at the northern limit of their range (such as some British butterflies) could benefit from warming conditions – evidence from monitoring by the Environmental Change Network shows peacock (*Inachis io*), green-veined white (*Pieris napi*) and dark green fritillary (*Argynnis aglaja*) butterflies increasing their numbers (Morecroft *et al.*, 2009). On the other hand, some invasive species – that is, fast-reproducing and underpredated non-native species which are successful competitors – may also benefit from warmer or changed conditions.

By heightening awareness of the environment, and promoting research and technology development, climate change has stimulated interest in approaches implemented through the spatial planning system which can improve our management of the environment – these include risk assessment, regulatory and fiscal measures, and also 'soft' (non-regulatory) measures. Examples relate to the introduction of green infrastructure (see Chapter 9) and sustainable urban drainage systems (SUDS – see Chapter 11, Section 11.4.2), both of which have corollary potential benefits for wildlife. Greater interest in environmental management within the construction industry has led to research and development in green roofs – with benefits for the urban heat island, for water management and also for biodiversity (see Chapter 9.9).

Finally, acknowledgement of climate change impacts, and recognition of the need to plan for this and make funding available, does also present an opportunity for a review of planning processes, for renewal and improvement of approaches such as EIA (Environmental Impact Assessment), SEA (Strategic Environmental Assessment) and SA (Sustainability Appraisal), and for better integration of objectives across sectors and boundaries (see *inter alia* Saavedra and Budd, 2009, p. 248). There is better recognition of the need to integrate planning for other impacts that may be occurring simultaneously and cumulatively – these may be indirect effects of climate change upon other components of an economic or environmental system, or they may not be associated with climate change, e.g. demographic change and economic cycles. In addition there is evidence that a longer-term view will be taken in policy and planning. The nature of climate change – gradual change punctuated by extreme events – is such that this long-term element, often lacking in the past, must now be included. These planning-related aspects are taken forward in Section 2.4. A number of authors have also seen climate change as providing 'an opportunity' for the focus of development agencies to be modified and expanded, so as to address links between climate change and development. Whilst this book focuses on the EU/UK situation, we recognize the links between developed and developing countries, and consider there is scope for shared learning in approaches to mitigation and adaptation. Klein, Eriksen *et al.* (2007) and Halsnaes and Shukla (2008) have investigated how synergies can be achieved when bringing together sustainable development policies and mainstreamed climate change policy, and have identified opportunities in alternative national development policies for infrastructure and water supply that provide resilience against climate variability and change. We address the issues of cross-national learning in Chapter 13.

2.3 The case for mitigation and adaptation

2.3.1 Climate change mitigation and adaptation responses

In addition to the direct and indirect impacts of climate change (such as increased temperatures, sea-level rise or changes in growing seasons), both beneficial and adverse impacts may result from attempts to mitigate climate change on the one hand, and adapt to it on the other. However, as past impacts on the atmosphere will inevitably cause continuing change in forthcoming decades, adaptation strategies must be designed to plan for all three types of adaptation defined in Box 2.1 (that is: proactive (advance) adaptation, spontaneous and planned) because mitigation and adaptation strategies may act in complex and interacting ways. It is necessary to assess these interactions, integrate responses and seek synergies where achievable.

Research amongst climate scientists and other experts for the IPCC identified a set of beliefs about adaptation and mitigation responses, and assessed the levels of confidence in those beliefs (Klein, Huq *et al.*, 2007). These researchers state that:

- effective climate policy aimed at reducing the risks of climate change to natural and human systems requires a portfolio of diverse adaptation and mitigation actions (very high confidence);
- different governance levels are involved in decisions on adaptation and mitigation, and that interrelationships exist within and across each of these levels (high confidence);
- creating synergies between adaptation and mitigation can increase the cost-effectiveness of actions and make them more attractive to stakeholders, including potential funding agencies (medium confidence).

Klein, Huq *et al.* (2007) also observe that it is not yet possible to answer the question as to whether or not investment in adaptation would buy time for mitigation (high confidence) but that people's capacities to adapt and mitigate are driven by similar factors.

2.3.2 Mitigation and adaptation: interrelationships and interactions

Preparation for living in a world with a changed climate does not have the choice between mitigation and adaptation. It is recognized that there are limits and barriers to adaptation (Adger *et al.*, 2007). The two strategies must work together (in addition to other measures taken), so mitigation and adaptation policies and approaches need to be assessed at a range of spatial levels for their fit with problems, and a combination of these is needed to confront the threats and risks of climate change. The routes to doing this are being sought at supranational level (global and international, such as the EU), at national and local levels of governance (legislation, planning policy), but also at the level of institutions and individuals.

However, mitigation and adaptation measures are not necessarily substitutes or complementary – they can also interact. Four types of interrelationship between mitigation and adaptation have been identified as part of the IPCC Fourth Assessment Report (AR4) (Klein, Huq *et al.*, 2007, p. 747); examples of these interactions are shown in Table 2.1. These four types are:

- adaptation actions that have consequences for mitigation;
- mitigation actions that have consequences for adaptation;
- decisions that include trade-offs or synergies between adaptation and mitigation;
- processes that have consequences for both adaptation and mitigation.

Both mitigation and adaptation responses may be made across the scale from individual household decisions to global policy, and there are interactions, including conflicts, between these levels. In other words, mitigation/adaptation responses at one level may lead to unexpected responses at another level, and these may be detrimental or beneficial to the overall response. For example, many individual decisions to change urban surfaces from permeable to impermeable (e.g. car parking spaces) can lead to increased flood risk and the need for new drainage infrastructure. Similarly, the effect of many individual decisions to adapt to higher temperatures by installing air-conditioning is to lead to increased carbon-intensive energy demand, and so failure of local or national attempts towards mitigation. Another type of unintended consequence may be the displacement of adverse impacts to other sectors (or regions) and so cause a neutral or negative impact upon adaptation to changed conditions overall – this is also known as 'maladaptation' (see also EEA, 2007a, p. 21).

In Section 2.4 and Part III we outline how these consequences (both adverse and beneficial), trade-offs and synergies may occur across a range of sectors

Table 2.1 Examples of interactions between climate change responses (mitigation and adaptation)

Adaptation actions that have consequences for mitigation	Mitigation actions that have consequences for adaptation
Individual responses to climatic hazards that increase or decrease greenhouse gas emissions More efficient community use of water, land, forests Natural resources managed to sustain livelihoods Tourism use of energy and water, with outcomes for incomes and emissions Resources used in adaptation, such as large-scale infrastructure, increase emissions	More efficient energy use and renewable sources that promote local development CDM projects on land use or energy use that support local economies and livelihoods Urban planning, building design and recycling with benefits for both adaptation and mitigation Health benefits of mitigation through reduced environmental stresses Afforestation, leading to depleted water resources and other ecosystem effects, with consequences for livelihoods Mitigation schemes that transfer finance to developing countries (such as a per capita allocation) stimulate investment that may benefit adaptation Effect of mitigation (e.g. through carbon taxes and energy prices, on resource use)
Decisions that include trade-offs or synergies between adaptation and mitigation	**Processes that have consequences for both adaptation and mitigation**
Public-sector funding and budgetary processes that allocate funding to both adaptation and mitigation Strategic planning related to development pathways (scenarios) to mainstream climate responses Allocation of funding and setting the agenda for UNFCCC negotiations and funds Stabilization targets that include limits to adaptation (e.g. Tolerable Windows Approach (TWA) to integrated assessments of climate change) Analysis of global costs and benefits of mitigation to inform targets Large scale mitigation (e.g. geo-engineering) with effects on impacts and adaptation	Cultural values that promote both adaptation and mitigation such as culturally valued forests (e.g. the restoration of the 'Caledonian forest' in Scotland of which about 1% remains) Management of socio-ecological systems to promote resilience (e.g. fisheries licensing) Ecological impacts, with some human element, drive further releases of greenhouse gases (e.g. methane from exposed peat) Legal implications of liability for climate impacts motivates mitigation (e.g. Carbon Pollution Reduction Scheme Bill – Australia, 2009) National capacity-building increases ability to respond to both adaptation and mitigation (e.g. UKCIP programme) Monitoring systems and reporting requirements that cover indicators of both adaptation and mitigation (e.g. National sustainable development indicators) Management of multilateral environmental agreements benefits both adaptation and mitigation (e.g. ECCP II, Natura 2000 sites)

Source: adapted from Klein, Huq et al., 2007, p. 762

within the remit of spatial planning, and the way in which planning for sustainable development (or sustainability) may help. Interactions between mitigation and adaptation measures is a topic that has been the subject of a good deal of work, such as chapter 17 (Adger *et al.*, 2007) and chapter 18 (Klein, Huq *et al.*, 2007) of the IPCC's Fourth Assessment Report (IPCC, 2007a). Moreover, a range of sectors in both developed and developing countries have been reviewed to seek interrelationships between the two approaches (Klein and Huq, supplementary material to Klein, Huq *et al.*, 2007). Similar work was undertaken by researchers working on the MACIS project to consider interaction between mitigation and adaptation, and the ultimate consequences of these for biodiversity (Berry, 2009).

2.4 The role of spatial planning in the synergy between mitigation and adaptation

2.4.1 Introduction

We have seen that there are complex possible interactions between strategies and measures to address climate change mitigation and adaptation, including synergies and potential conflicts, giving rise to what Pizarro (2009) calls a mitigation–adaptation 'conundrum'. As spatial planning has a remit to coordinate and integrate 'the spatial dimension of sectoral policies through a territorially based strategy' (Cullingworth and Nadin, 2006, p. 91), we consider that it has a useful – if not vital – role to play in assisting in the process of minimizing conflicts and identifying synergies between mitigation and adaptation. This is consistent with the move at European level to achieve integration of environmental policies and to integrate the environment into other sectoral policies of the EU (Lenschow, 2002), as committed under the Single European Act of 1996 and the Amsterdam Treaty. However, spatial planning enables us to move beyond the emphasis on integrating across sectors, and towards integration at territorial and spatial levels, for instance between cities and their hinterlands, between coastal zones and the marine environment, and between rural and urban areas within river catchments. Moreover, as spatial planning is a statutory function at a number of levels of governance – national, regional and local – it has a role in vertical integration. At all these levels, there has been commitment to planning's role on delivering sustainable development. As we argued in Chapter 1, addressing climate change can be seen as both an extension of addressing sustainability and an exemplar of more sustainable development. It also allows opportunities to address cumulative impacts not just over space but over time – particularly important, as we shall argue in Chapter 6, for foresightedness with respect to climate change. In addition, the EU has adopted specific procedures in the form of *ex ante* assessment tools to anticipate the impacts of other policies, plans and projects, and in many countries (such as the UK, Netherlands and Australia) the procedures of environmental impact assessment fall within the spatial planning function (Glasson *et al.*, 2005), providing a significant opportunity within spatial planning for anticipatory integrated assessment of policies and actions for climate change mitigation and adaptation to aim for synergies and avoid conflicts.

Nevertheless, we recognize that such integration is not easy and that there are many barriers to it. We therefore briefly review the argument for policy integration, and some of the barriers to achieving it. Further chapters in Part III examine in detail some of the opportunities and barriers in substantive sectors and spatial areas.

2.4.2 Explanations for lack of integration of mitigation and adaptation

This chapter has shown that there are concerns about the risks of maladaptation and increased costs or vulnerabilities to climate change through policies and measures for mitigation and adaptation being developed separately. Nevertheless, it is clear that, over the recent historical period within which governments and institutions have been attempting to address the issue of climate change, initially the focus was on mitigation measures, and that the two responses have developed differently in their epistemologies and institutions. Biesbroek *et al.* (2009) suggest some of the reasons for this. They argue that part of the explanation lies in the different areas of technical expertise: focusing on the 'different ways in which knowledge is produced' (p. 231), they suggest that the IPCC was initially dominated by climate modellers, employing and generating complex and specialist scientific knowledge of the drivers and sources of anthropogenic climate change. It was therefore inclined to frame mitigation syntheses for policymakers in terms of these sectoral drivers, with responses framed as technological or fiscal measures targeted at those sectors. Adaptation responses, on the other hand, have required a more cross-disciplinary approach, recognizing the socio-economic context and a wider set of actors at different scales, consistent with broader sustainability objectives. Biesbroek *et al.* (2009) suggest furthermore that there are different timescales of action, with (at least in the early part of climate policy development) mitigation actions being adopted as proactive, short-term actions to produce long-term outcomes, whereas adaptation was more reactive. Moreover, mitigation and adaptation have been addressed at different scales of government and governance, and by different types of stakeholders, with mitigation actions requiring essentially international and national level action in negotiating and reaching binding agreements. On the other hand, they argue, adaptation has been seen as requiring more locally focused action, as the impacts of climate change are experienced locally. They also suggest that there are differences in the ability to monitor and measure the outcomes of mitigation and adaptation actions, and to assign costs and liabilities, and that the already-complex institutional structures of policy and cross-sectoral integration have struggled to take on the further complexity of integrated climate change responses.

Another reason for the apparent dichotomy might be the reluctance of governments to acknowledge that their efforts of negotiation and commitments were not likely to deliver sufficient, and sufficiently timely, reductions in carbon emissions, given the time-lags in the carbon cycle, to avoid inevitable changes. Pielke *et al.* (2007) refer to 'lifting the taboo' on adaptation, a taboo reflecting fears that adaptation is seen as an ethical compromise which might even promote acceptance of activities generating further carbon emissions.

2.4.3 Expectations of integration through spatial planning

We argue in Chapter 5 that this conception of local and short-term adaptation is only partially true, with many examples of national-scale adaptation actions and local mitigation actions – but it has undoubtedly been a dominant conception amongst some of the climate change policy community. Biesbroek *et al.* (2009) acknowledge that now there is a paradigm shift in many of the propositions explaining the dichotomy, with greater cross-disciplinarity in knowledge, understanding and institutional responses, and a greater acceptance that mitigation and adaptation do not divide neatly along governance or administrative boundaries. Spatial planning, in its coordination of spatial and sectoral dimensions, has an important role in reducing this dichotomy. For instance, in the UK, the 2004 guidance on *The Planning Response to Climate Change* specifically included policies and implementation tools at local, national and regional scales for mitigation and adaptation (ODPM *et al.*, 2004), and in the US, Saavedra and Budd (2009) analyse some examples of municipal initiatives in addressing both mitigation and adaptation. Biesbroek *et al.* (2009) suggest that planning at the river basin management level has particular capacity to provide some of this climate response integration.

While integration sounds a noble objective, and is a key element of spatial planning, it is worth rehearsing and reviewing some of the reasons for this. Integration is particularly argued for in environmental policy, with the underlying assumption that the environment is indivisible and interconnected, possibly in ways we do not yet understand, and therefore addressing it as a discrete phenomenon risks ignoring this complexity. Reasons for integration include the perceived need to avoid the silos of inevitable departmental and decision-making structures – narrow remits adopted for reasons of manageability, for reasons of governance, or even for reasons of divide-and-rule, with budgets and power bases not so large as to challenge the centre. Integration should avoid the problem of externalities (costs or consequences being displaced to other sectors) and professional or departmental protectionism (Bryner, 2008), and can involve integration across policy domains, levels of government (vertical or horizontal) or governance (across stakeholders), and between policymaking and implementation or delivery (Scrase and Sheate, 2002).

Enjoining integration can risk becoming a mantra without serious attention to why we invoke it (Kidd, 2007) or much evidence of its efficacy: indeed, there is some evidence that integration at a superficial, policy level can obscure or even promote tactics of safeguarding narrower sectoral interests. There are two elements to integrating climate change into spatial planning: the integration of climate change into the sectors influenced by spatial planning, and the integration within spatial planning of mitigation and adaptation. Most economic sectors are influenced by non-climate drivers such as competition, market share and regulatory systems, and it has become increasingly clear that to achieve changes in production and consumption activities, climate change needs to be taken systematically into account. A useful review of the extent of this integration has been undertaken in the PEER project on climate policy integration, coherence and governance (Mickwitz et al., 2009). It found that, while climate change has become much more prominent in the countries they studied (Denmark, Finland, Germany, the Netherlands, Spain and the UK), with cabinet level and multi-departmental commitment, and is being reframed in terms of opportunities rather than just threats, its full integration needs to move beyond strategy commitments to specific policy areas and instruments across different levels of governance, and greater evaluation of, and learning from, policy outcomes. They cite the UK Climate Change Act 2008 as an example of more formal requirements for budgeting and reporting (we provide more information in Chapter 3, Section 3.4.3). The study makes the point that, while climate policy is now commonly integrated into spatial planning, more attention needs to be paid to outcomes. They found significant differences between countries, with the Netherlands (as we show in Chapters 3, 4 and 10) adopting new policies for water and flood management, in contrast with Germany where adaptation to climate change has not been a major concern in flood management.

For the second aspect of integration, the PEER study found that implementation within spatial planning was difficult: 'the capacities to respond are frequently shrinking because of the rigidity of administrative and political borders, the stability of departmentalism, and the strength of sectional interests and preference for small-scale solutions' (Mickwitz et al., 2009, p. 60). Even those countries such as the UK which have sought innovative structures separate out responsibilities. Responsibility for domestic adaptation lies with Defra (the Department for the Environment, Food and Rural Affairs), whilst international climate change policy, including mitigation and adaptation, is the responsibility of DECC (the Department for Energy and Climate Change); spatial planning is the responsibility of DCLG (Department for Communities and Local Government) and transport that of DfT (Department for Transport). The UKCIP, established in 1997 to promote a stakeholder-led adaptation capacity (West and Gawith, 2005), takes the view that national policy frameworks are not yet sufficiently developed to integrate adaptation and mitigation actions.

But it is important to recognize the conflicts that can occur in responding to mitigation and adaptation. Swart and Raes (2007) argue that, while for many sectors the potential of direct and indirect synergies in mitigation and adaptation is low, some sectors (such as land use, urban and spatial planning, agriculture, forestry and water) are important for both mitigation and adaptation, and there are opportunities for synergies and trade-offs. If they are not assessed together, trade-offs can be obscured, synergies lost and resources competed for unnecessarily (Tol, 2005). Some of the synergies in these sectors identified by Swart and Raes are shown in Table 2.2.

In spatial planning, specific examples include the possible tension between the need for urban regeneration for social, economic and environmental reasons, maximizing use of sustainable transport access as a mitigation measure, with the need to adapt to climate change by avoiding exacerbating flood risk. Hamin and Gurran (2009) illustrate some of these conflicts in their review of US and Australian case studies, where a substantial proportion of the planning actions could lead to significant conflicts between adaptation and mitigation. More examples are given throughout this book, and in Chapter 14 we indicate ways in which spatial planning can minimize these conflicts. As we saw in Chapter 1, the sustainable development 'lens' of spatial planning requires express attention to the interactions of economic, social and environmental dimensions of climate change, and it is in this light that we argue for their joint assessment. Given the likelihood that climate impacts will fall disproportionately on the most vulnerable in society, a sustainability perspective reinforces Swart and Raes's (2007) point about the need to build adaptive capacity without increasing those groups' vulnerability.

We acknowledge that spatial planning is not the whole answer – we discuss more fully in subsequent chapters the other powerful policy interventions (such as economic and fiscal policy) with and within which spatial planning operates. But we argue that, despite such reservations, it is important to integrate mitigation and adaptation, and that spatial planning has a role in doing this. An additional reason for not keeping them separate is that spatial planning needs to engage the public in participating in planning decision-making, and the general public is a vital player in addressing climate change, but is unlikely to be familiar with the climate change policy community's distinct terminology of mitigation and adaptation.

Whereas the UK Climate Change Act 2008 (HMG, 2008a) lays down separate reporting requirements for adaptation and mitigation, government policy for planning explicitly promotes the integration of the two: for instance, the PPS1 Supplement (the principal planning guidance on climate change for England) states that 'mitigation and adaptation should not be considered independently of each other, and new development should be planned with both in mind' (DCLG, 2007a, para. 10). Moreover, the Planning Act 2008 requires regional and local development plans to include policies to contribute to climate change mitigation and adaptation (HMG, 2008b, sections 181, 182). However, these policy requirements do not suggest how this integration might be achieved. It is our hope that this book, although not a 'how to' manual, will provide some

Table 2.2 Examples of synergies and trade-offs between direct adaptive and mitigative responses to climate change

Mitigation / Adaptation	Actions decreasing GHG emissions, enhancing sinks, protecting carbon stocks	Actions enhancing GHG emissions, reducing sinks, destroying carbon stocks
Actions decreasing exposure and sensitivity (vulnerability) to climate change	*Synergies (also contributing to wider sustainable development goals)* • Increase energy efficiency/reduce energy dependency • Increase water use efficiency/reduce water consumption • Protect soils, plant trees, develop agro-forestry (carbon storage) • Improve forest fire management • Produce crops matching local climate and local needs • Improve health through clean energy with less pollution • Enhance ecosystem resilience by reduced air pollution • Design urban areas with high levels of protection, high density and low energy use • Expand parks and other green spaces in/around cities • Design appropriate building codes/standards (climate-resistant and energy-efficient, e.g. natural ventilation or renewable energy for cooling)	*Trade-offs of adaptation ('adaptive emissions')* • Use fossil-based electricity for air conditioning, cooling of buildings and water supply (e.g. desalinization) • Strengthen coastal protection infrastructure (energy use) • Expand fossil-fuel-energized irrigation of lands • Adapt temperate farmers competing with tropical farmers • Expand crop area/number of annual crops to capture benefits of warming in relevant areas • Include mitigation in development aid or research programmes at expense of adaptation
Actions increasing exposure and sensitivity (vulnerability) to climate change	*Trade-offs of mitigation ('new vulnerabilities')* • Building low-emissions facilities (e.g. renewable/nuclear power plants) in vulnerable areas • Implement mitigation policies with costs that affect income of the vulnerable poor • Establish large-scale biofuel production driving locals to vulnerable areas • Include adaptation in development aid or research at expense of mitigation	*Actions contributing to unsustainable development* • Destroy forests, emitting carbon and increasing vulnerability to drought • Develop urban areas in low-lying areas with little natural cooling or long travel distances, and high vulnerability to flooding

Source: Swart and Raes, 2007 p. 298

suggestions in this respect. We point here to some of the principal tools and techniques which we explore in more detail later.

2.5 Integrating mitigation and adaptation (approaches and tools for spatial planning)

A number of tools exist that can be used by spatial planners to help integrate climate change considerations into spatial planning. Here we discuss briefly one important tool – climate risk assessment – and the ecosystems approach. Both are key elements in anticipatory environmental assessment in spatial planning, and are discussed at greater length, with appropriate case studies, elsewhere: environmental assessment and risk assessment in Chapters 7 and 14, and the ecosystems approach in Chapter 12. Although we present them here as tools and approaches that might require expert technical inputs, we strongly believe that the response to climate change requires the full engagement of the public and civil society: such tools can be used in community visioning and futures thinking, using public or vernacular knowledge and learning from experience. These aspects are discussed further in Chapters 6 and 13.

2.5.1 Risk assessment

The nature of risk

Schneider *et al.* (2007, p. 781) define risk associated with climate change as a concept which 'combines the magnitude of the impact with the probability of its occurrence, [and] captures uncertainty in the underlying processes of climate change, exposure, impacts and adaptation'. The risk triangle, as discussed by Crichton (2001, p. 17), sees risk as a space defined by exposure, hazard and vulnerability; Figure 2.4a illustrates this. As any of the three components/sides is reduced, the extent of risk declines towards zero. An alternative view of risk is that used by UKCIP in Willows and Connell (2003), which sees risk as determined by probability of hazard and magnitude of consequence (or impact) (shown in Figure 2.4b).

Other characteristics of risk have also been recognized, some more relevant to disaster or extreme events than to gradual change (Box 2.3).

Amongst the characteristics listed in Box 2.3, is outrage, which is relevant to decision-making. These authors (Geoscience Australia, 2008) note that outrage becomes particularly evident after a disaster, as a community expresses its outrage at what it believes to have been an inadequate response or lack of preparedness on behalf of the authorities. As a result, time is spent addressing community outrage rather than community safety (p. 38).

Outrage has been expressed, for example, following severe flooding in the UK.

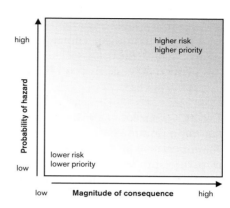

Figure 2.4

Two concepts of risk, hazard and vulnerability
Source: (a) Crichton, 2001. Fig. 2.4b; (b) Willows and Connell, 2003, p. 44

Box 2.3 Characteristics of risk

- frequency of the hazard;
- its seriousness or relative impact (in physical, social or economic terms);
- how manageable is the hazard and how effectively and conveniently the affected community can be dealt with (e.g. through warnings and emergency management plans);
- awareness within the community of the risks;
- urgency, or how critical it is to address the risk and implement mitigation measures;
- growth: the potential or rate at which the risk will increase (perhaps resulting from development or population growth); and
- outrage: the political dimension of risk.

Source: adapted from Geoscience Australia, 2008

International policy

The IPCC, in its Fourth Assessment Report,
key vulnerabilities (Schneider *et al.*, 2007, ch
studies as a tool in climate adaptation. These

- Given the uncertainties in factors suc
  climate change, vulnerability to climate
  likelihood of bringing such capacity to k

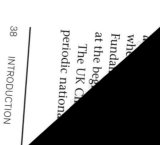

emerges as a useful framework to address key vulnerabilities. However, the assignment of probabilities to specific key impacts is often very difficult, due to the large uncertainties involved.

- Actions to mitigate climate change and reduce greenhouse gas emissions will reduce the risk associated with most key vulnerabilities. Postponement of such actions, in contrast, generally increases risks. (Schneider *et al.*, 2007, p. 782).

The IPCC concept of a risk management framework has been taken up by the European Commission. The 2009 EC White Paper *Adapting to Climate Change: Towards a European Framework for Action* (CEC, 2009a), in its section 5 (Working in partnership with the member states), states that to support cooperation on adaptation and with a view to taking forward its framework for action, the Commission intends to set up an Impact and Adaptation Steering Group (IASG). Together with other work, 'The Steering Group will provide a coordinated approach to building the evidence base on the impact of climate change, assessing the risks of climate change for the EU, the scope for increasing climate resilience and costing risks and opportunities' (p. 14). The European Directive on the assessment and management of flood risk (2007/60/EC) provides for a preliminary flood-risk assessment process to be undertaken for each river basin district or unit of management, by December 2011. This Directive notes that various human activities, together with climate change, 'contribute to an increase in the likelihood and adverse impacts of flood events' (CEC, 2007a; see also this volume, Chapter 11, Section 11.4).

Risk assessment guidance

The UK Climate Impacts Programme (UKCIP) was established in 1997 to help coordinate UK scientific research into the impacts of climate change, and to help organizations adapt to unavoidable impacts (West and Gawith, 2005). As the need for guidance on risk assessment became apparent, UKCIP was commissioned to work with others to produce guidance, eventually published as *Climate Adaptation: Risk, Uncertainty and Decision-Making* (Willows and Connell, 2003). This report defines risk assessment as 'the process, by which hazards and consequences are identified, characterized as to their probability and magnitude, and their significance assessed'. Willows and Connell distinguish between *climate adaptation decisions*, where climate change is a key element; *climate-influenced decisions*, where it is of low to moderate importance, and *adaptation constraining decisions* (called maladaptations in IPCC literature) where a decision has the capacity to constrain future adaptation approaches. mental concepts of the risk assessment process are defined in the glossary inning of this book, based on the UKCIP terminology.

imate Change Act of 2008 (see Chapter 3, Section 3.4.2) calls for l risk assessment: paragraph 56 of the Act states that it is the 'duty of the Secretary of State to lay reports before Parliament containing an assessment of the risks for the United Kingdom of the current and predicted impact of climate change'. The first Climate Change Risk Assessment (CCRA) report is to be presented in 2011 and thereafter at five-yearly intervals. This CCRA will inform assessments of hazards, vulnerabilities and exposures at regional and eventually at local level (see Chapter 3, Section 3.4.1 for further details). Whereas probabilities have been well known for some areas of hazard under conditions of climate change (such as slope collapse or flooding), past confidence levels may be inappropriate and new probabilities must be ascertained. For example, work by Reynard *et al.* (2007) has considered changes to flood risk in the UK under climate change; they have concluded that 'there is no clear message about the size, or even the direction of change in flood flow magnitudes in the UK. Changes in flood flows are catchment-specific, being driven by hydrological variability, such as geology, and the seasonal distribution of rainfall' (p. 299). Other uncertainties surround the choice of which Global Climate Model is used to derive scenarios of change, as well as how coarse-resolution climate changes (from global climate models) may be downscaled to the catchment level; there is also uncertainty associated with hydrological modelling. Flood-risk assessment is discussed further in Chapter 11, Section 11.4.

Figure 2.5 illustrates the iterative process recommended by UKCIP for risk assessment (Willows and Connell, 2003, p. 7), with stages of problem identification and objective setting, selection of criteria, risk assessment and options appraisal, leading to implementation and monitoring. This approach, UKCIP's Adaptation Wizard, is designed for businesses, local authorities or other decision-makers (UKCIP, 2008a. The guidance lists questions to be addressed at each of the six principal stages. The sequence matches the SA and SEA tools used during plan-formulation (see Chapter 7, Section 7.3). Brookes (2009) has discussed the 'cross-fertilization' of EIA and environmental risk assessment, though without touching on climate change. The figure illustrated in Figure 2.5 was also included in the UK Government's 2004 advice on the planning response to climate change, where the advice was to consider both consequences and probabilities of particular events: 'For instance, the consequences of flooding are well known. Hence the outcomes of an increase in flood frequency and magnitude can be determined with considerable confidence even if the probability of such an event is itself very uncertain' (ODPM *et al.*, 2004, p. 20). The guidance recommended seeking no-regrets and low-regrets outcomes, distinguishing between climate and other factors influencing plans, putting in place specific climate adaptation planning policies, and avoiding climate-adaptation constraining policies. Further approaches to risk assessment for spatial planning are discussed in Defra (2002) and in ESPACE project documents (ESPACE, 2008a).

A later publication by UKCIP (Johnstone *et al.*, 2009) suggests it is useful to distinguish between vulnerability, resilience and adaptive capacity (with a distinction between actions that build adaptive capacity and those that deliver

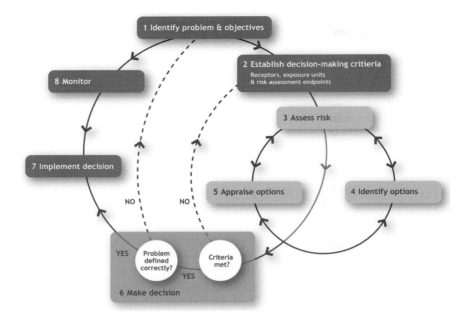

Figure 2.5

UKCIP Risk, uncertainty and decision-making framework
Source: Willows and Connell, 2003, p. 7

adaptation actions: spatial planning has an important role in both). Box 2.4 explains these concepts: while the guidance publication was intended for organizations and businesses generally, the concepts are useful ones for spatial planning. The guide also makes the point that we should aim for adapting well as opposed to aiming to be well adapted, as climate change is essentially dynamic, and the process of adapting should be continuous.

Work by Greiving *et al.* (2006a) has compared three methodologies of risk assessment leading to mapping of multiple hazards, including some associated with changing climates. Techniques include the Total Place Vulnerability Index and the Natural Hazard Index for Megacities. These authors propose an integrated risk assessment methodology for multiple hazards for spatial planning as they see this as indispensable to addressing responsibilities for a particular geographical area. They note that 'All approaches struggle with a lack of data on hazards and vulnerability and exhibit (in some cases comparable) methodological problems' (p. 17). Other research by Greiving *et al.* (2006b) explored the relationship between spatial planning and risk assessment in connection with disaster risk in eight EU member states (including the UK) and found that the role that might be played by spatial planning in risk assessment and management had been overstated. This position may now be changing. In the UK, risk assessment in connection with climate change is most common with

Box 2.4 Concepts in adaptive capacity

Vulnerability is defined by the IPCC as 'the degree to which a system is susceptible to, and unable to cope with, the adverse effects of climate change'.

Resilience is the capacity of a system to continue to function in the face of change or to transform an existing system. Adaptation can be seen as the process of improving resilience to climate change.

Adaptive capacity is defined by IPCC as 'the ability of a system to adjust to climate change (including climate variability and extremes), to moderate potential damages, to take advantage of opportunities, or to cope with the consequences'. This capacity depends on resources and institutional frameworks. Much adaptation aims to build adaptive capacity.

Building adaptive capacity means putting in place all the support systems and legislative and policy frameworks which will encourage, allow or require organizations to deliver adaptation actions.

Delivering adaptation action involves putting in place physical or managerial arrangements that respond to opportunities or threats presented by the changing climate.

Source: adapted from Johnstone *et al.*, 2009

respect to flood risk (see Chapter 11, Section 11.4). For example, at regional level in the Regional Strategy for South East England (the South East Plan, GOSE, 2009), Policy NRM4 is concerned with sustainable flood-risk management. This policy responds to PPS25 (on Development and Flood Risk), which calls for iteration between the different levels of flood-risk assessment and for climate change impacts to be taken into account, as well as outlining a flood-risk vulnerability classification for receptors such as transport infrastructure, hospitals and schools, residential care homes, etc. The PPS25 classification has four classes: essential infrastructure, highly vulnerable, more vulnerable and less vulnerable receptors. Chapter 11, Section 11.4 provides further discussion of flood-risk assessment as an example of risk assessment. The South East Plan also refers to 'risk' in connection with climate change, but this is adaptation to unquantified risks, and not risk-based assessment.

Lindley *et al.* (2007) have undertaken work on risk in the built environment under the ASCCUE project. Lindley *et al.* (2007) use an 'explicitly spatial' methodology, representing each of these three components of risk as individual data map layers and using Geographical Information System (GIS) overlay analysis and case studies in Manchester and Lewes. An urban system layer represented urban morphology types with similar biophysical properties (e.g. high, medium and low residential density, town centre, etc.). This approach was used to represent risk of heat stress in the 2050s experienced by vulnerable groups (such fours and the over seventy-fives). They compared, using a set of mptions, the increase or decrease in risk under the four UKCIP mic scenarios (World Markets, Global Responsibility, National 1d Local Stewardship – explained in Chapter 6, Section 6.6). The irios provide a means of exploring alternative potential development paths and consequent climate change impacts. In the ASCCUE analysis, increases in vulnerability resulting from, say, deprivation, are balanced against density of vulnerable populations at increased levels of exposure (indicated by maximum August temperatures). In the worked example, the Local Stewardship scenario was associated with lower vulnerability, as the scenario assumes relatively low increases in emissions and, *inter alia*, an increase in greenspace from derelict land and warehouse areas, as well as maintained protection of flood plain open space. These measures help balance any tendency towards an increased heat island effect. The researchers stress that the value of the analysis is that it indicates where elements of a scenario may help to reduce exposure and vulnerability successfully.

2.5.2 Ecosystems approach and ecosystem services approach

Two other related approaches have important potential within spatial planning for integrating climate change mitigation and adaptation, and in achieving sustainable development. The ecosystems approach recognizes the need to manage land and water for multiple purposes in order to respond to human needs. This approach, finding ecological solutions and innovation, involves seeking non-technological routes to resolving problems. Managed realignment (setting back sea walls and restoring intertidal habitats to provide natural flood protection, with other advantages) is often given as an example of this. Another approach is increasing green infrastructure as a means to multiple benefits (moderated temperatures, biodiversity connectivity, aesthetic and property values) in higher-quality urban areas (Natural England, 2009a, p. 16). Its current promotion through spatial planning is discussed in detail in Chapter 9.9.

Natural England (2009b), in discussing the ecosystems approach (p. 25), suggests that such solutions 'can be very beneficial – delivering very favourable benefit-cost ratios over a relatively short period of time (25 years in some cases)'. This inclusion of economic costs and benefits is usually known as the ecosystem services approach.

The Millennium Ecosystem Assessment (WRI, 2005) outlined four types of ecosystem services: provisioning (e.g. food and water), regulatory (flood and disease control), supporting (e.g. nutrient cycling to maintain the conditions for life) and cultural services (e.g. spiritual and recreational). The concept that ecosystems provide services that are essential for human well-being is long-standing; attempting a valuation of the benefits derived from those services has been seen as a route to better understanding their importance and also of improving protection. Egoh *et al.* (2007) provide a review of assessments in specific environments. In 2007 the TEEB study (The Economics of Ecosystems and Biodiversity) was initiated by the EC, and an interim report presented in 2008 (Sukdev, 2008). The purpose of the TEEB study is to evaluate the costs of the loss of biodiversity and the associated decline in ecosystem services worldwide, and compare these costs with those of effective conservation and sustainable use. It is hoped that this should lead to better recognition of the value of biodiversity and ecosystem services, with the subsequent development of more cost-effective policy responses. A 'valuation toolkit' is also to be developed.

Whilst there has been controversy amongst conservation planners and scientists about the wisdom of adducing economic values to ecosystem services (hedonic pricing methods proposed in the 1990s), the 'cost of loss' approach seems likely to give a more holistic account of their value, and is perhaps more widely supported (Tew, 2009). An example of the approach for supporting decision-making on coastal realignment can be found in Luisetti *et al.* (2008) where the ecosystem services approach was used to provide a framework for the cost-benefit analysis of multifunctional coastal schemes in the Blackwater estuary (Essex, UK). Using this method, a wide range of welfare impacts (such as carbon storage, fish nurseries, and recreation and amenity) could be considered on a common monetary scale.

Integration of ecosystem services valuation into spatial planning could take place via EIA or SEA, but it will clearly call for new skills amongst both assessors and planners. We explore these questions further in Parts III and IV.

2.6 Conclusions: mitigation and adaptation working together

There are circumstances where pursuing a mitigation agenda can interact positively with adaptation efforts, to produce synergies for climate change response. There may, at the same time, be 'co-benefits' for other aspects of the environment or human quality of life. On the other hand, adverse impacts may be incurred if proposals for, say, options for technologies or locations are not adequately assessed. Potential for maladaptation or increased vulnerability may arise where institutions and their knowledge bases differ, or where technical expertise is not shared. A cross-disciplinary approach, awareness of the socio-economic context, involvement of all relevant stakeholders and consideration of multiple timescales and cross-boundary effects are all elements of an effective approach to integration of mitigation and adaptation. In order to achieve this, the discipline and practice of spatial planning can deploy tools such as impact assessment, climate risk assessment, futures thinking and the ecosystem approach, always within the perspective of sustainability.

3 International, European and national policy frameworks

··

3.1 Introduction

In 1979 a first World Climate Conference organized by the World Meteorological Organization (WMO) acknowledged that human activity could lead to 'significant extended regional and even global changes of climate'. By 1985 research into emissions and likely impacts was presented at a joint conference in Villach, Austria, on the 'Assessment of the Role of Carbon Dioxide and of Other Greenhouse Gases in Climate Variations and Associated Impacts' (WMO, 1986). Also in 1985, a paper in *Nature* (Farman *et al.*, 1985) alerted policymakers to a different but related problem, the existence of an ozone hole in Antarctica, with potential adverse impacts for human health and the environment. Growing international concern and understanding of what the implications of these changes and impacts might mean led to the drafting of the *Montreal Protocol on Substances that Deplete the Ozone Layer* (1987). This Protocol was designed to control the emission to atmosphere of an array of ozone-depleting substances (including halogenated hydrocarbons or chlorofluorcarbons – CFCs) which were seen as causing the opening up of the Antarctic ozone hole and, subsequently, another over the Arctic Ocean. The process of negotiation and signing of the Montreal Protocol (1987–90 from opening for signature to entering into force) was an important example for subsequent global policy development concerned with protection of the atmosphere (Oberthür and Ott, 1999). Ozone-depleting substances are also greenhouse gases, contributing to climate change.

The process of building policy frameworks to address climate change has gathered pace since the 1980s, internationally, nationally and locally, with differing time horizons. The focus of climate policy has evolved over time; whereas initially it was predominantly linked with energy policy, it has now come to 'have a large interface with sustainable development' (Klein, 2006). (In Chapter 1, we explained that this is the approach taken in this book.) The early link to energy policy derived from the perceived importance of emissions reduction, as energy generation is a major source. Continuing evolution of this policy field has led to increasing emphasis on adaptation to climate change, but adaptation, suggests Klein (2006), had earlier been considered a 'politically incorrect' approach (as discussed in Chapter 2, Section 2.4). The role of carbon sequestration in 'carbon sinks', such as forests, soils, peatlands and oceans, has been the subject of increasing research from the 1990s. Other concepts coming more recently to the fore in policy are *building resilience* and *mainstreaming*, i.e. integrating policies and measures to address climate change into the planning and management of other sectors (transport, health, etc.).

In this chapter, we set out in some detail the policy frameworks as they provide such an important context for the spatial planning response to climate change, in addressing actions to mitigate and adapt to climate change, in extending planning horizons in time and space, and in changing governance relationships, as internationally agreed targets are cascaded down from national to regional and local planning levels. The influence and implications of the frameworks are explored in Parts II and III. Here, we describe briefly the principal international climate change policy development institutions, the UN Framework Convention on Climate Change, and the Kyoto Protocol (Section 3.2), then consider the EU framework building process (Section 3.3) and evolving national and regional policy (Section 3.4).

3.2 United Nations Framework Convention on Climate Change

3.2.1 Introduction

The UN Framework Convention on Climate Change (UNFCCC) was drafted and adopted in May 1992, then signed by more than 150 nations attending the 1992 Earth Summit in Rio de Janeiro. The Framework's principal objective is the 'stabilisation of greenhouse gas concentrations in the atmosphere at a level that would prevent dangerous anthropogenic interference with the climate system' (UN 1992). (Some greenhouse gases occur in nature, others are exclusively human-made and these are covered by the Montreal Protocol – see Section 3.1). The UNFCCC entered into force in 1994, leading in 1997 to the adoption of the Kyoto Protocol. A timeline of significant policy-related events is shown as Figure 3.1.

Climate change is a 'global commons' issue, an example of Hardin's (1968) 'tragedy of the commons' hypothesis, where individuals who benefit from a shared property resource such as either a pasture or the atmosphere, can act as 'free riders' on the efforts of others, making it difficult to ensure all parties contribute fairly to mutual benefit. Past emissions have largely been generated

International institutions and events – regular font; European action – *italics*

Year	Events, reports and actions
1979	First 'World Climate Conference', organized by the WMO, expressed concern that 'continued expansion of man's activities on earth may cause significant extended regional and even global changes of climate'.
1985	UNEP/WMO/ICSU Conference (Villach, Austria) on the 'Assessment of the Role of Carbon Dioxide and of Other Greenhouse Gases in Climate Variations and Associated Impacts' Ozone hole identified by British Antarctic Survey (Farmer *et al.*, 1985)
1987	Montreal Protocol opened for signature
1988	WMO and UNEP established the Intergovernmental Panel on Climate Change (IPCC) in 1988
1989	Montreal Protocol entered into force, 1 January (subsequently revised periodically)
1990	Montreal Protocol First IPCC Assessment Report (subsequently abbreviated as FAR)
1991	*First European Community strategy to limit carbon dioxide (CO_2) emissions and improve energy efficiency*
1992	United Nations Framework Convention on Climate Change (UNFCCC) adopted in May in New York and signed in Rio at Earth summit IPCC Supplementary Reports (energy, six IS92 scenarios of climate change, forestry, sea-level rise, vulnerability, etc.)
1994	UNFCCC entered into force in March IPCC Special Report Radiative forcing of climate change
1995	First Conference of the Parties to the UNFCCC (COP-1) met in February in Berlin, and laid foundations for the Kyoto Protocol Second IPCC Assessment Report (abbreviated as SAR)
1997	Adoption of the Kyoto Protocol
2000	*First European Climate Change Programme (2000–2004) launched*
2001	COP-7 Marrakech Accords, resolving many remaining Kyoto issues and leading to faster ratification Third IPCC Assessment Report (abbreviated as TAR)
2002	*EC ratifies Kyoto Protocol in May*
2004	COP-10 Buenos Aires. Programme of work on adaptation and response measures
2005	Kyoto Protocol entered into force in February. Three mechanisms proposed: Emissions trading; clean development mechanism (CDM); and joint implementation (JI) *Second European Climate Change Programme (ECCP II) launched*

Year	Events, reports and actions
2006	CDM (Clean Development Mechanism, within Kyoto Protocol), operational
2007	COP-13 Bali. Bali Road Map and Action Plan: enhanced action on adaptation Fourth IPCC Assessment Report (AR4) *Upgraded EU commitment: independent 20% reduction; 30% reduction if others also commit to higher reduction levels*
2008	COP-14 Poznan. Kyoto Protocol's Adaptation Fund. Progress on issues affecting developing countries: adaptation; finance; technology; reducing emissions from deforestation and forest degradation (REDD); and disaster management
2009	*EU White Paper 'Adapting to climate change'* COP-15 Copenhagen

Forthcoming dates:

2010	COP-16 Mexico
2012	End of first commitment period of Kyoto Protocol and year by which a new international framework will need to have been negotiated and ratified
2014	Fifth IPCC Assessment report (AR5)
2050	Projected recovery of ozone layer, *provided that* Montreal Protocol is adhered to
??	Stabilization of atmospheric composition, given current policy

Figure 3.1

Timeline of significant events in climate change policy development

by the developed countries (as explained in Chapter 1, Section 1.2.3), but the effects of climate change and the consequences of any responses are unevenly distributed within and between nations. (The implications of this are explored further in Chapter 6.) For this reason, a good deal of the international level of policymaking has been concerned with the impacts of both climate change and policy responses to it upon developing countries.

The evidence background for the UNFCCC is provided from many national and international sources, but principally by the Intergovernmental Panel of Climate Change (IPCC), established in 1988 by the United Nations Environment Programme (UNEP) and the World Meteorological Organization (WMO). UN General Assembly Resolution 43/53 of 6 December 1988 listed as the first tasks of the IPCC: the preparation of a comprehensive review and recommendations with respect to the state of knowledge of the science of climate change; studies of the social and economic impact of climate change, and recommendations on possible response strategies and elements for inclusion in a possible future international convention on climate (UN, 1988).

3.2.2 Kyoto Protocol

The Kyoto Protocol is a legally binding international treaty under which the major industrialized countries will reduce their collective emissions of greenhouse gases by 5.2 per cent compared with the year 1990 (but note that, compared with the emissions levels that would be expected by 2010 without the Protocol, this target represents a 29 per cent cut). The goal is to lower overall emissions from six greenhouse gases, calculated as an average over the five-year period of 2008–12. National targets were negotiated on the basis of national levels of development and other characteristics and so vary, ranging from 8 per cent reductions for the European Union and some others to 6 per cent for Japan, 0 per cent for Russia, and permitted increases of 8 per cent for Australia and 10 per cent for Iceland. The USA target was set at 7 per cent but the USA then withdrew from the Kyoto Protocol in 2001.

By signing this Protocol countries *commit* to their specified emission reduction targets (under Article 3), whereas under the Convention (in force from 1994) they were merely *encouraged* to make the reductions. The text of the Kyoto Protocol was adopted at the third session of the Conference of the Parties (COP 3) in Kyoto, Japan, in December 1997. The Kyoto Protocol came into force in 2005. Subsequently, individual nations and blocs, in the light of continuing emerging information on climate change impacts, have made new and more stringent commitments.

The measures by which each signatory country is to achieve its emissions limitation and reduction commitment are outlined in Article 2 of the Kyoto Protocol as: control of emissions; protection and enhancement of carbon sinks and reservoirs (e.g. forests are specified); sustainable forms of agriculture; research on forms of renewable energy and of sequestration technologies as well as 'environmentally sound' technologies; increases in energy efficiency and removal of 'market imperfections' such as fiscal incentives and subsidies that promote emissions; and sectoral reforms to limit emissions (specifying the transport, waste management and energy sectors) (UN, 1998).

Under Article 10 of the Kyoto Protocol signatories agree to 'Formulate, implement, publish and regularly update national and, where appropriate, regional programmes containing measures to mitigate climate change and measures to facilitate adequate adaptation to climate change'. The programmes would cover sectors such as energy, transport and industry, agriculture and waste management. This text also recognizes the role of spatial planning, stating: 'Furthermore, adaptation technologies and methods for improving spatial planning would improve adaptation to climate change' (UN, 1998, p. 9).

The Parties to the Convention and Protocol are classified into three main groups: Annex I (industrialized countries including specified Economies in

Transition), Annex II countries (OECD countries from Annex I but excluding the Economies in Transition (EIT) countries) and non-Annex I countries (generally the developing countries); this last group includes Brazil and China. By mid-January 2009, 183 countries plus the European Community had ratified or otherwise accepted the Protocol. This meant that 63.7 per cent of Annex I Parties' emissions were included, so preset conditions for the Protocol to become valid were met.

3.2.3 Kyoto mechanisms

Three interlocking mechanisms form the basis for achieving the targets of the Kyoto Protocol in a cost-effective manner, as outlined below.

Emissions trading (ETS): Article 17 of the Protocol sees greenhouse gas emission reductions or removals as a 'new commodity' to be exchanged in the market. It allows countries that have not reached their emissions limit to sell this excess 'capacity' to countries that exceed their targets. This is referred to as trading in carbon on the 'carbon market'.

Joint implementation (JI): An investing country (typically, developed) invests funds in clean technology or emissions-reducing activities in a 'host' (typically, developing) country, because a higher return on investment can be achieved there in terms of emissions reduction. Each emission reduction unit (ERU) is equivalent to one tonne of CO_2 and counts towards the emissions reduction target of the investing country (Article 6 of the Protocol).

The *Clean Development Mechanism* (CDM) (Article 12 of the Protocol): An industrialized country needing to cut its emissions 'transfers' this reduction to another country – typically, a developing country – promoting sustainable development there and providing a certified emission reduction (CER) to the industrialized country. An example might be a rural electrification project using solar panels. Another approach to offsetting and trading is the removal unit (RMU), which is based on land use, land-use change and forestry (LULUCF) activities such as reforestation. Mitigation achieved in these ways is seen as relatively cost-effective, though the resulting carbon stocks are not permanent (for example, when forest fires release carbon). Moreover, the stocks may be affected by environmental change including climate change. A further mechanism, Reducing Emissions from Deforestation and Forest Degradation (REDD), is not yet incorporated into the UNFCCC framework, but this was approved at the 2009 G8 meeting in L'Aquila and 'the immediate establishment' of a REDD-plus mechanism was supported by Article 6 of the Copenhagen Accord (UNFCCC, 2009, Decision -/CP.15), though this is not a legally binding agreement.

The negotiations over the adoption and effectiveness of these measures have been highly contentious: besides the complexity of the negotiations and bargaining over the Protocol, between and amongst countries, a number of interests have argued against the principles and the details of Kyoto (such as Lomborg, 2007). Sunstein (2007) has pointed to the related challenges facing international agreements to reduce risks. Nations appear to gain from cooperative action (such as technological innovation, intergenerational equity and development of poor nations). Nevertheless, whereas the Montreal Protocol has proved to be successful, in 2007 Sunstein suggested that the Kyoto Protocol seemed to have 'failed', stating: 'the benefits of the [Montreal Protocol] were anticipated to be substantial in the short-term and long-term while [those of the Kyoto Protocol] were perceived to be zero in the short-term and modest in the long-term' (p. 64). Sunstein attributes this difference partly to the 'radically different self-interested judgements of the United States' as well as to the 'pay-off structures' of the two agreements. The United States had signed the Protocol in November 1998 and then withdrew from it in March 2001. A change of policy was signalled by President Obama in November 2008, as evidenced by the USA contribution to COP-15 in Copenhagen in December 2009.

3.2.4 International funding for climate change responses

A UNFCCC technical paper (2008) has reported on investment and financial flows to address climate change. With regard to mitigation spending, estimates of cost are relatively precise: it is suggested that additional investment and financial flows of US$200–210 billion would be necessary to reduce CO_2-eq emissions by 25 per cent below 2000 levels in 2030 (UNFCCC, 2008). For adaptation measures, financing and investment requirements are less precise, estimated to be 'tens of billions, possibly hundreds of billions of US dollars per year'. A significant share of this will be needed in developing countries and the UNFCCC proposes that developed countries should take a lead in combating climate change and should determine how they can help developing countries. Parry *et al.* (2009) have subsequently suggested that the real costs of adaptation are likely to be much greater than estimates made by the UNFCCC, as sectors such as ecosystems, energy, manufacturing and tourism had not been included in the earlier analysis, others had been only partially included, and additional costs of adaptation had sometimes been calculated as 'climate mark-ups' against low levels of assumed investment (Parry *et al.*, 2009, p. 7). They conclude that

> for coastal protection the factor of under-estimation could be 2 to 3. For infrastructure it may be several times higher, at the lower end of the cost range. For health the 'intervention sets' that were costed relate to a disease burden that is approximately 30–50% of the anticipated total burden in low- and middle-income countries (and do not include interventions in high-income countries). Including ecosystems protection could add a further $65–$300 billion per year in costs. Furthermore, estimates are not made for sectors such as mining and manufacturing, energy, the retail and financial sectors and tourism.
>
> (Parry *et al.*, 2009, p. 17)

At the UNFCCC COP-15 meeting in Copenhagen a fund of US$100 billion to support climate protection policy in developing countries was proposed. Although this was eventually not agreed, an accord was reached which it is hoped will lay the basis for future financing (Box 3.1).

3.2.5 Requirements for action and reporting

Membership of the UNFCCC requires signatories to launch national strategies for addressing greenhouse gas emissions and adapting to expected impacts, including the provision of financial and technological support to developing countries. By committing to the UNFCCC, countries undertake to report on progress to the Conference of the Parties (COP). Report contents depend on status (Annex I or Annex II countries). All signatory countries must provide information annually on emissions and removals of greenhouse gases and details of the activities they have undertaken to implement the Convention. These national communications also usually contain information on national circumstances, vulnerability assessment, financial resources and transfer of technology, along with education, training and public awareness. Annex I countries' national communications, submitted at specified dates, additionally contain information on policies and measures. For Annex II countries, submission dates are not fixed, though a time limit is given. (A set of forty-eight Least Developed Countries are also funded to prepare National Adaptation Programmes of Action, or NAPAs, in order to focus on enhancing their adaptive capacity to climate variability.)

3.3 European climate change action

3.3.1 ECCP I (Mitigation)

Within the European Union the process of introducing action on climate change was also aimed at first mitigating climate change by reducing emissions, with adaptation to change incorporated later. Recognizing that action by both member states and the European Community needed strengthening to reach the Kyoto Protocol target, a further programme of priority actions and policy measures was launched in 2000 as Phase I of a European Climate Change Programme (ECCP), covering the years 2000–04. Stakeholders working towards this ECCP I included representatives from the Commission's different Directorates General (DGs), plus the member states, industry and environmental groups. ECCP I focused in particular on renewable energy and energy demand management. Working groups were established to explore the three UNFCCC flexible mechanisms (ETS, CDM and JI) as well as energy efficiency and supply and demand; transport, agriculture, industry, etc., and also forest-related 'carbon sinks'. Directives as well as measures and policies have been put in place, such as Directive 2009/29/EC on the EU Emissions Trading system (CEC, 2009b), Directive 2000/28/EC on Renewable Energy Sources (CEC, 2009d), and Directive 2009/31/EC on the geological storage of carbon dioxide (CEC, 2009e).

3.3.2 ECCP II (Adaptation)

ECCP II, launched in 2005, set out to explore further cost-effective options for reducing greenhouse gas emissions in synergy with the EU's 'Lisbon Strategy' of 2000, for increasing economic growth and job creation. New working groups were set up, covering carbon capture and geological storage, CO_2 emissions from light-duty vehicles, emissions from aviation, and adaptation to the effects of climate change. ECCP II is distinct from ECCP I, however, in that it recognizes the urgency and importance of adaptation to climate change, and that decisions about adaptation policy require assessments of risk and of costs and benefits; moreover, it recognizes that measures need to be taken at different levels (international, national, regional and local). At the same time, ECCP II recognizes that action taken now could adversely affect future climate resilience in the EU, and that such maladaptation is to be avoided. Examples of mal-adaptation, as described in Chapter 2, range from using air conditioning (and so, increasing emissions) to planned development policies and measures that, despite delivering short-term gains or economic benefits, actually exacerbate vulnerability in the medium to long term.

ECCP II working groups (WGs) have reported on impacts affecting sectors and assets (such as water and marine resources, human health; agriculture, forestry, biodiversity and tourism; regional and urban planning, built environment, public and energy infrastructure, structural funds, etc.) and reported on building national strategies for adaptation (country reports). These WG reports, published via the European Climate Change Programme website, summarize baselines across the EC, measures taken and ongoing research strategies, and (briefly) possible avenues in adaptation for the future. Research into adaptation and mitigation projects, and consultation exercises, have accompanied ECCP II.

The EU Climate Change Programme of 2006 indicated how CO_2 emissions will be cut across sectors, principally the energy sector (Table 3.1). The table demonstrates that many of these measures are either directly or indirectly influenced by the spatial planning process.

The current EU commitment is unilaterally to reduce EU-27 greenhouse gas emissions by at least 20 per cent by 2020 compared with 1990 levels; more-over, to reduce it by 30 per cent once other major emitters commit themselves to comparable emission reductions (CEC, 2008e). These levels of reduction were seen as consistent with staying below a 2°C rise in global temperature, a level identified as 'dangerous' (Anderson, 2009, p. 1) (see also Chapter 1, Section 1.2.4). Although the Copenhagen meeting (COP-15) did not see agreement on the higher levels of emission reductions, nevertheless the EU commitment still stands, as enunciated by EC President Barroso at the close of the meeting: 'the European Union remains ready and willing to move from a binding 20% reduction to 30% from 1990 to 2020 if others are also ready to move on ambitious deals' (Barroso, 2009).

3.3.3 EU White Paper on adaptation to climate change

The EC White Paper *Adapting to Climate Change: Towards a European Framework for Action* (CEC, 2009a) followed a Green Paper on this subject (CEC, 2007b) which had been consulted upon widely. A White Paper is a document con-taining proposals for Community action in a specific area, presenting detailed and closely argued policy for discussion and for decision. This EC White Paper presents the basis of the need for an adaptation strategy in terms of expected impacts, and the economic case for a strategic approach as consisting of the 'clear economic, environmental and social benefits' to be derived from anticipating impacts. At the same time, threats to ecosystems, human health, economy and infrastructure are to be minimized. The White Paper points to the need to take action at national, regional and local level in view of the regional

Table 3.1 Examples of ECCP emissions reduction measures relevant to the spatial planning system

Energy supply	To promote electricity produced from non-fossil renewable energy sources (such as wind, solar, geothermal, wave, tidal, hydroelectric, biomass, landfill gas, sewage treatment gas and biogas energies).
	• Indicative target of 21% in the share of EU gross electricity consumption to be reached by 2010 (currently: 14%).
	• Biofuels (liquid or gaseous fuels used for transport and produced from biomass). Indicative target: 5.75% in the share of fuels sold to be reached by 2010.
	• Cogeneration of heat and electricity (Directive 2004/8/EC).
	• Biomass Action Plan aims to more than double the use of biomass energy in the heating, electricity and transport sectors.
Energy demand	To improve the energy performance of buildings (Directive 2002/91/EC). Buildings account for around 40% of EU energy demand.
	• Minimum performance standards set for energy use by buildings (applicable from 2006); Energy Performance Certificates.
	• Promotion of end use efficiency and energy services (e.g. lighting equipment).
	• Action plan on energy efficiency (Green Paper on Energy Efficiency COM (2005) 265).
	• Inclusion of energy efficiency requirements in the permit system for industrial and agricultural installations.
	• Green Public Procurement considering energy efficiency.
	• Climate Change Awareness Campaign.
Transport	Emissions from transport account for 21% of the EU's greenhouse gas emissions (transport emissions rose by 22% between 1990 and 2002).
	• EU strategy to reduce CO_2 emissions from new passenger cars (voluntary commitments by international carmakers; information to consumers about fuel economy; proposal to base car taxation rates on CO_2 emissions to further influence consumer behaviour).
	• Shifting the balance between transport modes from road to rail and water.
	• Thematic strategy on the urban environment – related mainly to urban transport.

Source: CEC, 2006a

variability and severity of expected impacts, but emphasizes the role of the EU in supporting the necessary measures. The White Paper on adaptation notes the need to support adaptation in developing countries and refers to work through the Global Climate Change Alliance (GCCA) launched in 2008, by which means the EU will support developing countries and, in particular, the Least Developed Countries and Small Island Developing States. The principal action to be taken by the EU and member states is: 'To promote strategies which increase the resilience to climate change of health, property and the productive functions of land, *inter alia* by improving the management of water resources and ecosystems.' The White Paper identifies the areas of greatest risk:

- *regions*: (within Europe) Southern Europe, Mediterranean Basin, outermost regions and Arctic, mountain areas (especially the Alps), islands, coastal areas, urban areas, densely populated flood plains;
- *sectors*: agriculture, fisheries and aquaculture, buildings infrastructure, transport infrastructure, water resources and infrastructure, energy supply, human health, animal and plant health;
- *ecosystems*: coastal and marine ecosystems, forests;
- *ecosystem services*: carbon storage (peat, soils, forests), drinking water, food production. (CEC, 2009a)

Significantly, the White Paper highlights the importance of natural resources and ecosystems in responding to climate change: the response to their vulnerability and the need for protection are seen as a means to minimize the effects of change. The timetable of the White Paper is for a Phase I (2009–12) to build a solid knowledge base on impacts and consequences; to integrate adaptation into key EU policy areas/sectors (health and social policies; agriculture and forests; biodiversity, ecosystems and water; coastal and marine areas; production systems and physical infrastructure); to develop funding policy instruments for effective delivery of policy and avoid maladaptation; and to increase international cooperation on adaptation (partnership working). Phase II, from 2013, would implement the adaptation strategy.

Outlining impacts of climate change upon infrastructure, the White Paper (as noted in Chapter 1) identifies spatial planning as a route to adaptation: 'A more strategic and long-term approach to spatial planning will be necessary both on land and on marine areas, including transport, regional development, industry, tourism and energy policies' (p. 4). Past planning decisions are said to have 'rendered ecosystems and socio-economic systems more vulnerable to climate change and thus less capable of adapting' (p. 5). In discussing policy instruments, the White Paper focuses on instruments as a source of financing to fund adaptation, referring to the Stern Review (2007) as evidence of financing being a major barrier to adaptation. The better use of financial resources and instruments is seen as key to improved implementation of adaptation, while taking care to avoid maladaptation. The potential in the European Economic Recovery Plan of November 2008 (CEC, 2008c) to support climate change investments is noted. The fourth strategic aim of this recovery plan is to 'speed up the shift towards a low carbon economy', whilst the second 'pillar' of the plan consists of 'smart investment' (that is, investing in skills, energy efficiency and saving, clean technologies, infrastructure and interconnection). This plan covers the modernization of European infrastructure, improved energy efficiency within buildings, and a move towards 'green products', e.g. those meeting environmental performance requirements on energy or water use. The Adaptation White Paper highlights the use of market-based instruments and Payments for Ecosystem Services (PES). It is suggested that revenues generated via the EU Emissions Trading System (EU ETS) should be utilized to fund adaptation – a public–private sharing of adaptation costs. The White

Paper also states that external cooperation beyond the EU should contribute to promoting adaptation in partner countries, including by bilateral and regional financial assistance, again attempting to integrate climate change adaptation into all relevant/affected sectors. The EU has proposed a Framework for Action on Adaptation which would apply to the planned global agreement that will come into force from 2012 (i.e. after the end of the first commitment period of the Kyoto Protocol).

3.3.4 EU and member state competences

Climate change (together with the majority of policy areas) is an area of shared competence for the EU and member states: the Kyoto Protocol was concluded as a so-called mixed agreement. Behm (2008) indicates that some member states are calling for a stronger EC climate change policy, and there is the risk of creating competitive disadvantage where national measures to bring about emissions reduction differ from a European average. Behm notes that 'mixity' may lead to claims of failure to implement, but, on the other hand, it could also serve to reinforce a sense of individual (national) responsibility with respect to administration and policymaking. She suggests that the combination of shared competence and the member states' duty of cooperation provides space for research into and testing of the best instruments for climate change mitigation.

Spatial planning, in contrast, is an area within which the European Commission has no competence. Nevertheless, other areas in which the EC does have competence impinge upon spatial planning, and the European Spatial Development Perspective (see Box 3.2) is influential as a framework for balancing sustainable development across the EU territory.

There is a clear distinction between EU strategies, policy and legislation. Only directives require complete compliance, with their transposition into the domestic laws of each member state. European Union strategies, such as the ESDP, have no force of law and only gain authority as a result of common agreement on broad principles. Although it was approved by all EU member states as the framework for future planning in Europe, the ESDP notes that the EU does not have a land-use planning remit and that such matters must be dealt with on the principle of subsidiarity – the principle that policy, laws and regulations should be made at the most appropriate level of the Union; issues of only local importance should be legislated for at the local level. Whilst this position reduces the weight or importance of the ESDP as a policy instrument, as explained in Chapter 1, Section 1.3, the ESDP has been influential in reframing spatial planning, certainly within the UK, in shifting from a narrow land-use regulation to a broader, more spatial approach (Davoudi, 2009).

Faludi (2006) describes how the ESDP is aimed towards rectifying spatial imbalances in development; he sees the ESDP as an early version of territorial

Box 3.2 European Spatial Development Perspective (ESDP)

The ESDP (CEC, 1999) was developed to provide coherence and complementarity between the spatial development strategies of the Member States as well as addressing spatial planning aspects of EU policies. It provides a vision for the future territory of the EU. It is intended as a frame of reference for spatially effective measures and provides public and private decision-makers with a basis for policies and actions. It promotes the integration of different territorial structures and requirements of the EU into spatial policies as well as the coordination of different administrations – according to their respective competences – without impairing the diversity of the European territory.

The three objectives of the ESDP are: to promote a spatial dimension in Community and national policies; to improve knowledge and research on spatial development (e.g. via Interreg III); and to prepare for the enlargement of the European Union. Amongst other aims, the twelve-point ESDP action programme

- promotes a vision of polycentric and balanced spatial development;
- promotes competitive cities;
- acknowledges the need for 'wise management' of natural heritage; and
- acknowledges water resources as a special challenge.

The ESDP has had an influence on the structure and framing of regional and spatial planning in Europe. It currently fails to recognize climate change adaptation issues, whilst at the same time the EU Climate Change Programme currently fails to recognize the ESDP. There are at present no plans within the Commission to review or update the ESDP.

Source: adapted from Piper *et al.*, 2006, p. 50

cohesion policy which, under the 2004 proposed Constitution for Europe, would have been a shared competence of the EU and member states. Whilst territorial cohesion is not clearly defined, claims Faludi, it is said to complement 'the economic and social cohesion goal and harmonious and balanced development of the Union' (p. 669). Thus whilst it would not be significantly different from existing policies, territorial cohesion would focus on encouraging cooperation and networking, supporting the Lisbon Strategy aim of making Europe 'the most competitive area of sustainable growth' (Faludi, 2006). Zonneveld suggested in 2005 that spatial planning in Europe had 'reached new frontiers'. Despite having an informal, non-binding status, spatial planning was seen by Zonneveld as gradually entering the regulatory frameworks of the European Union (p. 137), as work proceeds at transnational level to define visions for larger areas, such as a Central European Space and North Sea region.

3.4 National policy frameworks

3.4.1 UK climate change strategies

The UK has taken the issue of climate change seriously at political levels and in developing a research and knowledge base. In 1989, the then UK prime minister, Margaret Thatcher, in speeches to the Royal Society and to the UN, called for international action to tackle climate change. Subsequently, research capacity was enhanced by the establishment of the Hadley and Tyndall Centres. UK government action on climate change, since signing the UNFCCC in the mid-1990s, has consisted of a number of programmes, measures and campaigns, culminating in the Climate Change Act 2008. Strategic approaches and commitments were set out in the UK Climate Change Programmes, published in 1996, 2000 and 2006. For instance, the 2000 programme (DETR, 2000a) committed the government to producing guidance on planning and climate change (of which a full account is given in Chapter 4). The Programmes focused primarily on mitigation (with measures introduced over time, ranging from raising building standards, increasing fuel costs to providing grants for home insulation, and support for action by regional, local and community-based organizations), but also acknowledged the necessity for adaptation. Climate change projections for 100 years (supported and disseminated from 1997 by the UK Climate Impacts Programme (UKCIP), as explained in Chapter 2) have played an important role in raising awareness of the impacts of climate change and hence the need for mitigation. The 2009 UK Climate Projections (known as UKCP09 – see Box 2.2 in Chapter 2) were published in 2009 and are designed to be used to guide responses by sectors, companies and government at all levels. UKCIP also provides research, policy guidance and a range of tools for adaptation, risk assessment, etc.

Government-backed campaigns include the Act On CO_2 initiative, which is working with businesses and individuals in order to reduce CO_2 emissions, and is supported by three relevant ministries (DECC, DfT and DCLG). The campaign provides web-based advice on reduction of individuals' and companies' carbon footprints. The most recent *UK National Strategy for Climate and Energy* (HMG, 2009a) sets out the government's Low Carbon Transition Plan in response to the requirements of the far-reaching Climate Change Act 2008.

3.4.2 UK climate change-related legislation

Important as strategies have been in coordinating and initiating action, a number of political groups and NGOs considered that progress to meet Kyoto targets and beyond was unlikely to be sufficient to prevent dangerous climate change, without a stronger, statutory foundation. The Big Ask campaign, initiated in 2005 by Friends of the Earth, with approximately 200,000 individual supporters, demanded legislation. The call was taken up by the Stop Climate

Chaos coalition: over two-thirds of MPs signed a petition for legislation, and a commitment was made in the Queen's Speech in November 2006. During the course of the campaign, the demands for an 80 per cent cut by 2050, five-year budgets, and the inclusion of aviation and shipping, were met and enacted in the Climate Change Act (for England, Wales and Northern Ireland) in November 2008. The Act was heralded as the world's first long-term legally binding framework for climate change. A Climate Change Bill for Scotland proposes a 42 per cent reduction in greenhouse gases by 2020 – an even more ambitious target. The Big Ask campaign has now extended to other European countries.

Legislation in 2008: Climate Change Act, Planning Act, Energy Act, and Planning and Energy Act

The public consultation document on the initial bill described the context of a warming climate system and the need for 'early and decisive action' to move towards a low-carbon economy 'over time'. The bill and subsequent Act are concerned very largely with mitigation responses, and to a lesser extent address adaptive responses. The UK-wide framework of the Act is chiefly intended:

- to establish an effective carbon management framework which is transparent and accountable;
- to establish a strong and independent Committee on Climate Change;
- to implement the Carbon Reduction Commitment and related measures to ensure impact upon emissions; and
- to adapt to the consequences of climate change via risk assessment and an adaptation programme.
- Other provisions in the Act relate to Community Energy Savings Programmes, waste, carrier bags, renewable transport fuel obligations, etc.

Section 56 of the Climate Change Act requires that a series of Climate Change Risk Assessments be carried out (incorporating the advice of the Committee on Climate Change). The first is to be presented within three years of the Act, followed by others at not more than five-year intervals. Programmes addressing the risks identified are to follow, and they must also conform to the requirements of sustainable development in their objectives, proposals and policies (section 58). Shortly after the establishment of the Committee on Climate Change, it set out the levels of the first three carbon budgets and recommended an emissions reduction path to 2022 (CCC, 2008). The government published policies and proposals to meet these first three carbon budgets through the 2009 Low Carbon Transition Plan (see Section 3.4.3). The Committee on Climate Change subsequently (in October 2009) published its first assessment of progress in *Meeting Carbon Budgets: The Need for a Step Change*; despite its title, this report argues strongly that, while the UK has ambitious policies, more drastic action is needed (CCC, 2009a). This has significant implications for spatial planning, discussed in Chapters 8 and 9.

Three other Acts, together with the Climate Change Act, form a 'package of action' to take forward the UK's transition to a low-carbon economy. The Energy Act of 2008 contains *inter alia* provisions relating to the generation of small-scale low-carbon electricity and the storage of carbon dioxide (e.g. in offshore sites). The 2008 Planning Act is concerned with the authorization of projects for the development of nationally significant infrastructure, including projects related to energy generation, and energy users such as transport (roads, airports, rail and ports); water; waste and wastewater treatment. (Chapters 4 and 5 provide a fuller analysis of the contentious genesis of the Act, and its implications for spatial planning for climate change.) The Planning Act also proposes the publication of national policy statements for specified 'descriptions of development' – taken to cover the infrastructure types mentioned above. National policy statements (NPSs) are to include an explanation of how the policy in question takes account of government policy relating to the mitigation of, and adaptation to, climate change (as an element towards achieving sustainable development). Moreover, this stipulation also applies to regional strategies and local plans (discussed further at Chapter 3.4.4). The final piece of legislation, the Planning and Energy Act, a private members' bill, gives further statutory support to allow local planning authorities to set targets in their area for on-site renewables, on-site low carbon electricity, and energy-efficiency standards.

3.4.3 UK Carbon Reduction Commitment and Low Carbon Transition Plan

Part 1 of the Climate Change Act deals with the carbon target and budgeting. A target is set for 2050 (i.e. beyond the current horizon of the Kyoto Protocol). This is: 'at least 80% lower than the 1990 baseline' (the baseline covers both carbon dioxide and other targeted greenhouse gases). To meet the target, five-year budgetary periods are established, starting with 2008–12, and in each of these a 'carbon budget' is to be set to ensure that the net UK carbon account for a budgetary period is not exceeded. By 2020 a reduction of 26 per cent of the 1990 baseline is to have been achieved. (Annual equivalents are to be used, i.e. an average of the five years in each budgetary period.) A consultation process and matters to be taken into account in connection with the setting of the budgets are also specified in the Act (e.g. evolving knowledge, available technology and circumstances at international and EU level). Arrangements for annual statements of UK emissions are detailed. Provision is also made for amendment of the target. The budgets recommended by the Committee on Climate Change were approved by Parliament in May 2009, including a target reduction of 34 per cent on 1990 levels by the 2020 period.

In order to achieve these budgets, the UK national strategy for climate and energy, published as *The UK Low Carbon Transition Plan*, sets out a five-point plan: protecting the public from immediate risk; preparing for the future; limiting the severity of future climate change through a new international climate agreement; building a low-carbon UK; and supporting individuals, communities and businesses to play their part (HMG, 2009a). The plan is intended to 'deliver cuts of 18% on 2008 levels by 2020', covering measures for government departments, targets for renewable electricity, building nuclear power stations, making homes 'greener' (with energy efficiency measures, smart meters, clean energy cash-back schemes, etc.), helping 'the most vulnerable' with price supports, and promoting green industry.

In view of the rate of emissions reduction set out in the Climate Change Act, it is useful to consider the rate of increase of emissions in the preceding years. Factors influencing emissions include population growth, economic growth and choices in power generation. In the period 1990 to 2008 the UK population increased by 6 per cent, with a further 27 per cent growth projected for 2050. GDP increased by 48 per cent; electricity use increased by 26 per cent, and transport energy use rose by 11 per cent (POST, 2008). The *Meeting Carbon Budgets* report from the Committee on Climate Change (CCC, 2009a) indicates that over the period 1990–2007 greenhouse gas emissions fell by 18 per cent, an average annual rate of 1.2 per cent, despite increasing energy demand in most sectors; the 13 per cent reduction in power sector emissions resulting from the replacement of coal with gas-fired power generation was significant in this. Emissions reductions have slowed to 0.95 per cent on average per year

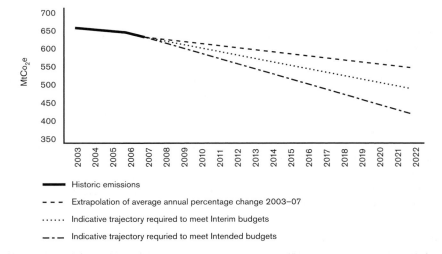

Figure 3.2

Recent UK GHG emissions and indicative reductions required to meet legislated carbon budgets
Source: CCC, 2009, p. 14

in the years 2003–07. The report notes that "given the relatively flat emissions trend in recent years, reduced potential for reductions from non-CO_2 and limited progress reducing emissions through implementation of measures [...] a fundamental step change is required in order that deep emissions cuts are achieved going forward" (CCC, 2009a, p. 40).

Figure 3.2 shows rates of UK greenhouse gas emissions since 2003, and indicates what future reductions are required to meet the legislated carbon budgets. Key sectors identified in *Meeting Carbon Budgets* to achieve these reductions are power, buildings and industry, and transport, and high-level policy options are proposed (CCC, 2009a).

For a number of reasons (discussed in Chapters 4, 5, 8 and 9), the UK has struggled to achieve its renewable energy targets, but a new Renewable Energy Strategy (HMG, 2009b) was published at the same time as the Low Carbon Transition Plan and underlines a commitment to a target of 15 per cent of energy consumption derived from renewable sources by 2020 (p. 80); this is an increase from 1.3 per cent in 2005. The commitment responds to EC Directive 2009/28/EC on renewable energy, which confirms a binding overall EU target of 20 per cent of energy consumption to come from renewable sources by 2020 (CEC, 2009d, para. 13).

3.4.4 UK national, regional and local planning policy frameworks

Planning Policy Statements

Planning Policy Statements (PPSs) are the means of communication for government planning policy, and cover topics including housing, biodiversity and geological conservation and sustainable waste management. PPSs are prepared by the government after public consultation; they explain statutory provisions and give guidance to local authorities and others on planning policy and the operation of the planning system. The PPS of particular relevance here is PPS1, *Delivering Sustainable Development* (ODPM, 2005a), and its supplement, *Planning and Climate Change* (DCLG, 2007a). PPS1 sets out six principles as a basis for ensuring that development plans and decisions taken on planning applications contribute to the delivery of sustainable development. These principles guide regional planning bodies and local planning authorities pursuing sustainable development in an integrated manner, in line with the UK Strategy on Sustainable Development (HMG, 2005). Moreover, they are designed to ensure that development plans contribute to global sustainability by addressing the causes and potential impacts of climate change (i.e. by reducing energy use and emissions, and developing renewable energy sources), whilst also taking climate change impacts into account with regard to the location and design of development. The third principle states that a spatial planning approach should be at the heart of planning for sustainable development – this entails a

Box 3.3 Decision-making principles for planning for climate change

Regional planning bodies and all planning authorities should apply the following principles in making decisions about their spatial strategies:

- the proposed provision for new development, its spatial distribution, location and design should be planned to limit carbon dioxide emissions;
- new development should be planned to make good use of opportunities for decentralized and renewable or low-carbon energy;
- new development should be planned to minimize future vulnerability in a changing climate;
- climate change considerations should be integrated into all spatial planning concerns;
- mitigation and adaptation should not be considered independently of each other, and new development should be planned with both in mind;
- sustainability appraisal (incorporating strategic environmental assessment) should be applied to shape planning strategies and policies that support the Key Planning Objectives; and
- appropriate indicators should be selected for monitoring and reporting on regional planning bodies' and planning authorities' annual monitoring reports. Such monitoring should be the basis on which regional planning bodies and planning authorities periodically review and roll forward their planning strategies.

Source: DCLG, 2007a, p. 10

clear vision and strategies for delivery, consideration of the needs and participation of communities, and the integration of a wide range of activities relating to development and regeneration, drawing on a robust evidence base and other plans (ODPM, 2005a). Other principles in the PPS relate to good design, inclusive access and community involvement.

Two years after the publication of PPS1, the supplement on planning for climate change (DCLG, 2007a) provided a set of 'decision-making principles' (see Box 3.3). (The complex story of the climate change supplement and its 2010 successor is described more fully in Chapter 4). The PPS supplement gave guidance on preparing regional spatial strategies, integrating climate change, managing performance and providing the evidence base. With regard to local development documents, the supplement provided guidance on the authority's core strategy, on the generation of renewable and low-carbon energy as well as decentralized energy for new development, and other local requirements for sustainable buildings. It advised on a set of considerations to be taken into account in the selection of land for development (potential contribution of low-carbon energy, transport links, the capacities of the range of types of physical infrastructure, the prospects for building and sustaining socially cohesive communities, impacts upon and response of biodiversity, etc.).

Chapter 4 gives an account of the campaign by the Planning and Climate

Change Coalition, led by Friends of the Earth and the Town and Country Planning Association (TCPA), to upgrade the policy framework, culminating in the publication in March 2010 of a consultation draft (DCLG, 2010a).

Regional and local requirements

The UK regions are required under the Planning Act 2008 (para. 181) to include in their Regional Spatial Strategies, 'policies designed to secure that the development and use of land in the region contribute to the mitigation of, and adaptation to, climate change'. Moreover, at the local level, the Act states: 'Development Plan Documents must (taken as a whole) include policies designed to secure that the development and use of land in the local planning authority's area contribute to the mitigation of, and adaptation to, climate change.' Further commentary on regional and local planning frameworks in connection with climate change is given in Part III (Chapters 8–12) for transport, built environment, water, flooding and biodiversity.

3.4.5 National climate change policy frameworks elsewhere

National policies on climate change are increasingly 'falling into line' as impacts of climate change are identified and threats become more widely acknowledged. Political change in government in at least two countries (USA and Australia) appears to have led to significant policy change. Whereas significant differences existed between countries at national level in the recent past, increasingly similar policy statements are being prepared at national level. 'Building resilience' and 'reducing vulnerability' are concepts that have emerged in policy fields in the early–mid-2000s and relate variously to communities, to buildings, to infrastructure and to habitats.

By 2010, national climate change policies are increasingly covering a common set of components (see Table 3.2), and are based on a set of climate change principles. For example, those of the EU Adaptation Green Paper (CEC, 2007a) were: Synergies, No regrets, Precautionary principle, Solidarity, Flexibility and subsidiarity, Knowledge-based, Proportionality, Sustainability.

Compston and Bailey (2008) have reviewed approaches taken across a group of 'affluent democracies', and identify a set of current political strategies now being pursued by these nations. These include attempting to reach global agreements including on reporting and targets, focusing on climate policies on which all major stakeholders can agree, advancing gradually and incrementally across many fronts with small-scale reforms, taking advantage of weather-related natural disasters to achieve consensus and action, and also framing climate policy in terms of other socio-economic objectives – to achieve co-benefits and wider support. For the future, Compston and Bailey suggest that further measures will include the closer adjustment of existing strategies

Table 3.2 Standard components of national climate change policy frameworks

Programme or policy on	Policy and measures for
Emissions reduction	Emissions reduction commitments; energy generation and supply; energy efficiency; renewable energy; transition to low-carbon economy
Adaptation	Climate change scenarios and mapping; resources identification and protection; housing and infrastructure; use of natural resources; health, planning, etc.
Mainstreaming	Inserting CC into range of policy sectors
Carbon capture and storage	Sinks: forests, peatland, soils; technology development
Building resilience/reducing vulnerability	Risk assessment; enhancing resilience
Cross-sectoral policy integration	Linking policy sectors with common programmes, indicators, timelines
Biodiversity and ecosystem services	Protection and enhancement; assessment of CC response
International obligations	Supporting developing countries
Budget and financial allocations	Supporting mitigation and adaptation; support for non-government initiatives (e.g. insurance)
Legislation, regulation, guidance	CC response across the board
Awareness, communications	Raising CC profile with officials, stakeholders, general public
Research and development	CC impacts by region, sector, etc.; models, methods, databases; technologies (energy generation and use, metering, etc.); changing behaviour
Monitoring	Emissions reduction, adaptation and all other programmes and policies

but also reform via new policies and governance, including increasingly radical policies that could target (or compensate) specific groups, or policies that can be applied more widely or that 'create pressure for their own strengthening' (2008, pp. 285–6).

Netherlands

Throughout this book, as explained in the Preface, particular attention is paid to the Netherlands. That country's approach to spatial planning for climate change is described more fully in Chapter 4, but here we outline the principal elements of national climate change strategy. The Netherlands provides regular reports under the UNFCCC reporting procedures, focusing principally on mitigation, but it has also committed significant resources to research and capacity building in adaptation. The Dutch government established the National Programme on Climate Adaptation and Spatial Planning (ARK) in 2007: under that programme, it produced a memorandum for policy discussion entitled *Make Room for the Climate!* (VROM *et al.*, 2007), followed by the national strategy which outlined the approach to climate-proofing the Netherlands. The work of the Delta Commission (2008) has taken further the national approach to climate-proofing. The government also established the Knowledge for Climate research programme in 2007.

3.5 Policy options for implementation

A set of implementation policy options was established as a framework in connection with the preparation of the EU's Climate Change Adaptation White Paper of April 2009 (CEC, 2009a). This array of options is also consistent with the Sixth Environmental Action Programme, which refers to horizontal integration measures as including EIA, SEA and Integrated Coastal Zone Management (ICZM), and vertical measures (that is, across levels of governance and within sectors). There may be some overlap between types: some actions could be described as falling into more than one of these categories. The characteristics of these policy options are shown in Table 3.3.

Table 3.3 Implementation policy options for climate change

Option	Characteristics/aims	Level (typically)
Regulation	Command and control – enforceable policy, widely applicable.	EU, national
MBIs and financial instruments	(Private sector involvement) Introduce measures and policies which preserve and extend choice, but direct choice towards 'desired' ends, working with the grain of the market. Includes fiscal and financial measures.	EU, national
Insurance	(Private sector involvement) Reduces risks associated with actions which are desired, e.g. 'biodiversity friendly' actions.	National
Soft options	(Potential NGO/civil society involvement) Provide guidance, support governance, raise awareness and skills.	EU, national, sub-national
Research and development	Identify models, methods and data which will improve effectiveness of future approaches.	International, EU, national

Whilst spatial planning corresponds most clearly to the 'Regulation' option, it is increasingly the case that it links, through partnerships and other measures, to other options to address climate change. For instance, planning bodies may play a role in identifying the spatial areas where financial instruments (such as habitat compensation payments) are applicable, or in finding ways of promoting green infrastructure (see Chapter 9.9). In Chapter 4 and throughout this book, we identify the partnerships and units set up to address climate change, employing examples from across the English regions (the North West, Yorkshire and Humber, West Midlands, East of England and the South East) and Scotland. Regional bodies and local planning authorities have become involved in research and development of specific approaches to address climate change: for instance, Hampshire County Council was a partner in the EU-funded ESPACE (European Spatial Planning Adapting to Climate Events) programme with, amongst others, the South East England Regional Assembly and Waterschap Rivierenland, a Netherlands water board. The ESPACE project was significant in demonstrating Europe-wide collaboration which has fed directly into regional and local spatial planning, including recommendations, case studies, and policy-guidance tools and mechanisms for integrating adaptation into planning. The project outputs from ESPACE can be found at www.espace-project.org.

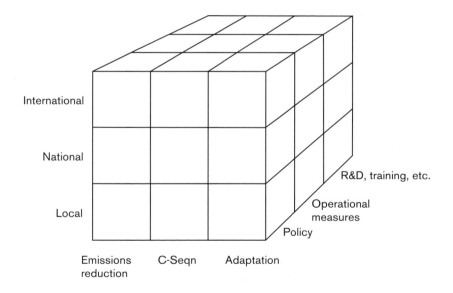

C-Seqn: Carbon sequestration
R&D: Research and development

Figure 3.3

Dimensions of action on climate change

3.6 Conclusions

This chapter has attempted to sketch the policy frameworks surrounding climate change work internationally and at EU and national levels. The global – and the 'global commons' – nature of this environmental, social and economic hazard demands action from many directions towards numerous goals. This action may be taken across all levels of the government and planning hierarchy (see Figure 3.3).

Aims and measures discussed within the various frameworks have been presented and some indication of the scope, advantages and disadvantages of different policy options has been discussed. What has been shown is that there is a good deal of activity within the climate change and spatial planning policy field, at many levels and pursuing different lines of approach. There seems to be no shortage of potential measures, of potential research topics, of proposed means of funding. Where political commitment is claimed but binding agreement cannot be reached, as happened at Copenhagen, the process inevitably loses credibility. Nevertheless, it is also true that slow progress is probably to be expected where there are multiple stakeholders and nations, and very many – and sometimes conflicting – views from experts.

As shown in Chapter 2, climate risk assessment should be undertaken in spatial planning, and the precautionary principle has a role here: there are circumstances where it is more appropriate to begin to take action rather than to wait for final and incontrovertible evidence. Many steps and measures put in place have the potential to make a contribution towards either mitigation or adaptation (or both). The position of climate change on the political agenda of all nations has changed unrecognizably over the past five years or so, and it is clear that policymakers now have a better understanding of the issues and are willing to take the actions that they can to address climate change. In Copenhagen in December 2009 there was little dissent about the problem or the necessary responses, though there was disagreement about burden-sharing and financial commitments. Some of the changes this growing consensus has wrought for the development of policy for spatial planning are discussed in Part II (Chapters 4–7). Part III (Chapters 8–12) then addresses interactions between spatial planning policy and sectoral practice. Part IV pulls together a number of issues: Chapter 13 explores social learning and the scope for other partners to become involved via community engagement; and Chapter 14 offers some principles for spatial planning to integrate climate change more fully into its decision-making.

Part II

Perspectives on spatial planning and climate change

4 Discourses of climate change and spatial planning

4.1 Introduction

Chapters 1 and 2 have shown the apparent legitimacy and reasonableness of the convergent calls for spatial planning to have a role in addressing climate change. But we must recognize that both planning and climate change are highly contested and complex labels, open to expression and framing by interests with divergent objectives and agendas. These interests are formed within a wider context (political, scientific and professional) and at different scales (global, national and local). The relationship of planning and climate change is relatively recent and uncharted territory, and it is worthwhile reflecting on its pattern of evolution in a number of different national contexts. The chapter focuses on the UK as an interesting example of the tensions between and within the climate change and spatial planning discourses, but also briefly provides a comparison with the contrasting developments in the Netherlands.

4.2 Discourse analysis

This chapter uses the perspective of discourse analysis as a loose framework to help with understanding some of these patterns. It can show insights into how actors and interests in policy formulation and implementation construct stories and meanings around problems. In a context such as that of climate change and spatial planning, there are many uncertainties around science, knowledge and conceptions of the public interest. Discourse analysis can be especially useful in pointing to the ways in which we conceptualize climate change as a problem and entertain possible solutions (Dryzek, 2005; Bryner, 2008). Dryzek argues that environmental issues are doubly complex, being at the intersection of ecosystems and human systems, both of which present a complex array of interconnected problems. He employs the notion of discourse, 'a shared way of apprehending the world' (2005, p. 9), to understand this variety of perspectives. Discourses rest on shared assumptions and language, and both reflect power and can be used to exercise or gain power. Dryzek analyses environmental discourses against four elements: the basic entities recognized or constructed within the discourse; the assumptions about natural relations; agents and their motives, and key metaphors or rhetorical devices employed (2005, p. 19). These criteria are useful for trying to understand and explain the climate change and spatial planning discourses (although we do not provide a systematic analysis against these criteria). As we have seen in Chapter 2, the different strategies for climate change mitigation and adaptation have employed different sets of knowledge, and different ways of framing the problem and hence solutions. These have generated different policy communities and networks of actors and stakeholders around climate change institutions and policy as described in Chapter 3. These groups can harness and disseminate certain discourses to mobilize support (Bryner, 2008). But these discourses also reflect their own view of the decision-making process and potential for action. For example, the discourses employed by the climate change policy communities indicate attitudes and beliefs about the scope for an incremental change or a more radical set of transformations.

Ecological modernization is an example of such a discourse. The thesis of ecological modernization represents a powerful set of assumptions about the ways of framing the problem of economic production within ecological limits and conceiving solutions within a paradigm of neoliberal economic restructuring (Hajer, 1995). For instance, it has been argued that ecological modernization can explain the way in which national interests in Australia have responded to the negotiations around the Kyoto Protocol in restructuring the national economy away from its current heavy dependence on fossil fuels (Currel, 2009)). In a very different political context, in the Netherlands, Smith and Kern (2007) suggest that the discourse of ecological modernization has particular appeal in resonating with the business and government storyline of innovation and efficiency in the energy sector. We can see that the ways in which climate change is framed as a problem, and the scope of possible solutions, relate strongly to other beliefs and value systems.

Climate change is therefore more than a physical phenomenon. Hulme (2009) argues that we need to see climate change as a 'kaleidoscopic' idea, a concept rooted in environmental, political and cultural terms, and a narrative that mobilizes 'very different sets of ideologies, meanings, values and goals' (p. 325). Indeed, he argues controversially that climate change is not even 'a problem that can be solved' in the same way as, for instance, the problems of ozone depletion were addressed. Rather, it is an 'idea of the imagination', which can be used to meet a range of objectives and fulfil a number of tasks (p. 341), particularly to 'rethink and renegotiate our wider social goals about how and why we live on this planet' (p. 361). The strength of this approach lies in the fact that action to address climate change is needed not just by government and business interests (as emphasized in the ecological modernization model), but by civil society and individuals.

These concepts of discourses and discourse coalitions have been familiar in the field of spatial planning, perhaps because of its more long-standing recognition of the importance of power. As a primarily state-led activity of regulation, planning has inevitably raised issues of legitimacy and the distribution of power (Forester, 1989; Flyvbjerg, 1998). In Europe, and particularly in the UK, the move towards spatial planning, with a more complex, intersectoral and integrated conception than that simply of land-use regulation, has extended the sphere of governance, encompassing a wider set of stakeholders. Nevertheless, questions of legitimacy and power remain. Rydin (2003) argues that discourse analysis offers a valid alternative to both the rationalist approach to legitimizing planning, and the more recent environmental governance approach. The rationalist ideal, still a powerful model, employs concepts of expert assessment, objective knowledge, the public interest and due process, to legitimize interventions which may ignore or disguise uneven distributions of power. Claims to rationality can therefore themselves be seen as socially constructed, expressing particular values, assumptions about norms and ways of framing knowledge, problems and possible solutions. Explicit acknowledgement of this potential for bias has led to calls for greater transparency, inclusion of a wider set of stakeholders and more attention to deliberative processes (Healey, 1997). But, as Rydin argues, the commitment to reach consensus through deliberative processes may ignore real and messy conflicts: consensus ideals themselves are socially constructed. Rydin therefore suggests that analysis of the discourse of these claims to legitimizing planning is useful in critically assessing the claims and own styles of presentation. Partly drawing on Dryzek's framework, she argues that three dimensions of analysis are needed: the context within which language is used and patterned; the use of the policy process and other arenas to communicate; and the active use of language through discursive strategies. She employed the approach specifically to examine the discourses and rhetoric around the concept of sustainable development.

This chapter takes these three dimensions to explore the evolution of the relationship between spatial planning as a form of intervention in the public interest, and the more recent discourse networks around the idea of climate change. It first reviews the discourses in the UK, and then examines the differing experiences in the Netherlands.

4.3 The United Kingdom

4.3.1 The planning response to climate change

The UK has a long tradition of climate change science and research, and has also paid attention to the relationship of spatial planning and climate change for over ten years. In this, it differs from experience in other countries, where it seems the relationship is only recently being explored (Biesbroek *et al.*, 2009). As explained in Chapter 3, the UK government has for some time taken the issue of climate change seriously, as evidenced by Mrs Thatcher's speech to the Royal Society in 1988, and the founding of the Hadley Centre for climate change research in 1990. The first national report for the UK under the UNFCCC was submitted in 1994. Consistent with its commitment to firm science and evidence-based policy, the government established the UK Climate Impacts Programme (UKCIP) in 1997, and created a Global Atmosphere Division within the environment ministry.

The UK therefore had a strong institutional and scientific base for both international policymaking and domestic response in both mitigation and adaptation. Government had already commissioned a report (ERM, 2000) that had pointed to the role that spatial planning could play in adapting to climate change. It had concluded that 'there is a need to make planning for climate change impacts more explicit in guidance documents; raise awareness of those undertaking other strategic planning exercises; [and] improve tools and information for those responsible for implementation of climate-sensitive day to day planning decisions' (ERM, 2000, p. 142). The UK government accordingly commissioned a project to research the responses of planning to climate change, and to make recommendations for good practice. The Climate Change Programme of 2000 (DETR, 2000a) was able to state that work had already begun 'on a best practice guide to help those involved in land use planning focus on its role in responding to climate change'. But the process of issuing such guidance revealed a conflict between different discourses of the planning and climate change policy communities. The divergence of views was exacerbated by the UK's simultaneous devolution agenda, and by exogenous events such as the serious floods of autumn 2000 and more 'wild card' events such as the outbreak of foot-and-mouth disease (Wilson, 2006a). Three years elapsed between the drafting and the final publication of the guidance (ODPM *et al.*, 2004). The delay can be explained partly in terms of these exogenous events diverting policymaking attention from the wider issue of climate change, and partly by the different and competing discourses of the climate change policy community – committed to urgent and firm action for both mitigation and adaptation – and the opposing and contrasting discourses within the spatial planning community itself. The research amongst planning practitioners had shown their desire for a firm commitment from central government that climate change was a 'material consideration' for planning. In other words, local authority and other practitioners required explicit confirmation that it was a legitimate concern that would be supported by central government in its scrutiny and approval processes of regional and local policymaking, and in decisions on specific developments. This included especially any challenges that might be made by proponents of development in the exercise of their right of appeal to the central government.

This was a discourse of legitimation: clear and explicit guidance in the form of national statements of policy was needed from the centre to legitimize the status of climate change as a material consideration. But the discourse also reflected the institutional structure of centralized decision-making and the relative weakness of regional and local tiers. This structure became more pronounced during the first ten years of New Labour from 1997 (Marshall, 2009a). We show in Chapter 5, Section 6.4 that not all practitioners at subnational level took this view of the relative incapacity of local government (Wilson, 2007). But, for the most part, the discourse of practitioners came up against the strongly held and prevalent discourse of the New Labour administration that there were already enough, if not too many, statements of national planning policy. Already in 2004 there were twenty-five guidance notes on planning policy, the latest that on development and flood risk (DETR, 2001). This flood-risk policy had been adopted quite rapidly in response to the floods in 2000. But such explicit policy advice was at odds with the prevailing belief that planning interventions should be light touch, flexible and enabling, rather than prescriptive, command-and-control injunctions. *The Planning Response to Climate Change* (ODPM *et al.*, 2004) was therefore published as a practitioner advice document, rather than as a statement of policy.

The advice set out the urgency of climate change mitigation and adaptation, recommending five key principles (Box 4.1):

Box 4.1 Key principles in planning for climate change

Key principles:

- Act now
- Make the links (for win–win solutions)
- Spread the word (an important function of spatial planning in its relations with politicians and the public)
- Make the best use of existing tools (such as EIA)
- Make the best use of existing instruments such as planning agreements

Source: adapted from ODPM *et al.*, 2004

The document addressed the ten topics shown in Box 4.2, and cross-cutting issues such as assessment including sustainability and environmental appraisal at plan, project and building level, and implementation.

The publication gave examples of some developing good practice, and listed the appropriate national statements of policy guidance, such as (for England) those on flood risk, renewable energy and coastal planning, and their equivalents for Scotland and Wales. It stated clearly that climate change was a material consideration in planning – and pointed out that Scotland and Wales, with their newly devolved powers and hence newly formulated policies, did have the policy and legislative framework to support this. For instance, the national planning framework for Scotland stated firmly that 'it is essential that the implications of climate change are factored into the decision-making process'

Box 4.2 Topics in planning for climate change

- Infrastructure
- Flooding
- Coasts
- Water resources
- Biodiversity, land and landscape
- Economic development and tourism
- Transport
- Waste and resources
- Energy systems
- Built environment

Source: ODPM *et al.*, 2004

(Scottish Executive, 2004a, para. 55). In Wales, the national spatial plan stated that response to climate change was one of the principal spatial challenges (Welsh Assembly Government, 2004). It is worth noting that the discourse of national plan-making has not been favoured within England: such a national spatial plan has never been adopted for England, despite some lobbying by professional planning groups and others, although the idea has been revived with the new system of national policy statements (discussed further in Chapter 5). Both in Edinburgh and Cardiff, new coalitions of interests were able to take on the issue of planning for climate change with much less controversy than in England. This may be because of their smaller policy communities, with closer interrelationships between policymakers, academics and practitioners at local level. Partly for these reasons, there was not the antagonism between the central and local government that has been evident in England (Peel and Lloyd, 2009; Tewdwr-Jones and Allmendinger, 2006). Within Whitehall, however, there was evident concern that practice advice should not be taken as promulgating policy, or as anything that could be construed as a policy statement: such statements needed to be made by ministers and reported to Parliament.

The central government planning ministry, which had commissioned the planning response study, therefore adopted a cautious position, but this generated conflict with the very different discourse of the sounding board established for the project (Wilson, 2006a). This comprised representatives from other government departments (such as Defra), non-departmental public bodies such as the Environment Agency and UKCIP, environmental NGOs such as RSPB, Friends of the Earth and National Trust, and the Association of British Insurers (ABI) as representative of the financial services sector. (In Britain, the onus of responsibility for flood protection and hence insurance lies with householders, and hence the insurance industry has been active in agenda-setting and policymaking on the spatial planning responses to climate change through its knowledge of the consequences of flood risk: it has entered into agreements with government to continue to provide insurance cover, provided the government adopts certain flood-risk policies and commits funds to flood protection.) All these organizations were active in promoting the vital importance of the role of planning in responding to climate change, and argued for a much clearer and firmer statement of policy from government. The ABI, for instance, had published a series of reports and position statements (such as ABI, 2002) urging stronger planning policies in areas of flood risk. The NGOs were also able to adopt a common position through their engagement in a number of networks and coalitions, such as the Wildlife and Countryside Link. The diverse groups were therefore able to use the formal policy process and informal networking to share and communicate their normative position, and achieved some success.

4.3.2 Reluctant prescriptions

Despite its initial reluctance to add to policy, the ODPM became persuaded to make clear that climate change was a material consideration. In the foreword to the advice publication it stated that 'It is the intention to remove any remaining ambiguity on this matter when PPG1 General Policy and Principles is revised' (ODPM *et al.*, 2004, p. 8). A draft of this had been published early in 2004, but it did not accord climate change any priority as an issue, and the advice for the role of planning was minimalist (ODPM, 2004a). Some of the climate change policy networks, including the regionally based climate change partnerships (such as that for the South East – see Section 4.3.3), argued that the government's continued commitment to the discourse of flexibility, minimalist intervention and voluntarism was not adequate to the challenge of climate change. The PPS1 as eventually published did give it more prominence, making climate change its second key principle (ODPM, 2005a). But the issue continued to present major problems for the government during the latter part of the decade in relation to its overt commitment to a conception of the national interest construed as a leader in global finance and capital. This required, as we shall see in the following chapter, both neoliberal approaches to deregulation and also the reframing of the spatial planning system to service these interests.

4.3.3 Discourse coalitions and networks

While central government was fending off calls for more prescriptive policy statements, other discourse networks were forming which ultimately led to a change of stance through a remarkable association between the government and one particular discourse, that of the Town and Country Planning Association's conception of sustainable communities (discussed further below). We have already suggested that, in Scotland and Wales, such networks developed their own discourses. At the regional level in England, another network comprised the regional climate change partnerships, encouraged and supported as stakeholder-led networks by the UKCIP (West and Gawith, 2005). Established as 'bottom-up' partnerships, they nevertheless in some cases worked cooperatively across regions, and in some areas had quite close relationships with elements of central government. The three regional partnerships for the area loosely called the 'Greater South East' (that is, the regions of London, the South East and the East of England) were particularly concerned at the lack of government advice specifically on adaptation to climate change. Following stakeholder-led regional studies on the possible impacts of climate change for the South East (Wade *et al.*, 1999) and London (LCCP, 2002), the three regions together commissioned and published a series of more detailed advice documents for planning (Box 4.3).

Box 4.3 Three Regions Climate Change Partnership publications

- *Adapting to Climate Change: A Checklist for Development. Guidance on Designing Developments for a Changing Climate* (LCCP et al., 2005)
- *Adapting to Climate Change: A Case Study Companion to the Checklist for Development* (LCCP et al., 2007)
- *Adapting to Climate Change: Lessons for London* (LCCP, 2006)
- *Adapting to Climate Change Impacts: A Good Practice Guide for Sustainable Communities* (LCCP et al., 2006)
- *Your Home in a Changing Climate: Retrofitting Existing Homes for Climate Change Impacts. Report for Policy-makers* (Three Regions Climate Change Group, 2008)

The contents comprised checklists, case studies, comparisons with other cities' and countries' experiences of climate change adaptation, recommendations for the Sustainable Communities Plan growth areas, and advice on adaptation in existing buildings. They reflect the changing focus over the decade from new development, especially that proposed in the government's growth areas identified in the government's Sustainable Communities Plan of 2003, to a greater attention to existing urban areas and buildings. These publications were disseminated through a series of high-profile events, such as the launch of the growth areas guidance by the then Mayor of London at a Thames Gateway Forum in November 2006. In these three regions, the initiatives therefore had political support at that time, particularly through the role of Ken Livingstone as Mayor of London, a strong advocate of local and global action to respond to climate change. (The London Mayor possesses more strategic spatial planning powers than any other planning authority in the UK.) Moreover, in London and in East of England, the regional government offices (with some staff having moved from working in climate change policy issues in central government departments) played a significant role in commissioning and aiding publication. There was also an exchange of personnel between government offices and the regional partnerships.

The outcome of these networks' political processes was a significant raising of the profile of climate change within regional spatial plans, particularly within London, and a discourse of practical implementation and innovation within an active planning and development process. The partnerships were also engaged with research and European networks (such as in London on the topic of urban heat island) (see Chapter 9.6.2), and in the South East with the EU-funded ESPACE and BRANCH projects (see Chapter 3, Section 3.5). At the local level, other networks comprised members of ICLEI (Local Governments for Sustainability), the signatories to the Nottingham Declaration, and participants in European-funded projects under the INTERREG programmes. As we shall see in Chapters 5 and 13, these all generated considerable policy innovation for both adaptation and mitigation at regional and local levels.

But perhaps one of the most significant discourse networks has been the convergence of the discourses of the Town and Country Planning Association (TCPA), and to a lesser extent, Friends of the Earth (FoE), with central government. The engagement of the FoE with such discourse coalitions to influence government directly is consistent with its highly successful Big Ask campaign (see Chapter 3) which led to the 2008 Climate Change Act. At an event in early 2006, at which TCPA launched their own advice on planning for energy (TCPA, 2006a), ministers of state from both Defra and the ODPM were invited to set out ministerial positions on planning and climate change. Baroness Andrews, from ODPM, initially maintained the minimalist approach: she argued that 'regional planning bodies and local authorities do not have to wait for more guidance from government in order to put this issue higher up the agenda. They need to listen and to learn from what's already happening around them in developments such as the Nottingham Declaration and the initiatives of authorities such as the London Borough of Merton' (Andrews, 2006). (The reference to Merton as good practice supported by government could be construed as somewhat ironic, as we shall see in Chapter 5.) But she also acknowledged that something further was needed, and invited comments on three possible alternative strategies: a new, free-standing PPS; a shorter ministerial statement expressly endorsing the current PPS1; or an update of the 2004 practice guidance. During the course of 2006, the government reached a compromise solution, drafting policy specifically on climate change to be adopted as a supplement to the principal planning policy statement, PPS1. But TCPA and FoE were not content with the progress in implementing this compromise option. They took the view that the PPS1 of 2005 still gave far too little express attention to what the government itself had identified at the Gleneagles G8 Summit as the most serious issue for international attention. In particular, they were concerned that any statement coming from government would be too late for the round of regional spatial strategies and local development frameworks being prepared under the 2004 Planning Act. Accordingly, at the round of party conferences in 2006, TCPA and FoE launched a mock planning policy statement ('PPS26') on planning and climate change (TCPA and FoE, 2006). In the mock PPS, they set out what they saw as the essential sequence of addressing climate change in planning through baseline assessment (for instance, of carbon emissions and vulnerability to climate change), option appraisal, target-setting, monitoring and review.

But, despite their efforts, when the government's first draft of the PPS1 supplement was issued (DCLG, 2006a), it was criticized for its feebleness. It demonstrated the continuing caution and timidity of central government's conception of spatial planning. We need to ask why this was so. One possible explanation lies in the dominance of the Treasury's view of planning at this time. In the early part of the first decade of this century, at the start of New Labour's second term of office, the government had published its Sustainable Communities Strategy, setting challenging housing targets for the regions to deliver in newly designated growth areas (ODPM, 2003), shown in Figure 4.1. The additional houses were needed to provide more affordable housing, to meet people's aspirations for home ownership and to ease labour mobility. This was accompanied by a critique that 'too often planning is reactive and defensive' (ODPM, 2002, p. 2). New Labour had set out to modernize local government and local planning, and introduce a new tier of regional planning, with a greater focus on strategic, spatial planning, more participation and engagement with other local agencies. The new system was given legislative effect through the 2004 Planning and Compulsory Purchase Act. But, despite this, there was criticism that the planning system was failing to provide sufficient houses. The Treasury commissioned the Barker report (from an economist and member of the Bank of England's monetary policy committee) into the housing market, which was highly critical of the ability of the planning system to deliver the houses required (Barker, 2004). However, as we will see in Chapter 7, the government's growth area plans initially were not framed with climate change objectives in mind, or assessed against them, leading to strong criticism from the House of Commons Environmental Audit Committee (2005).

There were, therefore, competing discourses around the notion of spatial planning. A discourse around a conception of planning's role as strategic and active intervention in mediating complex sectoral interests in a democratically accountable way across different territorial scales was at variance with one that saw it as serving the Treasury agenda. During the decade, the Treasury became a powerful player in central government, with a particular commitment to what is sometimes labelled as 'UK plc'. It was strongly argued by the Treasury (under the Chancellorship of Gordon Brown) that the interests of business, and particularly the needs of the City of London as a global player in financial and capital markets, required a permissive planning system which would also provide the considerable numbers of new homes in the Greater South East. This was partly to meet the needs of housing for key workers to service the booming financial economy. At the same time, the deregulatory liberalized approach to the financial markets was reflected in a view that planning was a burdensome constraint on business enterprise and initiative. The role

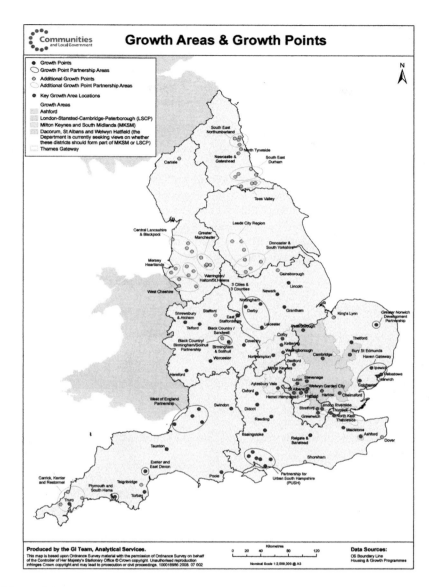

Figure 4.1

Sustainable Communities Growth Areas and Growth Points
Source: DCLG, 2009a

of planning was therefore seen as 'at best a means of facilitating the smoother functioning of markets, and otherwise as a regulatory burden' (Inch, 2009). (The implications for the relationship between central and local government are explored further in Chapter 5, and for the planning of development in climate-sensitive locations, in Chapter 8.) These two opposing conceptions of the purpose and scope of planning have been reflected in the shifting and uncertain development of the response to the issue of climate change.

But the TCPA claims to have succeeded in persuading government that a strong planning framework was needed, and in altering government's stance on the planning response to climate change, and it continues to press for greater commitment. For instance, in 2009, it initiated with the FoE a campaign for a new PPS, combining the PPS1 supplement with the PPS on renewable energy (Donatantonio, 2009). This led to a government commitment to merge the two (TCPA, 2009a; HMG, 2009c), a decision explored more fully in Chapter 5. In support of its position, the coalition published a Position Statement setting out the key principles it hoped to see in the new policy guidance (Box 4.4), and five recommendations for the PPS (covering the importance of climate change, the central role of adaptation, streamlining evidence and targets, community justice and energy planning, with a further two non-PPS recommendations on skills and education, and a climate and planning delivery group).

Box 4.4 Planning and Climate Change Coalition's key principles

- A restatement of the importance of sustainable development as the key objective for the planning system
- A strong commitment to the plan-led system, which can produce certainty and transparency for all sectors
- A commitment to make climate change a vital factor in all planning decision-making
- A strong commitment to environmental justice and open, transparent and participative decision-making
- A recognition of the importance of adaptation and the need to integrate mitigation and adaptation solutions
- The creation of a new technical advice body to ensure the integration of data sets, methodologies and target regimes
- The introduction of a new energy paradigm which requires a holistic and positive approach both to minimizing energy demand and to large-scale, community level and micro-renewables energy opportunities.

Source: TCPA and FoE, 2009, p. 4

To explain this discourse coalition, we need to understand the wider objectives of the TCPA. Founded by Ebenezer Howard in 1899, its currently stated aims are to campaign for the reform of the UK's planning system to make it more responsive to people's needs and aspirations and to promote sustainable development (TCPA, 2009b). It has retained a specific conception of the ideal settlement, of the garden city and people's housing needs. In the late 1990s, for instance, the TCPA had been associated with an idea of linked cities, new settlements linked by public transport routes with high levels of accessibility from residential areas (Hardy, 1999). This conception ran somewhat counter to the urban renaissance discourse, as expressed by the report of the Urban Task Force (1999), which argued for greater attention to be paid to existing urban areas. In response, the government published an Urban White Paper (DETR, 2000b), in which it adopted a target for brownfield land (a target of 60 per cent of all new houses to be built on previously developed land was set in 2000: the proportion in 2008 is 73 per cent. More details are given in Chapter 9). The TCPA therefore saw the opportunity of the government's Sustainable Communities initiative, which required an increase in housing numbers and hence the release of land, to promote the idea of new settlements on brownfield land. Part of its argument arose from the need to adapt to climate change. The TCPA had taken the role of the active principal stakeholder in involvement with the ASCCUE research project on adaptation strategies for climate change in urban areas. Funded by the EPSRC (one of the UK research councils) and UKCIP under the Building Knowledge for a Changing Climate research programme, ASCCUE had provided some evidence (described in more detail in Chapter 9) that an increase in urban greenspace could materially reduce urban temperature rises and contribute to flood attenuation. This evidence was readily taken up and promulgated by TCPA, enabling it to argue that climate change considerations required a reduction in the urban consolidation pressures, and hence provided an additional incentive for the planning and creation of new settlements.

4.3.4 The eco-towns initiative

The discourse of sustainable communities, meeting housing needs and addressing climate change considerations was a powerful one. The government for its part saw the TCPA as an ally in its wish to deliver higher housing numbers, against the reluctance of (for instance) some of the politically conservative shire counties represented on the Regional Assemblies. But the discourse coalition of the government and TCPA engendered a distinctive outcome in the form of the eco-towns initiative, first proposed early in 2007. TCPA has been closely involved with the formulation of both policy (in the original eco-towns prospectus) and advice. The TCPA chairman, David Lock, was appointed by government to report on the criteria appropriate for the ambitions of low- or zero-carbon developments (Cooper, 2007). The eco-towns have been conceived as exciting, innovative and radical ways of enabling entirely new communities to experiment with urban form and design, with new live–work and transport patterns, community infrastructure and open space, and new models of the development process. The substantive arguments about the response of urban areas and the built environment to both climate change mitigation and adaptation, and the claims and counterclaims about the efficacy of the eco-towns in fulfilling these requirements, are dealt with in Chapter 8, Section 8.6.

But the example illustrates the power of discourse coalitions to use climate change issues to further specific interests. Although the eco-towns initiative suffered from the banking crisis, and the collapse of the housing market and developers in 2008–09, it nevertheless demonstrated a remarkable alliance between central state and a planning pressure group. The government's objective has been to show its eco-credentials and yet to meet its economic agenda of delivering more houses in a process initiated outside the statutory regional and local planning system. The TCPA has used the opportunity of the eco-towns initiative to promote its own preferred form of settlement, a view promulgated through its *Town and Country Planning* journal (such as Lock, 2009). This is not to argue that there has been institutional capture of the agenda of one group by the other. But it does show that to understand the complex arena of the spatial planning response to climate change requires a much more nuanced understanding of discourses, discourse coalitions, and the arenas for debate and promulgation of these discourses, than mere injunctions to better practice.

4.3.5 Planning: fit for purpose?

There has therefore been ambivalence in attitudes to the role of the planning system in addressing climate change. The eco-towns ideal has seen the government committed to high standards of low- or zero-carbon developments, reflecting a shift from its initial formulation of the Code for Sustainable Homes as a voluntary measure to be internalized by the key economic sector of housing, to deciding to issue mandatory guidance (DCLG, 2006b; 2008a). This is discussed further in Chapter 9. A parallel but very different set of discourses around planning and climate change was also evident through the latter part of the decade. In this agenda, planning and the planning system, far from being seen as part of the necessary response to climate change, became labelled by certain interests as part of the problem. A powerful coalition of interests was led by the Treasury, given expression also by DTI and its successor, BERR (the Department for Business, Enterprise and Regulatory Reform), with the apparent support of the DCLG, and reinforced by the BWEA (British Wind Energy Association), the trade association representing British wind developer interests. This coalition forcefully argued that planning was a constraint on the delivery of a substantial part of the government's own climate change mitigation agenda, specifically renewables and specifically onshore wind. (The details of the government's commitments under Kyoto and under its own domestic obligation to deliver carbon-free energy are given in Chapters 3, 8 and 9.) Perhaps even more than with the housing agenda, the government chose to label planning as 'the problem'. The language of bureaucratic obstruction and delay was frequently used by these interests in support of an agenda of speeding up the planning process by removing decisions on key infrastructure projects – including low-carbon energy infrastructure – from local or regional democratic control. The planning system was singled out, for instance, in Energy White Paper of 2007 as 'becoming ever more challenging to potential investors' (DTI, 2007). The White Paper cited problems that it was taking too long, and creating uncertainty, with difficult and costly opportunities for participation, and knock-on effects for the energy markets and the wider economy. It acknowledged that not all delays could be attributed to 'planning hold-ups' (p. 254), but reiterated the view that 'obtaining planning permission can be a significant problem and that the current planning system is a key contributing factor' (p. 255).

The BWEA's position is equally clear: even while welcoming the opening of the largest onshore wind farm in the UK (the 322 MW Whitelee farm in Scotland), the BWEA pointed out that 7.1 GW of onshore wind is still awaiting planning permission, and that 'local planning decisions can take up to two years and have only a 40% approval rate' (BWEA, 2009a). The substantive arguments around onshore wind, and the attempts by other players (such as the RSPB) to move the debate forward, are discussed in Chapter 5. But here it is the use of the discourse which frames planning as an obstacle to the delivery of the UK's national commitments to climate change mitigation through the development of renewables that illustrates the positioning of producer interests and the power of labels to promote certain views.

Expectations of the planning system therefore vary from its being seen as a constraint or obstacle to addressing climate change to its being seen as a vital part of meeting the challenge. This ambivalence reflects the wider politics of climate change within the UK. Lorenzoni *et al.* (2008) argue that there are three principal constraints to improved or more effective national progress on climate change. They suggest that the gap in Britain's progress between the 'hot air' of its expressed political intentions and the 'cold feet' of actual delivery can be explained by the government's adherence to the discourse of ecological modernization, by fragmented and disjointed departmental portfolios and decision-making powers, especially under a devolution agenda, and by a failure to build on growing public concern about the issue of climate change with action within government to set a programme to require more radical change in people's behaviour. Some of these issues are being addressed – for instance, through the formation of the Department of Energy and Climate Change (DECC) in late 2008, and (as we shall see in Chapters 8 and 9) in the support for behavioural change in travel through the Sustainable Travel Demonstration Towns, and interventions in existing as well as new built environments. The Climate Change Act 2008 is undoubtedly an innovative and potentially powerful driver of clearer carbon targets and budgets. There still remain issues of split or overlapping portfolios, with domestic adaptation (and, for instance, the oversight of the Environment Agency and policy for flooding and water resources) remaining with Defra, while domestic and international mitigation and international adaptation are at DECC.

The wider political context was therefore one of ambivalent discourses: regulatory requirements were seen as onerous or an opportunity to claim the status

resented by statutory limits on carbon emissions under the
ct); market-based instruments (such as carbon trading or
re promoted as consistent with deregulated liberal markets
politically challenging. Institutional innovation occurred at
artmental level, but the importance of spatial planning has
contention. Discourses around planning as either too obstruc-
ital source of competitive opportunities for new development
pa.... as eco-towns have meant that sectional interests and networks
have been auie to promote particular positions and solutions. It is therefore
understandable that there are very different discourses around the role of
spatial planning in addressing climate change. In this complex field of environmental and political systems, different discourse coalitions have formed
which have employed similar language about planning, sharing storylines, and
thereby gaining political space and power. The role of the TCPA has been to
offer apparent solutions to government to achieve its house-building targets,
to generate support for its Sustainable Communities initiative, and to set the
standard for high-quality low-carbon communities. The TCPA can be seen to
have gained considerable leverage in offering new settlements as a solution
to government, at the same time as gaining access to policymakers in arguing
initially for a PPS on planning and climate change (eventually published in
2007) (DCLG, 2007a), and in 2009/10 for more visionary and transformational
planning. However, it has needed to tread a fine line between support for a
strong and participative statutory planning system, and the government's
framing of the eco-towns initiative as a competition for the private sector. The
coalition enterprisingly employed different policy arenas to communicate its
position and provide a platform and a negotiating table: public conferences,
dissemination through its own journal, and the work commissioned by government on eco-town standards, as well as privileged access to policymaking,
and the interchange of personnel.

Other discourse coalitions and partnerships, especially around the climate
change adaptation agenda in cities and regions, have shared an outlook and
language, and exchanged personnel, but have achieved their ends by direct
influence on the plan-making process with less media publicity. By contrast,
although the BWEA's views about planning as an obstacle have shared a storyline with government business and energy departments, and hence supported
the case that planning needed further major reform beyond the 2004 Act, the
outcomes of the 2008 Planning Act (as we shall see in Chapter 5) have not met
its requirements. Other coalitions, locally based but with a national political
presence, have presented alternative and powerful stories of the importance of
local support, local landscapes and the ineffectiveness or unreliability of wind:
although not all local opposition is sustained in the ultimate decision (Aitken,
McDonald and Strachan, 2008), the discourse of localism and participation
remains a powerful one.

In some ways – not all consistent – climate change has therefore wrought
significant changes to spatial planning in the UK.

4.4 The Netherlands

4.4.1 Experience and innovation: national water planning

The Netherlands provides an instructive contrast with the UK. Sometimes cited as a good comparator, with its well-established regime of planning powers at national, regional and municipal level, its high population density, urban settlement pattern and its experience of planned new towns, the Netherlands nevertheless possesses very different physical and socio-political characteristics. These characteristics reflect its place in, and relationship with, mainland Europe, its tradition of coalition politics, and its consensual and corporatist approach to public policy. The discourses of climate change, spatial planning and wider environmental policy have also been significantly different from those of the UK. The Netherlands is well known for its innovative series of national environmental policy plans which, since 1989 (VROM, 1989), have promoted a systematic integration of environmental issues and solutions. We discuss these in more detail below. But, perhaps surprisingly, the development of these National Environmental Policy Plans (NEPPs) has not been seen as an opportunity for further integration of climate change mitigation and adaptation measures. The emphasis on transitions to new energy systems and technologies within a conventional economic approach has been consistent with, and further justified by, the country's international climate change obligations, but the NEPP process has not employed the discourse around climate change to engage directly with the Dutch spatial planning systems.

However, outside the NEPP process, there has been a significant paradigm shift in the Dutch approach to water planning in the later 1990s and into the twenty-first century, which has impacted directly on spatial planning (as we shall see in Chapters 8, 10 and 11). This was a response to the serious floods of 1993, 1995 (in which over 100,000 people had to be evacuated) and 1998 (de Vries, 2006). A long-standing cultural and historical tradition of managing water by keeping it out has been overturned through the Room for Rivers policy of 2000. The Dutch already based their flood defences on more exacting risk assessment factors than the UK (based on 1:10,000 year events rather than 1:1,000), and it was held that Dutch society generally felt secure behind these defences, and, if they were concerned about climate change, considered it to affect other low-lying countries. But, following the recommendations of expert committee studies, in 2000 the government adopted a different approach to water, citing climate change as one of the principal reasons for the change, and also citing the experience of the serious floods in the UK of 2000 (MVenW, 2000). This new approach comprised policies and measures to accommodate water, representing a major change in the Dutch approach to fluvial flood risk (Woltjer and Al, 2007), and competition between the former water management discourses and the new discourses of accommodation (Wiering and Immink, 2006). In keeping with the Dutch pragmatic and consensual approach to policy coordination, it has been integrated into the national spatial strategy of 2006

Nota Ruimte (VROM *et al.*, 2006), to be implemented through a spatial planning key decision (SPKD), (MVenW, 2006), given legislative force through the Water Test, and given spatial expression through plans such as Rotterdam's Waterplan 2030 (City of Rotterdam, 2007; Wilson, 2009a). More details of this policy shift are given in Chapters 10 and 11. In December 2009, the Dutch Cabinet approved a new Water Strategy, based on new legislation on water and spatial planning, to cover the period 2009–15, and to coordinate with the work of the Delta Commission, endorsed by the Cabinet in 2008. The discourse around water is a powerful one in the Netherlands: 'Water is wonderful and the Dutch love it. The aim is crystal clear: the Netherlands, a safe and liveable delta, now and in the future' (MVenW, 2009). From 2009, a new national spatial structure covers specific areas at risk from climate change: the coast, the large rivers and the Ijsselmeer lake area, and, for those areas, the National Water Plan makes a major modification to the provisions of *Nota Ruimte*. The discourse of climate change has entered into spatial planning discourses via the water management community with their language of safety, liveability and well-being, and has been able to draw on the long-standing Dutch commitment to long-term horizons. Perhaps because the water management network in the Netherlands is so well established through the powerful Water Boards and the ministry, the shift in water management policy had not originally been seen as part of a wider attempt to build adaptive capacity across other sectors and impacts, but this is now changing. However, the extent of this reconception has also been criticized, such as by de Vries and Wolsink (2009) who argue that it retains too much of the technocratic discourse of engineered defences, with insufficient attention to community resilience with respect to uncertain futures.

4.4.2 The Climate changes Spatial Planning initiative

The coalition around this new discourse of climate change and planning has comprised a different policy community than that in the UK: in the Netherlands, the government has taken responsibility for flood protection, and so financial (insurance) interests (as represented by the ABI in Britain) have not been so active in agenda-setting. There has been no equivalent of the TCPA acting as a planning NGO to pressure government, although FoE Netherlands has latterly taken up the Big Ask campaign for legally binding greenhouse gas emissions targets. Nevertheless, the Netherlands has systematically looked to spatial planning as an activity with a significant role to play in addressing climate change. Consistent with the Dutch tradition of the very close relationship between academic research, government policymaking and private consultancy communities, this has been given force through the establishment of the Climate *changes* Spatial Planning (CcSP) initiative. This was established in 2004, with a budget of 80 million euros, jointly funded by government under the programme to invest in knowledge infrastructure (BSIK) and the increased capacity of stakeholders. The reasoning was that 'Although the co-dependency of spatial planning and climate change has largely been accepted, spatial planners and the climate change community have had mostly isolated (research) agendas so far. A major goal of the programme Climate *changes* Spatial Planning is to enhance joint-learning between the land use sectors, water management and spatial planning practitioners and communities' (CcSP, 2009). The programme was established by research institutes in a number of universities, and has the support of central government ministries for spatial planning, environment, water, economic affairs and science (respectively, VROM, LNV, MVenW, EZ and OCenW), as well as regional and local authorities, such as the province of South Holland, private sector interests such as the Port of Rotterdam, and NGOs such as Birdlife International. Unlike the UK, where there has been a fragmented approach to climate change and spatial planning research (with separate studies commissioned by different ministries and different research councils), the coalition of interests around the CcSP programme suggests greater consensuality and cooperation. It reflects the Dutch understanding of physical spatial planning, with a much more explicit integration of spatially extensive sectors such as agriculture, nature interest and water than is to be found in the UK.

Figure 4.2 shows the themes for the programme, and it is evident that integration is a key element to securing both comprehensiveness and consistency across the programme.

1 Climate Scenarios	2 Mitigation	3 Adaptation	Involved sectors:
			Agriculture Fisheries Water Management
4 Integration			Insurance Energy Construction
			Nature Recreation Institutions
5 Communication			

Figure 4.2

Climate *changes* Spatial Planning: themes

This is not to say that the programme has not been contentious. The ideas of competition are embedded in the funding of projects, and the mid-term evaluation found that coordination between projects could be improved, more progress was needed with the integration theme, and the involvement of spatial planning practitioners and decision-makers at regional and municipal level was unsatisfactory (Hordijk *et al.*, 2007). For instance, while the mitigation theme was commended for the scientific quality of its outputs, with internationally reputable knowledge and innovation, the research was not being translated into policy relevance for society, and was criticized for not having any spatial planning approach and insufficient social science input (p. 16).

4.4.3 NEPP tradition

It is possible that the explanation for this disconnect between climate change mitigation and planning lies in the particular discourses of climate change mitigation in the Netherlands. As indicated above, since 1989, the Dutch have pioneered attempts to develop a comprehensive and systematic environmental strategy through NEPPs, the latest being dated 2001 (VROM, 2001). These had adopted a systems approach to pollutants and resources, with a long-term (thirty-year) time horizon, and implementation through a range of policy measures across production and consumption sectors such as agriculture, waste and energy. Energy generation and demand were given attention in terms of resource efficiency and decoupling energy use from economic growth, and in a sense the climate change prompt has been additional to, rather than a driver of, the policy measures. Many observers (such as Weale, 1992; Hajer, 1995; Smith and Kern, 2007) have cited the implementation of this approach as a classic example of ecological modernization, emphasizing the role of technology, technical innovation and voluntary measures as an alternative to more market regulation. Smith and Kern (2007) suggest that even the more radical transition envisioned in the NEPP4, which aimed for a 40–60 per cent cut in CO_2 emissions by 2030, has maintained the strong business representation and emphasis on research and development for innovation and international competitiveness, with evidence of strong discourse coalitions around these themes. The mitigation theme in CcSP, for instance, emphasizes land uses such as agriculture, forests, soils and water, and the projects focused on supply-side measures (such as reduction of greenhouse gas emissions in the agricultural sector and the development of biomass), rather than demand management or energy efficiency. It is therefore not surprising that the CcSP project has not had a strong urban spatial planning input. Moreover, despite the innovation of policy instruments in the NEPPs, implementation has been an issue (Tuininga, 2007). For instance, just as in the UK (as we shall see in Chapter 5), where there has been considerable public media attention to the role of planning as either an inhibitor or enabler of alternative forms of energy supply, distribution and efficiency, the same problems with delivering renewables targets through planning for onshore wind have been experienced in the Netherlands. Breukers and Wolsink (2007) argue that the policy to promote wind energy as a form of ecological modernization was strongly influenced by the Ministry of Economic Affairs within the traditional energy policy and economics domain. But this centralized approach lacked a wider discourse and forms of knowledge amongst other stakeholders, such as environmentalists, spatial planners and turbine manufacturers. Moreover, Breukers and Wolsink (2007) argue that the dominant, top-down project planning discourse alienated local groups and helped to create local resistance.

As in the UK, central government has put in place reforms of the spatial planning system which have been designed to overcome some of the perceived drawbacks of Dutch planning, such as lack of clarity between the different levels of plan-making (national, provincial and municipal), lack of horizontal integration (for instance, between spatial planning and water management), perceptions of inconsistency and delay, and failure to implement national plans (Needham, 2006). Needham explains these in the context of other changes in Dutch society, such as the privatization of new housing and the liberalization of energy networks, the centralization of decision-making and the need to meet European Union requirements. All these are familiar issues in the UK, explored further in Chapter 6. The discourse coalitions around climate change and spatial planning in the Netherlands are different from those of the UK, but share some of the same language. The arenas have been partly shared, with participation in major European projects (such as ESPACE, BRANCH and GRaBS and the ESPON network). But, rather more than in the UK, climate change has been seen as an opportunity for the Netherlands to offer its expertise and experience of river delta management under conditions of a changing climate on a global stage, with domestic funding and support for domestic and international research, disseminated through international conferences.

4.5 Conclusions

Although this chapter has not attempted a direct comparison of the UK and Dutch approaches to integrating climate change considerations into spatial planning, it has shown some interesting overlaps and contrasts in the discourses employed, and the coalitions formed around these discourses. In both countries, there have been tensions between discourses of strong prescriptive standards for development and more permissive, light-touch planning regimes, and between uniformity and local variation and discretion. The coalitions around these have included NGOs, practitioners, governments and researchers, which have used the opportunity of the climate change challenge to make different claims on the planning system. In contrast with the UK, there has not been a coalition of climate change mitigation interests around spatial planning in the Netherlands, either as an enabler or as an obstacle to new energy systems. On the other hand, the discourse of climate change has significantly and successfully modified spatial planning practice for water management in the Netherlands in a very different way from the less prescriptive, more discretionary discourse of flood-risk planning in the UK.

We need, therefore, to be alert to the power of institutional and cultural discourses that frame the ways in which calls for spatial planning to respond to the issue of climate change are expressed. Institutional arrangements matter – the existence of a national spatial strategy in the Netherlands has enabled a more prescriptive expression of the response to climate change in the spatial strategy. But for all countries the issue of climate change throws up opportunities for some radical rethinking of the relationship and function of spatial planning. In the following two chapters, we examine two particular aspects of this, spatial and temporal: shifts in the scale and levels of governance at which the issues are addressed, and a revival of long-term and futures thinking in planning.

5   Multi-scalar spatial planning for climate change

· ·

5.1 Introduction

Climate change is a challenging issue for spatial planning in part because it raises particular problems of understanding 'the public interest'. Most planning systems, as explained in Chapter 1, have developed as an intervention in the free operation of land markets and development rights, with conceptions of the public interest lying both in the national interest and in local or community interests. In many countries, national governments have retained their powers of central- or national-level decision-making through legislating for the right to set policy for the use of land and space, and for powers to determine applications for consent for certain types of development (especially energy, minerals, transport and defence), in the national interest. At the same time, countries within the EU espouse the principle of subsidiarity, that is, the taking of decisions as closely as possible to the community directly affected. There has therefore always been potential for conflict between these scales for defining the public interest.

But the issue of climate change raises different questions about the nature of citizenship and responsibilities to others. A stable climate may be seen as a global public good, and its loss as a tragedy of the global commons (see Chapter 3). Therefore, in addition to the Brundtland Commission's sustainability arguments for equity in meeting the needs of the world's poor, threats to a stable climate posed by climate change reinforce the arguments, both altruistic and selfish, for action at a global scale. To an extent, the concept of sustainable development, as we have seen in Chapters 1 and 4, has brought about a recognition of the duties and responsibilities of nations and of citizens. Sustainability has become a dominant objective of spatial planning in European countries, and issues of distributive and environmental justice have become more significant. However, consideration of the issues of global equity and the rights of those in other countries initially did not figure strongly in national or local planning decision-making. But climate change raises specific questions about the global distribution of costs and benefits of measures to reduce that change, the impacts of unavoidable climate change and the distributive consequences of any adaptation measures. For instance, in the negotiations around the Kyoto Protocol, much of the most contentious debate (as explained in Chapter 3) has concerned the relative obligations of Annex I and Annex II countries (broadly the developed and developing nations), and the imbalance between the industrialized countries responsible for most greenhouse gas emissions and the countries more vulnerable to the consequences of climate change (Davenport, 2008; Adger *et al.*, 2006).

It is not our intention in this book, with its focus on spatial planning, to rehearse these arguments, but we need to recognize the force of the arguments in influencing national stances on climate change and hence national climate change policies (Compston and Bailey, 2008; Stern, 2009; Giddens, 2009). Inevitably, therefore, the expectation that spatial planning will play a part in both reducing and adapting to climate change is influenced by the global scale of problem-recognition. In this chapter we explore some of the complex terrain of how multiple scales of governance and multiple scales of justification for climate change action are mediated through spatial planning, using illustrative examples at different levels of policies regarding energy and aviation developments.

5.2 Multi-level governance and appeals to the global scale

Climate change has widened the locus of argument as to what are deemed material considerations in spatial planning, moving into the global level. The possibility of appealing to this level in both the perception of the problem and the conception of solutions has enabled interests and actors to lay claim to arguments and justifications beyond those of the national or local conception of the public interest. These scales of justification overlay what is already a complex multi-level governance for spatial planning. Theories of multi-level governance gained prominence in the last decade of the twentieth century to characterize the networks of actors and interests around the more formal processes of state policy, in particular in response to globalization, the power of multinational companies and the international movement of capital. As the power of the state in many industrialized countries of the West has diminished, with neoliberalizing and deregulatory tendencies, governments have needed to engage with wider networks of interests at international and national level. The wider governance therefore comprises the institutions of state and the surrounding networks of interests and stakeholders from business and civil society: policy formulation and implementation require negotiation vertically and horizontally across these multiple levels (global, national and local). Within the sphere of climate change politics, as well as economic policies, it has been argued that understanding the outcomes of subnational efforts to address climate change requires a recognition of the ways in which the boundaries of these levels are blurred 'by meshing the global and local in the presence of the nation-state' (Bulkeley and Betsill, 2005, p. 43).

But in addition to the multi-level governance that has developed around the issue of climate change, the issue itself has been used as an argument by different levels to challenge the role, interpretation or actions of other tiers. The environmentalists' adage of 'Think global, act local' has been replaced by a more complex set of arguments and action across all scales. Climate change justifications have been used to challenge higher tiers, in some cases to bypass intervening levels seen from a conventional hierarchical perspective, and in some cases successfully to promote actions as solutions from the bottom up which have been taken up by higher tiers. But the picture is not straightforward: the climate change card can be played both to strengthen and to moderate claims for action. For instance, as we shall explore at Section 5.6.2, levels of governance have used the issue of climate change to take away power from other tiers, and in other cases to give tiers responsibilities without also providing the requisite powers. The need for concerted effort on global climate change can also be used as a reason to stall on personal or local community actions. There is some evidence from public opinion surveys that a proportion of the public (25 per cent of respondents in a survey in the UK [Thornton, 2009]) believe that national or personal mitigation action is futile without all countries signing up to immediate action. A survey of European public opinion found that the EU's proposal for a post-Kyoto international target of 30 per cent reduction of greenhouse gas emissions by 2020 compared with a 1990 base was seen as too ambitious by 22 per cent of respondents (Eurobarometer, 2008, p. 52). The figures in the UK and the Netherlands (both countries with an ambivalent public attitude to climate change, which we explore in Chapter 13.4.2) were even higher, at 32 per cent and 35 per cent respectively.

The picture is further complicated by the bifurcated focus of climate change policy on mitigation and adaptation, and the different ways in which multi-level governance tries to integrate these two elements of a climate change response. Before we turn to examples of the way in which climate change is used as a justification for specific spatial planning interventions, we examine this dichotomy more closely.

5.3 Mitigation and adaptation: global and local?

We saw in Chapter 2 that the climate change policy community has subscribed to a conventional wisdom that mitigation actions are the responsibility of national government through its role in international negotiations, whereas adaptation has been seen as the remit of local levels of governance. This was a view adopted from the perspective of those engaged in international forums in establishing the science, and in negotiations amongst national governments, which understandably drew on knowledge and experience limited to that level of discourse, but it failed to recognize activities at other levels of governance. It was a view perhaps reinforced by the fact that the IPCC focused initially on mitigation, and by the fact that international and national mitigation initiatives, such as the EU's Emissions Trading Scheme, did indeed require a national scale of agreement and administration across economic sectors.

But there are both conceptual and empirical objections to this assumption that mitigation and adaptation are the remit of separate levels. Conceptually, policy analysis points to problems with the notion that these different levels – international, national and local – are static, impermeable and one-directional. The model of top-down policy implementation in its idealized form implies a cascading of policy measures (for instance, in the form of targets) down to lower tiers, with limited scope for bottom-up initiatives to influence higher levels of governance. But there are many barriers to this ideal, such as conditions not being met for agreement on the framing of the problem and solutions, and the existence of barriers at every stage of implementation (Trudgill, 1990; Hill, 2005). Moreover, actions at one level can dynamically affect actions at other levels, in both directions. In any case, the distinctions between local and higher levels are inevitably arbitrary, often reflecting historical–political divisions and the conventions of administrative boundaries, and are themselves in flux (such as the significant devolution agenda in the UK, empowering Scotland, Wales and Northern Ireland with different forms of self-government, and allowing different domestic climate change, environmental and spatial planning policies).

The literature on multi-level governance suggests that the shift towards it has occurred partly through the way 'formally-nested and clearly demarcated hierarchies between levels are giving way to more fluid, problem-focused networks based at one level, but seeking to draw in help from other levels' (Smith, 2007, p. 6267). Formal structures remain, with levels of government having clearly defined powers and functions, often imposed from the national level in cases where it is the ultimate legislative authority. But around certain issues – such as climate change – roles and accountabilities are more fluid and open to new initiatives.

The issue of climate change raises distinctive objections to the assumption of clearly demarcated responsibilities. First, there is much evidence that at subnational level provinces, regions, cities and municipalities have been taking climate change mitigation action. In federal or commonwealth systems, this action has often been in place of, or in advance of, the reluctant position of national governments, such as action by California, New York State and Oregon in the USA, as well as that by cities and municipalities through networks such as ICLEI and the Seattle-led Mayors' Climate Protection Agreement (Betsill, 2001; Alber and Kern, 2008). Chatrchyan and Doughman (2008) argue that, in the US, 'the political and popular framing of climate change in key states as both an imminent, proximate threat and an economic opportunity (coupled with negative portrayals of the federal government response) has been pivotal in gathering broad-based political support for climate leadership' (p. 253). Similarly, in Australia, before the new Labour government of Kevin Rudd endorsed the Kyoto Protocol in 2008, state and territory governments had developed their own emission reduction schemes (Currel, 2009). Even where governments had signed up to Kyoto, many municipalities nevertheless adopted their own targets. In some cases, this might be because there was doubt about the efficacy of central government actions: Alber and Kern (2008) suggest this is the case in Italy. In other countries, municipalities had adopted mitigation measures building on prior commitments to energy efficiency and energy saving as a part of general environmental policymaking even before the Rio Summit.

In the UK, for instance, energy generation had been highly centralized under state ownership before being privatized in the 1980s. Local action on energy had nevertheless been encouraged by the local authority associations (such as ACC et al., 1990). Local authorities adopted strategies reflecting their role as major employers, procurers of services and planning authorities for new developments (as we explore in Chapters 8 and 9), with a few innovative municipalities (such as Newcastle, Woking, Newark and Sherwood, and Leicester) leading the way in local energy planning. In Sweden, by contrast, from the 1970s municipalities owned and managed power and heating sources under the Municipal Energy Planning Act, and also adopted policies to reduce energy consumption (Granberg and Elander, 2007; Lundqvist and Biel, 2007). Similarly, in Norway, local climate policy development has reflected the municipalities' dual role as independent actors with their own initiatives, as well as having an agency role for implementing national obligations for carbon reductions (Aall et al., 2007).

The motivations for local level action may be both pragmatic and principled. Greenhouse gas emissions arise at the local and subnational level. In particular, emissions from the built environment, transport and land uses such as agriculture (as we explore in more detail in Chapters 8 and 9) account for a significant (and, in the case of transport, a growing) proportion of total emissions. Cities and municipalities, therefore, have acknowledged that action is needed at these levels as well as each nation state's focus on the production sectors of major industrial resource and energy production and processing industries. Local authorities can also argue that they play a vital role in translating targets into community-level support and commitment, and therefore can argue for the retention or allocation of powers and resources to perform this function. There are also many examples, such as the Slow Cities and the Transition Towns movements (which we discuss in Chapter 13), of communities taking their own initiatives to become more sustainable and low-carbon.

Second, within the field of mitigation actions, at least within the EU, the power and significance of the national level may be diminishing. As the EU develops its own Emissions Trading System (ETS), there are likely to be pressures for more harmonization of actions across Europe. Moreover, it can be argued (for instance, Hulme *et al.*, 2009) that the EU sees the climate change project as part of its *raison d'être*, taking action at this level partly as a justification in response to evidence of popular loss of support for the EU set of institutions. The EU also has a major role in agricultural policy – agriculture is a major land user and source of greenhouse gases. This reinforces the EU's sense of being an active and leading player in international negotiations around the UNFCCC (Damro and Mackenzie, 2008).

Third, although the effects of climate change may be experienced directly by citizens in their homes and local employment, and these effects may be very localized and variable, adaptation (either planned or autonomous) to those impacts is not wholly an action at local level in isolation. The researchers on the ADAM project (a European project on mitigation and adaptation), for instance, repeat the view that 'much adaptation will have to take place at a local scale', but they also make the point that the tiers of national and regional government set the regulatory and fiscal context (Hulme *et al.*, 2009, p. 11). In the UK, for example, the case for a national climate change risk assessment has been made on the grounds that national policy needs to set a framework for lower tiers.

> Much of the literature on adaptation identifies it as intrinsically local (partly in response to the global policy framework and global action which is needed for successful reduction of impacts through mitigation). In practice, in all policy areas, actions are usually local in nature, but the development of these options is set within a national policy framework [...] In looking to mainstream adaptation, there is clearly a need for a coherent national policy that sets the framework, and then cascades down to regional bodies, local government, as key delivery partners.
>
> (Watkiss *et al.*, 2009, p. 40)

Moreover, developing policy for adaptation to certain climate change impacts, such as those associated with water resources, flood-risk management and urban cooling, requires a catchment or subregional response. For instance, major water resource developments such as reservoirs are likely to serve a larger catchment than a single local authority or municipality. The case for the proposal by Thames Water in Oxfordshire, England, for a major new reservoir has been justified on the grounds of adaptation to climate change, as well as being necessary to serve the growing populations of the Upper Thames area (Oxfordshire in the SE region and Swindon in the SW region) and London, in the east of the catchment (Thames Water, 2006) (see Box 14.1). The administrative boundaries of distinct tiers or levels, drawn up for historical, pragmatic or practical reasons, determine scales of action which are not necessarily appropriate for addressing many aspects of climate change, such as river catchments, landscape-scale ecosystems and air quality.

Even at the local level, while it is necessary to build adaptive capacity through engaging stakeholders with the issues at the local scale, it is also necessary to legitimize at national level actions that may have a negative impact on some parts of some communities. Adaptation investment, for instance in flood defences, can favour some communities over others (see Chapter 6). Such actions will need to be legitimized through a claim to wider social good at different scales. Similarly, national financial support for research and development in mitigation actions (such as for renewables or nuclear technologies) is likely to have an uneven distributive impact. It is also at the local level that the consequences of maladaptation are experienced. These might include actions to mitigate climate change which have negative consequences for adaptive capacity or which increase vulnerability (examples are shown in Table 2.1).

Furthermore, national-level policymakers are also interested in adaptation responses to climate change at a national scale in terms of the vulnerability of critical national assets. For instance, the Pitt Review into the UK floods of 2007 distinguishes a category of critical national infrastructure. It defines this as infrastructure 'the loss or compromise of which would have a major impact on the availability or integrity of essential services leading to severe economic or social consequences or to loss of life' (Pitt, 2008, Section 14.9). In addition, the size and physical characteristics of individual countries mean that adaptation actions need taking at the national scale: in the Netherlands, for instance, the work of the Delta Commission, tasked by the Dutch government with addressing long-term flood risks in the Delta, did not restrict its remit to the coastal or river-basin areas, but drew up a plan for the whole country (Delta Commission, 2008) (more details are given in Chapter 8). As we explained in Chapter 2, the Dutch have a long history of national-scale spatial planning, which has not been the case in the UK. The Dutch response to climate change adaptation has reinforced the key role given to national spatial planning in the country: Make Room for the Climate (VROM et al., 2007a) was published as an output from ARK (the national programme for the adaptation of space and climate), to constitute the first steps towards a national adaptation strategy. The document made clear that, to make the Netherlands climate-proof, the two key principles of risk control and recovery of natural processes needed to be taken into account in a new strategic spatial planning task. (We explore subsequent developments in Dutch national planning in Chapter 9.)

However, the UK government, in the absence of a national plan, has since 2005 used both climate change adaptation and mitigation as reasons for centralizing decisions on key infrastructure (in addition to more usual arguments from the business case for speedier decision-making). More details of these examples are given at Sections 5.5.2.1 and 5.5.2.2. National levels of government also are concerned not just with climate change impacts within their borders, but (besides the ethical issue) with second-order global impacts of climate change such as disruptions to trade and food supplies, and international migration.

The picture is therefore one of a 'complex multi-level texture' (Hulme *et al.*, 2009, p. 22) in which different levels of governance use the climate change argument to act and claim legitimacy at different scales. Mitigation and adaptation are not being addressed solely or even wholly at one level, and there are extensive opportunities for mediation of interests across all scales.

5.4 Multi-scale governance networks

The existence of these multiple scales of action and legitimation provides opportunities for actors (proponents of action or inaction) to frame the problem and justification for their position. Lindseth argues that these scales are not predetermined, but can be used by groups to position their arguments and appeal to a particular agenda through 'scalar strategies' (Lindseth, 2006). Lindseth distinguishes between what he calls spaces of dependence and spaces of engagement. The former (spaces of dependence) include the interrelationship of local conditions and local interests, the latter including those broader sets of relations actively constructed to overcome or secure local spaces of dependence. He suggests that actors can and do build discourse coalitions around different scales in order to frame the debate in their terms. This is a particularly fruitful analysis for explaining the varied strategies of actors in framing and using the climate change debate. In the case he examined, in Stavanger in Norway, he found that both at national and local levels there were opposing discourses about the degree to which the exploitation of natural gas – a vital part of the national and local economy in Norway – was compatible with the national commitments to climate change mitigation. It might have been expected that this global scale would be used to reinforce arguments against further exploitation of fossil fuels. However, the outcome was that the appeal to the global scale in effect opened up a new space of engagement, and widened the decision-space, such that locally adopted commitments to climate change mitigation were outweighed. (A very similar argument is used in the SEA of UK offshore energy, as discussed in Chapter 7, Section 7.6.2.)

As we saw in Chapter 4, in the sphere of spatial planning and climate change, different coalitions have combined around different discourses and conceptions of the role of advice or prescriptive policy. In the absence of formal policy requirements, formally elected local levels of government have been able to engage with a wider network of governance, with evidence of advocacy coalitions and networks being formed around the climate change agenda, engaging elected representatives, members of the professions and civil society. Considerable attention has been paid (Betsill, 2001; Bulkeley and Betsill, 2003; Allman *et al.*, 2004; Betsill and Bulkeley, 2004; Alber and Kern, 2008; and Eckerberg and Baker, 2008) to the ways in which cities and municipalities have engaged with these multiple levels, both on their own initiatives and through networks and coalitions, such as the International Council for Local Environmental Initiatives (ICLEI), Cities for Climate Protection, C40, the

Seattle-led Mayors' Climate Protection Agreement, Zero Regio and, within the UK, the Nottingham Declaration.

Moreover, as we shall see in Part III, there is evidence that cross-national learning is already taking place, through the interest from the UK in lessons from abroad, in areas such as community-based energy systems, the promotion by the Netherlands of the concept of ecological networks at national and regional scales, and the adoption of the 'making space for water' principle in the UK following the Netherlands paradigm shift. Cross-national learning in spatial planning has also been evident in EU-funded projects such as ESPACE and BRANCH, which have looked particularly at climate change and spatial planning processes.

5.5 Implications for spatial planning

We therefore have a complex picture of the intermeshing of mitigation and adaptation across governance levels, and a complex set of coalitions and networks operating at and across different scales. This complexity has meant that the issue of climate change has raised a new set of dilemmas and opportunities for spatial planning in the definition of the public interest. The actors in planning systems comprise not just professionals and elected politicians but, crucially, the public in all its dimensions. Perhaps more than other public policy interventions, spatial planning has needed to legitimize its intervention in the public interest through express provisions for public participation in decision-making (Healey, 1997; Campbell and Marshall, 2002). Climate change as a global, national and local issue has therefore provided a platform for actors at different levels to appeal to higher or lower scales of issue-recognition and resolution. The wider public, civil society, NGOs, and other stakeholders such as business interests, have been able to use the argument of climate change to influence the policy and practice of more formally constituted levels of government.

But climate change has also raised many questions about how far spatial planning systems are fit for this climate change-responsive purpose. Although there is, as shown at Section 5.3, much evidence of activity at local level in both mitigation and adaptation, this does not necessarily translate into regulatory functions such as land-use spatial planning. Local powers to regulate the use and development of land are only one aspect of local governance. Bulkeley and Kern (2006) discern four governing modes for local authorities' climate change governance: self-governing, governing through enabling, governing by provision and governing by authority. There is a risk that many commentators on local authority or municipal action conflate these roles, and fail to recognize the significant constraints on autonomy of regulation – especially of spatial planning and land use – that some local councils perceive (although not all, as we see in Section 5.5.4). Moreover, in some planning systems, the regulatory function only covers new development, and therefore operates only at the margins – we argue in Chapter 9 for ways to change this. Zetter (2009) makes the point that the British planning system has been destabilized by the frequency of reforms, its position anomalous, at a time of deregulatory zeal, with the constraints of the immobility of land and land markets at odds with the free movement of capital. He argues that, compared with other countries' systems, central government has a more dominant role, and reforms have frequently paid more attention to efficiency rather than effectiveness, without resolving the lack of ability of local government generally to capture betterment value from development.

Moreover, as we shall see in Chapter 13, spatial planning can appear isolated from the climate change actions of wider local government corporate commitments to climate change action, and overburdened by too many publications advising on good practice (Phillips, 2008). The spatial planning system is sometimes perceived as lacking commensurate powers of action to implement change, for instance with respect to funding sustainable transport improvements and retrofitting existing development. In addition, at least in England, it has been faced with the cautious, discretionary approach taken by central government, with a presumption in favour of development and developer interests, and a concern not to 'gold-plate' any regulatory requirements (Wilson, 2009b).

Spatial planning has, accordingly, become a particularly contested arena over its fitness for purpose in addressing climate change, which we explore through a number of case studies at different scales.

5.5.1 Appeals to the climate change issue as a case for supranational planning

It is possible that, over the next decade, climate change might be used as an argument to justify further policy interventions, at the supranational level of the EU, into spatial planning. Although, as we have seen in Chapter 3, Section 3.3.4, the EU does not have a remit in spatial planning, some of its past initiatives, such as the ESDP, have been influential on planning concepts and practices amongst member states. The process of Territorial Impact Assessment might also have potential. It is possible that the issue of climate change will engender similar perspectives. The EU's Adaptation White Paper in 2009, for instance, justifies the need for EU adaptation action on four grounds: where the impacts of climate change transcend national boundaries; to provide 'solidarity' amongst member states to ensure support for disadvantaged or most vulnerable regions; to enable coordination and sharing of good practice amongst member states; and because many sectors where adaptation action is needed (such as agriculture, biodiversity and energy) are already the subject of significant EU regulation and financial support. As we have seen in Chapters 1 and 5, the White Paper expects that more strategic and longer-term spatial planning will be needed, on land and sea, for a range of sectors.

The implementation of the Habitats and Water Framework Directives has already had a direct influence on spatial planning for the allocation of land and land uses in member states (Wilson, 2009b); any revision to the Directives expressly to address climate change might reinforce this. Already, the ICZM policy, Flood-Risk Directive 2008 and Marine Policy Strategy will have more profound effects, as discussed in Chapters 10 and 11.

5.5.2 Appeals to the climate change issue as a case for national planning

In this part of the chapter, we examine primarily the case of the UK, where the Devolved Administrations of Scotland and Wales differ from England in adopting a national spatial framework. This is in contrast with the Netherlands: the tradition of strong national infrastructure planning as part of the national spatial plan (Marshall, 2009b) is already being adjusted to take account of the increased flood risk associated with climate change, through the new Water Plan (described in Chapter 4) and the work of the Delta Commission (see Section 5.3 and Chapter 8).

The Infrastructure Planning Commission and national policy statements in England and Wales

In England, climate change justifications have been used for the centralization of decision-making on national infrastructure for climate change mitigation and, to a lesser extent, adaptation. The 2007 Planning White Paper cited climate change and the need to move to a low-carbon economy as reasons for major changes to the planning system: 'The long-term challenges for planning are increasing. Over the coming decades, debate and decisions about where development should take place are likely to become more difficult. We must ensure that the whole planning system, including both the town and country planning system covering residential and commercial development and some infrastructure, and also the range of separate consent regimes for specific types of infrastructure, is fit and able to cope with [...] meeting the challenge of climate change' (HMG, 2007, p. 10). The resulting Planning Act of 2008 established an Infrastructure Planning Commission (IPC) which will decide on applications for a range of nationally significant infrastructure projects. These include projects in the fields of energy, transport, water, waste water and waste. The IPC will make its decisions in the framework of national policy statements (NPSs). These, to be 'designated' (that is, adopted) from 2010, will cover the fields of overarching energy (with separate NPSs on renewables, fossil fuel, electricity networks, oil and gas infrastructure, and nuclear), national networks (i.e. roads and railways), airports, waste water, water supply and hazardous waste. There is, however, to be no overarching NPS on transport (an issue discussed further in Chapter 8). Table 5.1 sets out the intended timetable (which has slipped from its original timing) for these NPSs.

The NPSs, which have cross-party support, are to set out government policy on the need for nationally significant infrastructure, so the issue of need cannot be excluded from debate at public inquiries. The intention is to give the IPC and proponents greater certainty. The Airports and Nuclear NPSs, however, will also be location-specific. The Planning Act requires NPSs to contribute to sustainable development, and to have regard to the desirability of integrating mitigation and adaptation. Such centralization of strategic planning raises profound questions of legitimacy and justification: what the rights are of local communities in decision-making on major projects; whether the scale and significance of infrastructure is such as to require a national-level decision; and whether this brings with it a better ability to provide consistency, coordination, integration and a longer time horizon (the advantages usually claimed for strategic decisions). The Planning White Paper indicated that the NPSs would take a ten to twenty-five-year horizon for need and demand studies, but would be

Table 5.1 Intended timetable for NPS for England and Wales

NPS	Consultation date (*to be published*)	Expected formal approval	Department
Overarching energy EN1	November 2009	2010	DECC
Fossil-fuel electricity-generating infrastructure EN-2	November 2009	2010	DECC
Renewable energy infrastructure EN-3	November 2009	2010	DECC
Gas supply infrastructure and gas and oil pipelines EN-4	November 2009	2010	DECC
Electricity networks infrastructure EN-5	November 2009	2010	DECC
Nuclear power generation EN-6	November 2009	2010	DECC
Ports	November 2009	2010	DfT
National networks (i.e. strategic roads and railways, including strategic rail freight interchanges)	*Early 2010*	Late 2010	DfT
Waste water (e.g. sewage treatment infrastructure)	*Spring 2010*	2011	Defra
Hazardous waste (e.g. high temperature incineration)	*Summer 2010*	2011	Defra
Water supply (e.g. reservoirs)	*Late 2010*	Early 2012	Defra
Airports	*Early 2011*	Late 2011	DfT

Source: DCLG, 2009b

required to take a longer-term view where the impacts of climate change might affect the location of infrastructure. Since then, the Prime Minister's statement of policy for 2009–10 (the final year in office before a General Election in 2010) proposed the establishment of an advisory body, Infrastructure UK, which will identify long-term (five to fifty years) needs (HMG, 2009c).

The question of what constitutes a scale for national significance has been resolved through the use of thresholds. These are set out in the Planning Act Part 3, largely based on pre-existing thresholds for decisions by central government on major projects: for instance, the construction or extension of a generating station onshore of greater than 50 MW, and offshore of greater than 100 MW. New thresholds were set for other forms of infrastructure which had previously been decided at the local planning level, such as a threshold for dams and reservoirs of greater than 10 million cubic metres. The electricity transmission and distribution system for lines of more than 20 kV had always been decided by central government, but the new IPC decision-making process removes previous provisions under which, if a local planning authority objected, a public inquiry had to be held. Electricity distribution networks are likely to become of even more national significance as decarbonizing of energy-generation systems was argued by the government as requiring a larger contribution of renewable energy through a more localized network of generation (and, more controversially, a new round of nuclear power stations). The decision in 2010 by the Minister for Enterprise, Energy and Tourism in the Scottish government to allow, on appeal, the upgrade of a 132 kV line to a 400 kV double circuit overhead electricity line from Beauly to Denny in Scotland, passing through some nationally designated landscapes, illustrates the possible tensions between different conceptions of the national interest (Scottish Government, 2010).

Non-climate justifications

Climate change has been one, but not the only, justification for this radical change in decision-making on major projects. The other justifications are to achieve speedier planning decision-making and the simplification of multiple consenting procedures, and energy security. The proposal for the IPC was made formally in the Planning White Paper of 2007, but it followed a number of reviews of the decision-making process for major projects. The White Paper claimed that 'the planning system is too bureaucratic, takes too long and is unpredictable' (HMG, 2007, p. 13). The aim of establishing the IPC was therefore to streamline decisions, avoid long-running public inquiries and make decisions more predictable. The government and media frequently cited the period of time taken to approve the fifth terminal at London's Heathrow Airport as an example of planning delay. This argument needs to be seen as part of the much wider anti-planning discourse (Zetter, 2009), one which castigated local-level planning in particular for its slowness and, to some extent, its parochialism. It is not possible here to detail all the arguments put forward by the proponents of this position, but the context was one in which a series of studies commissioned by the government had been seen to support the case for reform. The McKinsey review of productivity in the UK economy in 1998 had identified the planning system as an obstacle to greater economic growth, enabling the departments of state tasked with promoting business interests to influence government thinking. This theme had been taken up in the context of housing by the Barker Report of 2004 and the subsequent review of the Planning System in 2006, which made recommendations to improve the speed, responsiveness and efficiency of spatial planning. A similar conclusion was reached by reviews into major transport infrastructure (Eddington, 2006), and the Killian Pretty report (2008) into ways to make the local planning system faster and more responsive to the needs of business. All these reports were commissioned in rapid succession, even while the new Planning and Compulsory Purchase Act of 2004 implemented radical changes to the preparation of plans at regional and local level, changes intended to bring about more strategic and responsive planning.

There are many arguments as to the accuracy of the picture painted of the fitness of the planning system. For example, the Barker review failed to address the significant structural problems in the housing market (which were revealed by the exposure of the mortgage market and UK banking system to the global credit crisis, leading to a sharp decline of the house-building sector in 2008–09). Moreover, decisions for many infrastructure projects (for instance, ports, any power station over 50 MW and electricity transmission) were already made at central government rather than local level. Other major infrastructure projects, such as the Channel Tunnel Rail Link, had been approved under special parliamentary legislation. It can be argued (as has Levett, 2007) that major infrastructure decisions should, indeed, take time for consideration, especially to allow a full public debate of the needs case.

Energy developments

However, additional urgency for the government's case lay in the recognition of Britain's exposed position on energy security: in 2007, the UK had moved from being a net exporter of energy to being a net importer. North Sea oil and gas production had passed its peak, and a generation of ageing coal, oil and nuclear power stations was reaching the end of its life. Nuclear power provides some 19–20 per cent of electricity generation, and 3.5 per cent of overall energy used (BERR, 2008): but by 2023, all but one of the nuclear plants are due to close. For the fossil fuel-based power stations, this end-of-life date is being brought forward by their inability to meet European environmental standards for both sulphur emissions and carbon emissions. When the Labour government was first elected in 1997, it opposed new nuclear power, a commitment made partly to protect the interests of the coal-mining communities in the traditional Labour heartlands (from 1998–2000, it also had a moratorium on new gas-fired power plants). But in the early part of the twenty-first century, it has become clear that there will be a major shortfall in generating capacity, exposing the UK to more dependence on imports, and hence vulnerability to uncertain decisions by the exporting countries, Russia in particular. It has been estimated that, without demand management, by 2020 some 60 per cent of gas used could be imported (compared with 25 per cent in 2008) (HMG, 2009a, p. 28). The 2007 Energy White Paper (DTI, 2007) therefore put nuclear generation back into consideration, and the separate White Paper on Nuclear Power (BERR, 2008) concluded that, as part of an overall energy mix, nuclear power was low-carbon, affordable, dependable, safe and capable of increasing diversity and reducing dependence. The 2009 Low Carbon Transition Strategy envisages the new plants operating from perhaps 2018, 'but will look to accelerate timescales where possible' (HMG, 2009a, p. 64). The government had already undertaken a strategic siting assessment, and the draft NPS for nuclear power indicates potentially suitable sites for nuclear deployment (DECC, 2009a). The legitimacy, sequence and speed of decision-making had already been challenged by Greenpeace, leading to a revised consultation process, but concerns remain about the legitimacy of the siting process (Blowers, 2009, calls it 'inadequate, flawed and unfair' [p. 37]).

The combined challenges of climate change, energy security and economic development have therefore together provided support for major changes to decision-making in planning.

Responses of the planning community

It might have been expected that local government and planning practitioners would have opposed the wider governance challenge represented in the establishment of the IPC and NPS process. However, the RTPI (the professional planning institute in the UK) broadly welcomed the proposals, subject to a number of criteria concerning the independence of the IPC and the framing of NPSs – indeed, the former Secretary General of the RTPI was, in 2009, appointed a member of the Commission, as was the former director of the TCPA. The body representing local government was also on balance in favour, arguing that most projects within the scope of the IPC were already decided by central government; but it expressed serious concerns about local democracy, and feared that the scope of projects deemed to be of national significance might expand into local matters. It also considered that the NPSs and any approved projects should be assessed for their robustness with respect to climate change (LGA, 2007).

On the positive side, some of the planning community in England saw the NPSs as going part way to meeting the need for a national spatial plan. Chapter 4 has shown that, in Scotland and Wales, climate change has been used as part of the justification for the adoption of a national spatial planning framework. The chair of a TCPA-led inquiry into the case for a national spatial plan for England

(TCPA, 2006b) sees the NPSs as being a step in the right direction, but doubts that 'the sum of their disparate parts adds up to a rational overall strategy or development framework for England' (Hetherington, 2009, p. 306). By contrast, the National Planning Framework for Scotland 2 (Scottish Government, 2009) to 2030 contains an indicative map of national developments (such as power stations and electricity grid reinforcements) and national landscape designations (Figure 5.1). Contribution to climate change targets is one of the criteria against which such projects in Scotland are being assessed.

Aviation and airports policy

NGOs such as Friends of the Earth (who generated a large proportion of the 31,000 responses to the consultation on the Planning White Paper) objected to the White Paper on the grounds of lack of democratic accountability and loss of rights of public and community participation (Ellis, 2008), while also supporting stronger action on climate change. With other environmental NGOs, the FoE was also concerned that economic considerations would be given undue weight, that biodiversity and historic conservation interests would be neglected, and that carbon-intensive projects – such as airports and ports – would be promoted (DCLG, 2007b). Both international aviation and shipping are currently excluded from the domestic greenhouse gas inventory, although their emissions are growing rapidly, and aviation fuel generates high levels of pollutants. Air travel has doubled since 1990, and the government expects this trend (even allowing for the economic downturn) to continue (HMG, 2009a, p. 145). Accordingly, it favours airport capacity expansion both near London and in the regions (see Chapter 9). The controversial decision by the government in January 2009 to allow a third runway at Heathrow Airport (in the face of opposition by the Mayor of London, local authorities and some business groups) might confirm the expectation that the airports NPS will oblige the IPC to decide in favour of such expansion schemes.

Although the airports NPS is not due for consultation until 2011, the current policy framework is set by the 2003 Aviation White Paper (DfT, 2003), which has provided considerable and controversial support for the expansion of airports for passengers and freight. There have been many objections to individual schemes (such as Stansted, Manchester, Bristol, and Lydd in South East England) on grounds of inconsistency with climate change policies as well as on local grounds. The Aviation White Paper was published at a time of rapidly expanding demand for air travel, but has consistently been criticized for its business-as-usual approach to predicting and providing for growth. Cairns and Newson (2006) challenged many of its assumptions. They argued that CO_2 emissions from aviation had doubled during 1990–2000, but that the Aviation White Paper had underplayed the impact of other climate-forcing emissions. The CO_2 targets at that time were for a reduction of 60 per cent by 2050: even to reach that lesser target, other sectors would need to make huge reductions

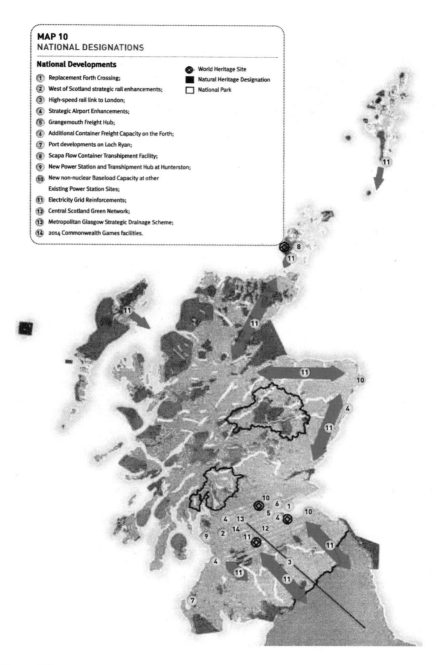

MAP 10
NATIONAL DESIGNATIONS

National Developments

1. Replacement Forth Crossing;
2. West of Scotland strategic rail enhancements;
3. High-speed rail link to London;
4. Strategic Airport Enhancements;
5. Grangemouth Freight Hub;
6. Additional Container Freight Capacity on the Forth;
7. Port developments on Loch Ryan;
8. Scapa Flow Container Transhipment Facility;
9. New Power Station and Transhipment Hub at Hunterston;
10. New non-nuclear Baseload Capacity at other Existing Power Station Sites;
11. Electricity Grid Reinforcements;
12. Central Scotland Green Network;
13. Metropolitan Glasgow Strategic Drainage Scheme;
14. 2014 Commonwealth Games facilities.

◈ World Heritage Site
■ Natural Heritage Designation
☐ National Park

Figure 5.1

Scotland National Planning Framework 2: National Developments
Source: Scottish Government, 2009, map 10

in emissions to offset those from aviation planned under the Aviation White Paper. They argued that the contribution of aviation to the UK economy (such as employment benefits) was partly offset by the tourism deficit, as the bulk of travel growth had been for leisure from the UK to other countries (rather than for business or inbound tourism). They also pointed to the risk of 'air-dependence', in which travel patterns become locked in to air travel, and to the unproven assumptions about the effectiveness of carbon-trading under the EU's ETS.

The Sustainable Development Commission (SDC, 2008) aimed to provide a way forward for government in proposing a special commission on aviation, and that no further proposals for major airport expansion should be considered by government until the commission had reported, and the Aviation White Paper had been revised. However, this recommendation has been overtaken by the establishment of the IPC and the Committee on Climate Change. The latter has found that there could be capacity for increase at Heathrow (CCC, 2009b) through the construction of a third runway, concluding that growth in air travel can continue to 2050, but at a greatly reduced rate (60 per cent compared with the 'business-as-usual' rate of 200 per cent). It considered alternative ways of reducing emissions (Box 5.1).

Box 5.1 Policy options to reduce aviation emissions to 2050

- Carbon pricing with capacity constraints
- Modal shift to rail/high-speed rail
- Communications technology substitution, e.g. video-conferencing
- Improvements in fleet fuel efficiency
- Use of biofuels in aviation

Source: CCC, 2009b, p. 7

The Committee concluded that, making prudent assumptions about technological improvements to fuel efficiency and use of biofuels, a maximum demand growth of 60 per cent would meet the CO_2 target. This implies a constraint on capacity expansion at different airports: however, the Committee decided not to assess the factors determining optimal capacity at these regional and smaller airports.

These factors raise essentially regional and local issues. The coalitions of interests around aviation do not fall neatly along political or spatial dimensions. Mander and Randles (2009) argue that aviation growth has been fuelled by two linked processes: the social practices of leisure travel (especially 'celebratory' travel) benefiting from cheap flights, and the coalition of actors around the Aviation White Paper. The latter comprises multinationals, national and regional economic and political interests (shown in Figure 5.2).

As we shall see in Chapter 8, regional support for airports is often part of a development package reflecting the fact that airports are major business

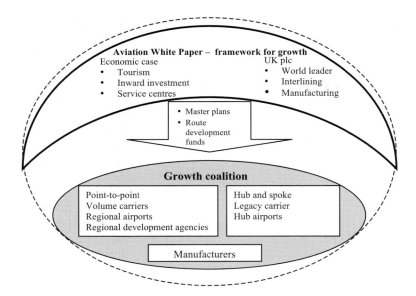

Figure 5.2

UK aviation growth coalitions
Source: Mander and Randles, 2009

and retail enterprises besides their transport interchange function, generating considerable associated pressures for development (Freestone, 2009), and policies of support challenge other local policies promoting sustainable travel and reduced travel dependency. Mander and Randles (2009) argue that the airport expansion coalitions have made strategic use of non-statutory airport master plans to embed airports in the statutory regional and local plan-making processes, even though master plans are required under the Aviation White Paper. It is clear that airport expansion and aviation policy raise issues of global, national, regional and local significance, and that climate change, while highly significant, is not the sole consideration. All scales of government and governance can appeal to the consideration of climate change, and the distinction between nationally significant and other airport infrastructure is blurred. Yet the issue of climate change is being interpreted by government agencies as one for national decision. This is illustrated in the decision of the Planning Inspector into the appeal on the increase of numbers at Stansted Airport:

> In conclusion on climate change policy, I consider that questions of the appropriateness and effectiveness of Government policies on aviation and climate change and their compatibility, while undoubtedly of great importance, are matters for debate in Parliament and elsewhere rather than through this appeal.
>
> (Boyland, 2008 para. 14.80)

NPSs and mitigation and adaptation

Questions also arise over how the requirement that NPSs contribute to sustainable development, and have regard to the desirability of integrating mitigation and adaptation, will be achieved. The NPSs constitute policy, and are not required to be subject to a formal *ex ante* SEA (the issues of climate change and SEA are discussed in Chapter 7). Instead, the government is committed to a new form of sustainability appraisal, labelled Appraisal of Sustainability (AoS), which is being undertaken alongside the drafting of the NPSs. They will provide an indication of the weight to be given to climate change considerations (both decarbonization and adaptation) in the new policies. The indications are that climate change, having been used overtly as an argument to justify the creation of NPSs and the IPC, will be reserved as a concern for central government and hence less open to alternative conceptions or ambitions. The draft NPS on Ports, for instance (DfT, 2009a), does require the applicant and decision-maker to consider the impacts of projected climate change over the lifetime of the port. However, in setting out the mitigation considerations for applicant and decision-maker in assessing schemes, it confines the scope of assessment by stating that, as international shipping is outside the national carbon budget, the decision-maker does not need to consider this aspect; the possibility of carbon impacts from significant inland transport is acknowledged, but the decision-maker 'should attach limited weight to the estimated likely net carbon emissions performance of port developments'. As Marshall (2010) argues, the NPS is premised on market choice of location within the given of overall predicted growth in port capacity, with no consideration of the wider sustainability or climate change issues, or of the new transitions to low-carbon consumption and production.

Renewable energy: national benefits and local impacts?

Climate change is therefore not the only argument being cited by central government to justify the new arrangements for nationally significant infrastructure, but it has particular force as a moral imperative, reinforcing wider arguments about the planning system as being unfit for purpose. This argument was used by government and the onshore wind development industry in the context of the role of the planning system in delivering or constraining more renewable energy. The UK has had a long-standing commitment to increase the proportion of renewable energy. Advice for planning authorities was published in 1993 in the form of one of the early national planning policy guidance notes. Over time, the renewables target has been raised: the target in the Low Carbon Transition Plan and Renewable Energy Strategy is for 30 per cent of electricity to come from renewables by 2020 (HMG, 2009b). This accords with the EU Renewables Directive target for 15 per cent of energy (that is, for electricity, heat and transport) to be generated from renewable sources by 2020. The target

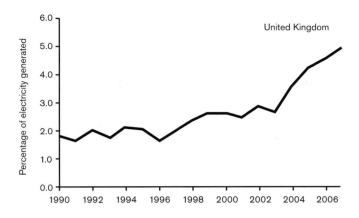

Figure 5.3

Renewable electricity as a percentage of total, 1990–2007
Source: Defra, 2009b

represents a significant increase on the 2007 renewables share of some 5.5 per cent (Figure 5.3).

Despite the evident increase in renewables, the proportion generated from onshore wind has increased only slowly, and the target of 10 per cent by 2010 looks unattainable. The high-profile debate over the causes of failure to reach this target has riven the planning and environmental policy communities. Onshore wind had been deemed to be the easiest technology to use, as the UK has an abundant wind resource and it requires relatively low start-up and capital costs. But the Planning White Paper repeated the arguments of the Energy White Papers that the local planning system was a source – if not *the* source – of unacceptable delays in obtaining consent for such schemes. The wind and marine renewables trade lobby group, the BWEA, argued in its response to the Planning White Paper that 8,250 MW of onshore wind capacity, amounting potentially to 6 per cent of the UK's electricity supplies, was awaiting decision in the planning system, and that, if only a quarter of it were built, the UK would meet its 2010 renewables target. They made the point that around half of this comprised schemes of more than 50 MW (that is, for decision by central government), equating to 3 per cent. BWEA also argued that there were serious 'blockages' in the planning system: in 2006, fewer than 5 per cent of schemes had been determined within the statutory period, compared with the national average for major infrastructure schemes of 70 per cent. They considered that these renewable energy projects were therefore of such national significance that decisions on all wind schemes should be consistent across scales, and the threshold for government decision should be lowered to 25 MW (BWEA, 2007).

Although the government did not accept this argument (it argued that thresholds should not be set so low as to capture projects that were not of national significance), it retained the right to decide projects where cumulative impacts give rise to more than local effects. Nevertheless, the argument has brought the planning system into the spotlight as a source of delay and obstructionist localism. There have been many studies of planning decision-making for, and public attitudes towards, onshore wind schemes (such as Cowell, 2007; Ellis *et al.*, 2007; Toke *et al.*, 2008; Aitken *et al.*, 2008), and of the wind energy industry (such as Strachan *et al.*, 2006), and it is not our intention here to review these studies. Instead, we draw attention to the implications for multi-level governance in the balance of power between central and local levels, and the structural constraints on offsetting perceived adverse community impacts with community benefits. The combination of wind resource availability, fiscal support through the Renewables Obligation, and national designations for protected upland landscapes has meant that schemes have been proposed across a wide area of the country (BWEA, 2008), requiring planning decision-making by rural districts. This has exposed the policies for the protection of non-designated countryside and landscape, and local governance issues in the relationship of locally elected councillors with their constituents and planning advisers. The Secretary of State for Energy and Climate Change, for instance, has argued that it should be socially unacceptable to object to such projects, but that instead there should be popular mobilization in their favour (Stratton, 2009). However, in England, as well as fiscal disincentives in the absence (before 2010) of a feed-in tariff (guaranteed payments for renewably generated electricity fed into the national grid), there are currently legal constraints on obtaining community benefits in the form of goodwill payments, through the planning process, because of concerns about the buying of planning permissions. Unless wind farms are community-owned, they do not necessarily bring local benefits (except for aspects such as public access or habitat enhancement), and yet they do not meet the strict criteria for planning obligations where some of the development value can be used to support local infrastructure. This contrasts with more supportive policies in Wales and Scotland, where community trust funds are actively encouraged.

The experience of the Netherlands is interesting here. Breukers and Wolsink (2007) show that the implementation of policies for onshore wind energy were 'cumbersome', suffering from overcentralized policy prescription which failed to consider other spatial and environmental planning issues, and the question of local acceptance: as a result, local objections had increased. They conclude that such objections reflect not just attitudes to local landscapes, but disaffection with decision-making. However, where there was local ownership – which they describe as an unintended consequence of the liberalization of energy markets – and local involvement, genuinely making use of vernacular knowledge and values, support can be enhanced. This suggests all sorts of lessons for less confrontational practice in England.

The high profile of the debate in Britain has prompted other environmental organizations that have opposed many schemes in sensitive habitat or landscape areas to rethink their position. The RSPB, for instance, commissioned a report (IEEP, 2009) examining different policy incentives in continental Europe and ways of reconciling developments with biodiversity interests. The report compared practice within the UK and with Germany, Denmark and Spain. It found (only partly consistent with Breukers and Wolsink) that a number of elements are needed to meet commitments to both wind energy and biodiversity conservation (Box 5.2).

Box 5.2 Key elements in planning for wind power and biodiversity conservation

- Early engagement of stakeholders
- Clarity over nature conservation concerns
- Appropriate institutional resourcing and retention of central pools of knowledge
- Being spatially explicit
- High quality environmental impact assessments
- Maximizing local benefits from wind developments
- Ensuring effective ongoing management
- Political will to deliver new onshore capacity

Source: IEEP, 2009, pp. 3–4

The report described a gradation of indicative planning policies within the UK, with Wales being the most structured, and England the most ad hoc (IEEP, 2009, p. 25). Wales has identified Strategic Search Areas in which larger-scale (over 25 MW) schemes could be located, each with an indicative target (WAG, 2005). In Scotland, planning guidance promotes the use of a spatial framework based on agreed criteria (SEDD, 2007). The report commended such 'structured, spatially explicit and pro-active' planning approaches (p. 4); but it also recommended that more responsibility for achieving national priorities should be given to the local level, perhaps through greater use of regional and local targets. It found that Scotland approved the largest capacity, with larger developments and a higher proportion of capacity approved overall (IEEP, 2009, p. 22). Because of the size of schemes, more were over the 50 MW threshold and therefore decided by the Scottish Executive. The report acknowledged the fact that, as wind turbine technology changes, generation capacity will increase, and more schemes might exceed the threshold for central decision. In response, the RSPB has called for

- a strategic approach from the planning system, identifying areas of priority for wind deployment and areas of conflict;
- clear and detailed information such as bird sensitivity maps;
- strong leadership from the government to tackle lack of technical know-how in local authorities, and make clear that wind energy is a national priority;

- an expectation that developers discuss proposals with other stakeholders before making applications, in order to reduce conflict. (RSPB, 2009a)

In some ways, the UK Renewable Energy Strategy (HMG, 2009b) follows this model. The government has resisted calls for taking all wind applications away from the local level, and allocating them to the IPC for decisions. Instead, it intends to alter its own interventions – such as the ability to 'recover' for ministerial decision appeals for schemes under 50 MW, and to prioritize appeals in the Planning Inspectorate for renewable schemes (p. 77). The strategy proposes a raft of additional sticks and carrots for LPAs: the use of funded Planning Performance Agreements (PPAs) to encourage prompt decision-making; changes in costs awards against LPAs; and more flexibility for existing renewables permissions to allow for technological changes. It also has published a revised version of the toolkit on obtaining community benefits from wind energy projects (CSE, 2009).

The problems with onshore wind have already caused a major shift towards offshore deployment (DECC, 2009b) (discussed further in Chapters 7 and 11). It is clear, however, that the onshore wind crisis has dominated the debate and possibly diverted attention from other renewables options which are likely to generate equal controversy, including renewables schemes such as tidal and wave power. The Severn Barrage could potentially deliver 5 per cent of the UK electricity supply, but conflict has already emerged between the government's climate change objectives and commitments to sites designated as of European significance for biodiversity. In 2007 the government announced its intention to designate the whole of the Severn, Dee and Humber Estuaries as Special Areas of Conservation under the Habitats Directive. It recognized that this designation might bring about direct conflict with any barrage scheme, especially the Cardiff–Weston option, the largest scheme under consideration for the Severn Estuary (DECC, SWRDA and WAG, 2009). The government's shortlist does not include the alternative put forward by environmental groups for a tidal reef scheme, on the grounds of its insufficiently advanced technical specification, although it is supporting further research into the scheme as an embryonic technology. Any barrage will need to meet the three Natura 2000 tests: whether there are alternatives, whether it is of overriding public interest, and whether it is possible to provide compensation (it is estimated that up to 14,500 ha of intertidal habitat would be lost in the Cardiff–Weston scheme [SDC, 2007]). Chapters 11 and 12 provide further discussion of these tensions.

5.5.3 Appeals to the climate change issue as a case for regional planning

It might be expected that regions are the most coherent level for resolving some of the national–local tensions over renewable energy (and indeed, as we discuss in Chapters 8 and 9, for mitigation and adaptation more broadly). Renewables also include hydropower, geothermal, biomass and waste-to-energy schemes: the latter are likely to be as contentious as onshore wind, and assessment of opportunities, capacity and strategic decision-making might be undertaken most appropriately at a regional level. Smith (2007) explored the devolution of some previously highly centralized aspects of energy policy to the regions in England. He concluded that 'regional governance for renewable energy is in a weak and uncertain position': although targets were set, and allied with more formal powers (what he calls Type I governance), it proved difficult to implement them in competition with other targets (such as housing and economic development targets), without the necessary resources of finance and skills, and especially where there is a lack of political will at regional level. This picture of ambivalence towards devolving powers to regions was continued by the 2007 policy guidance on planning and climate change. This requires regional planning bodies to:

> Set regional targets for renewable energy generation in line with PPS22, and ensure their ambition fully reflects opportunities in the region, are consistent with the government's national targets, and where appropriate in the light of delivery, are periodically revised upwards.
>
> (DCLG, 2007a, p. 13)

The guidance also states that the compelling case for renewable energy means that applicants for renewable energy should no longer have to justify the energy need for their project, either in general or in particular locations (DCLG, 2007a). But achieving these targets remains problematic, and research by the BWEA shows that these targets are likely to be 'comprehensively' missed: across the regions of England, on average only half of the 2010 target for 10 per cent of electricity generation to come from renewables will be met (BWEA, 2009b). However, the report concludes that sufficient generating capacity has in fact been approved, so the 10 per cent target can be met, if not by the target year. A parallel study for the DCLG reached similar conclusions, but also drew attention to the inconsistencies in assessing renewable capacities across regions, with some regions including offshore capacity in their targets (Ove Arup, 2009). The Arup study found that, while policies and targets for renewables were set fairly comprehensively in the strategies, not only was there a gap in the necessary rate to achieve the targets, but some of the targets were very modest in relation to the renewables resource available, and well below the targets necessary to deliver the government's 30 per cent renewables target for 2020. Moreover, those regions where renewables resources were more plentiful would need to make higher provision in order to meet the overall target for England.

Such a lack of ambition might be partly explained by the fact that the Regional Spatial Strategies (RSSs) were not formally adopted until 2008–09, and that much of central government spatial planning thinking in England is phrased in terms of permission rather than obligation. The PPS1 climate change supplement made clear that, although strategic targets can be set, they should be strategic tools, and not directly applied to applications for planning consent (DCLG, 2007a, p. 13). This illustrates the reluctance to strengthen powers at regional level. However, the 2009 Renewables Strategy states that the new NPS on renewable energy and an updated combined PPS1 climate change supplement and PPS22 will 'set a clear and challenging framework for delivering energy infrastructure and cutting carbon emissions consistent with national ambitions' (HMG, 2009b, p. 76). Moreover, the Labour government changed the institutional arrangements for regional-scale spatial planning in England. Part of the justification for integrating the former Regional Spatial Strategies with the Regional Economic Strategies has been to allow greater integration between the capital budgets of the latter and spatial plans: this might offer potential to promote a regional green economy and low-carbon economic areas (see Chapter 9). The new integrated Regional Strategies (RSs) are to contain 'ambitious targets for renewables, as well as some forms of low-carbon energy' (HMG, 2009b, p. 79), with a more strategic approach to regional potential and constraints. The ambition will be supported by funding, and new institutional and investment arrangements in the Office for Renewable Energy Deployment and Renewables Deployment Task Force.

The new RSs may therefore have more devolved powers and resources to deliver and enforce renewables targets. But it remains to be seen whether there is the political will to drive the changes through. Undoubtedly, ambivalence about the larger regionalization project (which, under Labour, gave powers to the regional tier, but met resistance from some local authorities and did not have cross-party support) has played a role, and there is uncertainty over the future of regional governance after 2010.

5.5.4 Appeals to the climate change issue as a case for local planning

While the discussion above has focused on the use of the climate change imperative to reconfigure the planning powers at national, regional and local level, there has been considerable capacity in the system for the local level to take the initiative, and indeed to influence national policy. The case of the 'Merton Rule' has been discussed in full elsewhere (such as Wilson, 2009b). In brief, the London Borough of Merton pushed through a requirement that any non-residential development over $1,000\,m^2$ should meet 10 per cent of its energy requirements from on-site renewables. To do this it overcame the objections of the Government Office for London, which had ultimate power of approval of the plan. The policy was taken up and expanded by the London Borough of Croydon, to cover all new developments, and ultimately found its way into paragraph 8 of PPS22 (ODPM, 2004b). Following representation from the property and development industry, paragraph 8 both weakened and widened the scope of the policy to state that LPAs may (rather than should) include policies to require a proportion of a development's energy needs to come from renewable and low-carbon sources (i.e. both on- or off-site). However, a significant proportion of LPAs had already taken up a Merton-style policy (TCPA, 2006c), and central government's own study of the implementation of paragraph 8 found that 90 per cent of the new-style plans incorporated such a policy (ODPM, 2006). The PPS1 Supplement therefore adopted the more forceful requirement that LPAs should set targets (DCLG, 2007a, p. 16), a move which the Planning White Paper claimed as a 'radical development' of the Merton Rule (HMG, 2007, p. 105). Statutory support for the requirements for local energy targets was given in the Planning and Energy Act 2008.

In this case, claims of the need and urgency of addressing climate change came from active local government, which showed how policy and practice could be extended to the national scale, despite initial opposition. The London Borough of Merton was able to build support for this policy by use of professional and political networks (amongst London Boroughs), personal efforts and campaigns, and promotion through the TCPA. Moreover, as Merton argues, the policy offers many benefits in terms of creating a market for renewables technologies, and hence employment (Merton estimates a value of £750 m). It should also assist in climate change adaptation through decentralizing energy generation and reducing vulnerability to any power outages under extreme weather events. In addition, the policy can bring about the behavioural change and community-level action needed to decarbonize energy generation. It ties in with applications for change of use or small householder extensions, and so affects the existing built environment as well as new build. This is a key element of the retrofitting, microgeneration and community energy-saving strategies for existing areas, discussed further in Chapter 9.

5.6 Conclusions

Climate change is reconfiguring the governance of spatial planning, and the relationship of national, regional and local levels. This is not, however, a one-way move towards greater centralization. Climate change has provided the opportunity for all levels to claim that they are the most appropriate scale at which both the benefits and costs of action should be addressed. The issue of climate change has moral force which can add weight to these claims. But these claims need to be understood in the context of wider issues of power and powers, and the use of discourses of 'fitness for purpose'. In terms of the different modes of governance for local authorities' climate change actions (Sections 5.4 and 5.5), the climate change agenda is bringing about a shift in the regulatory powers of local spatial planning, but it is also prompting greater integration with other interventions and across other scales through enablement and direct provision. The transition to a decarbonized society, spatial pattern and economy which is also resilient to climate change clearly requires action across all modes and at all levels. We explore these issues further for particular policy areas in Part III.

6 Just transitions

Horizons, timescales and equity

6.1 Introduction

The spatial planning response to climate change needs to be seen in the wider context of the principles of sustainability. We suggested in Chapter 1 that this requires an understanding of society's duties and obligations to both future and current generations. The costs of mitigating climate change might be justified on the grounds that we owe a duty of care to future generations not to expose them to the consequences of dangerous climate change in which tipping points (such as melting of ice caps and release of methane hydrates from the tundra or under the seabed) might trigger further irreversible climate change. Hence, it is argued, the current generation is morally obliged to take action to reduce the causes of climate change, and especially to limit the absolute amount of carbon in the atmosphere. But we must also consider the distributive impacts of the means used to achieve this on the present generation. Climate change adaptation also entails complex justifications, in that it can be argued that the impacts of climate change are already affecting more vulnerable groups, both globally (World Bank, 2009; Oxfam, 2008) and within countries. But adaptation is not a one-off set of actions, but a process of adaptation actions over time and building adaptive capacity over time (as explained in Chapter 2). Adaptation actions are therefore justified in terms of our obligations to the future as well as the current generation.

In this chapter, we explore some aspects of thinking about spatial planning's response to these issues. We ague that the issue of climate change has had the effect of radically altering the horizons in spatial planning, with revived attention being given to the longer-term future. There is a renewed commitment to the interests of future generations. However, climate change considerations are throwing into greater relief the problems of ensuring equitable outcomes of plans and planning decisions both now and in the future. We suggest that one way in which more systematic assessment can be made of these impacts is through the use of longer time frames and the use of future socio-economic as well as climate change scenarios.

6.2 Futures thinking in spatial planning

We saw in Chapter 2 that the IPCC's climate change scenarios are based on a set of assumptions (the SRES scenarios) about future levels of emissions of greenhouse gases, which were produced expressly to provide input into the development of climate models. In the UK, climate modelling (UKCIP02, UKCP09) shows results at different timescales representing the decades around the 2020s, 2050s and 2080s. Other models have estimated the impacts of climate change for much longer periods (such as Tyndall Centre's work on climate change on a millennial timescale (Lenton *et al.*, 2006)) for aspects such as the melting of ice sheets, sea-level rise, and the slowing or reversal of the North Atlantic thermohaline circulation, under which north-western Europe experiences warmer conditions than would be expected at its latitude.

By contrast, most spatial plans drawn up by local, regional and national authorities have a much shorter time frame (although, as we shall see, there are differences between countries). For many people, this is paradoxical, as spatial planning as a public policy intervention might be associated with long-term thinking and utopian ideals (although utopianism itself is seen as discredited, as Giddens (2009) argued). But in the latter part of the twentieth century, its horizons foreshortened. The previous chapter has suggested that the more strategic the scale (national and regional), the greater the expectation that time horizons would be longer: but, in the UK at least, even these have been modest. The first RSSs had horizons of fifteen to twenty years, and their successors are also tasked with looking to this horizon; similarly, the national spatial frameworks for Scotland and Wales extend only to twenty years. By contrast, as we saw in Chapter 4, the Netherlands has planning horizons of fifty years for the national spatial plan and the NEPP and, for the Randstad area, thirty to forty years.

There are a number of possible explanations for this shortening of planning horizons in the UK. One might be the particular interpretation of sustainability that has been dominant in much planning discourse, of meeting the three dimensions of social, economic and environmental objectives. Much of the debate in both sustainable development and planning discourses has centred on the extent to which these three can be balanced, traded off or shifted fundamentally (see, for instance, Owens and Cowell, 2001; Baker and Eckerberg, 2008; and Adger and Jordan, 2009). The planning profession has claimed a role in sustainability consistent with its ability to engage with such issues as trade-offs and community participation, and the emphasis has been on the present rather than the future.

Second, the postmodernist emphasis on 'indeterminacy, incommensurability, variance, diversity, complexity and intentionality' (Allmendinger, 2009, p. 32) has challenged the notion of a controllable future. Connell (2009) suggests that the practice of planning might be seen as a way of 'making the future a visible part of present decision-making processes' (p. 86); he reviews a number of statements from planning theorists such as Friedman, Forester and

Healey that suggest that an orientation to the future is a fundamental tenet of planning. But, with Allmendinger, he argues that a loss of faith in notions of progress, scientific determinacy and technical solutions has led to a loss of confidence in the modernist project of increased control over the future. Theorists such as Beck (1992) argue that in a risk society, even as governments have become more committed to managing risk, those risks have become amplified and inherently unmanageable. By contrast, Marshall (1997) argues that the use of futures-thinking techniques such as horizon-scanning and scenario exercises by the industrial-military complex has tarnished by association the use of scenarios and storylines (which we discuss further at Section 6.6). Connell suggests that the response of the planning profession has been to move away from attempts to plan the future towards managing processes and planning for liveable cities, emphasizing diversity rather than a conception of a single public interest. Such approaches are consistent with the collaborative notions of planning discussed in Chapter 1.

Third, planning has been expected to give more attention to implementation and delivery; this itself may be for political reasons, such as New Labour's emphasis on modernizing planning in a managerialist mode, with targets, performance audits and monitoring. It may also be the result of disenchantment with the more ambitious, longer-term projects of the post-war redevelopment schemes and post-war (called Mark II) new towns. As a profession, planning in the UK has been criticized for overambition and the apparent failure of these larger-scale planning projects (Giddens, 2009), while at the same time the media treatment of planning portrays it as an activity akin to environmental health and neighbour dispute resolution.

Fourth, the acknowledgement that planning is significantly a political activity, as much as a professional one, has reinforced the association with short-term electoral cycles, often of only five years. A survey for the SECTORS project (SEECCP, 2004) showed that the large majority of planning respondents in both public and private sectors thought in terms of five-year horizons, for this reason.

Finally, it may be that the European notion of spatial planning, perhaps in stressing the need for integration of land use with other policy sectors and those sectors' decisions on the use of land, has placed more emphasis on space and spatial relationships at the expense of the dimension of time.

6.3 Sustainable development and planning for future generations

However, as we saw in Chapter 1, one of the essential principles of sustainability thinking is the regard for future generations. While this has become something of a mantra, it is worth recognizing that it is in itself a philosophically contentious principle. There are those, such as Beckerman and Pasek (2001), who argue that it is incoherent, under a welfare-maximizing utilitarian ethic, to owe a duty of care to future generations, on the grounds that they might not exist; and, if they do exist, we cannot know what they will value. Therefore, it is argued, it is illogical to defer current consumption (for instance of resources) or to reduce present welfare or happiness in favour of possible future generations who might place very different values on those resources. Some object to this argument on the grounds that this is a distortion of utilitarianism, and that the moral obligations under sustainability and justice to future generations imply a duty of care: 'Sustainability obliges us to think about sustaining something into the future, and justice makes us think about distributing something across present and future' (Dobson, 1999, p. 5). The philosophical debate is sharpened when considering climate change (Page, 2006), and hinges on offering defences to what may be seen as a morally distasteful conclusion that we do not have such obligations to future generations.

While spatial planning in a postmodernist world may emphasize the present, planning has subscribed to a wider conception of sustainable development. The word 'sustainable' can mean both that development (in the form of human cultural, economic and social activity) needs to be sustained by ecosystem functions, natural processes and natural resources (such as climate regulation, the water cycle and food products), and that such activity should be capable of being sustained into the future. The UK's conception of sustainable development has changed over the two decades since the Rio Summit, with varying emphases on the social dimension (introduced as an explicit principle in the first sustainable development strategy of the new Labour government), and on the notion of environmental limits (explicitly mentioned as a key principle in the 2005 Strategy [HMG, 2005]). The overarching planning policy guidance from 2005 (PPS1) is that planning plays a key role in supporting the achievement of sustainable development (ODPM, 2005a).

6.4 Planning, climate change and the future

While planning still retains its commitment to sustainable development, the issue of climate change has reoriented its attention to the future. We argue that the discourse of climate change in terms of future conditions, the emphasis on possible futures from climate modellers, as well as the representation of those different futures as associated with degrees of global temperature change (such as *Six Degrees* [Lynas, 2007]), have prompted a new orientation to the future. This has been reinforced by debates about peak oil and the finite and time-limited resources of other fossil fuels. It is argued that global oil production from conventional sources will start to decline within the next twenty years (IEA, 2009). Another prompt has been reappraisal associated with the turn of the century and a new millennium, instigating millennial assessments such as the Millennium Development Goals of the UN Development Programme (UNDP), and the Millennium Ecosystem Assessment of the UN Environment Programme (UNEP) (this latter is discussed in Chapter 12).

A significant implication of these new frames of thinking for planning for the built environment, infrastructure and natural environments has been a refocusing on the planned or expected lifetime of development. As we argue in Chapters 8 and 9, the availability of climate change scenarios for different time-periods has enabled estimates to be made of the climatic conditions that the built environment might experience. This has, in turn, drawn attention to the age and condition of the existing stock of houses, buildings and infra-structure, and to the lifetime of the newly built environment. It has raised questions of responsibility for planning authorities, designers, developers and the financial institutions who will both finance and insure such developments for the next sixty years (the average lifetime of new dwellings). This forward-looking activity has been reinforced in the UK by a revision to population forecasts, under which a significant growth in population is expected (from a population of 60.5 million people in 2006 to one perhaps of 85 million by 2081), after a period of relatively stable population in the 1970s to 1990s (ONS, 2008).

The outcome has been a reimagining of the future – both as a future to be avoided (in the sense of dangerous climate change) and as a future to be planned for and adapted to in the sense of a relatively high probability and degree of certainty about the impacts of at least a 2°C change in global temperature by the 2050s.

6.5 Climate change and intra-generational equity

Spatial planning has a commitment to different conceptions of the public interest: in some conceptions, this entails an obligation to consider the distributional impacts of planned actions, or to minimize the inequitable consequences, or, more overtly, to increase equity. In some ways, the issue of climate change has blurred the distinction in sustainable development between inter-generational and intra-generational equity (that is, both between and within generations). A number of studies have shown that, under the changes currently being experienced, the poor and disadvantaged are significantly more vulnerable than the wealthy and better-resourced. This is the case at an international level, with countries such as Vietnam and those of sub-Saharan Africa both more exposed to the physical changes (in temperatures, rainfall patterns, sea-level rise and water resources) and having less adaptive capacity in the sense of wealth and resources (Oxfam, 2008; Adger et al., 2006). It is also the case within countries and, indeed, within cities and rural areas, with the well-documented experience of the inequitable impacts of and responses to Hurricane Katrina in New Orleans in 2005 (Olshansky, 2006), and the severe impact of the 2003 heatwave in Europe on the elderly, especially those in urban areas experiencing social isolation (EEA, 2004).

6.5.1 Climate change and social justice

Although none of these events can be attributable incontrovertibly to climate change, they do indicate the sort of impacts that are expected under the climate change scenarios. Within the UK, the most obvious example of the sorts of conditions or extreme events that might be experienced under a changing climate is that of flooding (fluvial, urban and coastal). The experiences of floods in the twenty-first century (see Chapter 11) have raised fundamental questions about the impacts of flooding events and about the impacts of planned choices to adapt to such events (through, for instance, the funding and provision of flood defences). A number of studies (such as Round Table on Climate Change and Poverty, 2008, and SNIFFER, 2009) have reviewed the potential impacts of climate change on a currently inequitable society. The first report argues that those most affected by climate change will be the 1.5 million people in the UK who live in poverty. They live in poorer housing, have poorer health, less access to home insurance and fewer resources to adapt to rising prices (such as of fuel or food). Moreover, there is evidence that the most deprived populations already experience poor environments: for instance, the most deprived populations in South Yorkshire are two to three times more likely than the average to be living near a waste or landfill site, and most likely to be living next to multiple waste sites and near an industrial plant (Fairburn, Butler and Smith, 2009). The Health Protection Agency suggests that, while wintertime pollution episodes might decrease under climate change, summertime episodes of photochemical ozone pollution will become more frequent, although possibly less intense (Kovats, 2008). While there has been considerable coverage of the issue of flooding and equity (see Section 6.5.2), there has been less discussion of the impacts of climate change on air quality and health. The Round Table report also argued that the credit crisis has raised doubts as to whether environmental protection can be afforded at the same time as addressing the economic crisis, but the report argues that what is needed in response are virtuous circles which reduce poverty and address climate change: 'Addressing poverty is the most effective way of ensuring that communities have the resources they need to adapt to climate change' (RTCCP, 2008, p. 38).

The SNIFFER report on differential impacts (2009) similarly concludes that climate change will 'widen existing inequalities, unless social impacts are actively addressed across the range of adaptation and mitigation measures' (p. 1). The report identifies the factors affecting people's vulnerability to climate change as the relationship between places at risk, social deprivation and dis-empowerment (see Figure 6.1).

In terms of places at risk, the 2009 climate projections for the UK do allow more localized impacts to be estimated (for instance, for cities, administrative regions or catchments). Understanding of the exposure of such places to climate change is therefore a little more informed: as we shall see in Chapters 8 and 9, the understanding of local vulnerability requires more localized assessments,

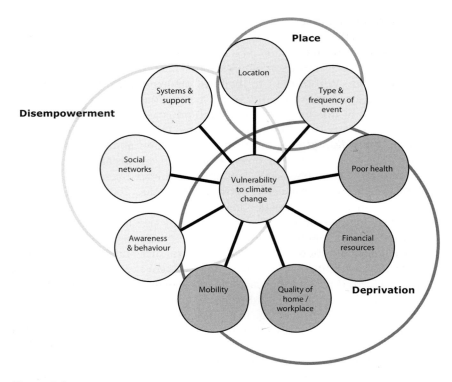

Figure 6.1

Factors affecting vulnerability to climate change
Source: SNIFFER, 2009, p. 10

especially with regard to the built environment and (for instance) to the incidence of urban and ground-water flooding.

Nevertheless, the SNIFFER report cites evidence from the reviews undertaken for the Environment Agency that suggests weather-related vulnerabilities are greatest for socially deprived areas (that is, experiencing multiple deprivation such as poverty and low educational attainment). Walker *et al.* (2006) argue that households within areas of deprivation experience cumulative vulnerability with lower levels of flood awareness, fewer resources in the form of social capital to cope with the flood and its consequences, and health impacts aggravating existing poor health. Older people may possess resources (including experience of coping with floods or other events), but they may have other disadvantages of mobility problems, isolation and lack of financial resources (Pitt, 2008).

In response, the SNIFFER report recommends an adaptation framework for social vulnerability to climate change, which proposes action at national, local and community levels, and concludes that measures are needed in policy and management, as well as building social resilience and adaptive capacity. Spatial planning has a role to play in all these approaches, such as through setting national, regional and local policy objectives for the built and natural environments, through the use of tools such as sustainability appraisal and strategic environmental assessment, through monitoring and auditing the distributive outcomes of policy implementation, and through providing opportunities for participation and community engagement. We address these issues in Chapters 7–11.

6.5.2 Equity in flood risk and coastal erosion management

Both these RTCCP and SNIFFER review reports recommend that social and distributive questions be formulated during the consideration of policy and in the assessment of options. But adopting a normative stance towards the promotion of social and environmental justice does not resolve some of the difficulties in implementation, such as the exposure and vulnerability to flooding. Policies for flood-risk management (as we shall see in more detail in Chapter 11) have shifted from a hard-engineering, scheme-led approach to a broader conception of making space for water, managing flood risks and consequences, and a wider consideration of sustainability principles of economic, social and environmental benefits and costs. Johnson *et al.* (2007) examine the extent to which the different elements of this new approach – structural works (such as flood diversion or alleviation channels, or dredging), flood storage and non-structural interventions (such as insurance, flood warnings, awareness-raising, land-use controls and planning, homeowner adaptations and emergency management) – meet criteria for social justice. They argue that the practical realities of implementing all these approaches at national, regional and local scales still give rise to issues of fairness (to those funding the measures, to their beneficiaries, and to those who are excluded from the schemes and may even have an increased flood risk as a result). The sustainability imperative might suggest that we should favour those who are most vulnerable or already experiencing social and environmental inequality (a principle Johnson *et al.* [2007] derive from Rawlsian conceptions of social contract [Rawls, 1972]); however, other principles of justice relate to equality of access or opportunity, or procedural justice – the degree to which citizens are positioned with respect to planning and decision-making, including the existing distribution of power. The authors conclude that all of the interventions present difficulties, although spatial planning, through the provisions of PPS25 (DCLG, 2006c), meets most of the criteria. For instance, they suggest that it offers nationally consistent criteria (for England), and hence procedural equality; it includes an exceptions test, under which some development in flood-risk areas is allowed for wider social, environmental or economic benefits, such as regeneration, to avoid socio-economic blight and retain the value of past investment in urban infrastructure. It also accords special consideration to the vulnerable – such as homes for the elderly and children's homes – in excluding such developments from the categories of development allowed in a flood plain.

The 2009–10 revision to the PPS25 to encompass coastal flooding (see Chapter 11) also gives rise to issues of procedural and distributive justice. Serious issues arise at the coast where the decision not to hold the line of the coast entails that certain properties, or even communities, over time will need to be abandoned, and therefore questions arise of society's responsibility to provide compensation or resettlement. There are already inequities in that, while flood insurance may be part of standard packages, it does not generally cover coastal erosion (Stallworthy, 2006). The reallocation of public funds for flood defences, or the shift away from coastal defences, might encourage the government to take a different view of its role with respect to insurance, perhaps becoming an insurer of last resort (more akin to the position in the Netherlands), especially in areas such as the Thames Gateway where the development is being promoted by government itself. In this context, the role of spatial planning in allocating land for development is intimately bound up with issues of burden-sharing. Stallworthy comments that it is surprising that the shift towards more sustainable coastal zone management 'has so far failed seriously to engage the question of disproportionate impacts upon these individuals and communities at the most vulnerable locations' (2006, p. 370). He concludes that, in order to reflect some of the new realities of climate change, one might prohibit private sea defences, but observe procedural equity by acknowledging property rights through the provision of advance notice of a receding shoreline (indeterminate but over an estimated time period), or by the state selectively purchasing land, even if at a discounted rate to reflect the new risks. However, he acknowledges that in many places there is insufficient time available to establish such an equitable scheme, but he concludes that 'government, in pursuing sustainable responses to climate change, must recognise and address distributional issues' (p. 373) through, for instance, the structured discounting of property values, but especially through open participatory processes in establishing strategic priorities.

As with fluvial flooding, there are very real issues of distributive and procedural justice that might be addressed through the spatial planning system and the interaction of land-use plans with flood-risk management. These issues are beginning to be addressed in the revised PPS on development and coastal change (due to be published by DCLG in 2010) (see Chapter 11). The PPS lays considerable stress on the roles of the statutory agencies – Environment Agency, Natural England, English Heritage and local authorities – in terms of establishing an evidence base about coastal processes and a range of possible options for coastal defences, managed realignment or community resettlement. There are proposals for a Coastal Change Fund to reduce hardship and support communities where relocation is planned within Coastal Change Management Areas. The PPS acknowledges the importance of community links in allocating any suitable land for relocation, but perhaps underplays the importance of full engagement with the local community. Agyeman *et al.* (2009) argue that 'managed retreat interventions need to take full account of people's attachment to place as part of their self-identity, and use citizen knowledge: involving residents and making an effort to understand how they relate to places can both enrich the value of restorative/managed retreat efforts and alleviate potential conflict throughout their implementation' (p. 510). Such interventions 'are more likely to be accepted if they are interpreted by those involved in it as a process that is fair, transparent and inclusive or that leads to positive and fair outcomes for the groups and individuals involved' (p. 512). They warn that more research is needed on the process of place detachment as part of relocation, where the planning actions need to engage fully with community values and develop conditions of trust.

6.5.3 Social justice for current and future generations

Issues of climate change have therefore to some extent blurred the distinction in the Brundtland conception of sustainability between meeting the needs of the present generation and those of future generations. Issues of distributive and procedural justice cross the boundary. In many areas likely to be affected by climate change, the distribution of risks – such as risks of flood or erosion – is already inherently unfair, through either natural or anthropogenic causes, and therefore outcome equality may be impossible. The role of flood-risk and coastal-zone management, as well as air-quality and waste management, should therefore be to mimimize relative inequalities (Johnson *et al.*, 2007) and to ensure a more transparent discussion of equity and the distribution of costs and benefits. Paavola *et al.* argue that it is unlikely that distributive justice 'will provide a sufficient foundation for climate change justice because of the heterogeneity of involved parties' (2006, p. 267). They contend that procedural justice is needed to give legitimacy to climate change policy regimes, provided questions of recognition of the rights and ability to participate and the effective distribution of power are addressed (p. 268).

6.6 Futures thinking: socio-economic and climate change scenarios

The ability of climate change science to make projections (with increasing degrees of confidence) of future conditions has driven the policy responses of mitigation and adaptation. It has also raised the salience of the future, with organizations, individuals and campaigns now standardly referring to targets such as that to produce 20 per cent of energy by renewables by 2020, or to reduce greenhouse gas emissions by 80 per cent by 2050.

Yet we need to consider just how we think about the future, and what tools are available to us to enable us to do so. The climate scenarios from the IPCC and, in the UK, from UKCIP, are the outcome not just of extensive modelling effort and scientific scrutiny, but also the result of debate and negotiations amongst a range of different interests, representing scientists, decision-makers, politicians and funding bodies (Hulme and Dessai, 2008). Moreover, the socio-economic conditions that will obtain at those periods are likely to be different – possibly very different – from current conditions. The IPCC's climate change projections (as described in Chapter 1) themselves are based on a set of assumptions about the future economic and social conditions with which certain levels of emissions might be associated. The Special Report on Emissions Scenarios (SRES) projected a set of scenarios based on consistent assumptions about globalization, economic growth and societal values, contrasting continued global economic growth, with different storylines representing greater use of fossil fuel or technological developments, with a set of scenarios around less material-intensive and more efficient consumption. Scenarios have been defined as 'coherent, internally consistent and plausible descriptions of future states of the world, used to inform future trends, potential decisions or consequences' (UKCIP, 2001, p. 4).

6.6.1 Socio-economic scenarios: opportunities and barriers

Socio-economic scenarios are useful in a number of ways. They can

- sensitize an organization to a range of possible futures;
- offer a plausible representation of the future;
- remove filters we impose on our thinking which exclude possibilities outside current trends;
- build networks of common concerns and shared understandings;
- handle uncertainty and complexity;
- highlight discontinuities and ruptures;
- suggest reactive (anticipating risks) or normative (suggesting desired opportunities) courses of action.

These various purposes determine the approaches used in the scenarios, but also raise questions about the use of, and audience for, the scenarios. Scenarios have been extensively developed in the last few years, but there has been much less *post hoc* analysis of their utility. Table 6.1 shows the drivers and principal features of a number of socio-economic scenarios developed at European level for both research and policy purposes. It will be seen that there are some common drivers of change. The MACIS project (a European project to examine the impacts of climate change for biodiversity, both mitigation and adaptation) reviewed a number of these scenarios. Part of the project involved exploring the range of environmental change scenarios that has been developed within the European context to explore climate change impacts on biodiversity. Interviews were undertaken with scenario users in the EEA, EC and Scottish public bodies; it was found that users considered scenarios useful for visualization, debate and communication, thinking about non-linear events, decision-making, through visualizing futures where specific uncertainties have been resolved, and hence

Table 6.1 Socio-economic scenarios

Scenario analysis/scope	Timeframe	Justification	Driving forces	Scenarios
EEA PRELUDE (Prospective environmental analysis of land use and development in Europe) EU-25 plus Norway & Switzerland	2005–35	Impacts of future development on EU landscape & biodiversity	• environmental awareness • solidarity & equity • governance & intervention • agricultural organization • technology & innovation	• Great Escape (contrasts) • Evolved Society (harmony) • Clustered Networks (structure) • Lettuce SurpriseU (innovation) • Big Crisis (cohesion)
PESETA (Projection of economic impacts of climate change in sectors of EU based on bottom-up analysis)	2011–40, 2071–100	Multisectoral assessment of climate change impacts, and monetary valuation	Global emissions driven by: • demographic change • economic development • technological change	Two global scenarios: • IPCC A2 (national enterprise) • IPCC B2 (local stewardship)
ALARM (Assessing large-scale risks for biodiversity with tested methods) EU-25	2020/2050	Exploration of forces behind pressures to develop effective biodiversity protection and EU public policies	• CAP • Chemicals, energy, transport, trade & biotechnology policy • structural funds • ESDP • Natura 2000 • Climate change	• BAMBU (business-as-usual) • GRAS – growth applied strategy • SEDG – sustainable European development goal

(continued)

Table 6.1 (cont.)

Scenario analysis/scope	Timeframe	Justification	Driving forces	Scenarios
ACCELERATES (**Assessing climate change effects on land use and ecosystems: from regional analysis to European scale**) EU-25	2080	Assess vulnerability of European land use and ecosystems (agriculture, forestry, species distribution and habitat fragmentation) to climate change in context of UNFCCC and CBD	Drivers for socio-economic context of agro-ecosystems: • geographical situation • demography (population growth and migration) • economic, agricultural, social and environment policies • land market regulation • resource competition • farm structure and function of rural areas	Two GCM climate scenarios SRES emissions scenarios: • A1 World Market • A2 Regional Enterprise • B1 Global Sustainability • B2 Local Stewardship
ESPON EU-25 plus Norway & Switzerland	2006–30	Spatial scenarios in context of EU enlargement	Disparities in wealth at enlargement External factors: • globalization • energy price-rise • climate change • immigration Internal factors: • population change • EU policies	• Trend scenario • Globally competitive Europe • Economic, social & territorial cohesion • Prescriptive scenario
SENSOR EU-25	2005–25	Impact assessment tools to support decision-making for multifunctional land-use	• oil price • world demand • population growth	• Reference – trend • High growth • Low growth

Scenario analysis/scope	Timeframe	Justification	Driving forces	Scenarios
SENSOR (cont.) EU-25	2005–25		• Labour participation rates • R&D efforts	
SCENAR 2020 EU-27	2020	Agricultural and rural economy	• Rural demography • Agricultural technology • Agricultural markets • Natural & social constraints on land use • Exogenous and policy-related (e.g. EU enlargement, WTO, CAP)	• Trend-based reference scenario • Regionalization • Liberalization
EURURALIS EU-27	2000–30	Develop a tool to support long-term changes and policy challenges in rural areas of Europe	• Continuation of globalization • Government intervention • Agriculture • Land use • Rural development	• Global economy • Global cooperation • Continental markets • Regional communities
EEA Urban Sprawl in Europe EU-27	2005–100 City case studies 2020; 2025	Examine drivers for sprawl in context of EU policies of Internal market, competitiveness, sustainable development Cohesion Structural funds	• Macroeconomic • Microeconomic (e.g. price of land) • Demography • Housing preferences • Transportation • Regulatory framework (e.g. poor enforcement or coordination)	• Business-as-usual • Compact development • Scattered development

the opportunity to test a decision. However, barriers to use included difficulty in envisioning different futures; documentation of scenarios; debate over probabilistic scenarios; relevance to policy, policy cycles and level of governance; and inherent uncertainty (such as the failure to envisage the banking and credit crisis of 2008–09).

At the national level, the UKCIP, as part of its early work on climate change projections, had recognized that the climate scenarios needed to be considered in the context of changed socio-economic conditions, which might by the 2050s or 2080s significantly affect both sensitivity to climate change and the potential for adaptive responses. UKCIP therefore commissioned a set of socio-economic scenarios from the Policy Studies Institute; they identified two key dimensions on which to generate a set of possible futures: social values and governance systems (UKCIP, 2001). The social values dimension represents community and individual attitudes, with more individualistic, materialist and short-term values at one end of the spectrum, contrasted with concerns for greater sustainability and social equity at the other. The governance dimension represents aspects of the scale and structure of political authority, with regionalization (possibly represented by nationalism or protectionism) at one end and global political institutions at the other (Eames and Skea, 2002) (see Figure 6.2).

UKCIP has promoted the use of the scenarios as a tool in support of its role to develop stakeholder awareness and understanding of climate change adaptation, and to develop tools to support understanding. UKCIP had advised on how the scenarios could be paired with the UKCIP02 climate change scenarios (see Table 6.2), pointing out that in future the socio-economic pathway might

Figure 6.2

Four socio-economic scenarios for the UK
Source: UKCIP, 2001, p. 19

diverge from the global climate emission scenario on which it is based (for instance, where countries such as the UK might be moving towards a Local Stewardship, low-carbon economy and society, but global greenhouse gas emissions were still increasing with the economic growth of countries such as China). UKCIP therefore recommended (UKCIP, 2006) combining a range of climate change and socio-economic scenarios, but ensuring that full account is still given to the range of uncertainties and possible sudden changes.

The socio-economic scenarios have been used in a number of studies of relevance to spatial planning, both research projects (such as MONARCH and ASCCUE) and policy applications (such as *Foresight Future Flooding*, Evans *et al.*, 2004) and in regional climate change adaptation studies (such as for the East Midlands and London). The Foresight Flooding study, for instance, evaluated future flood risks and their economic, social and environmental costs under different IPCC emissions and socio-economic scenarios. It found that, under a World Markets scenario, although emission levels might be high, the wealth generated might fund more effective flood defences; however, a Global Sustainability scenario incurred higher urban damage costs than a Local Stewardship scenario (even though it was matched by lower emissions), as property values were projected to be lower. The study recommended a range of measures consistent with the move towards more sustainable flood-risk management as outlined in *Making Space for Water* (Defra, 2004a).

There are, therefore, practical applications of scenarios of future socio-economic conditions which can help to highlight issues and identify possible courses of action – some examples in spatial planning are given below. The UKCIP commissioned a study of the lessons learnt from the development and use of the scenarios (Hughes *et al.*, 2008). The study suggests that, in order to make such judgements, it is important to understand whether socio-economic

Table 6.2 Possible combinations of climate change scenarios and socio-economic scenarios

		Socio-economic scenario			
		Global sustainability (GDP=2.25%)	Local Stewardship (GDP=1.25%)	National Enterprise (GDP=1.75%)	World Markets (GDP=3%)
UKCIP02 climate change scenario	Low	S C	S		S
	Medium– low		C		
	Medium– high			C	
	High	S	S		S C

Source: UKCIP, 2006

Key: S = combination used in sensitivity analysis; C = combination used if consistency is considered scenarios are being used reactively or proactively, and the relationship between actors, their motivations and power of agency. Other important features of scenarios are the ways in which they handle the uncertainties of the future, achieve a detailed understanding of the present, and succeed in grounding the scenarios in the experience and knowledge of stakeholders; moreover they provide an opportunity for new language and concepts beyond current world views and mental maps. It can be seen that some of these features – for instance, the need for grounding but the chance to think beyond conventional trends and concepts – might be in opposition to each other. The review examined a number of studies which had actually used the UKCIP scenarios, and those which considered doing so but did not; it interviewed researchers and policy-makers who has been involved in the studies, and it drew on these to identify some key issues.

The study found that many studies using the scenarios overemphasized the values dimension and underplayed the governance dimension As the govern-ance dimension was characterized by globalization versus the independence of the nation-state, it proved hard to relate to the subnational (regional) focus of many of the studies. This emphasis risked exaggerating the values axis, and pre-senting a caricatured polarization of green futures versus growth. For regional and local authorities, this overlooked their own commitment to sustainable development under which they were aiming to meet multiple (environmental, economic and social) objectives. The review found that, for near-term decision-making (ten–twenty years), regional planning policies (at that time, represented by the Regional Planning Guidance, the forerunners of the Regional Spatial Strategies) were used as an independent, contrasting reference scenario, rather than as an input into the scenarios themselves (Hughes *et al.*, 2008, p. 34).

In general, however, there were a number of reasons why the socio-economic scenarios were not more actively used in the studies reviewed. One reason lay in the lack of clarity of purpose of the scenario process – especially the question of how far they were to be used in informing the decisions likely to be taken by regional actors. Second, the studies using the socio-economic scenarios were focused on climate change adaptation, and yet they did not enable easy identi-fication of agency or causation, and so were less helpful in identifying either decisions and choices that could increase adaptive capacity or reduce vulner-ability, or the roles of different tiers of actors and authorities. Given that the climate change scenarios were determined by global emissions, this limited the range of actions open to regional or local levels. A third concern was the polar-ization of the scenario spaces by the use of a 2×2 matrix. Finally, while UKCIP had intended the high level scenario to provide a consistent framework, the regional users had selected or adapted them according to their own concerns and stakeholders' interests. This meant that consistency and comparability were harder to achieve.

Nevertheless, it was clear that the existence of such scenarios had helped to prompt a wider consideration of possible alternative futures, and in this sense fulfilled some of the functions of scenario exercises. Despite the difficulties found in practice in both the MACIS and UKCIP reviews, the researchers concluded that socio-economic scenarios have potential, provided that they are developed with stakeholder engagement and a clear understanding of the concerns and policy-action space of users of the scenarios.

6.6.2 Application of scenarios in spatial planning in the UK

In UK spatial planning practice, the UKCIP02 scenarios have been applied in regional impacts studies and in research studies which have influenced some of the thinking about climate change in the preparation of regional plans, such as that for the north-west, and the spatial plan for London. The socio-economic scenarios were developed, with specific quantitative indicators such as GDP and GVA up to 2060s, for the regional level, for both the north-west and south-east regions, under the BESEECH project, part of the Building Knowledge for a Changing Climate (BKCC) project (Walsh *et al.*, 2007). The ASCCUE project then combined them with more localized climate change scenarios generated by the BETWIXT research project, and used the resulting scenarios to explore a number of socio-economic variables. For instance, they drew attention to the possible impacts of climate change for those already suffering levels of deprivation in terms of poor health, housing and poverty (Lindley *et al.*, 2007). The ASCCUE study also, in its exploration of the implications of climate change for human external thermal comfort, suggested that the use of open space might change under a changing climate, and such spaces could assist people's agency and capacity to adapt. Social surveys were undertaken of users of open spaces in Manchester city centre and Lewes in South East England, and it was found, as expected, that humans are capable of adapting to different thermal conditions, through a range of actions including choice of location, activity and clothing. Comparing the results with those of a Europe-wide study, it was found that there is in fact a remarkable tolerance – expressed as perceptions of personal thermal comfort – of widely different climatic conditions, from south-east Europe to north-west Europe. It was concluded that, provided that climate change is not too abrupt, people will be able to adapt given certain contextual conditions. These include freedom of opportunity to adjust behaviour, which raises questions about the socio-economic conditions which will obtain in the future under a changed climate (Wilson *et al.*, 2008).

There is already concern at the privatization of open space and shopping precincts under which hard-pressed local authorities enter agreements with private developers or town centre management companies to manage spaces. Some of the outcomes of this are an emphasis on footfall and consumer spending, with a consequent tendency to limit rights of access to certain groups deemed to be 'suitable' (Minton, 2006; 2009). Under socio-economic scenarios such as World Markets and National Enterprise, where community interests are favoured less than individualistic action, this tendency to privatization of space might intensify; under conditions of increased summer temperatures or more intense or prolonged heat waves, there may be limits placed on access to open space and the opportunities for thermal comfort that it offers. Moreover, under a major intensification of the urban heat island effect, it was suggested by stakeholders involved in the ASCCUE project that certain groups who have recently been attracted to central area residential accommodation (especially younger, high-income households) might move out to cooler, suburban areas, but those households (especially the elderly or disadvantaged) without such resources might experience more severe thermal discomfort.

The implications of this for social justice, social inclusion and the equitable spatial planning of urban spaces are significant. Planning policies might be needed expressly not just to incorporate climate-responsive provision and design of such open spaces, but also to ensure the maintenance of free public access to such spaces. The policies in the London Plan go some way towards this. The London Plan itself had (as explained in Chapter 9) drawn on work undertaken using the socio-economic scenarios in *London's Warming* (LCCP, 2002), the study of the impacts of climate change in London. This had led to further studies of the impacts of increased temperatures and more frequent heat-waves, and to specific policies for urban cooling and for the creation and maintenance of public open space in the London plan (further explained in Chapter 9).

Scenario sets with a more specific focus have been developed in other sectors and areas of resource use, such as the VIBAT (Visioning and Backcasting for Transport in London) study (Hickman *et al.*, 2009), and a UK Foresight study of sustainable energy management in the built environment (Foresight SEMBE, 2008; Rydin, 2009), which are discussed further in Chapters 8 and 9 respectively. The UK Foresight initiative has followed up its study of future flooding (Evans *et al.*, 2004) with studies of future land use (Foresight Land Use Futures Project, 2010). The SEMBE project did not use the UKCIP SES, but developed its own 2×2 matrix with dimensions of the geopolitical context for energy (similar to the SES axis of autonomy and interdependence), contrasted with attitudes to innovation and investment on new or existing built environment and energy systems (thus, an axis indicating preference for either optimizing existing, or developing new systems). The resulting scenario spaces – characterized as carbon creativity, resourceful regions, sunshine state and green growth – were used to highlight key issues, such as the extent of refurbishment or replacement of the existing built environment (especially the residential stock) (Rydin, 2009). This is discussed in greater depth in Chapter 9.

6.7 Socio-economic scenarios in the Netherlands

Just as the UK had developed a set of socio-economic scenarios for use with the climate change scenarios, the Netherlands has also adopted a set of scenarios employing a 2×2 matrix. In this study, the two key drivers are the degree of

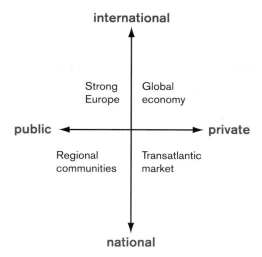

international

| Strong Europe | Global economy |

public ← → private

| Regional communities | Transatlantic market |

national

Figure 6.3

Socio-economic scenarios in the Netherlands
Source: Janssen *et al.*, 2006

international cooperation contrasted with action at the scale of the nation-state, and the degree of individualism compared with public action (Janssen *et al.*, 2006). The resulting scenarios from the matrix are Strong Europe, Global economy, Transatlantic market, and Regional communities: the scenarios are understandably similar to those of UKCIP, but with a stronger European perspective (Figure 6.3).

The scenarios have been used in the CcSP research project (see Chapter 4); scenarios have also been examined by the Delta Commission study (Deltacommissie, 2008) on future flood risk and the implications for national and provincial planning in the Netherlands (see Chapter 8). As with the Foresight studies in the UK, the Delta Commission considered that social, socio-economic, demographic and growth factors for this century and beyond were as significant as the physical changes likely under climate change. The study assessed a range of sources for scenarios up to 2040s, including that of the National Environmental Assessment Agency (MNP, 2007), which used the scenarios to project a population of between 15 million under a Regional Communities scenario, and more than 20 million under the Global Economy scenario. Under the latter scenario, from about 2035 to 2050, population might continue to grow slightly in the Randstad cities, but higher rates of migration to less urban adjoining regions might occur; some 500,000 to 1.5 million new dwellings might be needed. GNP per capita in 2040 might have grown by between 30 per cent and 120 per cent: 'increased prosperity and population growth will thus greatly increase the potential flood risk in this part of the country' (p. 32). The Commission concluded that 'the dominant long-term variables are pressure on space and the preparedness to invest' (p. 33), the latter depending heavily on the state of economic development and prosperity.

6.8 Other tools for futures thinking in spatial planning

In addition to the more systematically developed scenarios of the IPCC and national governments, there are many other futures thinking tools which have been used in spatial planning, such as Delphi and Monte Carlo techniques, expert judgement and participative visioning (Glasson *et al.*, 2005). Marshall (1997) suggested that, in the 1990s, a renewed interest in strategic planning, especially at the European scale, and a commitment to environmentalism, had prompted greater use of futures techniques (although the argument of this chapter is that there has been a reluctance in British spatial planning to engage with the medium- to long-term future). Such tools include trend-based forecasting, and visioning exercises, used quite extensively in Local Agenda 21 exercises (Baker and Eckerberg, 2008), or at the European scale in more strategic visioning exercises (Nadin, 2002), although all of them have their drawbacks (Shipley (2002).

Alternative futures have also been used for community engagement in land-scape visualization of future conditions under climate change, to assess climate impacts and develop community-based adaptation (such as Sheppard, 2008, in Canada). These applications are discussed further in Chapter 13. They can also be used for considering mitigation options, such as the proportion of land to be needed for renewables (biomass, solar, wind, hydro-power), conventional electricity generation or nuclear. The Northmoor Trust Project Timescape has developed a spreadsheet in which given population growth and extension of the built environment in the area around Didcot in Oxfordshire, and varying proportions of renewables and other energy sources converted into land-take, can be used in participatory exercises up to 2050 to show the implications of various policy choices. Something similar at national scale is undertaken by Mackay (2008) in which he estimates the land area needed across the UK for different combinations of energy sources. Mackay estimates that the UK will need a plan for energy production which will meet future consumption: he estimates current energy consumption at 125 kWh/day per person: applying efficiency savings in conversion and consumption, but allowing for increased demand, he estimates that any plan for 2050 will need to increase electricity supply by between 18 and 48 kWh/day per person. He suggests five different ways of meeting this supply: Mackay shows a mid-range 'plan', including nuclear power, a range of renewables (tidal, wave, pumped heat, wood, wind, hydro, solar and photovoltaics), biofuels, clean coal and 16 kWh/day of imported desert solar. While these alternative plans are not specifically developed as scenario exercises, they can be used to generate participation in thinking in radically different ways about energy futures.

The significance of all these socio-economic scenarios and alternative future visions is that we can explore the implications of different sets of values, and be conscious of their outcomes for more socially just or less socially just societies. Many of the sets of socio-economic scenarios used in several EU research projects shown in Table 6.1 (such as PRELUDE and ACCELERATES), as well as those of UKCIP and the Netherlands, identify equity or community cohesion as a key dimension in exploring the future, and hence allow us to consider systematically the implications of planning actions on justice and fairness. This will be particularly important in the way in which society responds to climate change.

6.9 Conclusions

The use of socio-economic scenarios with climate change projections enables us to 'orientate' ourselves to the future, in a way which is consistent with the sustainability principles of intra-and inter-generational equity. The socio-economic scenarios suggest that, in addition to considerations of equity between generations, which obliges us to think of the future, we should also consider issues of intra-generational equity within future generations: the distribution of vulnerability needs to be taken into account in moving to a low-carbon economy and building adaptive capacity over time. Ultimately, decisions about the future require political choices, and the decision to owe a duty of care both to future generations and to current generations is a normative one. Although much socio-economic scenarios work has been undertaken with a specific intention of aiding adaptation assessments, the close relationship of levels of emission with socio-economic conditions suggests that they could be used more extensively to evaluate both mitigation and adaptation actions. In this way, they have potential to re-engage spatial planning with the future. The use of socio-economic scenarios as internally consistent storylines offers a more systematic way of exploring the future, with the opportunity to identify key variables and drivers (not necessarily on a quadrant matrix, however visually appealing this might be) and to recognize the issues of equity within and across generations.

The following chapter explores the field of environmental assessment and suggests that current tools such as SA and SEA could be much improved if more attention were given to testing the resilience and robustness of plans and projects with respect to uncertain futures, and which address the relationship between mitigation and adaptation.

7 Environmental impact assessment for climate change in spatial planning

7.1 Introduction

Climate change is already having an impact on development and land use, and is likely to have further effects in two ways: through the impact of a changing climate itself on the built and natural environments, and through the policy decisions to provide both emissions mitigation and adaptation responses. All the first order effects might also have second-order effects: for instance, the impact of climate change mitigation measures (such as biofuels) on biodiversity, or the consequences for energy demand for transport of abandoning certain developed areas as an adaptation response to climate change impacts. Chapter 2 has shown that these mitigation and adaptation responses do not necessarily act in concert or synergy: there will be both conflicts and opportunities. It is therefore important to integrate decisions across these areas of public policy. We argued in Chapter 5 that policy to shape these decisions should take into account the different scales of justification for action and of impacts, and in Chapter 6 that such policy needs to have regard to inter- and intra-generational equity. These arguments reinforce the case for an anticipatory, *ex ante* assessment of the possible impacts of climate change and other policies. Environmental impact assessment can address first and second order impacts, and cumulative and synergistic effects, and lead to actions which can prevent or minimize any expected adverse consequences. In particular, such assessments need to include the impacts of the plan or project on the causes of climate change (such as the contribution of the plan or project to the emission of greenhouse gases) and the impact of any unavoidable climate change on the plan or project.

This chapter reviews the arguments for environmental impact assessment in addressing climate change, examines the available guidance (in Section 7.4), and reviews a number of case studies at strategic plan level (Section 7.6). We use the term environmental impact assessment (EIA) for convenience (except where EA or IA are used in direct quotations), although we acknowledge that climate change is more than an environmental issue alone, that EIA is conventionally used just for project-level assessments, and that EIA has a wider focus which includes socio-economic impacts, as well as health and social impact assessment. For the sake of clarity in an area of potential terminological confusion, we also distinguish between climate change mitigation (as discussed in Chapter 2) and impact mitigation (the term used in EIA to indicate measures to reduce the adverse consequences of a plan or project).

The chapter explores the potential of the EIA process to address climate change, and the extent to which practice needs to change even in advance of any revision to the EU guidelines on EIA (promised for 2011 [CEC, 2009a]).

7.2 Environmental impact assessment processes

Within Europe and in many countries around the world, potentially useful processes for undertaking this assessment have been adopted through requirements for policy impact assessment, sustainability appraisal, strategic environmental assessment of plans and programmes, and project-level assessment (Glasson *et al.*, 2005). The EU has adopted a formal process of EIA of its own proposals (policies and expenditure) and the plans, programmes and major projects of member states (this is simply 'Impact Assessment' in the Commission's terminology). EIA of major projects has been required under the EIA Directive since 1988 (CEC, 1985, amended in 1997 and 2003), and of plans and programmes (CEC, 2001) since 2004 (this latter Directive is known as the SEA Directive). The aim of the EIA Directive is to ensure that certain public or private projects, likely to have significant effects by virtue of their nature, size, or location, are subject to EIA prior to development consent. The Directive sets out the minimum requirements, the obligations on developers, the involvement of the public and the role of decision-making authorities. The SEA Directive requires an assessment of environmental effects in the preparation of and prior to the adoption of plans and programmes in certain sectors which set the framework for future development consent for projects under the EIA Directive. The sectors are agriculture, forestry, fisheries, energy, industry, transport, waste management, water management, telecommunications, tourism, town and country planning, and land use; the provisions also apply to plans and programmes requiring assessment under the Habitats Directive (CEC, 1992). The intention of the SEA Directive is to take a strategic and proactive view of alternative options, and of cumulative and synergistic impacts. Both Directives require assessment of the direct and indirect effects of a project on human beings, fauna and flora, soil, water, climatic factors, air, material assets, cultural heritage, the landscape, and the interaction between those factors.

In European countries, impact assessment should be undertaken for sectoral and spatial plans, and for the major projects to which the plans give rise. Its importance lies in being an evaluative process carried out in advance of decision-making. The SEA Directive requires the publication of a report showing the likely significant effects of the plan or programme, the reasonable alternatives and consultations with the public and agencies. The SEA Directive does not set out precisely how the SEA should be carried out. By 2009, all Member States had transposed the Directive into domestic legislation (CEC, 2009f), although in practice, implementation of the Directive varies amongst and within countries. For instance, in Scotland, the SEA Directive applies to all sectoral and spatial plans; in England, for spatial plans at regional and local level, SEA is instead incorporated into Sustainability Appraisal, which has extended the focus of environmental assessment from the biophysical environment to a wider set of economic and social considerations.

7.3 Environmental impact assessment and climate change

It would therefore seem prima facie that EIA has a potentially powerful role to play in integrating climate change considerations into sectoral and spatial planning decision-making. For spatial plans and strategies, where it is important to assess the climate resilience of the plan, EIA should have considerable potential 'as it can be used to ascertain the contribution of plans and projects to abating greenhouse gas emissions, and the feasibility of responding to the impacts of climate change' (Draaijers and van der Velden, 2009). However, the issue of climate change has not been readily taken up until the latter part of the 2000s. The EU, in its five-year monitoring reviews of the EIA Directive, concluded that:

> The EIA Directive does not expressly address climate change issues. Most of the MS recognise that climate change issues are not adequately identified and assessed within the EIA process. Any review of the impacts of climate change is often limited to CO_2 and other greenhouse gas emissions from industry and from increases in transport as part of air quality studies or as indirect impacts . . . In addition, the effects on global climate, the cumulative effects of an additional project and adaptation to climate change are not sufficiently considered.
>
> (CEC, 2009g, para. 3.5.4)

For SEA, similar conclusions were reached, but the CEC also found that 'the lack of a well-established methodology to determine impacts has been mentioned as a key problem by many MSs' (CEC, 2009f, para. 4.4).

Outside the EU, Canada has had a similar experience. A report for the Canadian Environmental Assessment Agency concluded that

- climate change has not been adequately acknowledged or addressed in most EAs
- uncertainties about climate change have been addressed even less well
- climate change is addressed inconsistently between similar types of project, and
- more recent EAs are not necessarily better with respect to these concerns.
(Byer and Yeomans, 2007, p. 85)

But, even where practice has developed, there are still limitations, in particular with respect to adaptation and futures thinking. The Dutch report on climate adaptation in the Netherlands concluded that time horizons are still short: 'so far, little attention has been given to spatial planning for the long run, i.e. for the period beyond 2050' (PBL, 2006, p. 2). It is worth exploring the reasons why there have been these limitations, examining the explanations under two aspects: factors external to and those internal within environmental assessment.

7.3.1 Factors external to EIA

We suggest there are three principal external reasons why EIA has not systematically addressed climate change. One frequently cited reason is the uncertainty of climate change and the difficulty of making predictions. For instance, Byer and Yeomans, having reviewed a number of EIAs in Canada, explain that 'A major difficulty for EAs has been to determine how the uncertainties about changing climatic considerations can impact projects, and how these uncertainties can be effectively incorporated into the analysis' (Byer and Yeomans, 2007, p. 85). Perhaps as a result of this reluctance to address uncertainty and uncertain futures, time horizons taken in most EIAs are short, focusing more on contextual plan periods (such as ten–fifteen years) than on the lifetime of the project. Moreover, although a standard stage in all EIA guidance is description of the baseline, and its likely evolution in the absence of the plan or project, for most EIAs there has been an assumption that this baseline will not change significantly over the plan or project period (Morris and Therivel, 2009). This may be surprising, given that some sectoral and spatial plans have extended horizons. In the Netherlands, for instance, the NEPPs and national spatial and infrastructure plans have horizons of some forty–fifty years (and, in the case of the Delta Commission, up to 2200); in the UK, some schemes have extended horizons (such as the Thames Estuary 2100 project with a horizon up to 2170

– see Section 7.6.3). By contrast, most spatial plan horizons in the UK, as we saw in Chapter 4, are short term – for instance, local plans have a ten-year horizon, and even regional plans only a twenty–twenty-five year horizon.

The lack of futures thinking in spatial planning may also be explicable as timidity with respect to constructing grandiose alternative visions; it may also reflect a focus on the present, on fulfilling social, environmental and economic objectives to meet current and pressing needs. For projects requiring a formal EIA, assessments have been poor at explicitly examining the lifetime of the project: only recently has attention been paid to the end-of-life and decommissioning stages. It is understandable that, within broader political and economic conditions which favour short-termism (Kay, 2009), policy and project appraisal communities have not been required by regulators or clients to extend the scope of their assessments. The consequence has been that there has been a reluctance to envisage radically different futures. One of the techniques for doing this, the use of scenarios or storylines, has been available but has not been much used in EIA (Byer and Yeomans, 2007; Sheate *et al.*, 2008).

A second set of possible explanations for the lack of consideration of climate change in plan and project appraisal lies in the institutional context within which such plans are framed or projects developed. While the ideal of integration is promoted, we need to recognize that it is difficult to achieve. Lenschow (2002), in reviewing sectoral policy areas such as agriculture, transport and energy, shows that policy fragmentation and inconsistency remain, even with explicit provision for environmental policy integration in the EU treaties. It may be unreasonable, therefore, to expect EIA processes fully to counter this tendency. Thirdly, the EIA and climate change practitioner communities have developed separately, with significant terminology, such as the term 'mitigation', having very different meanings. While this may seem an insignificant and not insuperable barrier, it has generated some confusion (Kirwan, 2005).

7.3.2 Factors internal to EIA

In addition to the external factors, there may be reasons internal to the EIA profession and policy community. Climate change, as we have argued, is not solely a physical phenomenon, but a social and economic one, requiring interdisciplinary approaches to problem identification and assessment of options for solutions. But the EIA community has, if anything, become more fragmented with specialist disciplines and interest groups, for instance within the International Association for Impact Assessment (IAIA). Burdge (2009), in arguing that climate change now offers a 'window of opportunity' (p. 618) for impact assessment, makes a parallel comparison with the failure of social impact assessment to be integrated with other assessments. He suggests that, within the US, there are different knowledge bases, with the historical biophysical emphasis of both impact assessment and land use planning not being ready, in his view, to employ social science. He considers that climate change offers a chance for the EIA disciplines to reaffirm the value of assessment in the decision-making process (reaffirming the substantive goals, so it is seen as less of an administrative hurdle to be overcome). The actual processes of assessment should include more recognition of vernacular as well as expert knowledge, and pay more attention to the monitoring of implementation of impact mitigation measures as a form of adaptive management. This is a persuasive argument: standards set through legislative or EIA professional bodies would be needed to achieve this.

This fragmentation might also explain why, even though a consideration of interaction between impacts is required by the EU Directives, and most EIAs are undertaken by multidisciplinary teams, interactive impacts are not well handled (CEC, 2009a).

It is also possible that the EIA process has become somewhat formulaic, relying too much on guidance or precedent, and focusing on process rather than substantive content. As explained above, the implementation of the EIA Directives has led to the publication of various national guidelines to assist different tiers of government and plan or project proponents, and to ensure consistency. Such guidance needs to strike a balance between conformity and flexible innovation. In the UK, guidance on practice in SEA was prepared jointly by national governments (ODPM *et al.*, 2005), in the context of climate change being a priority in the UK sustainable development strategy (HMG, 2005). The guidance made the point that climate change is an example of cumulative or synergistic effects most appropriately handled in the SEA process rather than on a project EIA level. (This raises contentious issues of the relationship between decision-making at national level on nationally significant projects, as discussed in Chapter 5.) It suggested an objectives-led approach to SEA, with climate factors as one such SEA objective, with their associated indicators. The SEA Directive also requires assessments to include short, medium and long-term effects. The UK guidance suggests that, for climate change, timescales could be five, twenty and one hundred years. Methods for handling uncertainty over the longer timescale are not given, although the UKCIP is mentioned as a source of climate change scenarios.

Plans falling within the scope of the SEA guidance include river basin management plans (see Chapter 10, Section 10.3), oil and gas licensing and offshore wind licensing (see Section 7.6.2). Spatial plans at regional and local level in England are required by the government to undergo sustainability appraisal (SA) (which, since 2004, incorporates the requirements of the SEA Directive) (ODPM, 2005b). Guidance on SA follows the SEA Directive in taking a fairly narrow interpretation of climatic factors. In Scotland, where qualifying plans including spatial plans are subject to SEA, guidance is based on ODPM *et al.*, 2005, and follows an objectives-led approach (Scottish Executive and Natural Scotland, 2006), but more consideration is given to adaptation (Table 7.1).

Other advice on implementing the SEA Directive has come from consultancies (for instance, Scott Wilson *et al.* 2006 on Habitats Regulations Assessment

Table 7.1 Examples of SEA climate change objectives

SEA topic	Possible SEA objectives	Possible SEA indicators
Climatic factors	• To reduce the cause and effects of climate change • reduce greenhouse gas emissions • reduce vulnerability to the effects of climate change, e.g. flooding, disruption to travel by extreme weather, etc.	• electricity and gas use (proxy indicator) • electricity generated from renewable energy sources and CHP located in the area (proxy indicator) • energy consumption per building and per occupant (proxy indicator) • carbon dioxide (CO_2) emissions by sector/per capita • amount of development in the flood plain • flood risk

Source: Scottish Executive (Natural Scotland), 2006

[formerly called appropriate assessment]), which includes a specific section on climate change considerations (Box 7.1), and from NGOs such as the RSPB on SEA (2007) and on Habitats Regulations Assessment (Dodd *et al.*, 2007).

A review of some early sustainability appraisals and environmental assessments of the regional development plans in England found that, although some climate change issues were incorporated in the EIA reports, mitigation measures were given more attention than adaptation (Kolodnytska, 2006). Specific topics such as flooding (Carter *et al.*, 2009) are addressed, but make no systematic consideration of climate change. A more recent review of the practice of sustainability appraisal in the spatial planning system of England and Wales emphasized process issues of evidence-gathering, judgements of significance of impacts identified, and integration with different forms of assessment (such as SEA, Habitats Regulations Assessments and Health Impact Assessments) and recommended further research into ways of 'forecasting sustainability trends and outcomes into the future' (Land Use Consultants and RTPI, 2008). It seems therefore the guidance might have constrained SEAs and SAs to treat climate change as a set of limited objectives – such as reduction of greenhouse gas emissions or of flood risk – amongst other objectives, rather than as an opportunity to assess impacts holistically and over time.

The separation of the EIA and climate change policy and practice communities from each other, mentioned already as an external factor also has implications within EIA. Policy requirements have been set out by separate departments: for instance, at the EU level, different divisions within DGEnv and DG TREN; within the UK, EIA has been the responsibility of DCLG rather than Defra or DECC; and in the Netherlands the Netherlands Commission for Environmental Assessment has been separate from the Netherlands Environmental Assessment Agency. Moreover, as we saw in Chapter 2, the climate change policy community itself has until recently tended to separate mitigation and adaptation.

The growth in private sector consultancies undertaking the EIAs has perhaps led to teams specializing in EIA and to a certain uniformity or house style of approach, reinforcing the separation of communities of discourse (as argued in Chapter 4) between the climate change impacts communities (which have included promotion of the concept of integrated assessments) and the EIA professionals, working within separate sets of assumptions and frames of knowledge. Owens *et al.* (2004) suggest that in the broader field of impact assessment (that is, not specifically for issues of climate change and develop-ment), approaches to appraisal have derived from assumptions of procedural rationality rather than from a basis of normative values. There has understand-ably been a focus within the EIA community on procedural and methodological issues such as the difficulty in the treatment of cumulative impacts, and the relationship of the EIA to decision-making. It may be that, with the high profile in the media in the early part of the twenty-first century of argument over climate change science, the coverage of the climate scepticism position (Boykoff and Mansfield, 2008) and the emphasis on uncertainty, climate change assessment had been seen by EIA professionals or proponents as too value-laden and contestable. (We discuss these issues further in Chapter 13.)

7.4 Specific guidance on climate change within EIA

Nevertheless, despite the limited requirements of the EU Directives in terms of consideration of climate change, specific advisory guidance on how to address climate change issues within EIA has been available. Such guidance is very important in that, certainly at the individual project level, there are real challenges and difficulties in actually assessing the relationship of the project to global emissions, or to likely or possible future local impacts of climate change. For instance, the Canadian Environmental Assessment Agency issued guidance in 2003 for the incorporation of climate change considerations into environmental assessment. The CEAA had been amongst the first agencies to address this question, having commissioned a study in 2000 (Barrow and Lee, 2000). The 2003 guidance had to tread a fine line between taking up the issue as one of major global, national and local importance, and the federal government's alignment with the US position of reluctance towards the Kyoto Protocol – although Canada had adopted a Climate Change Plan in 2002, there were as yet no legally binding greenhouse gas targets or benchmarks at federal level. The guidance also stressed the uncertainty of understanding of impacts and how they should be assessed. But it argued that giving consideration to climate change in project EAs will:

- be consistent with broader climate change policy;
- increase attention to, and awareness of, GHG [greenhouse gas] emissions from projects subject to EA;
- stimulate consideration of less emission-intensive ways to design and operate projects;
- help proponents manage or reduce the potential risks associated with climate change impacts on projects; and
- assure the public that climate change considerations are being taken into account (CEAA, 2003).

The guidance makes the point that, 'unlike most project-related environmental effects, the contribution of an individual project to climate change cannot be measured'; nor is detailed local information on climate impacts likely to be available. However, it argues that, to address the former challenge, practitioners might set the project within the policies of higher jurisdictions, where perhaps an SEA might have been undertaken; and, to address the latter challenge, they might use scenarios employing traditional ecological knowledge while more systematic climate change projections are developed. The guidance emphasizes the important role of adaptive management, a long-standing tool of project management within Canada, which it suggests can be useful both for the project itself, especially those with long life-times, and for climate change action more generally through learning from other projects' experiences of vulnerabilities and risks. The guidance cites a number of case study projects (one from as early as 1993) at federal and provincial level where climate change considerations have already been assessed within the EIAs. It suggests considering the sensitivities of different phases or components of a major project – such as construction, operational and decommissioning phases, and transport, raw materials and waste disposal – to climate-related parameters such as average temperature and precipitation, and frequency or severity of extremes.

The Canadian guidance was drawn on in the UK in the preparation of specific guidance on the treatment of climate change in SEA. A coalition of non-departmental public bodies (the Environment Agency, UKCIP, Countryside Council for Wales, and English Nature (subsequently Natural England)) commissioned in 2004 a guide on SEA and climate change, which was revised in 2007 (Levett-Therivel Sustainability Consultants *et al.*, 2004 and 2007). The guidance sets out in parallel the stages of SEA in accordance with ODPM *et al.*, 2005, with possible ways in which climate change could be considered at each stage (Table 7.2). It provides suggestions for possible indicators and sources of information, and gives some examples of possible mitigation measures and adaptation measures for spatial plans and other plans. Despite the endorsement of these statutory agencies, a review (Kirwan, 2005) had shown that the 2004 version had not become widely disseminated: some sixty responses were received from public sector practitioners surveyed amongst local authorities, regional planning bodies and consultee agencies, of whom only 50 per cent were aware of the guidance and only 29 per cent had used it. The study employed interviews to establish views on improvements – such as more guidance on indicators and case studies – which were incorporated in the 2007 revision.

At the project EIA level, IEMA, the professional body for EIA practitioners in the UK, in late 2009 published draft principles on climate change mitigation and EIA (IEMA, 2009). A survey of practitioners in summer 2009 had found that some 90 per cent considered that greenhouse gas emissions should be addressed in the process and reporting of EIA. The guidance sets out overarching principles, assessment principles (shown in Box 7.2), and principles for reporting and follow-up.

As we saw in Chapter 4, the discourses of planning within the UK in any event favoured discretionary and voluntary measures, such as the publication of advice, whereas in the Netherlands there is a tradition of more formal compacts between state and developers or infrastructure providers (Marshall, 2009b). In the UK, the guidance on SEA simply drew attention to climatic factors as one amongst many objectives. *Make Room for the Climate!* (VROM *et al.*, 2007a), the precursor to the adaptation strategy in the Netherlands, requires spatial plans to be made 'climate-proof', and the EIA process is one way of aiding in this. The Netherlands is unusual (Glasson *et al.*, 2005) amongst EU member states in having an independent body of experts to determine the quality of assessments undertaken. The Netherlands Commission for Environmental Assessment (NCEA) has a mandatory role (statutorily required under the Dutch Environmental Management Act) in all EIAs for projects and more recently, since the implementation into national law of the SEA Directive, considerable involvement in SEAs. The Commission is specifically involved in the scoping stage of EIA, and in reviewing the quality of the report of the environmental assessment (NCEA, 2009). Through this role, it can indirectly enforce the assessment of certain issues such as climate change impacts, and it can also issue

Table 7.2 Climate change (mitigation and adaptation) in the SEA process

Stage of SEA process	How climate change should be considered in the process
Stage A: Setting the context and objectives, establishing the baseline and deciding on the scope • Identifying other relevant plans, programmes and environmental protection objectives • Collecting baseline information • Identifying environmental problems • Developing SEA objectives • Consulting on the scope of the SEA	• Describe the current and likely future **climate change baseline** • Identify the likely significant **problems and constraints caused by climate change**: e.g. English authorities should refer to the Regional Flood Risk Appraisal or Strategic Flood Risk Assessment required by Planning Policy Statement (PPS)25. Other impacts may relate to, e.g. water quality, biodiversity, health, or buildings • Develop **climate change objectives and indicators** that take account of (the uncertainty of future) climate change: • Consult with SEA Consultation Bodies: 　—Environment Agency – in particular on flood risk, water availability and quality 　—Natural England and Countryside Council for Wales – on the natural environment 　—English Heritage and CADW – cultural heritage • Consult with other organizations
Stage B: Developing and refining alternatives and assessing effects • Testing the plan or programme objectives against the SEA objectives • Developing strategic alternatives • Predicting the effects of the plan or programme, including (realistic) alternatives • Evaluating the effects of the plan or programme, including (realistic) alternatives • Avoiding and minimizing adverse impacts	• Suggest plan alternatives (related to both mitigation and adaptation) to deal with key climate change related problems • Assess the **effects of plan alternatives** on the climate change objectives and indicators • Refer to, or summarize the findings of, the Regional Flood Risk Appraisal or Strategic Flood Risk Assessment in the Environmental Report • Consider the alternatives' impacts on greenhouse gas emissions, and their ability to integrate climate change adaptation measures when selecting the preferred alternatives • Integrate **climate change mitigation and adaptation measures** into the final plan
Stage C: Preparing the Environmental Report • Preparing the Environmental Report	• Explain in the Environmental Report how climate change issues have been identified and managed, including how uncertainty has been managed

(continued)

Stage of SEA process	How climate change should be considered in the process
Stage D: Consulting on the draft plan or programme and the Environmental Report • Consulting the public and Consultation Bodies on the draft plan or programme and the Environmental Report • Assessing significant changes • Making decisions and providing information	• Consult authorities responsible for climate change management and others who can provide advice on good practice
Stage E: Monitoring the significant effects of implementing the plan or programme on the environment • Developing aims and methods for monitoring	• Monitor the effectiveness of mitigation measures in reducing greenhouse gas emissions. The effectiveness of adaptation measures is likely to be difficult to monitor, but whether such measures are put in place/implemented can be monitored • Be prepared to respond to any adverse impacts identified

Source: adapted from Levett Therivel Sustainability Consultants *et al.*, 2007

Box 7.2 IEMA Draft Principles for GHG emissions assessment in EIA

• Scoping GHG emissions should consider the relevant policy framework (global to local) and review the mitigation findings in any associated SEA/SA
• When assessing alternatives, a basic consideration of the likely GHG emissions performance of each option should be considered
• Baseline considerations related to GHG emissions should refer to the policy framework, current situation and, where possible, trends for the sector
• Quantification of GHG will not always be necessary, but any qualitative assessment must be effectively described and justified
• Assessment of GHG emissions must consider the whole-life effects, including embodied energy, and emissions relating to construction, operation, and decommissioning
• Evaluation of the significance of GHG emissions should include positive (reduced) or negative (additional) emissions
• Where avoidance of GHG emissions is not practicable, the EIA should aim to reduce the residual significance at all stages (materials, construction, operation and decommissioning)
• Where GHG emissions remain significant, approaches to compensate should be considered

Source: IEMA, 2009, pp. 1–2

advice on improvements to EIA processes. For instance, a working group of the NCEA was set up in 2007 to advise on how climate change should be dealt with in EIA/SEA. The conclusions were incorporated in guidance published in 2009 (Draaijers and van der Velden, 2009). The Dutch arrangements differ from those of the UK where there is no equivalent body overseeing the quality or approach of SEA and EIAs.

7.5 Integrating mitigation and adaptation in EIA

The guidance documents are valuable in pointing to the need for integrating emissions mitigation and adaptation, but less firm on ways in which this integrated assessment should be done. The non-governmental British guidance suggests that mitigation measures 'should all take account of projected changes in the future climate, and aim to set a complementary context for adaptation measures' (Levett-Therivel Sustainability Consultants *et al.*, 2007, p. 11). The Dutch NCEA also argues for integrity and synergy: as adaptation is implemented across different sectors and areas, 'there is a danger that one measure will negate another, so a complete assessment of the various interests at stake is important' (p. 18). It calls for synergies to be identified also between adaptation and mitigation measures, giving the example of home insulation aiding adaptation to hotter ambient temperatures as well as saving energy and hence reducing greenhouse gases.

Larsen (2008) offers a useful diagram of how this might be done in SEA of River Basin Management Plans in Denmark (where the Danish Ministry of the Environment had decided not to consider climate change in the first round of RBMPs) (Figure 7.1).

More recently, OECD/DAC (2008) has issued guidance on adaptation within SEA, of particular importance to many developing countries where adaptation

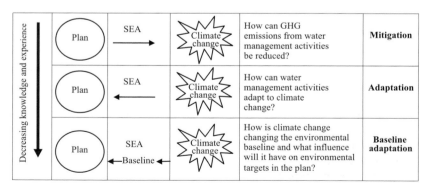

Figure 7.1

Climate change in SEA of RBMPs
Source: Larsen, 2008

rather than mitigation is the priority, as there is significant evidence that they are more at risk from climate change and moreover are responsible for a much smaller proportion of greenhouse gases (as explained in Chapter 6). The guide acknowledges that mitigation and adaptation are 'complementary aspects of climate change risk management, and that synergies between these activities exist' (p. 6), but, citing the IPCC, argues that, as there are major differences in time and spatial scale, stakeholder interests and decision processes, it is reasonable to address adaptation separately.

We therefore consider that there is scope for some innovation and practical development in the ways in which EIA can integrate mitigation and adaptation considerations, and in handling uncertainty, and we explore some possible ways of doing this in Section 7.7. First, we provide some examples of EIAs which have expressly addressed climate change.

7.6 Case studies: SEA and climate change

It can be argued that the complexity of interactions of climate change and sustainability makes assessment at the strategic level particularly appropriate (OECD/DAC 2008; NCEA, 2009). We therefore examine three case studies of SEAs – one for large-scale terrestrial spatial planning, one for a marine energy sectoral plan, and one an estuarial adaptation (flood risk) plan – to review the ways in which they addressed climate change considerations in assessing integration, synergistic and cumulative impacts, and baseline projections over a longer time horizon. (We consider the treatment of climate change in SAs of spatial plans in England in Chapter 8).

7.6.1 Case study 1: Randstad 2040

The Randstad (sometimes called Delta Metropole) is the heart of the urbanized part of the Netherlands, comprising the major cities of Rotterdam, Amsterdam, The Hague and Utrecht. It is a vital part of the national economy, and the government in its national spatial plan has been keen to secure decisions on future developments of the area, particularly the future of the ports (Schiphol Airport and the Rotterdam Mainport), as well as housing and employment provision, and other infrastructure. The Dutch government has also been keen to promote the role of the region as a world city, competitive with London, New York and Tokyo. In 2005 the government resolved to draw up a strategic plan for the whole region. The plan was subject to SEA. Although EIA in the Netherlands had principally been applied at the project level, changes to the legislation on EIA, and the new Spatial Planning Act of 2008, have shifted this focus to the more strategic level. The Planning Act requires all levels of government (that is, national, provincial and local) to formulate long-term 'structural design plans' for their areas; as such plans are likely to lead to developments which

Table 7.3 Sustainability assessment matrix in the Netherlands

	People	Planet	Profit
Here and now			
Later			
Elsewhere			

Source: van Eck, 2009, p. 12

themselves require EIA, an SEA is now required (van Eck, 2009). Such an SEA was therefore undertaken for the Randstad strategic vision.

Initially, three models of development for the future of the Randstad area up to 2040 were generated, named 'World city' (enlarging space through consolidating developments in existing urban areas), 'Coastal city' (creating space beyond the current coast-line), and 'Outer city' (developing beyond the Randstad rim), from which a fourth option evolved. The SEA adopted an integrated, sustainability perspective, using a matrix (Table 7.3) employing the 'people, planet, profit' interpretation of sustainability derived from the business conception of 'triple bottom line', and endorsed in the Dutch national adaptation strategy (VROM *et al.*, 2007b).

The SEA showed that, on the initial appraisal, the best option was the World City model (i.e. it ranked most highly for most of the assessment parameters); but the Dutch government took the opportunity to draw up a vision of its preferred option (the Cabinet's vision) combining some of the features of all the options (see Table 7.4). It is reported that, on the final assessment, the latter development model did not perform as well as World City, but 'the cabinet's vision is more adaptable to possible future unexpected developments and fits in better with the Dutch people's housing wishes, because it entails less high rise' (van Eck, 2009 p. 12). This is the development plan which has been adopted: 'This vision is a stimulus for a Randstad that can measure up in all respects to other urban areas in Europe, while at the same time being sustainable and climate-resilient' (VROM, 2008a).

The indicators and rankings used in the assessment for the 'here and now' period up to 2040 are shown in Table 7.4.

The use of the SEA to help formulate policy, as well as the advice of other interests (such as the Council for Housing) and the involvement of the public, nicely illustrates the argument that spatial planning and environmental assessment are value-laden processes, not ones simply of expert, rational assessment (Weston, 2000).

7.6.2 Case study 2: UK offshore energy SEA

The difficulty of addressing climate change holistically in an SEA is demonstrated in the policy of the UK government to institute a process of SEA for

Table 7.4 Assessment table for 'here and now' of Randstad 2040 options

		World city	Coastal city	Outer city	Cabinet's vision R2040
Subsurface/ water	Flooding & safety; water storage	1	3	3	3
	Extent to which functions fit in with the properties of the subsurface	1	4	2	2
	Probability x as a result of calamity (flooding)	3	4	1	2
Energy & raw materials	Potential to approximately halve CO_2 vis-à-vis 1990	1	4	1	2
Mobility	Accessibility of other people & facilities (shops, school, sport, etc.)	1	4	2	2
	Accessibility of businesses	1	2	3	3
	Quality and linkage of networks (public transport, cars, bikes)	1	3	3	2
Nature	Conservation of the quality of Natura 2000/National Ecological Network	2	4	1	2
	Space for new nature in the Randstad	1	4	1	1
Landscape quality	Opportunities for improving spatial quality, restructuring	1	2	4	2
	Opportunities for improving spatial quality, fragmentation	1	4	1	1
	Recognizability of historical landscapes	1	4	3	2
Quality of residential environment	Noise nuisance	4	2	1	3
	External safety (controlling the risks to the environment from the use, storage and transport of dangerous substances)	2	1	4	3
	Social cohesion/ engagement of people in their residential environment	4	3	1	2
	Safe residential environment	4	1	1	3

Source: van Eck, 2009, p. 13

offshore energy projects. The effort is commendable for a number of reasons: the UK government has not always undertaken *ex ante* assessments of its own planning policy initiatives (such as in the lack of an initial assessment of the Sustainable Communities Plan, explained in Chapter 4). This may be partly to retain the prerogative of responsive policymaking to perceived immediate problems or crises (such as a housing shortage), a position adopted by the UK government in the early discussions on the need for SEA (Therivel *et al.*, 1992). But in the case of offshore oil, and gas, the UK in 1999 instituted the first SEA of licensing rounds in the North Sea, anticipating the SEA Directive of 2001 which did not take formal effect until 2004. Moreover, the SEA has a very large scope, encompassing plans for different energy sources, and across a very large area, with a complex environment and many different sets of users. Figure 7.2 shows the spatial extent of SEAs for former licensing rounds. Comprehensive environmental information has been lacking with some major gaps in the knowledge and science base, for instance of marine archaeology, and the SEA has commissioned specific new studies to fill some of these gaps.

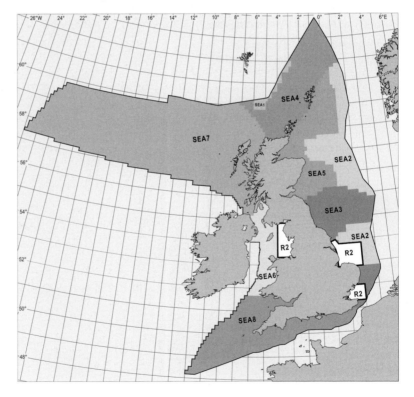

Figure 7.2

Past SEA sequence of licensing in offshore waters
Source: DECC, 2009c, Map 1

The same procedure was followed when the UK shifted its focus for renewables from onshore wind (as we discuss in Chapter 5) to offshore. This experience of SEA can be seen as an important precursor to some of the arrangements for marine planning under the Marine and Coastal Access Act 2009 (see 11.6.3), in taking a strategic view of a range of activities and pressures on the marine environment, and attempting to address the problems of lack of coordination, or planning 'at the margins' (Jay, 2008) of formal terrestrial planning processes. In 2008, the UK created a new Department for Energy and Climate Change (DECC) to which responsibility for the SEA of offshore energy passed from the trade and business department formerly responsible for the energy sector. The draft plan for both the leasing of offshore wind and the licensing of offshore oil and gas exploitation and gas storage was drawn up in response to the UK Energy White Paper of 2007 (DTI, 2007). The objectives for the plan are, therefore, to ensure security of supply, both for climate change reasons (meeting the UK's commitments to reduction of greenhouse gases) and more general reasons of diversity of supply (DECC, 2009c). These objectives are to be met without compromising other objectives such as protecting ecosystem functions, nature and heritage interests and human heath and other material assets. For wind energy, the plan has a specific target of delivering twenty-five GW of additional generation capacity for England and Wales by 2020 (that is, excluding Scotland and Northern Ireland, which have their own renewable energy targets). The plan estimates that this will require 'several thousand' wind turbines, which might require an area of up to $10,000 \, \text{km}^2$. (The UK has the largest offshore area with potential for wind-energy sites within the EU – $120,000 \, \text{km}^2$ within 50 km of the shore [EEA, 2009a]).

The Off-shore Energy SEA follows regulatory requirements in assessing two alternatives (the do nothing and business as usual options) to the plan:

- Not to offer any areas for leasing/licensing (do nothing)
- To proceed with a leasing and licensing programme (business as usual)
- To restrict the areas offered for leasing and licensing temporally or spatially (the preferred option).

The SEA process undertook an initial scoping for the study through consultation with a Steering Group and other stakeholders, and formal public consultation in 2007. The SEA follows the requirements of the SEA Directive in identifying potentially affected receptors and climatic factors. It acknowledges the richness of the marine biodiversity, and its current vulnerability to human activities such as fishing and aggregate extraction.

It is instructive to focus on two areas of the SEA: the assessment of the plan's contribution to climate change mitigation, and the assumptions it makes about evolution of the baseline under conditions of unavoidable climate change, and hence the scope for adaptation. The policy context includes international commitments, such as the OSPAR Convention for the protection of the north-east Atlantic, the EU Marine Strategy Framework Directive 2008, and the UK Marine and Coastal Access Act 2009 and Marine (Scotland) Bill. The latter legislative proposals promote the concept of marine spatial planning partly in order to address climate change in an integrated way (the wider implications of these policies are more fully examined in Chapter 11). However, the Off-shore Energy SEA interprets climatic factors principally in terms of the contribution of activities implemented following the plan to local, regional and global CO_2 and other greenhouse gas emissions. It argues that, while it may not be consistent with UK and EU commitments to reduce greenhouse gas emissions, in the short term the new hydrocarbons policy would be neutral in the attainment of UK climate change policy objectives (Table 7.5). This is argued on the basis that, in the short term, alternative imported sources might involve more gas-flaring and hence higher greenhouse gas emissions.

The report on comments received following the publication of the SEA (DECC, 2009d) made clear that many respondents had challenged this interpretation: not only were the downstream greenhouse gas implications excluded (such as the use of the hydrocarbons), but other alternatives (such as greater energy efficiency or more renewables) were not considered to be appropriate options for comparison.

The second area where climate change might specifically be taken into account is the evolution of the baseline: here the SEA makes clear that many of the factors will be affected – for instance, in describing the baseline water environment, the SEA considers that a global sea-level rise of 1–2 mm per year is possible. Under climatic factors, the SEA acknowledges that there are many long-term changes in climate at different scales; it states that future trajectories are uncertain, but refers to sources of information such as the IPCC, UKCIP and UK Marine Climate Change Impacts Partnership (MCCIP). In assessing actual impacts, serious attention is given to the IPCC Fourth Assessment Report (AR4) of 2007. The SEA states that:

> Future climate change may generate alterations which threaten ecological and social systems . . . Industries and settlements in coastal locations may

Table 7.5 SEA of UK offshore energy: assessment of greenhouse gas emissions

SEA Topic climatic factors				
	Altve 1	Altve 2	Altve 3	Narrative
Contributions to greenhouse gas emissions positive or negative	Potential minor negative impact	Positive impact	Positive impact	Incremental contribution of oil and gas and gas storage neutral (replacement of reserves) or negligible; [offshore windfarm] development would contribute to significant reduction in emissions

Source: DECC, 2009c, p. 211

be disrupted due to changes in sea-levels and coastal erosion and therefore will be more prone to flooding. Increased storminess at sea may also negatively affect off-shore operations, with shorter weather windows and increased 'down-time'.

(DECC, 2009c, pp. 183–4)

The SEA pays particular attention to the impacts on marine ecosystems, such as changes in benthic and zoo plankton communities being due to rising sea temperatures. It draws on the IPCC reports (2007e) to give confidence levels for issues such as:

- the resilience of ecosystems likely to be exceeded if greenhouse gas emissions and other pressures continue (high);
- substantial changes in the structure and functioning of marine and aquatic ecosystems with global warming of more than 2–3 degrees C (high);
- ecosystems and species are very likely to show a wide range of vulnerabilities to climate change, depending on imminence of exposure to eco-system specific, critical thresholds (very high). (p. 184)

The SEA already addresses complex interactions between marine and coastal zones, and between the many users of the marine environment. It may be unreasonable to have expected a more systematic attempt to assess the interactions of the plan with respect to both mitigation and adaptation. The MCCIP is responsible for considering the impacts of climate change on the marine environment: while the Partnership contributed to the SEA, its major report on ecosystem linkages and marine impacts (MCCIP, 2009) was published after the SEA. The Off-shore Energy SEA proposes employing the precautionary principle in the absence of a firm evidence base for informing an adaptive management approach for ecological receptors for offshore wind, a position which was opposed by a number of offshore operators in their responses, but supported by the RSPB (DECC, 2009d).

The SEA therefore demonstrates some of the difficulties of assessing complex interactions, assessing impacts over specified timescales and relying on evidence and a knowledge base. These issues were picked up by some of the respondents to the consultation on the SEA. WWF, for instance, welcomed the greater attention to climatic factors in this SEA compared with previous ones for oil and gas licensing, but had serious reservations:

WWF-UK welcomes the acceptance of the likely impact of this plan/program on climatic factors, notably climate change and the identification of many potential impacts from climate change on people and nature. However, WWF-UK finds that the SEA fails to properly assess the impacts on the environment and people, as well as the scale, importance, significance and reversibility of potential impacts. The SEA also fails to offer methods to reduce such impacts or mitigate/offset them, as required by the SEA Directive. For these reasons, we believe that the SEA is inadequate and fails to fulfil the requirements of the SEA Directive.

(WWF, in DECC, 2009d)

In response, the Post Consultation Report (DECC, 2009e) argued that wider energy policies were not subject to SEA. The outcome of the SEA is that the DECC considers 'there are no over-riding environmental considerations to prevent the achievement of our draft plan/programme of leasing for offshore wind, and licensing of oil and gas production, and gas storage, if mitigation measures are implemented to prevent, reduce and offset significant adverse effects'. The government's policy document for offshore wind (DECC, 2009b) provides for such measures, including spatial restrictions on criteria relating to other users such as military and shipping routes.

7.6.3 Case study 3: SEA of Thames Estuary 2100

The third SEA case study we examine is one which has, through the terms of the plan it is assessing, necessarily a long-term horizon. The strategic aim of the Environment Agency's Thames Estuary 2100 plan (TE2100) is:

> To develop a flood management plan for London and the Thames Estuary that is risk based, takes into account existing and future assets, is sustainable, includes the needs of stakeholders and addresses the issues in the context of a changing climate and varying socio-economic conditions that may develop over the next 100 years.
>
> (EA, 2009a, p. 33)

The SEA was undertaken alongside the preparation of the plan: this helped both to develop and assess strategic alternatives. The final estuary-wide options considered are shown in Box 7.3.

The SEA assessed key existing problems against a future situation without TE2100; it looks at synergies and conflicts with other plans in the estuary area. Options are then compared for short and medium term (roughly to 2070), long term (from 2070 to 2170), temporary, permanent, secondary, cumulative/synergistic impacts of each option and for specific 'reaches' of the estuary, and for beyond the estuary.

The options were assessed for effectiveness and efficiency in meeting the plan objectives. The SEA used a set of objectives to compare the effects of alternatives (and with the intention of guiding future monitoring of implementation of the Plan) to:

- reduce the risk of flooding to people and minimize the impacts of flooding to property and the environment
- adapt to the challenges we will face from climate change

- support and inform the land use planning process to ensure appropriate, sustainable and resilient development in the tidal Thames flood plain
- protect the cultural and commercial value of the tidal River Thames, its tidal tributaries and its flood plain
- enhance and restore estuarine ecosystems to contribute to biodiversity targets and maximize the environmental benefits of natural floods.

(EA, 2009a, Table 4.2)

The SEA concludes that the two preferred options (option 1.4 and option 3) could manage flood risk into the twenty-second century: on current assumptions of flood risk, option 1.4 provides acceptable risk management up to 2135, but a new barrier would provide a plan to 2170.

Unlike the Off-shore Energy SEA, this SEA scoped out air and climatic factors. This was decided on following consultation on the scoping report: the reason given is that 'Climatic factors were felt to be a policy driver for TE2100, but TE2100 itself was felt to have little impact on the climate' (p. 55). Nevertheless, estuary-wide problems had been identified in the baseline studies which are of relevance both to climate change adaptation and mitigation, including issues of consumption of non-renewable resources (fossil fuels in transport, and the associated high emissions of CO_2).

A distinctive feature of the plan is its explicit attention to dealing with uncertainty and planning for the long term. To address the first aim, it proposes continuing monitoring, throughout the 100-year life of the plan, of ten

Box 7.3 TE2100 Estuary-wide options

Option 1 Improve the existing defences
1.1 raise defences when needed
1.2 allow for future adaptation of defences
1.3 raise defences when they are replaced
1.4 optimise defence repair and replacement

Option 2 Tidal flood storage
Four potential sites have been identified to store tidal waters and reduce the level of storm surges

Option 3 New barrier
3.1 Tilbury or 3.2 Long Reach (after 2065)

Option 4 barrier with locks
4.1 Tilbury
4.2 Long Reach
4.3 Barrier with locks at Thames Barrier

Source: EA, 2009a, p. 48

key indicators, or 'triggers of change'. To address the second aim of ensuring the plan is adaptable and fit for purpose throughout its life, the time horizon adopted for the assessment of changing climate extends to 2170.

The SEA explicitly acknowledges uncertainties, with respect to climate change, socio-economic conditions, and the dynamism inherent in a natural system such as an estuary. The options appraised are based on current guidance, but the SEA points out that the guidance on SLR and on acceptable levels of risk 'could change over the lifetime of the strategy as the effects of climate change unfold, combined with greater scientific knowledge and the development of more accurate sea level prediction techniques' (p. 58). This is consistent with UKCIP's approach to adaptive management.

One example of synergies with climate change mitigation measures is the emphasis on redevelopment of brownfield sites through expansion of Thames Gateway, and emissions reduction through promotion of sustainable modes of transport (such as the Channel Tunnel Rail Link, CrossRail, an extension to Docklands Light Railway, and new rail crossings). The SEA concludes that 'flood risk to existing and planned infrastructure will increase' (p. 165). Moreover, while TE2100 has developed options to manage the risk, and would bring long-term and permanent benefits, 'it may indirectly promote development in the area that is not flood-compatible or flood-resilient. In the case of failure or overtopping of any flood defences, the resulting consequences could be significantly worse than under a business-as-usual scenario' (EA, 2009a, p. 167). This reinforces our argument that issues of equity need to be considered in integrated assessment of mitigation and adaptation.

This SEA demonstrates a systematic attempt to address interactions between the plan and many other related policy objectives, recognizing the complex changes likely to take place both with and independently of the plan, and the implications of residual flood risk. Even so, it does not explicitly address either the greenhouse gas implications of the hard and soft flood-defence measures proposed in the plan, nor does it systematically explore the relationship between spatial planning mitigation measures (such as development and transport infrastructure) and flood management as adaptation.

7.6.4 Strengths and weaknesses in SEA case studies

The SEAs demonstrate a range of strengths: they all set out clear objectives. They address the possibility of the baseline changing over time, and two SEAs adopt extended time horizons from 2040 to the end of the twenty-second century. They identify a number of options which are assessed in the light of these possible changes. They look at cumulative impacts and interaction between factors. The spatial plan for the Randstad takes a broad view of climatic factors to include aspects of both mitigation and adaptation, but none of the SEAs systematically assesses interactions between these.

7.7 Risk assessment and uncertainty in EIA

As explained above, Byer and Yeomans (2007) concluded that climate change uncertainty is not well handled within EIAs. They recommend exploring the scope for scenario analysis, sensitivity analysis, or probabilistic analysis. Scenario analysis, using data for a range of possible future climates and socio-economic factors, as we have seen in Chapter 6, has become much more commonly used in the UK in research projects (for instance for energy, transport, urban development and flood-risk futures). It could well be adapted for greater use in SEA or project EIA. Sensitivity analysis can identify sensitivities in a system and any climatic factors that affect those sensitivities (such as the sensitivity of hydro-power schemes to stream flows, likely to be affected by a changing climate). Byer and Yeomans argue that focusing on the question of what change in parameter x would cause a certain level of impact, for instance, can help to identify threshold vulnerabilities. Asking whether, if parameter x changed by a certain amount, what would be the effect, can help to identify the most significant elements. They argue that scenario and sensitivity analysis can provide information on consequences, but not on the likelihood of changes: to address this, they suggest the use of probabilistic analysis such as Monte Carlo or simulation methods.

Sensitivity analysis is already widely used in other climate change work, such as to explore regional climate change probabilities (Dessai *et al.*, 2005), whilst in biodiversity conservation Hannah *et al.* (2002a) have used regional climate models, biotic response models and sensitivity analysis to identify climate change impacts on biodiversity at a regional scale to guide choices in conservation planning. Hannah *et al.* argue that sensitivity analysis can help address the considerable uncertainty inherent in projecting future climates and biodiversity response. In a similar way, sensitivity analysis might be used to test how sensitive spatial planning goals are to variation in climate-related parameters – this could include for example the sensitivity of house-building programmes to flood frequency, or the choice of transport mode as affected by temperatures within the urban heat island. Sensitivity analysis can thus help with building models of future behaviour and can reduce uncertainty about models' forecasts – and so can build confidence in the projections made for the future.

Sensitivity analysis in connection with risk of flooding in the Thames Estuary area for the ESPACE project showed that the estuary-wide annual average flood damage values are relatively insensitive to the sea-level rise prediction, changing from 7 mm/year to 8.9 mm/year for the strategic option to maintain a 1:1000 year standard of protection; it showed that damages in this case increase by only 5 per cent, whilst other flood defence options led to faster increases in damage values (Reeder *et al.*, 2005). Whereas scenario-based assessments often consider significantly changed circumstances overall, sensitivity analysis takes a more focused approach and investigates responses by modifying one parameter at a time, and at a measured rate.

These approaches are consistent with the UKCIP's risk, uncertainty and decision-making framework (Willows and Connell, 2003), which has evolved into UKCIP's Adaptation Wizard (see Chapter 2, Section 2.5). The UKCIP guidance on managing climate change adaptation in organizations (Johnstone *et al.*, 2009) reinforces the point that, while there is a high degree of certainty that climate is changing, there is uncertainty about the rate, distribution and impact of the projected changes. Expressing these potential impacts in terms of risk – the combination of likelihood and magnitude of consequence – is useful in that it can be incorporated into existing risk management processes. Such approaches should be readily integrated into SEAs and project-level EIAs. They could also offer a way of assessing adaptation and mitigation interactions through adopting certain principles advocated in the 2004 guidance on planning and climate change (ODPM *et al.*, 2004), and on SEA and climate change (Levett Therivel Sustainability Consultants *et al.*, 2007):

- keep options open and flexible
- avoid decisions that will make it more difficult to manage risks in the future
- implement no-regret options that will deliver net benefits whatever the extent of climate change
- find win-win options that contribute to climate change mitigation, adaptation and wider plan objectives.

Brookes (2009) offers a comparison between EIA and environmental risk assessment (ERA) which could be adapted to include climate risk assessment (Table 7.6) using the UKCIP framework for handling risk and uncertainty. He makes the point that there is great scope for better integration and cross-fertilization of

Table 7.6 Comparison between EIA and ERA

Framework for EIA	Framework for ERA
Screening	Screening for risks
Scoping	Prioritization or ranking
	Hazard identification
Baseline studies	Hazard analysis
Impact prediction	Consequence analysis
	Risk determination
Assessment of relative importance of effects	Risk evaluation
Evaluation of acceptability of proposal or project	Risk management options
Monitoring and audit	Monitoring and audit

Source: adapted from Brookes, 2009, p. 427

EIA and environmental risk assessment, which have developed separately from each other. This development could be particularly important for addressing uncertainties, as perceived by both experts, stakeholders and, importantly, the public. We return to this issue in Chapter 14.

7.8 New regulatory requirements for addressing climate change in EIA

We have shown that, during much of the first decade of the twenty-first century, there has been a good deal of guidance on the treatment of climate change within EA, but no statutory requirement to address climate change systematically. However, the EC is now committed to producing guidelines by 2011 to make sure that climate impacts are addressed in the EIA Directive (CEC, 2009a), and consideration is being given to extending the scope of the SEA Directive to address climate change issues (CEC, 2009b). This is partly also in relation to the implications of the SEA Protocol of the Espoo Convention on Transboundary EIA, which also requires evaluation of the effects in a domestic context of policies and legislation as well as plans and programmes. In the UK, the Climate Change Act imposes an obligation on public bodies to address climate change, and the Planning Act 2008 requires regional and local spatial plans to take action on climate change.

As we saw in Chapter 4, the discourses of planning within the UK have favoured discretionary and voluntaristic measures, such as the publication of guidance and advice, but the new statutory obligations under the 2008 Climate Change Act should give greater force to systematic assessment. The Act requires a national risk assessment to be published by 2012, and formal regional and local level assessments are likely to follow. In the Netherlands, by contrast, a national adaptation strategy has already been adopted (VROM et al., 2007b). Such a framework sets the context for the work of the independent Dutch Commission for EIA (described above at 7.4). In the UK, it will be interesting to see how EIA is treated in the Infrastructure Planning Commission: although this is an independent body, its remit is constrained by the National Policy Statements on significant infrastructure (as we saw in Chapter 5). However, the combination of EC and domestic statutory requirements should significantly raise the profile of climate change in EIA in the 2010s in the UK and the Netherlands.

7.9 Conclusions

We have seen that, even in the absence of formal, statutory requirements for assessing climate change within SEA and EIA, there has been considerable innovation and experimentation, and professional bodies such as IEMA are developing appropriate guidance. This innovation is in the way the SEAs address mitigation and adaptation, in their approach to handling uncertainty in evolution of the baseline environment, and in the prediction of impacts, through the use of different time-frames. SEAs provide an opportunity for plans drawn up with a particular policy driver in mind (either climate change adaptation or mitigation) to be assessed more holistically. For spatial plans, with a broader remit than just energy sources or flood-risk management, SEAs do need to address both mitigation and adaptation. Over time, as plans become more climate-aware in their objectives and their choice of alternative options, the task of SEAs should become more straightforward. But in the meantime, 'the integration of climate change into strategic planning through the application of SEAs should lead to better-informed, evidence-based policies, plans and programmes that are more sustainable in the context of a changing climate, and more capable of delivering progress on human development' (OECD/DAC 2008, p. 6).

In the next chapters, therefore, we explore ways in which spatial plans for development and urban areas, in meeting energy, water, and biodiversity objectives, can take account of climate change considerations, and adopt policies and proposals which address these in a way which minimizes conflict and maximizes synergies.

Part III

Spatial planning in practice

8 Strategic planning for low-carbon and resilient development patterns

8.1 Introduction

We have seen in previous chapters some of the opportunities that the challenge of climate change has presented for more long-term and holistic strategic planning. Climate considerations have had to secure their place amongst a pre-existing set of planning concepts, some of which represent long-standing professional and political assumptions – for instance, about sustainable settlement patterns and ideal urban forms. While some of these may satisfy the objectives of both climate change mitigation and adaptation, the new agenda may also challenge the justification and evidence base for these assumptions. Planning outcomes are also expected to serve other objectives, as we saw in Chapters 4 and 5, such as housing provision, economic growth and international competitiveness.

This chapter explores some of the tensions and synergies encountered in accommodating these multiple objectives. Chapter 5 has looked at the national and regional scales of planning for low-carbon energy sources. Here we look at one of the key users of energy – transport – and at the relationship with strategic policies at the regional and subregional scale for the location of development and for climate change adaptation. A key thesis is that we need to consider the relationship between mitigation and adaptation policies. In the next chapter, we explore the issues in planning for and retrofitting existing urban areas to be low carbon and resilient to climate change (see Glossary). Over time, of course, the distinction between new and existing development becomes blurred (see Figure 9.6). Therefore, policies for mitigation and adaptation within the built environment from 2010 to the 2050s and beyond will need to address both new and existing development. We conclude the two chapters with a discussion of some of the planning initiatives in which such integration is occurring, such as through the provision of green infrastructure.

8.2 Patterns of development

8.2.1 Trends in location of development in Europe

Spatial planning at the regional and subregional scale can influence the location and scale of new development: in moving towards a low-carbon and climate-resilient society, we need to consider the complex relationship between changes in land use patterns and activities and transport, their associated greenhouse gas emissions and their vulnerability to climate change impacts. Greenhouse gas emissions in the transport sector have been growing faster than in other sectors of the economy, and therefore it might seem that decisions on the location of new development would be of critical importance in mitigating climate change. However, transport is largely a derived demand: the spatial pattern of development can be expected to both respond to and influence this demand, although there are many other factors at play in influencing travel patterns and travel behaviour.

Since the European Commission's Green Paper on the Urban Environment (CEC, 1990), policies in many countries of north-west Europe have promoted the consolidation of urban areas. The reasons have been primarily to maintain urban quality of life, to aid regeneration for social reasons, to sustain investment in existing urban infrastructure and demand for urban services, and to conserve rural land for agricultural or horticultural production, as well as biodiversity and ecosystem functions, landscape qualities, access to recreational areas, or flood absorption or storage. In some countries, such as the UK and the Netherlands, these objectives have been supported by policies to contain urban extensions through protective measures such as green belts, green wedges, strategic open spaces of the Dutch 'green heart', a thinly populated area within the Randstadt (Hall *et al.*, 1973; Amati, 2008), and by policies to steer new development to urban areas. In general, these policies have not been adopted with climate change objectives expressly in mind.

Despite such policies, in many countries the socio-economic drivers of counter-urbanization, which create pressures to accommodate new development and to respond to the housing market, have led to high rates of urban development around and beyond existing settlements. Within Europe, urban growth had historically been driven by population growth and migration from rural areas, stimulated in the late nineteenth century by the advent of mass forms of transport such as suburban railways, and in the early part of the twentieth century by motorized transport (Ward, 2004). But since the mid-1950s, urban expansion has occurred even without population growth. There are many reasons for this: demographic change in household composition, socio-economic factors relating to work patterns and the role of women, lifestyle choices and, in particular, the advent of private personal mobility. The different perceptions of people and planning professionals about the character and consequences of these different patterns of growth are summed up in the labels of 'urban sprawl' or 'town cramming' – labels which hint at the assumptions of the users, and their use in discourses and agenda-setting, as much as any consistent analysis. A report from the European Environment Agency, for instance, argued that 'Sprawl threatens the very culture of Europe, as it creates environmental social and economic impacts for the cities and countryside of Europe. Moreover, it seriously undermines efforts to meet the global challenge of climate change' (EEA, 2006, p. 5).

That report offered an analysis of the drivers of this trend towards urban expansion (Table 8.1). To this list should be added the consequences of structural trends in European economies, changes in manufacturing processes to more spatially extensive forms of production requiring more land (such as car manufacture and storage), changes in logistics and distribution, shifts to campus-style service and quaternary industries, the centralization of facilities such as medical services and retail outlets, and national or regional level support for major traffic generating uses such as airports.

The most evident impacts of urban extension are well distributed across Europe: in countries with already high population densities and economic activity (such as Belgium, the Netherlands, south and west Germany, northern Italy and the Paris region), or in areas with rapid economic growth (such as Ireland, Portugal, east Germany and around Madrid). Other areas are around smaller towns and along transportation corridors, particularly river valleys and coastal zones (such as the Rhone Valley, and the Compostela to Lisbon motorway) (EEA, 2009b). The interrelationship of transport provision, suburbanization and lifestyle changes is complex, but it is clear that the provision of transport infrastructure has both responded to the increase in personal mobility and has stimulated it. The length of the motorway network has tripled in thirty years, increasing the attractiveness of more distant locations for certain land uses (EEA, 2009b). Economic growth is also associated with other transport infrastructure such as airports and railway junctions. A complex feedback of transport provision – some of it funded by the EU through its cohesion programme – and urban development results, independent of population growth (Figure 8.1).

8.2.2 Location of development and transport energy use

There are many environmental, social and economic impacts of these complex trends, and there has been much debate over urban form, especially the merits

Table 8.1 Drivers of urban sprawl

Macroeconomic factors	Economic growth
	Globalization
	European integration
Microeconomic factors	Rising living standards
	Price of land
	Availability of cheap agricultural land
	Competition between municipalities
Demographic factors	Population growth
	Increase in household formation
Housing preferences	More space per person
	Housing preferences
Inner city problems	Poor air quality
	Noise
	Small apartments
	Unsafe environments
	Social problems
	Lack of green open space
	Poor quality schools
Transport	Private car ownership
	Availability of roads
	Low cost of fuel
	Poor public transport
Regulatory frameworks	Weak land use planning
	Poor enforcement of existing plans
	Lack of horizontal and vertical coordination and collaboration

Source: EEA, 2006, p. 17

of compact cities, urban extensions, smaller towns, and free-standing settlements (such as Jenks, Burton and Williams, 1996; Williams, 2005; Echenique *et al.*, 2009a). There are still many uncertainties over the relationship of the strategic location of development and transport, and the efficacy of different policy objectives. We first explore the relationship between development patterns and transport energy use, before looking at location and climate change adaptation, and regional policies to address these.

In a review of the available studies of the relationship between urban settlement pattern and energy use in transport in Australia, Rickwood *et al.* conclude that 'it is clear that, on aggregate level, densely populated cities use less transport energy per capita, and per passenger kilometre, than do sparsely populated ones' (2008, p. 74): but, because transport and land use are not independent, and there are positive feedbacks between land use structure and

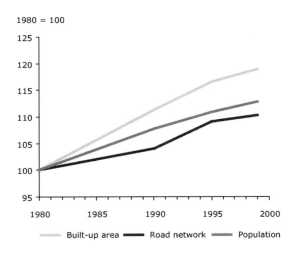

1980 = 100

——— Built-up area ■■■■■ Road network ——— Population

Figure 8.1

Built-up area, road network and population increase in selected European countries
Source: EEA, 2006, p. 13, fig. 3

public transport use and feasibility, it is difficult to establish a causal link. The relationship is further complicated by demographic and socio-economic factors, such as household composition and income, car-ownership, car use and propensity to travel. A number of commentators on sustainable energy futures (Mackay 2009, for instance) suggest that spatial planning has a major role to play in promoting urban settlement patterns which encourage sustainable modes of transport. But the legacy of the predict-and-provide model of transport planning, which extrapolated growth in private vehicles and road freight and made provision for further such growth, and the relative lack of investment in more sustainable alternative modes, has meant that, despite the policy of urban consolidation, spatial planning has had a relatively weak influence on travel behaviour (Headicar, 2009). This point is significant for policies to move towards low-carbon transport (see Section 8.3 below). The pattern of peri-urban development and the complex commuting patterns seen across much of England (Green, 2008) seem to confirm the dispersal of live-work functions, a pattern which suggests to some (for instance, Hall and Pain, 2006) a polycentric structure of urban development, which they see as similar to the planned concentrated dispersal of the Randstad in the Netherlands (discussed in Chapter 7).

However, there is still debate over the appropriate policy responses (as we shall see in the discussion of the Yorkshire and Humber regional plan – see below in Section 8.5). Considerations of climate change – especially the urgency of the obligations to mitigate climate change – add another layer to this already complex relationship, making it a challenge to assess sectoral and spatial policy and plans.

8.2.3 Transport and greenhouse gas emissions

Given this complexity of patterns and types of urban development, and transport and travel behaviour, it is equally difficult to establish the causal links between transport and trends in greenhouse gas emissions.

But it is important to try to understand these relationships, as the transport sector is not only a major contributor to greenhouse gas emissions, but represents a growing proportion of the total, as emissions from other sectors fall. Within the EU, it is estimated that in 2006 it was responsible for 19 per cent of greenhouse gas emissions (primarily CO_2) (Figure 2.3 in Chapter 2), and 21 per cent of those of the EU-15 member states (EEA, 2008c). (Transport here includes all land-based modes and national aviation, but excludes international aviation and shipping: these are addressed in Chapter 5 in the discussion of national planning for major infrastructure such as ports and airports). There are statistical estimates of emissions of greenhouse gases associated with motorized transport, but no estimates on the indirect consequences of soil sealing from the construction of transport infrastructure itself (such as the road network and hard-surfacing for the manufacture and storage of vehicles and their parking that reduces the capacity of soil to act as a carbon sink). Neither do the statistics include a life-cycle analysis of the carbon footprint of the vehicles' manufacture and disposal.

Road transport comprises 93 per cent of the total for the sector (EEA, 2008c). There was a 26 per cent increase in emissions over the period 1990–2006 in the

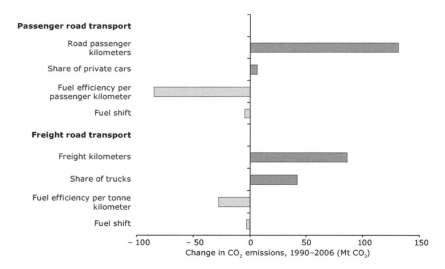

Figure 8.2

Factors affecting development of EU-15 emissions from passenger road and freight road transport, 1990–2006
Source: EEA, 2008c, Fig 4.11

EU-15, and this increase has been largely attributable to an increase in road passenger and freight kilometres, despite improvements required by the EU in fuel efficiency (Figure 8.2).

The EU has strengthened its measures to alter the technologies of road transport, requiring clean fuels and promoting biofuels (see Chapter 2), enforcing regulations for fuel-efficiency ratings of cars and imposing obligations on car manufacturers. Further technical and labelling measures were proposed in the Commission's 2009 communication on sustainable transport (CEC, 2009f). These policies were adopted partly but not wholly for reasons of greenhouse gas reductions. Recently, the increase in emissions has been decoupled from the growth in kilometres travelled, and it is projected that the rate of increase will stabilize over the next few years. It is uncertain how far this reflects a long-term shift, or a short-term response to the price of fuel, and therefore what pattern will emerge after any recovery from the economic downturn of 2008–09. Nevertheless, there are other strong environmental and social reasons to reduce the growth in road transport. Such considerations include its negative impacts on health, accidents, community severance, equity, land-take, resource use, biodiversity, water resources and water quality, air quality, impact on buildings, quality of life, noise and vibration (Royal Commission on Environmental Pollution (RCEP), 1994).

8.2.4 EU regional policies for climate change mitigation

In response to this range of policy objectives for transport, the EU has also adopted strategic policies to promote modal shift, in particular for freight, through its financing of TEN-T (Trans-European Network – Transport) projects promoting rail, and short-sea shipping and inland waterways (although these are not without their environmental problems, such as the proposal for the Danube-Oder-Elbe Canal under the TEN-T VII corridor). DG-Regio has evaluated the outcomes of the Cohesion Programme spending up to 2009, and has found that some projects supported by the fund are likely to have led to increased greenhouse gas emissions. It has already amended its funding to support the low-carbon economy, investing in sustainable energy and transport, and the domestic buildings sector (DG-Regio, 2009). It is therefore reviewing the objectives for the next budget (post 2013) to align them more closely with the EU's own climate change policies for climate change mitigation and adaptation. The EU has also addressed intraurban transport through its Thematic Strategy on the Urban Environment (CEC, 2006b), and the sharing of best practice among different cities and municipalities through networks and events. Nevertheless, it is clear that, to meet the EU's target of a 30 per cent reduction of greenhouse gas emissions by 2020 (see Chapter 3), substantial further efforts need to be made in the transport sector, especially the demand for travel. Transport demand for food, education, business and leisure activity is still increasing, and there is a need for transport planning to shift its focus to accessibility to services rather than mobility (EEA, 2008d). The EEA argues that spatial planning has a significant role in making destinations more accessible and journeys shorter; this will also help to moderate the rebound effect, under which energy-efficiency savings might not lead to overall reduction in energy use (through, for instance, more fuel-efficient but longer journeys being made). It recognizes that steering new development to more sustainable locations works only over the medium–long term (EEA, 2009c). As we explain in the next chapter, only a small proportion of the built environment changes in any year (most estimates are of the order of 1 per cent turnover to account for new builds and refurbishment). However, it is still open to question just how far coordinated spatial planning can achieve changes in travel patterns and behaviour even over the period 2010 to 2050. The UK offers some interesting experience and cautionary tales in these approaches, which we explore in the following section.

8.3 Strategic planning, transport and climate change mitigation in the UK

8.3.1 Transport and greenhouse gas emissions: trends and targets

As with other countries, the UK is struggling to deliver climate change mitigation targets within the transport sector. The Climate Change Act of 2008 (HMG, 2008a) commits the country to a series of carbon budgets to reach the long-term goal of an 80 per cent reduction of greenhouse gases by 2050. The first Low Carbon Transition Plan was published in 2009 (HMG, 2009a) and included an obligation on the transport sector to reduce its 2008 levels of emissions by 14 per cent by 2020.

Transport in the UK represents some 21 per cent of total UK domestic greenhouse gas emissions (in line with the EU-15's average). Whereas total greenhouse gas emissions have declined since 1990, transport emissions have grown, albeit slowly (Figure 8.3). ('Other' end users in Figure 8.3 comprise mainly public, industrial and agricultural sectors.)

The growth in personal private motorized travel (a significant element of transport emissions) has moderated since 2005, and its relationship to household expenditure has weakened since the mid-1990s (Figure 8.4).

However, there has been significant growth in road freight tonne-kms, and CO_2 (Figure 8.5). On a per capita basis, road transport emissions (passenger cars, LGVs, HGVs, buses and coaches, and mopeds/motorcycles) fell by 0.7 per cent between 2005–07 (AEA, 2009), but this masks large differences in the absolute levels. Greater London produced 1.2 tCO_2 per capita compared with 2.9 in Northern Ireland, 2.6 in the South East, and 2.0 in the North East. Figure 8.6 maps the pattern for the UK, and shows the contrast between lower levels in cities (not just the metropolitan cities, but smaller free-standing settlements

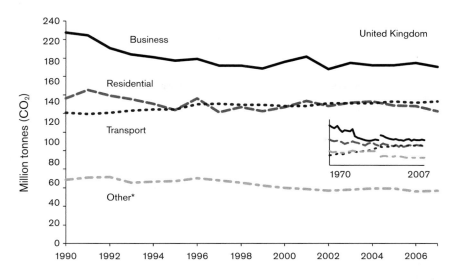

Figure 8.3

CO$_2$ emissions by end user
Source: Defra, 2009b

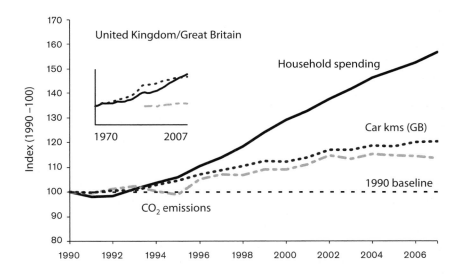

Figure 8.4

Private car use, household spending and CO$_2$ emissions
Source: Defra, 2009b

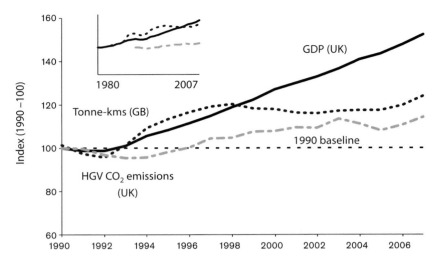

Figure 8.5

Road freight 1990–2007
Source: Defra, 2009b

such as York), and the commuting areas of the outer South East and South West, and the more remote rural areas. One argument for an urban containment policy is that urban dwellers have both the opportunity but also the propensity to travel in more sustainable modes.

8.3.2 National and regional policies for strategic location of development and transport

The change in personal travel has to some degree been influenced by the policies for spatial planning, housing and transport planning that the UK has had in place since the 1990s. The objectives of the planning policy guidance on transport to regional bodies and local authorities (DETR, 2001) have been to reduce the need to travel, to reduce the length of any necessary travel, and to encourage any such journeys to be made by more sustainable modes than the private car. When the Labour Government came to power in 1997, it promised a New Deal on Transport (DETR, 1998) which set transport in the context of other environmental, economic and social objectives, and passed a Road Traffic Reduction Act. The thrust of the policy was to reinforce the location of residential development in urban areas and major travel generators in existing centres (Headicar, 2009). Parallel with these transport policies has been a strong steer for new housing towards existing urban areas, following the report of the Urban Task Force in 1999. In its Urban White Paper (DETR, 2000b), the government adopted a target that, by 2008, at least 60 per cent of all residential

2007 Road Transport Emissions (tonnes Carbon Dioxide per capita)

- < 1.39
- 1.39 - 1.96
- 1.97 - 2.48
- 2.49 - 3.50
- > 3.50

There is an equal number of Local Authorities in each category

Figure 8.6

Per capita road transport CO_2 emissions by Local Authority, 2007
Source: AEA, 2009

development should be located on previously developed land. Given formal expression in planning policy guidance for housing (DETR, 2000c) and reinforced in guidance for the preparation of regional and local plans, this has had a significant effect on the pattern of new residential development. The percentage of dwellings built on previously developed land or converted land has risen from 54 per cent in 1990 to an estimated 78 per cent in 2008 (Figure 8.7). Around half of all development (not only residential) is now taking place on such land, although Figure 8.7 suggests a sharp drop from 2005.

From 2004–09, strategic plan-making has been a function of the new regional arrangements in the English regions. In formulating the regional spatial strategies (RSSs), the regions were guided by PPS11 (Planning Policy Statement 11). This reaffirmed this policy direction towards urban areas, and also made clear that RSSs were to comprise an integrated planning and transport spatial strategy.

> By shaping the pattern of development and influencing the location, scale, density, design and mix of land uses, planning can help to reduce the need to travel, reduce the length of journeys and make it safer and easier to access jobs, shopping, leisure facilities, and services by public transport, walking and cycling. Conversely, good public transport can provide access to economic and leisure activities, support or initiate regeneration, and promote sustainable land use choices.
>
> (ODPM, 2004c, para. 2.16, p. 11)

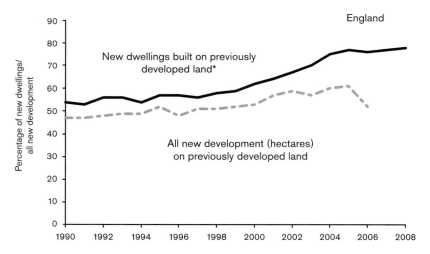

* Includes conversions. Up to 2002 the conversion of existing buildings was estimated to add three percentage points, from 2003 the process of estimation has been elaborated

Figure 8.7

Recycled land
Source: Defra, 2009b

The later guidance on planning for housing (DCLG, 2006c) required the RSSs to identify broad locations for new housing to meet sustainable development criteria including a contribution to cutting carbon emissions. (We shall review below in Section 8.5 the extent to which this worked in practice in a regional example).

The policy guidance from 2007 on planning for climate change continued this policy steer, albeit in a moderated form; it asked that regional planning bodies should, in integrating climate change considerations into the plan,

> pay attention to the location of major generators of travel, the effect of differing patterns of urban growth and sustainable rural development on the movement of goods, and . . . provide a framework for subregional and local planning to focus substantial new development on locations with good accessibility by means other than the private car.
>
> (DCLG, 2007a, p. 12)

It is clear that such policies of urban consolidation have made it easier to maintain and promote more sustainable forms of travel in the face of pressures of counter-urbanization and freedom of choice (Headicar, 2009). There have been some significant recent changes in travel: car availability has remained steady since 2005 (25 per cent of households do not have access to a car); and trips per person by car have levelled off (Figure 8.8); the distance travelled by surface rail has increased by 54 per cent, and the number of trips by rail has increased since 1996 (DfT/NS, 2009a). Since the mid-1990s, there has been growth in local bus and light rail use (especially bus use in London), but substantial falls in other English metropolitan areas (DfT/NS, 2009b). There has been a large increase in London underground journeys. But despite long-standing planning

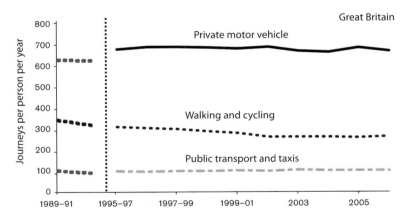

Figure 8.8

Trips per person per mode, 1989/91–2006
Source: Defra, 2009b

and sustainable transport policies, it has proved difficult to shift travel to more sustainable modes: walking and cycling (both average number and percentage of all trips) have declined since 1995 (although cycling rates, especially in London, have increased since 2002), and overall there has been no growth in the proportion of trips by public transport. Domestic freight moved by road has increased by 86 per cent from the 1980s, and road freight has increased its share of all goods moved (DfT/NS, 2009a).

The problems of the Labour transport policy have been catalogued (Vigar, 2002; Docherty and Shaw, 2008; Headicar, 2009): transport has had a low political profile in the Cabinet (with a rapid turnover of departmental ministers), and the transport function in government has been separate from the planning or environment departments. Political pressures from road users were exerted in 2000 through the fuel duty protests, and there has been a continued emphasis on consumer choice and freedom. The effects of the privatization of the railways, and the deregulation of buses, combined with the lack of an overall national programme to reduce traffic volumes, have contributed to policy conflict (Headicar, 2009), and a number of local authorities (such as Manchester and Edinburgh) have failed to gain popular support for proposed road pricing schemes.

There is therefore some disagreement as to how far policy can influence a shift from past patterns. Conclusions from studies which have modelled land use and transport are influenced by initial assumptions and conditions. The SOLUTIONS study, for instance, modelled, to 2031, current trends compared with three alternative development patterns (compaction, market-led dispersal and planned expansion) for two regions of England – the wider South East, and the Tyne and Wear city region in the North East. It concluded that 'the differences between them are overwhelmed by long-run socio-economic trends' (Echenique *et al.*, 2009a, p. 380). Moreover, they concluded that current policies will not materially reduce future increases in CO_2. To some extent, their conclusions are influenced by the assumptions they make about the desirability and social costs of different urban forms, as well as about labour, congestion and production costs (Echenique *et al.*, 2009b). They favour technological solutions over behavioural changes as being more feasible.

The Commission for Integrated Transport, by contrast, argues that transport policies need fundamental change, and that rethinking is needed at the level of strategy development and policy development (CfIT, 2009a) (Box 8.1).

Since that report, the CfIT has published further guidance on the integration of spatial planning and transport planning (CfIT, 2009b). At the strategic spatial scale, it addresses the themes of size and strategic location, and argues that larger settlements can reduce car travel, as there is broadly an inverse relationship with an increased average distance travelled as settlement size decreases. It recommends locating development in urban areas with a population of at least 25,000, rather than leapfrogging dispersal or replicating existing urban patterns, and ensuring strategic traffic generation considerations should allow a review of urban containment policies (such as green belts).

Other suggestions (Headicar, 2009) are that we need to address the issue of traffic growth through conventional demand management, and through additional measures to lessen individual car ownership (such as travel plans for new residential developments, improving non-car travel for work and school journeys, and extending personalized travel planning). We also need to rethink interurban travel in the longer term, for instance, interchanges between different modes for long-distance (e.g. high speed linked vehicles) and urban modes, and, in the shorter term, to promote greater density of passengers (through promoting multi-occupied vehicles or coaches, and catering explicitly for intertown express coaches, suitable for a polycentric urban pattern and new city-regions).

8.3.3 Spatial planning policies for transport demand management and travel behaviour

Given the weight of car dependence in existing development, there are strong arguments for supplementing strategic planning policies to reduce travel demand and to shift travel mode by measures to change behaviour more directly, through physical provision of more sustainable modes within or at the edge of urban areas (such as transport interchanges and increased provision of cycle networks and pedestrian links), through fiscal measures (road user charging or fuel duty escalation) or through softer measures. Some interesting findings are emerging from research on the relationship between these initiatives and overall inter- and intraurban travel.

Research for the DfT has suggested that a range of soft measures known collectively as 'Smarter Choices' could achieve significant reductions in traffic, depending on the degree of other policy support. Policy has been redirected to support these (Table 8.2).

As Headicar (2009) argues, not all of these measures require the intervention of public agencies, but spatial planning can influence the demand for and mode of travel through its ability to require such measures as workplace and residential travel plans, as well as accessibility assessments for locating and appraising new developments. One recent initiative, the Sustainable Travel Towns project, has promoted a sustained programme of smarter choice travel measures in which three demonstration towns (Darlington, Peterborough and Worcester) have adopted individualized travel marketing and a range of other measures such as workplace and school travel planning, car-sharing schemes, and improved provision and marketing of public transport). Under the five-year programme, car journeys (by driver) have reduced by 9%, and increases in cycling by 12–113% and walking by 14% have been achieved (DfT, 2009b p. 14). The scheme is now being extended to cities (through competitive bidding for funding).

As indicated above, there has been much less political will to institute fiscal measures, with the exception of London. London already has a significantly higher share of travel by public transport modes than other cities. The

Table 8.2 Typical measures for sustainable travel packages

Introduce travel plans	Promote public transport	Active travel choices	Influencing demand	Marketing and branding	Sustainable car use
Workplace	Fare incentives & smart ticketing	Walking support & infrastructure	Tele-working/ teleconferencing	Information on travel choices	Car clubs & car sharing
School	Improved service	Cycle training	Home shopping	Travel awareness campaigns	Car sharing where possible
Personalized travel planning	Better access/ interchange	Business cycle facilities & initiatives	Parking restrictions	Branding	Eco-driving
Station travel plans	Better integration	Cycle hire schemes	Traffic management		Electric vehicle infrastructure
		Cycle & walking route maps	Integrated land use planning		Vehicle choice

Source: DfT, 2009b, p. 12

congestion charge in central London, introduced in 2003 through the particular (and unique to London) powers of the elected mayor, was intended to
reduce congestion, improve bus services and journey time reliability for cars,
and make the delivery of goods and services more efficient. Despite significant
initial reductions, it seems that the early benefits of decongestion have recently
been moderated by the reallocation of space to sustainable modes (such as bus
lanes), and CO_2 emissions in the central zone have reduced by only 1 per cent
per annum 2003–06 (TfL, 2008, p. 105).

Fiscal measures such as the congestion charge or road user charging are
much advocated as effective interventions in tune with the market, behavioural
change, personal responsibility and freedom (see Echenique *et al.*, 2009), but
the outcomes in London indicate some of the difficulties in predicting the
interactions in practice. This very brief review shows that the interrelationship between planning policy, transport policy, travel behaviour and new and
existing development is extremely complex. One conclusion to be drawn is
that we need to consider the location of new development as part of a wider
assessment of travel patterns and behaviour in existing built environments.
Headicar (2009) argues that we must consider future transport in its context of
spatial development, and the question of interurban transport in the context of
the 'whole journey' of trips which originate within towns and cities. In other
words, we need an assessment which relates interurban and intraurban travel;
the additional requirement to reduce the CO_2 emissions from transport (from
2008, an explicit objective of government sustainable transport strategy [DfT,
2008a]) has to be considered in the same assessment.

8.3.4 National and regional targets for low-carbon transport

Chapter 3 has described the UK's domestic and international commitment to
reduce carbon, and the principal means to achieve this. The Climate Change
Act 2008 and the subsequent Low Carbon Transition Plan impose a new obligation on transport to reduce transport-related CO_2 by 14 per cent by 2020. The
transport strategy (DfT, 2008a) already expected cities and regional networks
to contribute by delivering quantified reductions in greenhouse gases; local
authorities and local authority partnerships are also subject to performance
assessment under National Indicator 186 (reduction of per capita CO_2 emissions, including road transport). It might be expected that this will herald a
new impetus to shift transport to more sustainable modes through stringent
transport and spatial planning policies, and the use of carbon targets as a met-
ric in assessing regional and local transport proposals. However, the plan for a
transition to low-carbon transport by 2022 (DfT, 2009c) favours technological
measures to improve fuel and vehicle efficiencies for cars, vans, buses, freight,
aviation, shipping, and proposes actions for new technologies and to promote
sustainable biofuels. It acknowledges that these on their own are insufficient
to reduce transport emissions to reach the reduction target of 14 per cent and

therefore proposes other measures to promote lower carbon choices (Box 8.2), although it is clear that the role of spatial planning is subsidiary.

> **Box 8.2** Non-technological measures in Carbon Reduction Strategy for Transport
>
> - Providing lower-carbon public transport.
> - Promoting the integration of transport modes (such as through improving interchanges).
> - Promoting other sustainable modes (such as extending the Sustainable Travel Towns to Cities, and developing a national cycle plan and an active transport strategy).
> - Working further with regions and local authorities (through strategic and local transport planning).
> - Promoting change through better information.
> - Reducing CO_2 from business-related travel and the distribution of goods.
> - Reducing the need to travel through information technology and through spatial planning.
>
> Source: adapted from DfT, 2009c, pp. 8–11

The Department claims that the impact of these measures should be to reduce transport emissions by $15\,MtCO_2$ in addition to the expected trend reduction by 2020, and make a saving of 85 Mt in the carbon budget period 2018–22 (DfT, 2009c).

The Campaign for Better Transport (2009) is highly critical of the emphasis in the plan on technological solutions, claiming the government overstates the speed and effectiveness with which any benefits from technology would be gained, and underestimates the impact of the types of smart choice options indicated in Section 8.3.3. They argue that the plan pays little attention to the wider sustainability objectives of equity, health, community cohesion, resource and land use efficiency and environmental protection which strategic spatial planning for transport needs to address. The VIBAT back-casting study (Hickman and Banister, 2007), briefly mentioned in Chapter 6, concluded that carbon reduction targets can be achieved by 2030 through significant behavioural changes (including reducing the need to travel through compact or polycentric patterns and public-transport-oriented development), but that behavioural changes must happen now. They considered that technological innovation is a risky strategy to rely on. The study was extended to 2050 for London, and for an overall 80 per cent reduction, which reinforced the conclusion that the necessary policies and measures will be very difficult to implement, and that 'the huge challenge of delivering the necessary trend-break is currently being seriously under-estimated' (Hickman, Ashiru and Banister, 2009, p. 68).

Such a view is reinforced by the Committee on Climate Change in its progress report on Meeting Carbon Budgets (CCC, 2009a). The Committee argued that reductions in greenhouse gas emissions over the period 2003–07 fell by less than 1 per cent per annum (and by even less for CO_2), and that any fall over 2008–09 was the result of the recession, and unlikely to be sustained once the national economy recovers. They argue that 'a step change will be required to achieve deep emission cuts' for road-based transport. They propose a radical programme of infrastructure to service electric vehicles (to serve three-quarters of car-owning households), the training of almost 4 million drivers in eco-driving, stricter enforcement or even reduction of the motorway speed limit, and recommend that the government develops 'an integrated land use planning and transport strategy' which fully addresses the risk of increasing transport emissions (CCC, 2009a, p. 28). However, it seems that there is little thought being given at such climate change policy-formulating levels to different patterns of development. Nevertheless, there is much interest and enthusiasm within the broader sustainability policy field (such as Jackson, 2009; Green New Deal Group, 2008) in radically changing the live-work relationship, with different modes of production and distribution of goods and food, such as in the Transition Towns movement or local eco-community initiatives, with their potential to benefit society and to reduce transport emissions. We return to this theme in Chapter 14.

8.4 Strategic planning and climate change adaptation in the UK

8.4.1 National adaptation planning

The previous section has indicated some of the issues in selecting strategic locations for development to meet low carbon transport objectives and targets. But, as we have seen in Part I, we need also to ensure development locations are resilient with respect to future climate change. This presents different challenges for strategic plan-making at regional and subregional scales. Firstly, there are no legally binding targets to set a framework against which to judge actions. The UK has as yet no national risk assessment or adaptation plan (although these are being prepared in conformity with the Climate Change Act 2008, for adoption by 2012: see Chapter 3, Section 3.4.2), and Scotland published a climate change adaptation framework in 2009. Secondly, whereas Scotland's national spatial framework states that one of the principal elements of the spatial strategy to 2030 is 'to promote development which helps to reduce Scotland's carbon footprint and facilitates adaptation to climate change development', and addresses flood risk, drainage and water resources (Scottish Government, 2009), England lacks such a national spatial plan. Thirdly, plan-making needs to have regard not just for climate change scenarios for projected future conditions, but also for socio-economic scenarios (as we saw in Chapter 6). Fourthly, in England, until the 2007 PPS1 Supplement on climate change (DCLG, 2007a), formal policy guidance from the government on the location of development with respect to natural hazards was dispersed amongst separate PPSs, such as those on flood risk and coastal planning. As we shall see in Chapter 10, water resource issues have had patchy coverage in government guidance but have proved a major issue in the preparation of regional spatial strategies. On the other hand, a significant amount of work (described in Chapter 5) has been undertaken at the regional scale on the impacts of climate change, and it can be argued that this strategic scale is an appropriate one for assessing impacts and formulating adaptive responses in relation to development patterns.

8.4.2 Adaptation in regional planning

The PPS Supplement on climate change (DCLG, 2007a) indicated some links between patterns of urban growth and climate change adaptation (Box 8.3).

Box 8.3 Guidance on climate change adaptation in regional spatial strategies

Key principle: New development should be planned to minimize future vulnerability in a changing climate (p. 10).
  Roles of RPBs:

- Consider the region's vulnerability to climate change using, for example, the most recent scenarios from UKCIP, and specifically the implications for built development, infrastructure and services and biodiversity (p. 12).
- Consider and take account of the availability of water resources.
- Consider the desirability of avoiding new development in those areas with likely increased vulnerability to the effects of climate change, particularly where it is not viable to manage likely risks through suitable measures to provide resilience (p. 13).

Source: adapted from DCLG, 2007a, pp. 10–13

This was more specific than the earlier guidance for the preparation of regional spatial strategies, which made only indirect reference to the need to adapt to climate change (ODPM, 2004c). But the former guidance did point to the large number of studies at regional level on the impacts of climate change on the regions, and the scope for adaptation. These had been produced by the regional climate change partnerships set up under the auspices of UKCIP (described in more detail in Chapter 4). The studies highlighted different regional vulnerabilities (UKCIP, 2001): for instance, that for the North West, with its still-significant manufacturing employment base, identified the impacts of warmer summers on the conditions for its production processes and workforce, as well as impacts on its important tourism and agricultural sectors, and its coastal areas, landscapes and biodiversity. Most of the regional studies drew

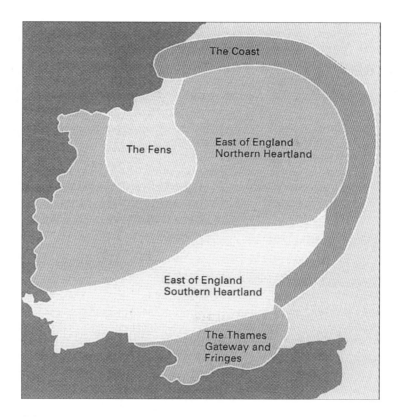

Figure 8.9

Climate change subregions in East of England
Source: EESDRT, 2004

attention to the impacts on water resources, flood risk, thermal comfort and biodiversity, but few mapped the combined impacts in terms of the combined vulnerabilities for the location of future development. An exception was the study for the East of England (EESDRT, 2004). This identified five climate change subregions with similar socio-economic and environmental characteristics that also shared similar climate change impacts: the coast, the Fens, the Thames Gateway and fringes, the southern heartlands and the northern heartlands (Box 8.4; Figure 8.9). The study suggested that adaptation responses in the subregions might be guided by UKCIP principles – keep options flexible; avoid foreclosing future adaptation; and seek no-regrets options – to optimize the location of development and reduce vulnerabilities.

Chapters 10 and 11 look in more detail at issues of water resources and flood risk, and Chapter 12 at biodiversity and ecosystem implications, and their role in climate change adaptation and mitigation through incorporation in regional and local plans. We examine below the case of one region – Yorkshire and

Humberside – to explore the extent to which it has been able to incorporate both mitigation and adaptation objectives within an RSS. We also draw attention to the challenges presented to the new regional strategies in addressing these issues and the need to mitigate climate change at the same time as a series of new initiatives came from the government for strategic locations for development.

8.5 Climate change mitigation and adaptation at the regional level: the Yorkshire and Humber Plan

In Chapter 7, we have suggested that the sustainability appraisal (SA) represents a good vehicle for a holistic and integrated assessment of climate change mitigation and adaptation in regional spatial plan formulation. We showed that sustainability appraisals have advanced considerably in their treatment of climate change issues – partly in response to the changed profile of targets (such as renewable energy and carbon reduction targets), and partly from innovations among the professional assessment community and environmental groups. Notwithstanding this, tensions still exist between the desire for economic growth and house-building at national and regional levels, and the ability to respond to climate change. One example of the complex interaction of SA, regional plan-making and central government policy initiatives in practice is the Yorkshire and Humber Plan (the RSS for Yorkshire and Humber).

8.5.1 Context and process of plan preparation and sustainability appraisal

When the first Yorkshire and Humber Regional Spatial Strategy (RSS), building on an earlier RPG, had been adopted in 2004, work had already commenced on a fully revised RSS which included explicit attention to addressing climate change. Relevant studies were already in progress (WS Atkins *et al.*, 2002; Land Use Consultants (LUC) and Wilbraham, 2005). The new RSS was adopted in May 2008 following the Examination in Public (EiP); its drafting had been accompanied by a full sustainability appraisal (incorporating strategic environmental assessment), commissioned and approved by regional government. Work then started on an update responding to government targets for more house-building (through the Sustainable Communities Plan, discussed in Chapter 4) and extending the time-horizon to 2026. Long-term infrastructure needs (including green infrastructure) and climate change were additional reasons for the update (Yorkshire and Humber Regional Assembly, 2008). Box 8.5 shows the expected climate change impacts in the region.

Box 8.5 Climate change vulnerabilities and opportunities

Widespread/generalized impacts:

- Sea-level rise, coastal erosion, increased flooding.
- Increased temperatures, pressure on water resources.
- Changing agricultural landscapes, habitats and species distribution.
- Impacts on property, industry and infrastructure (such as ports, road and rail) from effects such as subsidence, and risk of storm damage.

Impacts in particular locations:

- Heat island effect on inland urban areas such as Leeds.
- Increased flood risk along Humber estuary, Vale of York, and in urban areas adjoining the Pennines such as Bradford, Keighley, Leeds and Sheffield.
- Water shortages for areas relying on Lower Derwent and Doncaster/Selby Sandstone aquifer.
- Coastal squeeze on habitats.

Opportunities: for tourism, the agricultural sector and technological innovation.

Source: adapted from LUC and Wilbraham, 2005, based on WS Atkins *et al.*, 2002

Three scenarios were used during preparation of the adopted Plan: responding to market-forces, matching needs with opportunity and managing the environment as a key resource. The adopted spatial vision contained elements of all three, although with a strong element of intervention to address needs. Counsell *et al.* (2007) have described the tensions arising in the attempts to integrate the RSS with other regional strategies (the Regional Economic and Housing Strategies, and the Regional Sustainable Development Framework: the latter set the aims for the region which were to be used in the SA of the developing Plan).

The 2008 SA had identified increasing mobility, climate change (greenhouse gas emissions), water demand and waste production as key sustainability problems for the RSS. Yorkshire and Humberside is a region with areas of concentrated socio-economic deprivation, but with some significant assets in its population, economic base, cultural heritage and landscapes. It has an above-average level of greenhouse gas emissions – the region provides 18 per cent of the nation's electricity production; moreover, transport-related emissions were rising. The region has experienced major flooding, for instance in the Selby and York area in 2000, and in Hull, Doncaster and Sheffield in summer 2007.

8.5.2 Climate change policies in the Plan

The approved Plan's spatial vision is:

> Over the next 15–20 years, there will be more sustainable patterns and forms of development, investment and activity, and a greater emphasis on matching needs with opportunities and managing the environment as a key resource.
>
> (GOYH, 2008, pp. 7–8)

The Plan's intentions are to reverse the trend of population and investment dispersal from the region's cities and towns, to transform those towns into cohesive and attractive places, to reduce inequalities, improve accessibility, address the growth in transport-related emissions and raise environmental quality. The region also intends to respond proactively to the global and local effects of climate change and to optimize the use of land, social and environmental (including green) infrastructure. A policy (YH2) to support the climate change aim, which was backed by selected indicators and targets (principally relating to energy use and flooding), is shown in Box 8.6.

8.5.3 Mitigation objectives: location and transport elements

The SA took an objectives-led approach to appraising the Plan (in line with national guidance in ODPM, 2005b). The relevant objectives included

Policy YH2: Climate change and resource use
Plans, strategies, investment decisions and programmes should:

A Help to meet the target set out in the RES to reduce greenhouse gas emissions in the region in 2016 by 20–25% (compared to 1990 levels) with further reductions thereafter by:
1. Increasing population, development and activity in cities and towns.
2. Encouraging better energy, resource and water efficient buildings.
3. Minimizing resource demands from development.
4. Reducing traffic growth through an appropriate location of development, demand management, and improving public transport and facilities for walking and cycling.
5. Encouraging redevelopment of previously developed land.
6. Facilitating effective waste management.
7. Increasing renewable energy capacity and carbon capture.

B Plan for the successful adaptation to the predicted impacts of climate change by:
1. Minimizing threats from and impact of coastal erosion, increased flood risk, increased storminess, habitat disturbance, increased pressure on water resources, supply and drainage systems.
2. Maximizing opportunities from increased growing season, greater tourism potential and warmer urban environments.

Source: GOYH, 2008, p. 15

'Minimis[ing] greenhouse gas emissions and a managed response to the effects of climate change. If environmental impacts are a significant result of the activity consider an environmental impact assessment' (EDAW *et al.*, 2008).

The Plan acknowledges that many of the measures required to achieve reductions of greenhouse gases are outside its scope, but pointed to the potential through increasing urban density and use of the public transport network, especially in the Leeds City Region, helping in the transformation of urban areas (GOYH, 2008, para. 2.21). Improved public transport is indeed a theme of the Plan, although other proposals (new road links and motorway junction improvements, and some elements of the implementation of the Northern Way Growth Strategy) run counter to this commitment. The final SA of the Plan concluded that there was particular concern over connectivity and the expansion of business facilities in rural locations. Assessing the plan policies against the SA objectives, it concluded that policies for the provision and distribution of housing, and for airports, were likely to have a very negative impact (EDAW *et al.*, 2008). Overall, the SA judged that meeting the greenhouse gas objective was finely balanced between negative and positive outcomes (p. 33). The SA suggested some alternative approaches to mitigating climate change:

although the final policy YH2 did not go beyond national targets, it did propose some complementary measures, such as the support for smart travel. The region has also tried to address climate change mitigation targets through its Climate Change Action Plan (GOYH, 2005), supporting clean coal, although there was disjunction between the regional ambition and its powers, its lack of support for renewables and implementation through local-level planning (Drake, 2009).

8.5.4 Adaptation objectives

The Plan amplifies its overarching policy for climate change with adaptation through policies on development and flood risk (ENV 1) (Box 8.7), green infrastructure (YH8) and biodiversity (ENV8). For the coastal sub-area, the Plan proposes to 'Avoid the risk from flooding, erosion and landslip along the coast, through roll-back approaches to relocate existing uses' (GOYH, 2008, Policy C1).

Box 8.7 Development and flood-risk policy in Yorkshire and Humber Plan

A The region will manage flood risk proactively by reducing the causes of flooding to existing and future development, especially in tidal areas, and avoiding development in high flood-risk areas where possible.

B Allocation of areas for development will follow a sequential approach and will be in the lowest risk sites appropriate for the development (identified by Strategic Flood Risk Assessments).

C Flood management will be required to:
1. Facilitate development in the cities of Leeds, Bradford, Sheffield, Hull and York; coastal towns including Bridlington, Grimsby, Scarborough and Whitby; inland urban areas including Doncaster, Goole, Halifax, Scunthorpe, Selby and Wakefield (where there is little development land available outside high flood-risk zones) and land on the south bank of the Humber, provided the sequential approach has been used to inform decisions regarding flood risk.
2. Protect parts of the strategic transport network, especially the Selby-Hull, Doncaster-York and Doncaster-Immingham transport corridors.
3. Provide flood storage, habitat creation and managed realignment in areas around the Humber, and other river corridors as required.
4. Provide positive land management for flood alleviation, particularly in the upland areas of the Yorkshire Dales, the North York Moors, the Howardian Hills and the Pennines.

Source: GOYH, 2008, Policy ENV1

The SA did not address climate change adaptation holistically. Acknowledging policies on water resources and subregional policies, the SA concluded that, while the policy on development and flood risk had been strengthened in the final RSS, flood risk will continue to be a significant issue for the region, and sustainable development options with consideration of flood risk will need to be identified (EDAW *et al.*, 2008).

8.5.5 Prospects from 2010 onwards

The Plan Update will itself be subject to an SA which will be expected to challenge and provide an independent critical appraisal of the approach to the options. The Scoping Report for the Spatial Options Plan Update shows that, while, as might be expected, total CO_2 emissions are correlated with density of population, per capita emissions are highest in rural areas, demonstrating the greater propensity to travel by car (LUC, 2008). The report recognizes that the relationship between housing demand, employment growth and reducing the need to travel is a complex sustainability issue.

In responding to the consultation on the spatial options, the Environment Agency points out that there is a much better evidence base – recent work on the national climate change projections, and regional work on River Basin Management Plans under the Water Framework Directive, the Green Infrastructure and Critical Infrastructure Studies, etc. – to support the Plan Update in improving on the RSS. However, the Agency considers that a regional flood-risk appraisal should be undertaken, with subregional appraisals for the Humber, Leeds City Region and South Yorkshire sub-areas, looking more closely at the capacity of development locations to accommodate 'existing as well as increased housing numbers' (EA, 2009b).

This example shows the difficult sustainability challenges of going beyond merely 'taking climate change into consideration' in regional and subregional planning for new development. There is a complex and currently changing multi-level governance at the regional scale: the adopted plan was prepared by the Regional Assembly, representatives of elected local councillors, in tandem with the Regional Economic strategy prepared by Yorkshire Forward, the government-funded and nominated Regional Development Agency. This provides an opportunity for integration across scales, but also exposes the process to initiatives from the centre which can render ineffective efforts at radical policymaking and appraisal. This complexity is exacerbated by the Treasury-led decision to abolish Regional Assemblies, and to amalgamate the RSS and RES from 2010 into a single regional strategy prepared by a Local Government Leader Board with the RDA. The consequences are likely to be a more narrowly economics-driven interpretation of growth (Glasson and Marshall, 2007). Yorkshire Forward has inherited responsibility for the Regional Transport Strategy from the Regional Assembly. It was expected that in Yorkshire and Humber the new Leaders' Board would be established from 2010, but the future of regional governance and regional planning is in doubt following the General Election of 2010.

8.6 Eco-towns

By contrast with the statutory processes for regional plan-making, and the formal opportunities for assessment of climate change considerations, the Labour Government proposed a programme of new settlements somewhat outside the formal plan-making process, but which were explicitly linked to aspects of climate change. While the national commitment to mitigating climate change and to reducing transport emissions was becoming more ambitious over the plan-making period, the government's agenda for higher rates of house-building has thrown into question the basis of a number of regional plans. This has been exemplified in the eco-towns initiative.

8.6.1 Objectives and Prospectus

The eco-towns programme was announced by Gordon Brown in April 2007 when he was still Chancellor of the Exchequer. As explained in Chapter 4, the initiative arose out of an alliance of Treasury thinking on sustainable housing with the TCPA's enthusiasm for new settlements and garden cities. It was also consistent in style with the government's belief in competition and challenges, and its expectations that the private development sector was more able to identify suitable sites for development than the formal planning process. The idea was given more formal status in the Housing Green Paper (DCLG, 2007c) (at which time new settlements of up to 20,000 homes were envisaged). The objectives of eco-towns were for new growth to help housing affordability, and to achieve significantly higher standards of development, especially zero carbon and sustainable living across the whole settlement. The requirements were set out in the *Eco-towns Prospectus*, with broad criteria for suitable locations (Box 8.8).

The somewhat back-to-front process was illustrated by the fact that a draft PPS on eco-towns was not published by DCLG until after the first 57 submissions were received, and that no Sustainability Appraisal or Strategic Environmental Assessment of the plan was published until 2008. The *Prospectus* quoted from the TCPA's study for government of urban extensions and new settlements which had commented, following PPS 3 Housing (DCLG, 2006c), that:

> Ideas about town and country, urban and rural, and their differences and complementarities, are going through another period of change [...] In some areas the point is reached where existing towns 'must have stop', and a bold new step will have to be taken to meet the need for housing and urban development in such a way that the distinction between town and country is not confused by sprawl.
>
> (TCPA, 2007, pp. 38–9)

The *Prospectus* cited previous new settlement proposals at Northstowe in Cambridgeshire and Cranbrook near Exeter, and argued somewhat disingenuously that these had been planned before the full-scale of climate change was clear – an example of the discourse of climate change being claimed in support of particular policy positions. The *Prospectus* also cited the reputation of the UK for new settlements such as Letchworth Garden City, as well as a selection of exemplars of Vauban, near Freiburg in Germany, Malmo and Hammarby Sjöstad in Sweden, and Nieuw Terbregge near Rotterdam. The *Prospectus* did not offer a systematic assessment of the wider context of policies, institutional frameworks, development and financing of infrastructure which had supported them. The criterion for location for eco-towns was therefore given little substance other than being 'separate and distinct from but well-linked to existing towns'. The expectations for transport focused primarily on intraurban features, but did also mention that they should include:

- An area-wide travel plan, showing how it would achieve a significantly higher proportion of journeys on foot, bicycle and by public transport than comparable settlements in size.
- High quality public transport links (and easy access to a wide range of subregion employment and leisure facilities), and reduced car-dependency including cycling and walking.
- Consideration of impacts on roads and congestion when siting the eco-towns, and planning infrastructure requirements.

(DCLG, 2007d, p. 15)

For employment, the *Prospectus* required as an outcome a clear economic strategy, relating business potential in the settlement to nearby towns and economic clusters, and 'above all, sustainable locations which relate well to the existing network of surrounding towns and villages' (p. 18). There was encouragement for the sites to make use of surplus public sector or brownfield land – many possible sites were somewhat isolated ex-military airfields, recently declared as surplus by the Ministry of Defence. The emphasis was very much on the place-making rather than strategic locational features of the eco-towns. Practical guidance was to be prepared by David Lock and the TCPA.

The DfT published its own requirements for the eco-towns in April 2008, acknowledging that new roads might be required to access the developments:

> Plans for new roads to developments should only be considered where they are essential for improved access or the town's economic sustainability and where they would provide more sustainable access for residents and/or businesses. Any road-building should be designed with a high priority assigned to sustainable modes of travel.
>
> (DfT, 2008b, p. 6)

The TCPA's *Transport Worksheet*, published in tandem with the DfT's guidance, suggested that an overall CO_2 emissions target for the entire development should be set, with a specific target for transport (TCPA, 2008). No precise target was given, but as a proxy it suggested, for exemplar towns, a maximum of 25 per cent of all journeys by private car, compared with no more than 40 per cent as general good practice in all eco-towns, although this had to be realistic given other objectives such as equality of access (TCPA, 2008).

8.6.2 Eco-town outcomes

In the event, some 57 submissions were received: a short-list of 15 then reduced to 13 as schemes dropped out. The draft eco-towns PPS, and the short-listed locations, were subject to a Sustainability Appraisal and Habitats Regulations Assessment (HRA), published in November 2008. The final PPS, published as the second Supplement to PPS1, in July 2009, reduced the modal shift target to demonstrating 'how the town's design will enable at least 50 per cent of trips originating in eco-towns to be made by non-car means, with the potential for this to increase over time to at least 60 per cent' (DCLG, 2009c, p. 9). The government assessed the schemes against five criteria (Box 8.9).

Only four locations were considered in this assessment to have the potential to be eco-towns, of which two (Whitehill-Bordon, Hampshire, and NW Bicester, Oxfordshire) are urban extensions, both of which have local authority support (DCLG, 2009d). Others, including Rossington near Doncaster, a growth point in the Yorkshire and Humberside region, were deemed to merit further work on deliverability in relation to access to the road network. Flood risk was an issue in a number of the short-listed sites. In December 2009, the government announced funding to support nine further expressions of

Box 8.9 Criteria for judging eco-town proposals

- Scope for the location to exemplify high sustainability gains (in terms of PPS standards) in relation to its context and surrounding area.
- Infrastructure proposals for the location, such as transport, sufficiently developed to be able to achieve sustainability standards of the type set in the PPS.
- Infrastructure proposed for the location likely to be deliverable, taking account of affordability and public sector constraints.
- Location likely to work well in terms of economic and employment links and impacts on neighbouring settlements.
- Going forward, the deliverability of an eco-town in this location likely to fit well with current or emerging policies on planning and wider growth and regeneration issues.

Source: adapted from DCLG, 2009d, pp. 10–11

interest from local authorities and city-regions across fourteen locations; the list again included Northstowe in Cambridgeshire, but no others from the earlier shortlist.

The wider governance issues of the eco-towns initiative are not our concern here, except in relation to the evident lack of ownership of the greenhouse gas emissions and wider climate change implications of strategic locations for new development, which is dispersed between the DCLG, DfT, TCPA, the Challenge Panel of Experts, the RAs and LPAs. In particular, it is not clear how far the DCLG's agenda has been integrated with ongoing DfT thinking towards low-carbon and sustainable transport (as described in 8.3.4) from the 2007 Transport White Paper (DfT, 2007a) to the Low Carbon Plan (DfT, 2009b), and subsequent guidance to regions on delivering sustainable transport (DfT, 2009c). The eco-towns programme was pushed forward by an alliance of DCLG with TCPA, which was enthusiastic for the opportunities for place-making and urban design in low-carbon communities, but perhaps underplayed issues of strategic or subregional transport planning. Similar issues arose from the enthusiasm for citing developments from continental Europe as models, without sufficient analysis of the wider carbon emissions from transport experienced in these cases.

8.7 Learning from Europe

The *Eco-towns Prospectus* illustrated some of its enthusiasms with examples from continental Europe, but without including a systematic appraisal of their location, delivery and management. Studies undertaken by TCPA and others (such as Falk and Hall, 2009; HCA, 2008) rectified this. They argue that continental Europe is a good comparator, as many areas have provided high levels and standards of new housing. It has also experienced some of the same economic shifts out of manufacturing, and issues of integration of internal and international migration, but generally has achieved higher quality of life and levels of happiness (PRP *et al.*, 2008). We take the case of the Netherlands here.

8.7.1 The Netherlands: context

The Netherlands has long been associated in the minds of British planning professionals with an emphasis on strategic national infrastructure planning (Marshall, 2009b), sustainable modes of interurban transport and high quality residential environments (Falk, 2008a). But despite its reputation for high levels of sustainable intraurban transport, such as cycling (Figure 8.10), and its good public transport accessibility to key traffic generators such as Schiphol Airport, the Netherlands has experienced a significant growth in transport-related greenhouse gas emissions over the last 16 years above the EU-32 average: it had a 37 per cent increase in transport greenhouse gases from 1990–2006, compared with an EU average of 27 per cent. (The rate of increase in the UK was 15 per cent, and 165 per cent in Ireland [EEA, 2009c]). Passenger car-km increased by 22 per cent over the period 1990–2003 (although this was less than the growth in GDP), but the growth in freight tonnes-km on roads was 44 per cent, higher than the growth rate of GDP (VROM, 2008b). Policies operating

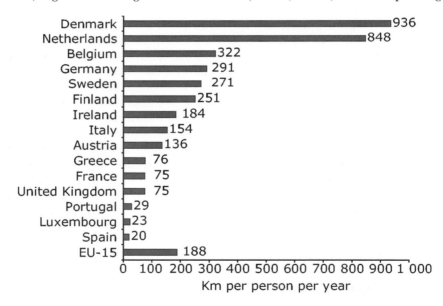

Figure 8.10

Cycling rates in 2000 (EU-15)
Source: EEA, 2008c, fig.11.2

in the later half of this period included, besides fiscal, technological, energy-labelling and behavioural change measures, policies to encourage modal shift to lower-carbon modes through short journeys and the successful promotion of bicycle and public transportation (VROM, 2008b).

8.7.2 The Netherlands: urban developments

Amersfoort, near Utrecht in the Netherlands, was one of the sites chosen for comparison by TCPA and URBED in arranging study visits of comparative practice. It is one of the VINEX schemes under the Fourth Memorandum on Spatial Planning for the country from 1993–2000. VINEX schemes were to deliver 455,000 houses, mostly in the Randstad area bounded by Amsterdam, Utrecht, Rotterdam and The Hague (see Chapter 7, Section 7.6.1). They were partly intended to stem the flow of middle-income households from the larger cities into more rural locations. Developments were to be close to settlements with a population of over 100,000, relatively compact and with good transport systems (HCA, 2008). Vathorst, a free-standing development of 11,000 new homes to be built 2000–14, also forms part of the new Amersfoort. Vathorst had to face four challenges: extending beyond the motorway that had formed a clear boundary; incorporating an existing village; building on land occupied by farming and industry; and dealing with polluted and floodable land. Prior to development commencing in 2001, agreement had been reached with central government on contributions to connections to the motorways and the construction of a new railway station on the line to Amsterdam. There has been a higher than expected use of private cars, with accessibility to the motorway network and employment in the Amsterdam area, which has required the allocation of more land for car parking than originally planned (Falk, 2008b).

While Vathorst is physically separated from Amersfoort, most other study-locations more closely approximated the urban extensions at Upton, Northamptonshire and Ashton Green, Leicestershire, rather than the TCPA's ideal of eco-towns as being clearly distinct from existing settlements. The key lessons are not wholly supportive of the eco-towns initiative. The study report concluded that 'the implications of [our] findings need to be applied more widely and engrained in a wholly new approach to large-scale sustainable development, much of which will inevitably take the form of regeneration or urban extensions rather than in stand-alone new communities' (PRP et al., 2008, p. 6).

Similar lessons are drawn by the HCA, which appraised evidence from what it considered the most advanced eco-towns and cities in the EU against four criteria: climate, connectivity, community and character (HCA, 2008). For connectivity, it concluded that building in the right places should mean:

- Choose the right locations which have ready access to jobs, education and services.

- Draw on the strengths of existing conurbations and add to them, rather than draw resources away from them.
- Build on and add to committed infrastructure, such as rail and bus routes, rather than starting from scratch.
- Work within the framework of RSSs and LDFs.

(HCA, 2008, p. 32).

The Netherlands is an interesting comparator because its recent house-building rates are much higher than those in the UK, and conform to higher environmental standards. But it has a national spatial plan, a much larger social housing sector, significantly different local municipality powers of land assembly and development, and a tradition of local energy generation, often with CHP (we examine the lessons for planning existing urban areas in the next chapter). A broad conclusion to be drawn from the lessons from Europe studies is that the conditions examined are closer to the growth area model under the Sustainable Communities Plan, with public sector resources allocated to planned provision and multi-agency coordination – similar to Northstowe in Cambridgeshire with its guided bus links to Cambridge. Falk and Hall (2009, p. 28) suggest that, in contrast, most of the eco-town proposals 'may easily degenerate into car-dependant commuter dormitories'.

8.8 Conclusions

If we are to meet the challenge of climate change, including reducing greenhouse gas emissions from new development, we need not just to focus on the energy-characteristics of the developments themselves (the building and urban form), but to evaluate systematically the implications of different locations – within cities, and medium and smaller urban areas, city and urban extensions, and new settlements. We need to consider the role of such new development in assisting existing urban areas to address energy use and climate change adaptation. We also need to be aware of the risks of 'lock-in' to unsustainable patterns of transport, and the possibilities for very different forms of food production and distribution if society moves towards reducing food miles and promoting local sourcing of materials. In this evaluation, we need to consider mitigation and adaptation in an integrated way, and to assess in sustainability terms the social implications of radical restructuring of settlement patterns in the UK.

The following chapter looks at the role of existing urban areas – new build and retrofit – in mitigating and adapting to climate change. Succeeding chapters look in more detail at the role of integrating natural systems for water and biodiversity/ecosystems, through terrestrial and marine spatial planning. We then bring together the issues in integrating climate change mitigation and adaptation in Chapter 14.

However, we also need to be aware of the wider context of central government policymaking and financing decisions. Chapter 5 has shown how central government in England (and to some extent in Scotland) has gained more decision-making powers on transport infrastructure and major generators of trips (such as through the NPSs on ports, airports, road and rail) and housing. At the same time, there are arguments for stronger city-regions to address transport demand management on the London model (Anable and Shaw, 2007). Moreover, the banking crisis and economic recession of 2008–09 have undermined significant parts of the construction industry, especially the volume house-builders, with serious consequences for the funding of new infrastructure via the Community Infrastructure Levy to support new development. The high level of public sector debt is also likely to reduce government funding for sustainable transport infrastructure. It remains to be seen whether recovery from the economic recession will lead to a pattern of development more consistent with an economy which is low carbon and resilient with respect to future climatic changes. We discuss this further in our concluding Chapter 14.

9   Climate change and the built environment

····································

9.1 Introduction

This chapter explores the role of the built environment in mitigating climate change and in adapting to climate change, and the scope of policy and practices to integrate these two goals. It focuses especially on issues of energy, infrastructure (especially local transport systems), heat and open space within existing urban areas. The need to plan at the wider water catchment and flood management scale, and to plan for ecosystems and biodiversity, are addressed in succeeding chapters. We look at the position for mitigation and adaptation across the EU, and focus on the UK and the Netherlands, as illustrations of different national issues and planning approaches.

9.2 The built environment and infrastructure: definitions

The built environment is hugely important in human society, culture and economic activity. Over 50 per cent of the world's population now lives in areas classed as urban, and in the industrialized European countries (the focus of this book) the proportion is 80 per cent (CEC, 2006b). Urban areas are generally the drivers of economic activity and innovation. It is also acknowledged that, from a socio-economic and cultural perspective, we live in an urbanized and networked society, less dependent on place (Graham and Marvin, 2001).

By built environment, we use a wide definition used by the Foresight Sustainable Energy Project:

> The built environment includes all buildings places and settlements that are created or modified by people. It includes, for example, homes, shops, schools, workplaces, hospitals, parks and recreational areas, green and blue spaces. The built environment is defined partly by its physical makeup

and partly by the ways in which people use it. Both aspects change over time.

(Foresight, 2008, p. 1)

We add to this definition the built infrastructure of energy services, water supplies, flood defences and waste infrastructure, which have both linear and point-based networks.

This broad definition brings advantages and disadvantages. The advantages lie in allowing the possibility of a holistic exploration of the buildings, spaces and use of land, in particular, urban, suburban and rural built forms. The disadvantages are that this scope may make for unmanageable analysis, with considerable differences between the elements – for instance, between the relatively standard uses of domestic dwellings (although their form, location and tenure vary) and the wider range of activities and types of use of non-domestic buildings sectors. Spatial planning powers to regulate this wide range of built environments vary across national, regional and local levels. There is also erratic provision of data or evidence base (for instance, less authoritative information is available on the use of energy in certain non-domestic buildings). However, we consider that our broad focus is justified in that spatial planning responses to climate change are leading to a recognition of the importance of linkages and networks – for instance, between built-up urban areas, their open spaces and upstream catchments, transport links and food, materials and utility supply networks.

9.3 Reducing emissions from the built environment

9.3.1 Introduction

Energy use in the built environment is a major contributor to greenhouse gas emissions and hence to climate change. There are many different – and not always consistent – ways of measuring this. But on some estimates, the use of energy in buildings in developed, industrialized economies constitutes a significant proportion – some 40–50 per cent – of carbon emissions (Foresight, 2008).

The early negotiations around the UNFCCC addressed the major energy-users and producers such as chemicals, steel and electricity supply industries. Chapter 1 has shown how policy, regulatory measures and market-based instruments focused on these as economic sectors. Chapter 5 showed how regional and local government has also taken action to promote alternative forms of energy generation, to reduce energy consumption and to improve energy-efficiency. The built environment is a significant part of their responsibilities, and hence particularly of spatial planning, but this needs to be understood in the context of supranational and national policies.

There is a complex set of interrelationships between energy demand and use in buildings and greenhouse gas emissions. It is nevertheless clear that, even for the limited part of the built environment comprising the household sector, there are significant opportunities for greater reductions in greenhouse gases, and this can be extended to the wider built environment. Although energy-efficiency of buildings is governed in most countries by building codes, spatial planning has a role in setting aspirations for future development through urban design, layout and building design, and through policies to promote energy-efficiency and low carbon development.

9.3.2 The EU context: energy use and emissions reduction

At EU level, there is no consistent measurement of greenhouse gas emissions from buildings: measurements tend to be by user and sector rather than more broadly defined by buildings or the built environment. Data is available for households as some sort of proxy for the built environment. The proportion of energy consumed by households (this includes heating, cooling and lighting) across the EU is estimated at almost 27 per cent (as shown in Figure 9.1). Between 1990 and 2005 energy use increased by 1 per cent per annum. The principal reasons for this are decreasing household size and increasing acquisition of household electrical appliances. Space heating accounts for some 67 per cent of energy use in households across all EU countries.

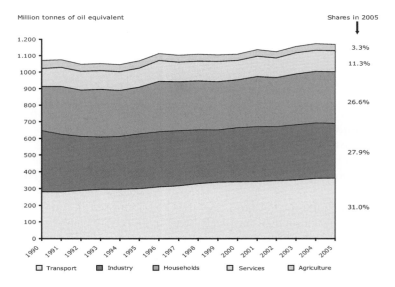

Figure 9.1

Final energy consumption by sector in 2005 (EU-27)
Source: EEA, 2008a, fig 2.6

Energy consumption and greenhouse gas emissions are not exact correlates. CO_2 emissions per dwelling have decreased by 17 per cent in the EU-15, and by 23 per cent in the EU-27 (EEA, 2008a), while total household emissions have remained fairly stable, despite a 19 per cent increase in the number of dwellings (EEA, 2008c). This decoupling is partly a result of policies – such as the Energy Performance of Buildings Directive – to improve the thermal efficiency of buildings and to increase the efficiency of appliances, and partly the result of a different fuel mix (with more use of natural gas and district heating) (Figure 9.2). The EEA warns that this apparent decoupling across the EU is principally a result of shifting from domestic fuel combustion to electricity production and combined heat and power and (since much of this still comes from coal-fired power generation) does not necessarily imply an overall reduction in total greenhouse gases (EEA, 2008a).

The EEA reports do not provide data on non-domestic buildings at EU level, but these come within the scope of the Energy Performance of Buildings Directive (CEC, 2002a) which sets minimum energy requirements for new construction and large refurbishments, and requires a mandatory energy certificate for new and existing buildings when they are constructed, sold or rented (Sunikka, 2005). For commercial office buildings, although electricity use for IT appliances has increased and thermal comfort standards are higher, there have been energy savings overall.

Estimates of future demand for and use of energy and/or electricity vary under different scenarios (see Chapters 6 and 8) of population growth, household size,

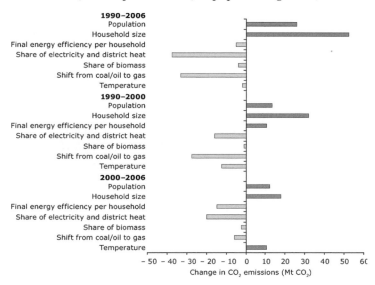

Figure 9.2

Factors affecting CO_2 emissions from households, 1990–2006 (EU-15)
Source: EEA, 2009c, fig. 4.9

economic activity, work patterns and sociocultural conditions. But climate change itself will have an impact on energy supply and demand. The changing water regime under conditions of climate change will impact on hydropower (a significant part of energy generation in Scandinavian countries) and on cooling water for conventional fossil-fuel generation. Sea-level rise might also affect coastal thermal power stations. Energy demand will also be affected: while there may be a decrease in demand for space heating in winter, there may be an increase in demand for space cooling in Mediterranean countries and in temperate climates (EEA, 2008a). This might alter the energy mix, as base-load and peak demand are met from different energy sources. Even with measures to reduce energy use and carbon sources, increases in energy demand are expected in many areas (Figure 9.3).

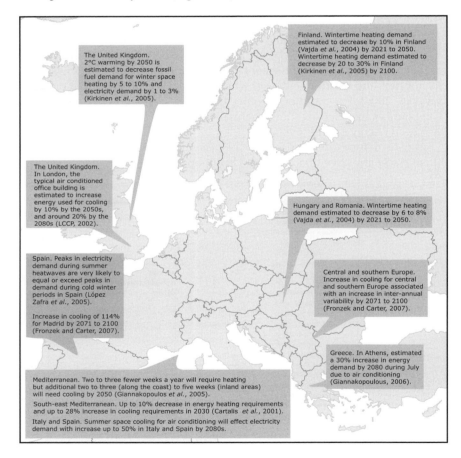

Figure 9.3

Projections of energy demand for several time horizons in Europe
Source: EEA, 2008a, fig 1.16

This reinforces the arguments for action for emissions reduction. In addition to the EU's adoption of the ETS as its principal mechanism for reducing carbon emissions, and targeted measures such as the Energy Performance of Buildings Directive, the EU has also adopted a 'softer' measure in the Thematic Strategy for the Urban Environment which promotes integrated environmental action at the local level, including efforts to achieve a low-carbon built environment (CEC, 2006b). The intention of this strategy is to support regional and local authorities through cross-national sharing and learning, and to reinforce awareness of the interconnectedness of challenges facing the urban environment. It affirms the role of urban areas in responding to climate change mitigation and adaptation, and promotes sustainable urban design and land use planning to reduce urban sprawl and to prevent loss of habitats and biodiversity and soil-sealing. It also recognizes the problem of retrofitting existing buildings (which we address in Section 9.4.2). Proposed under the Sixth Environmental Action Plan, the thematic strategy for the urban environment was adopted by the Council and Parliament in 2006. Although, as we have explained in Chapters 1 and 5, the EU does not have a remit in spatial planning, these policy initiatives are important in providing the context for spatial planning at national and subnational levels. We therefore examine some examples at these levels in the UK and the Netherlands.

9.4 Reducing emissions from the built environment: the UK

9.4.1 Introduction

It is estimated that 50 per cent of the UK's energy use can be attributed to space heating and cooling, water heating, lighting and appliances in buildings (Foresight, 2008), the larger part of which (some 53 per cent) is in domestic dwellings. Greenhouse gas emissions from buildings and industry in 2006 were around 380 $MtCO_2$, or 70 per cent of total UK emissions (Figure 9.4). Of these, residential buildings accounted for around 40 per cent and public and commercial buildings for 20 per cent.

The UK Low Carbon Transition Strategy (HMG, 2009a) draws on the conclusions of the Committee on Climate Change that, in order to meet the country's target of 80 per cent reduction in greenhouse gases by 2050, the UK needs to reduce emissions from households almost entirely by 2050. This is an immense challenge. The government proposes that first the carbon budget requires a 34 per cent reduction from1990 levels: to reach this target, emissions for heating in houses should fall by 29 per cent by 2020 compared with 2008 levels, which would constitute 13 per cent of the total savings needed. The measures to achieve this are shown in Figure 9.5.

What role should spatial planning therefore play in achieving these reductions?

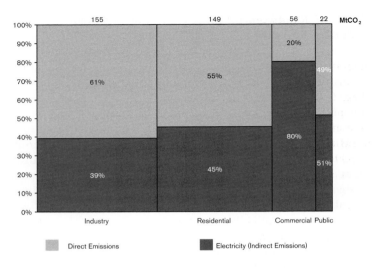

Figure 9.4

Direct and indirect emissions from energy use in buildings and industry in 2006
Source: CCC, 2008, p. 214, fig 6.1

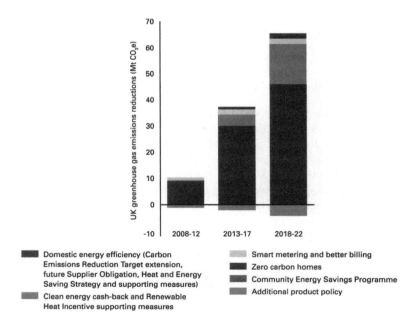

Figure 9.5

Domestic energy efficiency package
Source: HMG, 2009a, p. 81, chart 4

9.4.2 National spatial planning context: new and existing built environment

The urgency of climate change has already brought about a transformation in the way in which spatial planning addresses energy. As explained in Chapter 5, in the later twentieth century the only specific government planning policy for energy planning had merely enjoined the planning system to deliver more renewable energy, and was targeted principally at non-domestic generation. The ODPM advice on the planning response to climate change more radically advocated adopting an energy systems approach (including action on energy efficiency as well as decentralizing energy generation through microgeneration) (ODPM *et al.*, 2004). But the government at that time still took the view that planning should not overlap with the role of building control in thermal efficiency standards, and (as discussed in Chapter 4) that it should not impose undue burdens on the house-building sector. For instance, it took four years for the Code for Sustainable Homes to become adopted as a mandatory requirement (this requires new housing association and owner-occupied dwellings to be carbon neutral by 2016, and likewise all new buildings by 2019 (DCLG, 2008a) – see Section 9.4.8). It was left to organizations such as the TCPA in its energy advice of 2006 to promote more comprehensive planning approaches to energy (TCPA, 2006a). The influential TCPA guide suggested a number of planning approaches (Box 9.1).

Box 9.1 Actions for local energy planning

- Create a sustainable energy plan.
- Promote whole-life funding.
- Promote energy services such as through ESCos.
- Involve community.
- Reduce energy demand at neighbourhood, street and building scale.
- Promote energy-efficient supply at all scales.
- Promote renewable energy at all scales.

Source: adapted from TCPA, 2006a

The government guidance on planning for climate change (DCLG, 2007a: a draft revision was published in 2010 [DCLG, 2010a]) to some extent confirmed this approach of local energy planning. The Foresight project on sustainable energy management also considered that spatial planning should incorporate an energy-system perspective to achieve a low-carbon built environment (Rydin, 2009). This perspective requires that the scope of planning extend to encompass existing development as much as new development. We have in Chapter 5 looked at the role of regional planning for renewable energy generation, and in Chapter 8 at the role of regions in planning for low-carbon economic development and transport. Here we focus on the role of the city-regional, urban and local level in planning for a low-carbon built environment, looking at the relationship of new and existing development. The rate of turn-over in UK domestic property, even in the boom years of the early twenty-first century, was only 1 per cent. At past turnover rates, two thirds of the housing which will be in use in 2050 (the date by which the UK is to have reduced its carbon emissions by 80 per cent) already exists (Foresight, 2008). We there-fore consider that as, over time, new build becomes the future existing stock, both mitigation and adaptation measures need to be considered as applying to development through time (shown schematically in Figure 9.6).

A number of reports (such as Boardman *et al.*, 2005) controversially proposed that the very low levels of thermal efficiency of the existing housing stock in the UK meant that, to meet the target set for 2050 (at that time, a 60 per cent reduction target), a greatly increased demolition rate would be needed. Boardman *et al.* suggested some 14 per cent of existing stock be removed, a demolition rate four times the current rate, rising to 80,000 dwellings per annum by 2016. A total of 3.2 million houses (those with a SAP rating of below 33 points) would need to be demolished. The argument was that the extent and condition of older property, especially pre-WWII property, was such that it could never be upgraded to the necessary energy-efficiency standards (i.e. an average SAP [Standard Assessment Procedure] rating of 80) by 2050. Figure 9.7 shows the age and condition of the UK housing stock.

Such rates of demolition would have had immense social, economic and cul-tural impacts, which were only partly examined in the Boardman report (2005). The case for demolition provoked some opposition. Research for the Foresight

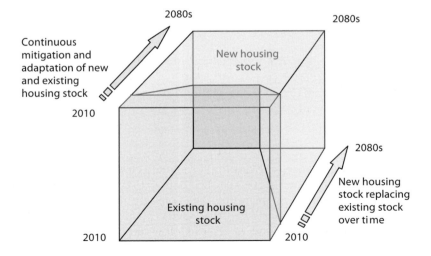

Figure 9.6

Relationship over time of existing and new housing stock: mitigation and adaptation

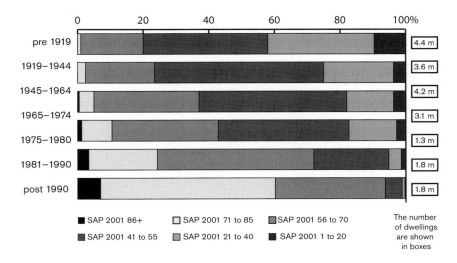

Figure 9.7

Energy performance of existing dwelling stock, 2004
Source: DCLG, 2006, p. 5

project on sustainable energy futures in the built environment argued that a more systematic review of the advantages and disadvantages of demolition is necessary (Power, 2008). Power reviewed evidence from a number of studies, including a major programme in Germany to retrofit all pre-1984 homes (some 30 million units) by 2020. A pilot exercise had already achieved significant cuts of 80 per cent in energy consumption. She concluded that, from a regeneration and renewal perspective, there are significant disadvantages to demolition (Box 9.2).

Other reports, such as the Sustainable Development Commission (2006), House of Commons Communities and Local Government Committee (2007), Three Regions Climate Change Partnership (2008) and the UK Green Building Council (2008), have all addressed issues of integrating planning for new development with regeneration of the existing stock. A revised report (Boardman, 2007), based on the 80 per cent carbon reduction target, amended the estimates of demolition required and instead recommended a major programme of retrofitting through a combination of measures: a legally binding target for housing, strict minimum legal standards for houses and products, concentrated new development meeting mandatory Code for Sustainable Homes and retrofitting through Low Carbon Zones. These zones would extend from an initial coverage of fuel-poor households to all areas. Other initiatives exist which vary from the small neighbourhood scale to very high-density, mixed use areas such as Soho in central London (see Max Lock Institute, 2008). The political and professional commitment to retrofitting and refurbishment is discussed further in 9.4.5.

Box 9.2 Impacts of demolition and retention of existing homes

Regeneration and renewal disadvantages:

- The actual loss of the home.
- The cumulative blight to neighbouring properties and investment.
- The tendency to scope out larger areas than necessary would take out some viable properties.
- The consequential impacts on local public services.
- The risk of post-demolition delay and blight.
- The loss of social capital.
- The pressure for further urban sprawl.

Environmental disadvantages:

- The implications for the embodied carbon in new and replacement build.
- The loss of or destruction of scarce building materials.

Social arguments for retention of existing stock:

- Benefits to poorer and older households.
- Shorter building process.
- Investment in local economy.
- Retention of social capital.
- Promotion of interest in previously marginal sites and consequent investment.

Source: adapted from Power, 2008

9.4.3 Existing urban areas: the historic environment

A particular category of spatial planning for existing development involves those assets deemed to be of historic and cultural value. It is suggested that a quarter of the homes existing in 2050 will have been built with traditional construction methods (that is, largely buildings built before 1919, with solid-wall construction, single-glazed bay or sash windows, and without a damp-proof course) (English Heritage, 2008a; 2008b). Questions arise as to the extent to which such homes can be modified to adopt mitigation measures, either directly (such as the installation of microturbines or solar panels on listed buildings or in conservation areas), or indirectly through the contribution of historic landscapes and gardens to larger-scale renewables such as biomass production, or through their role in urban cooling. (Similar issues arise over adaptation measures, such as to increased flood risk – see Chapter 11). The planning system in the UK has come under fire both from residents who wish to demonstrate their personal commitment to climate change action, and believe this has been prevented by insensitive and not fit-for-purpose conservation policies, and from those who object to such alterations to historic buildings. English Heritage in response has published studies showing that traditional buildings are often more energy-efficient (partly because of their high thermal mass) than buildings from the early twentieth century. They argue also that older buildings have value as exemplars: 'the past has witnessed significant climatic change and today's historic buildings, sites and landscapes provide an unparalleled source of information on these long-term fluctuations, on human responses to them, and on living in a low-carbon economy' (English Heritage, 2008a, p. 9). Partly in response to the suggestions indicated above that demolition rates should increase, English Heritage advise that any appraisal of existing stock should consider a number of aspects (shown in Box 9.3).

Box 9.3 The historic environment: aspects for the appraisal of existing buildings

- The cultural and social significance of the existing stock.
- The whole-life energy costs of new stock, its lifespan and durability.
- The residual life energy costs of the existing stock, allowing for strategies to increase its thermal efficiency.
- The sustainability of new stock in terms of both energy and materials.
- The effect of the generous green spaces associated with many historic buildings, in mitigating some climate change effects.

Source: English Heritage, 2008a, p. 8

Principally as a follow-up to proposed reforms to provide a unified approach to heritage protection policy, but partly in response to the perceived policy gap for climate change mitigation and adaptation in historic buildings and conservation areas, the government is revising the planning policy statements on the historic environment and archaeology. The consultation draft argues that keeping historic assets (such as buildings) in use reduces the consumption of building materials and hence energy: it acknowledges that there may be conflicts, but argues that 'there will normally be opportunities for enhanced energy efficiency, improved resilience to weather, greater use of renewable energy, or sustainable drainage and use of water' without such conflict arising (DCLG and DCMS, 2009, p. 16).

9.4.4 Local energy planning: reduction in energy demand, and renewables

Together, these debates have contributed to a more strategic approach to the scope for action in existing homes and buildings. The government's PPS1

Supplement acknowledged the importance of considering the relationship between existing and new developments (DCLG, 2007a), and requires LPAs to prepare local energy plans to identify potential for decentralized renewable or low-carbon energy generation. In Chapter 5, we described the genesis of the Merton Rule, which had eventually been adopted by central government in a revision to PPS22 (on renewable energy). The progenitors and supporters of the Merton Rule argue that it has a number of advantages:

- It promotes energy efficiency through providing an incentive to reduce energy consumption (the smaller the energy demand, the lower the proportion of energy demand under obligation to meet a percentage from renewables).
- It can apply to existing dwellings and non-residential buildings through application of smaller size thresholds (such as extensions).
- It will, through its visibility, persuade neighbours that this is a worthwhile exercise.
- It can generate a substantial market of small-scale renewables and hence jobs in manufacture, supply, fitting and maintenance.

Its detractors argue (Foresight, 2008) that it has enabled local authorities to ask for significant percentages of on-site renewables without fully appraising other off-site options. It is argued that the Rule illustrates the dangers of a target-driven rather than outcome-oriented process and is ill-conceived, and that it should be left to developers and the market to propose appropriate solutions (Brooke *et al.*, 2007). However, it is clear that developers can and should appraise different ways of achieving the goal. Moreover, a very localized, decentralized renewables system can meet the objectives of a climate-change-resilient distributed system less vulnerable to disruption from outages – an argument for integrating mitigation and adaptation considerations (see Chapter 14).

Local planning authorities with a range of urban characteristics and scales had by 2007 adopted policies for comprehensive energy planning (Box 9.4) which went beyond the Merton Rule.

Box 9.4 Examples of local authority planning for energy

Uttlesford, a District Council in Essex, with a population of some 70,000, has since 2005 had Supplementary Planning Guidance on house extensions that requires the remainder of the house to meet energy-saving measures as a condition of obtaining planning permission. The policy applies to extensions such as conversions of lofts or garages, and the addition of annexes. The approach has been unusual but successful, and has been accepted locally. It demonstrated close working between building control and planning functions, when proposals for a 'consequential improvements' category of the Building Regulations Part L were dropped (Clare, 2008). The District is a signatory to the Nottingham Declaration, and adopted its own Climate Change

---

Strategy in 2007 (Uttlesford DC, 2007). It also opposes the second runway at Stansted Airport and the proposed eco-town at Elsenham.

Milton Keynes, a new (post-1970) city with a population of 230,000, and part of the Milton Keynes-South Midlands growth areas under the government's Sustainable Communities Plan, has since 2005 had a planning policy amounting to a carbon tariff, under which developments of over five dwellings or 1000 m² floor space had to achieve carbon neutrality or contribute to a carbon-offset fund, via a tariff linked to agreements under S106 of the planning legislation. Contributions are put towards a fund managed by the MK Energy Agency towards schemes which include retrofitting some of the existing stock (much of which was built in the 1970s to low insulation standards), renewable energy or carbon-absorption planting. The Council considers it as an effective way of using the planning system to secure funds for CO_2 reduction (Clare, 2008). It is expected that it will generate about £800,000 per annum in carbon offset payments and save 4000 tonnes of CO_2 per annum. (Milton Keynes Council, 2007; Milton Keynes Partnership and English Partnerships, 2007)

Woking Borough Council has received much attention (e.g. TCPA, 2006a) for its innovative Energy Supply Company (ESCo) (a 'private wire' energy distribution network based on a town centre CHP system) set up in 1999 as a public/private venture by the local authority. But less attention has been paid to the consequences of this initiative for wider local authority functions, including its planning policies. In 2002, the borough, an early signatory to the Nottingham Declaration, adopted a Climate Change Strategy: through leadership by example, and work undertaken by the local authority on its own building stock (such as installation of fuel cells, solar panels, and retrofitting its own housing stock and promoting community retrofitting and microgeneration), it has been able to engage the community and raise expectations. A part of the strategy is a voluntary code for climate neutral developments which will become a mandatory requirement as part of the council's commitment to an 80 per cent CO_2 reduction by 2050 when the local plan is adopted. The Climate Neutral Development Good Practice Guide contains guides for five areas: location and transport, site layout and building design, energy, SuDS, and water conservation and recycling (Woking Borough Council, 2008).

9.4.5 Local energy planning: community energy

The tightly controlled planning system had therefore found a way to get beyond what might be seen as the strait-jacket of central government's narrow interpretation of local planning authority powers and arguments about *ultra vires*. National policy has confirmed the approach of working through spatial planning and building regulations to deliver low-carbon communities. The government's strategy for household energy management was published in 2010 (HMG, 2010b). Shortly after the draft strategy had been published (DECC, 2009f), the Energy Saving Trust and WWF, with Grand Designs, launched the 'Great British Refurb' campaign.

This focus on existing stock has clear implications for the urban regeneration agenda, especially for some of the peripheral housing estates which have lacked community-level investment. One of the sponsors of the campaign, for instance, is working with a community in Liverpool to refurbish an estate, achieving a reduction in carbon emissions of 74 per cent of the average household.

The draft strategy proposes the ambitious target that by 2050 emissions from all buildings should be as close to zero as possible. It suggests an indicative pathway with milestones to reach this 2050 target (Box 9.5), including proposing that all homes by 2030 should have undergone some form of 'whole house' package of measures. The strategy is supplemented by a £350m community energy saving programme, for energy companies to work with local authorities and community organizations across low-income areas. This calls for the wider conception of spatial planning.

Box 9.5 Indicative milestones to reach 2050 target

2015: all lofts and cavity walls insulated.

2020: up to 7 million houses to have chance to take up more substantial 'whole-house' packages (such as solid wall insulation or small-scale renewables); all houses to have smart meters.

2030: all homes to have received a package of the most cost-effective measures.

2050: emissions from buildings as close to zero as possible.

Source: DECC, 2009f, box 1.2

Besides the raft of financial support for individual homes and groups of homes, the strategy proposes significant further support for district heating (DH) and combined heat and power (CHP), beyond the encouragement given in PPS1 Supplement (DCLG, 2007a). According to the UK Low Carbon Transition Plan, at present community heating provides only 2 per cent of heating needs in the UK, but the government believes that it could contribute up to14 per cent (HMG, 2009a). The Transition Plan looks to the planning system to work in partnership with community groups or local suppliers through its knowledge of local conditions to identify opportunities for more DH and CHP. The Plan states that it will 'examine the case for local authorities to have greater ability to require existing developments to connect to heating schemes, to complement their ability to require new developments to connect' (p. 96). (The HESS consultation strategy had indicated that such further regulation might be an unwarranted burden on investment in energy [para. 7.24]). Nevertheless, the draft HESS recommends the stance of Uttlesford, and also proposes (para. 1.29) changes to energy services markets to encourage more local authorities to follow the Woking Borough Council route of setting up an ESCo or Municipal Supply Company. These measures comprise a significant part of the Low Carbon Transition Plan.

The Low Carbon Strategy provides further encouragement to refurbishment through budgetary support measures, and the use of tools of urban area heat mapping (an example is DECoRuM, a GIS-based method of estimating carbon reduction potential in urban dwellings [Gupta, 2008]). Such mapping can constitute an important part of the engagement with the public in community energy planning. However, the ability to evaluate developers' claims about the energy-performance of buildings, and to undertake and interpret heat mapping, will require a considerable extension of the skills of professional planners and elected councillors. These issues are discussed further in Chapter 13.

Community energy schemes are supported in the NESTA Big Green Challenge 2010: the winners of the competition include rural community schemes in the Three Valleys, Brecon in Wales (community-owned renewables and actions to reduce households' emissions using local expertise), the Isle of Eigg in Scotland (a scheme for local renewables, local food and low-carbon transport) and Ludlow in Shropshire (a community-based ESCo). Low Carbon West Oxford (see Chapter 13, Box 13.6) was a runner-up.

9.4.6 Local energy planning: new build

Sustainable construction and development has been a theme of spatial plans which predated the 2004 Planning Act, responding to the sustainability agenda with a range of policies, supplementary planning guidance and sustainability checklists governing topics such as energy- and water-efficiency, materials, waste and ecology. There is also a tradition of authorities of different characteristics adopting energy plans, such as Newcastle, Newark and Sherwood District, and Kirklees (ODPM *et al.*, 2004). The climate change issue has heightened the importance of these policies and plans, but has reinforced some of the tensions between local innovation and central government's wish for a consistent regime which was not unduly onerous on the development industry. Local planning authorities are required to have a firm evidence base for the policies they include in their local plans on energy and climate change. As the urgency of the shift to a low-carbon built environment has increased, LPAs have wished to go beyond the time scale envisaged in the government's Code for Sustainable Homes (CSH).

The CSH was intended to provide a single standard to benefit home-builders, consumers, social housing providers and the environment, to complement the Energy Performance Certificates required under the European Energy Performance of Buildings Directive. Originally conceived as a voluntary measure, under which builders were simply encouraged to follow the Code, the CSH became mandatory for all new homes from 2008 (DCLG, 2008a). It requires that all homes are assessed against a set of nine standards (covering energy and

CO_2 emissions, water, materials, surface water run-off, waste, pollution, health and well-being, management and ecology) on the basis of a 'whole home' approach, with a resultant rating against levels 1–6. Minimum standards are set at each level for energy and water use and CO_2 emissions. The government has as a target that all new homes will be zero carbon (Level 6) by 2016 through raising standards in the Building Regulations (Table 9.1). All new social housing from 2008 was to be at least Level 3.

The 2007 PPS1 Supplement made clear that LPAs should support innovative building designs, and that 'there may be situations where it could be appropriate to anticipate levels of building sustainability in advance of those set out nationally' (DCLG, 2007a, para. 31). However, LPAs have needed to provide a secure evidence base on which to argue that all new homes (or just those in growth areas, where substantial new-build is planned) should be Level 4 with immediate effect. Providing such an evidence base involves a considerable commitment of resources – one example is Bristol City Council, which commissioned a study of the opportunities and constraints for renewable, sustainable and low carbon energy in the city (CSE, 2009).

9.4.7 Local energy planning: eco-towns

Chapters 4 and 8 explained that part of the argument for new settlements such as eco-towns was to allow urban areas to be designed from the start with climate change in mind, and so to set high standards for energy within the development. It was also intended that experience of meeting the eco-town standards could help to raise standards within the development industry generally, although, as we have seen, some LPAs favour setting standards beyond CSH requirements for major developments (such as greater than 10 houses or over 1000 ha in area) and strategic urban extensions. All new homes in eco-towns are to meet CSH Level 4, and part of the requirement is that 'over a year, the net carbon dioxide emissions from all energy use within the buildings on the eco-town development are zero or below' (DCLG, 2009c). Concept schemes prepared for the four locations which have been selected by the government for inclusion in the eco-towns PPS have all included innovative energy plans. One of the sites, NW Bicester, in Oxfordshire, was promoted by the local

Table 9.1 CSH carbon improvement over time

Date	2010	2013	2016
Energy efficiency improvement of the dwelling compared to 2006 (Part L Building Regulations)	25%	44%	Zero carbon
Equivalent standard within the Code	Code level 3	Code level 4	Code level 6

Source: DCLG, 2008a

authority, Cherwell District Council, as offering more opportunities to benefit existing communities in the area than a larger, freestanding proposal at nearby Weston on the Green. The council commissioned a firm of consultants to establish the viability and practicability of the proposal, and their proposals are shown in Box 9.6. The effect of the strategy would be that the layout of the development is to some extent determined by the zero-carbon energy requirements, with certain functions concentrated in the core zone around the energy centre.

Box 9.6 NW Bicester eco-town: concept energy strategy

Supply side measures:
Use of local energy assets: biomass, solar, wind, ground-source and waste district heating system from central energy centre (biomass boilers and biogas CHP).

Demand side measures:
Core zone: district heating system.
Periphery zones: *PassivHaus* design to minimize heat demand.
Residential development: wood fuel; non-residential: ground source heat.

Source: adapted from Halcrow, 2009

9.4.8 Spatial planning and energy planning: future prospects

The Foresight report on the future of energy in the built environment makes the point strongly that we need to adopt a 'co-evolution' approach, that is, one that recognizes that buildings on their own do not consume energy – rather, energy generation, distribution and use need to be seen as the result of interactions between users, technologies and infrastructure systems, all of which operate within a framework of public policy interventions in energy markets, spatial planning and building codes (Foresight, 2008). It is therefore important to see the role of spatial planning as one of the drivers of urban development, but to recognize that other drivers may not always be consistent or synergistic. The focus of UK policy for the built environment in the past has been to reduce its energy demand by improving its thermal efficiency, to address issues of fuel poverty and energy insecurity, and more recently to assist recovery from the economic downturn by promoting low-carbon economic initiatives. Because of the very different powers at a municipal level in the UK compared with continental European cities, spatial planning in the UK has had to rely largely on enablement rather than prescriptive interventions such as requiring district heating (PRP *et al.*, 2008). However, the new Low Carbon Transition Plan and the debate generated by the eco-towns initiative suggest that spatial planning will see radical changes in its ambitions for new and existing development, beyond the innovative examples shown in Box 9.4.

Changes will also be required of the development industry. Local planning authorities need to work with private sector developers who have their own objectives, and, especially at times of economic downturn and uncertainty, a tension is generated between their investment strategies and their environmental commitments. A report by a partnership including WWF, Insight Investment, Bank of Scotland, the Housing Corporation and Jones Lang Lasalle found that eight of the ten largest home-builders have a climate change policy (compared with none in 2007); over half measure their energy use, and 45 per cent set targets to reduce it; and two-fifths have developed tools to help deliver the Code for Sustainable Homes (Next Generation, 2008). However, these represent a particularly active set within the industry, and the report therefore argues that all house-builders should align climate change mitigation and adaptation more closely to their core business risk analysis, and that more government analysis of the costs of meeting the CSH, fiscal incentives for home-buyers and support in innovation is needed. (The government is considering further revisions in 2010 to the CSH to make it both more effective and user-friendly). An interesting development is the AIMC4 consortium of house-builders, BRE, product manufacturers and Oxford Brookes University (funded by the Technology Support Board) to construct and monitor twelve zero-carbon, sustainable homes that use only energy-efficient materials, without relying on renewables.

The UK Green Building Council has also been instrumental in raising the aspirations of the construction industry, publishing a report that makes the case for a mandatory Code for Sustainable Buildings (i.e. not just houses) (UK-GBC, 2009). As with the CSH, it would be based on a regulatory escalator through the building regulations. The government is proposing, in line with possible changes to the Energy Performance of Buildings Directive, to clarify the definition of low or zero carbon, and to set further targets for low or zero carbon in new and refurbished dwellings, commercial buildings and public authorities' buildings (HMG, 2010a).

The government has included climate change in its set of indicators to measure local authority performance: by 2009, 130 out of 150 Local Area Agreements in England already included carbon reduction targets (HMG, 2009a). Spatial planning is therefore working within wider local authority networks, such as the Nottingham Declaration Partnership, and with Local Strategic Partnerships, to deliver these energy aspirations. At the regional level, as discussed in Chapters 5 and 8, energy plans will be prepared jointly by the Regional Development Agencies (RDAs) and local authorities in the new integrated Regional Strategies from 2010 (although this regional institutional framework may have an uncertain future as it is not supported by the Conservative Party. This is discussed further in Chapter 14). The Planning and Climate Change Coalition (TCPA and Friends of the Earth, 2009) stressed that, despite innovation and progress, 'a new (zero-carbon) energy planning paradigm is required' (p. 14). They argue that a comprehensive response is required, addressing the three areas of opportunity within the influence of spatial planning shown in Table 9.2.

Table 9.2 Energy opportunities and planning

Energy opportunity	Delivery mechanisms	Likely delivery partners
Stand-alone generation and other CO_2 reductions (e.g. wind farms)	Planning policy and targets Local Development Orders Public sector policy and targets Allowable solutions	Energy developers Community organizations
Community integrated generation and infrastructure (e.g. district heating networks)	Planning policy and targets CIL and S106 Local Development Orders Powers of well-being Conditions to LA land sales Allowable solutions	LAs LSPs Regional and national public bodies Energy developers House-builders/developers/RSLs Home/building owners Others (e.g. ESCos)
Building or development integrated CO_2 reductions and generation (e.g. building-mounted PV)	Building Regulations Interim planning targets Conditions to LA land sales Local Development Orders Allowable solutions	LAs LSPs House-builders/ developers/RSLs Home/building owners Others (e.g. ESCos)

Source: TCPA and FoE, 2009

Thus we can conclude that spatial planning at regional and local levels in the UK is undergoing a transformation in its approach to energy planning for both new and existing development. Despite the differences in municipal powers, this brings it rather closer to some aspects of energy planning elsewhere in Europe, such as in the Netherlands.

9.5 Reducing emissions from the built environment: the Netherlands

9.5.1 National spatial planning context

Compared with the UK, the Netherlands already has an energy-efficient housing stock. Although much of the housing built rapidly after WWII had high energy consumption, and suffered damp and heat-loss, a major insulation programme in the 1980s brought about a significant reduction in energy use. Household energy consumption per capita reduced 1990–2005, but household electricity consumption rose by over 25 per cent (EEA, 2008a Fig. 6.1), due primarily to greater consumption for appliances and lighting. Over the same period, there has been a high rate of residential construction – some 80,000 units per annum since 1990 (although this has declined since 1998) – as well as a decrease in household size. For the purposes of UNFCCC reporting, the Netherlands includes within the buildings sector households, trade and services. Relevant policies address the energy performance of new buildings, retrofitting existing buildings and energy-efficient appliances (VROM, 2008b), with the intention of reducing CO_2 emissions by 2015 (contributing 13 per cent of the national total reduction). Measures include regulations such as raising the Energy Performance Standard (part of the Building Code), fiscal measures and information campaigns. The Netherlands has a Climate Covenant with provinces and municipalities and, under the Sustainable Buildings Covenant, with housing developer trade associations (VROM, 2008b). The Climate Covenant, signed in 2002, is aimed at reducing emissions through municipalities' housing programmes and greater use of renewables, and is supported by a subsidy scheme. This programme is consistent with the Energy Transition Policy for the 4th NEPP (see Chapter 4). The Netherlands also has an Energy Performance of Location (EPL) classification system for new housing developments, part of the government's Optimum Energy Infrastructure programme. A voluntary process, EPL classification allows actors in the development process (local authorities, energy companies and developers) to assess the energy infrastructure appropriate for the development (such as cogeneration or other supplies), building orientation and design (Huibers *et al.*, 2002). The model has been extended from the original Vinex new development sites (see Chapter 8) to include redevelopment of existing areas.

For the near future, the Netherlands estimates that, under two different socio-economic scenarios (Strong Europe and Global Economy), developed in the Climate *changes* Spatial Planning project (see Chapter 4), greenhouse gas emissions will grow after 2010, although the rate of building will decline; however, with additional measures, it is expected that the Kyoto target for this sector will be met by 2012 (VROM, 2008b).

9.5.2 Municipal spatial planning responses

A significant element of the approach to spatial planning for urban areas in the Netherlands has been, at least until the 1990s, to design higher density developments in comparison with the UK, to a higher thermal efficiency standard, but also to incorporate cogeneration or Combined Heat and Power (CHP). This reflects the model of the economics and management of the development process, with a large social rented housing sector and different forms of involvement of the municipalities in land acquisition and property ownership (PRP *et al.*, 2008). This is a very different model from that in the UK, and partly explains why the introduction of CHP in the UK has been problematic. These differences mean that in the Netherlands decisions on new development can be better integrated with those for existing development. CHP was promoted during the period 1985–95, encouraged by exemption from energy taxes. Although, with liberalization of the energy markets, this growth has declined, it nevertheless still provides some 40–50 per cent of Dutch electricity, with thermal efficiencies of 85 per cent (VROM, 2008b). Much of the CHP is in industrial plants, but one quarter is in use for District Heating. There are therefore significant links to the local and municipal spatial planning scale. With many CHP plants being owned by municipal companies, it also has the consequence that the Netherlands has a well-distributed and decentralized energy supply system, in contrast to the centralized energy system of the UK.

Perhaps for these reasons, the Dutch national spatial strategy, *Nota Ruimte*, (VROM, 2006) did not address the role of spatial planning in moving towards a low-carbon economy in urban areas, although it did promote more renewable energy sources. It did not address the issue of new development or retrofitting, as the onus for these activities lies with provincial and municipal levels. Examples of municipal spatial and energy planning are given in Boxes 9.7 and 9.8.

Box 9.7 Spatial planning for energy in Rotterdam

Rotterdam, a city with a population of over 500,000, and 1.5 million in the wider city-region, has established the Rotterdam Climate Proof initiative for the city and the port. In addition to adaptation actions (see 9.8.3), it proposes that Rotterdam be the first CO_2 free city, with an ambitious target of 50% reduction of CO_2 by 2025 (Project Rotterdam, 2007). The programme includes an objective of 3% annual reduction in CO_2 in the residential sector. Part of the drive for this partnership initiative is in response to the likely negative impacts of changes in climate and power supplies to the industrial and port/trading functions of the city. While there is an element of place promotion in the initiative, it does reflect very real concerns abut the exposure of the city to future energy costs and to climate change impacts. Accordingly, the city council has established a Strategic Energy Policy portfolio. The Rotterdam City Development Corporation is responsible for economic and spatial development and land management in the city, and has an industrial heat company. As part of this strategy to promote innovation, the city and universities are also proposing a carbon-neutral campus. This is coordinated in the Rotterdam City Vision 2030 (City of Rotterdam, 2007), which proposes that the target will be delivered through:

- New renewable energy, energy savings and biomass.
- Efficient supply networks.
- Sustainable mobility through alternative fuels and behavioural change.
- Renewable electricity.
- An energy-neutral built environment.

The Climate Initiative is aimed at changing the scale of intervention from individual buildings to neighbourhoods and districts and, ultimately, the city. As part of the initiative, the REAP (Rotterdam Energy Approach and Planning) programme proposes a change in the approach to energy planning. It considers that the current approach of reducing consumption, using renewable energy, and then supplying the remaining

---

demand as cleanly and efficiently as possible has not delivered sufficient change. It proposes instead a stepped strategy:

- Reduce consumption.
- Reuse waste energy streams (waste heat, waste energy and waste water).
- Use renewable energy sources and ensure that waste is reused as feedstock.

This strategy can be extended to a cluster of buildings, or a neighbourhood, to determine whether energy can be exchanged, stored or cascaded. REAP shows how the principles could work in the Hart van Zuid area of the city (Tillie *et al.*, 2009)

Box 9.8 Spatial planning for energy in Almere

At a different scale, Almere is a planned new town on the Flevoland polder, 25 km east of Amsterdam. It is a partner with Milton Keynes in the CRRESCENDO consortium (Combined rational and renewable energy strategies in cities, for existing and new dwellings and optimal quality of life). It currently has a population of 185,000, with the intention of expansion to 350,000 by 2030. It has been built at a much lower density than major Dutch towns, at 1500 per km^2 compared with 4400 per km^2. Owner-occupation is also significantly higher (at 63%) than most Dutch towns. Under the Crrescendo project, the municipality aims to reduce its CO_2 emissions by 20% by 2010, focusing on two development areas for 2,000 eco-homes, 600 solar homes and 100 passive houses. It is currently constructing (with Nuon, the Dutch energy company) a solar energy collector on an artificial island which will serve 10% of the city's hot water needs. The city's structural vision for 2030 comprises four growth areas, of different characters and densities, but all intended to be carbon-neutral.

Source: adapted from Crrescendo, 2008

The principal lesson from the Netherlands is that the municipal energy and spatial planning systems operate in a way to support action beyond the level of the individual building, and therefore align more fully with concepts of planning at the neighbourhood or wider scale, and of integrating new with existing development.

9.6 Climate change adaptation in the built environment

9.6.1 Introduction

Chapter 2 has shown that we need to adapt to climate change (both to unavoidable and possible further changes) as well as acting to reduce its causes, in order not to experience dangerous increases in global temperatures. The impacts of this current and future unavoidable climate change on the built environment and infrastructure are particularly significant in urban areas, given the concentration of population and economic wealth-generation there. Adaptation needs to be considered alongside mitigation – climate change will impact on both the demand for and provision of energy.

Chapter 8 has already looked at the national and regional impacts and spatial planning policy. Here we focus on urban areas and infrastructure.

9.6.2 EU policy

Urban areas are already experiencing impacts similar to those which would be expected under climate change (EEA, 2008b). The EU White Paper on Adaptation (CEC, 2009a) argued that urban areas and densely populated flood plains would experience significant direct impacts of climate change, as well as indirect impacts on the essential infrastructure of buildings, transport, energy and water supply. Although it is notoriously difficult to put a cost on such impacts, the Stern report (2007) estimated that a 2–3°C rise would reduce global output by up to 3 per cent. In Europe, the EEA estimated that the principal vulnerabilities are to extreme floods and storm events, heat waves and drought. The costs of floods are partly the result of increases in population, wealth and urbanization. Storms are particularly costly: the costs of damage from a 100-year storm event could double by the 2080s (EEA, 2007a). It is estimated that the costs of the *canicule* in France in summer 2003 (impacts on power generation, the transport system, biodiversity and agriculture, as well as significant loss of life) was 0.1–0.2 per cent of GDP (EEA, 2007a). Second-order impacts include physical damage such as landslips and erosion, as well as social, health and unequally distributed impacts. The White Paper therefore argues for action across different sectors, including spatial planning.

As we have seen in Chapter 6, many reports estimate the impacts of future climate change under different scenarios: there will be negative impacts on society and health, which may impact most severely on vulnerable populations, and there will be some benefits, such as reduced need for space heating in winter in northern Europe, and possibly a reduction in fuel poverty in the UK. But it is expected that, overall, the costs hugely outweigh the benefits.

9.7 Climate change adaptation in the built environment: the UK

9.7.1 Impacts on infrastructure: a case for national planning?

The latest projections for climate change in the UK (Defra, 2009a) suggest that headline changes are of warmer, wetter winters, hotter and drier summers, sea-level rise and more extreme weather events. UKCIP suggest that it is helpful to distinguish between climate change events, impacts and consequences (Table 9.3).

It will be evident that, not only is it difficult systematically to estimate impacts and consequences, but it is difficult to distinguish between impacts and their consequences; moreover, impacts can interact with each other (for instance, heavy rain can cause erosion and landslips, erosion can lead to more downstream flooding, high temperatures or heat waves can cause fires which can lead to erosion).

The impacts of these changes on buildings and built form would be largely of overheating, thermal discomfort affecting users, flood damage, erosion and

Table 9.3 Climate change impacts and consequences for infrastructure

Climate change and related events	Example impacts on infrastructure	Consequences
• Hotter, drier summers —Heatwaves —Droughts	• Damage to physical assets from expansion of metals and contraction of clays outside previous range	• Disruption to services • Overheating • Thermal discomfort • Increase in demand for service (e.g. water or energy) • Inequity • Health and safety
• Milder, wetter winters • Storms and greater proportion of rain in heavy downpours —Heavy rain —Fewer cold snaps —High winds	• Erosion and landslip damaging property • Subsidence • Flooding of property • Damage to physical assets from storms • Overburdening of infrastructure (electrical, drainage) • Change in biological/chemical processes affecting structures	• Loss of access to services • Health and safety implications • Loss of property (temporary or permanent) • Loss of life • Costs • Inequity
• Sea-level rise —Inundation —Higher storm surge	• Erosion • Damage and loss of physical assets from storms and high water and debris • Salt water intrusion and damage	• Loss of access to services • Health and safety implications • Loss of property (temporary or permanent) • Loss of life • Costs • Inequity

Source: based on Johnstone *et al.*, 2009, Fig 1.3

subsidence. There has been a large number of studies on the impacts of climate change on the built environment in the UK: many of the early generation of UKCIP stakeholder-led regional studies identified the built environment as particularly at risk of flooding, water-stress and heat (West and Gawith, 2005). More detailed studies have been undertaken on the impacts on infrastructure (IME, 2009), on buildings and built form (such as Graves and Phillipson, 2000; Wilby, 2007; Roberts, 2008), as well as on particular urban areas (see LCCP, 2002; Walsh et al., 2007).

Chapters 3 and 8 have outlined some of the national adaptation response in the work of UKCIP. Here we focus particularly on interdependencies. The Pitt Review, conducted after the floods of 2007, suggested that the country's infrastructure is vulnerable through the interdependencies of its networks. The Review highlighted the exposure of the electricity supply, water treatment and sewage infrastructure and the failure of emergency planning (Pitt, 2008). For example, flooding can lead to loss of water and waste-water treatment and pumping plants; simultaneous loss of electricity can expose serious loss of function. Loss of a bridge may also disrupt telecommunications links or even water/drainage pipes. In England, following the UKCIP 2009 projections, the Environment Agency estimated that, without more funding for flood defences to protect communities from fluvial or coastal flooding, economic damage of £4bn per year could be experienced. One in six homes – 5.2 million properties – are at risk of flooding. Of these, 2.4 million homes are at risk from fluvial and coastal flooding, 1 millioon of which are vulnerable to surface water flooding; a further 2.8 million properties are susceptible to surface water flooding. Essential infrastructure is at risk, especially water-related services (as shown in Chapter 11): over 55 per cent of water and sewage pumping or treatment works are identified as being in flood-risk areas, and 34 per cent are at significant risk. One sixth of the country's electricity infrastructure (generating plants, pylons, sub-stations) is situated in flood plains (EA, 2009c). Community infrastructure, such as schools, hospitals, care homes and community centres, is also at risk, as shown in the Local Climate Impact Profiles (see Box 9.10).

The age profile of the housing stock in the UK, as we saw in 9.4.2, suggests that by 2050 the larger part (80 per cent) will need to have adapted to a changing climate. While there has been considerable focus on the longevity of buildings, and in particular on residential properties, less attention had perhaps been paid to infrastructure until the serious floods of summer 2007. However, the UK (characterized by Wright [1985] as an 'old country') has an aged stock of civil infrastructure: 70 per cent of assets are over 100 years old, 13 per cent 50–100, 10 per cent 20–50 and 7 per cent less than 20 years old (CIRIA [Construction Industry Research and Information Association], 2009). CIRIA argues that assets such as tunnels, embankments and bridges were over-engineered at the time of construction, which has given them endurance and resilience over the last century (it also suggests that in many cases they are more robust than structures built in the 1970s). But many of them (such as the rail network) are experiencing stresses from increased demand and use, and from more extreme climatic conditions. The engineering profession itself has issued major warnings about the lack of resilience: the IME suggests that, even with vigorous action to limit carbon emissions, there will be serious impacts in the short, medium and long term (beyond 100 years) on energy, water, transport and buildings infrastructure. They propose a fundamental move towards a greater decentralization of energy production and more international connectivity: more resilient sources of water (such as underground capture and storage and desalination) and distribution systems, increased water recycling, master planning for new transport routes, and master planning for urban areas, including addressing issues of the long-term viability of some settlements (IME, 2009).

Table 9.3 shows the possible consequences of climate change for the services supplied by that infrastructure: there will also be consequences for demand such as increased demand for energy for cooling, or for water for irrigation and cooling (Walsh *et al.*, 2007). Given that most of the utilities in the UK are privatized, the need to adapt to climate change presents a challenge for government in its long-term and contingency planning. As explained in Chapter 5, there is no national spatial plan for England (in this, England differs from the Netherlands and Scotland). However, under the Climate Change Act 2008, the government has to report to parliament every five years on the risks to the UK from climate change, and to draw up plans to address them. Public bodies and statutory undertakers such as utilities can also be required to undertake such risk assessments. Such an assessment will need to be consistent with the Low Carbon Transition Plan (HMG, 2009a), and the new system under the Planning Act 2008 of NPSs (National Policy Statements) and the decisions of the Infrastructure Planning Commission (discussed in Chapter 5). It will be interesting to see how this complex institutional framework for decision-making will take climate change into account, and how far it will approximate to a national spatial plan. In Scotland, the list of nationally significant projects in the National Planning Framework (discussed in Chapter 5) includes two where climate change adaptation is part of the justification (Green Infrastructure and the Metropolitan Glasgow Strategic Drainage Scheme).

9.7.2 Regional and local spatial planning policies and practice for adaptation

Given this lack of a national policy for adaptation, central government planning policy has responded to the need for adaptation in an incremental way. The advisory guidance (ODPM *et al.*, 2004) made explicit the need to consider adaptation but, as explained in Chapter 4, this did not constitute authoritative policy. Nevertheless, the guidance set out five principles that should be followed: act now, make the links with other objectives, spread the word, make the best use of existing tools (such as SEA) and instruments (such as conditions and agreements). Under 'making the links', it argued for taking a holistic view in assessing uncertainty: no-regrets actions, which are worthwhile now in meeting other non-climate objectives, and low-regrets actions, where the costs are low and the benefits are large, even if uncertain. It gave examples where regional planning bodies and LPAs were already adopting policies to respond to climate change, such as for water resources and biodiversity. The new form of regional and local plan-making under the Planning and Compulsory Purchase Act 2004 provided the opportunity to pay more attention to the issue. But a review of local planning policy responses up to 2006 (Wilson, 2006b) showed that, while most authorities had changed their policies for flood risk, there was much less attention paid to other impacts of climate change, such as biodiversity, water supplies, historic assets (both built and natural), subsidence, erosion, open space, air quality and overheating. Partly to provide more local support, the regional climate change partnerships under the auspices of UKCIP (see Box 4.3) and the TCPA (Shaw *et al.*, 2007) published more detailed guidance to encourage a proactive stance from LPAs.

The government's PPS1 Supplement on climate change (DCLG, 2007a) set out a range of principles and expectations for regional and local levels, but (as explained in Chapter 5) these were expressed in terms of enablement and encouragement rather than obligation, avoiding duplication with other regimes such as building control, and asking developers only for 'proportionate' information. Nevertheless, in recent years spatial planning has made significant shifts in policies for adaptation at regional and local level, with policies for all the issues mentioned above – including surface water management, water supplies and urban heating – now being framed. The regional climate change partnerships and networks such as the Nottingham Declaration Partnership have been instrumental in bringing about this change. Chapter 8 has explored regional planning policies to guide new development for both climate change mitigation and adaptation. The following sections review some of this progress at three scales for new and existing development within urban areas: at regional to local level, climate-resilient transport infrastructure; at metropolitan scale (London), climate-resilient spaces; and at local scale, climate-resilient building (Bilston Urban Village, West Midlands). We look particularly at the issues of transport, urban heating, open space and green infrastructure, as the adaptation issues of water resources, flood risk and biodiversity are addressed in detail in Chapters 10, 11 and 12.

9.7.3 Regional to local scale: implementing climate-resilience in South East England

The South East region of England is likely to experience some of the largest changes in climate and some of the most significant impacts (Wade *et al.*, 1999; SEECCP, 2004; SEEPB, 2009). The UKCP09 projections show that, under a medium emissions scenario (see Chapter 2 for explanations of the climate models) summer mean temperatures in the region by 2080s may change by up to 4.2°C (the central probability estimates) (Defra, 2009a). In parts of the

South East, mean daily maximum temperature increases in the summer might be 5.4°C. Changes in summer precipitation by 2080s might be a reduction of 40 per cent. UKCP09 projections for relative sea-level rise (that is, taking account of isostatic adjustment) are given for four locations; for London, under the medium emissions scenario, the estimate is 41.6 cm over 1990 levels by the 2090s.

The South East is also a region seeking to accommodate new development and its supporting infrastructure, and LPAs' local plans are drawn up within the framework of the regional plan. The South East Plan (GOSE, 2009) proposes to deliver 654,000 additional houses over the plan period to 2026. The Plan has a cross-cutting policy for climate change (see Chapter 11), and proposes a series of measures to reduce the vulnerability of infrastructure. As regional plans do not have direct powers of development control, the South East regional planning body has needed to consider how the plan will be implemented. The South East England Regional Assembly (SEERA) was a partner in the EU-funded ESPACE (European Spatial Panning: Adapting to Climate Events) project. Drawing on the experience of partners in the project from Belgium, the Netherlands and Germany, the ESPACE project and SEERA published an Implementation Plan for the draft South East Plan (SEERA and ESPACE, 2007). The report recognized that the Assembly needed support from other stakeholders in delivering the plan, and proposed a number of priority actions. For infrastructure, it argued that transport, energy, utilities and telecommunications need to be designed to minimize impacts and consequential disruption from storm events, landslides, subsidence, changes in mean and extreme temperatures and flood events, and hence responsibility lay with a wide set of public and private stakeholders.

Once the regional plan was formally adopted in 2009 (although the process has been subject to legal challenge), the SEEPB (the successor to the regional assembly) published advice to LPAs on integrating climate change considerations into LDFs (SEEPB, 2009). The advice adapted the UKCIP Adaptation Wizard (UKCIP, 2008a; see Chapter 2) to propose a sequence of tasks at each stage; this is illustrated in Box 9.9.

Publication of these supporting documents at regional level illustrates the role of regional planning in providing a framework for other tiers of planning to implement; it also reflects the strength of the regional networks and partnerships, with participation in cross-tier and cross-national research, cooperation in overcoming barriers, and recognition of the value to be gained in maintaining links under the new regional planning arrangements from 2010. What the advice also shows is the need for planning to be well-integrated with other local authority functions and commitments. For instance, a number of local authorities have undertaken Local Climate Impacts Profiles to help authorities better understand their vulnerability to past weather and hence their vulnerability to future climate change (Box 9.10).

Local and subregional transport provision is therefore important, and adaptation needs to be considered alongside mitigation. Chapter 8 has shown the many efforts now underway to move to low carbon modes of transport,

Box 9.9 Tasks in implementing adaptation policies in LDFs

Task 1: Evidence base: characteristics of the area
Such an assessment will meet the requirements of the PPS1 Supplement, the reporting obligations under the Climate Change Act 2008, and the National Indicators 188 and 189 under the Comprehensive Area Assessment. It suggests that a LCLIP, although not planning-based, might be useful in showing vulnerability and preparedness.

Task 2: Issues, problems and challenges
This will address level 2 of NI 188, which requires a risk-based assessment of future vulnerabilities.

Task 3: Vision and objectives
Alignment with Sustainable Community Strategy and Local Strategic Partnership.

Task 4: Spatial Strategy
Use ESPACE Decision Support Guidance Screening tool.

Task 5: Delivery

Task 6: Monitoring

Source: adapted from SEEPB, 2009

particularly within urban areas. Much of this action continues recent work to promote more sustainable travel, with significant changes in highway engineering and street design in line with the publication of a revised *Manual for Streets* (DfT, 2007b). This promoted concepts of home-zones and shared space, to restrain the interests of traffic movement in favour of those of a wider set of street users and quality of life objectives. Further encouragement for such use of space is given in CABE's sustainable cities initiative (CABE, 2009a). Sustainable transport needs not just to meet carbon targets but also to be resilient to future climate change. The Transport Planning Society, UKCIP and the Nottingham Declaration Partnership have published guidance on adaptation for those preparing Local Transport Plans (Transport Planning Society *et al.*, 2009). The guidance includes a checklist of issues to consider for network vulnerability to climate change (Table 9.4), and recommends measures to strengthen resilience, especially at scheme and option appraisal and design. LTPs should be more closely aligned with spatial plan-making at local and regional levels. The guidance makes clear that adaptation must be considered alongside carbon reduction measures (such as schemes to promote walking and cycling), as there is a risk that, with more intense weather events, there will be a modal shift away from sustainable modes. We return to this issue in the conclusions to this chapter.

Box 9.10 Local Climate Impact Profiles (LCLIPs)

LCLIPs are an initiative of UKCIP to help local authorities better understand their vulnerability to weather and hence their vulnerability to future climate change. Through focusing on how past events have affected both local communities and the authority's assets and capacity to deliver services, a LCLIP can be a useful tool in raising awareness of the need to adapt among members and officers. The technique involves a scan of media and council reports on events and their consequences including costs. Such profiles can be of direct relevance to spatial planning through showing the vulnerability of transport infrastructure such as roads, cycle paths, pavements and rail (to buckling or surface melting under heat, subsidence, tree falls, erosion and floods) and the vulnerability of community infrastructure such as schools, care homes and health centres. Consequently, important messages for the spatial planning of accessibility and critical thresholds for service functions can be incorporated in vulnerability assessments for LDFs.

An early LCLIP for Oxfordshire found that key issues were flooding, heat waves, subsidence and consequent costs to the LA, including rising insurance costs.

A more recent LCLIP for London (Standley et al., 2009, for the LCCP) has identified that more than half the weather impacts reported in the media and by interviewees related to transport.

Source: UKCIP, 2008b

9.7.4 Metropolitan scale: implementing climate change adaptation in London

London is a good example of a city with a high proportion of travel by sustainable and lower-carbon modes, but which is taking very seriously the issue of the impacts of climate change on its transport systems. Since the publication of *London's Warming* (LCCP, 2002), an assessment of climate change impacts on London, the city has recognized the possible implications of this for its role as a leading world-city financially and culturally, and the largely negative impacts this will have on the health and welfare of its citizens.

A study of the potential impacts of climate change on its transport network (Mayor of London and LCCP, 2005) had identified significant concerns about aspects of flooding, heat stress and infrastructure. The research took a case-study approach in examining tidal and flood risk in the London Thames Gateway, infrastructure damage and station closure caused by local flooding, infrastructure damage in hot weather and passenger comfort on the London Underground. The study recommended adopting the UKCIP principles of:

- Incorporating climate risks into routine risk management.
- Building in adaptation at planning, upgrading and reviewing stages to avoid impacts of sudden events or costs.

Table 9.4 Checklist of issues to consider for transport network vulnerability to climate change

Weather/climate and its impacts	Roads/pavements	Cycling/walking	Buses/trains/trams	Structures
Coastal erosion and storm surges	• Realignment of routes • Collapse of cliffs taking down infrastructure • Temporary or permanent inundation of infrastructure • Communities and/or services cut off (e.g. homes, hotels, roads, beach access routes, ports and harbours)			• Surface and structural damage
Heatwaves – increase in extreme temperatures	• Surface damage such as melting tarmac • Subsidence and heave	• Surface damage such as melting tarmac • Overheating of paths and discomfort • Modal shift away from walking and cycling due to discomfort	• Buckling rails, speed restrictions & emergency timetables • Overheating and discomfort/health risks for passengers (especially underground) • Modal shift to cars due to discomfort	
Increases in average daily temperatures	• Longer growing seasons and increased verge/embankment maintenance • Drought and lower water tables causing ground shrinkage, unstable ground, subsidence, landslides, etc.			
Heavy rainfall and flooding	• Network failures due to flooding/flash flooding • Landslips • Damage to pavements	• Pedestrian subways more likely to flood and take longer to clear	• Higher risk for underground networks • Flooding of train/tram power sources	• Embankment unsafe or collapse • Landslides bringing down structures • Bridges damaged or washed away

(continued)

Table 9.4 (cont.)

Weather/climate and its impacts	Roads/pavements	Cycling/walking	Buses/trains/trams	Structures
High winds and storms	• Unsafe buildings and consequent transport diversions • Fallen trees and associated debris – blocking routes/safety risk	• Modal shift to cars and public transport	• Damage to overhead power lines	• Vulnerability of/danger from movement of lightweight structures (traffic signs, lighting, street furniture)
Severe weather generally	• Disruption to normal traffic flows • Risks to passenger safety • Impact on outdoor workforce and public transport staff • Failures of 'just-in-time' supply chains, mostly food supplies			
Indirect impacts	• Increase in tourist visitors from overseas and UK visitors staying in UK • Changes in visitor travel patterns – especially to coastal locations • Population movements away from urban heat islands and locations that suffer frequent floods • Changes in economic sectors/employment patterns • Inward migration from other countries that are suffering more severe climate change			

Source: Transport Planning Society et al., 2009

- Ensuring risk management measures are flexible.
- Avoiding actions which will make it more difficult or expensive to cope with future changes.

(Mayor of London and LCCP, 2005)

Current actions to implement these principles include mapping drainage infrastructure, testing surface water management plans, preparing an inventory of vulnerable assets (such as the electrical bulk supply points to the Underground, essential for any safe evacuation), designs for larger carriages to improve air circulation and making better use of natural assets (such as, at Victoria Station, the use of ground-water for system cooling through heat exchange) (Transport Planning Society *et al.*, 2009).

As an extensive built-up area, London already experiences a significant urban heat island effect which, during the August 2003 heatwave, reached 8–9°C above surrounding rural areas (Mayor of London, 2006). Under conditions of climate change, with warmer average summer temperatures and more frequent heat waves, there may be both an increase in heat from air-conditioning units and reduced opportunities for evaporative cooling. Air quality is a significant issue: episodes of air pollution are associated with low wind and low temperatures in winters and hot summers. With climate change, winters might be wetter, which might reduce air pollution episodes, but hotter summers are likely to exacerbate the severity and frequency of pollution. In the heat wave of 2003, there were an estimated 700 additional deaths because of the ozone and particulate pollution (Mayor of London, 2009a).

Possible ways of addressing the urban heat island issue at different scales are shown in Table 9.5, and are being implemented through the London Plan (the spatial strategy for London).

Table 9.5 Adaptation actions for urban heat islands

Physical scale	Policy scale	Urban climate scale
City plan (arrangement of commercial, industrial, residential, recreational and greenspace)	Subregional spatial strategy	1–50 km City/metropolitan scale, UHI form and intensity
Urban design (arrangement of buildings, roads, green space)	Urban design strategy Area Action Plan Local Development Framework	10–1000 m Neighbourhood scale, suburban variations of climate
Individual building/street (façade and roof construction materials, design and orientation)	Building regulations and building control Urban design strategy Local Development Framework	1–10 m Indoor climate and street canyon

Source: Mayor of London, 2006

Measures in central London include preserving greenspace and planning for new greenspace: at street and building scale promoting green roofs, green walls, cool roofs, seasonal shading, cool materials and thermal mass; and at regional scale promoting green infrastructure (see Section 9.7). The London Plan Review of 2009 Adaptation to Climate Change theme proposes to maintain some of these approaches by following the principles shown in Box 9.11.

Box 9.11 Principles for adaptation in London Plan Review

- Minimize overheating in buildings and excessive heat generation, and offset the contribution of development to the urban heat island.
- Encourage and support the promotion of urban greening through the development and the enhancement of open space, green infrastructure and green (living) roofs and walls.
- Strengthen the policy approach to adaptation and resource efficiency in the design of new buildings.
- Strengthen policies to minimize and manage flood risk in London and its risk to development and infrastructure and provide the basis for a coordinated approach by the mayor, boroughs and other organizations to manage strategic flood risk.
- Continue to promote sustainable drainage across London through the use of the established drainage hierarchy and investigate solutions to address existing areas through the Drain London project.
- Protect and conserve water supplies and water resources through improved infrastructure and maximum water use targets for new development. The mayor will also explore the concept of water neutrality.
- Support improved sewerage infrastructure, in particular the principle of the Thames Tideway Sewer, and ensure that the water quality of London's water bodies and rivers is protected and improved.

Source: Mayor of London, 2009b, p. 57

The consolidated London Plan of 2008 (Mayor of London, 2008a) includes a policy that expects developments to incorporate living roofs and walls (Box 9.12).

Box 9.12 London Plan policy on living roofs and walls

The mayor will and boroughs should expect major developments to incorporate living roofs and walls where feasible and reflect this principle in LDF policies. It is expected that this will include roof and wall planting that deliver as many of these objectives as possible:

- accessible roof space
- adapting to and mitigating climate change

The definition in London of living roofs and walls includes green roofs and walls, roof terraces and roof gardens, and the Assembly has provided technical guidance to support its policy (Mayor of London, 2008b). The report reiterates the benefits of living roofs (Box 9.13). It also argues that the perceived barriers – lack of a national and local policy framework, lack of a common technical standard, maintenance, cost, structural issues, leakage and damage to water-proofing and lack of expertise and skills – can all be overcome. An additional benefit is improved air quality, for which the GLA has strategic responsibility.

Box 9.13 Benefits of living roofs and walls

- Helping London adapt to climate change.
- Improving energy balance and reducing CO_2 emissions.
- Reducing urban heat island effect.
- Enhancing amenity value.
- Conserving and improving biodiversity.
- Improving storm water attenuation.

Source: adapted from Mayor of London, 2008b

9.7.5 Urban neighbourhood scale: Bilston Urban Village, West Midlands

UKCIP has worked with Advantage West Midlands (the RDA for the West Midlands) and Wolverhampton City Council to promote climate change adaptation in the development of proposals for Bilston Urban Village. The 43 ha site lies close to Bilston town centre, but is separated from it by a major urban road; it comprises former industrial and derelict land, crossed by the Bilston Brook and has frontage to the Bradley Arm of the Birmingham Mainline Canal. The site's topography and network of watercourses makes it vulnerable to flood-ing, but the Development Brief incorporated wider aspects of climate change adaptation. Advantage West Midlands and the City Council have invested £20 m in preparing the site, and drawing up the Development Brief; in 2009 a development partner was appointed. The master plan proposes some 500 dwellings, employment uses, public open space, sports facilities and sustainable transport networks. In addition, the public authorities are providing a pedestrian link to Bilston town centre, a new school, community centre and leisure centre. The Design Brief for the leisure centre requires an Adaptation Strategy to identify any vulnerabilities over the lifetime of the scheme up to 2070, and to meet BREEAM 'very good' standards. The issues addressed in the adaptation strategy are shown in Table 9.6.

The examples above show what significant changes have come about in spatial planning policies at different scales of planning in response to the need to adapt to climate change. Just as in strategic mitigation, one of the themes in many reports and studies on adaptation is the benefit of cross-national learning. An example often cited is the longstanding policy of planning based on climatic factors in Stuttgart in Germany. Areas are protected for unimpeded air flow, in order to improve air quality and reduce the UHI, with building and urban greenspace managed proactively to this end (CABE, 2009a). Here we explore some of the Dutch approaches to national and municipal level adaptation planning for the built environment.

Table 9.6 Bilston Urban Village Leisure Centre impact assessment and options appraisal

Theme	Recommendation
Site layout, materials, structure	Clarify extent of Flood Risk Assessment incorporation of climate change
	Take account of PPS25 allowance for 30% increase in flow
	Assess cost of increase in gutter capacity
	Ensure design of building fabric prevents ingress of driving rain
	Take account of possible decrease in soil moisture (up to 35% by 2080)
Ventilation and cooling	Use UKCP09 scenarios for Design Summer Years and Test Reference Years
SuDS	Incorporate additional water handling storage capacity to accommodate drier summers and more intense events
	Install maximum green roof areas
Water use on site	Water efficient fittings, rainwater harvesting and grey-water recycling
Outdoor space and shading	Provision of green space and tree cover to ameliorate future conditions
Landscaping and ecology	Select appropriate tree and longer-life shrub species to be drought tolerant and deciduous

Source: Jacobs Engineering, 2008

9.8 Climate change adaptation in the built environment: The Netherlands

9.8.1 National adaptation planning: the Delta Plan

The Netherlands is likely to experience significant changes in the future, with the impacts of climate change adding to existing subsidence from isostatic adjustment and soil compaction in a densely populated country dominated by rivers and the sea. Because of serious concerns about recent flooding and the impacts of future climate change, the government commissioned the Delta Commission (previously convened after the floods of 1953 – see also Section 11.3.3) to advise government on the planning and development of the Netherlands to protect against climate change in the long term, addressing both safety and environmental (spatial) quality. The Commission estimated that 9 million people (over half of a total population of 16.5 million) live in the Delta area, which generates 65 per cent of the GNP of the Netherlands (Deltacommissie, 2008). The coastal conurbations of the Randstad are the heart of the country and of great significance in the national culture. Expected impacts from climate change in this region include rising sea levels (an earlier estimate of 0.2–0.6 million by 2100 has been revised by the Commission to 0.65–1.13 million; the Commission also expects a rise of 2–4 million by 2200). Other changes are forecast in river discharges (perhaps 40 per cent higher in winter, and 30 per cent lower in summer), increases in winter precipitation and heat waves. Second-order impacts on the built environment, water resources and water quality, transport, electricity production, agriculture, recreation and biodiversity are significant (VROM, 2008b).

The Delta Commission suggests that in the short-term socio-economic changes will exacerbate the possible economic costs from climate change, as investment in housing, industrial areas and infrastructure are already planned for the region, with an estimated 400,000 more dwellings in the coastal conurbations up to 2030. Due to the complexity of the interaction of river discharges and coastal sea-level rise, there are major implications for spatial planning of all land uses, and for fresh water and agriculture. Additional pumping – for instance, from the Ijsselmeer into the Wadden Sea – might be needed. The Commission concluded that, despite the high levels of historic flood-defence standards, and the shift in the twenty-first century to accommodating water, there are weak links along the coastal zone, and not all diked areas comply with the standards. Accordingly, the Commission concluded that '[t]he Netherlands is unprepared for climate change' (Deltacommissie 2008, p. 29).

9.8.2 National spatial planning response

At a national level, *Nota Ruimte*, the national spatial strategy (VROM *et al.*, 2006), recognizes the need for adaptation, and makes explicit provision that water and soil should be the 'structuring principles' of all planning. Although detailed planning is the responsibility of provincial and municipal tiers, national government has responsibility for major rivers, the coast and the Ijsselmeer; the national spatial strategy therefore sets out spatial plans for the main rivers, the coastal zone, the Ijsselmeer and the National Ecological Network (see Chapter 12.6.2). The paradigm shift in approaches to planning with water is described in more detail in Chapters 4, 10 and 11, including the mandatory water test (or water assessment), introduced in 2000. Because of the historic importance of water in the Netherlands, a system of regional water boards has primary responsibility for regional water management. The provinces have to incorporate these management measures in spatial plans and supervise municipalities' zoning plans. All municipalities are required to prepare a water plan: some 25 per cent had done so by 2008, and many of these specifically incorporated adaptation to climate change (VROM, 2008b). However, some have challenged the extent to which municipalities actually implement all the provisions of the regime (such as de Vries and Wolsink, 2009).

The Netherlands already has a programme entitled ARK (National space and climate adaptation programme) (see Chapter 4). A cross-departmental programme approved in 2006, it aims to climate-proof spatial planning through researching both the ways in which planning can respond to the consequences of climate change, and any barriers to this response, then exploring ways to overcome them. The Delta Commission has been able to take the issues further in making recommendations for the whole country. It proposes that two guiding principles be observed: water safety (both flood protection and water supplies) and sustainability. On the basis of its analysis of current and future risks to human life and economic activity under a number of scenarios, the Commission proposes 'an integral vision of the long-term protection of the delta and the spatial planning of the coast and the hinterland. Regional considerations related to specific issues must always be weighed against an integral, national view' (Deltacommissie 2008, p. 38).

The national-scale vision for a climate-proof Netherlands is moderated by sustainability considerations: the Commission concludes that it is unnecessary to relocate all development from the coastal conurbations. It argues that all proposals for the location of large-scale projects, regional development and investment programmes should be assessed against this national view. New urban development in low-lying areas should observe the principle that present and future costs and benefits must be assessed, and costs must not be passed on to other administrative tiers but borne by those who benefit. Nevertheless, extensive and costly programmes of flood protection are to be implemented in the Delta and other regions. For the Delta area of the Netherlands (which, in comparison with British risk-design standards of 1:1000, already meets very high [1:10,000] risk standards), the Commission proposes that the level of flood protection be raised by a factor of 10. Attention is also to be paid to areas upstream, such as integration with the earlier Room for the Rivers initiative in the Rhine basin (Figure 9.8). The works will be funded by a Delta

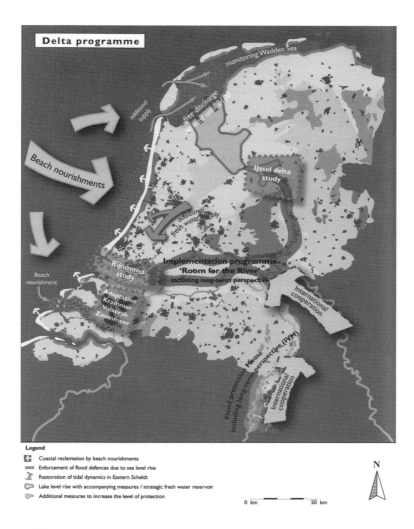

Figure 9.8

Delta programme
Source: Delta Commissie, 2008

Fund partly funded by revenues from natural gas from the Dutch fields of the North Sea.

9.8.3 Regional and municipal spatial planning response

The principles are already being implemented at the provincial and municipal level. The Randstad 2040 Structural Vision (VROM, 2008a) includes two structuring principles of living in a safe, climate resilient and green-blue delta, and creating quality through greater interaction between green (landscape), blue (water) and red (urbanization) aspects. The national government's vision for the Randstad includes developing green living and working environments linked to the green-blue setting, and promoting the provision of metropolitan parks in the cities.

In Rotterdam, water has been a guiding principle through the Waterplan 2040, prepared alongside the city-wide spatial plan (Wilson, 2009a). Further details of the Waterplan are given in Chapter 11, Box 11.2. Figure 9.9 illustrates some thinking on integrating water into the city spatial framework. Moreover, the REAP initiative in Rotterdam is aiming to reduce urban heating under conditions of climate change by ensuring that all waste heat from energy-generation and space and water heating is reused rather than being wasted to the atmosphere (see Box 9.7 above).

We will see in Chapters 10 and 11 how Dutch water-planning works through detailed development decisions through the water test. The Dutch experience of planning for blue and green infrastructure is contributing to the EU-funded GRaBS project (Henderson, 2009) on the role of green and blue infrastructure in aiding adaptation. But a key argument for such an approach is that green and blue infrastructure and sustainable drainage can also contribute to climate change mitigation.

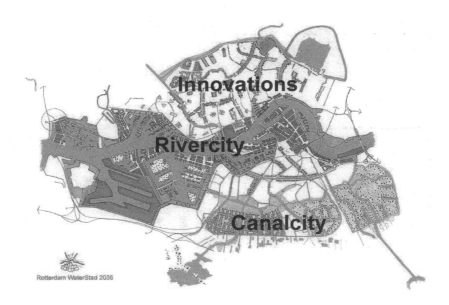

Figure 9.9

Rotterdam Water Plan
Source: Tillie, 2007

9.9 Bringing adaptation and mitigation together: green infrastructure

9.9.1 Benefits of green and blue infrastructure

Green infrastructure is defined in government planning policy guidance as 'A network of multi-functional green space, both new and existing, both rural and urban, which supports the natural and ecological processes and is integral to the health and quality of life of sustainable communities' (DCLG, 2008b, p. 5). While there are many definitions of green infrastructure, some including blue infrastructure (that is open water), it can be argued that they all involve 'natural and green areas in urban and rural settings, are about the strategic connection of open green areas, and should provide multiple benefits for people' (NECF, 2006). Enthusiasm for the provision of green infrastructure as a critical part of urban and interurban infrastructure has arisen for a number of reasons. It offers opportunities for joined-up thinking and so better decision-making. Climate change has provided additional justification. Research undertaken by the Centre for Urban Ecology at the University of Manchester as part of the ASCCUE project (see also Chapters 6 and 13) developed models of urban morphology and climate change scenarios, adjusted for Greater Manchester: projections showed that a 10 per cent increase in green spaces can significantly moderate flood risk and higher temperatures (Gill *et al.*, 2007; Walsh *et al.*, 2007). Climate change considerations of flood attenuation and urban cooling have therefore reinforced arguments for the multifunctionality of green infrastructure: landscape, food production, social interaction, recreation, safe transport routes, biodiversity, air quality and health benefits.

But green and blue infrastructure can also meet climate change mitigation objectives: through its shading and evaporative cooling effect, it can reduce the need for artificial cooling of buildings (and hence reduce the need for artificial ventilation [CABE, 2009b]). Cooling can also reduce the need for water. Green infrastructure can also play a role in carbon sequestration. Indirectly, it can also provide attractive open spaces which can encourage sustainable modes of transport such as walking and cycling. Some of the multifunctional benefits of urban green and blue space are shown in Table 9.7.

9.9.2 Policy context

Accordingly, government policy for some years has been supportive (Table 9.8) of green infrastructure in providing these multiple functions, to which climate change adaptation is an additional benefit.

Green infrastructure is already a key part of many adaptation and mitigation strategies. Early work on improving the landscape of the subregional area of the Thames Gateway (a major expansion area planned and underway since the late

Table 9.7 Benefits of green infrastructure

Environmental	Social	Economic
• Resilience to climate change impacts • Urban cooling • Rainfall absorption and flood alleviation • Water cleansing • Carbon storage • Biodiversity conservation and enhancement • Improved air quality	• Health benefits • Mental well-being • Sense of place • Passive and active recreation and sport • Inclusivity • Accessibility • Safe and sustainable transport routes • Local food or fuel production in allotments, gardens or horticulture • Environmental education	• Employment • Land and property values • Economic growth and investment • Labour productivity • Tourism • Products from the land

1990s) led to a green infrastructure plan for the subregion (Defra and ODPM, 2004). The concept has since been promoted by statutory agencies such as the Environment Agency and Natural England (Land Use Consultants *et al.*, 2009), advisory bodies such as CABE (2009b), regional bodies such as One North West, Yorkshire and Humber Regional Assembly and the South East Partnership, metropolitan areas such as Greater Manchester, and boroughs such as Milton Keynes (2007) and Woking (2008).

9.9.3 Regional and local practice

The North West Region has made a significant contribution to the understanding of green infrastructure. A study for Natural Economy North West estimated that the broader environmental economy, including green and blue space, provided economic benefit to the regional economy of a gross added value (GVA) of £26m, and supported over 100,000 jobs (Natural Economy North West, 2008). As with other regions, the RSS for the North West (GONW, 2008) includes a policy for green infrastructure. A regional think tank has been established, drawing on academic and practitioner expertise, including the Red Rose and Mersey Forests, and guidance drafted on implementing green infrastructure at subregional level. Work by the Community Forests North West (Gill, 2008) identified eight climate change mitigation and adaptation functions of green infrastructure (see Box 9.14), estimated thresholds for each function, and mapped areas of the region where each function should be preserved and protected, or increased and enhanced. The intention is that such mapping can lead to regional priorities and action plans.

In the urban context, the provision of greenspace can help to sustain city centre and central area living and working; as these areas have a higher modal

Table 9.8 National planning policy supporting green infrastructure in England

Policy	Relevance for green infrastructure planning
Strategy for Improving Quality of Place (HMG, 2009b)	Provision of green space and GI (including green and blue infrastructure) as one of four key elements in quality of place: a vital role in combating climate change and tackling its effects
Forthcoming (2010) PPS on Green Infrastructure	Combining elements of PPSs on open space and recreation, and biodiversity
Consultation Policy Statement on Regional Strategies (DCLG and BIS, 2009)	Policies and priorities to show how plans for sustainable economic growth, housing and other development have taken account of available infrastructure, including environmental (and green) infrastructure
PPS1 Supplement on Climate Change	Spatial strategies and development should deliver GI as part of any strategy to address CC mitigation and adaptation
PPS 12 Local Spatial Planning	LPAs to plan for infrastructure, including GI
Sustainable Communities Plan Growth Areas	10% of first round funding for Growth Areas ring-fenced for green space projects
Sustainable Communities Plan Growth points	GI strategy required
PPS on eco-towns (DCLG, 2009)	Eco-town standards for 40% of total land to be green space, of which at least half to be public; multifunctional network to connect to wider countryside; local production of food
TCPA worksheet on GI (TCPA et al., 2008)	Guidance on how to design, incorporate and manage GI, and how it can be factored in to land values

Source: based on Land Use Consultants, 2009

split to public transport, it can help reduce overall transport emissions. Green routes can also provide safe and accessible routes for more sustainable modes of travel such as cycling and walking, including for the journey to school, with consequent multiple benefits. However, as we saw in Chapter 8, the provision of such routes and corridors does not necessarily achieve the desired modal shift without further household-level intervention (Jones, 2008).

While the subregional scale is important for a strategic view of linking green infrastructure, there is much scope at the local level. Under the forthcoming revision of PPS25, all developments should now consider the provision of SuDs which provide many of the benefits of green infrastructure at a local scale (discussed further in Chapter 11). Natural England (2009a) cites a number of local case studies, including those where climate change adaptation and community involvement are complementary activities: Mayesbrook Park, in Barking and Dagenham in East London, where river restoration as part of the Thames

Wetland Vision scheme and Natural Connections initiatives will meet objectives for biodiversity, climate change and community engagement in design and management; and Brickies Pond in Stockton, part of the Tees Valley green infrastructure strategy, where habitat improvements will meet biodiversity and climate change objectives through movement corridors, and improved public access (Natural England, 2009a).

Climate change adaptation, as for mitigation, is therefore as much about improving the resilience of existing urban areas as it is about new development. Nevertheless, it is important to recognize that there may be winners and losers from the provision of new forms of green and blue infrastructure: for instance, in urban areas, providing blue corridors – setting flood defences further back in order to alleviate flooding elsewhere in the urban area – would increase the functional flood plain (as defined in PPS25 – see Chapter 11) and impact on existing land uses, property interests and future regeneration plans. Participative implementation – as in some of the urban river projects described in Chapter 13.2.4 – is vital.

Thames Gateway

A much-cited example of the difficulties of implementing an equitable adaptation policy is the major new development planned in the Thames Gateway. Chapter 4 has briefly explained the government's commitment to development in the Thames Gateway, and the concerns of the Environmental Audit Committee about the lack of prior assessment of flood risk in the area. The issue of climate change adds weight to these concerns. Chapter 7, Section 6.3 has given an account of the approach to risk and uncertainty under conditions of climate change taken in the SEA of the TE2100 project for strategic tidal flood-risk management in London and the Thames Estuary up to 2100. As explained above, there are longstanding proposals in the Gateway for green and blue infrastructure to shape the development, help to manage flood risk, and benefit existing and future residents. Nevertheless, despite these intentions, concerns remain about the extent to which the new development planned in the Thames Gateway will be designed and maintained at urban or at building scale to be resilient to future floods (Hall *et al.*, 2009). Flood risks remain in the defended flood plain. Developments have to follow the sequential test in PPS25 (see Chapter 11), but the implications of the policy in shifting some responsibility to individual householders to ensure the resilience of their own property to a possible flood remain untested. There has been much talk of replicating the Dutch practice of floating houses (and floating greenhouses), such as Terry Farrell's concept of a cluster of islands in the Thames Estuary, incorporating floating homes. The government appointed Terry Farrell as Parklands Design Champion, and the green landscape elements have been worked up in the *Thames Gateway Parklands Vision* (DCLG, 2008c; figure 9.10). The government intends the vision to provide further momentum as a framework for further regeneration and improvement of the urban and natural environments in the Gateway: but issues remain of coordination and implementation in the new 'soft spaces' of such subregional plans (Haughton *et al.*, 2010). The differences in implementation are revealing of the differences in the Dutch and British approaches to ambitious amphibian spatial planning.

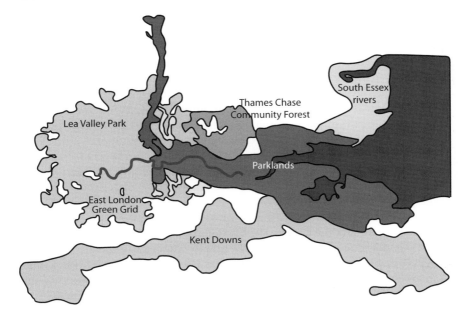

Figure 9.10

Thames Gateway Parklands
Source: DCLG, 2008c

9.10 Conclusions: spatial planning for mitigation and adaptation

This review of practice in the UK and the Netherlands demonstrates the importance of taking a holistic view in the context of wider sustainable development objectives. The built environment has a significant role in climate change mitigation and adaptation and we need to adopt an integrated approach to the planning of new and existing built development. It is evident there is scope for both innovation and cross-national learning in low carbon, carbon-neutral and energy planning. However, it is clear there are barriers to implementation of initiatives in different countries. Chapter 13 will look at some of the issues of social learning and acquisition of skills for this new challenge of low carbon planning. Chapter 14 then suggests some principles and procedures for integrating mitigation and adaptation.

Spatial planning in its plan-making and development-consenting functions has undergone a significant shift in the last few years in response to climate change. In both the Netherlands and the UK, spatial plans are being drawn up specifically to increase the resilience of existing and new urban development. More attention is being given to longer time horizons in seeking to promote resilience with respect to expected future changes in climate, and to achieve targets for low-carbon development. The new focus of planning on existing as well as new development provides an opportunity for more consideration of social equity and the distributional consequences of development. The need for spatial planning to work with other areas of public policy, and with communities and households, is increasingly acknowledged.

The revived enthusiasm for green infrastructure demonstrates the ways in which climate change mitigation and adaptation can provide win-win solutions and increase adaptive capacity through satisfying other sustainability objectives. But, although the principles outlined above are being incorporated in plans and decisions, it is not yet clear that sufficient attention is being paid to identifying and avoiding any conflicts, or adapting policies to promote synergies. The PPS1 Supplement on climate change stated that 'mitigation and adaptation should not be considered independently of each other, and new development should be planned with both in mind' (DCLG, 2007a, p. 11) – but it does not refer to the links with existing development, nor does the practice guide accompanying the advice (HCA Academy, 2009) give much insight into how this can be done. Chapter 7 showed how *ex ante* assessments are also struggling to integrate mitigation and adaptation assessments. The following three chapters show how wider conceptions of planning within natural processes of water and ecosystems can assist with promoting this more synoptic approach. Chapter 14 then draws together some of the principles to achieve this.

10 Planning for water resources under climate change

··

10.1 Introduction

Integrating the planning and management of water (both resources and floods) and use of land (built areas, agriculture, coastal and semi-natural areas) is one of the greatest challenges in building resilience to climate change. Water is a component (as either a resource or pathway) of probably all natural and human systems. The complexity of interaction means that, while integrated water and spatial planning for climate change addresses strategic to local levels, management must extend to the simplest level – e.g. the household. Advances in technology for representing and monitoring the systems involved are making feasible both better informed planning and closer management. Government policy on water resources was reviewed in Defra's policy document for England, *Future Water* (Defra, 2008a); the sector regulator in England and Wales is the Environment Agency, which published its water resources strategy *Water for People and the Environment*, in 2009 (EA, 2009d).

The water resources topic is covered here at some length partly because little guidance on this is currently available in Planning Policy Statements – although a National Policy Statement on water infrastructure is expected to be published (in line with part 2 of the Planning Act, 2009) in late 2010 – see Chapters 5.2.1, 8.4.2 and 9.8. In this and the following chapter we can address only some of the many water-related issues associated with spatial planning and climate change. These issues are concerned with water supply and quality on the one hand, and flood (fluvial, pluvial and coastal) on the other. Other issues will be mentioned more briefly (such as energy use in the water sector, wastewater and the interaction with biodiversity, etc). In view of the complexity of legislation and policy, we have covered water issues in two chapters: water resources in Chapter 10, then flood risk together with marine and coastal planning in Chapter 11.

However, it will be understood that there is a good deal of meshing between these topics, and related policies and measures, and between approaches to mitigation and adaptation for climate change as they relate to water.

As a most vital resource, water is particularly affected by climate change impacts: the risk of both flooding and drought is increased by climate change. Other pressures also affect access to safe, sustainable and sufficient supplies: growing populations and increasing use per head, coupled with pollution, have pushed supplies in densely populated areas of Europe towards scarcity (EEA, 2009d) and there are areas of water stress across England (Defra, 2008a) (see Figure 10.4). Similarly, other factors have increased flood risk: increased sealing of surfaces reducing infiltration, with impermeable or hard surfaces or simply by compacting soil. Water supply on the one hand, and drainage and flood defence on the other, are systems requiring major infrastructure and wise planning and management. Nevertheless, in the past both systems have been rather fragmented in their institutional structures, and separate from each other. During the second half of the twentieth century, increasing demands upon water supplies, and decreasing quality led to recognition of a need for institutional and policy change with respect to water resources. Subsequently, awareness of climate change has accelerated action to move towards integration of the planning and management not only of water resources but also flood risk. This has led to the concept of large-scale river basin management planning and the question of how this might be integrated with spatial planning to respond to climate change.

Water infrastructure (for supply, drainage, sanitation and irrigation) is built at a scale which reflects both need and the historic reliability of precipitation, but now both more frequent precipitation extremes and incremental change need to be incorporated into development plans. The planning period for these major infrastructure systems is long and the design life of the infrastructure is typically 50–100 years or more, so they will persist as climates change. At the same time, changes in management, practice and behaviour at the local level can also contribute to appropriate adaptation to changed climate. A series of European Directives (subsequently transposed into national legislations) is relevant to these major issues, particularly the Water Framework Directive 2000/60/EC (CEC, 2000b) and the Floods Directive 2007/60/EC (CEC, 2007a), together with the Habitats Directive Council Directive 92/43/EEC (CEC, 1992), as well as others dealing with pollution.

Section 10.2 outlines the range of pressures and impacts on the water environment, then 10.3 explores the legislation and strategies involved in delivering water to consumers at EU to local levels, including integrated water resources management. Tools for policy integration are introduced in Section 10.4 – these include water neutral development policy and assessment studies.

10.2 Water resources: use and climate change impacts

10.2.1 Abstraction and use

Globally, humans appropriate more than 50 per cent of all renewable and accessible freshwater (EEA, 2009d). In Europe, where water is relatively abundant, only approximately 13 per cent of the resource is abstracted. But this figure masks considerable variation in availability, and overexploitation by a range of economic sectors poses a threat to Europe's water resources. Irrigation is a major use in southern Europe and is a consumptive use (i.e. water is consumed and not returned to the environment – see following section); irrigation demand often exceeds availability (EEA, 2009d). Not only is the resource itself – in the form of lakes, rivers and streams on the surface and groundwater below the surface – at risk, but many other environmental elements are affected through subsidiary pathways of change. Biodiversity and soils, for example, are strongly reliant on broadly stable water relations, and many human systems (drinking water, sanitation, health and agriculture) depend on a supply of water which is reliable (though the amount varies from place to place). Some European water statistics are given in Box 10.1, showing uses and current pressures.

Box 10.1 Water resources statistics – Europe

Across Europe abstraction is about 500 m^3/person/year, and of this 44% is abstracted for energy production, 24% for agriculture, 21% for the public water supply and 11% for industry (there is considerable variation between countries and regions). In eastern and western Europe abstraction for electricity generation predominates, whereas in southern Europe irrigation water may account for 60–80% of abstracted water. In general, climate change – in particular higher temperatures and drier summers – is likely to increase the demand for irrigation in the summer (EEA, 2009d).

- 20% of all surface water in the European Union is seriously threatened with pollution.
- Groundwater supplies around 65% of all Europe's drinking water.
- 60% of European cities overexploit their groundwater resources.
- 50% of wetlands have 'endangered status' due to groundwater overexploitation (CEC, 2002b).

The population of the EU-27 has risen from 400 million in 1960 to 497 million in 2007, and is projected to increase further to 521 million by 2035 with a gradual subsequent decline to 506 million in 2060 (Eurostat, 2008a).

Abstraction for human use and consumption is the main pressure on the water environment – abstracted water may be consumed (incorporated into vegetation and products) or it may be recycled or drained to the river or sea after treatment. Statistics for England and Wales show abstraction rates of 356,000 m³ per day. Table 10.1 shows the breakdown of water abstracted in England and Wales by major sectoral uses, with public water supply accounting for almost half of all water supplied. Household water use (litres/head/day) varies between suppliers, and metered households use less than unmetered households. Average use in England and Wales was 148 l/head/day in 2006–07, though the extremes of the range are from 117 (Severn Trent, metered) to over 170 l/head/day unmetered use in parts of the Thames valley, depending on water supply company (Ofwat, 2007). Approximately one third of each household's consumption is used for showers and baths, another third for lavatory flushing (Welsh Water, undated).

Of water abstracted for supply, electricity generation, industry and fish farming, 80 per cent is returned to the river, whereas the water used in agriculture (less than 1 per cent) is not. European policy (e.g. the Urban Wastewater Treatment Directive 91/271/EEC [CEC, 1991] amended 1998, and the Habitats Directive, 92/43/EEC [CEC, 1992] protecting wild plants, animals and habitats), has meant that both abstraction and wastewater treatment works have been moved downstream – to reduce impacts on the environment and to amalgamate small, poorly performing treatment works into larger more efficient works which discharge closer to the sea. However, this means that abstraction and wastewater treatment are at a greater distance from the point of consumption, so the return of this water has little benefit for the freshwater environment (returning it upstream by pumping would have high economic and carbon costs).

Population change is a significant factor in future water demand and the UK population is projected to rise by a further 20 million by 2050 (EA, 2009d). Household size also affects water use: smaller households use more water per head than larger households. UK figures suggest per person use is 38 per cent less in five-person households than in single-person households (GLA, 2007). Other influences on use are income (and ownership of appliances) and consumer behaviour, for example in using water-efficient appliances (see Sections 10.4.3 and 10.4.4).

Table 10.1 Licensed abstractions, England and Wales (%)

Water abstracted for	% of total
Public and private water supply	48.5
Electricity generation	28.1
Industry and other	12.0
Fish farming, cress growing and amenity ponds	10.3
Agriculture, spray and other	0.8

Source: Defra, 2008a

10.2.2 Climate change impacts on water resources

Direct impacts

Early indications of climate change effects on water can be seen in precipitation statistics: rainfall/snowfall in Europe generally increased over the twentieth century, rising by 6–8 per cent on average between 1901 and 2005. This overall trend masks major differences between European regions, in particular a pre-cipitation reduction in the Mediterranean and eastern Europe (EEA, 2008a). The consequences of climate change for water resources (availability and quality), as briefly introduced in Chapter 2, are likely to include less water and a less reliable supply through the seasons, with an increased risk of pollution events. The seasonal distribution of precipitation is expected to change: projections suggest that there will be fewer months with high precipitation (these occur over the winter) while in the summer months rainfall amounts will decline though rainfall may be more intense. Intense rainfall may thus provide a higher proportion of total precipitation.

IPCC projections show milder, wetter winters for much of the NW Europe region, and hotter, drier summers (IPCC, 2007a). By 2020 demand for water could increase by 5 per cent in England and Wales. By 2050, climate change may have reduced the amount of water available in England and Wales by 10–15 per cent, with average summer river flows down by 50–80 per cent. While summer rainfall decreases, agricultural irrigation demand in England and Wales could increase by about 20 per cent by 2020, and 30 per cent by 2050 (Defra 2008a). Change of crop type, species and variety would impact on this. Table 10.2 summarizes the broad impacts of climate change upon water gathering and consequently upon water storage and supply infrastructure.

Options for reducing supply shortages relate to new resources (such as build-ing new reservoirs or increasing reservoir capacity) and more efficient use (water neutrality, efficient appliances) and demand management; these options are discussed in Section 10.4. Physical restriction of use and rebalancing use between sectors (agriculture, industry, public water supply, energy) are further options. As water heating is a major component of household energy demand, improving the efficiency of use would contribute to reducing greenhouse gas emissions and could make a significant contribution towards the UK Carbon Reduction Commitment. In *Future Water*, Defra (2008a) claims this reduction could amount to 27 to 40 per cent of current use in public water supply, if water metering were near universal. Moreover, more efficient use of water would reduce the volume of water treated for supply and passing through wastewater treatment systems, thus further cutting energy use. This is an example of an adaptive action also bringing benefits for mitigation.

Water quality may be degraded by both drought and flood and so may be affected by climate change. Environment Agency modelling work has shown that there is an impact upon river quality in England and Wales, indicating that climate change may downgrade the ecological status of 190 km of rivers

Table 10.2 Impacts of climate change on water resources and infrastructure needs

Changes in climate variables	Water supply impacts
Greater % of annual precipitation in winter	Pattern of natural supply changes over course of year. • Provide more storage capacity • Increase efficiency of use
Faster snowmelt	Risk of loss of potential stocks at earlier period.
Rainfall more intense	Overwhelmed drainage systems may lead to water contamination and impacts for supplies. Increased erosion and sediment content.
Greater % of rainfall in intense episodes	Need to build more headroom into water storage facilities, to capture rain when it falls. Also, need to encourage recharge of groundwater.
Higher summer temperatures	Exacerbation of supply problems with higher potential evapotranspiration and higher use rates. Also, greater catchment demand (vegetation).
	Increased demand and changes to location of demand, e.g. from increased rural tourism. Water quality impacts (algal bloom) and low oxygen levels affect biodiversity.
Long dry periods cause 'soil sealing' and lower infiltration	Proportion of precipitation lost to run-off increases, so need for measures to increase infiltration (e.g. diversion to washlands).
Less predictable (more erratic) weather patterns	Increased drought risk – need to build additional storage or promote more efficient use.
	Need to increase infiltration and drainage capacity.
Milder winters	Less snow and faster snowmelt – less storage of rainfall to feed rivers later.

by 2020 (Grayling, 2009). There are short-term risks to water quality, however, where drainage systems are overwhelmed and overflow, or where extra high 'pulses' of agro-chemicals (or other pollutants) reach water courses following rain after a period of drought. The Pitt Review (2008, p. 72) notes that there is an automatic right of connection of new developments to public sewers once planning permission has been given, and points to the risks of surface water flooding where sewers are overwhelmed, as in the 2007 floods. The report states 'we do not consider it sensible to allow new connections of surface water drainage to the sewerage system to take place unchecked', and goes on to recommend (in Recommendation 10) that this automatic right should be removed (Pitt, 2008, p. xvi). In its response to the Pitt Review, the government agreed that this automatic right to connect surface water drainage to the public sewer should be removed and undertook to incorporate this into law (Defra, 2008c, p. 45), stating this change would be introduced via the Floods and Water Management Act. However, this appears not yet to have been assured.

In its response to the Defra consultation on the Draft Bill of April 2009, Water UK (responding on behalf of the water industry) pointed out that the Bill had been drafted so as to permit developers to drain new developments via a SUDS feature that discharges to the public sewer, subject to the approval of the SUDS design by the Suds Approving Body. (The consultation document suggests that in unconstrained green field sites, connection to the public sewer should be unnecessary as 'a range of SUDS techniques' should obviate this, whereas on more constrained sites, 'National Standards will set requirements for reducing peak run-off of surface water' [Defra, 2009d, p. 47].) Water UK states that as a consequence, water companies will therefore still have 'no control over the quantity or quality of flows discharged to the public sewers they are responsible for, with likely risk of downstream property flooding or pollution incidents that are effectively beyond the control of the water company will therefore continue' (Water UK, n.d., p. 2).

Indirect impacts of climate change (mitigation and adaptation)

Policies and measures taken to respond to climate change may also have impacts upon water resources quantity and quality. For example, a switch to biofuels could have an impact upon infiltration rates and crop water use, affecting river flows. On the other hand, a change in energy generation technology that meant a lower requirement for cooling water in power stations would reduce abstraction, though as almost all this water is returned, it would not significantly affect river flows.

Measures which increase or maintain water levels in wetlands could affect organic decomposition, possibly changing methane emissions (the direction of change would depend on local circumstances). Increases in irrigation – especially in the drier south-east and east of England – could affect water resources significantly. In East Anglia an increase of 30 per cent in the volume of water is forecast to be needed in 2050 to irrigate the same area of crops (Weatherhead, 2008).

10.3 Integrating planning for land and water: water resources

10.3.1 EU Water Framework Directive

It is the expressed intention of the EU and its member states to move towards integrated planning for land and water through the 'river basin planning approach', which brings together primarily water resources and spatial planning, but which also recognizes the interaction with flood risk. The principal legislation governing river basin planning is the Water Framework Directive (WFD) of 2000.

It is the purpose of the WFD 'to deliver an integrated approach for the protection and sustainable use of the water environment' (Defra, 2006a, p. 6). In addition to sustainable use, other purposes of the WFD are: to enhance the status and prevent further deterioration of aquatic ecosystems and associated wetlands, which depend on the aquatic ecosystems; to reduce pollution of water, including groundwater, and to preserve protected areas. A further purpose is 'to contribute to mitigating the effects of floods and droughts' (Article 1 (e) of CEC, 2000b). The WFD is thus an integrating instrument aimed at all aspects of water-related policy. Woltjer and Al (2007) describe the process of negotiation which led to the WFD as 'difficult', highlighting conflicting aims and constraints upon parties. The final Directive is seen as a compromise reflecting the influences of both the environmental lobby and agricultural interests.

The WFD puts in place an iterative process across the EU to raise both the ecological status and the chemical status of all water bodies, i.e. rivers, lakes, groundwater, etc. (Special arrangements are put in place for artificial or modified water bodies such as canals and harbours.) The Directive calls for a series of cycles of reporting leading to identification of needs and proposals for improvements (Programmes of Measures). The central concepts of the WFD are the River Basin District and the related Management Plan (RBMP). The contents of RBMPs are indicated in Box 10.2. The first cycle of the river basin management process was completed in 2009 with the publication of RBMPs for all River Basin Districts (i.e. fifteen in the UK). Eventually, by 2027 and the end of the third RBD planning cycle, the WFD's ultimate goal of 'good status' (which covers both good ecological status and good chemical status) is to be achieved for all water bodies, together with principal environmental objectives (subject to conditions). Under the WFD provisions and the transposed legislation England and Wales are divided into eleven River Basin Districts; most of Scotland is a single RBD, plus the cross-boundary Solway Tweed RBD (see map, Figure 10.1) and Northern Ireland shares three RBDs with Ireland. RBMPs are drawn up by the Environment Agency (SEPA in Scotland) in consultation with stakeholders (including representatives of ports, consumers, business and industry, farming, recreation, water companies, freshwater fisheries and riparian owners, and environmental NGOs plus government bodies and agencies such as regional and local authorities and Natural England). Other plans and strategies prepared in the sector – such as Catchment Abstraction Management Strategies (CAMSs), Water Resources Management Plans (WRMPs) and Drought Plans – share the objective of sustainable water use, and so feed into this process. Both WRMPs and Drought Plans are produced by water companies, CAMSs are produced by the Environment Agency.

Item 6 of Box 10.2 refers to changing conditions, including development. The scale of this development to be incorporated in assessments for RBMPs is considerable. The draft RBMPs for each of these RBDs indicate planned development (e.g. a further 200,000 new homes by 2026 in the South East RBD, a further 900,000 homes by 2026 in the Humber RBD, and a further 500,000 new homes by 2021 in Anglian RBD (EA, 2009e). Other associated development will

Box 10.2 Contents of River Basin Management Plans

RBMPs are to include:

1. The essential characteristics of the River Basin District
   population, with maps).
2. The expected outcomes of planned changes (principal (
   for example: improving rural land management, reducing t
   and the built environment managing future development
   supply of water, improving wildlife habitats with river rest
   addressing point source pollution via control regimes or en
   regimes). This set of planned actions (or 'programmes (
   is to be operational by 2012.
3. What objectives are being set the RBD for 2015 (and be,
   good ecological status objective cannot be met by that d
4. The status of individual catchments within the RBD by
   Thames RBD is made up of 18 catchments). Also, progr
   the objectives.
5. A summary action plan, by sectors (e.g. industry, local g
6. Other changing conditions: climate change, developmen
   erosion (for climate change related conditions, see Table
7. Plans for SEA and Habitats Regulations assessments fc

Source: adapted from Defra, 2006, p. 62

include transport and energy infrastructures, etc. Clima
considered in RBMPs, though WFD does not explicitly ac
nevertheless its cyclical and stepwise approach is seen as
the long-term implications of climate change' (EEA, 2
effectiveness in leading to appropriate adaptation is see
the long-term perspective of the RBMP. The EEA suggest

> Adaptation could be explicitly incorporated into
> of the WFD in various ways, for example throu
> impact assessment for each river basin district an
> ated catchment-wide actions in the programmes (
> of climate change impacts and adaptation indicato
> activities could also be considered.

10.3.2 England/UK: legislation and strategy – wat

Responses by European and national planning and polic
tion of planning for water with spatial planning are set i

RBMPs)

RBD) (size, location,

utcomes will include,
he impact of transport
securing sustainable
eration strategies and
ironmental permitting
f measures' – PoMs)

ond 2015, where the
ate)?
2015 (for example,
ess towards achieving

vernment).
, flooding and coastal
10.2).
the RBD.

e change is also to be
dress climate change;
well-suited to handle
07a, p. 7) though its
n as dependent upon
s that:

the implementation
gh a climate change
l inclusion of associ-
f measures. Inclusion
s in WFD monitoring

(EEA, 2007a, p. 7)

r resources

makers to the integra-
the context of a wide

lopment agenda and
legislative and policy
vith the most recent
s to England only; a

esources

and treatment, and
lex. In England and
sibility of the water
id the Environment
these roles are filled

ds

East of
England

don

t

Table 10.3 UK legislation and planning policy affecting UK water resources

Legislation or strategy	Aimed at	Significant elements for spatial planning
Water Environment (Water Framework Directive) Regulations (England and Wales) 2003 and in Scotland by the Water Environment and Water Services Act (WEWS) 2003 (transposes WFD)	Ecological health of water bodies	River Basin Management strategies (RBMPs): iterative cycles of improvement of basin management. LPAs are seen as key delivery partners for this policy.
The Conservation (Natural Habitats, etc.) Regulations 1994 (transposes Habitats Directive 92/43/EEC)	Protection of wildlife	Identification of sites suitable for designation as having Community importance. Encouragement of planning policies for linear features valuable for biodiversity.
UK Water Act, 2003 Statutory water company plans	To improve: water conservation, public health and the environment, service to customers	Makes significant changes to the abstraction licensing process. Areas/abstractors affected are mainly: small abstractors, abstractions for mining/quarrying and engineering works, transfers from canals and harbours, transfers into internal drainage districts, agriculture and the water industry.
Flood and Water Management Act (HMG, 2010c) (transposes 2007/60/EC)	(in part) to enable better management of water resources and quality	See also Chapter 11.3.3.
Future Water (Defra, 2008) (strategy for England)	Presents Government vision for water to 2030	Quality: improve pollution control. Surface water: promote infiltration and reuse, rather than drainage via sewers. Flooding: flood-risk management. Emissions: reduce greenhouse gas emissions (1% of UK total from water industry). Charging: increase penetration of metering.
Water for people and the environment (EA, 2009a) (applies to England and Wales)	A better place for people and wildlife, for present and for future generations	Objectives and measures: Good water management contributes to sustainable development by supporting people and the economy in an improved environment. New and existing homes and buildings to be more water efficient.

(continued)

Table 10.3 (*cont.*)

Legislation or strategy	Aimed at	Significant elements for spatial planning
Water for people and the environment (*cont.*)	(see above)	Water resources to be allocated efficiently and are shared within regions where there are areas of surplus.
		The needs of wildlife, fisheries, navigation and recreation, as well as the environment and abstractors, are fully taken into account when allocating water resources.
		Introducing 'slow water' and SuDS.

Planning policy statements relevant to water resources planning (England)

Statement	Relevance for water resources. Planning authorities should:
PPS1 Delivering Sustainable Development (ODPM/DCLG, 2005)	• take account of availability of water resources • promote the sustainable use of water resources and the use of SuDS
PPS1 Supplement on Climate Change (DCLG, 2007)	• consider water resources, supply and water efficiency • set local sustainability levels, such as higher Code for Sustainable Homes levels for water, through Local Plan policy
PPS3 Housing (DCLG, 2006)	• assess environmental constraints, including water
PPS12 Local Spatial Planning (DCLG, 2008)	• apply soundness test of coherence, consistency and effectiveness (as well as correct procedure and conformity with relevant plans) • have particular regard to policies that safeguard water resources
PPS23 Planning and Pollution Control (ODPM/ DCLG, 2004)	• have regard to the requirements of the Water Framework Directive (impacts on water quality are a material consideration for planning) Interfacing with drainage responsibilities of Water Service Companies is set out, as is interface with Integrated Pollution Prevention and Control regime (IPPC).
PPS25 Development and Flood Risk (DCLG, 2006) now revised: DCLG, 2010d	• manage surface water so as to improve water quality and reduce pressure on water resources • promote SuDS and Surface Water Management Plans • promote partnership working (see also Section 11.4.2)

by the Water Industry Commission for Scotland (WICS) and SEPA. The quality of public supply is overseen by the Drinking Water Inspectorate in England and Wales, the Drinking Water Quality Regulator in Scotland. Water privatization in 1989 (England and Wales) has been credited by some (e.g. Rachwal,

2007) with benefits including increased capital expenditures, better water quality and a greater security of supply. Different structures exist in Scotland and Northern Ireland, where the water sectors remains in public ownership: Scottish Water is the water supply and sewerage authority for the whole of Scotland. Its obligations were defined by the Water (Scotland) Act 1980 and the Sewage (Scotland) Act 1968, as amended. The Environment Act 1995 also created the Scottish Environmental Protection Agency (SEPA) with similar powers to the Environment Agency in England and Wales. In 2007, under the Water and Sewerage Services (Northern Ireland) Order 2006, responsibility for Northern Ireland's water supply and sewerage services was transferred to the government-owned company, Northern Ireland Water.

In England and Wales, whilst the water industry has a '*duty* to supply' (water) to consumers under the Water Act 2003, the water companies are not statutory consultees on all developments, though they are to become statutory consultees where nationally significant infrastructure (see Chapter 5.5.2) is proposed in areas that they cover (EA, 2009f). The Environment Agency has this role partly to ensure that plans for development do not lead to excessive demands placed upon water resources within a catchment (and consequently, the ecosystems that depend on those resources). The EA's Restoring Sustainable Abstraction programme (initiated in 1999) catalogues sites which may be at risk from over-abstraction, particularly those affected by the EC Habitats Directive, Sites of Specific Scientific Interest or local sites.

The elements of Defra's *Future Water* strategy (2008a) which interact with the spatial planning function are, in particular, sustainable use and amenity benefits, attractive waters (that is, water bodies that may attract development) and the use of land for flood storage (which is seen as a means of reducing flooding in urban areas downstream). Thus the achievement of this vision (see Box 10.3) effectively requires better integration of spatial and water planning functions and depends on the integrated water resources management approach to be implemented via the River Basin Management Plans.

10.3.4 Integrating planning for land and water at River Basin District level

River Basin Management Plans respond to the need for integration of different forms of planning at the strategic level. Other approaches are being developed at a district level such as the Integrated Water Resources Studies and Water Cycle Studies (Section 10.4.1). Work by Kidd and Shaw (2007), and by Woltjer and Al (2007) for the Netherlands, explores how planning for land-use and water might be brought together. Kidd and Shaw compare two models of governance: the *centralized model*, with unified public organization for management of river basins, and the *decentralized* (or *polycentric*) *model*, involving the coordination of actions of existing organizations in relation to river basin management. Kidd and Shaw recognize that water resources management is usually a combination

- improved quality of the water environment and the ecology which it supports, and continued provision of high levels of drinking water quality from our taps
- sustainable management of risks from flooding and coastal erosion, with greater understanding and more effective management of surface water
- ensured sustainable use of water resources, and implemented fair, affordable and cost-reflective water charges
- reduced greenhouse gas emissions associated with water sector
- embedded continuous adaptation to climate change and other pressures across the water industry and water users
- improved governance and regulation.

RBMPs, WRMPs, Ofwat and the Drinking Water Inspectorate all have significant roles in delivering the vision.

Source: adapted from Defra, 2008a

of these two approaches (p. 313). In England it is the decentralized, partnership-based approach that is pursued. Kidd and Shaw list seventeen different types of partners to be involved (including government agencies, unitary and district authorities, regulators, water and sewerage undertakers, etc.).

Gaps in understanding between water managers and spatial planners and politicians, the complexity of ecosystem functioning and of interactions between people and the environment, together with institutional weaknesses, are seen by Kidd and Shaw as major challenges to achieving integration. If water and spatial planning are to work together then to these natural system dimensions must be added the further dimensions of the 'human system' which may be grouped as sectoral, territorial and organizational. Figure 10.2, redrawn from Kidd and Shaw 2007, sets out the framework of these dimensions. This framework, they argue, demonstrates that integration of water and spatial planning must entail significant changes in organization culture and practice.

Kidd and Shaw (2007) do not discuss climate change in their analysis, but Woltjer and Al (2007) – working in the Netherlands – acknowledge the impact of climate change upon water issues. Although flooding risk is a priority concern for them, Woltjer and Al conclude that 'Climate change and the new regionalism are converting water into a stronger strategic instrument, giving planners interesting opportunities for combining uses and finding innovative solutions' (p. 221). They describe four approaches to integrating water management and spatial planning in terms of two styles of governance (regulatory and strategic), and two types of focus or competence (functional and sociocultural regions). The four approaches are described as shown in Table 10.4.

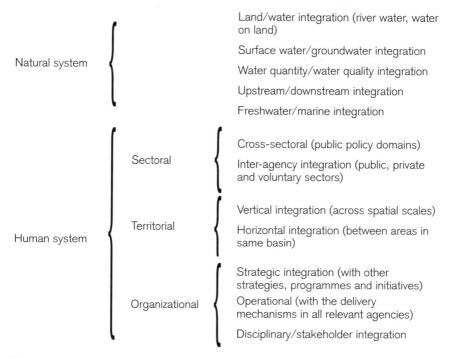

Figure 10.2

Dimensions of an integrative framework
Source: adapted from Kidd and Shaw, 2007

Woltjer and Al (2007) see opportunities for planners to facilitate the move towards the 'New water culture', where new capacities and identities are created, together with new coordinating institutions, in a social environment in which water is seen as an important component of attractive living and working conditions. However, they acknowledge the tensions that may arise from this attempt to integrate two distinct professional cultures – the technical orientation of water agency staff compared to the more political and economic visions of spatial planning. Their New Water Culture approach encompasses all the dimensions noted by Kidd and Shaw (2007), and in addition, there is a strengthening of the use made of water as a promotional element in development, for example as seen in Birmingham's Canalside developments, the work of the Mersey Basin campaign and Rotterdam's Water Plan (see Section 9.8 and Box 11.2). The WFD and river basin planning is a step towards the 'new water culture', though without the element of new development identities. The new National Water Plan in the Netherlands (see Sections 4.4.1 and 11.3.3) seems to exemplify this cultural shift (MVenW, 2009).

Table 10.4 Four approaches to integrating water management and spatial planning

	Functional regions	Sociocultural regions
Regulatory	**Conventional** *Key objective:* Public management of water quantity and quality	**Spatial Planning** *Key objective:* Water integrated into broader policymaking
Strategic	**Water Planning** *Key objective:* Making water management more important politically and socially	**New Water Culture** *Key objective:* Water as a source of social coherence and participation and 'new identities'

Source: adapted from Woltjer and Al, 2007, p. 220

10.4 Tools for policy integration: water resources

Examples of policies and approaches which should help with integrating water resources management and spatial planning are briefly outlined below: integrative studies (integrated water resources studies and water cycle studies), catchment abstraction management strategies, pricing and the use of scenarios as a tool in planning for new water resources capacity.

10.4.1 Studies of planning for new development and water

Studies have been undertaken in the UK in connection with the proposal for 45 New Growth Points (DCLG, 2006f) identified in response to pressures for development, and especially housing and eco-towns. These growth points were important drivers in the preparation of the Regional Spatial Strategies. These studies (Integrated Water Resources Studies and Water Cycle Studies) have several similarities and represent an approach for a better integration of water resource management into the spatial planning processes. Two case studies are illustrated. The first, in Box 10.4, summarizes an IWRS for part of South Hampshire, for PUSH (Partnership for Urban South Hampshire).

The PUSH IWRS study was completed before the publication of the relevant RBMP under the WFD (planned for the end of 2009) and was based on existing research and information (from Environment Agency and water company assessments, plans and appraisals) to identify and assess the options for delivering the water management requirements associated with the levels and locations of development under the South East Plan. The authors note that the potential impacts of WFD implementation were poorly understood at the time of the study, but expect that this position will have changed by the second

Box 10.4 IWRS of Urban South Hampshire as New Growth Point

The PUSH IWRS was commissioned in view of plans for an additional 80,000 homes in the subregion by 2026 (PUSH, 2008). Its objectives were to:

- Guide and inform the level and location of development to be accommodated in South Hampshire in accordance with the Draft South East Plan.
- Identify a preferred high level strategy for water management for the period to 2026, including the general location and timing of infrastructure requirements, the agencies responsible and the means of funding the necessary work.
- Identify the further work necessary to implement the preferred strategy and to monitor its effectiveness over the plan period.

Criteria for the options appraisal included contribution of the option to facilitating the planned development (i.e. its effectiveness), environmental sustainability, economic viability, carbon footprint, robustness to climate change and social equity.

The priority issues in the PUSH subregion were identified as water supply, waste-water treatment and flood risk. The flood-risk element of the report drew largely on an existing Strategic Flood Risk Assessment, the water supply and wastewater assessments undertook new analysis. Biodiversity and fisheries were given 'more general consideration', and climate change was taken into account with respect to changes over a 20–30 year period.

Planning policy recommendations were developed to provide the PUSH Partners (eleven local authorities plus key external partners) with a set of methods to influence the current regulatory system to provide more integrated water management. These recommendations cover lobbying and responding to consultations, developing subre-gional policies and guidance, LDF preparation by individual authorities, determination of planning applications, working with partners, funding infrastructure provision and targeted research. PUSH recognizes for itself a role in coordinating policy develop-ment and sharing good practice across the subregion: 'This includes the development of consistent policy approaches, and undertaking subregional research studies to provide the evidence base for subsequent individual LDFs and planning applications' (p. 153). Four draft policies were consequently proposed:

1. To promote incorporation of water efficiency and demand management meas-ures in new developments.
2. To promote SuDS, Surface Water Management and Groundwater Protection.
3. To facilitate the provision of necessary water management infrastructure.
4. To ensure sufficient water management infrastructure exists, or can be made available to serve new development.

Source: adapted from PUSH, 2008

round of plans, in 2015. Comparing the PUSH IWRS with Woltjer and Al's four approaches to integration (shown in Table 10.4), it is clear that the strategy study makes reference to issues beyond water planning, including quality of life, economic growth and sustainable development, habitat enhancement and environmental capacity. This may be seen as a step towards the 'new water culture' they propose, though it does not go as far as 'Using water strategically to create [...] new identities.'

A related study process for Water Cycle Studies (WCS) process has been proposed by the Environment Agency to bring together development and planning; it is required where the development area is a proposed eco-town or where a WCS is a condition of growth point status and it is a requirement of the Regional Spatial Strategy or Core Strategy (for example, WCSs are required under Policy NRM 2 Water Quality in the South East Plan [GOSE, 2009]). How the WCS process fits with local planning is shown in Figure 10.3.

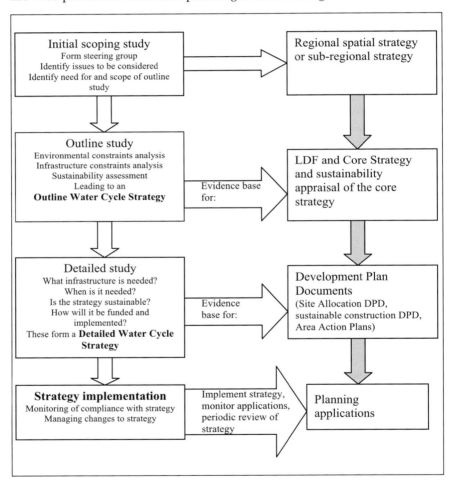

Figure 10.3

Relationship between Water Cycle Studies and Spatial Planning
Source: based on figure in EA, 2009d, p. 52

The WCS process is intended to identify tensions

between growth proposals and environmental requirements, and identify potential solutions to addressing them. Effective planning and close cooperation between all parties involved is essential to the success of a water cycle study. One of the most important benefits of a WCS is that it allows all the key organizations to work together in the planning process and builds confidence between parties.

(EA, 2009g)

The elements to be covered in a WCS are flood-risk (and drainage) management, surface water management planning, water resources, wastewater and water quality, Water Framework Directive and river basin planning, and urban pollution management. Thus, there is a good deal of overlap between the two study types, IWRS and WCS, though the former focuses on resources and incorporates flood risk whereas the WCS is intended to investigate and analyse the whole water cycle.

By bringing together all water and planning evidence under a single framework the WCS should promote better understanding the environmental and physical constraints to development. The approach is risk-based and works together with green infrastructure planning (see Chapter 9.9) to identify opportunities for more sustainable planning. A case study, for Basingstoke (Box 10.5)

Box 10.5 Case study – Basingstoke Detailed Water Cycle Study

Project Group
Basingstoke and Deane Borough Council, Hampshire County Council, Environment Agency, Natural England, Thames Water, South East Water, Southern Water.

Key Driver for Study
The outline water cycle study identified key concerns with respect to water quality standards and environmental capacity in the receiving water. The detailed WCS will provide the evidence base for the core strategy with respect to environmental capacity for growth.

Key Features of Study

- Informs core strategy preferred options.
- Detailed modelling of impact of growth on water quality and ecology.
- Detailed ecological surveys.
- Climate change impact assessment.
- Sustainability appraisal of water cycle options.
- Assessment of flood risk through a complementary Strategic Flood Risk Assessment.

---

illustrates the range of partners involved, the purpose and issues addressed, and outcome with respect to constraints upon development.

Both the PUSH IWRS and the Basingstoke WCS go some way collaboratively to contribute to the aims of Defra's Future Water strategy, in that they refer to issues of quality (environments and water), infiltration, water and flood risk management, as well as sustainability options relating to energy use, and other criteria. They demonstrate, in terms of process but also involvement of partners and use of data sources, the complexity of integrating of land and water planning. The value of these studies lies to a great extent in the opportunity for raising awareness among partners – awareness of the policies and restrictions of other stakeholders, but also of wider issues, in particular, climate change and its impacts.

10.4.2 CAMS and water-stress area mapping

Across the UK, Catchment Abstraction Management Strategies (CAMSs) prepared in line with the WFD by the Environment Agency (and SEPA) permit the mapping of areas of water stress. Catchments are categorized into four groups, as outlined in Box 10.6.

> **Box 10.6** Water resource availability status categories
>
> Water available: Water is likely to be available at all flows including low flows. Restrictions may apply.
>
> No water available: No water is available for further licensing at low flows. Water may be available at higher flows with appropriate restrictions.
>
> Over-licensed: Current actual abstraction is such that no water is available at low flows. If existing licences were used to their full allocation they could cause unacceptable environmental damage at low flows. Water may be available at high flows with appropriate restrictions.
>
> Over-abstracted: Existing abstraction is causing unacceptable damage to the environment at low flows. Water may still be available at high flows with appropriate restrictions.
>
> Source: EA, 2008, p. 5

The CAMS and water-stress mapping will feed into the WFD RBMPs for each River Basin District, and they are also scoped in as relevant policy documents in the sustainability appraisals of local plan documents. Areas of most widespread and serious water stress ('over-abstracted') are scattered across south-east England, eastern England and in the Midlands, as shown in Figure 10.4.

10.4.3 Pricing policy

The Water Framework Directive indicates that water pricing can be a key mechanism for achieving sustainable public use of water (EEA 2009a). Water pricing is controlled by Ofwat in England and Wales and the WCIS in Scotland, so it is beyond the control of spatial planning, but as pricing policy is expected to play a role in efficient use of water resources it may interact with development and impact upon spatial planning, for example by supporting water neutral development or affecting investment in new water resources (see subsequent sections). Water pricing is associated with social equity issues on the one hand (see Chapter 6) and discretionary use (e.g. garden watering) on the other hand, which can lead to tensions between the positions of Ofwat and the EA: whereas the EA would wish to see high levels of household water metering, Ofwat's role is to restrain costs to consumers. The *cost-effectiveness* condition of Programmes of Measures (PoMs) within the RBMPs is intended to lead towards better pricing policy, providing 'adequate incentives for users to use water resources efficiently' (CEC, 2000b, Article 9) and ensuring operational PoMs in each river basin deliver environmental objectives. The implementation of the WFD is seen as providing the 'necessary impetus for formulating water-price

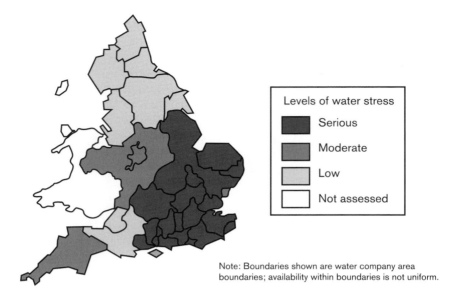

Levels of water stress

■ Serious

■ Moderate

□ Low

□ Not assessed

Note: Boundaries shown are water company area
boundaries; availability within boundaries is not uniform.

Figure 10.4

Broad indication of water resources availability status (surface and groundwater)
Source: redrawn from Defra, 2008c

policies' in line with factors such as all relevant financial, environmental and
resource costs (CEC, 2000a).

At the European level, further measures to support the WFD might include
the integration of water pricing policy with other European Union policies
such as the Common Agricultural Policy or the structural and cohesion policies
which can also provide incentives for better use of water.

10.4.4 Containing demand, seeking water neutral development

Demand management is an important route to sustainable use of water and the
options available here include labelling of appliances, metering, installation
of rainwater harvesting and reuse. Metering and level of charges for water use,
and the technology of water-using appliances, plus recycling and domestic rainwater harvesting can reduce water use and abstractions from rivers. Research
data suggests metered households use 10–15 per cent less than those without
water meters (EA, 2009d), though there was a 2 per cent increase in use by both
types from 2000–01 to 2005–06.

For new housing, the Code for Sustainable Homes (DCLG, 2006b) (see
Section 9.4.6), introduced from 2008 mandatory minimum standards for water
efficiency and set standards for household water use, with a rating of code level

1 or 2 for a designed usage of 120 litres per person per day, rising to code level 5 or 6 for a designed usage of 80 litres per person per day (which is approximately half the current use rate in the Thames region.) The UK-GBC campaign for a Code for Sustainable Buildings seeks to take this approach further and include not only non-domestic buildings within a rating process, but also existing buildings, with all buildings be reassessed periodically to drive forward the refurbishment of existing buildings (UK-GBC, 2009).

Spatial planning policies to improve the water efficiency of buildings are beginning to be seen at regional and local level. Encouraging change towards water efficient buildings is an element of core strategy YH2 (Climate Change and Resource Use) of the Yorkshire and Humber Plan (see Chapter 8, Box 8.11). Among the Yorkshire and Humber Environment policies, ENV2 Water Resources calls for the safeguarding of water resources in the region and the encouragement of water efficiency, noting in particular the need to avoid depleting a sandstone aquifer. A target is set for all new publicly funded housing to meet at least level 3 of the Code for Sustainable Homes (i.e. daily per person use of not more than 105 litres). In line with the ENV2 policy, developers 'should consider development in terms of water resource availability; provide adequate design and mitigation measures (e.g. water efficiency, rainwater harvesting) as appropriate, especially in water-sensitive areas, in line with best practice (e.g. BREEAM, Sustainable Drainage Systems, Code for Sustainable Homes)' (GOYH, 2008, p. 97). As a district level example, South Norfolk's Supplementary Planning document on the Norwich Research Park calls for reduction of water use and water efficiency as part of the guiding principle of sustainability for the development. SUDS (see Chapter 11.4.2), rainwater harvesting and greywater recycling are some of the ways mentioned to meet the design principles for the Park, but no volume targets were set.

Water neutrality, that is to say where development does not lead to an increase in total water demand, is an approach that responds to both the sustainable development and the climate change agendas. In the UK the concept dates from a one-year feasibility study initiated in November 2006 in London's Thames Gateway area, which is projected to expand its population to a total of 1.45 million people, outlined in Box 10.7. The feasibility study modelled a number of pathway scenarios that move towards and potentially achieve water neutrality. Preliminary findings reported by Every and Styles (2007) indicate that achieving water neutrality in the Gateway may be technically feasible, and moreover 'that existing residents may be receptive to the goal of greater water efficiency' (p. 585).

Water neutrality is discussed in the draft Planning Policy statement on eco-towns (DCLG, 2008c) which acknowledges that this is a challenging aim,

> only likely to be achieved through a combination of measures. A key component is to make the new development water efficient, through utilising the most water efficient products and where appropriate looking at water reuse options. (p. 18)

Box 10.7 Case study: Towards water neutrality in the Thames Gateway

The Thames Gateway is billed as Europe's largest regeneration project and a major growth area, with 160,000 new homes planned for development between 2001 and 2016.

Like much of the south-east, with low rainfall and high water demand, the Gateway area is identified as one of 'serious' water stress, and water supply options are restricted to ensure there are no serious cost and environmental implications. The Environment Agency, in partnership with DCLG and Defra, led a study to explore the feasibility of achieving water neutrality, leaving water in the environment for wildlife and for people to enjoy. Water neutrality in the area would be achieved: *if the total water used after new development was equal to or less than total water use in the Thames Gateway before the development* (in the baseline year of 2005/06: 521 million litres per day). Assuming business-as-usual water use rates, and the building programme (homes and other development) completed, by 2016 water demand would increase by 8% to 563 million litres per day. Seven scenarios of change were assessed: non-households accounted for a third of the water saved in each neutrality scenario and existing households accounted for between 23 and 47 per cent of total water saved. The way to reach water neutrality was seen as a combination of:

- making new developments much more water-efficient;
- 'offsetting' new demand by retrofitting existing homes and other buildings with more efficient devices and appliances;
- expanding metering and introducing innovative tariffs for water use to encourage water more efficient use.

With regards to costs:

- The total costs for households range from £127 million to £181 million, which accounts for around two-thirds of the water savings needed to achieve neutrality. The range of costs for new homes is £275 to £765, averaged across all homes built in the Gateway between 2005 and 2016.
- The cost for existing homes (to pay for retrofitting, fitting a meter and applying tariffs where applicable) is £135 to £154 per house, with costs averaged across all existing households in the Gateway in 2005–06.

(These represent one-off capital costs for all measures except metering and tariffs, where replacement costs and operational costs are included. Costs for the non-household sector are stated to be 'far less certain'.)

The study suggests that it is technically possible to achieve water neutrality, even with the forecast new development, population growth and increases in water demand. This study is seen by its commissioning partners as demonstrating how growth and sustainable management of water resources can go hand in hand. Further work by the Environment Agency with Communities and Local Government (DCLG), Defra, Ofwat and water companies will explore the necessary costs and delivery mechanisms in more detail.

Source: adapted from EA, Defra and DCLG, 2007

Modification of existing built stock towards water neutrality is recognized as more difficult. Other measures to be taken would need to be explored in partnership with the water companies and might include the extent of metering, variable tariffs to encourage water efficiency, retrofitting existing buildings with water efficient products and reducing demand from 'non-households' (DCLG, 2008d). Waterwise, a water industry lobbying group, has pointed out in a response on the UK eco-towns programme that water neutrality – particularly in areas of water stress – does not redress the balance of water use and could possibly make it more difficult to reduce net extractions in the future. Waterwise suggests that instead efforts should go into improving water resources. The Environment Agency has provided further information on water neutrality (EA, 2009h; 2009i). Its guidance is aimed at local authorities, developers and others, and sets out how to calculate the 'water neutrality gap' for developments. Potential sources of funding for action on water neutrality include the *Decent Homes* scheme, *New Growth Point* schemes and the proposed *Community Infrastructure Levy* under the Planning Act 2008. The London Climate Change Partnership (LCCP, 2009) explores potential economic incentives schemes for retrofitting London's housing stock for climate change, to cover water, green roofs and flood-risk management.

10.4.5 Scenarios of change and planning for new resource developments

Storing water during the winter months for use in dry periods remains a favoured alternative for water companies, despite high investment costs. Recently new reservoirs have been considered at a number of sites, e.g. in south west Oxfordshire (Abingdon) and Broad Oak, Kent for south-east England, and also near Clitheroe, Lancashire, to supply the North West. Alternatively, the dam height of existing reservoirs may be raised to increase their storage capacity (e.g. at Bewl and at Abberton, also for the south-east). Obstacles to be overcome include obtaining water abstraction licences and planning permissions, as well as funding. Both new reservoirs and extensions mean significant impacts as land is submerged and major temporary disruption is caused. As many other factors interact to affect water demand (e.g. population growth, greater efficiency of use and changes in demand as industrial sectors expand and decline) there needs to be a robust examination of the costs and benefits of any investment from the spatial planning as well as the financial viewpoint. Thames Water, which based its proposal for the Upper Thames reservoir upon the UKCIP02 scenarios, is in 2010 reassessing the implications of the UKCP09 projections, given that from 2025 the company believes that demand management will be insufficient to balance demand and supply as well as 'the wider uncertainties' (Thames Water, 2009b). A public inquiry into the scheme is to be held in 2010 (see Section 14.2.2). Alternatives to new storage, such as desalination plants, leakage control and wastewater recycling might be the preferred options under the least-cost approach to decision-making. Following a previous refusal of permission (by Newnham Borough, at the direction of the then mayor of London on grounds of high energy use and emissions) Thames Water was in 2008 given planning permission for a desalination plant at Beckton, East London. From spring 2010 the plant will produce around 140 million litres of water a day, sufficient for 400,000 people (Owen, 2008).

The fragmentation of water supply companies' supply areas in South East England is an obstacle to efficient water resources management, but the group Water Resources in the South East has brought together the water companies, the EA, the regional assembly (SEERA) and Ofwat and has completed modelling work for SEERA as part of the development of the draft South East Plan, in an attempt at better coordination of regional water resources planning.

10.5 Conclusions: water resources

Climate change is likely to have many diverse direct and indirect impacts upon water resources, and these impacts may 'cascade' to create secondary impacts – e.g. for biodiversity and rural tourism. There is a need for adaptation measures to 'embed' water-related adaptation into the wider national/European policy field, and integrate approaches across sectors. This means that objectives must coincide, i.e. policy fields should not pull away from each other, with one advocating (say) development in an area, another advocating reduced vulnerability to climate change. Consequently, policies also need to coincide across levels (national, regional, sectoral, local); this will require the sharing of not only objectives but also time horizons and indicators. Partnerships and the involvement of civil society and business sector organizations (e.g. the UK-Green Building Council) are seen as important to this process. Transboundary issues on water resources need to be addressed at the European or international level with treaties and agreements monitored for impacts and changing needs.

'No regrets' approaches may include, for example, designating washlands for water storage and infiltration thus supporting biodiversity and enhancing blue and green infrastructure (see Chapter 9). Other priorities (EEA Briefing 01, 2007a) are to reduce the vulnerabilities of people and societies 'to hydro-meteorological trends, increased climate variability, and extreme events'. Ecosystems – and particularly in this connection, freshwater, wetlands, peatlands and forests, all of which are important in local hydrological cycles – must be protected and where necessary restored so that they can continue to provide their specific services, such as the collecting, storing and cleansing of water.

While additional storage capacity (reservoirs) or infrastructure and institutions to share water across regions may help increase availability, the reduction of demand for water is an important priority identified by EEA Briefing 01 (2007a). Planning-related strategies here may include sharing losses, research into uncertainties and adaptive measures, and technological development as well as regulatory and institutional changes, such as higher water efficiency standards for appliances or homes. EEA Briefing 01 suggests that at the time of publication (2007) measures related to the management of water scarcity and drought 'do not yet seem to be widespread', even though these impacts were recognized in national vulnerability assessments.

In the past water (resources and supply) has not been a significant factor in UK planning: drought has led to street stand pipes only rarely. But the spatial planning perspective, a significant drought in 1996 (particularly in Yorkshire) and climate change projections, have changed this to give greater awareness of the need to integrate water planning with planning for growth. Barriers to better policy integration include the non-coincidence of groundwater, catchment and administrative boundaries, the absence (until recently) of any requirement to consider the water resources issues, the privatized status of the water industry and the industry's 'duty to supply' water, as well as the profit motive which may have encouraged maximizing the 'sale' of water (and acquisition of assets like reservoirs) above wise use. With the legislative change and new powers and duties under the WFD and the Water Act of 2003, greater integration is likely to follow. Kidd and Shaw (2007) have suggested that an integrated process of water resources planning and spatial planning, rather than parallel processes, would improve aspects such as political support, democratic accountability, independent review, community recognition and implementation authority for water resources planning, as it is brought into line with standard spatial planning practice. However, the risk of extended plan preparation timescales is recognized. As also noted in Chapter 11, institutions and responsibilities associated with water (both as resource and as flood risk) are complex and interacting, as are the impacts upon water and water bodies of both climate change and measures aimed at mitigation and adaptation. The need for closer integration of planning for water and spatial planning is now fully recognized, though routes to achieve this are still to be developed. This is a significant area for research and for implementation of measures.

11 Flood risk, and marine and coastal areas

··

Planning for climate change

11.1 Introduction

As a most vital resource, water is particularly affected by climate change impacts; the risk of both flooding and drought is increased by climate change, although other changes (demographic, development) also affect flood risk, such as the increased 'sealing' of soil under impermeable surfaces. While the institutional basis of drainage and flood management is long established, it has been fragmented; institutional reform is now aiming to simplify flood management. Research undertaken under the Foresight Future Flooding Project (Evans *et al.*, 2004, see also Section 6.6), in response to flood events, used a scenarios-based approach to projecting the severity and likelihood of UK flood events during the twenty-first century under changing climates. This research provided much of the evidence base for the new government strategy for flood-risk management in England, *Making Space for Water* (Defra, 2005, see also Section 11.3.3 below and Table 11.2). Awareness of climate change has accelerated action to move towards better management of flood risk, and its integration with spatial planning. Flooding types are distinguished as fluvial (from rivers), from land (surface-water run-off or pluvial flooding), from water bodies including groundwater and from the sea. The DCLG (2006c, p. 18) states that it is difficult to define precisely what constitutes a flood-risk area, 'as floods with similar probability may result from different combinations of weather, sources, rainfall patterns, local topography and patterns of development'.

A series of European Directives (subsequently transposed into national legislations) are relevant to these major issues, particularly the Water Framework Directive 2000/60/EC (CEC, 2000b) and the Floods Directive 2007/60/EC (CEC, 2007a), together with others dealing with pollution. Coastal zone management and marine spatial planning are concepts under development which will also play an important role in responses to climate change – a Marine Strategy Framework Directive was adopted in 2008 to protect the marine environment (see Section 11.6).

11.2 Flood risk and climate change

11.2.1 Flooding in the EU and UK

Since 1990, 259 major river floods have been reported in Europe, and 64 per cent of these have occurred since 2000. Catastrophic floods along the Danube and Elbe rivers in summer 2002 were followed by further severe floods in 2005. There was very unusual and significant flooding in central England in the summer of 2007 following sustained periods of 'unprecedented' heavy rain, with the 'total cumulative rainfall in May, June and July 2007 averaging 395.1 mm across England and Wales' (Pitt, 2008, p. 3). In other words, more than twice the normal rainfall fell on saturated ground during this period. Better reporting and land use changes have contributed to increased numbers of reported floods. In part the increased social and economic loss is the result of greater encroachment of buildings and infrastructure onto floodplains, but also the value of property and assets held in any buildings affected by flood is likely now to be greater than in the past. These episodes of intense rainfall are consistent with climate change projections, although it is more difficult to establish directly that impacts of climate change, such as those set out in Table 11.1, are contributing to increased flood frequency. Since 1998 floods in Europe have caused some 700 deaths, while around 500,000 people have been displaced – sometimes for periods of over a year, and insured economic losses have risen to over € 25 billion (EEA, 2005, p. 2). In the Netherlands, possible damage due to flooding in a country in which over half the population lives below mean sea level, is estimated to vary between € 300 and € 800 billion (Kortenhaus, 2009). (At the world scale, according to Kortenhaus, 15 of the 20 megacities are located at the coast and are 'more or less directly subject to floods'.)

The EEA publication *Impacts of Europe's changing climate – 2008 indicator-based assessment* (EEA, 2008b) has noted that:

- Although a significant trend in extreme river flows has not yet been observed, twice as many river flow maxima occurred in Europe between 1981 and 2000 as between 1961 and 1980.
- Nevertheless, global warming is projected to intensify the hydrological cycle, as a warmer atmosphere can hold more moisture, and may increase the occurrence and frequency of flood events in large parts of Europe, although estimates of changes in flood frequency and magnitude remain highly uncertain.
- Projections suggest that warming will result in less snow accumulation during winter and therefore a lower risk of early spring flooding.

While flooding over river floodplains is a natural (and beneficial) seasonal event in a lightly populated valley, dense and growing settlement along many European rivers means that flooding has severe economic and social consequences. Evans *et al.* (2004) estimate that, by the 2080s and under different emissions scenarios, the number of people in the UK at high risk of a 1 in 75 year flood will be between 2.3 million under the low emissions Local Stewardship scenario, to 3.6 million under the high emissions National Enterprise scenario. This compares with 1.6 million at the same level of risk in 2002 (Evans *et al.*, 2006, p. 54). In terms of their economic value, flood and coastal defence work in England and Wales has been credited with preventing annual average damages of approximately € 4 billion, while the value of the assets at risk of river and coastal flooding are assessed as amounting to over € 300 billion. Box 11.1 presents statistics on flood risk in England and Wales.

Box 11.1 Flood risk in England and Wales

England
Regions: Greater London has the highest number of people across the three levels of risk (1.2 million are in low, moderate or high risk flood plain areas), but of these, 84 per cent of properties are in the 'low' category. Many properties in the Yorkshire and Humber region are at high or moderate risk (about 240,000) whilst in SE England these two categories account for approximately 260,000 properties. (The highest number of properties in the 'high' risk category is in the South East Region: about 112,000 properties).

Properties: Around 5.2 million properties in England, or one in six properties, are at risk of flooding; 2.4 million properties are at risk of flooding from rivers and the sea. Preliminary assessment of surface water flood risk also suggests that one million of these are also at risk of surface water flooding with a further 2.8 million properties susceptible to surface water flooding alone. The expected annual damages to residential and non-residential properties in England at risk of flooding from rivers and the sea is estimated at more than £1 billion.

Infrastructure: Over 55% of water and sewage pumping stations/treatment works are in flood-risk areas, with 34% at significant risk; 14% of electricity infrastructure, 2,358 schools and 2,363 doctors' surgeries in England are in flood-risk areas, together with 4,000 km of roads and 2,500 km of railway.

Cost of risk reduction: Improvement and maintenance of 25,400 miles of flood defences is the EA's major budget item: £427 million in 2008–09. 'Most' new flood defence schemes being built reduce expected damage by £8 for every £1 spent. A budget increase to £1.04 billion annually by 2035 (before inflation) is sought – to give a total spend of £320 billion over 25 years.

Source: adapted from EA, 2009c

Wales
Properties: About one in six Welsh buildings are at risk of flooding. More than 357,000 people live in 220,000 properties that are at risk of flooding from rivers or the sea. Nearly half (97,000) are also at risk of surface water flooding. A further

---

137,000 properties are at risk of surface water flooding alone. Expected annual damages to residential and non-residential properties in Wales at risk of flooding from rivers and the sea is estimated at about £200 million. The 2004 Foresight Future Flooding study (Evans *et al.*, 2004) suggested that the annual economic damages in Wales will rise from £70 million in 2004 to £1,235 million in the 2080s under the 'most likely' scenario.

Infrastructure: Over 80% of water and sewage pumping stations/treatment works are in flood-risk areas, with 67% at significant risk. Approximately 22% of all electricity infrastructure sites are at flood risk, as are nearly 800 police, fire and ambulance stations, and about 11% of main roads and 33% of railways.

Source: adapted from EA Wales, 2009

Figure 11.1 presents mapping derived from the Foresight Future Flooding research (Evans *et al.*, 2006), demonstrating projected flood risk increases across England and Wales, under one of the Foresight futures, based on UKCIP work (see Section 6.6.1 for more discussion of these scenarios). These maps suggest a countrywide increase in flood risk under a scenario of largely unrestrained use of fossil fuels.

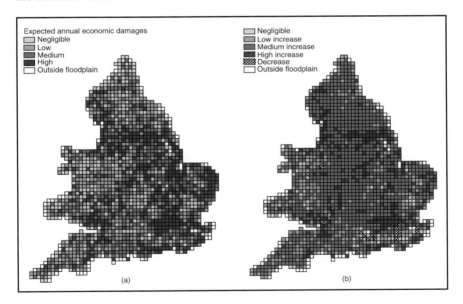

Figure 11.1

Schematic maps showing: (a) annual average economic damage, 2002; and (b) increase in baseline annual average economic change 'world markets' scenario, 2080s compared with 2002

Source: Evans *et al.*, 2004, fig. 4.10

11.2.2 Impacts of climate change upon flood risk

Many of the expected changes to climates in Europe and elsewhere are concerned with precipitation – its intensity, frequency and distribution through the year as well as total amount. In some regions (e.g. South East England), although total annual amount is not expected to greatly change as a result of climate change, a shift in distribution from summer to increased winter rainfall can increase flooding risk, as can an increase in rainfall intensity. Impacts of changes in climate indicators for flood risk and drainage are summarized in Table 11.1.

11.3 Integrating spatial planning and flood-risk planning

11.3.1 EU Floods Directive

Although there is reference to floods in the Water Framework Directive (CEC, 2000b, discussed in Section 10.3.1), the planning and management of flood risk are not its prime purpose. The EU Floods Directive of 2007 (Directive 2007/60/EC on the assessment and management of flood risks, CEC 2007a) fills this role and strengthens policy responses to the flood risk aspects of integrated land and water planning. The Directive aims to help member states prevent and limit floods and their damaging effects on human health, the environment, infrastructure and property. In England and Wales this Directive has now been transposed in national legislation as the Flood and Water Management Act 2010 (HMG, 2010c). Acknowledging the impact of climate change and that the WFD does not specifically address climate change, the Floods Directive calls for assessment and mapping of flood risk along all water courses and coastlines. The Floods Directive requires various management tools to be prepared:

- Preliminary flood-risk assessments are to be made (and completed by year end, 2011).
- Flood hazard and flood-risk maps are to be drawn up by 2013, using a set of probability scenarios (low, medium and high probability floods) and indicating the extent, depth and other details of such floods as well as their consequences (inhabitants potentially affected, economic activities affected, installations likely to cause pollution, etc.).
- Flood-risk management plans (FRMPs) focused on prevention, protection and preparedness are to be complete by 2015. These are to take into account relevant matters such as costs and benefits, conveyance routes and washlands, and the information of the flood maps.

In accordance with the Floods Directive, people and assets at risk are to be assessed, and adequate and coordinated measures are to be taken. These may include the use of flood retention washlands and sustainable drainage systems

Table 11.1 Impacts of climate change for flood risk and drainage and responses

Type of change	Impacts for flood risk and drainage, actions required
Greater % of annual precipitation in winter	Risk of overwhelming of drainage systems, especially where hard (impermeable) surfaces area has increased. Increased risk of river flooding.
Faster snowmelt	Less predictable and higher peak flows in rivers. Risk of overwhelming of drainage systems, especially where hard surfaces area has increased.
Rainfall more intense	Higher peak flows in rivers and shorter time to peak (need to implement flood prevention faster).
Greater % of rain falls in intense episodes	Risk of overloading drainage systems, especially where area of hard surfaces has increased. Increased erosion of bare (unprotected) surfaces and risk of landslip. Need for flood protection. Assess risks and prevent impacts on dams. Need to increase drainage capacity and more frequent maintenance of schemes needed.
Higher summer temperatures	Higher risk of thunderstorms and flash flooding – enhance drainage systems.
Less predictable (more erratic) weather patterns	Need to increased drainage capacity – investment costs. Increased investment costs, for flood protection infrastructure.
Milder winters	Possibility of overwhelmed drainage systems where precipitation previously fell predominantly as snow. If less precipitation is 'stored' as lying snow, more risk of winter flooding.

(SUDS) (see 11.3.3 and 11.4.2). Rights of access to information on risk, and a voice in the planning process, are also reinforced by the Directive. Provision is made for transboundary river basins, and those shared with non-EU countries: no measures are to be taken which might increase flood risk for any other parties. Flood-risk management plans (FRMPs) are to be periodically reviewed and updated, taking into account the impacts of climate change upon the occurrence of floods. It is a requirement that work under the Floods Directive must be coordinated with that for the Water Framework Directive (CEC, 2000b, Article 9).

11.3.2 UK legislation and planning policy: flood risk

Table 11.2 lists UK legislation and planning policy relevant to flood risk and management, with the aims of the policy and the ways in which it links to spatial planning.

Table 11.2 UK legislation and planning policy: flood risk

Legislation or strategy	Aim	Spatial planning relevance
UK Flood and Water Management Act (Transposing EU 2007/60/EC)	To reform legislation to give a simpler, more effective regime for flood management.	Local Authorities (LAs) given more powers to manage surface water SUDS; national standards, approval system, also, adoption of SUDS by LAs. Sewer connection: rights to connect surface water to sewers removed.
Making space for water (Defra, 2005a)	To firmly embed the concept of sustainable development in all flood-risk management and coastal erosion decisions and operations.	Surface Water Management Plans Catchment flood management plans

Planning policy statements relevant to flood risk (England)

Statement/guidance	Aim	Flood risk relevance
PPS25 Development and flood risk (2006)	To ensure that flood risk is taken into account at all stages in the planning process to avoid inappropriate development in areas at risk of flooding, and to direct development away from areas of highest risk.	Establishes flood-risk assessment. Where new development is, exceptionally, necessary in areas unsuitable for development, policy aims to make it safe, without increasing flood risk elsewhere, and, where possible, reducing flood risk overall.
PPG20 Coastal Planning (1992)	To reconcile development and other pressures at the coast.	Discusses measures to protect, conserve and, where appropriate, improve the landscape, environmental quality, wildlife habitats and recreational opportunities of the coast.
Supplement to Planning Policy Statement 1 Planning and Climate Change	To contribute to the delivery of sustainable development, providing a full and appropriate response on climate change.	Regional planning bodies (RPBs) and Local planning authorities (LPAs) should take account of known flood risk and take a precautionary approach to increases in risk that could arise as a result of likely changes to the climate. (p. 15) Also, LPAs should expect new development to recognize 'opportunities for flood storage'. (p. 20)

(continued)

Statement/guidance	Aim
Revision of PPS25	Following consultation on proposed amendments clarifying aspects of the spatial planning policy on development and flood risk, revision published as DCLG 2010d. These amendments affect policy on essential infrastructure, including water and sewage treatment works, emergency services facilities, bulk storage facilities, wind turbines and the identification of functional flood plains.
PPS 25 Supplement Development and Coastal change	The new PPS25 supplement emphasizes the importance of 'understanding of coastal change over time' and preventing 'new development from being put at risk from coastal change' by avoiding inappropriate development in vulnerable areas and directing development away from such areas (DCLG 2010b). Risk to development which must be located in coastal areas is to be 'managed over its planned lifetime', and by so doing ensure the long-term sustainability of coastal areas.

It is intended that the Flood and Water Management Act of 2010 (HMG, 2010c) will improve security and sustainability, clarify responsibilities, encourage more sustainable forms of drainage in new developments, and make it easier to resolve misconnections to sewers.

11.3.3 Shifting flood-risk policy: UK and Netherlands

UK/England

A significant shift in UK flood-related policy occurred in the mid-2000s. Defra's *Making Space for Water* strategy of 2005 was in part a response to greater awareness of climate change risks and an increase in serious flooding events, as well as the new focus of policy on sustainable development, but it also built on a similar shift of policy in the Netherlands. The Foresight Future Flooding report (Evans *et al.*, 2004), looking at flood and coastal defence, pointed to considerable increases in risk unless there was policy change, and the need for a broadly based response. *Making Space for Water* introduced a 'more holistic approach' to ensure adaptability to climate change is incorporated in all flood and coastal erosion management decisions. A whole-catchment and whole-shoreline approach, consistent with the WFD, would be adopted, involving stakeholders at all levels of risk management. The 2009 national assessment of flood risk, *Flooding in England* (EA, 2009c), clearly states the consequences of this policy shift:

> Flooding is a part of nature. It is neither technically feasible nor economically affordable to prevent all properties from flooding. The Environment Agency's aim is to reduce flood risk and minimize the harm caused by flooding. (p. 5)

The Agency uses a risk-based approach to floods. Moreover, to increase the possible range of implementation responses to flood and coastal erosion risk, the use of rural wetlands and washlands and managed realignment of coasts and rivers are promoted as routes to more sustainable forms of development (Defra, 2005). Research into the possible contribution to managing flood risk of rural land management techniques such as cultivation methods and creating woodlands has also been carried out (Read *et al.*, 2009).

With respect to development control and spatial planning, the Environment Agency (2009b) acknowledges that 'locating property outside the flood plain is a prime way to reduce flood risk' (p. 5). Where this is not always a practical approach, areas of lowest risk should be chosen. Local planning authorities must consult the Agency on planning applications 'where the proposed development is at risk from flooding or is likely to increase the risk of flooding elsewhere' (p. 5).

In England, Planning Policy Statement 25 (PPS25) was published in 2006 by the DCLG to replace the previous (2001) guidance and specifically respond to the increased awareness of flood risk resulting from climate change. The key aim of this PPS was 'to ensure that flood risk is taken into account at all stages in the planning process to avoid inappropriate development in areas at risk of flooding, and to direct development away from areas at highest risk' (DCLG, 2006c, p. 2) – a sequential test and an exception test are outlined to assist with this. PPS25 calls for a precautionary and partnership-based approach. This is to be achieved by a process of Regional Flood Risk Appraisal (RFRA) and the management and reduction of risk. Partners include the Environment Agency, other operators and other stakeholders (such as Internal Drainage Boards, British Waterways, etc.), and planning authorities. The responsibilities of the partners are set out in PPS25. Broad principles to guide the preparation of planning strategies for flood risk relate to the consideration of flood risk in the Regional Spatial Strategies prepared by Regional Planning Bodies. This consideration is to be consistent with RFRAs and Strategic Flood Risk Assessments (SFRAs) as well as other plans and appraisals including the WFD plans and SMPs. Policies for the allocation of sites and control of development in ways that avoid flood risk are to be included within Local Development Documents. The sequential test is essentially is a sieving process, preferentially allocating development sites into areas of lowest risk (see Box 11.3 on SFRA). Moreover, consistency is required between the levels of the planning hierarchy so that local area strategies support government objectives for development and flood risk, at the same time as being 'integrated effectively with other strategies of material significance, such as Regional Economic Strategies' (DCLG, 2006c, p. 4). This is to be achieved via a sustainability appraisal process – see Chapter 7 and also Section 11.4.3. PPS25 also specifically refers to those cases where climate change is expected to increase flood risk to the extent that some existing development may not be sustainable in the long term. In such cases, the local planning authority is to consider whether opportunities exist – when preparing LDFs – to relocate development to more sustainable locations at lower flood risk (DCLG, 2006c). Carter *et al.* (2009) have reviewed examples of sustainability appraisal of regional spatial plans with respect to flooding issues and recommend, for example, a tiered hierarchy of assessment procedures and a 'dedicated [Sustainability Assessment] objective tied to flooding' (see below, this section). Recommendation 18 of the Pitt Review concluded that surface water management plans should provide the basis for managing local flood risk (Pitt, 2008, p. 90).

Local planning agencies must now consult the EA on planning applications in flood-risk areas: figures for 2007–08 suggest that, in the main, EA advice is accepted, and that 'where the Agency has objected on flood-risk grounds, fewer than 4% have gone ahead' (EA, 2009j). The Agency is objecting on flood-risk grounds to an increasing number of planning applications (4,750 in 2006–07 rising to 6,232 in 2007–08) (EA, 2009j). In the case of the sixteen major developments given planning permission against EA advice (2006–08), six were wholly in areas of the highest flood risk. The Town and Country Planning (Flooding) (England) Direction, 2007, requires the LPA to notify the Secretary of State of such a proposal so that the application's general compliance with the policies in PPS25 may be checked. The Agency sees this provision (the Flooding Call-in Direction) to be successful, but highlighted a continuing need for improvement in site-specific flood-risk assessments that accompany planning applications.

The consultation on proposed amendments to PPS25 clarified aspects of the spatial planning policy on development and flood risk, in response to the findings of the Pitt Review. These amendments would change the identification of the 'functional floodplain' and affect the application of the policy to essential infrastructure. Functional floodplain is land where water 'has to flow or be stored in times of flood' (DCLG, 2009e, p. 8) and is identified as 'land which would flood with an annual probability of 1 in 20 (5%) or greater in any year'. In future, it was proposed, the delineation should start with this definition, but also take into account local circumstances. Additionally, the consultation on PPS25 (DCLG, 2009e) proposed certain changes to the allocation of critical utility infrastructure (e.g. sewage treatment works, electricity substations, police, ambulance and fire stations, and transport hubs) within the vulnerability classification system (which uses the classes: 'less vulnerable', 'more vulnerable', 'highly vulnerable', as well as specific classes for 'essential infrastructure' and 'water-compatible development'). For example, wind energy infrastructure becomes 'essential infrastructure', as do water treatment and sewage plants. These changes have been published as DCLG, 2010d.

In addition, a Coastal Supplement to PPS25 was proposed by the DCLG (DCLG, 2010b), coinciding with a review by Defra of coastal change policy. A PPS25 coastal supplement would propose a planning framework for the continuing economic and social viability of coastal communities in areas of coastal change. The policy would be aimed at balancing economic prosperity and reducing the consequences of coastal change on communities. Planning principles to achieve this would cover the agreed evidence base (to include coastal erosion and projected sea-level rise), climate projections (including storm frequencies and intensities), as well as the avoidance of inappropriate development in areas vulnerable to coastal change. The new PPS25 Supplement emphasizes the importance of 'understanding of coastal change over time' and preventing 'new development from being put at risk from coastal change' by avoiding inappropriate development in vulnerable areas and directing development away from such areas (DCLG 2010b). Risk to development necessarily located in coastal areas is to be 'managed over its planned lifetime', and the long-term sustainability of coastal areas ensured. See also Section 11.6 on spatial planning in the coastal zone.

Netherlands

Chapter 5 has already described the *Make Room for the Climate!* initiative (part of the National Adaptation Strategy in the Netherlands). This acknowledged that 'the increasing threat of flood risk makes our country one of the most vulnerable regions in Europe' (VROM *et al.*, 2007a, p. 3). Within the Netherlands 'embankments protect nine million people and 70% of the Dutch gross national product is earned below sea level' (ten Brinke *et al.*, 2008, p. 93). The *Make Room for the Climate!* approach is an additional strand in Dutch flood prevention measures. We have also (in Chapter 9, Section 9.6.3) examined one response in the reconvening of the Delta Commission, whose comprehensive and authoritative report is being given policy force through the National Water Plan. The National Water Plan proposes a three tier or layer approach: the first is prevention of flooding, but as flooding cannot be entirely ruled out, the second layer is 'to create a sustainable spatial layout of the Netherlands and the third seeks to improve the organisational preparations for a potential flood' (MVenW, 2009, p. 3). The shift in flooding policy outlined above for the UK reflects policy developments in the Netherlands where the Spatial Planning Key Decision (SPKD) '*Room for the River*' (*Ruimte voor de rivier*) was introduced in 2006 (MVenW, 2006). The SPKD has two major policy elements: ensuring that the ecological functions of the water system provide the foundation of spatial planning decisions (using a Water Test, to consider issues of water storage and retention within a plan area) and the proactive designation of areas for the permanent or temporary storage of water (ESPACE Partnership, 2007).

Thus the spatial planning approach is aimed at creating more space for the river and lowering high water levels, by deepening the forelands of the rivers, displacing dikes further inland, lowering groynes in the rivers and enlarging summer riverbeds. The case of the Rotterdam Water Plan 2 is briefly described in Box 11.2. Referring back to the four categories of integration of water and spatial planning distinguished by Woltjer and Al (2007 – see Table 10.5), planning for water and flood risk in Rotterdam might be said to fall into the *New water culture* category, where water has become 'a source of social coherence and participation', helping to define the city. Aspects of planning for Rotterdam are also discussed in Chapters 8 and 9.

Box 11.2 Case study: Water Plan 2 Rotterdam

This plan sets out the objectives of the City of Rotterdam and the water boards, updating the current plan in view of ongoing major development, new knowledge and climate change. The city needs not only to cope with climate change but also to develop as an attractive 'water city', but it is threatened by 'greater quantities of water [coming] from the sea, the rivers, the air and the ground'. The time horizon of Rotterdam's City Plan is 2030.

The three themes of the Water Plan 2 are water storage, stringent water quality standards (under the WFD) and flood protection. It is estimated that the current need for storage already surpasses the capacity by some 600,000 m³, but in a dense and ancient built up area, the estimated additional 80 ha of flood storage area is not easily found. Water Plan 2 states:

> Perhaps the most important decision concerns the question as to how the city's appeal can further be enhanced as a place to live, work, study and spend leisure time, while at the same time solving the water management issues. Traditional solutions are inadequate. In the city centre and the old neighbourhoods, for example, it isn't possible to tackle the problems of water storage by digging extra facilities. The costs are exorbitant and existing buildings can't simply be demolished. Innovations such as green roofs, water plazas and alternative forms of water storage are, therefore, essential for the further development of the city. (p. 7)

The Plan attempts to study these impacts on Rotterdam, and to explore how available approaches for coping with the extra water can be used to make the city more attractive.

Suggestions are made for four different areas of the city and include improving inner city travel with water transport, a recreational route along the Maas/Meuse, reinforcement of canals and storage basins in Rotterdam North (residential and commercial districts), and in Rotterdam South (ports and other urban areas) the reinforcement and extension of the water structure, and the creation of new water networks and links.

Source: adapted from City of Rotterdam, 2007

The Netherlands 'Water Test' is intended to give specific guidance about how to deal with water in spatial plans, as part of a process between spatial planners and the water board. The Water Test requires that every spatial plan have a water paragraph in which the spatial planner answers two questions:

1) Does your plan now or in the future have negative effects on the water system?
2) If yes, how do you (within your plan) compensate for this negative effect?

The usefulness of the Water Test has been investigated as part of the ESPACE project and results showed widespread satisfaction with this mechanism amongst respondents (ESPACE Partnership, 2007).

Significant differences between UK and Netherlands policy and practice on flood risk are noted by ten Brinke *et al.* (2008), who highlight differences such as: the greater role of UK local authorities; the central role of cost/benefit analysis of implementation measures; the use of insurance as an instrument for deterring undesirable development; and stress placed on the responsibility of businesses and the public to undertake their own measures for preventing or limiting flood consequences. These differences, state ten Brinke *et al.*, are largely accounted for by variations in the extent of flood risk: risk is very much more widespread in the Netherlands, so insurance is not an effective measure. The promotion of greater awareness among the UK public, however, and experience acquired by local authorities in the preparation and response phase are seen as a useful pointers to future Netherlands practice. Jonkman *et al.* (2008) have investigated the case of the dike ring area of south Holland – using different flood scenarios they estimate the potential number of fatalities. Given the large area and dense population, a flood here could, without sufficient notice of evacuation, mean hundreds to thousands of fatalities. Jonkman *et al.* clarify that, while the risk level faced by an individual is small, the 'societal risk' of flooding is relatively large in comparison with sectors such as chemicals or aviation. The authors argue that the societal risk of flooding is unacceptable and that an 'acceptable level' of flood risk for the Netherlands needs to be established, as a basis for introducing further risk-reducing measures (p. 1357).

The emphasis on societal safety and environmental (spatial) quality in the Delta Programme and the National Water Plan aims to provide this, although some commentators (such as de Vries and Wolsink, 2009) suggest that it still places too much emphasis on prevention and not enough on resilience to climate change.

11.4 Tools for integration of flood risk into spatial planning

Both Integrated Water Resources Studies and Water Cycle Studies (see Section 10.4.1) seek to address flooding issues by incorporating Strategic Flood Risk Assessments.

11.4.1 Strategic Flood Risk Assessment (SFRA)

SFRAs are required by the EU Floods Directive, UK legislation and PPS25. SFRAs are compiled by all local authorities as part of the LDF process. The purpose of the SFRA is to enable LPAs to fully understand flood risk in their area, from all sources, including surrounding areas in the same catchment. Local Authorities also have the role of being the drainage authority for all ordinary watercourses in their district where there are no Internal Drainage Boards. This is to permit informed decision-making when land use allocations are determined. A range of partners are involved, including water companies and Internal Drainage Boards, where appropriate (see Section 11.4.4). SFRAs contribute to the evidence base of local development documents and also inform Sustainability Appraisals. The role of the Environment Agency here is to advise on technical aspects of flood risk, such as providing data and advising on local proposals for flood management. LPAs must use SFRAs and the results of the Sequential Test (see Box 11.3) to allocate development sites and revise flood and planning policy. They must avoid risk and propose sustainable and long-term solutions – such desirable solutions may include SUDS, and avoid 'urban creep', rather than 'hard' flood defence measures.

First a preliminary ('level 1') SFRA is conducted to establish relationships, review the planning context, gather and analyse data, produce strategic flood-risk maps, GIS deliverables and a technical report and provide suitable guidance to the SFRA partners. Within each of the three flood zones, land should be allocated as shown in Box 11.3.

The key characteristics of the SFRA are therefore its partnership approach and use of all relevant evidence, and the 'living' nature of the assessment (in that it is subject to ongoing update as necessary and that, in addition to text, an SFRA consists of maps including a series of GIS layers, which can be interrogated to assist in decision-making). Following the preliminary desk-based level 1 assessment, a level 2 SFRA involves a more detailed review of flood hazard (probability, depth, flood velocity and rate of onset of flooding) taking into account existing flood-risk management measures such as flood defences. A level 2 study may also be required to give a more detailed assessment of flooding from 'other sources' in development areas. In addition to identifying which areas should not or might be developed, SFRA also identifies existing developed areas at risk of flooding both now and at modified risk under climate change.

11.4.2 Surface Water Management Plans and SUDS

Urban flooding caused by the overwhelming of drainage systems by rainfall is estimated to cost £270 million a year in England and Wales; an estimated 80,000 homes are at risk (POST, 2007). It has been projected that the costs of urban flooding could rise considerably – a very broad range of £1–10 billion each year by the 2080s is hypothesized by the Parliamentary Office of Science and Technology (POST), if no action is taken to reduce the risks (POST, 2007). Surface Water Management Plans (SWMPs) are a response to the Pitt Review and the recommendation that 'local surface water management plans as set out under PPS25 and co-ordinated by local authorities should provide the basis for managing all local flood risk' (Pitt, 2008, p. 90).

Box 11.3 Choosing locations for development under the SFRA

- New development should be directed away from sources of flood risk and towards the area of lowest probability of flooding, as indicated by the SFRA maps, i.e. preferentially to zone 1 land and only to zones 2 (and, eventually zone 3 – 'highest flood risk') if no reasonably available sites are available in zones of lower risk. Within a zone, the areas of lowest risk should be allocated first.
- The flood vulnerability of the development should be matched to the flood risk of the site, e.g. higher vulnerability uses should be located on parts of the site at lowest probability of flooding. The Sequential Test is to be used to demonstrate that there are no reasonably available sites in areas with a lower probability of flooding that would be appropriate to the type of development or land use proposed. PPS25 and indeed the SFRA summarizes the appropriate uses of each zone, as well as FRA requirements and policy aims for each.

Source: adapted from DCLG, 2006c

Documentary evidence from many sources underlies an SFRA, including:

- Strategically important documents including the Regional Flood Risk Appraisal, the Pitt Report and *Making Space for Water* (Defra, 2005).
- Historical flooding information from Environment Agency historic fluvial flood outlines and various datasets from water companies, the councils, the Highways Agency and British Waterways, detailing flooding experienced from 'other sources'.
- Environment Agency Flood Zone maps and detailed flood-risk mapping outputs, including fluvial climate change outputs. Information on flood-risk management infrastructure, including defences and culverts (supported by information from the Councils and the Environment Agency's National Flood and Coastal Defence Database [NFCDD]).
- Existing flood-risk management reports including Catchment Flood Management Plans (CFMPs).
- Environment Agency flood warning and flood watch information.

Source: adapted from Gloucestershire County Council, 2008

Guidance on SWMPs is under development by Defra, and available as a living draft (Defra 2009d). SWMPs are designed to achieve better integrated and cost effective urban drainage management, and are the responsibility of local authorities working with partners (water utilities, the Environment Agency and Internal Drainage Boards); other stakeholders include developers and any property owner vulnerable to flooding. The new guidance is based upon a series of fiteen Integrated Urban Drainage pilots and refers to other sources of good practice and research in surface water management. The four phases of SWMP production are: preparation, risk assessment; options appraisal and action plan implementation.

Appropriate actions for flood management may include the installation of SUDS (Sustainable [Urban] Drainage Systems) to manage increases in flood risk from new development as well as providing water quality and amenity benefits. They are designed to deal with run-off close to where the rain has fallen, to manage potential pollution and to protect water resources from point pollution (i.e. such as accidental spilling or leaking of oil) or from more diffuse sources, such as drainage from a heavily used urban area. By introducing opportunities for infiltration rather than immediate drainage to sewers, SUDS may permit further new development in areas where existing sewerage systems are currently close to full capacity. SUDS options include: green roofs, pervious/permeable pavements, infiltration ponds, soakaways, rainwater harvesting, swales and trenches, and bioretention systems as well as tank-based geocellular storage systems (CIRIA, 2007). (A communications network, known as LANDFoRM has been set up by CIRIA for local authorities, to provide information and training on drainage and flood-risk management.) An example of a SUDS proposal, for Fairleigh Park, Sheffield, is shown in Figure 11.2, where an alternative method of surface water management was needed for a housing scheme in the Manor and Castle area, but also to provide better access and recreation opportunities. Design criteria included attenuations of flows, water quality management, safety, enhancement of biodiversity, integration into the park, aesthetics and manageability. The topography of the 25 ha site has a 20 metre height change; it is described as a retrofit example (Nowell and Bray, 2009).

There has been continuing concern over the actual implementation of SUDS and surface water management. White and Alarcon (2009), for instance, in the case study area of Greater Manchester (comprising ten LAs), argue that, despite the strong policy context for SUDS through PPS25, SWMPs and water cycle strategies, considerable barriers to implementation remain. These relate to the whole development process, with issues still over adoption and maintenance of SUDs, stakeholder perceptions (even if unfounded) of extra costs, as well as difficulties with adjusting design standards. They found lack of coordination and communication between stakeholders was exacerbated by insufficient evidence base, expertise or experience. Nevertheless, they found examples where successful local champions or meeting BREEAM standards had ensured implementation. Some of these issues have been addressed in the Flood and Water Management Act, 2010 (HMG, 2010c) (see Table 11.2).

11.4.3 Sustainability appraisal

Carter, *et al.* (2009) have evaluated the benefits of sustainability appraisal of spatial plans with respect to flooding. They identify systemic and procedural benefits (see Box 11.4). Carter *et al.* (2009) also reviewed the SAs of the nine Regional Spatial Strategies, in 2006, for a set of thirteen criteria covering the treatment of flooding issues within SA reports. They identified a set of barriers to a more effective contribution of SA/SEA to deliver flood-risk management

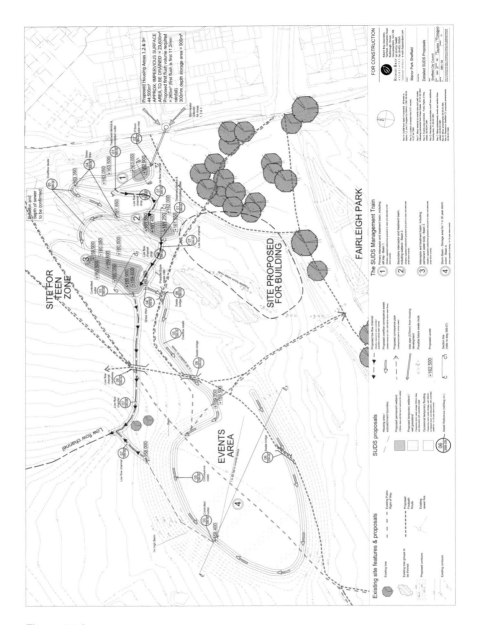

Figure 11.2

Example of a SUDS proposal, Sheffield
Source: With kind permission of R. Nowell, Sheffield City Council

goals, such as failure to give flooding sufficient priority in SA objectives, lack of integration between the SA and the spatial plan/RSS and the fact that such plans do not specify development sites, so flooding impacts cannot be predicted. Carter *et al.* then make recommendations for improving the contribution of spatial plan SAs to flood-risk management.

Box 11.4 Benefits of the SA of spatial plans to flood-risk management

Systemic benefits associated with the application of SA

- SA provides a route to introduce flooding concerns into the planning system. SA can raise awareness and knowledge of flooding and the impact of spatial plans on flooding issues amongst planners and decision-makers.
- SA can encourage planners to take a strategic, holistic, balanced and long-term view of the relationship between spatial plans and flooding issues.
- SA can enable planning policy development to proceed more sustainably where flooding impacts are identified.

Procedural benefits associated with the application of SA

- SA can encourage an objective assessment of the potential flooding impact of spatial plans during the plan-making process.
- SA facilitates the assessment of flood-risk impacts concerning policies not automatically thought to have a relationship with flood risk.
- SA can aid the identification of planning options and development sites that lessen flood risk. Statutory consultation procedures undertaken during SA provide an opportunity to introduce specialist flooding knowledge into the plan-making process.
- Recommendations and mitigation measures proposed during SA can positively influence the content of spatial planning policies in terms of flood risk.
- SA can encourage planning authorities to gather baseline data on flooding issues.

Additional benefits, associated with consultation and participation

- *Awareness raising*: SA can raise awareness of the problem of flood risk among stakeholders engaged in the process.
- *Generating consensus*: Consultation and participation can help to generate debate and consensus on flooding impacts and options for managing impacts via spatial plans.
- *Facilitating joint working*: SA provides an ideal opportunity to encourage joint working.
- *Bringing knowledge and experience into the plan preparation process*: Involving stakeholders during the appraisal of a spatial plan can enhance the availability of data concerning flooding and its potential impacts.

Source: adapted from Carter *et al.*, 2009

11.4.4 Integrating flood control and other benefits

Flood-risk adaptation policy promotes approaches to adapting river manage-ment which bring together urban and rural areas, for example reducing the height of floods by increasing groundwater recharge by infiltration, using diver-sion onto rural land on the one hand and into designed and engineered systems (SUDS) within urban areas on the other hand (see Section 11.4.2). Within both urban and rural areas measures which increase green areas and water storage will have additional benefits for biodiversity – see Section 9.8 and Chapter 12. The Rotterdam case study above (Box 11.2) signposts some potential benefits within a major city. However, within urban areas, some flood management measures for renaturalizing rivers within their flood plains – sometimes referred to as 'blue corridors' – give rise to profound issues of feasibility and equity. We have seen in Chapter 9 some examples of ways to accommodate blue and green infrastructure within urbanized areas but, where the scope for making space for water is limited, allowing an extension to the flood plain might reduce overall flood-risk exposure, but might at the same time (even if well-planned and designed) conflict with plans for regeneration and lead to a reduced flood-defence levels expenditure for some properties. An example of a proposed UK urban blue corridor is for the Lower Derwent, Derby, where an Environment Agency-led scheme proposes constructing new flood defences set further back from the river than the existing defences to allow greater water conveyance through the river corridor (Gosden and Ive, 2009). Up to 120 m wide, the corridor will offer improved flood defence for large parts of the city, but is likely in due course to mean less protection for land within the blue corridor.

Rural storage of flood surges may be increased by additional retention on land and within soils by reducing the efficiency of drainage through field drains and ditches (i.e. impeding drainage, raising weirs) or introducing buffer strips to impede surface run-off. Raising the water level in wetlands may have the additional benefit of carbon sequestration, though methane production may also increase, with detrimental effects. The diversion of river flows onto rural land at times of flood is an approach being introduced in both the Netherlands

---

Box 11.5 Case study: Itchen Valley Living Landscape

A scheme promoted by the Hampshire and Isle of Wight Wildlife (HIWW) Trust provides an example of multiple benefits to be derived from a sustainable approach to flood management. The HIWW Trust aims to restore and reconnect over 66 hec-tares of flood plain, grazing marsh, fen, reedbed and wet woodland at Winnall Moors nature reserve, in addition to key areas along over 20 kilometres of the 300-year-old Itchen Navigation.

The HIWW Trust believes that restoration will also provide crucial ecosystem serv-ices, due to the improved water storage potential of the Itchen's wetland systems.

Moreover, the Trust claims that in addition to carbon sequestration in peat, this will reduce flooding and provide better resources for drinking water. Other benefits include improved health and well-being, recreation-related benefits and better awareness of the landscape's history and value.

A wide range of important species are expected to benefit from the scheme. Re-wetting of meadows will enhance conditions for wading birds such as snipe and rare invertebrates such as Desmoulin's whorl snail. River management, says the HIWW Trust, will improve the habitat for the southern damselfly, water vole and otter. The increased connectivity between river systems will also enable species to migrate within and between floodplains as climatic conditions change.

Source: adapted from The Wildlife Trusts, 2009

and the UK (see Box 11.5 – Itchen Valley scheme) In England and Wales, Water Level Management Plans (WLMPs), which are required for SSSIs and the European sites of nature conservation interest, provide a means whereby water level requirements for flood defence, as well as agriculture and conservation, can be balanced and integrated (Defra, 2004b). Whereas in England and Wales the Environment Agency is the responsible body for 'main river' flooding and drainage issues, along minor watercourses the responsible body is the Internal Drainage Board (IDB). IDBs are supervised by Regional Flood Defence Committees within each of the Environment Agency's eight regions; SEPA is the responsible body in Scotland.

11.5 Conclusions: flood risk

Increased risks of flooding, resulting from both land development and weather conditions associated with climate change, call for far-sighted responses from the spatial planning system in partnership with others, in a chain from awareness to flood management. A great range of measures needs to be undertaken, requiring investment in both the software and hardware of flood prevention and defence. Understanding of options which work with nature, such as SUDS and green roofs, is growing but will not be sufficient fully to address the problem. Large-scale infrastructure – from storage basins to flood walls – will no doubt also remain necessary, and planning for these requires long time scales. NW Europe, including the UK, is a region spared major geological catastrophic events, and flooding is perhaps the most common disaster experienced, one that may increase unless appropriate measures are taken. The consequences of flooding involve great personal, social and economic costs. In planning and working to prevent or minimize flooding it is also possible to improve opportunities for recreation, biodiversity and social welfare, as well as to improve the attractiveness of urban areas.

11.6 Marine and coastal spatial planning

11.6.1 Introduction

At the interface of land and sea, the coastal zone is often the site of intense human use of the environment: industry, settlements and tourism on the land and fisheries, dredging, shipping routes, recreation, etc. on the sea. One-third of the coastline of England and Wales has some form of shoreline protection, i.e. around 1,200 km, mainly in southern and eastern England. Typically, this is in the form of hard engineering structures – from earth embankments to the Thames Barrier (De La Vega-Leinert and Nicholls, 2008, p. 343). Recent estimates of protected assets (from the late 1990s) suggest that in England around 1.5 million people, 1.1 million properties and 400,000 ha of land – in all, a total capital of £137 billion – were protected by tidal/sea defences from sea or tidal flooding and coastal erosion (De La Vega-Leinert and Nicholls, 2008, p. 383). In the past decade there will have been considerable increases in these assets, as populations and investment in coastal areas have continued to increase. A more recent estimate given by the Flood Risk Management Research Consortium for all assets at flood risk (rivers, coastal, etc.) is £238 billion (FRMRC, 2008).

Beyond the coast there is also competing use for marine resources and space: the *EC Roadmap for Maritime Spatial Planning: Achieving Common Principles in the EU* (CEC, 2008a) points to increased activity on Europe's seas, and the need for spatial planning to control and coordinate these uses. Between 3 and 5 per cent of Europe's Gross Domestic Product (GDP) as well as five million jobs, are

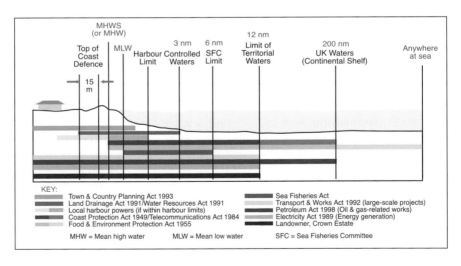

Figure 11.3

Geographical extent of principal marine controls in England and Wales
Source: RCEP, 2004, p. 232

estimated to be generated by maritime industries and services. Some of these are seen as having high growth potential (CEC, 2008a). Figure 11.3 shows the complex and overlapping boundaries of spatial planning systems in the territorial, coastal and marine environments in England and Wales.

Conflicts arise between specific uses and the environment (e.g. tidal barrage and nature conservation areas) and between different uses (e.g. fisheries, oil and minerals extraction, wind energy and shipping). It has been argued (see Huggett *et al.*, 2003) that the marine environment around Europe is severely degraded and that its capacity to recover is under threat – the lack of strategic coastal planning is seen as a root cause of this, leading to consenting authorities making decisions which demonstrate a lack of forward planning and do not coordinate sectoral interests. Huggett *et al.* (2003) argue that other needs to be met include participation and inclusiveness and a plan-led system based on the assessment of environmental capacity. Increasing demand for the natural resources of seas and oceans, argues Maes (2008), has led to loss of biodiversity, habitat depletion and irreversible damage to the marine environment. Peel and Lloyd (2004) point to 'evolving awareness of the marine problem' and an incremental approach to meeting concerns. Coastal planning guidelines and strategic planning framework in Scotland resulted in a view of the relationship between land and sea which was 'essentially land-based' (Peel and Lloyd, 2004), but this has developed towards the 'more sophisticated' approach of Integrated Coastal Zone Management (ICZM) and more recently, marine spatial planning. This latter has been given legislative force in the Marine and Coastal Access Act 2009 (see 11.6.3).

11.6.2 Climate change impacts upon coastal and marine areas

The impacts of climate change in coastal areas are associated with increased flood risk from rivers, in places exacerbated by sea-level rise at the coast. The IPCC estimates that as a global average the sea has risen by about 150 mm during the past century, and sea level will further rise by between 180 and 590 mm in the next 100 years; the EEA estimates that SLR is proceeding at 1.2 – 2.5 mm per year around the Atlantic and North Sea coasts of Europe (sea level is predicted to fall within the Baltic and within the Mediterranean) (EEA, undated, Sea-level rise dataset). Rising sea levels are largely a consequence of the thermal expansion of the ocean, the melting of low latitude glaciers across the world and many other factors. There is the additional complicating impact of isostatic readjustment (the process whereby the Earth's crust regains equilibrium, or 'rebounds' after the retreat of glacial ice).

In the UK, isostatic readjustment means that the southern and eastern regions of England are 'sinking' while northern and Scottish coasts are rising from the sea. Work at the UK Proudman Oceanographic Laboratory indicates a rise in historic mean sea level, ranging from 0.6 mm per year at Aberdeen to

2 mm per year at Sheerness in Kent (Woodworth and Horsburgh, 2008). This reflects a UK sea-level rise of approximately 1 mm per year plus the long-term geological movements. De La Vega-Leinart and Nicholls (2008) have discussed the potential implication of SLR for the UK. They note that of the UK's 12,000 km coastline, Scotland's coast (7,000 km) is the least vulnerable while the coasts of east and south England are the most vulnerable because they are more susceptible coastal types and have a concentration of both populations and assets (London is a 'hotspot of exposure'). Nevertheless, 'Compared to most European countries, Great Britain appears [...] to be better prepared to face and adapt to potential impacts of [climate change] and [accelerated] SLR]' (De La Vega Leinert and Nicholls, 2008, p. 352). At the coast, SLR and high freshwater flows in rivers and estuaries following storms can combine to increase flood risk. Future peak freshwater flows for the Thames, at Kingston for instance, could increase by around 40 per cent by 2080 (Met Office, 2008). Conditions of particular risk occur where high tides coincide with cyclonic conditions (depressions), giving a localized area of higher sea level under the low pressure cell and causing a sea surge. The Thames Estuary 2100 project's 'worst case scenario' (see Chapter 7.6.3) is for a maximum water level of 2.7 m aod (a downwards revision from a previous estimate of 4.2 m) (EA, 2009a, p. 23). In severe conditions flooding may also cause losses to transport and other infrastructures. Storms and flooding hasten coastal erosion, which is occurring along 17 per cent of the UK coastline – along as much as 30 per cent of the coastline of England, 23 per cent of Wales, 20 per cent of Northern Ireland and 12 per cent of Scotland (Marine Climate Change Impacts Partnership, MCCIP, 2008).

Further into the marine zone, the interaction of measures to mitigate climate change via emissions reduction interacts with marine spatial planning where renewable energy systems are installed (wind, wave, tidal, etc.) in order to reduce reliance on fossil fuels. These may lead to further impacts upon coastal zone biodiversity. In these cases there is a particular need for the assessment of the many impacts, appropriately weighing costs and benefits of alternatives. Table 11.3 outlines the range of climate change impacts upon coastal and marine areas. It also indicates how strategies aimed at mitigation of and adaptation to these impacts may further affect coastal and marine resources.

11.6.3 Spatial planning responses in the marine and coastal zones

Legislation and institutions, EU and UK

Since 1996, the European Commission has worked to promote Integrated Coastal Zone Management (ICZM) as an approach to integrated planning and management, in which all policies, sectors and interests are taken into account to achieve sustainable coastal development. An EU Integrated Marine Policy was adopted in 2007 and marine spatial planning for the EU is promoted via

Table 11.3 Climate change impacts in marine areas and coastal zone

Changes	Coastal zone and marine areas
Greater % of annual precipitation in winter Faster snowmelt Rainfall more intense and/or higher % of rainfall in intense episodes	Changes to precipitation and river-flow patterns may change water quantity and quality flowing out through river mouths and estuaries into the sea, at sensitive times, with consequences for: • coastal biodiversity, including fisheries • tourism (availability of water in hot summers) with need for alternative supply (inc. desalination)
Higher summer temperatures	Impacts upon tourism patterns at coast ('Climate change is increasing the frequency of months when conditions are more comfortable for tourists in north-west Europe than in the Mediterranean.' MCCIP, 2008, p. 7) Impacts upon marine/coastal biodiversity, affecting tourism and fisheries Likelihood of establishment of non-native species (often introduced by human intervention) could be increased by climate change (MCCIP, 2009))
More severe (or more frequent) storms	Damage to flood defences, salt contamination of soils and marshes, etc. Impacts on coastal landscape features (including cliffs, beaches, lagoons) with impacts for flood risk and for tourism Risks to coastal transport routes (road, rail)
Milder winters	Impacts upon tourism patterns at coast Impacts upon marine/coastal biodiversity, affecting tourism and fisheries
Sea-level rise and acidification	Increased flood risk or loss of sites: residential and industrial Continuing loss of nature conservation sites ('At least 40–100 ha of saltmarsh is being lost every year' (MCCIP, 2008, p. 5)) Impacts upon coastal landscape features (inc. cliffs, lagoons) Risks to coastal transport routes (road, rail) Changing coastal currents and patterns of sedimentation Impacts upon marine ecosystems, aquaculture, fisheries (and feedback to climate regulation, MCCIP, 2009)
Arctic sea ice	Significant decreases in Arctic summer and winter sea ice in recent decades has affected habitats and ecosystems (MCCIP, 2009)
Mitigation measures	Where renewable energy generation projects are implemented at the coast, these may have impacts for nature conservation areas and wildlife (e.g. tidal barrages, windfarms)
Adaptation measures	Adaptation strategies such as resettlement away from an eroding coast may lead to the loss of biodiversity sites, as may the re-routing of transport to avoid coastal storms or erosion

the Marine Strategy Framework Directive of 2008 (2008/56/EC, CEC 2008b) which is concerned with environmental issues. Marine spatial planning is aimed at the sustainable development of the marine environment, involving holistic management covering the effects of use and development. Table 11.4 lists the relevant EU and UK legislation and planning guidance, its aims and relevance.

Table 11.4 above shows specific coastal and marine legislation; other legislation that applies includes the Water Framework Directive (which also applies in coastal and transitional waters), the SEA and EIA Directives, the Habitats Directive, as well as the Common Fisheries Policy, *inter alia*. The proposal for an ecosystem approach builds on work under the OSPAR Convention of 1992 for the protection of the North East Atlantic (Baltic Marine Environment Protection Commission *et al.*, 2003).

EU Marine Strategy Framework

The EU's Marine Strategy Framework Directive (CEC, 2008b) is intended to protect more effectively the marine environment across Europe. This directive provides the environmental component of the Union's future maritime policy while also having regard to economic and social issues (Annex IV, Clause 9). Several European countries are now implementing marine spatial planning to control activities at the coast or in marine areas including new development (e.g. offshore wind farms, minerals and oil extraction – see also Chapter 7.6.2) plus nature conservation, coastal defence and shoreline management, dredging, shipping and fisheries.

Marine spatial planning is seen as a process which allocates space for specific uses, helps to avoid conflicts between the various users of this environment to improve the management of activities making claims upon resources (including offshore wind and wave energy) (Maes, 2008). Douvere and Ehler (2007), reporting on an international workshop held in Paris in 2006, highlight the importance of marine spatial planning, arguing that it is the component of an overall ecosystem-based management that can influence the location of human activities. They acknowledge that zoning is only one tool of marine spatial planning, sea use management and other tools are also needed, in particular: the early and continuing engagement of stakeholders in a transparent management process, and appropriate monitoring and evaluation. A multidisciplinary approach is needed, it is suggested, to incorporate both the human dimension and the ecosystem approach. Douvere and Ehler argue that marine spatial planning, its implementation tools and benefits need to be focused more closely on finding solutions to problems. Gilliland and Laffoley (2008) have emphasized the importance of marine spatial planning for delivering an ecosystem approach, and discuss elements of the process: time frame, boundaries, objectives and priorities; they also recognize the importance of stakeholder consultation. De La Vega-Leinert and Nicholls (2008) also stress

Table 11.4 EU and UK legislation and planning policy for marine and coastal areas

Legislation or strategy	Aim	Spatial planning relevance
Marine		
Marine Strategy Framework Directive 2008/56/EC	Member states must achieve good marine environmental status by 2020	Proposes an ecosystem approach, and ensuring that pressure from human activities is compatible with good environmental status
Also note: OSPAR Convention (1992) (covering the north-east Atlantic)	To conserve marine ecosystems and safeguard human health by preventing and eliminating pollution; by protecting the marine environment from the adverse effects of human activities	Collaborating with EC on maritime spatial planning
Coastal		
European Strategy for ICZM: Communication from the Commission to the Council and the European Parliament on Integrated Coastal Zone Management: a Strategy for Europe (COM/2000/547), adopted 27 September 2000	Improved management of coastal zones; integrated, participative territorial approach to coastal planning	Directed towards an approach which is 'environmentally and economically sustainable, as well as socially equitable and cohesive'
UK Marine and Coastal Access Act 2009	To set out a framework to manage demands on the marine environment, improve marine conservation and open up public access to English coast	Establishes a new system for marine planning (see note below)
Planning policy statements relevant to marine and coastal planning		
PPG20 Coastal Planning (1992)	To reconcile development and other pressures	Discusses measures to protect, conserve and, where appropriate, improve the landscape, environmental quality, wildlife habitats and recreational opportunities of the coast
Planning policy on coastal change as a supplement to PPS25	To set out a planning framework for the continuing economic and social viability of coastal communities	Consultation (to October, 2009): recognized that climate change is likely to exacerbate erosion and

(continued)

Table 11.4 (*cont.*)

Legislation or strategy	Aim	Spatial planning relevance
Supplement to PPS25 (*cont.*)	(as above)	coastal flooding through projected sea-level rise, together with the potential increase in coastal storms over the next century (UKCP09). New policy is to be developed to assist in managing the impact of coastal erosion and flooding in a sustainable manner, 'ensuring that (. . .) spatial planning policies shape sustainable communities that are resilient to the risks presented by climate change'

Note: The Marine and Coastal Access Act (2009) makes no reference to marine 'spatial' planning, and refers to marine planning throughout, as Defra sees planning as containing a spatial element.

that regional analyses of changes in coastal ecosystem stocks are a further component of marine spatial planning. Douvere and Ehler (2007) point to the EC's recognition of marine spatial planning 'as a core aspect to manage a growing and increasingly competitive maritime economy, while at the same time safeguarding biodiversity' (p. 582).

The EC Roadmap on Maritime Spatial Planning emphasizes that maritime spatial planning can help coastal areas to prepare for climate change impacts such as rising sea levels, floods, altered marine ecosystems and investments in coastal protection (CEC, 2008a, p. 2). Marine spatial planning is promoted as part of a strategy for sustainable growth in the use of both marine and coastal resources. Climate change interactions with marine spatial planning can be expected in the following sectors in estuaries and in offshore areas: renewable fuels (as an option for climate change mitigation), and in connection with carbon storage at sea. Marine spatial planning is also important to protect coral reefs and coldwater reefs; biodiversity issues are discussed in Chapter 12.

UK Marine and Coastal Access Act 2009

In the UK a longstanding campaign orchestrated by environmental protection NGOs including the Marine Conservation Society, the RSPB, WWF and the Wildlife Trusts has sought a new marine legal framework, leading to the Marine and Coastal Access Act 2009. The MCA Act maps the UK marine area and where specific activities may take place, and it introduces a system for licensing marine works and activities together with a mechanism for marine nature conservation. It, moreover, makes provisions with respect to fisheries of all kinds as well as a new enforcement system. Separate but consistent arrangements are being made for Scotland, Wales and Northern Ireland.

A Marine Policy Statement, with short- and long-term objectives for sustainable use of the marine environment, is to be drawn up by Defra for adoption by the end of 2011 to facilitate an integrated approach to marine management, setting the framework for marine plans and licensing decisions. It will need to be consistent with the NPSs for nationally significant infrastructure in England and Wales (see Chapter 5). A series of marine plans will be devised in a second stage, implementing the policy statement in specific areas, informed by evidence about spatial uses and needs in those areas. The Act establishes a Marine Management Organisation (MMO) which will be responsible for marine mapping and also for licensing marine activities. New provisions are also made for marine nature conservation and for fisheries. Climate change is seen as a driver of the Act, which is intended to lead to better decisions in the marine areas affecting climate change mitigation, for example through renewable energy projects.

UK planning policy for coastal areas

PPG20 on Coastal Planning provides guidance for England and Wales (DoE & WO, 1992). It discusses types of coasts, policies for conservation, development flood risk, erosion and land instability, as well as coastal protection and defence. PPG20 also presents policies for developments using coastal locations, including tourism, recreation, minerals extraction, energy generation and waste water and sewage treatment plants. (In Scotland, *NPPG13 Coastal Planning* was published in 1997. It distinguishes between the developed, undeveloped and the isolated coast; it does not refer to climate change.) The Department for Communities and Local Government has recently considered the need to update PPG20 in the light of climate change and the forecast sea-level rise, in view of increased erosion rates and risk of changes to the coastline. PPG20 has been revised and republished as the Development and Coastal Change Supplement to PPS25 (DCLG, 2010b).

With regards to management of coastal activities, strategies were published for each UK administration in 2008, for example the publication: *A Strategy for Promoting an Integrated Approach to the Management of Coastal Areas in England* (Defra, 2008b). Stakeholders in coastal management and planning are indicated in this strategy which strongly advocates partnership working as an essential part of the strategy, for example including the coastal towns working group, and the coastal towns network. Figure 11.4 outlines the policy and strategic direction links relevant to coastal areas.

Over the past decade and in line with European trends, the UK approach to coastal protection has changed from 'construct and defend' to 'managed

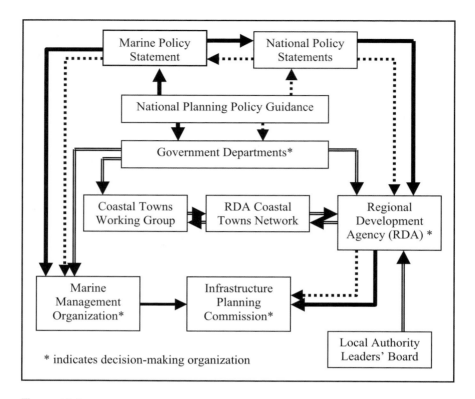

Figure 11.4

Policy and strategic links for coastal areas
Source: based on Defra, 2008b, p. 13

realignment', i.e. leaving low-lying natural coastal features (marshes, salt-marshes, mud and sand flats, etc.) to flood and absorb impacts. This approach is also referred to as 'working with dynamic coastal processes'. The change has been motivated by an awareness of the inevitability of losing land to the sea (in some cases this is reclaimed land) because it is no longer feasible to meet the cost of continued defence maintenance (EA, 2004). Consequences of this change of policy for coastal biodiversity are discussed in Chapter 12. Here we focus on the implications for society, after first summarizing the existing SMP process.

Shoreline Management Plans

Planning approaches to coastal management in the UK have included Shoreline Management Plans (SMPs), addressing sea flooding and coastal erosion. The shoreline of England and Wales is covered by forty-nine SMPs and there are eight for Scotland. The first round of SMPs of the late 1990s is now (2009–10) under review, integrating climate change impacts and responses. The review process consists of scoping, strategic environmental assessment and review of coastal, geomorphologic and estuary processes (under climate change these could be affected by changes in storm tracks, in storm swells, in wave environments, etc.). SMPs are high-level documents which provide a large-scale assessment of the risks associated with coastal processes and present a long-term policy framework to reduce these risks to people and the developed, historic and natural environment in a sustainable manner. They thus constitute an important part of the strategy for flood and coastal erosion risk management. It has been pointed out that SMPs provide guidance but are not legally binding for local authorities. Nevertheless, as 'they are tied to grant aid for sea and coast defence projects, they generally have much more influence than Estuary Management Plans and Coastal Zone Management Plans' (De La Vega-Leinert and Nicholls, 2008, p. 350). SMPs are developed by coastal groups, made up primarily of coastal district authorities and other bodies with coastal defence responsibilities and are overseen by the Environment Agency. An example is given in Box 11.6.

Box 11.6 Case study: SMP review: Poole and Christchurch Bays

Poole and Christchurch Bays (sub-cell 5F of the English coast) cover 190 km from Durlston Head in the west and Hurst Spit to the east, and within the SMP are divided into seven Process Units, subdivided into a total of forty-one Management (or Policy) Units. The SMP aims to balance flooding and erosion risks with natural processes and the consequences of climate change. It will enable planners and regulators to plan for and manage the way that the coast will change by maintaining or improving defences, by enabling the natural processes to play a greater role, by creating new natural habitat or by helping areas that are at risk of flooding at some point in the future to cope with and limit the impact of flooding events.

The SMP review (SMP2) will enable landowners, residents and businesses to know how the coast will be managed by regulators during the next 100 years, so that they can plan ahead and make decisions about investments, homes, development and the management of their resources. The review process will prepare a sustainable policy framework, assessing change along the coast at future points (twenty-five, fifty and 100 years) and identifying risks to the developed, historic and natural environments as the coast changes.

The SMP review will identify one of four shoreline management policies for each Policy Unit:

- No active intervention.
- Hold the existing line.
- Advance the line (building defences to the seaward side).
- Managed realignment – allowing retreat (or advance) of the shoreline with management of that movement.

Shoreline management planning is inevitably conflictual, as significant assets (homes, farms, businesses) may be lost when defences cease to be maintained. The SMP process is one that requires active engagement from the range of stakeholders. Milligan and O'Riordan (2007) have examined the process in East Anglia, where they identified unresolved tensions between national strategic frameworks, emerging planning arrangements, changing economic assessments and the desirability of delivering, through a number of public and voluntary agencies, local flexibility in participation and in coastal design. Challenges for coastal governance were identified, such as achieving fairness and reasonably protecting land values as well as creating 'scope for creative partnerships between science, planning, policy delivery, and public acceptance'. The consultation document for the proposed coastal planning supplement to PPS25 (DCLG, 2009c) (see Table 11.4) stressed the need for partnership working, and stated that regional planning bodies should 'take into account the wider social, economic and environmental policy objectives', so it appears likely that some of the challenges identified by Milligan and O'Riordan (2007) will be considered.

As we saw in Chapter 6, the DCLG consultation on coastal change planning policy raised further issues of equity and social justice. The consultation proposed requiring LPAs to identify on their LDF map areas as Coastal Change Management Areas (CCMA), those areas likely to be affected by shoreline physical changes and where the SMP policy is not to hold the line. This raises significant issues of social justice in decisions on coastal defence funding, uncertainty and disruption to vulnerable communities, loss of economic function and viability, and loss of associations of place attachment: for instance, the Defra consultation makes reference to the 'inevitable' loss of specific historic buildings on the Norfolk coast as a result of sea-level rise and climate change (Defra, 2009c). Young (2009) comments that, while CCMAs can be a positive step in the engagement of spatial planning with integrated coastal management, planners must be provided with sufficient resources to become involved in the preparation of SMPs.

As part of a wider debate on responses to climate change and specifically sea-level rise, a study based on a design charrette hosted by RIBA Building Futures and the Institution of Civil Engineers (ICE) brought together a range of relevant sector professionals who considered three options for coastal and estuarine cities affected by sea-level rise. The options reviewed and visualized in their report for Portsmouth and Hull, are retreat, defend and attack – where 'attack' means building out into the coastal waters on new engineered structures. The study emphasizes the role of communication between stakeholders: thirty-seven types of stakeholder are mentioned, including government bodies and agencies, land and home owners, the rail regulator, navigation, harbour and port authorities and many more (RIBA-Building Futures and ICE, 2010). Figure 11.5, taken from that study, illustrates broadly what two of the options might entail at two major ports.

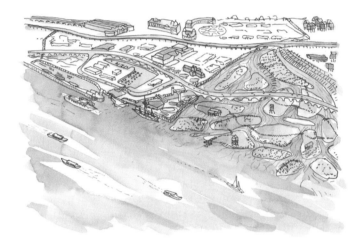

Figure 11.5

Visualizing options: Hull – retreat, Portsmouth – defend
Source: © RIBA Building Futures and ICE, drawn by Christophe Egret.

Integrated coastal zone management

The need to extend the reach of planning further over sea areas has long been recognized, and integrated coastal zone planning and management proposed. An early impetus came from the Habitats Directive (CEC, 1992) which required single schemes of management for the protection of designated European sites for the conservation of wild birds, plus other specified habitats. In 2002, European member states adopted a recommendation on implementing integrated coastal zone management (ICZM) in Europe. An evaluation of progress towards ICZM across the EU in 2006 (Rupprecht, 2006) found varying progress: at that point no country had implemented an ICZM National Strategy as prompted by the EU ICZM Recommendation but in seven countries (including the United Kingdom) the implementation of an ICZM National Strategy was pending.

Tompkins *et al.* (2008) have examined stakeholder engagement with CZM in the UK, where they believe it does not adequately incorporate changing stakeholder preferences, or effectively ensure that stakeholders are aware of the trade-offs inherent in management decisions. They applied a scenario-based method, involving stakeholder analysis, climate change management scenarios and deliberative techniques, in order to assess the necessary trade-offs associated with long-term coastal planning at two case-study sites (Christchurch Bay and the Orkney Islands). The analysis showed that stakeholders held conflicting preferences for ideal governance structures for coastal management under the scenarios. Moreover, the analysis showed that public understanding (and backing) of trade-offs that would need to be made in coastal management is critical if there is to be public support for long-term coastal decision-making. The scenarios approach is seen by these researchers as a useful tool for use with shoreline management planning.

In the UK the principles of ICZM are now incorporated within the Marine and Coastal Access Act 2009 (see below), but other planning-led approaches have been in position for some years, such as integrated strategies for estuaries, plans for harbours and shoreline management plans (see case studies, below). These processes increasingly involve approaches to ensure transparency (access to information), stakeholder participation and monitoring (Taussik, 2007). Taussik points out that integrated coastal management boundaries have in the past been set close to the coast, whereas wider boundaries (i.e. including marine areas) would mean that cumulative environmental effects would be more accurately considered.

Coastal Adaptation Action Plan

A Coastal Adaptation Action Plan is a (non-statutory) closely detailed local response plan addressing climate change, setting out objectives, baseline, targets, responsibilities, planned deliverables and, ideally, funding sources.

Box 11.7 summarizes a coastal adaptation action plan developed with partners through a European research programme.

Box 11.7 Case study: Manhood Peninsula (coastal planning and climate change)

Work to research and reconcile issues resulting from climate change in coastal areas was undertaken as part of ESPACE (European Spatial Planning: Adapting to Climate Events) research. The aim of the study was to raise awareness within the communities and decision-makers of the area of the impact of climate change, the implications for land use and spatial planning, and the need to adapt, with two subsidiary objectives:

• To set out locally agreed action plans that enable positive local responses to climate change.
• To provide a channel for influencing future planning and decision-making to account for effects of climate change locally.

The Manhood Peninsula is a low-lying area of land already suffering (in 2004) from coastal erosion, flooding (coastal and fluvial), housing pressures, poor infrastructure, and from supporting areas of environmental sensitivity as well as a climate-sensitive economy including horticulture, tourism and agriculture. All these pressures were considered likely to be exacerbated by climate change impacts. The Manhood Peninsula Partnership, or MPP, pursued an Adaptation Action Plan for the peninsula, to reduce its vulnerability to climate change impacts and to maximize the opportunities of a changing climate. The partnership received funding for this from the EU and West Sussex County Council. The action plan sets out the work and further research required for the Manhood Peninsula. The plan was developed in response to the visions of project participants of a 'successfully adapted peninsula in 2050'. The resulting action plan has a wide-ranging set of socio-economic and environmental actions that together form an integrated framework for adapting to climate change on the peninsula.

The MPP's Adaptation Action Plan contains six Action Programmes: Spatial and Development Planning, Water Supply and Management, Landscape and Land Management, Tourism and Recreation, Energy and Communication and Awareness. Each action programme sets out the 'project deliverables' made up of complementary and/or overlapping actions that contribute to its achievement. Priorities and timescales for each deliverable were established during the consultation phase of the action plan development.

Source: adapted from ESPACE, 2006

11.6.4 Conclusions: marine and coastal planning

The complex web of interactions between activities and processes in the three-dimensional environment of the coast and marine areas, interacting with climate change and with climate change mitigation and adaptation as well as international relations, has meant that marine spatial planning is a hotly contested area, with active development of strategy and policy. Plasman (2008) has reported on the implementation of marine spatial planning in Belgium and points to a set of ingredients for effective implementation, from a policy perspective. These include: using all available authorities at all levels of governance as well as 'all the cards in your hand', recognizing the importance of leadership, using science and scientists effectively and putting the pieces together, recognizing the importance of short-term accomplishments and communicating them and equally building trust and public support.

This experience points to the important issues in the implementation of the radical new marine and coastal regimes.

11.7 Conclusions

Conclusions for the major topics covered by this chapter are given above: for flood risk in Section 11.5 and for marine and coastal issues in Section 11.6.4. Here we simply wish to note that these are matters of vital current interest which are the subject of a great deal of active policy development at international, EU and national levels. Climate change impacts associated with water (whether it be freshwater or salt, flowing, flooding or stored) are recognized as particularly important for their ability to affect human systems. The consequences for the water environment of actions taken to reduce emissions or to adapt to climate change can mean further impacts upon water systems, and so need to be fully assessed. A number of assessment schemes and plans are now being introduced; new partnerships are being formed to assist in policy delivery. Given the complex and overlapping structure of responsibilities with respect to water as resource or threat, this plethora of new instruments has the potential to cause delays and confusion, so close attention must be given to training those involved and to monitoring outcomes.

We return to these issues in Part IV of the book.

12 Planning for biodiversity under climate change

· ·

12.1 Introduction

This chapter addresses the vital asset (and resource) that is biodiversity, discussing briefly its importance and role in maintaining life and how its protection can be enhanced by spatial planning in circumstances of changing climates. Biodiversity is a word of relatively recent coinage, an abbreviation of *biological diversity* which came into use in the 1990s, following the signing of the international Convention on Biological Diversity (CBD – see Section 12.2.1). A 2007 opinion poll across the EU showed that two-thirds of citizens did not understand the word 'biodiversity' or the main threats to it (EEA, 2009e, p. 8). The term encompasses a set of ideas:

- The diversity of plants, animals and microorganisms (with an estimated 3 to 100 million species on Earth (CBD, 2000)).
- Genetic diversity within species, including varieties and breeds.
- The diversity of ecosystems (forests, wetlands, agricultural landscapes, etc., each of which is constituted by a community of species and the physical attributes of soil, slope, water relations and air quality).
- The range of age classes of species, particularly with respect to long-lived, late-reproducing species.

Biodiversity treaties and legislation are concerned with species, communities of species and habitats. Biodiversity not only is life, it also maintains the continuing possibility of life on Earth as it is involved in the fundamental processes of cycling and purifying water and air, cycling nutrients, pollinating plants, building soils, plant pollination, detoxification of wastes, etc. (CBD, 2000). These processes are expected to be modified by climate change, but biodiversity and ecosystem functioning can contribute to strengthening resilience to change (Sankaran and McNaughton 1999; Tilman *et al.*, 2006).

The range of linkages between biodiversity and human welfare and activity has not always been well acknowledged. But as knowledge increases we see that

> if any part of the web [...] breaks down, the future of life on the planet will be at risk. Biological diversity – the variability of life on Earth – is the key to the ability of the biosphere to continue providing us with these ecological goods and services and thus is our species' life assurance policy.
>
> (CBD, 2000, p. ii)

Among the range of services they provide, ecosystems also offer cultural and aesthetic benefits, and space for leisure. In addition to all these life-sustaining benefits motivating its protection, an ethical basis for the preservation and protection of biodiversity is also widely acknowledged (e.g. CBD, 2000, p. 6; UKBP, 2007, p. 5).

The following sections outline first the variety of pressures affecting bio-diversity (Section 12.2), then briefly describe the range of institutions put in place internationally, at EU level and nationally to protect biodiversity; the level of success achieved, as indicated by the status of habitats and species, is also noted (Sections 12.3 and 12.4). Section 12.5 introduces the way in which spatial planning policy in England and Wales provides protection for and interacts with biodiversity planning at national, regional and local levels. A set of policy measures which will be important in future planning for biodiversity is then discussed; this includes climate space and connectivity, the ecosystem approach and the valuation of ecosystem services. Barriers to better biodiversity protection and the uptake of effective measures are outlined in Section 12.7. Finally, some conclusions are drawn for not only conservation of biodiversity but also its further creation and enhancement.

12.2 Pressures upon biodiversity

12.2.1 Climate change impacts

Table 12.1 summarizes the likely impacts of the expected climate change trends in Europe and the UK, and also indicates some indirect impacts result-ing from either mitigation or adaptation measures for climate change. A few opportunities that exist are also noted. If appropriately protected, however, biodiversity can itself help improve resilience to climate change – this role is outlined below the table.

Ecosystems help preserve capacity for resisting change; biodiversity can help with mitigation via the creation and maintenance of carbon stores in soils and biomass. Terrestrial and marine ecosystems are major reservoirs of carbon and integral components of the global carbon cycle. Significantly more carbon is

Table 12.1 Impacts of climate change on biodiversity, habitats and ecosystems

Changes	Impacts upon biodiversity
Greater % of annual precipitation in winter	Summer drought risk increased, affecting flora and fauna. Increased risk of flooding of habitats, waterlogging, etc. with risk of loss of young.
Faster snowmelt	Increased risk of flooding of habitats, waterlogging, etc. Summer drought risk increased, affecting flora and fauna.
Rainfall more intense and greater % of rainfall in intense episodes	Risks to vegetation and animals from intense rainfall, loss of seedlings and nests if occurring in the spring. Summer drought risk increased, affecting flora and fauna. Increased risk of flooding of habitats, waterlogging, etc.
Higher summer temperatures	Summer drought risk increased, affecting flora and fauna. Increased fire risk affecting vegetation and some fauna. Very high temperatures and drought may cause loss of organic matter from soils, affecting fertility. In soils with high organic content (e.g. peatlands) this may result in severe habitat change.
Warming	Individuals, in dispersing, move polewards or 'upslope' to regain suitable 'climate space'. (see Section 12.5.2)
Long dry periods cause 'soil sealing' and lower infiltration	Summer drought risk increased, affecting flora and fauna. Increased fire risk affecting vegetation of some fauna.
Changing seasonal onset	Disruption of phenology with of loss of synchrony of life events of prey and predator species, both flora and fauna (e.g. plant/insect emergence and hatching)
Less predictable (more erratic) weather patterns	Normal behaviour patterns (nesting, breeding, etc.) may be disrupted by 'unseasonable' cold, heat, flood and drought.
Milder winters	Mixed impacts on flora and fauna, with beneficial or adverse effects (e.g. survival of pests, but also better availability of food sources).
More frequent extremes (heat, cold, flood)	Extremes can lead to loss of unadapted species and habitats and can reduce the likelihood of successful adaptation.
Impacts of mitigation measures	Potential impacts of new energy-generating technologies upon sites and habitats (e.g. tidal barrages, windfarms).
Impacts of adaptation measures	Risk of new adaptive infrastructure (e.g. road, rail, water) occupying or affecting habitats (loss, fragmentation).
Opportunities	New SuDS green roofs and open spaces in urban areas providing opportunities for habitats. Floodplain protection policies (washlands, development restrictions) may restore/ create habitat space.

Source: BRANCH Partners, 2007 and Berry, 2009

stored in soils, vegetation and the oceans than in the atmosphere, and these carbon stores play a vital role in regulating the climate (Thompson, 2008); see also Figure 2.1. These reservoirs (in forests, wetlands, soils, etc.) are also, of course, potential sources of carbon dioxide if conditions change (through fire or drought). Biodiversity's roles with regards to adaptation to climate change include:

- Stabilization and moderation of the Earth's climate and microclimates, for example through evapotranspiration, cooling urban spaces, fixing CO_2 in oceans, etc.
- Moderation of floods and droughts by promoting infiltration to ground-water and retention in wetlands, moderating extreme temperatures and wind.
- Provision of genetic resources for crop development and medicines to meet future needs. ('Currently about 9% of European patent activity relates to biodiversity, or 16% if the full spectrum of pharmaceutical activity is included', [EEA, 2009e, p. 8].)

Actions taken to mitigate or promote adaptation to climate change may affect biodiversity (Chapter 14 suggests some possible ways of reconciling these).

12.2.2 Other impacts on biodiversity

Other pressures upon biodiversity which may interact with climate change include human population change and economic growth and the associated development of the built environment (including the infrastructure within and between urban areas), causing loss of habitat space or fragmentation of existing habitats. The result may mean that remaining blocks of habitat are either insufficient to support a local population, or cease to be linked to other essential habitat such as breeding or feeding habitat. Climate change impacts on other species can become a further interacting pressure, for example where climate change makes it possible for exotic or 'alien' species to invade these areas. Invasion potential is determined by characteristics such as tolerance of wide range of climate/weather conditions, absence of customary predators, or prolific seed production and dispersal.

Legislation or policy change in other sectors can also impact indirectly upon biodiversity. The case of biofuels is such an example, where an EU policy aimed at emissions reduction set a 10 per cent target for the contribution of biofuels to total fuel consumption. This led to pressures to convert semi-natural habitats (within Europe and in tropical forests) to crop monocultures (e.g. sugar beet, *Miscanthus* and oil palm) at the expense of local biodiversity. The target was later suspended as a result of lobbying from the European Environment Agency's Scientific Committee because of its impact upon not only biodiversity and environmental resources, but also upon food production (EEA, 2008f).

Other policy drivers affecting biodiversity include both those directed specifically at biodiversity and ecosystem protection at a range of levels (international to local) and others concerned with uses of land: agriculture, infrastructure, transport, etc., again, at levels from local to national or international. Thus we see that biodiversity, like water, is an environmental component with complex interactions across the range of human activities and interests, and can be indirectly impacted in many ways, particularly where there are changes in the water relations of soils and habitats.

12.3 International biodiversity protection: institutions and status

12.3.1 The Convention on Biological Diversity and global status assessment

International agreements containing provisions for establishing networks of protected sites include the Ramsar Convention (signed in Iran in 1971), the World Heritage Convention (1972) and the OSPAR Convention (1993). While in some countries there has been meticulous recording of wildlife species for centuries, research into the global picture has developed and accelerated since the UNCED Rio Earth Summit (1992). Almost all nations are parties to the legally binding Convention on Biological Diversity, which has been in force since 1993.

The objectives of the Convention on Biological Diversity (CBD) are essentially the conservation of biodiversity, the sustainable use of its components and the 'fair and equitable sharing of the benefits of genetic resources' (CBD, 2006). To achieve this, states have a right to exploit their own resources in line with their own environmental policies, but have also a responsibility to ensure that they do not damage the environment of other states. States undertake to develop national strategies, plans and programmes to achieve the CBD objective. A Strategic Plan published in 2002 established a global biodiversity target: 'to achieve, by 2010, a significant reduction of the current rate of biodiversity loss at the global, regional and national level, as a contribution to poverty alleviation and to the benefit of all life on Earth' (CBD, 2006, p. 2). Countersigning parties (including the EU and its member states) committed themselves to this target, which is to be updated at the CBD's COP-10 meeting in Japan in October 2010. The CBD Strategic Plan of 2002 identifies the obstacles that are perceived in achieving its goals, categorized as including political/societal obstacles; institutional, technical and capacity or information-related; the consequence of economic or financial policy; concerned with collaboration or cooperation, or legal/juridical impediments; or the result of socio-economic factors. Climate change is also mentioned in the CBD, together with natural disasters. Already by 2005 there was recognition in the Millennium Ecosystem Assessment (WRI, 2005) – which was prepared partly to advance the CBD process – that the CBD's

2010 target was unlikely to be achieved: 'An unprecedented effort would be needed to achieve by 2010 a significant reduction in the rate of biodiversity loss at all levels.' (WRI, 2005, p. vi). Longer-term goals (for instance goals to be achieved by 2050) are recommended as part of the Millennium Ecosystem Assessment in order to guide policy and action – this was proposed in view of the 'characteristic response times for political, socio-economic and ecological systems' (WRI, 2005, p. vi).

Global status assessment

Work for the Millennium Ecosystem Assessment for the UN (WRI, 2005) showed that changes in biodiversity due to human activities have been more rapid in the fifty years to 2005 than at any previous time in human history, with the drivers of change either steady or increasing in intensity; 'these rates of changes in biodiversity are projected to continue or to accelerate' (WRI, 2005, p. vi). In a widely quoted, rather controversial paper, Thomas *et al.* (2004) predicted, following modelling work for regions covering some 20 per cent of the Earth's surface and on the basis of mid-range climate-warming scenarios for 2050, 'that 15–37 per cent of species in our sample of regions and taxa will be "committed to extinction"' (p. 145). At the same time, some species have been shown to benefit, a few to the extent of becoming invasive.

The 2005 Millennium Ecosystem Assessment presented an overview of the status of biodiversity at the beginning of the twenty-first century, and of twenty-four *ecosystem services*, of which fifteen were rated as being 'in decline', including provision of fresh water, marine fishery production, the self-cleansing ability of the atmosphere, pollination and natural pest control in agricultural ecosystems (WRI, 2005). In its 2006 publication *Global Biodiversity Outlook 2*, the CBD reported on monitoring work towards the global 2010 biodiversity target (see Section 12.4.1 below). The *Global Biodiversity Outlook 2* report shows adverse trends for: extent of selected biomes, ecosystems and habitats; abundance and distribution of selected species; marine trophic index; connectivity; alien invasive species; area of forest, agricultural and aquaculture systems under sustainable management; ecological footprint and related concepts; and official development assistance provided in support of the convention. Only one indicator showed a positive trend: the indicator of coverage of protected areas. The report also indicates the level of confidence in each trend, and in most cases this is high. The report concludes:

> Overall, unsustainable consumption continues, as indicated by our grow- ing global ecological footprint. The global demand for resources now exceeds the biological capacity of the Earth to renew these resources by some 20%.
>
> (CBD, 2006, p. 3)

12.3.2 The European level: biodiversity institutions, policy framework and status

Institutions and policy responses affecting European biodiversity

The framework of biodiversity protection within the EU is built upon membership of the CBD and measures towards the 2010 target, as well as towards three major directives: the Birds Directive, the Habitats Directive and the Water Framework Directive. The Habitats Directive established the Natura 2000 network of sites of European interest. The principal measures introduced by the three directives and other policy documents are indicated in Table 12.2. There has been a development, over the course of time, from protection of sites and species towards greater recognition of biodiversity within interacting systems and the need for integration of objectives and 'mainstreaming' into policy for other sectors.

Rapidly growing understanding of the impacts of climate change generally led to the publication of a White Paper, *Adapting to Climate Change*, in 2009, that highlighted the importance of biodiversity protection and maintenance. A set of policy measures to protect biodiversity and ecosystems were listed in the White Paper, and near-term deadlines were set for these: for example, developing guidelines and tools to ensure that the River Basin Management Plans (RBMP) required under the Water Framework Directive are climate-proofed by the end of 2009 (see Chapter 10); ensuring that climate change is taken into account in the implementation of the Floods Directive (see Chapter 11) and drafting guidelines by 2010 on dealing with the impact of climate change on the management of Natura 2000 sites. Other measures include research aimed at safe exploitation of co-benefits of biodiversity while avoiding ecosystem feedbacks that may accelerate global warming, and exploring the potential for policies and measures to boost ecosystem storage capacity for water in Europe (CEC, 2009a).

The EU Biodiversity Action Plan (CEC, 2008d) outlines a set of objectives demonstrating the EU's commitment to the objective of halting the loss of biodiversity by 2010. These BAP objectives are grouped into four policy areas, which include safeguarding 'the most important' habitats and species, but also conserving biodiversity in the wider countryside and marine environment, integrating biodiversity into land-use planning and development (Objective 4) and reducing the impact of invasive alien species. The EU BAP also commits member states to protecting biodiversity beyond the EU via international measures and to improving the knowledge base. In addition, Objective 9 is concerned with supporting biodiversity adaptation to climate change. Plans for monitoring and reporting are also set out; other supporting measures are concerned with:

- Ensuring adequate financing for the Natura 2000 network and for biodiversity in the wider environment under the various financial programmes.

Table 12.2 EU policy documents supporting biodiversity protection

Policy document	Measures include:
Birds Directive, 1979 79/409/EEC	General scheme for protection of all wild birds; and requirement for their maintenance in 'favourable conservation status' across their range. Special Protection Areas for birds.
Habitats Directive, 1992 92/43/EEC	Natura 2000 network of sites of European interest. Appropriate assessment procedures (aka Habitats Regulations assessment) for developments affecting these sites.
Water Framework Directive, 2000 2000/60/EC	Introduces the target, for all water bodies, of achieving 'good ecological status'. Also introduces River Basin Management Plans to integrate objectives (see also Section 10.3.1).
EU *Biodiversity Action Plan* (BAP), 2006	Policy aimed at global commitment to halt loss of biodiversity by 2010 (see page 000).
EC White Paper *Adapting to climate change: Towards a European framework for action*, 2009	Objective: to improve the EU's resilience to deal with the impact of climate change. Seeks: a comprehensive and integrated approach towards the maintenance and enhancement of ecosystems and the goods and services they provide is needed. Emphasizes: importance of ecosystem services, stresses importance of relationship with water planning and management to protect biodiversity. Suggests that: 'In future it may be necessary to consider establishing a permeable landscape in order to enhance the interconnectivity of natural areas.' Also that coordinated EU action will be necessary in certain sectors (e.g. agriculture, water, biodiversity, fisheries, and energy networks) that are closely integrated at EU level through the single market and common policies (Section 3.3.3).

- Strengthening the EU decision-making process to integrate biodiversity concerns into all EU and national policies, and screening new initiatives for their potential impacts.
- Ensuring the active collaboration of all key stakeholder groups.
- Raising awareness and encouraging public participation in biodiversity conservation.

(CEC, 2008d, p. 7)

European level status assessment

The EEA report on progress towards the 2010 biodiversity target (EEA, 2009e) states that '40–85% of habitats and 40–70% of species of European interest have an unfavourable conservation status' (p. 8). The report states:

Our indicator-based assessment illustrates that European biodiversity remains under serious pressure and our policy responses have been insufficient to halt its general decline. It is disappointing that we have to conclude that the European 2010 target will not be met.

(EEA, 2009e, p. 5)

This EEA study used a set of twenty-six internationally agreed indicators (known as SEBI 2010) adopted at EU and pan-European levels. The indicators include: status and trends of the components of biological diversity; threats to biodiversity, ecosystem integrity and ecosystem goods and services; sustainable use; resource transfers and public opinion. Whilst only Indicator 11 (Impact of climatic change on bird populations) is directly concerned with climate change, the majority of other variables have potential to act in synergy with climate change to cause further impacts upon biodiversity; in particular habitat fragmentation, nitrogen (N) loading and ecological footprint. Monitoring of Indicator 11 shows that the impact of climate change is becoming visible and more species of birds are adversely impacted by climate change than are positively affected: 92 species compared with 30 species (EEA, 2009e, p. 8). Other trends and evidence highlighted by this report include:

- On land, urban sprawl and abandonment of agricultural land are putting pressure on natural and semi-natural areas. Forest cover is still slightly increasing in Europe, nevertheless forests have become more fragmented locally in certain places.
- Europe cannot sustainably meet its consumption demands from within its own borders. The Ecological Footprint indicator shows that demand exceeds the total capacity for biological production and absorption of waste; this gap between demand and biocapacity has been growing progressively since 1960.
- Estimates of EU spending on biodiversity are currently confined to expenditure on the LIFE programme, which amounts to less than 0.1 per cent of the EU budget in any one year. This, however, is not a comprehensive picture of total spending across the Member States.

(EEA, 2009e, p. 8)

The report notes that in future the ecosystem accounts approach will be applied more widely to provide a quantitative basis of information to guide policymakers (see Section 12.6.3).

With regards to protected habitats, the Natura 2000 network with its 'sites of European importance' is growing; up to 17 per cent of EU land area is now included in the Natura 2000 network and 16 per cent is protected under national instruments across thirty-nine countries. Within member states there are 26,000 Natura 2000 protected areas with a total area of around 850,000 km². Nevertheless, the EEA notes that 40–85 per cent of habitats (and 40–70 per cent of species of European interest) have an unfavourable conservation status (EEA, 2009e, p. 21). Progressive decline in grasslands and wetlands across Europe is also noted, while urban, woodland and open water habitats are increasing. Figure 12.1 indicates the distribution of Natura 2000 sites across the EU – note the greater density of sites in Spain, Germany and northern Norway than in the UK. Some sites are offshore (marine) sites, such as the Wadden Sea area bordering the Netherlands, Denmark and Germany, and the Wash, UK.

12.4 National level: UK biodiversity institutions and policy framework

12.4.1 Biodiversity planning and status

A UK Biodiversity Action Plan (UKBAP) was launched in 1994 in response to the CBD (1993) and drew up some 1,250 action plans for diverse species and habitats. A new strategic framework for UK biodiversity conservation was published in 2007 (*Conserving Biodiversity: The UK Approach*) founded on the principles of partnership of statutory, voluntary, academic and business sectors, nationally and locally, as well as the ecosystem approach (UKBP, 2007). The ecosystem approach is defined as a strategy for the integrated management of land, air, water and living resources that promotes conservation and sustainable use in an equitable way, and which recognizes that people with their cultural and varied social needs are an integral part of ecosystems (UKBP, 2007); the ecosystem approach is discussed further in Section 12.6.3. The biodiversity conservation framework complements the UK's framework for sustainable development (HMG, 2005). It lists UK and international priorities for action, plus a set of indicators for monitoring key issues. Targets for 2020 agreed under the UK BAP include restoration and creation of habitats such as grazing marsh, fen and reedbed, totalling 34,000 ha. The UK BAP targets will require additional habitat to be recreated to replace that lost at the coast due to sea-level rise. In addition, there is a commitment to establish eight new landscape-scale wetland complexes, though locations and sources of funding are not determined.

A good deal of biodiversity-related policy is directed to the protection of designated sites; designations include the network of Natura 2000 European sites: Special Protection Areas (under the Birds Directive) and Special Areas of Conservation (under the Habitats Directive). There are also various designations at national to local level, giving a total of around 3.6 million hectares of protected land (JNCC datasheet, 2009), which, in addition to biodiversity protection, also have a recognized role to play in maintaining water quality, flood alleviation, carbon storage and air quality. There is a good deal of overlap between designations: in England alone there are 4,115 SSSIs (Sites of Special Scientific Interest), occupying over 1 million hectares designated for habitats, wildlife or geology, and most of this is also designated as land, wetland or

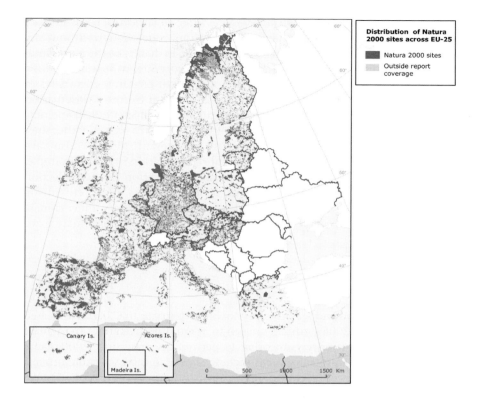

Figure 12.1

Distribution of Natura 2000 sites across EU-25

Source: www.eea.europa.eu/data-and-maps/figures/distribution-of-natura-2000-sites-across-the-27-eu-member-states

offshore SPA or SAC. Nevertheless, as designated sites amount to less than 20 per cent of the total area of the UK, clearly the 'wider countryside' (that is, countryside outside protected sites) is also very important. The importance of planning for biodiversity at the landscape level, i.e. considering the overall connectivity of habitats within the wider landscape, is increasingly recognized and referred to in policy statements at EU and UK level. Examples of this are given in Sections 12.6.2 and 12.6.3.

At the local level, Local Biodiversity Action Plans bring together partnerships to identify local priorities and to determine contributions to achieving the national Species and Habitat Action Plan targets. LBAPs often, but not always, conform to county boundaries. As part of a national public sector performance framework published in November 2007, a National Indicator has been chosen to provide information for biodiversity action and is monitored by local authorities. This is NI 197: *Improved Local Biodiversity – proportion of Local Sites where positive conservation management has been or is being implemented.* Local Sites are defined as 'sites of substantive nature conservation value' though without any statutory status. It is suggested that many are equal in quality to the representative sample of sites that make up the series of statutory Sites of Special Scientific Interest (SSSIs) (Defra, 2006b). Local Sites (35,000 in England) cover Sites of Importance for Nature Conservation (SINCs), Sites of Nature Conservation Importance (SNCIs) and Regionally Important Geological Sites (RIGS) and may contribute a significant area of biodiversity interest within a county. Other sites, for example, agri-environment sites such as Local Stewardship sites, also have biodiversity value. The fragility of local nature conservation sites – for example, in the light of climate change – is seen as a suitable criterion for their selection and protection. Another criterion (Defra, 2006b) is a site's role in enhancing connectivity, thus responding to a principal need for biodiversity under climate change – for habitats and species to be able to 'track' appropriate climate space (see Section 12.5.2).

UK biodiversity status assessment

The total area of land and sea protected for biodiversity in the UK has increased between 1996 and 2006 from 2.3 million to 3.5 million hectares – an increase of 50 per cent over twenty years or an 11 per cent increase since 2000 (Defra 2007b, p. 20). These protected areas include Sites of Special Scientific Interest (SSSI) (Areas of Special Scientific Interest in Northern Ireland, ASSI), Special Areas of Conservation (SAC) and Special Protection Areas (SPA); many sites have more than one designation but each site contributes only once to the overall total area. A national assessment of SSSI condition in 2003 showed that 57 per cent of SSSI were in target condition (i.e. in favourable or recovering condition). By 31 March 2009, the proportion of SSSIs' area in target condition had increased to 88 per cent. The target is to have 95 per cent of SSSIs in target condition by end of 2010. (Natural England, 2009d).

Across the UK, 1,150 species are priorities for national conservation action, among which 211 species (18 per cent) have populations in the UK that constitute a 'significant proportion' of the total population for the EU Atlantic biogeographic region (i.e. over 25 per cent). Bird species account for 23 of these, and higher plants for 52 (JNCC, 2009). The UK National Report to the CBD (JNCC, 2009) indicates that few of the diverse wildlife species occupying UK habitats are endemic (i.e. found only in the UK) and few are considered at risk of extinction. This UK fourth report to the CBD concludes that 'the rapid declines in biodiversity in the UK during the last quarter of the 20th century have been substantially slowed and in some cases halted or reversed' (JNCC, 2009, p. 5). Moreover, responses – such as financial support and volunteering by the public – have increased. Nevertheless, 'there is a lot more to do' (p. 6).

12.5 Spatial planning links to biodiversity

12.5.1 England and Wales – spatial planning policy affecting biodiversity

Planning policy relevant to biodiversity protection in England and Wales is shown in Table 12.3. DCLG is currently (2010) streamlining the present array of PPSs from 25 in number to 21. A consultation was launched (DCLG, 2010c) to consolidate planning policy on topics dealt with in PPS7, PPS9, PPG17 and PPG20 in a new PPS to be entitled *Planning for a Natural and Healthy Environment*, incorporating planning for green infrastructure. The Scottish Government's biodiversity strategy is set out in *Scotland's Biodiversity: It's in Your Hands* (Scottish Executive, 2004b) which includes objectives which refer to halting loss, increasing awareness, restoring and enhancing biodiversity through better planning, design and practice, as well as 'continue to revise previous losses through targeted action' (p. 36). The strategy recognizes that 'some changes due to climate change are inevitable and irreversible' (p. 36).

Among the guidance shown in Table 12.3, the PPS1 supplement on climate change (DCLG, 2007a) provided further advice on adapting to climate change and takes precedence over other PPSs. PPS9 (ODPM, 2005c) covers the protection of designated sites of both biodiversity and geological interest. The PPS updated a previous (1994) guidance note on nature conservation, PPG9. Surprisingly, given its publication in 2005, the PPS makes but a single reference to climate change, and this is in connection with Regional Spatial Strategies: 'Over time the distribution of habitats and species, and geomorphological processes and features, will be affected by climate change and such change will need to be taken into account.' (Environmental NGOs were critical of PPS9 at the time of its publication, especially with respect to the failure to require Habitats Regulations Assessment.) PPS9 emphasizes that the planning system has a significant role to play in addressing not only domestic policies for habitats, species and ecosystems but also the government's international commitments. PPS9 is now under review and is to be consolidated with PPG17 and the landscape aspects of PPS7. A consultation draft was published in 2010. The principles of PPS9 make reference to using an up-to-date evidence base to

Table 12.3 Planning policy and biodiversity, England and Wales

Policy document	Significant elements for spatial planning
PPS1 Delivering sustainable development (2005)	Development plan policies should take account of environmental issues such as: [...] the protection of the wider countryside and the impact of development on landscape quality; the conservation and enhancement of wildlife species and habitats and the promotion of biodiversity.

(continued)

Table 12.3 *(cont.)*

Policy document	Significant elements for spatial planning
Supplement to PPS1 Planning and climate change (2007)	Regional planning bodies and all planning authorities should prepare, and manage the delivery of, [...] spatial strategies that conserve and enhance biodiversity, recognizing that the distribution of habitats and species will be affected by climate change.
	RPBs should consider the region's vulnerability to climate change, including [...] implications for biodiversity.
	PAs should take into account [...] the effect of development on biodiversity and its capacity to adapt to likely changes in the climate; also [...] the contribution to be made from existing and new opportunities for open space and green infrastructure to urban cooling, sustainable drainage systems, and conserving and enhancing biodiversity.
PPS3 Housing (2006)	Matters to consider when assessing design quality include the extent to which the proposed development: [...] Provides for the retention or re-establishment of the biodiversity within residential environments.
	LDDs should set out a strategy which takes into account [...] the need to protect natural resources, e.g. water and biodiversity.
PPS7 Sustainable development in rural areas (2004)	Objectives include: to promote sustainable, diverse and adaptable agriculture sectors where farming achieves high environmental standards, minimizing impact on natural resources, and manages valued landscapes and biodiversity.
PPS9 Biodiversity and geological conservation (2005)	PPS under review, with amalgamation into new PPS: Planning for a Natural and Healthy Environment now under consultation (DCLG, 2010c)
PPS11 Regional spatial strategies (2004)	RSSs, in their role of contributing to sustainable development, must take into account priorities for the environment, such as countryside and biodiversity protection. (PPS11 is currently under review – see note below).
PPS25 Development and flood risk (2006)	RPAs and LPAs prepare strategies in which flood risk should be considered alongside other spatial planning issues such as transport, housing, economic growth, natural resources, regeneration, biodiversity, the historic environment and the management of other hazards.
	Owners/developers are responsible for preparing Flood Risk Assessments which identify (*inter alia*) opportunities to reduce flood risk, enhance biodiversity and amenity, protect the historic environment and seek collective solutions to managing flood risk.
	PPS25 has been revised and is published as DCLG 2010d, with recommendations affecting biodiversity broadly similar.

maintain, enhance, restore or add to biodiversity while attaching 'appropriate weight' to designated sites and protected species, to taking a strategic approach to biodiversity protection and to promoting opportunities for the incorporation of beneficial biodiversity within the design of development. It states that where the principal objective is to conserve or enhance biodiversity, then development proposals should be permitted and that the aim of planning decisions should be to prevent harm to biodiversity interests. However, if significant harm would result from planning permission then a staged response is set out staged response is set out in ODPM (2005c, p. 3):

> Significant harm caused to biodiversity: LPA will need to be satisfied that the development cannot reasonably be located on any alternative sites that would result in less or no harm.

> Significant harm, but no alternative sites: LPA should ensure that, before planning permission is granted, adequate mitigation measures are put in place.

> Significant harm, no alternative sites and adequate mitigation not possible: LPAs should seek appropriate compensation measures.

> Significant harm, no alternative sites, adequate mitigation not possible nor is compensation possible: planning permission should be refused.

Jenkins (2007) has reviewed the likely value of this PPS to local decision-makers; she notes that, while the destruction of SSSIs is an important indicator of government success in protecting biodiversity, in 2005 only 67 per cent of SSSIs were in a favourable or recovering condition. However, Jenkins attributes over half of the damage to overgrazing or moor burning, with planning permission responsible for only 3 per cent of damage, and consequently identifies the 'real problem' as the destruction of SSSIs in cases that do not require planning permission (e.g. agricultural activities) (p. 94). As a result Jenkins suggests that, while nationally and internationally protected sites have successful protection regimes in place, it is the protection of regional and local sites that requires further strengthening; she also notes that progress is being made in this direction via BAP measures and measures under the Countryside and Rights of Way Act 2000, section 74. Jenkins renews a call for 'the adoption of a unified and simplified development consent procedure applied to all plans or project affecting protected sites, whatever their nature' (Jenkins, 2007, p. 94).

12.5.2 Biodiversity at regional and local planning policy levels

Regional level

As an example of policy responses at regional level, Box 12.1 summarizes excerpts from the RSS for south-east England, the South East Plan of April 2009 (GOSE,

Box 12.1 Biodiversity policies in the South East Plan

Cross-cutting Policy CC1: sustainable development is specifically oriented towards mitigation and adaptation to climate change, stating that sustainable development priorities for the South East are:

iii. reducing greenhouse gas emissions associated with the region
iv. ensuring that the South East is prepared for the inevitable impacts of climate change . . . (p. 31)

This policy thus modifies policy on biodiversity which follows.

NRM5: Conservation and improvement of biodiversity. LPAs and other bodies shall avoid a net loss of biodiversity and actively pursue opportunities to achieve a net gain across the region. They will do this by:

- giving the highest level of protection to international sites.
- taking a precautionary approach and not approving applications where, after Appropriate Assessment, it cannot be concluded that there will be no adverse effect on European sites.
- ensuring appropriate access to wildlife areas and identifying areas for biodiversity. improvement and setting targets reflecting the Regional Biodiversity targets. Pursuing opportunities for biodiversity improvement, including connection of sites, large-scale habitat restoration, enhancement and recreation in the areas of strategic opportunity for biodiversity improvement.
- influencing and applying other schemes (agri-environment, forestry, flood defence, etc., to deliver biodiversity targets and increase the wildlife value of land.

Areas of Strategic Opportunity for Biodiversity Improvement are mapped in broad-brush terms and targets for habitat improvement (in hectares) are set for 2010 and 2026 by broad habitat type (e.g. coastal flood plain and grazing marsh, calcareous grassland). The areas of strategic opportunity within which these habitat types may be found are also identified.

Biodiversity is also part of the following core regional policies for the South East.

CC4: Sustainable construction and design. There is to be consideration of how all aspects of development form can contribute to securing high standards of sustainable development, including biodiversity.

CC8: Green infrastructure. Substantial networks of multifunctional greenspace are to be planned, provided and managed. The 'widest range' of environmental and social benefits is to be delivered, including enhancing and conserving biodiversity as well as landscape, recreation, water management, etc. The networks are to be created and managed as a framework of greenspaces that will increase the environmental capacity of the region as a whole, helping communities to be more resilient to climate change.

NRM4: Sustainable flood-risk management. Local authorities, together with the EA should 'consider the associated social and environmental costs and benefits to fisheries, biodiversity and the built and historic environment in assessment of new flood management schemes'.

NRM7: Woodlands. The region's woodland should be protected and enhanced in accordance with the Regional Forestry and Woodland Framework.

W14: Restoration. High quality restoration and aftercare of waste sites to help deliver the environmental and social objectives including biodiversity.

C5: Managing the rural-urban fringe. LDDs should:

- identify issues and opportunities that require action to deliver a sustainable multifunctional rural-urban fringe.
- target positive management on areas where urban extensions are planned to ensure early consideration is given to landscape and biodiversity enhancement.

Source: adapted from GOSE, 2009

2009) showing policies underpinned by measures to protect and enhance biodiversity. The South East Plan groups together the concepts of biodiversity, open space and green infrastructure and frequently refers to 'multi-functional green spaces', to include biodiversity. The Plan incorporates the principles set out in Section 12.6, such as protection of existing sites, increasing connectivity and mainstreaming biodiversity into wider sectoral policies. It also makes many references to 'valuing' the environment, landscape and wildlife – though not explicitly in economic terms.

Local level

In order to help embed the regional policies for climate change shown in Box 12.3 within Local Development Frameworks (LDFs), the SE England Partnership Board has issued guidance (SEEPB, 2009) on how the policies are to be reflected in the region's LDFs. It could be argued that this guidance does not take this much further forward as the recommendations are rather bland, and merely reiterate what is required under legislation. However, the third recommendation under proposed LDF policy NRM5 on biodiversity (see below) is a new departure: it calls for networks at a subregional level, while the proposed recommendation under NRM7 (Woodlands) calls for the creation of new woodlands 'where possible in accordance with green infrastructure frameworks' (SEEPB, 2009, p. 13) (see also Chapter 9.9).

NRM5 – Conservation and improvement of biodiversity

1. Designated international, national and local sites for nature conservation should be protected in the spatial strategy.
2. Policies should enforce the need to protect and enhance sites for nature conservation.
3. A network of sites should be created to enable species and habitats to adapt to climate change.

12.6 Concepts and principles for future biodiversity protection

Three important principles of biodiversity protection and adaptation to climate change are: the maintenance and enhancement of existing protected areas (see Section 12.6.1), improving connectivity at the landscape scale (Sections 12.6.2), and the use of the ecosystem approach (see Section 12.6.3) in order to both appropriately and adaptively manage ecosystems. This means valuing biodiversity and ecosystem services is a part of the ecosystem approach increasingly recognized by all levels of biodiversity policy but also is proposed as a way to 'mainstream' biodiversity into all policy sectors. Research, modelling and mapping underlie these principles. Sustainability appraisal is outlined in Section 12.6.4 and other guidance is mentioned in Section 12.6.5.

First, however, we consider the wider landscape context and its position linking people and biodiversity. While many of us spend the majority of our time within built-up areas (80 per cent of people in Europe's industrialized countries now live in towns and cities), nevertheless we remain inexorably linked to rural areas and open and wooded landscapes (both upstream and downstream in the local catchment, and others very distant) for our food, fibre, water (and oxygen) as well as for aesthetic benefits and recreation. The maintenance of what in the UK and Europe we perceive as the essential ingredients of countryside landscapes (geological formations, woods and trees, fields of crops and livestock, moorlands and wetlands) is vital to the biodiversity that depends on those landscapes – including humanity. While the pattern of landscape features may change to some degree, and has evolved over time in response to use, it is critical that overall natural and semi-natural areas but also productive land are protected and managed with climate change impacts in mind. By changing temperatures and patterns of seasonal warming, and by altering water relations, climate change is very likely to affect the structure and stability of soils and, consequently, everything that depends on them. Peatlands are vulnerable to drying, moorlands and forests to fire, while the fertility and stability of agricultural land and pastures may be affected by more variable soil moisture regimes as a result of climate change, and eroded by wind and overland flow. Pressures from overuse or poor management – including too many or careless visitors at rural sites – can act cumulatively under a changed climate to lead to risk of loss of habitats, but also of landscapes of which the value comprises their aesthetic and biodiversity interest as well as their economic values, and among these, their importance as water gathering grounds, as sources of food, biomass, timber and other outputs.

While, in the UK, many aspects of the rural landscape fall outside the authority of the spatial planning system, there are issues that planning must address in connection with economic activities, and these must raise awareness of the interaction between people and landscapes in the context of climate change. McEvoy, Handley *et al.* (2006) have emphasized the importance of sensitive management of landscapes, under climate change, with respect to the visitor economy of the north-west of England, discussing impacts upon dunes and moorlands as well as upon the city centre environment. They underline how, if climate change leads to increased visitor pressure, without additional protective measures the very sites that support this important economic sector could be endangered. The report identifies four different aspects of the capacity of a landscape to withstand pressures and continue to offer benefits for visitors: the physical capacity of facilities such as car parks and access roads, the ecological capacity beyond which soils and wildlife are endangered, the perceptual or social capacity which limits the recreational experience and the economic capacity, which is the 'threshold beyond which the investment needed to sustain environmental quality becomes prohibitive' (p. 7). Boxes 12.2 and 12.5 below give examples of particular landscapes and likely change within them.

12.6.1 Retention of existing designated sites, development of new sites

While much discussion of future planning for biodiversity discusses other approaches, it must be emphasized first that the retention, continuing protection and possibly extension or buffering of existing sites is seen by biodiversity interests (e.g. the RSPB and Natural England) as an important plank of future biodiversity policy (see, for example, English Nature 2005 on the protection of the Thames Basin Heaths). Recognizing that the species and habitat composition of these sites may well change over time as a result of climate change, it is generally agreed that such sites are, nevertheless, important in that they have been designated as the 'best' currently available (in terms of diversity of conditions, habitats and species), and this status is not likely to change. Moreover, given their current populations, these existing sites – especially the Natura 2000 network but also national and local sites – are likely to be important 'core' areas from which dispersing species can spread (Natural England, 2009c, p. 4).

New areas of protected sites will be necessary (Hannah *et al.*, 2002b) including buffering land around existing sites to provide space and further protection. This is a further important role for spatial planning: to safeguard from development those sites where relative biodiversity value may increase in the future.

The range and variability of species and variation within sites and habitats also need to be conserved and enhanced (Hopkins *et al.*, 2007).

12.6.2 Climate space and connectivity

Climate change has been inducing range shifts for many species as they follow their suitable climate space; further shifts are projected. In broad terms, the impact of climate change upon biodiversity habitat is to move it 'polewards and upslope', i.e. to higher altitudes and latitudes, in response to warming. Whether or not species will be able to colonize new regions of climate space as climate conditions become suitable depends on species traits and habitat fragmentation (Vos *et al.*, 2008) as well as other physical characteristics of sites (e.g. soils). Modelling future change for a set of species and ecosystem types into the mid-twenty-first century, Vos *et al.* (2008) showed that the amount of climatically suitable habitat in northwest Europe falls for all studied species for the 2020 and 2050 time slices, and isolation meant other significant portions of habitat could not be colonized. This research thus indicates a decline in the amount of suitable habitat protected in Natura 2000 sites. The method used makes it possible to select suitable locations for climate corridors where improving connectivity is most urgent and potential gain is highest. Other work in the Netherlands and elsewhere has shown that the large-scale ecosystem network is a major conservation strategy to reduce the risks of climate change for biodiversity.

Research studies, including the MONARCH, BRANCH and MACIS programmes have used modelling-based methods to identify change in species/habitat climate space in the UK and Europe. Thus MONARCH, for example, identified which species were more able to 'track' the climate space suitable for them. Modelling undertaken for BRANCH demonstrated how climate space will change in NW Europe, for example showing SE England becoming suitable for typically Mediterranean vegetation in the 2080s, under some climate change scenarios. As an example, Box 12.2 presents case-study material for species in

---

Box 12.2 Future prospects for lowland heath and chalk grassland, Hampshire UK

Lowland heath and chalk grassland species are likely to respond to climate change differently. They could gain and lose climate space in varying amounts. The response of these species to climate change is also likely to change over time. Some could find new climate space in the short and medium term. But they could have no climate space under the 2080s high emissions scenario of climate change.

Some may disappear unless they can adapt to new conditions. Species that still have climate space by the 2080s may still suffer because other species on which they rely have disappeared. For example, just four lowland heath species studied

---

two habitat types in southern England. This example is taken from the BRANCH research project and indicates prospects for species in these habitats.

Identifying the location of a species' climate space in coming decades is simply a first but valuable step towards identifying where it might be able to survive. Hannah *et al.* (2007), working within the MACIS programme, have used climate space mapping to propose methods for identifying protected area needs in a changing climate – and have found that where action is taken rapidly to secure appropriate sites, this can be more effective and achieved at lower cost than where it is delayed.

Netherlands ecological network

As suggested elsewhere, it is useful to consider UK practice with practice in the Netherlands as the two countries share similarities of the physical environment as well as high pressure from population and development. An important feature of recent Dutch nature conservation policy has been the establishment of the National Ecological Network (NEN) or Ecologische Hoofdstructuur (EHS), which is scheduled to be completed in 2018, as land is acquired and brought under nature conservation management. By that date the NEN should cover over 700,000 ha of land and 6.3 million hectares of water (including lakes, the Wadden Sea and parts of the North Sea). The NEN was originally planned as a response to the poor nature conservation position of the Netherlands, but an additional role for such networks is now also seen as its potential contribution to biodiversity adaptation to climate change (Opdam *et al.*, 2006). Tamis *et al.* (2005) found evidence of rapid response of the Dutch flora to climate change in the final decades of the twentieth century, with an increase in warmth-loving (thermophilic) species coinciding with a 'marked' increase in ambient temperature observed. While urbanization was an alternative explanation, this was found to explain only 50 per cent of the increased presence of this group of species.

Connectivity throughout the NEN is prioritized and transboundary (cross-frontier) movement is also ensured. NEN areas are designated by the Dutch provinces (each with its own approach), and this process is now almost complete. The NEN consists of both existing and new nature areas and management areas. The process of designating the NEN was initially covered by land development projects and later by an area-specific policy. In selecting the designated areas, account was taken as far as possible of current and potential natural features ('nature values'). A number of provinces also took account of water management in the areas. The NEN – with its non-binding ecological targets – combines conservation of existing sites, nature restoration, the linking-up of ecological corridors and conversion of agricultural land into semi-natural areas – often together with flood prevention measures (Notenboom *et al.*, 2006, p. 7). Such an approach was deemed necessary as many sites in the Netherlands are small and isolated, while local environmental and hydrological conditions are not suitable to the needs of species and habitats. However, Opdam *et al.* (2006) note that one of the main challenges of establishing ecological networks will be ensuring cooperation between administrative units and across ecological scales (p. 331).

The Netherlands Natura 2000 network is also being extended and improved and an evaluation of Dutch biodiversity in 2008 (van Veen *et al.*, 2008) suggests that biodiversity loss is slowing down, but at a low level in terms of mean species abundance. Since 1990, the loss of natural area has been reversed. Some remaining areas of the traditional agricultural system are protected as nature reserves; agri-environmental schemes are being established. At the species level, less vulnerable species show improvements, while the most vulnerable species show further decline (van Veen *et al.*, 2008, p. 12).

12.6.3 The ecosystem approach: integration with other sectors

The CBD defines the ecosystem approach (introduced in Section 2.5.2) as: 'a strategy for the integrated management of land, water and living resources that promotes conservation and sustainable use in an equitable way'. It is also seen as a means 'to mainstream biodiversity into all policy sectors'. 'Mainstreaming' means that apart from supporting traditional conservation initiatives, biodiversity conservation should be integrated into all levels (macro, sectoral and project) of economic planning, as part of a sustainable development strategy (Kumari *et al.*, 1997; Spangenberg, 2006). The principles of the ecosystem approach were agreed by the CBD in 2000, to seek the appropriate balance between and integration of conservation and the use of biological diversity (UK Biodiversity Partnership, 2007, p. 3).

Elements in achieving the implementation of an ecosystem approach will include stakeholder participation and good use of research and knowledge at appropriate spatial and temporal scales. Importantly, it means recognizing the economic contribution of biodiversity rather than simply exploiting economic externalities without compensation (for example, benefiting from the contribution of biodiversity to the 'quality' of a place, without ensuring the survival of that biodiversity). Thus the ecosystem approach is closely allied with sustainable development. Box 12.3 summarizes Defra's England Ecosystem Approach Action Plan with its core principles of holism, valuing ecosystem services, sustainable development, appropriate scale and adaptive management to changing pressures, such as climate change. Valuing ecosystem services is discussed further, below.

If integration into wider policymaking is the objective, then many policy areas must integrate ecosystems into their decision-making. It could be argued that some sectors such as water and the built environment are already beginning to do this but any development of tourism, energy, education, ports and further sectors also need to be brought into this process. A long-term strategy for the development of environmental valuation in transport appraisal, including the valuation of ecosystem services, is referred to as part of Defra's Ecosystem Action Plan Priority 4 (Defra, 2007c, p. 23). *An Introductory Guide*

Box 12.3 The England Ecosystem Approach Action Plan

The Ecosystem Approach Action Plan forms the basis for a more strategic approach to policymaking and delivery on the natural environment. The action plan sets out a strategic approach to policy and delivery on the natural environment. It sets out a number of actions to enable the UK Department for the Environment, Food and Rural Affairs (Defra), key partners and stakeholders to work together in applying an ecosystem approach to conserving, managing and enhancing the natural environment in England. These actions are based on a number of core principles including:

- taking a more holistic approach to policymaking and delivery, with the focus on maintaining healthy ecosystems and ecosystem services.
- ensuring that the value of ecosystem services is fully reflected in decision-making.
- ensuring environmental limits are respected in the context of sustainable development, taking into account ecosystem functioning.
- taking decisions at the appropriate spatial scale while recognizing the cumulative impacts of decisions.
- applying adaptive management of the natural environment to respond to changing pressures, including climate change. (p. 11)

Progress towards delivering the goals of the Ecosystem Approach Action Plan will be measured using the indicators which relate to water quality, biodiversity, air quality, marine health and agricultural land management.

Source: adapted from Defra, 2007c

---

to Valuing Ecosystem Services (Defra 2007d) was published to accompany the England Ecosystem Approach Action Plan. It builds on previous approaches to valuing the environment but is designed to take a more systematic approach to the assessment of impacts on the natural environment (p. 22–3).

Figure 12.2, based on a study on 'The Economics of Ecosystems and Biodiversity: Towards a Valuation Framework' (widely known as the TEEB study: Sukdev, 2008), attempts to demonstrate the links between biodiversity and the output of ecosystem services, leading to values (benefits). Note that benefits may in turn place additional pressures upon the biological structures, such as habitats.

Valuing/monetizing

Constraints on spatial planning action on biodiversity include the hard-to-quantify nature of non-market biodiversity benefits, especially as economic growth is a principal aim of planning systems. Slootweg and Beukering (2008) argue that SEA and planning processes are enhanced by the identification and quantification of ecosystem services, arguing that: 'economists often are not aware of the SEA instrument' and that SEA can embed economics methods and knowledge into the decision-making process. Environmental economists aim

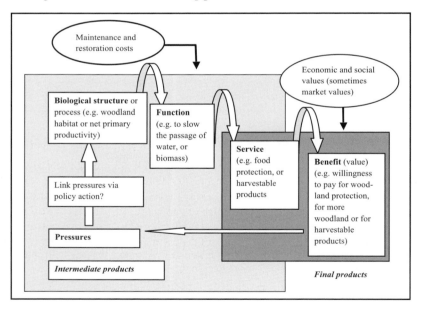

Figure 12.2

The link between biodiversity and the output of ecosystem services
Source: based on Haines-Young and Potschin, 2010

to represent the 'value' of environmental goods that are not traded directly in the market place (e.g. air quality) through a calculated surrogate value. This calculation is based on individuals' willingness to pay for a related traded good. There are concerns that this approach inaccurately represents social values and, moreover, reflects only social (human) values (see, for example, Foster, 1997, p. 108; Bowers, 1997, p. 154). 'Monetizing' ecosystem services could lead to the subsidizing of particular ecosystems via contributions from those who benefit from the services provided. An example of a valuation study of ecosystem services provided by wetland in central-southern England is given in McInnes *et al.* (2008). While economic valuation of biodiversity and ecosystem services is only one route to their protection, it seems that an accurate financial valuation, incorporating externalities, with appropriate monetization of services, may be useful in improving awareness of biodiversity's role in protecting social life, and so research in this area should be taken into account by spatial planning systems.

This area of policymaking demonstrates the linkages across the levels of climate change response – international and national – where biodiversity and ecosystem services are concerned. The concluding message from the EC-sponsored Athens meeting Biodiversity Protection: Beyond 2010 (CEC, 2009j) addressed funding, among other issues, noting that, while financial support is theoretically available from EU and national funds to help with biodiversity protection, actual financial resources committed to conservation are low. It was recommended that the findings of the TEEB study should be 'mainstreamed' to demonstrate the strong economic rationale for conserving biodiversity (EC, 2009c).

12.6.4 Sustainability appraisal and biodiversity

Natural England has published recommendations for a set of core actions and aspirations in relation to the preparation of Development Plans (Tyldesley, 2009), examining how adaptation may be incorporated into regional and local plans and also handled in sustainability appraisal. The guidance indicates that prerequisites for positively influencing the spatial planning system include a basis of good awareness of not only the impacts but also the legal and policy frameworks affecting climate change, together with a sound evidence base with regards to local (and neighbouring) biodiversity and projections over the long term, the identification of a 'no regret and low regret' policy framework, and full and continuing engagement with RSS statutory consultees and others. Box 12.4, taken from that guidance, suggests actions and aspirations for biodiversity planning and policy with regards to sites and links.

This Natural England guidance on biodiversity guidance and LDFs (Tyldesley, 2009) outlines a sustainability assessment process for a proposed plan, and Table 12.4 presents recommended measures from the guidance showing how biodiversity adaptation may be covered at the stages of scoping report and sustainability report. Chapter 7 has already commented on the broad treatment of climate change in sustainability appraisal, and Chapter 14 suggests ways of integrating mitigation and adaptation.

12.6.5 Other guidance on biodiversity and climate change

Other work from Natural England discusses how to build climate change adaptation into planning for *landscape character* areas. Recommendations which are relevant to spatial planning, taken from a report dealing specifically with the Dorset Downs (Natural England, 2008), suggest the measures shown in Box 12.5 as being relevant to species and habitats, in terms of working with partners and planning.

Other guidance document for local biodiversity policy, published on behalf of the UK Biodiversity Partnership by Defra (Hopkins *et al.*, 2007) presents guiding principles to assist terrestrial biodiversity to adapt to climate change (further guidance would be required for marine ecosystems). The guidance suggests ways to use the existing planning policy framework and wildlife legislation to full advantage to safeguard protected sites from harm, actively seeking opportunities to create buffers of semi-natural habitat through targeted site

Table 12.4 Sustainability appraisal of plans for biodiversity adaptation

Reporting stages	Measures to incorporate biodiversity adaptation
SA Scoping report	
Identify relevant EU and UK legislation, policy and commitment with regards to environmental assets	Review to include: • EC Adaptation Directive, Climate Change Act • PPS: PPS1 Sustainable Development and supplement (Climate change) and PPS9 on biological conservation • UK Biodiversity Action Plan and Local BAP • Relevant Biodiversity Strategy, e.g. England Biodiversity Strategy
Describe plan area environment and identify environment-related problems	Problems might include: • Changes in composition and abundance of ecosystems • Local changes in species (extinctions, in-comers) • Loss of sites and connections, limiting dispersal: 　—Loss of specific features of biodiversity value, such as isolated 'islands' or linear features 　—Isolation of high quality habitats 　—Landscape fragmentation
Project forward the 'without plan' situation	Recognize fully the need for a policy to help mitigate cumulative climate change and other stresses on the biodiversity character of the plan area and likely future adverse effects for biodiversity.
Sustainability report	
Assess likely and significant impacts of the plan upon biodiversity	Confirm that policy and proposal assessment against sustainability criteria is robust.
Make recommendations on amendment of plan as necessary to address sustainability issues identified	Confirm that proposals for plan changes accurately reflect the importance/significance of the environmental problems identified by the SA process, and that they are robust and auditable.

Source: adapted from Tyldesley, 2009, pp. 32, 33

acquisition, management agreements and encouraging take-up of agri-environment scheme options by other land managers. In addition, it is suggested that a more strategic approach to site protection should be developed through Local Biodiversity Action Plans and partnership arrangements with other conservation land managers, including development of local conservation forums, outreach programmes and countryside management schemes (Hopkins *et al.*, 2007, p. 16). The third recommendation, to develop ecologically resilient and varied landscapes, emphasizes habitat connectivity and landscape permeability in helping species dispersal and enhancing resilience.

> **Box 12.5** Planning for landscape character areas: biodiversity and climate change
>
> Working with partners in Dorset Downs and Cranbourne Chase to promote:
> - increased water storage on farms, particularly dewponds.
> - re-establishment of chalk grassland or native woodland adjoining water courses to improve recharge of the chalk aquifer and reduce downstream flooding.
> - on-farm protection of water quality and soil resources, such as maintaining vegetated field margins and avoiding bare fields in autumn and winter.
> - creation of more naturally functioning floodplains to allow greater water storage and the evolution of new wetland habitats.
>
> Planning for an uncertain future:
> - Adopt a partnership approach between statutory bodies and planning authorities to maintain adequate land for the natural environment and ensure resilience to climate change at all scales.
> - With 'growth points' as the priority, guide development away from sensitive environmental zones. Option appraisal should consider the value of ecosystem goods and services so that, for example, the full impacts of building on flood-plains can be assessed, and the full costs of conventional development versus development adapted to future climate can be compared.
> - Require installation of Sustainable Urban Drainage Systems (SUDS) in new developments to intercept and store water.
> - Ensure that renewable energy infrastructure is strategically planned. A landscape capacity study for the Character Area would help to ensure that infrastructure is sited in the best locations and would also help to develop markets.
>
> Source: adapted from Natural England, 2008, p. 11

In 2009 the TCPA published a worksheet on biodiversity planning (TCPA *et al.* 2009) for eco-towns, at a time when further eco-towns were under consideration (see Section 8.6) The guidance worksheet identifies six key elements in an effective strategy for eco-town biodiversity, shown in Box 12.6. Four of these relate directly to sites, flora and fauna and their management, but two others concern the equally important matters of funding and governance. Importantly, this guidance – prepared by TCPA, Natural England and DCLG – stresses the achievement of 'net gains for biodiversity', i.e. striving beyond the status quo.

12.7 Spatial planning, biodiversity and climate change: barriers and constraints

While the public's understanding of the term 'biodiversity' has been shown to be rather poor across the EU, interest in wildlife and recognition of the value

Box 12.6 TCPA guidance on biodiversity for eco-towns

Siting, location and context: Adverse impacts of development should be mitigated and compensatory measures should be taken to ensure overall gain in biodiversity.

Master-planning: Eco-town master plans should consider the conservation of existing habitats, the creation of new habitats. The scheduling of activities is highlighted.

Design: Detailed design of buildings and other structures should include specific measures for biodiversity, including trees in hard landscaping, living ('green') roofs and nesting sites.

Management: Positive and continuing management is needed for long-term sustainability as neglect and development can adversely affect habitats and greenspaces. Management should be planned and properly funded, and should involve local communities.

Funding: Allocation of funding for long-term management should be an integral part of the green infrastructure funding arrangements, including the provision of contingency funding.

Governance and accountability: Appropriate governance structures are required to ensure that standards are met, community engagement is continued, future development continues to meet eco-town standards and community assets are maintained.

Source: TCPA, Natural England and DCLG, 2009, p. 2

of natural systems is increasing amongst both policymakers and the public. Nevertheless, it is acknowledged that the CBD initiative to halt biodiversity decline by 2010 will not be achieved worldwide nor within Europe. In this section we consider what barriers or constraints may have contributed to this failure and how these may have impacted upon spatial planning. We argue in this book that the spatial planning system has an important role to play in addressing and building resilience to climate change, and this role is particularly significant in the case of biodiversity protection and enhancement. This is the case because:

- the primary aim of spatial planning (currently) is sustainable development, and the environment is a major theme of policy and action in this approach.
- spatial planning is an activity that brings together a range of interests, environmental, economic and social, and so parallels the multifunctionality of biodiversity (maintaining natural systems, underpinning health,

wealth and culture), which suggests that spatial planning might provide integrated approaches.

- in addition, spatial planning shares with biodiversity issues such as the significance of boundaries, and biodiversity has a fundamental connection with space/territory and movement across space – essential concerns of planning.

The following analysis uses the structure proposed by Trudgill (1990) for identifying barriers to better environmental policy implementation.

Agreement: there is international, regional and national agreement about the importance of and need to protect biodiversity, and commitments have been made to this at all levels since the signing of the CBD, specifically under the 'Halt biodiversity loss by 2010' policy. Nevertheless, an understanding of what is to be protected is still developing, moving from simply species and habitats towards ecosystems and their interrelated processes. It could be argued that there is no clear single agreed articulation of what the motivation for this policy is, however, rather than there being a single, clear threat, many 'small' threats exist (e.g. loss of individual species amongst many species, or loss of examples of habitats and ecosystems where other examples continue to survive). To an extent the threat is now crystallizing as a threat to the continued success of 'life on Earth', with biodiversity seen as 'life assurance'.

Knowledge and uncertainty: understanding of natural processes, their importance to life on Earth, the quantity of and interactions between species, habitats and processes is rapidly expanding – wildlife research and monitoring has accumulated quantities of data and understanding of status and consequences of change. However, there are still many areas of uncertainty: species and habitat responses, impact of invasive species, consequences of phenology change, likelihood of dispersal success, etc. While policy is frequently embarked upon in circumstances of uncertainty (as in trade policy), it may be that the many layers of uncertainty involved in biodiversity's adaptation to climate change have contributed to delayed and inadequate action though there has been a good deal of policy discussion, lobbying and advocacy.

A key approach to biodiversity protection, as mentioned in Section 12.6, is increasing connectivity between current and future (potential) sites, despite uncertainty about climate change and consequent environmental impacts on sites, and despite uncertainty about species interactions. Uncertainties about the status of future sites may relate to future water relations, soil characteristics, competing species, the breaking of prey-predator links, etc. Dispersal abilities vary and may be insufficient to cross barriers such as landscapes fragmented by intensive agriculture or urban infrastructure as well as mountains and deserts. To overcome such barriers increasing landscape connectivity is proposed, which includes making rural landscapes generally more wildlife-friendly over wide areas for example by introducing corridors and 'stepping stones' between protected areas and areas with future potential for colonization. Araújo *et al.* (2004) showed that common conservation planning approaches do not capture such retention and connection areas, and that new tools are needed for bio-diversity conservation to meet the rapid environmental and other changes. Attempts have been made to develop conservation planning tools to account for forecast changes in species distributions (for example, Hannah *et al.*, 2007). These studies identify minimum sets of areas that protect occurrences of the species currently and as forecasted according to ecological models and climate change scenarios – weaknesses with such methods have been discussed by Thuiller *et al.* (2008). These areas of uncertainty mean that the planning of con-servation areas must, at the very least, acknowledge uncertainty and provide flexibility to adapt and respond. The precautionary principle is relevant here – not waiting for 'complete' information, but acting on the basis of probabilities in advance of that.

Technology: technological developments seem unlikely to have been a bar-rier, but rather to have largely assisted the increased profile of biodiversity: computer modelling and mapping of population change and dispersal and climate change, technology for continuous and remote monitoring species and habitats, and research and communications technology to inform and permit analysis and discussion as well as to present information and trends graphically for wide dissemination of ideas. Examples here include the mapping of habitats and *Biodiversity Opportunity Areas in Kent* (Kent CC, undated) and the *Ecological Network for Cheshire* (Cheshire CC, undated). The Cheshire initiative aims, by 2020, to 'encompass nearly 4,000 hectares of new and restored peatlands, heathlands, woodlands, meadows and wetlands linked together with existing priority habitats to form a coherent and sustainable network that will improve conditions for many species of plants and animals'.

Economic and financial factors: these, particularly competition and funding, are more easily identified as barriers in biodiversity policy development. First, sustainable development and biodiversity protection – while acknowledged as priority issues – have to compete for both action and funding with the more pressing priority that is economic growth. Although habitats and ecosystems are important in making development attractive (or even possible) at specific locations, the connection is not always sufficiently recognized and rewarded.

Some funding to support biodiversity may be available from regional infra-structure funds or other sources, but development itself is a principal route to funding, through Section 106 agreements under the Town and Country Planning Act 1990. This act allows an LPA to enter into a legally binding agree-ment or planning obligation with a landowner in association with the granting of planning permission. Guidance published on improving biodiversity resili-ence to climate change rarely mentions funding.

Social: such barriers to biodiversity policy may arise again in connection with economic issues: for example, the need for a buffering strip around a designated site may be outweighed by the need for jobs or housing. The multiple oppor-tunities provided by green areas (on which we elaborate in Section 9.9) are a counterweight to this, though greenspace does not need to be wholly 'natural' to offer health benefits and improve the physical environment.

Political: finally, political (and administrative) factors which may act as obstacles to biodiversity policy include the lack of fit between, for example, catchment or habitat boundaries or migration routes with political boundaries; this can lead to dilution or downgrading of the policy. In the prioritization of sectors, biodiversity may be overlooked as, although biodiversity may be a subsidiary support to health, education, recreation, air and water quality policies, these are awarded priority standing by themselves, so subsidiary biodiversity–related benefits may not be specified as policy aims, and could be undervalued.

12.8 Conclusions – implications for biodiversity policy: conservation and enhancement

We have reviewed in the preceding sections a broad-brush integrated system, from international to national and local levels, designed to conserve and protect biodiversity. The rhetoric associated with these strategies and action plans acknowledges the value and importance of ecosystems as providing the feedback which supports life on Earth, and specifically, human life. Nevertheless, despite the strategies, some funding and the measures proposed, it is recognized that the 2010 target is not within our grasp (EEA, 2009e, p. 5), and that much stronger measures are needed in coming decades. Moreover, the static nature protection in isolated protected areas is no longer considered sufficient to adequately conserve biodiversity in the future and to overcome the accumulation of impacts from not only climate change but also development-induced habitat fragmentation. New approaches are needed – though protected areas continue to play a role as vital long-term sites for flora and fauna. Work by researchers such as Hannah *et al.* (2007) has shown that site protection remains an important conservation strategy under a 'moderate climate change scenario' and that site connectivity is important.

The central importance of biodiversity and ecosystems to human welfare and the full range of climate change impacts experienced are increasingly recognized – indeed, growing awareness of climate change risks may have improved awareness of the role of biodiversity in maintaining Earth's ecosystems and consequently may thus contribute to conserving biodiversity. Other researchers, including Lomborg (2007) also argue that climate change has 'hijacked' the wider agenda, which includes not only biodiversity but also poverty. We would, however, argue that the response to climate change is an essential part of sustainable development. Spatial planning has an essential role to achieve appropriate land allocations, integration across sectors and long-term spatial measures within a sustainability framework – various approaches have been recommended to achieve this at national, regional and local scales. Spatial planning can contribute to land management for climate change adaptation where it protects vulnerable land, for instance by protecting upland soils such as moorlands and peatlands – which play other roles as carbon sinks or for water retention. The economic valuation of biodiversity and ecosystem services, via appropriate monetization of services and a contribution to compensation, also has a role to play, as funding for biodiversity needs to be secured.

Part IV
Prospects

13 Climate change learning, knowledge and communication amongst spatial planning communities

······································

13.1 Introduction

A theme of this book has been that the spatial planning response to climate change needs to be seen in the context of the ideals and principles of sustainable development. To the complex and contestable precepts of sustainable development, climate change adds further complexity and uncertainty, which are magnified through the interaction with social, political and economic systems. In this chapter, we look at the scope for policy learning in supporting the development and implementation of climate-change responsive spatial planning policy. As Dryzek argues in the context of environmentalism, 'we need institutions and discourses which are capable of learning – not least about their own shortcomings' (Dryzek, 2005, p. 232). Responding to the challenge of sustainable development has required significant change in thinking and concepts within spatial planning, and responding to the particular issue of climate change represents a new challenge for policy learning.

For instance, spatial planning policy and practice now interacts with other policy communities, such as that of climate change policy. This latter is not homogeneous. On one hand, there has been a difference between the scientists and modellers, with their analysis of causes and consequences into the future, and their recommendations (such as those of the IPCC) for action, and the government and public to whom they make their recommendations. There are also disjunctions between the climate change mitigation interest groups, pushing for low-carbon futures, and the adaptation interests, pushing for a continuous process of adaptation and resilience. Spatial planning has needed to engage with and learn about this complexity; but the spatial planning community itself is not uniform as it comprises planning and other professionals, politicians, development interests and civil society.

We need to recognize that these interests are made up of individuals and groups with their own complex and possibly inconsistent beliefs and attitudes, who will respond differently to the issue of climate change.

This raises fundamental questions about the way in which climate change is presented and communicated, and the expectations of society about the response of spatial planning to climate change, and its scope for action. How does policy learning happen in this context? For instance, a firm expectation of the UK planning system comes from the TCPA and Friends of the Earth-led Coalition for Planning and Climate Change (TCPA and FoE, 2009), which has lobbied government to make more explicit and stringent the obligation on statutory planning to promote low-carbon and well-adapted futures, but claims that spatial planning lacks the knowledge, powers or will to act – all crucial aspects of policy learning. Following Glasbergen (1996), we can see policy learning as comprising technical, conceptual and social learning. The former, it is argued, can be seen as a form of searching for new or improved existing instruments and implementing them in an improved or more effective way – Ebrahim (2008) characterizes this as single-loop learning, in which fundamental premises are not challenged. The initial formulation of government policy on planning for climate change in England in 2007 could be seen as an example of this, where it was expected that the mere expression of intention and encouragement would deliver outcomes, without a fundamental re-evaluation of strategic approaches. Conceptual learning represents a double-loop, where the definition of the problem, the underlying assumptions and the scope of goals and objectives are reappraised and reformulated. One example might be the shift in attitudes among professionals to making space for water. The third element is institutional or social learning, which emphasises deliberation and dialogues among stakeholders and attention to the norms within which they operate, which offers scope to improve both technical and conceptual learning. Glasbergen suggests that environmental policy initially developed with a model of cognitive learning, where knowledge is a dominant variable, and insights are gained into both cause–effect relationships and policy processes (he gives environmental impact assessment as an example). But he argues that, as environmental policy matured and yet some problems seemed intractable, social processes of interdependence and communication amongst government agencies and civil society became recognized as necessary to generate 'multi-faceted problem-solving capacity' (p. 183), particularly under conditions of complexity and uncertainty. The three types of learning must be seen as complementing each other, but (following Glasbergen) Ebrahim (2008) also emphasises that the importance of the institutional context, and in particular social and political power and conflict, should be recognized.

This chapter will review some of the factors around these assertions, looking at the scope for social or institutional learning among planning communities, the production and communication of climate change knowledge, issues of attitudes and behaviour, and the political space for action. Of course, all the issues of knowledge, learning and communication are closely related, and the arguments could be structured differently. This interrelationship is especially complex to disentangle, given the prominence of climate change in the media and public discourse in the latter part of the first decade of the twenty-first century.

13.2 Institutional and social learning

We suggest that the institutional context for policy learning in planning for climate change is important in that it shapes the relations between actors and stakeholders. Through engagement and debate, there should be opportunities for iterations of policy development and for reflection about knowledge and experience, and their role in decision-making. A distinguishing feature of climate change awareness raising and policy development is the engagement of a range of stakeholders in the process; it needs to be both a bottom-up and a top-down process, with local communities taking an active role as well as government at all levels and private companies. As such, the field of spatial planning is an area that may be expected to use and demonstrate social learning as part of knowledge acquisition and policy formulation. By 'social learning' we understand a process involving public participation, polycentric and collaborative governance.

To date there are few studies of social learning within spatial planning for climate change; we pay particular attention to learning in planning for and the co-management of the built environment and natural resources. In this section we introduce examples of social learning within European and UK climate change adaptation communities of practice, within river basin management (a process required by EU Directive), and across the planning and construction sector. We distinguish here between *post hoc* analyses of institutional learning and specific exercises in providing opportunities for social learning. We draw out from the studies both the supporting conditions for and also the barriers to social learning.

13.2.1 Institutional learning

Glasbergen's analysis of policy learning was based on experience with the development of innovative environmental policy in the Netherlands, and reflected (although it did not draw upon) similar work on institutional learning in Weale's analysis (1992) of the capacity for learning in the formulating and implementation of the Dutch NEPP (see Chapter 4). Weale argued that the radical approach of the NEPP could be explained through both the theoretical logic of cognitive knowledge (its systems approach to environmental flows and limits) and the institutional conditions. These latter are themselves a reflection of the prevailing Dutch tradition of consensus, cooperation and coalition. This enabled the NEPP to be a means of social learning – 'learning by planning, (Weale, 1992, p. 146) – through a better, shared understanding of policy issues in pollution management. However, he recognized that such learning might be necessary but was certainly not sufficient to achieve the desired outcomes.

13.2.2 Social learning in adaptation

From these early foundations, there has been considerable interest in the concept of social learning as part of the development of environmental policy and, more recently, in its utility in understanding climate change adaptation (Pelling and High, 2005; McEvoy, Lonsdale and Matczak, 2008). Less attention has been given to the concept within the spatial planning response to climate change, but we consider that this approach might offer useful insights. Pelling and High explain the value of social learning for adaptation and lay stress on institutions not as organizational entities but as formal elements (such as legislation or guidelines) and informal elements (such as cultural norms and values). In their analysis, adaptation can be seen as learning, both by individuals and social groups, and can take the form of material or intangible adaptation strategies. The social context can influence the individual, and social organizations themselves can learn. Pelling and High conclude that, for climate change adaptation, there is a skills gap, especially among people who can 'operate at the boundaries of practice and facilitate communication and learning' (Pelling and High, 2005, p. 15). In the UK, this may be a particular issue for spatial planning given its broadly social science recruitment at present, and the general lack of trust between public, scientists and politicians (Jackson, 2009).

A study which looked at both mitigation and adaptation, including some spatial planning case studies, was undertaken as part of the ADAM project: participants in a number of learning examples across Europe were interviewed to understand the influences on learning (McEvoy, Lonsdale and Matczak, 2008). The authors found that actors valued opportunities for learning and reflection, and discovered the scope this offered for bringing about changes in institutions' management and behaviour. One example of social learning – the UK Local Climate Impact Profile – has been shown in Chapter 9, Box 9.10. Collaboration and mutual learning can be supportive (the study cites the example of Flood Liaison and Appraisal Groups in Scotland), or exclusive (where, for instance, top-down decision-makers are not aware of the knowledge of operational front-line staff).

13.2.3 Social learning in planning for sustainable construction

One example of a study of social learning specifically within a spatial planning context and set of institutions and norms is the study by Rydin *et al.* (2007), that explored social learning with respect to environmentally sustainable construction (ESC). There are lessons here for climate change adaptation. These researchers suggest that, as ESC is seen as part of the broader sustainable development agenda, within which planners are expected to play a role in delivering more sustainable patterns of both construction and development, this 'puts particular demands on the knowledge resources of planners since knowledge is implicated in the power relations between planners and developers' (p. 366). Noting that in practice ESC requires debate about different sustainability options at the scale of the development site, Rydin *et al.* suggest that planners may use their control over development rights to achieve ESC as a form of planning gain, but that planners will need to be knowledgeable in order to promote a shift towards more sustainable modes of construction (p. 366). However, 'recognised knowledge frames the policy problem and the possible solutions, while policy dynamics influence what counts as knowledge' (p. 367). Rydin *et al.* also consider the concept of communities of practice, where the coherence of such a community is based on mutual engagement of stakeholders, together with their shared past experience and activity including learning, the 'locally negotiated regime of competence', and 'the demonstrated ability to "read" the local context' (p. 367). Approaches such as training, guides and checklists, however, lead to tensions between the need for time efficiency and the need for wider knowledge, such as the economics of different options. The need for knowledge which would be robust against an appeal by developers, and which had clear links to Building Regulations, was also seen as essential. Many of these issues (knowledge and learning, applicability of guides and checklists, full understanding of options) will also apply to learning and action with respect to climate change adaptation.

The acquisition of new skills may therefore only be part of this social learning, although the London Borough of Haringey is reported as stating that, from 2015, all new planning staff will need to be BREEAM accredited (Gillman, 2009).

An example of a community of practice around the need for sustainable construction is that of the UK Green Building Council (Box 13.1).

13.2.4 Social learning in natural resource management

Social learning may be particularly important in natural resource management, and therefore of potential interest in planning for climate change, where there is interdependence of stakeholders and an awareness of the needs of resource management. This is especially the case for 'common pool' assets such as soils, river basins and biodiversity which are subject to overexploitation as

Box 13.1 UK Green Building Council

Work by the UK Green Building Council demonstrates what such a community of practice might be within the private sector. The UK-GBC (launched in February 2007) has as its stated mission: 'to dramatically improve the sustainability of the built environment, by radically transforming the way it is planned, designed, constructed, maintained and operated'. It works by bringing together developers, architects, investors, product manufacturers, cost consultants, energy suppliers, surveyors, civil and other engineering specialists, contractors, occupiers as well as academics and local government – all groups involved in planning, designing, constructing, maintaining and operating buildings. Much UK-GBC work is accomplished by time limited 'task groups'. These are working groups that bring together experts from within the memberships to tackle a particular issue – for instance, past working groups have tackled low carbon existing homes, defining zero carbon, carbon reductions in new non-domestic buildings and sustainable district infrastructure. Each group works over a limited 6–12 month period, during which member representatives meet regularly to discuss and prepare a report and recommendations, for example, on biodiversity and the built environment (UK-GBC, 2009). The task group outcomes, defined at the outset by a task group proposal from its membership, may then feed directly into the development of government policy, or set out guidance for the industry on a given issue but, while accepting the need for regulation, the GBC also seeks a non-prescriptive approach, 'allowing industry the flexibility to innovate and adapt accordingly'. The UK-GBC approach is perhaps remarkable for the way in which it brings together industry players who are in competition, secures their uncompensated input and achieves agreement on future action.

users cannot be excluded (see also Chapter 3.2.1 and Chapter 5.1). The social learning process can lead through the development of trust, joint problem definition and data collection, and the development and assessment of a set of alternatives, towards joint decision-making and joint planning for implementation (Grey 1989, quoted by Mostert *et al.*, 2007). The purpose and outcomes of the social learning process are not only better natural resources management but also 'social-relational outcomes such as better relations, increased trust, empowerment of stakeholders, and the establishment or strengthening of networks' (Mostert *et al.*, 2007, p. 2). The analysis by Mostert *et al.*, exploring social learning as a policy development mechanism for European river basins, identified a set of general themes among factors fostering or hindering social learning. These included clarity about stakeholder involvement and its impacts, extent of reliance on technical expertise and fear of losing control, opportunities for interaction, motivation and skills of leaders and facilitators, openness, representativeness, framing and reframing, and resources. The researchers point to building on positive experiences derived from participatory exercises as a route to overcoming resistance to social learning. Mostert *et al.* claim that social learning occurs when interdependent stakeholders with different interests and perceptions come together and manage to deal with these differences to the common benefit. It becomes an issue, however, when organizational settings are complex and cases are controversial. In such situations, they state 'social learning processes can become time-consuming and costly' and therefore 'should only be embarked upon for really important issues and when there is at least a slight chance of success' (p. 13).

Examples of active attempts at social learning within urban river environments in the UK include the River Tame in the West Midlands (Petts, 2007) and the River Dearne in South Yorkshire (Selman and Bailey, 2009). The latter (described in more detail in Box 13.2) was one of the projects supported by the Homes and Communities Academy and the Economic and Social Research Council in their Skills and Knowledge for Sustainable Communities Initiative which looked at innovative ideas and approaches. These might serve as useful models for extending participative social learning in spatial planning for climate change at the local level.

Box 13.2 Engaging local communities in sustainable river management and planning

The project aimed to build on current experiences of participation in river basin planning through the medium of imaginative writing and the creation of an anthology of local knowledge and experiences. The groups found they had changed awareness, shared knowledge and gained confidence, and the process was valued by participants. The project concluded that such an approach to social learning could involve local people in personal and community sustainable development actions.

Source: Selman and Bailey, 2009

13.3 Networks and learning

13.3.1 Networks and coalitions

One response to providing opportunities for mutual learning is the establishment of networks: we have already indicated (especially in Chapter 4) that there are a number of such networks in the field of spatial planning response to climate change, some of which are bottom-up in the sense of being led by stakeholders. These have tended to be focused either on mitigation or adaptation. The Nottingham Declaration in its early years provided an example of a network in mitigation, when 100 local authority members had signed up to action on climate change mitigation. This single focus possibly contributed to the low profile and slower take-up of adaptation actions at the local level (Wilson, 2006). The Nottingham Declaration was relaunched in 2005, and adopted an adaptation commitment. Some 300 councils are now signatories (90 per cent of all councils in England), as well as a number of other agencies such as the Audit Commission. The Declaration has been endorsed by the Local Government Association which, as part of its Small Change, Big Difference campaign, calls on all councils to sign (LGA, 2008). In line with the Declaration, many councils have produced climate change action plans, but there is little monitoring of their effectiveness (LGA Commission, 2007). Another example of mitigation networks is the partnerships established through the UK Carbon Trust in working alongside local authorities and other organizations. In the field of adaptation, the stakeholder-led regional climate change adaptation partnerships, as we have argued in Chapter 4, have played a significant role in raising awareness and supporting mutual learning. More recently, some of the regional adaptation partnerships – such as that for the North East – have altered their scope and are now expressly including mitigation activities within their remit.

There have also been more integrated approaches among campaigning groups, such as the alliances among the biodiversity and ecosystems community (for instance, the campaign for legislative protection for the marine environment, which bore fruit in the passing of the Marine and Coastal Access Act in 2009) and the planning community. The coalition led by TCPA and Friends of the Earth pressing for more stringent planning policy comprises a mixture of campaigning organizations and private sector companies; as an issue-focused coalition it is likely to be transient. It will be interesting to see how far its aims are met in the final revision of planning policy guidance, whether the group persists beyond that time and if so how its aims evolve.

13.3.2 Cross-national learning

Although, as we have seen, spatial planning is not a European Union competence, cross-national learning within the EU and beyond has been encouraged by the European Framework Programmes for Research and Technological Development (with FP7 launched in 2009). The aim is to create a unified area within which there is movement of researchers, knowledge sharing and cross-national research, addressing major challenges together. While conditions (social, economic and environmental) vary across the EU, the value of cross-national learning lies in the bringing together of broad and diverging understandings of theory and change, together with wide experience of options, approaches and consequences. Principles can be deduced and tested in many contexts, hopefully resulting in 'faster' and perhaps more robust learning, but also helping to knit together the European Union. Much of this process may also be described as social or institutional learning, in that it incorporates (to follow Siebenhüner and Suplie, 2005):

- communication structures that are intense, open and transparent.
- learning mechanisms such as regular evaluations, specific committees, workshops, etc.

- commonly shared values and norms contributing towards solving problems.
- a set of conflicts (or differing viewpoints) about resources, values and identities, which help spark and promote both demand for change and also learning.

Specific programmes for planning and climate change have included those funded by INTERREG funding under the EU's Cohesion Policy such as ESPACE (climate change and spatial planning) and BRANCH (biodiversity and climate change), and currently GRaBS, together with ALARM and MACIS (biodiversity and climate change) funded under the R&D Framework Programmes. The ESPACE project has been successful in drawing on experiences of climate change and planning responses in the Netherlands and Germany, leading to the publication of guidance for the implementation of climate change policies in South East England (SEERA and ESPACE, 2007; SE Leaders Board, 2009). It has also developed the PACT (performance acceleration for climate) tool, which assesses organizational capacity for addressing mitigation and adaptation, and has been used in public and private sectors. Similarly, the GRaBS project (Henderson, 2009) is intended to test and promote the risk and vulnerabilities tool being developed at the University of Manchester, building on the work of the ASCCUE and SKCC research projects.

Such cross-national work offers opportunities for learning among the participants. These opportunities have been particularly significant in the learning between the Netherlands and the UK, with shifts in attitudes to water, flood management and landscape-scale biodiversity conservation as part of extended planning responses to climate change. The Dutch are also seeing the opportunities for cross-national learning to benefit their economy through their specialist expertise in flood management in deltas, with links with New Orleans and the deltas of Southeast Asia.

13.3.3 Academic and practitioner networks

Throughout the book, we have drawn on a number of research projects which have involved the academic research community, consultancies, stakeholders and spatial planning practitioners. We showed in Chapter 4 that, in the Netherlands, the distinctions between these groups are less clearly delineated in practice than in the UK. Nevertheless, there have been examples in the UK of these academic and practitioner networks working together on climate change themes. Examples include the involvement of universities in modelling climate impacts on biodiversity and assessing their policy implications in the BRANCH project (see Chapter 12); the work of the Tyndall Centre for Climate Change Research Cities Programme at Newcastle University with the GLA in using the UK Climate Projections 09 to assess, using an integrated assessment model, how complex cities such as London can continue to grow under a changing climate

(Hall *et al.* 2009 – see Box 13.3); and the work of the University of Manchester with local authorities in Greater Manchester and the North West region in developing a campaign and actions for green infrastructure at different spatial scales (discussed in Chapter 9).

Box 13.3 *Engineering Cities* project

The Tyndall Centre worked with the stakeholders and the developing policy agenda in London to assess the implications of changes in climate, population and the economy up to 2100 for land use, buildings and infrastructure. Using the Urban Integrated Assessment Facility, the project modelled economic drivers, land use changes, carbon emissions, urban temperatures, water availability and flood risk under a number of scenarios. The project concluded that a portfolio of demand-and-supply side measures is needed. 'The research has demonstrated the central role of land use planning in guiding and constraining pathways to sustainable urban layout in the long term' (Hall *et al.*, 2009, p. 3). It pointed to certain synergies and trade-offs, which are being analysed further in preparation for the next London Plan.

The follow-up ARCADIA project 2009–12 will build on this project, including assessing the impacts of climate change on the urban economy, changing scenarios of socio-economic factors and a wider set of adaptation options.

Source: Hall *et al.*, 2009

13.3.4 Professional networks

In 2006, the RTPI (the professional planning institute in the UK) proposed a campaign for coordinated engagement with research and policy on spatial planning and climate change. In 2008–09, it reviewed its Vision for Planning (dating from 2001), and in 2009 it set out key principles and priorities to fulfil its commitment that 'Spatial planning must help communities at all scales to achieve sustainable development and particularly to respond to climate change' (RTPI, 2009). The institute has developed action plans for these principles: promoting behavioural change, adapting existing places, delivering climate change responsive legislation and policies, improving current practice, celebrating best practice, and developing climate change education and skills.

The RTPI also became a stakeholder in a number of EPSRC-funded projects: with the TCPA it was a stakeholder in the ASCCUE project under the Building Knowledge for Changing Climate programme (see Chapter 9), and currently it is a partner in two projects under the Adaptation and Resilience in a Changing Climate (ARCC) programme 2009–13 (part of the UK research councils' Living with Environmental Change programme). The RTPI is involved in ARCADIA (Adaptation and Resilience in Cities: Analysis and Decision making using Integrated Assessment) (see Box 13.3) and SNACC (Suburban Neighbourhood

Adaptation for a Changing Climate) – identifying effective, practical and accessible means of suburban redesign.

Its position as a professional institute which accredits higher education courses should give the RTPI the opportunity to promote learning within both the next generation and through lifelong learning. There are, however, other contenders for this role in upgrading the skills of current planning professionals, such as the Homes and Communities Academy with its involvement in the Skills and Knowledge programme mentioned above, and its endorsement (if not formal accreditation) of educational initiatives such as some master's programmes in regeneration and housing.

As a professional institute, the RTPI's role as a campaigning organization is limited. It is not, for instance, a member of the TCPA and Friends of the Earth's Coalition. On the other hand, the RTPI's commitment in its Living with Climate Change Vision to promoting behavioural change represents a shift to more substantive goals (such as carbon reduction) than the institute had formerly endorsed.

However, to all these networks there is an element of reinforcement rather than outreach, with the organizations and individuals participating being those already active in the field. Moreover, there is a question over the extent of representativeness in membership of such coalitions and networks – for instance, although the large majority of local authorities are now signed up to the Nottingham Declaration, this does not necessarily percolate through to all elements of an authority's remit and services. Where there are dedicated environmental departments within councils, climate change may still be seen as their specialist concern and not one of relevance to spatial planning. This was found in the SECTORS survey, where questions to district council local planning departments on their response to climate change adaptation were redirected to climate change officers or environmental departments (SEECCP, 2004). The internal politics of local government are also material. Indeed, there has been concern that spatial planning as a local authority function has been sidelined or not regarded as a key corporate commitment. Similar issues might arise at central government level in relation to DCLG, Whitehall and Westminster (see Chapter 4).

13.3.5 Guidance and good practice

In earlier chapters, we have referred to the wealth of advisory material which has been published by networks, professional bodies, advisory bodies such as CABE and pressure groups such as TCPA. However, there is evidence that the publication of guidance and advocacy of tools without the active opportunities for social learning and engagement that we have discussed in this chapter can be, if not counterproductive, at least not helpful in learning and changing habits and norms. The LGA's own Climate Change Commission (LGA Climate Change Commission, 2007) found that local authority officers expressed concern at guidance fatigue, with too many such documents published without attention to the political space for action or the resource-constrained realities of local authorities. Phillips (2008) found that there was considerable ignorance among the planners surveyed of the available published guidance, such as the Three Regions CC Partnerships' guidance (Three Regions, 2006) and the TCPA's guidance on adaptation (Shaw *et al.*, 2007). This suggests that we need to explore further the nature of knowledge among planning communities, and to recognize that communities of practice may exist which mutually reinforce constrained action or even inaction.

13.4 Climate change knowledge amongst planning communities

One possibility is that there are specific aspects of climate change knowledge which make social and policy learning among planning communities problematic, or at any rate not straightforward. Climate change is multidimensional – not just across the mitigation-adaptation dimension, but across the economic, social and cultural contexts of its causes and consequences. A key issue must therefore be how knowledge about climate change is communicated not just to professionals and experts but to civil society and the lay public.

13.4.1 Climate change communication and the media

There has been considerable attention paid in recent years to the challenge of effective communication of climate change (Moser and Dilling, 2007; Lorenzoni *et al.* 2007), much of which is premised on the need to communicate the urgency of action to the public. It is argued that we need to be aware of the targeted audience, how climate change is framed by the messengers, the language employed and the means of communication, all of which are filtered through issues of trust. We also need to be aware of the norms of media practice. For instance, certain tabloid newspapers in the UK claim to be providing balanced coverage when they portray the sceptics' view of climate change as mainstream, despite the majority scientific consensus. Boykoff and Mansfield (2007) used content analysis to show that some of the UK tabloid press, unlike either the US press or UK broadsheets, significantly diverged from the scientific consensus and consistently offered contrarian views. The importance of this distortion lies in the large readership of this press, which might be exposed to misrepresentation at a time when governments and NGOs are urging raised awareness in order to take personal action and press for more political action. Boykoff and Mansfield suggest that, in addition to the perverse use of the norm of balance, explanations might lie in the papers' lack of specialist scientific or environmental correspondents as well as other editorial and economic pressures.

13.4.2 Attitudes and behaviour

The press may, through such norms, reinforce attitudes of scepticism which might in turn extend to public views on the appropriateness or not of government action in the field of climate change. Surveys of public attitudes in Europe and the UK have shown some interesting paradoxes between apparent knowledge of climate change and expectations of either governmental or personal action. Citizens in Sweden, the Netherlands, Finland and the UK feel well-informed about climate change (with some three-quarters of respondents feeling informed about the causes and consequences of climate change) (Eurobarometer, 2009). These countries also have a high proportion of people who have taken some personal action to fight climate change. However, in Ireland, the UK and the Netherlands, opinion is evenly divided between those who think that CO_2 has a marginal impact on climate change and those who disagree. Moreover, in Luxembourg, the Netherlands and the UK, a significant proportion – almost 40 per cent – of respondents think that the issue of climate change has been exaggerated. Compared with the EU average of 67 per cent, the UK and the Netherlands have a lower proportion of the population (only around half) who classify climate change as a very serious problem. This paradox (of well-informed populations, a large proportion of whom do not see climate change as very serious) is sufficiently odd that the Eurobarometer report specifically remarks upon it, although it does not offer an explanation.

This finding of seemingly paradoxical views is consistent with a UK survey (Thornton, 2009), which found that, while knowledge of climate change terms was high, some 25 per cent of people thought that 'it is not worth Britain trying to control climate change because other countries will just cancel out what we do' (p. 12). Moreover, although there has been an increase in the proportion of people agreeing that climate change is caused by energy use, and that they were taking a number of actions, one in ten respondents were not prepared to change their behaviour (p. 18).

This is a fascinating area of social psychology which we do not have space to explore further here. But the point to emphasise is that planning communities of professionals and politicians are also citizens and users of the media for their information, which might strongly affect their attitudes and their learning. Moreover, they are also the targets of campaigns aiming at changing behaviour. Spatial planning is usually seen as a manifestation of public policy requiring regulation and legislation. But of course there is a choice of policy instruments to implement any policy, and there has been much interest in market-based instruments (such as the Landfill tax, the Aggregates tax and subsidies for renewables and energy-efficient homes), as well as in education and raising awareness to promote personal voluntary commitment and hence to change in both behaviour and self-motivating attitudes. This has been the premise of much of the campaigning to citizens as householders and as consumers of transport, based on conceptions of 'pro-environmental behaviours' (Defra, 2009e). The framework employs social marketing insights to segment the population and behaviours along dimensions such as willingness to act and ability to act and then aims to tailor campaigning to these segments.

Within the field of spatial planning, the individuals comprising any community of practice – professionals, politicians or public – might fall into any of these segmented categories; no single and consistent set of beliefs should be assumed.

13.4.3 Political engagement

There has recently been criticism of the social marketing approach on two grounds: firstly, that cumulatively doing a little will only achieve a little (Mackay, 2009), and secondly, that the simple and painless pro-environmental behaviours do not necessarily lead to more difficult or challenging actions (WWF, 2008; 2009). WWF concludes also that such simple changes in the personal sphere will not lead to the necessary public-sphere political pressure for government intervention. They argue that campaigning organizations need to find 'more effective ways to generate and mobilize public pressure for change' (p. 6) and that more effort must go into creating 'political space' through the mobilization of political demands for fundamental change. Ockwell *et al.* (2009), however, argue that it is possible that grassroots engagement could promote a demand for more regulation to require more pro-environmental behaviour. They suggest that climate change communication could actually stimulate pressure for regulation, through more explicitly engendering public acceptance of regulation, and through prompting grassroots activities. In this way, bottom-up and top-down approaches – both essential for addressing climate change effectively – can be employed.

This is particularly material to the activities of spatial planning as it has been essentially a regulatory intervention. The relationship of social learning, knowledge, communication of climate change as an issue, behaviour and attitudes is complex, and it is not possible to do more than point out the broad outlines of some of the debates here. But it is evident that, compared with Scandinavian countries which also have a strong tradition of public sector planning, the UK and the Netherlands represent challenges in that there are significant elements of the populations who take the view that climate change is exaggerated or not a serious issue. This might limit the extent to which spatial planning can, as argued by the TCPA and Friends of the Earth Coalition, drive a radical or transformational shift in behaviour. We return to this question in the book's final chapter.

However, one question not elicited in the studies is the relationship between the awareness of the need for adaptation and taking action to limit emissions through reducing carbon use or energy demand. In this field, there is considerable interest in extending some of the principles of community-level planning through visioning and visualizing the future to effect change.

13.5 Community engagement and visualization

13.5.1 The use of analogy

Environmental campaigning groups have long recognized that they have a dilemma in striking the balance between portraying the urgency and seriousness of an issue to gain media and public attention, and the risk of disempowering people through a sense of doom and inevitability. O'Neill and Nicholson-Cole (2009) found that images of human suffering (such as starving children) had this effect of disempowerment, but that 'images that stimulated the greatest feelings of personal efficacy were those clearly showing what people can do personally' (p. 374). Local impacts and icons of images selected by non-experts were found to empower people to act. This points to the importance of local engagement with the issues, and familiar experience. This might include the use of analogy (in the context of adaptation, it might involve reminding people of conditions of the hot summer of 2003 or the summer floods of 2007) or visualization. Using the imagery, for instance, of saying that the summer of 2003 might be the normal summer temperatures by the 2050s (as is done in the Defra 2009 projections) might attune with people's experiences and memories of how they adapted, and hence build preparedness and adaptive capacity. (Whether it would aid their motivation to take action to reduce carbon emissions to ensure that average global temperature changes do not exceed that is a moot point.) The Center for Research in Environmental Decisions at Columbia University is clear: 'in order for climate science information to be fully absorbed by audiences, it must be actively communicated with appropriate language, metaphor, and analogy; combined with narrative storytelling; made vivid through visual imagery and experiential scenarios; balanced with scientific information; and delivered by trusted messengers in group settings' (CRED, 2009). One problem is in agreeing on what is appropriate analogy. It is not necessarily helpful to extrapolate climate change variables such as average summer temperatures from one cultural context to another – especially in the field of the built environment. For instance, in the Netherlands and the UK, urban and building design has largely developed (at least in traditional building) to accommodate our maritime, temperate climatic conditions and not those of southern France, which has sometimes been used to suggest a model of north-west Europe's likely future climate.

On the other hand, some useful points can be conveyed, with images such as those showing the equivalent geographical location of Europe's capital cities by precipitation and temperature by 2070s (Figure 13.1). The authors of the map identified 'climate analogues', arguing that the study would help those who plan and design buildings and urban areas to consider the need for different designs for the future (Kopf *et al.*, 2007).

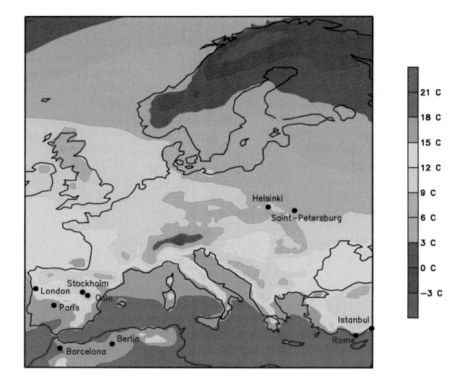

Figure 13.1

City analogue map to illustrate climate change scenarios
Source: Kopf *et al.*, 2008

13.5.2 Community and local visualization

An ability to visualize the future and assess likely impacts – and their consequences within that future – is a vital skill for decision-makers but also for
the stakeholders they may consult. We mentioned in Chapter 6 the scope for
such visualization of future scenarios as part of community visioning, and we
explore it further here.

Advances in software bring ever-better means of helping the public, stakeholders and decision-makers to visualize alternative futures and alternative
environments. Visual representations of changes at a local level – through
perhaps different scenarios of climate change, land use and landscape change,
and plans for built environments – show great potential for raising awareness of
the possible impacts of these plans, and so offer particular possibilities for participation in spatial planning. In Canada, Stephen Sheppard has pioneered the
use of landscape visualization techniques to the problems of communicating

climate change (Sheppard, 2005), and has put these into practice in local climate change visioning with local communities in British Columbia to build local adaptive capacity (Sheppard, 2008; Sheppard and Tatebe, 2009). Sheppard and Tatebe found that, while the visualization was positively received, there was concern about the extent of its outreach to the wider community, and that most councils lacked funding or a mechanism to undertake training or a visioning project. They conclude that councils should look for synergies with other plan-making and outreach processes at different levels of governance, that they could collaborate with others to promote demonstration projects at a neighbourhood scale and that more comprehensive capacity-building and training could be developed, to include community guidance or tool-kit, and consideration of the necessary policy changes for mitigation and adaptation.

In the UK, there have been a number of examples where projects have included visualization at the community scale. At the landscape scale, a project in Oxfordshire, drawing on the Canadian experience, developed maps of possible future land use to provide visual images for use in the work of the Northmoor Trust's Landscape Evolution Centre, which was aimed at engaging primarily with young people (Wood *et al.*, 2006) (Box 13.4).

Box 13.4 Northmoor Trust *Future Landscapes* scenarios

The project downscaled climate change and socio-economic scenarios using inputs from local stakeholders (from eight sectors of agriculture, surface water, flood management, urban and transport, biofuels, protected areas, forestry and business) and land use modelling expertise. The scenarios' work drew on the ATEAM and ACCELERATES European land use scenario projects (see Chapter 7) and UKCIP02 climate change scenarios for the 2020s, 2050s and 2080s. Four scenarios were generated across the dimensions of environmental-economic and global-regional; narratives were developed for each of the scenarios and discussed with the sector groups to generate spatial allocation rules in GIS. In the event, two scenarios – global economic and regional sustainability – were taken further to quantification, modelling and mapping.

The project has been developed by the Project Timescape team to include a workshop exercise on energy futures to 2050. The local area has varied generation potential, including the Didcot Power Stations (Didcot A is a 2000MW coal-fired station due to close by 2015, and Didcot B is gas-fired) and the River Thames. The JET project (Euratom's Joint European Torus, an experimental fusion facility) is also located here. The local area also includes Wittenham Clumps, a local high point and landscape feature, with an Iron Age hill fort. Before taking part in the energy workshop people are encouraged to walk up to the Clumps to see the landscape as it is now.

Workshop participants are then provided with the necessary data to enable them to calculate and 'see' (using materials and counters to represent, for instance, solar panel use or hectares of biofuels) the impact upon the landscape of different combinations of energy-generating technologies.

Source: adapted from Wood *et al.*, 2006

In East Anglia, there have been a number of exercises in representing coastal landscape changes as part of the Shoreline Management Plan process (Nicholson-Cole, 2008). These approaches involve downscaling global and regional climate change scenarios to a local coastal area, including impacts such as sea-level rise, storm surges and wave impacts, and linking them to models of coastal erosion and evolution with the intention of representing them in graphical images to engage communities in shoreline management options for the future.

There are also examples of visualization systems representing sustainable urban development which can also represent aspects of climate change (such as a flood risk) (see Box 13.5 and Figure 13.2).

Box 13.5 Modelling and visualizing sustainable urban environments

The sustainable city visualization tool (S-City VT) is a prototype decision-support tool using an analytical network process methodology to incorporate aspects of interacting social, economic and environmental sustainability factors. The tool is designed to allow stakeholders to understand and influence decisions that affect the sustainability of a development (such as the waterfront development in Dundee, Scotland).

The visualization tool converts two-dimensional plans to a 3D virtual world (with freedom of motion and view) enabling the comparison of materials (e.g. glass, steel), sustainability information and scenarios of change. Options which can be represented include layouts and design, traffic densities and also high to low sustainability options with respect to economic output, energy use, acceptability, air emissions to air, tourism and housing provision.

Coastal flood risk resulting from sea-level rise is also visualized.

The visualization can be seen at: www.scityvt.co.uk

Source: Isaacs et al., 2008

13.5.3 Capacity building through collaborative local working

Many examples can now be given of collaborative organizations working and learning together to address climate change through adaptation and mitigation. Some of these are community-based, perhaps set up locally by a small group of interested activists who may later achieve some funded support. ClimateXchange is an organization supporting and informing low carbon and adaptation groups across Oxfordshire. Provided with some government (Defra) funding to support a coordinator, the organization brings together ideas, speakers, the public and experts to discuss and act on measures to reduce emissions and promote more sustainable and climate-adapted lifestyles. Opportunities for 'eco-regeneration investment', social enterprise networks and the development of communicators ('climate explorers') are also within the overall range of activities. Also within the county, Low Carbon West Oxford (Box 13.6) and Low Carbon Wolvercote (like other similar groups) are active in seeking government and personal responses to climate change, providing information, training and

Figure 13.2

Visualization of waterfront development and flood risk
Reproduced with kind permission of John Isaacs, University of Abertay, Dundee

seeking responses on stakeholder consultations as well as providing opportunities for investment in a low-carbon lifestyle.

Moreover, the LCWO initiative is seen by SEEDA, the regional economic development agency, as being one element of its intentions for the Oxford region to be a 'diamond' for investment and growth around the subregion's skills in low-carbon technology and design. The Oxfordshire Economic Partnership is active in promoting sustainable construction and bringing university and research expertise together with the skills of small- and medium-sized enterprises.

Box 13.6 Low Carbon West Oxford

Low Carbon West Oxford (LCWO) was founded in 2007 by a number of residents concerned at the frequency of flooding in West Oxford in the twenty-first century (in 2000, 2003 and 2007), and at global impacts of climate change. They decided to take action at a local level both to make a contribution to abating climate change through reducing carbon emissions and to improve the community's resilience to climate change. Concern at the direct and local impacts of events such as flooding, and the prospect of greater risk in future (the UK climate projections of 2009 suggest that winter rainfall in the River Thames valley might increase by up to 30% by the 2050s) prompted local abatement action.

LCWO aims to achieve environmental benefits (by cutting the community's carbon emissions by 80% by 2050, through annual reductions in CO_2, generating local sources of renewable energy, sharing resources and reducing waste, and using low carbon sources of food and transport) and social benefits; strengthening the community through joint working; developing more secure sources of energy and food; reducing expensive household energy bills; developing partnerships between community, council, businesses and others; and influencing local and national government to adopt policies to help communities and businesses tackle climate change.

The initiative has established a not-for-profit company – WO Community Renewables – to raise funds for investing in:

- large-scale solar PV roofs on the local industrial estate.
- a micro-hydro scheme at Osney Weir on the Thames.
- small-scale wind turbines on hills to the west of the city.

The proceeds from the sale of the electricity generated will be used to help local households save energy and money, and ultimately support some carbon sequestration actions such as tree planting. LCWO has already succeeded in raising funds from the government's Low Carbon Communities Challenge, and is a finalist in the Big Green Challenge (organized by NESTA – National Endowment for Science Technology and the Arts).

Source: Low Carbon West Oxford, 2009

Such local community actions are to be found across the country, from the Energy Island campaign of Anglesey to the Town Centre Energy Action Plan in the London Borough of Barking (LBBD, 2006), in addition to the longer-established Transition Towns movement. For the most part, they represent a very positive form of community planning, and the question arises as to the role of spatial planning not just in support but in active promotion of such initiatives. The TCPA and Friends of the Earth Coalition 2009 position statement asks for such a role to be adopted. Despite the central government's assertions that spatial planning has a key role to play in the move to a low-carbon and well-adapted society, without clear confirmation from the centre that this is within its remit, the concern is that spatial planning might find that such lighter-footed plan-making leaves the statutory planning processes behind.

13.6 Conclusions

Successful policy learning requires conceptual, technical and social learning, but we also need to be aware of the institutional norms and values which might inhibit or support learning, and certainly of the wider political context and agenda setting. The TCPA and Friends of the Earth coalition identified as key factors better knowledge, skills and will. But we can see that improved provision of these factors will not in itself achieve the wider learning necessary for sustained and effective policy development.

This chapter has given just an outline of the many issues involved in furthering the role of spatial planning in responding to climate change. We conclude, however, that despite all the barriers to social learning and the contention around the multiple areas of knowledge involved in climate change, spatial planning has an important dual role: it should present opportunities for future visioning of local (and indeed subregional or regional) places, as part of engaging people with their future as low-carbon, well-adapted and resilient communities; and, as the regulatory framework, it should set ambitious parameters for the use of land, the activities which take place on it, and the relationship between those activities and the built, social and natural environments. For this framework to be sufficiently ambitious, changes will be needed in the attitudes and behaviour of professionals, public and politicians; the profession owes a duty to press for the political decision-making to ensure this.

In our concluding chapter we set out what we see as some of the essential principles and requirements for such climate responsive and responsible planning.

14 Integrating mitigation and adaptation for sustainable development

....

14.1 Introduction

The argument of this book has been that spatial planning has an important role to play in actions to mitigate the causes of climate change and to adapt to the impacts of unavoidable climate change. We have shown a number of examples where new planning approaches are being taken, in particular through the adoption of an ecosystems approach (see Chapter 12) to integrate environmental, social and economic aspects of development. Spatial planning is placing a new emphasis in its policies on the multiple benefits of sustainable development and of dynamic conservation. Planning is beginning to address the issues of the relationship between rural and urban areas, for instance in terms of flood management in river catchments, water resources, and the scope for biodiversity to play a role in climate change mitigation (through, for example, carbon fixing) and in adapting to climate change. This is being reflected in planning policies at all levels, and in the role expected of spatial planning.

These shifts in our understanding and practice have already been urged by a number of authors in emphasizing the ecosystem approach to urban areas (such as Hough [2004], White [2001] and, recently, Newman and Jennings [2008]). Sometimes the 'ecological turn' can employ a misplaced organic analogy in comparing the city to a self-sustaining organic body where flows of communication and transport are seen as veins and arteries, the city centre as the heart and greenspaces as the lungs. This book has tried to show instead that we need to acknowledge that cities are human constructs, open to political, economic and social forces, but that climate change is prompting us to acknowledge afresh their dependence on natural systems.

Despite this shift towards a greater recognition of natural processes and the interconnectedness of ecosystems, there is still a tendency for climate change to be seen as just an environmental or economic issue, and in particular for climate change mitigation and adaptation to be considered separately. However, the contention of this book is that both aspects need to be addressed at the same time, and that we need to integrate across different spatial scales and levels of governance. Spatial planning also needs to look further ahead. It is acknowledged that this is not straightforward. In the UK, in particular, it has proved very hard, for example, to integrate land use planning and transport planning at national, regional and local levels. As shown in Chapter 8, despite many arguments that integrated land use and transport planning is an essential element in reducing the growing emissions from transport, it has proved hard to achieve, with decisions on land use being taken by agencies such as central government (for instance, in favour of airport expansion) or health authorities (for centralized specialist health care services), with consequences which induce travel dependence and lock-in to less sustainable modes. Although such decisions may include provision for increased or improved public transport modes, they also generate additional fossil-fuel-based air or terrestrial journeys. The solutions in planning and acting for a low-carbon economy cannot be found only within adaptation but also require more direct action on mitigation.

In this chapter, we suggest two principal ways in which spatial planning can respond to climate change in order to integrate mitigation and adaptation: setting clear objectives and undertaking prior assessments. Spatial planning needs to adopt explicit objectives to achieve this integration; existing impact assessment tools (in particular, SEA and EIA, and – in England and Wales – sustainability appraisal or SA) can be used to ensure that this is done consistently. These objectives will influence the formulation and implementation of plans and projects. First, we review the reasons for integration.

14.2 Benefits of integration of mitigation and adaptation

14.2.1 Maximizing beneficial synergies and opportunities

Reinforcing this attention to integrating new and existing development is the cost-efficiency argument that the move to a low-carbon economy should not be seen as one of costs alone, but one where there may be other benefits in the form of opportunities for 'no regrets' or 'win-win' outcomes. These include recognition of the economic values of the natural environment (Natural England, 2009) and the cost-effectiveness of measures which both mitigate climate change and enable adaptation to unavoidable climate change up to the mid-twenty-first century. Green infrastructure, as discussed in Chapters 9, 11 and 12, is an example where multiple benefits can be achieved when provision of greenspaces (parks, avenues, gardens and riverbanks, etc.) creates opportunities for biodiversity, for walking and cycling, and for flood water management, among others.

14.2.2 Reducing conflict

The obverse of the above is the need to avoid or reduce conflicts, especially between mitigation and adaptation measures and between those receptors and people who are differentially affected by these measures. For instance, the projects to generate new forms of power through the development of tidal barrages have the potential to damage biodiversity (SDC, 2007; RSPB, 2009b). Not only will this run counter to the biodiversity commitments of the CBD, the EU and the UK Biodiversity Action Plan, but such decisions need to acknowledge the importance of ecosystems and the ecosystem approach for sustaining essential life-support services under a changing climate. Another example is the development of projects specifically to aid adaptation to climate change – for instance, schemes to respond to water stress and water shortage through new large-scale provision such as reservoirs. It is important both to assess the adaptation benefits of such a scheme throughout its lifetime, but also the carbon cost of the project in construction, operational phase and decommissioning phases. An example, referred to in Section 10.4.5, is given in Box 14.1.

Box 14.1 Proposed reservoir, Oxfordshire

The development of an Upper Thames Major Water Resource was originally proposed in 1990 to meet the expected demand for water in the Thames Valley arising from increased house-building, increased numbers of households and increased use of water-intensive domestic appliances. As work on the scheme and its alternatives of leakage reduction and demand management was undertaken in the 1990s, the justification was more explicitly based on meeting the anticipated shortfall between supply and demand under conditions of climate change, in which both the reliable supply of water is expected to diminish, and climate change induced demand (for instance, for cooling or gardening) might increase. The scheme originally included a multifunctional proposal for the body of water to serve also as a major recreational facility (in this case, a regional sailing centre). Such an activity would have been entirely car-dependent, likely to exacerbate congestion on existing trunk and local roads and certainly would have generated additional carbon emissions. This illustrates the importance of assessing the carbon emission implications over the lifetime of a development, even if that development is planned as an adaptation measure.

Thames Water's draft Water Resources Management Plan, in which the reservoir scheme is proposed, goes to Public Inquiry in 2010. Because of recent economic changes and revised demand projections, the scheme is currently on hold (subject to annual review). However, it is expected that the reservoir will still be needed, but after about 2026, rather than 2021 as previously thought.

Sources: Thames Water, 2006; 2009c

14.2.3 New and existing development

A theme of the book has been the importance of integrating planning for new and existing development, especially through using the development process to generate benefits for (and from) existing development. This is not just to convince reluctant host communities of the advantages of new investment in an area, or to 'buy off' potential objections to new development from existing residents or occupiers, but to utilize the investment that new development can bring. This should explicitly entail enhancing the public realm and refurbishing existing properties both to achieve low-carbon development and to ensure the existing built environment is more resilient to a changing climate. Examples include the use of development funds to retrofit existing properties for energy-efficiency, the provision of green infrastructure to benefit new and existing development (see Chapter 9) and ensuring that new development aims for water neutrality across a wider area than the immediate development project (see Chapter 10).

14.3 Methods for integration

14.3.1 Principles and objectives

There is a danger that addressing the climate change challenge may become a mantra in the same way in which many have argued that sustainable development has become debased through overuse and imprecise specification. We may also need to 'beware the hegemony of climate change' (a memorable phrase from Susan Owens), in which other potential issues and objectives are ignored, absorbed or diminished. There is a danger that, if everything is seen through the eyes of climate change, the associated policy communities will become larger and more dominant but with fewer alternative conceptions and perspectives and possibly less innovation. Conceptions of problems and solutions might become institutionalized and ossified and alternative voices become excluded. People might tire of the issue itself: as shown in Chapter 13, there is some evidence for this already. Nevertheless, the argument of this book is that there are some fundamental principles which spatial planning should adopt to respond to climate change.

These principles are those pertaining to sustainable development: the principles of inter and intra-generational equity, the recognition of the importance of an ecosystems approach (including valuing the underlying life-support services provided by ecosystems) and, finally, the commitment to community-level engagement. These principles derive (as described in Chapter 1 and 2) from elements of the definition of sustainability from the Brundtland Commission (WCED, 1987) and Jacobs (1991). From these should flow a number of actions:

- explicit objective-setting in spatial plans for stabilization of CO_2 and targets of at least 80 per cent reduction in CO_2 by 2050, and climate change resilience;
- integration of mitigation and adaptation actions;
- use of scenarios and futures thinking;
- use of tools such as IA to take a holistic assessment of impacts;
- taking a climate risk-based approach which considers gradual change over the long term, but also extremes in the short-term;
- using science and vernacular knowledge, through stakeholder and public engagement and opportunities for social learning and education.

The objectives of making the transition to a low-carbon society are clearly normative ones, based on value judgements and prescribing changes in processes and behaviour; we consider that the principles of sustainable development also imply adopting objectives for climate resilience and adaptation. 'Adaptation' was defined in Chapter 2 as the adjustment in natural or human systems in response to actual or expected climates and weather, or their effects, in order to moderate harm or exploit beneficial opportunities. Distinct types of adaptation are recognized: anticipatory, autonomous and planned adaptation. Climate resilience, on the other hand, is the ability to recover from climate impacts. There is some reluctance in the UK to using the term climate proofing (although it is used in the Netherlands), on the grounds that the term suggests too much analogy with weatherproofing, as though this were a one-off application of an exterior coat on a system which is in other respects designed conventionally. The contention of this book is that, just as moving to a low-carbon society requires radical change, so does the activity of adaptation.

The arguments for thinking ahead and taking a longer-term horizon in decision-making have been shown in Chapter 6: longer-term thinking offers scope for employing different methods such as storytelling, scenario analysis and visioning, and presents opportunities for community engagement. Different methods can be used for different purposes or contexts: community visualization exercises to promote community engagement (as illustrated in Chapter 13; see also Larsen and Gunnarsson-Östling, 2009), or more systematic appraisal of options against scenarios for decision-makers or spatial planning professionals. Longer-term thinking also has advantages in raising questions of distributive justice for future generations. Examples are to be found in many policy fields, such as transport (Hickman and Banister, 2007; Echenique *et al.*, 2009), land use (Swain and Konwitz, 2009; and the Foresight study on land use futures), urban energy (Rydin, 2009), and integrated urban assessments (Hall *et al.*, 2009). The challenge is to use the principles and findings of these scenario modelling exercises in ways which can be useful to the policy- and plan-making activities of spatial planning.

14.3.2 Critiques of conventional assessment and appraisal

These objectives would differ from the usual somewhat bland objectives adopted in many spatial plans. It has been argued by Clive George that plan objectives are often very unchallenging (especially if derived from governments' interpretations of sustainable development). He also criticizes the objectives-led approach for confusing the process of sustainability appraisal with the activity of regional-level plan-making. He contends that such appraisal is too often a circular process, in that the objectives merge, and that there is no challenging commitment to achieving sustainable development, but only to moving towards it. He proposes instead criteria for assessment based more directly on the principles of the Rio Declaration, including those for inter- and intra-generational equity, at different scales and at both weak and strong definitions of sustainability. We commend this approach, which would make clear that the criteria being used in appraisal are value-laden (that is, with the values of the Rio Declaration). The contention of this book is that, in addition, spatial planning needs explicitly to embed the values of minimizing the causes of climate change and adaptation to unavoidable climate change. But adding to responsibilities without increasing authority or capacity is unlikely to be effective.

In addition to the reasons for adopting objectives which seek to integrate mitigation and adaptation across new and existing development, and across spatial scales, we need also to employ some systematic method of assessing the likely impacts (direct, indirect, secondary and cumulative) of decisions of plans and developments.

Such assessments have had a critical press. It has been argued that they are conceived too much in the outdated rationalist mode, based on a model in which experts are in possession of objective facts which enable them to make value-free judgements to place before decision-makers. This has been a criticism of both strategic level assessments (such as Kørnøv and Thissen, 2000; Connelly and Richardson, 2005) and those for projects (for instance, Weston, 2004). At a more general level, policy appraisal has been criticized as lacking sufficiently explicit value-judgements (Owens *et al.*, 2004). There has perhaps been confusion between the employment of techniques by 'experts' and the need for a systematic and explicit (even if not transparent) appraisal. Moreover, in some cases it is clear that the assessment process has not just ticked boxes as a procedural minimum, but has made a difference to the framing of the policies or proposals in the plan (Therivel *et al.*, 2009).

Owens and her co-authors argue that the technical-rational model, based on implicit assumptions about inductive method and the influence of science on decision-makers, has proved remarkably tenacious in the face of practitioners' and theorists' critiques. These criticisms include technical factors (the inability to scope unintended consequences), political factors (where the technique implicitly embodies assumptions and values that lead to a desired outcome) and practical factors (where contention is simply shifted to later in the decision-making process). There has been much theorizing about the need to move to a more deliberative approach, where practical knowledge and negotiated learning can be recognized: 'towards practices of appraisal that seek not to depoliticise policy controversies, but to improve opportunities for deliberation in which open dialogue about difficult choices can occur' (Owens *et al.*, 2004, p. 1948). But Owens *et al.* argue that in practice there has been little change because there remain issues of representation and access, and the possibility of fundamental differences or conflict of positions, with little change in outcomes even if outputs differ.

Owens and her co-authors therefore propose a combination of approaches, perhaps along a continuum, where those undertaking such appraisals distinguish between the object of the appraisal – asking whether the problem is well-understood or our knowledge is unstructured – and the objective of the appraisal – asking whether it is to promote deliberative discussion and learning amongst participants (and, if so, what types of learning).

However, in the MATISSE study of *ex ante* assessment in policymaking within the EU and three European countries, Hertin *et al.* concluded that the processes have failed to provide opportunities for policy debate and deliberation, and have only rarely enabled any learning (conceptual or political) beyond instrumental learning from the knowledge generated by the assessment (Hertin *et al.*, 2009). Indeed, they conclude that 'when learning occurred in [our] cases, it was despite rather than because of the instrumental conception of the prevailing assessment procedure' (p. 1198). They conclude that improvements might lie in designing systems that more clearly acknowledge the processes of and barriers to the use of knowledge in framing policy decisions. Although their research was looking at assessment of policymaking rather than spatial plans, some of the findings no doubt are applicable to anticipatory SEA and EIA.

It is clear that there need to be explicit objectives to achieve desired end states, and that this involves value judgements on the part of decision-makers. It is important to acknowledge that climate change is a moral issue, as argued in Chapter 6, in that it is associated with unequal outcomes and adversely affects those social groups (and species) that did not cause it, and therefore there is explicit acknowledgement of the values underlying such actions. However, there is a need to assess the impacts of plans and projects before decisions are reached: it is in that context that this chapter suggests a number of ways in which, within an objectives-led commitment to challenging responses to climate change, systematic attempts can be made to assist integration. This can be done through assessment against different climate change impacts, or by more conventional sectoral or thematic objectives.

14.3.3 Assessment frameworks

As we saw in the previous chapter, there are a number of large-scale, integrated modelling approaches at present (such as ARCADIA – see Box 13.3) which aim to provide an integrated assessment of socio-economic and climate futures and land use options. Such assessments are impressive in their scope and development of sophisticated models and programmes in order systematically to examine interactions and test policy options. But they are resource- and time-intensive, requiring considerable multidisciplinary research capacity. It will not always be possible to commission or employ such assessments except at a strategic, metropolitan scale.

A number of more limited – but nevertheless useful – frameworks for assessment and presentation are suggested.

1. The first is a simple 'mileage chart' in which mitigation objectives and adaptation measures are assessed for their consistency and vice versa. Such basic mileage charts were proposed in the early days of the environmental appraisal of development plans (EADP) (DoE, 1993). While there is now greater sophistication of both quantitative and qualitative assessment tools, there is merit in the simplicity of such a matrix in getting started on the integrative assessment. At its most basic level, this might reveal areas of clear conflict or uncertainty where further analysis should be undertaken. The evidence from the rapid development of practice in the EADP is that such tools proved useful in developing capabilities and experience (Therivel and Partidario, 1996). A schematic example is given in Figure 14.1. The device is simple but works as a way to encapsulate and

	Mitigation action 1	Mitigation action 2	Adaptation action 1	Adaptation action 2
Mitigation action 1				
Mitigation action 2	·			
Adaptation action 1	?	·		
Adaptation action 2	·	x	x	

Legend: · = consistent   x = inconsistent   ? = uncertain

Figure 14.1

Mitigation and adaptation consistency mileage chart

represent the consequences of actions. Hamin and Gurran (2008) show, through a basic assessment of a selection of spatial planning policies from Australia, the US and the UK, where there might be conflict between planning policies for adaptation and mitigation objectives. An example is in New South Wales, where explicit policies to promote biodiversity (through maintaining eucalypt cover to preserve koala populations) to aid adaptation to climate change leads to low density housing, and hence car-dependent development. The suggested policy response might be a more radical decision to avoid development in such areas altogether.

2. A number of attempts have been made to chart the interactions of the impacts of climate change on the built environment, and the potential for mitigation and adaptation measures or responses to be in conflict or synergy (such as McEvoy *et al.*, 2006). Howard (2009) argues that mitigation is of overriding importance, and that there is a danger that an overemphasis on adaptation can undermine efforts to tackle the difficult problem (difficult politically and technically) of reducing carbon emissions. He proposes giving first priority to mitigation actions where mitigation is synonymous with adaptation; he draws a useful distinction between those actions where mitigation might have no short-term effect on adaptation (but does prejudice it in the longer term), and those actions where mitigation might in the near-term undermine adaptation, but support it over the longer term (Table 14.1 based on Howard in Davoudi, 2009).

   For those who are drawing up or implementing adaptation plans and actions, this approach requires more explicit attention to be paid to the first- and second-order impacts of climate change and adaptation responses, and importantly needs to give active consideration of links to mitigation measures over time. The chart could be adapted also to consider impacts at different scales such as settlement pattern, urban form or site, and building scale.

3. Alternatively, one might start from a different objective – such as biodiversity conservation – and adopt a schema (such as that used in the MACIS project) which shows in diagrammatic form the mitigation and adaptation actions which favour or disadvantage the objective (in this case, biodiversity conservation), as well as their synergies and conflicts (Figure 14.2). Such a diagram could be revised for a specific plan or (perhaps) region, indicating broad assessments of comparative impacts upon objectives. Such a representation, once agreed, could act as a summary statement of the consensus of understanding on options, to short-circuit their repeated reappraisal *ab initio*.

4. Sensitivity analysis and environmental limits
   Sensitivity analysis is used to show how 'sensitive' a model of a system is to changes in the value of the parameters of the model and to changes in model structure. Chapter 7 has suggested some ways in which sensitivity analysis could be incorporated as part of a climate risk assessment in EIA and SEA processes. Sensitivity analysis can also help with identifying

Table 14.1 Howard's five modes of adaptation

	A1 Mitigation is directly and immediately synonymous with adaptation	A2 Mitigation is adaptation-neutral in the short term but supports or obviates adaptation in the long term	A3 Mitigation undermines adaptation in the short term but supports or obviates it in the long term	C Adaptation is mitigation-neutral	E Adaptation hinders mitigation
	Priority: 1	Priority: 2	Priority: 3	Priority: 4	Priority: 5
Excessive heat	LEED-certified building standards	• Reducing overall levels of consumption;	Dense urban form in hot, humid climate		Increased use of air conditioning
Drought	Improved efficiency of water use	• LEED-EB renovation of existing buildings; Using construction materials with low embodied energy;	Hydropower (potential conflict with agricultural irrigation)	Local rainwater harvesting and floodwater storage	New conventional reservoirs; importation of water from distant regions
Rising sea levels	Relocating coastal residents inland to LEED platinum urban housing	• Reducing personal mileage;		Relocating coastal residents into existing conventional housing	Relocating coastal residents into new conventional suburban housing
Flooding	Restoration of wetlands	• Reducing reliance on air travel;			Building concrete dikes and levees
Degradation of urban air quality	Urban tree planting; open space and habitat protection	• Increasing reliance on mass transit and long-distance rail	Use of biodiesel (minor increase in NO_x emissions)	Passive filtering within buildings (e.g. via plants)	Active filtering within buildings via mechanical systems
Increase in incidence or severity of violent storms	Decentralized renewable energy generation; restoration of coastal wetlands			Improved storm warning systems and evacuation planning	Making structures storm-resistant through use of concrete and steel walls

Source: Howard, 2009, table 2.1

Note: LEED is US Green Building Council rating for Leadership in Energy and Environmental Design

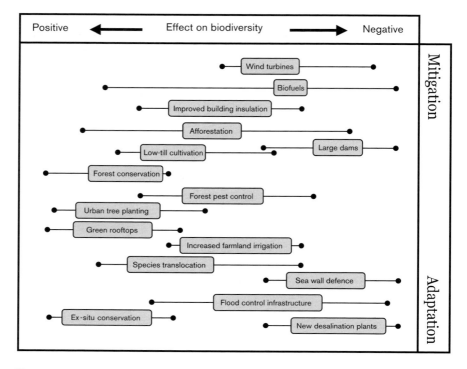

Figure 14.2

Known and potential relationships between mitigation and adaptation measures and their impacts on biodiversity

Source: Paterson *et al.*, 2008

thresholds beyond which response to a parameter becomes excessive or undesirable, and in this way can be linked to much of the work currently underway on environmental limits within spatial planning. In particular, it can be used as part of the ecosystems approach (Defra, 2007c) described in Chapter 12. Smith and Pearson (2008) give an account of the application of the approach in the context of concern about the environmental capacity of the East of England. Although the project was in the nature of a pilot, and was not yet robust enough for planning purposes, it showed the advantages of such an approach: it helped to systematize environmental capacity concepts; it could be used in SEA or SA, and help to identify mitigation measures; and it allowed stakeholder involvement, and allowed information to be brought together that was suitable for lay people. Such approaches have considerable potential in identifying the benefits derived from ecosystem services, distinguishing between environmental issues at different scales (global carbon emissions to local or subregional landscapes), and allows judgement of current limits and potential limits in the context of climate change. They might, for instance, be appropriate in assessing policies at different scales: from policies for retaining allotments in urban areas, and responding to suggestions from the Energy Technology Institute to search for 'under-used' land for biofuels.

5. Multi-criteria analysis
    Finally, it might be argued that the use of a comprehensive approach such as multi-criteria analysis (MCA) would demonstrate the conflicts and synergies, and potentially the trade-offs, between mitigation and adaptation measures. MCA is often used in transportation evaluation schemes as an alternative to monetized cost-benefit analysis (DCLG, 2009f), to provide an integrated way of addressing complex interactions. It has considerable potential in revealing the trade-offs between conflicting objectives, and showing the assumptions and perspectives of different stakeholders. Part of the intention of these techniques is for the process itself to provide an opportunity for learning among professionals, stakeholders and the public, and to make clear the assumptions and reasoning behind judgements of significance. As the issue of climate change raises questions of the scope of direct, indirect, secondary and cumulative impacts, and the interrelationship of mitigation and adaptation, it will be important to ensure that assumptions about these are explicit in any MCA in the field of spatial planning.

14.4 Understanding the development process

The argument of this book is that, in the context of spatial planning for climate change, plans for new development need to be seen in relation to existing development. For instance, while the indirect benefits through reduced global emissions of action on mitigation (such as investment in zero-carbon homes) might be imperceptible locally, such actions can also directly benefit existing development: an example is the Centre for Sustainable Energy's Warm Streets initiative in south-west Britain aimed at reducing fuel poverty through tackling cold homes and carbon emissions. Similarly, adaptation actions should benefit development directly and indirectly. This requires an understanding of the development process, the way in which land is owned, how it is allocated for development and how the development is financed and funds raised or provided. The review of comparative experience between new developments in the Netherlands and the UK (see Chapter 8) shows the importance of local municipality business models, under which cash flows are made available for the funding of timely infrastructure (PRP Ltd *et al.*, 2008). The review concluded that there is also greater collaborative working in the Netherlands, with less adversarial land allocation, and with long-term development agencies which draw on civic involvement and cooperate across administrative boundaries.

It is important not just to build links between the assessment processes mentioned above and the decisions on plan policies and proposals to ensure they maximize objectives but also to consider plan implementation and the development process. While local authorities in Britain (particularly in England) lack the powers of continental municipalities, there are good examples, illustrated in Chapter 9, where local authorities have developed innovative ways of addressing climate change in existing and new development. Elsewhere, the creation of special agencies such as the London Thames Gateway Development Corporation and the Olympics Delivery Authority have been able to take a longer-term view of the development of the area and the Olympics legacy, and to use the development process to achieve benefits for existing residents, such as through the restoration of the River Lea to a multifunctional green and blue space for recreation, flood absorption, biodiversity movement and urban cooling. Another example is the Thames Gateway eco-quarter, an area of some 2,000 new and existing homes where finance from the Homes and Communities Agency will provide revenue funding for low-carbon, energy-efficient and water-efficient homes and businesses. The project will trial the concept of water neutrality in the new developments (DCLG, 2009g), and this may include, for example, partially retrofitting existing developments (also discussed in Chapter 10.4.4).

One example of an organization going through quite a radical reappraisal of its approach to public policymaking, land management and the integration of actions to mitigate and adapt to climate change is the National Trust (Box 14.2). The Trust is an organization with a high public profile and a long-term perspective yet, as a land manager and developer, it is having to tackle climate change in practical ways. Its experiences offer a useful illustration of the way in which land has to be planned and managed for environmental and social reasons. Some of its future actions in greening its estate and its visitors' travel patterns will no doubt challenge the expectations of some of its public and members. Its role in educating its members and visitors, and in promoting social learning, will be crucial.

Box 14.2 The National Trust

The National Trust for England, Wales and Northern Ireland has a distinctive charitable status, and has over 3 million members and inalienable land ownership of some 300 houses, 250 gardens and 254,000 hectares of land. It is, of course, not a planning authority but, as a major landowner, it is engaging more directly than in the past with public policymaking, partly because of the issue of climate change. For instance, it was represented on the Steering Committee of the initial study of the Planning Response to Climate Change set up in 2000, and was a member of the Coalition led by TCPA and FoE urging further advances in the spatial planning response to climate change. It is experiencing first hand as a landowner the impacts of climate change, and is able to test out approaches to climate-resilient land management and public engagement on its own properties. For instance, the Trust is already changing its management practices to address the issues of sea-level rise

---

and coastal erosion (National Trust, 2005a; 2007). Changing growing seasons are affecting its land management (National Trust et al., 2002) and floods have affected the conservation of its historic buildings. Peat moorlands in its ownership include 1,350 hectares of exposed peat on its properties in the High Peak in Derbyshire, which are responsible for significant carbon emissions, and are in danger of further erosion causing further release of carbon, but also loss of water retention and risk of downstream flooding (National Trust, 2005b).

The Trust is therefore trying simultaneously to adapt to climate change and to tackle the causes of climate change, but this presents some dilemmas – the Trust's properties receive over 14 million visits per year, many of them car-borne visits (National Trust, 2009). While the Trust is promoting green travel plans and new sustainable routes such as ferry links, it depends heavily on fee-paying visits to generate income. It has adopted a Carbon Footprint project in Northumberland, and is promoting microgeneration and demonstration projects within its own properties and new-builds such as at Stamford in Cheshire and Cliveden in Buckinghamshire.

14.5 Prospects

Our argument has been that integrating climate change mitigation and adaptation into spatial planning is not just a matter of better plan-making or appraisal processes: we need to set challenging objectives, to think ahead and to understand the spatial planning processes of development and implementation. We need to utilize the expertise of integrated assessments, but also to acknowledge the limitations of political space and public engagement. This requires an understanding of the wider politics of development and of appraisal, and the influence on and drivers of the behaviour and attitudes of professionals, decision-makers and the public. For instance, we need to beware of adopting energy-efficiency or water-efficiency measures without considering the rebound effect, under which the advantages of resource conservation are lost in increased energy demand for other purposes (Herring and Sorrell, 2009).

We need also to be aware of the attitudes of professionals. As shown in Chapter 7, it is possible for professions to adopt standard conventions or protocols which inhibit experimentation or innovation. As planners, designers and users of the built environment, we also need to be aware of gaps between plan and implementation: for example, evidence from post-occupancy surveys of 'smart' office buildings shows that users seek personal control over their working conditions, introducing individual heaters or fans to gain control in temperature-controlled buildings (Roaf et al., 2009).

The themes of this book have been that spatial planning is changing in response to the urgent issue of climate change – climate changes spatial planning, the phrase used in the research programme in the Netherlands, is a telling one. We have shown that people's expectations of spatial planning, and the activities and skills of practitioners, are changing. Of course, we recognize – and hope to have shown in the book – that spatial planning is but one of many key interventions needed to address climate change. We have tried to indicate some of the extraordinary liveliness – if not frantic activity – within the research community (Betsill and Bulkeley, 2007), formal government initiatives and among the communities of civil society. However, we consider that such solutions considered and implemented need to be framed within the moral and scientific principles of sustainability. Within this context, we consider that climate change raises seven key and related themes for spatial planning:

1. *Norms and values in a post-postmodern world*
   We consider that the spatial planning debate has moved from its postmodernist phase of ambivalence and discretion to one where the normative principles of sustainability – especially those of equity – are explicitly acknowledged and argued over through political debate and action. While there are tools to help with this – such as the assessment and appraisal processes discussed in the book, or even monetization of environmental assets – the messy debates over the allocation of scarce resources are inevitably and rightly political ones.

2. *The relationship of science, scientific knowledge and expertise to the built and natural environment professions, the public and political decision-makers*
   While much of this book draws on the research and practice undertaken by academics and professional planners, nevertheless there is still disagreement over climate change (Hulme, 2009). Hulme's argument – and to some extent ours – is that climate change is an issue which does not lend itself to simple solutions: the process of transition to a low-carbon, well-adapting society will be continuous, difficult and contested. The relationship between expertise and public attitudes and behaviour will be crucial if spatial planning is to play a role in this transformation. This raises profound issues about the public's trust in and expectations of public policy, especially at a time when that trust is declining. This is especially important in relation to managing coastal retreat of whole communities, which will need a significant degree of trust to be built up. Even those actions which seem entirely beneficial, such as the provision of green infrastructure as an underlying structure worthy of capital and social investment, and the re-naturing of urban river corridors, will have direct benefits (such as the legacy of the London Olympics), but will also imply the indirect reallocation of costs and benefits, producing winners and losers.

3. *The conception of nature and the environment, and the relationship of people with their environments, natural and built*
   Linked to the point above is the issue of planning professionals' understanding of social, environmental and natural processes and their ability to work with other professionals and land managers (such as water managers). For instance, the concept of headroom, much employed by water engineers, might be a useful concept to adopt in planning our built environment and urban areas in order to build in the resilience and flexibility

that will be needed to address extreme and unpredictable events, as well as re-engaging urban areas with their rural catchments. The complexity of natural systems – especially water and biodiversity – suggests the need for utilizing sensitivity analyses, as suggested above. It might also suggest a need for revived landscape planning – a Dutch tradition, but one which has received less attention in the UK.

A further potential area for more thoughtful spatial planning is in the new regime of marine planning, as explained in Chapter 11, that is of vital importance to both the UK and the Netherlands.

4. *Time*

The time horizons over which we look and plan ahead, our ability to do so, and the commitment we make to future generations will necessarily extend, even while we recognize that our planning for distant times must remain tentative and exploratory. As Lafferty and Meadowcroft (1996) argue, it might be difficult within conventional electoral cycles for 'democratic decision-making processes effectively to be adapted to consider extended impact horizons' (p. 269), but the advantages of thinking ahead about 'preferred trajectories of social development' are that this can help to form collective responsibility and be a collective learning experience. Technology – for instance the modelling of the consequences of climate change and the use of GIS in mapping and visualizing the impacts – offers important tools for public communication. But we need to recognize that socio-economic changes are as important as technology in determining how well we respond to these changes in climate.

5. *The scale at which spatial planning is undertaken*

We need to be aware of significant changes in the wider governance of space and climate policy: political and community institutions are changing at transnational, national and local levels (Bulkeley *et al.*, 2009). At the same time, new territorial relations are developing, with soft spaces and fuzzy boundaries (as Haughton *et al.*, 2010 call them) around less formal spatial planning processes. But of course climate change is not the only driver of change, as we saw in Chapters 4, 5 and 13, there are still strong drivers for centralization (in order to give force to ideological values of globalization, privatization and liberalization, as manifested in the 'invitation to tender' style of the draft National Policy Statements for nationally significant infrastructure in England and Wales). There are also strong drivers to localization (again, for reasons of political principle favouring community or individual responsibility, cooperation and equity, or thrift and economy). There are, for instance, as we have seen, significant differences between the Netherlands and the UK (and, within the UK, between the Devolved Administrations and England), which reflect long-standing cultural and political traditions of the relations between state and civil society, and between different levels of governance (including the research and NGO communities). Some of these reflect physical differences – the Netherlands as a delta, compared with the British Isles as an archipelago

– and institutional differences. But it may be that the relationship of UK spatial planning and the research community could develop along the lines of the Dutch model of integration. We consider that these provide opportunities for social and institutional learning as experience develops and alternatives are tried.

6. *The relationship of local communities with their locally elected representatives*
Given that much activity – such as Transition Towns, local food networks and community energy schemes – is bottom-up, locally generated and sometimes deliberately outside existing governance and authority structures such as formal spatial planning. One example of the complexity of change is that, at the same time as the controls of conventional land-use planning are being loosened with respect to the installation of microgeneration capacity, households are also losing rights to pave over front gardens in response to the concerns about urban flood risk (and biodiversity loss) caused by 'urban creep'. Such changes need public understanding and support.

7. *Opportunities*
Nevertheless, the response to climate change presents many opportunities where public and domestic spaces can be enhanced by design and measures which can add to the beauty of the built environment as well as strengthening interdependence with rural environments. Many of these measures will be forms of green infrastructure, others will derive from urban design. Where awareness-raising and community participation and action are added to this, there may also be a reintegration of civic values. The evidence suggests that the costs of measures taken can be expected to be less than the cost of inaction.

We consider that, in all the above ways, the issue of climate change is changing spatial planning – this is a defining challenge for the present century, and the planning system must continue to respond to the challenge.

Glossary

· ·

In the following glossary, definitions related to climate change are chiefly taken from the IPCC Assessment Reports (IPCC, 2001 and IPCC 2007a).

Adaptation   Adjustment in natural or human systems in response to actual or expected climatic stimuli or their effects, which moderates harm or exploits beneficial opportunities. Various types of adaptation can be distinguished, including anticipatory, autonomous and planned adaptation:
   Anticipatory adaptation   Adaptation that takes place before impacts of climate change are observed. Also referred to as proactive adaptation.
   Autonomous adaptation   Adaptation that does not constitute a conscious response to climatic stimuli but is triggered by ecological changes in natural systems and by market or welfare changes in human systems. Also referred to as spontaneous adaptation
   Planned adaptation   Adaptation that is the result of a deliberate policy decision, based on an awareness that conditions have changed or are about to change and that action is required to return to, maintain, or achieve a desired state.
Adaptive capacity   The ability of a system to adapt to climate change (including climate variability and extremes) to moderate potential damages, to take advantage of opportunities, or to cope with the consequences.
Biodiversity   The total diversity of all organisms and ecosystems at various spatial scales (from genes to entire regional ecosystems).
Biofuel   A fuel produced from organic matter or combustible oils produced by plants. Examples of biofuel include alcohol, black liquor from the paper-manufacturing process, wood, and soybean oil.
Biosphere   The part of the Earth system comprising all ecosystems and living organisms in the atmosphere, on land (terrestrial biosphere), or in the oceans (marine biosphere), including derived dead organic matter, such as litter, soil organic matter and oceanic detritus.
Bud-break   Initiation of growth from a bud, in the spring.
CCS   Carbon capture and storage/sequestration. The process of increasing the carbon content of a reservoir/pool other than the atmosphere.
CDM (Clean Development Mechanism)   The CDM allows greenhouse gas

emission reduction projects to take place in countries that have no emission targets under the United Nations Framework Convention on Climate Change (UNFCCC) Kyoto Protocol, yet are signatories.

CFC   Chlorofluorocarbons – also known as Freon. Used as coolants in refrigeration and air conditioners, as solvents in cleaners, especially for electronic circuit boards, as aerosol propellants and in the production of foam (e.g. fire extinguishers).

CH$_4$ Methane. Odourless, combustible natural gas (fossil fuel); major constituent of landfill gas. Released the atmosphere from natural processes (30 per cent – e.g. marsh gas) and from human activities (70 per cent – e.g. cooking).

Climate   Climate in a narrow sense is usually defined as the 'average weather', or more rigorously, as the statistical description in terms of the mean and variability of relevant quantities over a period of time ranging from months to thousands or millions of years. These quantities are most often surface variables such as temperature, precipitation and wind. Climate in a wider sense is the state, including a statistical description, of the climate system. The World Meteorological Organization (WMO) defines the period of time typically used as thirty years.

Climate change   Climate change refers to any change in climate over time, whether due to natural variability or as a result of human activity. This usage differs from that in the United Nations Framework Convention on Climate Change (UNFCCC), which defines 'climate change' as: 'a change of climate which is attributed directly or indirectly to human activity that alters the composition of the global atmosphere and which is in addition to natural climate variability observed over comparable time periods'. See also climate variability.

Climate (change) scenario   A plausible and often simplified representation of the future climate, based on an internally consistent set of climatological relationships and assumptions of radiative forcing, typically constructed for explicit use as input to climate change impact models. A 'climate change scenario' is the difference between a climate scenario and the current climate.

Climate model   A numerical representation of the climate system based on the physical, chemical and biological properties of its components, their interactions and feedback processes, and accounting for all or some of its known properties. The climate system can be represented by models of varying complexity (i.e. for any one component or combination of components a hierarchy of models can be identified, differing in such aspects as the number of spatial dimensions, the extent to which physical, chemical or biological processes are explicitly represented, or the level at which empirical parameterizations are involved. Coupled atmosphere/ocean/sea-ice General Circulation Models (AOGCMs) provide a comprehensive representation of the climate system. More complex models include active chemistry and biology. Climate models are applied, as a research tool, to study and simulate the climate, but also for operational purposes, including monthly, seasonal and inter-annual climate predictions.

Coastal squeeze   The squeeze of coastal ecosystems (e.g. salt marshes, mangroves, and mud and sand flats) between rising sea levels and naturally or artificially fixed shorelines, including hard engineering defences.

Ecological community   A community of plants and animals characterized by a typical assemblage of species and their abundances. See also ecosystem.

Ecological corridor   A (relatively narrow) strip of vegetation used by wildlife, potentially allowing movement of biotic factors between two areas.

Ecosystem   The interactive system formed from all living organisms and their abiotic (physical and chemical) environment within a given area. Ecosystems cover a hierarchy of spatial scales and can comprise the entire globe, biomes at the continental scale or small, well-circumscribed systems such as a small pond.

Ecosystem approach   The ecosystem approach is a strategy for the integrated management of land, water and living resources that promotes conservation and sustainable use in an equitable way. An ecosystem approach is based on the application of appropriate scientific methodologies focused on levels of biological organization, which encompass the essential structure, processes, functions and interactions among organisms and their environment. It recognizes that humans, with their cultural diversity, are an integral component of many ecosystems. The ecosystem approach requires adaptive management to deal with the complex and dynamic nature of ecosystems and the absence of complete knowledge or understanding of their functioning. Priority targets are conservation of biodiversity and of the ecosystem structure and functioning, in order to maintain ecosystem services.

Ecosystem services   Ecological processes or functions having monetary or non-monetary value to individuals or society at large. There are (i) supporting services such as productivity or biodiversity maintenance; (ii) provisioning services such as food, fibre, or fish; (iii) regulating services such as climate regulation or carbon sequestration; and (iv) cultural services such as tourism or spiritual and aesthetic appreciation.

Exposure unit   The system considered to be at risk – could be a geographical area (city, region) plus the sets of receptors within it.

Externalities   Occur when a change in the production or consumption of one individual or firm affects indirectly the well-being of another individual or firm. Externalities can be positive or negative. The impacts of pollution on ecosystems, water courses or air quality represent classic cases of negative externality.

Extinction   The global disappearance of an entire species.

Extreme weather event   An event that is rare within its statistical reference distribution at a particular place. Definitions of 'rare' vary, but an extreme weather event would normally be as rare as or rarer than the 10th or 90th percentile. By definition, the characteristics of what is called 'extreme weather' may vary from place to place. Extreme weather events may typically include floods and droughts.

Green infrastructure   Green infrastructure is the physical environment within and between our cities, towns and villages. It is a network of multi-functional open spaces, including formal parks, gardens, woodlands, green corridors, waterways, street trees and open countryside. It comprises all environmental resources, and thus a green infrastructure approach also contributes towards sustainable resource management.

Greenhouse effect   The process in which the absorption of infrared radiation by the atmosphere warms the Earth. In common parlance, the term 'greenhouse effect' may be used to refer either to the natural greenhouse effect, due to naturally occurring greenhouse gases, or to the enhanced (anthropogenic) greenhouse effect, which results from gases emitted as a result of human activities.

Greenhouse gas   Greenhouse gases are those gaseous constituents of the atmosphere, both natural and anthropogenic, that absorb and emit radiation at specific wavelengths within the spectrum of infrared radiation emitted by the Earth's surface, the atmosphere and clouds. This property causes the greenhouse effect. Water vapour (H_2O), carbon dioxide (CO_2), nitrous oxide (N_2O), methane (CH_4) and ozone (O_3) are the primary greenhouse gases in the Earth's atmosphere. As well as CO_2, N_2O, and CH_4, the Kyoto Protocol deals with the greenhouse gases sulphur hexafluoride (SF_6), hydrofluorocarbons (HFCs) and perfluorocarbons (PFCs).

Harm   Synonymous with detrimental consequence or impact.

Hazard   A situation or event with the potential to cause harm. A hazard does not necessarily cause harm.

Mitigation   An anthropogenic intervention to reduce the anthropogenic forcing of the climate system; it includes strategies to reduce greenhouse gas sources and emissions and enhancing greenhouse gas sinks.

N_2O   Nitrous oxide (also known as laughing gas). Used in surgery and as a foaming agent.

No regrets policy   A policy that would generate net social and/or economic benefits irrespective of whether or not anthropogenic climate change occurs.

Phenology   The study of natural phenomena that recur periodically (e.g. development stages, migration) and their relation to climate and seasonal changes.

Radiative forcing   Radiative forcing is the change in the net vertical irradiance (expressed in Watts per square metre) at the tropopause due to an internal or external change in the forcing of the climate system, such as a change in the concentration of CO_2 or the output of the Sun.

Receptor   The entity that may be harmed or affected by a hazard or set of hazardous events. Examples: ecological community, social community; species, a school, a business.

Resilience   The ability of a social or ecological system to absorb disturbances while retaining the same basic structure and ways of functioning, the capacity for self-organization, and the capacity to adapt to stress and change.

Risk   A characteristic of a system or decision where the probabilities that certain states or outcomes have occurred or may occur are precisely known. Risk is a combination of the change or probability of an event occurring, and the impact or consequence associated with that event. Decisions that involve risk are those decisions where probabilities are precisely known: e.g. the size of a 1 in 200-year flood.

Scenario   A plausible and often simplified description of how the future may develop, based on a coherent and internally consistent set of assumptions about driving forces and key relationships. Scenarios may be derived from projections, but are often based on additional information from other sources, sometimes combined with a 'narrative storyline'.

Sea-level rise   An increase in the mean level of the ocean. Eustatic sea-level rise is a change in global average sea level brought about by an increase in the volume of the world ocean. Relative sea-level rise occurs where there is a local increase in the level of the ocean relative to the land, which might be due to ocean rise and/or land level subsidence. In areas subject to rapid land-level uplift, relative sea level can fall.

Sink (carbon sink)   Any process, activity, or mechanism that removes a greenhouse gas, an aerosol, or a precursor of a greenhouse gas or aerosol from the atmosphere.

Sustainable development   Development that meets the cultural, social, political and economic needs of the present generation without compromising the ability of future generations to meet their own needs.

Thermal expansion   In connection with sea-level rise, this refers to the increase in volume (and decrease in density) that results from warming water. A warming of the ocean leads to an expansion of the ocean volume and hence an increase in sea level.

Uncertainty   A characteristic of a system or decision where the probabilities that certain states or outcomes have occurred or may occur is not precisely known. Reflects a lack of confidence about baseline or forecasts.

Vulnerability   Vulnerability is the degree to which a system is susceptible to, and unable to cope with, adverse effects of climate change, including climate variability and extremes. Vulnerability is a function of the character, magnitude, and rate of climate change and variation to which a system is exposed, its sensitivity, and its adaptive capacity.

Water neutral development   A characteristic of new development, where for every new development, total water use across the wider area after the development must be equal to or less than total water use across the wider area before the development.

Bibliography

Aall, C., Groven, K. and Lindseth, G. (2007), The scope of action for local climate policy: the case of Norway, *Global Environmental Politics*, 7(2): 451–65.

ABI (Association of British Insurers) (2002), Insurers announce new principles for flood insurance. Available online at: http://www.abi.org.uk/Media/Releases/2002/09/Insurers_announce_new_principles_for_flood_insurance.aspx (accessed 23 June 2009).

ACC (Association of County Councils), ADC (Association of District Councils) and AMA (Association of Metropolitan Authorities) (1990), *Environmental Practice in Local Government: A Guide prepared by the Local Authority Associations*, London: ACC.

Adger, W. N. (2003), Social aspects of adaptive capacity. In: J. Smith, R. T Klein, and S. Huq (eds), *Climate Change, Adaptive Capacity and Development*, London: Imperial College Press.

Adger, W. N., Paavola, J., Huq, S. and Mace, M. (eds) (2006), *Fairness in Adaptation to Climate Change*, Cambridge, MA and London: MIT Press.

Adger, W. N. and Jordan, A. (eds) (2009), *Governing Sustainability*, Cambridge: Cambridge University Press.

Adger, W. N., Agrawala, S., Mirza, M. M. Q., Conde, C., O'Brien, K., Pulhin, J., Pulwarty, R., Smit, B. and Takahashi, K. (2007), Assessment of adaptation practices, options, constraints and capacity. In: M. L. Parry, O. F. Canziani, J. P. Palutikof, P. J. van der Linden and C. E. Hanson (eds), *Climate Change 2007: Impacts, Adaptation and Vulnerability*, Contribution of Working Group II to the Fourth Assessment Report of the IPCC, Cambridge: Cambridge University Press.

AEA (2009), *Local and Regional CO_2 Emissions Estimates for 2005–2007 for the UK. Report to Department for Environment, Food and Rural Affairs*, Harwell: AEA.

Agyeman, J., Devine-Wright, P. and Prange, J. (2009), Close to the edge, down by the river? Joining up managed retreat and place attachment in a climate changed world, *Environment and Planning A*, 41(3): 509–13.

Aitken, M., McDonald, S. and Strachan, P. (2008), Locating 'power' in wind power planning processes: the (not so) influential role of local objectors, *Journal of Environmental Planning and Management*, 51(6): 777–99.

Alber, G. and Kern, K. (2008), Governing climate change in cities: modes of urban climate governance in multi-level systems. Available online at: http://www.oecd.org/dataoecd/22/7/41449602.pdf (accessed 11 December 2008).

Allman, L., Fleming, P. and Wallace, A. (2004), The progress of English and Welsh Local Authorities in addressing climate change, *Local Environment*, 9(3): 271–83.

Allmendinger, P. (2009), *Planning Theory*, 2nd edn, Basingstoke: Palgrave Macmillan.

Amati, M. (ed.) (2008), *Urban Green Belts in the Twenty-first Century*, Aldershot: Ashgate.

Anable, J. and Shaw, J. (2007), Priorities, policies and (time)scales: The delivery of emissions reductions in the UK transport sector, *Area*, 39(4): 443–57.

Anderson, K. (2009), *Climate Change in a Myopic World*, Tyndall Briefing Note No. 36, Norwich: Tyndall Centre.

Andrews, Baroness K. (2006), speech delivered to the Planning for Climate Change Conference 26 January 2006. Available online at: http://www.communities.gov. uk/speeches/corporate/climate-change-conference (accessed 1 June 2009).

Araújo, M. B., Cabeza, M., Thuiller, W., Hannah, L. and Williams, P. H. (2004), Would climate change drive species out of reserves? An assessment of existing reserve-selection methods, *Global Change Biology*, 10(9): 1618–26.

Arctic Climate Impact Assessment (2004), *Impacts of a Warming Arctic: Arctic Climate Impact Assessment Synthesis Report*, Cambridge: Cambridge University Press.

B&CCWG (Biodiversity and Climate Change Working Group) (2009), 'Report to Plenary, Athens Conference Biodiversity Protection: Beyond 2010', paper presented at the conference on Biodiversity Protection: Beyond 2010, Athens, Greece, 27–28 April.

Baker, S. and Eckerberg, K. (eds) (2008), *In Pursuit of Sustainable Development: New Governance Practices at the Sub-national Level in Europe*, Abingdon: Routledge.

Baltic Marine Environment Protection Commission and the OSPAR Commission (2003), *Towards an Ecosystem Approach to the Management of Human Activities*. Joint statement. Available online at: http://www.ospar.org/content/content.asp?menu =00430109150000_000000_000000 (accessed 3 June 2010).

Barker, K. (2004), *Review of Housing Supply: Delivering Stability. Securing our Future Housing Needs. Final Report – Recommendations*, London: HM Stationery Office.

Barroso, J. M. D. (2009), Statement of President Barroso to the Plenary of the Copenhagen conference on climate change. In: *Copenhagen Conference on Climate Change COP 15*, SPEECH/09/587, 18 December 2009. Available online at: http://europa.eu/rapid/pressReleasesAction.do?reference=SPEECH/09/587&format=HTML&aged=0&language=EN&guiLanguage=en

Barrow, E. M. and Lee, R. J. (2000), *Climate Change and Environmental Assessment: Part 2: Climate Change Guidance for Environmental Assessments*, Research and Development Monograph Series, Ottawa: Canadian Environmental Assessment Agency.

Beck, U. (1992), *Risk Society: Towards a New Modernity*, London: Sage.

Beckerman, W. and Pasek, J. (2001), *Justice, Posterity and the Environment*, Oxford: Oxford University Press.

Behm, A. (2008), EC international relations under the Kyoto Protocol, *Environmental Law and Management*, 20(6): 340–52.

Berry, P (ed.) (2009), *Biodiversity in the Balance: Mitigation and Adaptation Conflicts and Synergies*, Sofia: Pensoft Publishers.

Betsill, M. M. (2001), Mitigating climate change in US cities: opportunities and obstacles, *Local Environment*, 6(4): 393–406.

Betsill, M. and Bulkeley, H. (2007) Guest editorial: Looking back and thinking ahead: a decade of cities and climate change research, *Local Environment* 12(5): 447–56.

Betsill, M. M. and Bulkeley, H. (2004), Transnational networks and global environmental governance: the Cities for Climate Protection Program, *International Studies Quarterly*, 48: 471–93.

Biesbroek, G. R., Swart, R. J. and van der Knapp, W. G. M. (2009), The mitigation-adaptation dichotomy and the role of spatial planning, *Habitat International*, 33(3): 230–7.

Blowers, A. (2009), Why dump on us? *Town and Country Planning*, 78(1): 33–7.

Boardman, B., Darby, S., Killip, G., Hinnells, M., Jardine, C. N., Palmer, J. and Sinden, G. (2005), *40% House*, Oxford: Environmental Change Institute, University of Oxford.

Boardman, B. (2007), *Home Truths: A Low Carbon Strategy to Reduce UK Housing Emissions by 80% by 2050*, Oxford: Environmental Change Institute, University of Oxford.

Booy, O., Wade, M. and White, V. (2008), *Invasive Species Management for Infrastructure Managers and the Construction Industry*, London: CIRIA.

Bowers, J. K. (1997), *Sustainability and Environmental Economics: An Alternative Text*, Harlow: Longman.

Boykoff, M. T. and Mansfield, M. (2008), 'Ye Olde Hot Aire': Reporting on human contributions to climate change in the UK tabloid press, *Environmental Research Letters*, 3(2): 1–8.

Boyland, A. (2008), *Report to the Secretary of State for Communities and Local Government and the Secretary of State for Transport: Appeal by BAA plc and Stansted Airport Ltd.: Stansted Airport*. Bristol: The Planning Inspectorate.

BRANCH Partners (2007), *Planning for Biodiversity as Climate Changes. BRANCH Project Final Report*, Peterborough: Natural England.

Breukers, S. and Wolsink, M. (2007), Wind energy policies in the Netherlands: Institutional capacity-building for ecological modernisation, *Environmental Politics*, 16(1): 92–112.

Brooke, R., Settles, P. and Tapley, B. (2007), The real cost of saving the world, *Gateway*, Winter(5): 47–8.

Brookes, A. (2009), Environmental risk assessment and risk management. in: P. Morris and R. Therivel (eds), *Methods of Environmental Impact Assessment*, 3rd edn. London: Routledge.

Bryner, G. C. (2008), Political perspectives on climate policy. In: H. Compston and I. Bailey (eds), *Turning Down the Heat: The Politics of Climate Policy in Affluent Democracies*, Basingstoke: Palgrave Macmillan.

Bulkeley, H. and Betsill, M. M. (2003), *Cities and Climate Change: Urban Sustainability and Global Environmental Governance*, London: Routledge.

Bulkeley, H. and Betsill, M. M. (2005), Rethinking sustainable cities: multi-level governance and the 'urban' politics of climate change, *Environmental Politics*, 14(1): 42–63.

Bulkeley, H. and Kern, K. (2006), Local government and the governing of climate change in Germany and the UK, *Urban Studies*, 43(12): 2237–59.

Bulkeley, H., Schroeder, H., Janda, K., Zhao, J., Armstrong, A., Chu, S. Y. and Ghosh, S. (2009), 'Cities and climate change: the role of institutions, governance and urban planning', report prepared for the *World Bank Symposium on Climate Change*, Marseilles, June 2009. Available online at: http://www.urs2009.net/docs/papers/Bulkeley.pdf (accessed 15 January 2010).

Burdge, R. J. (2009), The focus of impact assessment (and IAIA) must now shift to global climate change! *Environmental Impact Assessment Review*, 28: 618–22.

BWEA (British Wind Energy Association) (2007), *Planning for a Sustainable Future – White Paper. BWEA response*. Available online at: http://www.bwea.com/pdf/0708%20PWP%20Response.pdf (accessed 3 December 2007).

BWEA (2008), *Wind energy in the UK: A BWEA State of the Industry Report*. Available online at: http://www.bwea.com/pdf/publications/Industry_Report_08.pdf (accessed 12 December 2008).

BWEA (2009a), BWEA welcomes largest onshore windfarm coming on-line and securing extension. Available online at: http://www.bwea.com/media/news/articles/bwea_welcomes_europes_largest.html (accessed 11 June 2009).

BWEA (2009b), *England's Regional Renewable Energy Targets: Progress Report*. Available online at: http://www.bwea.com/pdf/publications/RRETProgressReport.pdf (accessed 6 August 2009).

Byer, P. H. and Yeomans, J. S. (2007), Methods for addressing climate change uncertainties in project environmental impact assessments, *Impact Assessment and Project Appraisal*, 25(2): 85–99.

CABE (Commission for Architecture and the Built Environment) (2009a), *Hallmarks of a Sustainable City*, London: CABE.

CABE (2009b), *Public Space Lessons: Adapting Public Space to Climate Change*, London: CABE.

Cairns, S. and Newson, C. (2006), *Predict and Decide: Aviation, Climate Change and UK Policy. Final Report*, Oxford: Environmental Change Institute, University of Oxford.

Campaign for Better Transport (2009), *Creative Accounting lets Transport Off the Hook*, press release, 31 July 2009, London: CBT.

Campbell, H. (2006), Interface: Is the issue of climate change too big for spatial planning? *Planning Theory & Practice*, 7(2): 201–30.

Campbell H. J. and Marshall, R. (2002), Utilitarianism's bad breath? A re-evaluation of the public interest justification for planning, *Planning Theory*, 1(2): 163–87.

Carter, J. G., White, I. and Richards, J. (2009), Sustainability appraisal and flood risk management, *Environmental Impact Assessment Review*, 29(1): 7–14.

CBD (Convention on Biological Diversity) (2000), *Sustaining Life on Earth*, Montreal, Canada: Secretariat of the Convention on Biological Diversity.

CBD (2006), *Global Biodiversity Outlook 2*, Montreal: CBD.

CCC (Committee on Climate Change) (2008), *Building a Low-Carbon Economy: The UK's Contribution to Tackling Climate Change*, London: TSO.

CCC (2009a), *Meeting Carbon Budgets: The Need for a Step Change. Progress Report to Parliament*, London: Committee on Climate Change.

CCC (2009b), *Meeting the UK Aviation Target: Options for Reducing Emissions to 2050*, London: CCC.

CcSP (Climate *changes* Spatial Planning) (2009). Available online at: http://www.klimaatvoorruimte.nl/pro3/general/start.asp?i=0&j=0&k=0&p=0 (accessed 10 June 2009).

CEAA (Canadian Environmental Assessment Agency) (2003), *Incorporating Climate Change Considerations in EA: General Guidance for Practitioners*. Available online at: http://www.ceaa.gc.ca/default.asp?lang=En&n=A41F45C5–1 (accessed 21 June 2009).

CEC (Commission of the European Communities) (1979), Council Directive 79/409/EEC of 2 April 1979 on the conservation of wild birds, *Official Journal*, L 103, 25 April 1979, pp. 1–8 (Birds Directive).

CEC (1985), Council Directive 85/337/EEC of 27 June 1985 on the assessment of the effects of certain public and private projects on the environment, *Official Journal*, L 175, 5 July 1985, pp. 40–8 (EIA Directive).

CEC (1990), *Green Paper on the Urban Environment*, Brussels: CEC.

CEC (1991), Council Directive 91/271/EEC of 21 May 1991 concerning urban waste water treatment, *Official Journal*, L 135, 30 May 1991, pp. 40–52 (Urban Wastewater Directive).

CEC (1992), Council Directive 92/43/EEC of 21 May 1992 on the conservation of natural habitats and of wild fauna and flora, *Official Journal*, L206, 22 July 1992, pp. 7–50 (Habitats Directive).

CEC (1997), *The EU Compendium of Spatial Planning Systems and Policies*, Brussels: CEC.

CEC (1999), *European Spatial Development Perspective: Towards Balanced and Sustainable Development of the Territory of the EU*, Brussels: CEC.

CEC (2000a), Communication from the Commission to the Council, European Parliament and Economic and Social Committee: Pricing and sustainable management of water resources. [COM(2000) 477 Final, Brussels: CEC].

CEC (2000b), Directive 2000/60/EC establishing a framework for Community action in the field of water policy, *Official Journal*, L 327, 22 December 2000, pp. 1–73 (Water Framework Directive).

CEC (2001), Directive 2001/42/EC on the assessment of the effects of certain plans and programmes on the environment, *Official Journal*, L 197, 21 July 2001, pp. 30–7 (SEA Directive).

CEC (2002a), Directive 2002/91/EC on the energy performance of buildings, *Official Journal*, L 001, 4 January 2003, pp. 65–71 (Energy Performance of Buildings Directive).

CEC (2002b), *The Water Framework Directive. Tap into it!* Luxembourg: Office for Official Publications of the European Communities.

CEC (2002c), Recommendation of the European Parliament and of the Council Concerning the Implementation of Integrated Coastal Zone Management in Europe, (2002/413/EC) *Official Journal*, L 148, 6 June 2002 , pp. 24–27.

CEC (2006a), *EU Action Against Climate Change: The European Climate Change Programme*, Luxembourg: European Communities.

CEC (2006b), *Communication from the Commission to the Council and the European Parliament on Thematic Strategy on the Urban Environment*, COM(2005) 718 Final, SEC(2006) 16, Brussels: CEC.

CEC (2007a), Directive 2007/60/EC of 23 October 2007 on the assessment and management of flood risks, *Official Journal*, L 288, 6 November 2007, pp. 27–34 (Floods or Flood Risk Directive).

CEC (2007b), *Green Paper: Adapting to Climate Change in Europe: Options for EU Action*, SEC(2007) 849, COM(2007) 0354 Final, Brussels: CEC.

CEC (2008a), *Communication from the Commission. Roadmap for Maritime Spatial Planning: Achieving Common Principles in the EU*, COM(2008) 791 Final, Brussels: CEC.

CEC (2008b), Directive 2008/56/EC of the European Parliament and of the Council of 17 June 2008 establishing a framework for community action in the field of marine environmental policy, *Official Journal*, 25 June 2008, L 164/19 (Marine Strategy Framework Directive).

CEC (2008c), *European Economic Recovery Plan*, COM(2008) 800 Final, Brussels: CEC.

CEC (2008d), *The European Union's Biodiversity Action Plan*, Luxembourg: Office for Official Publications of the European Communities.

CEC (2008e), *20 20 by 2020: Europe's Climate Change Opportunity*, COM(2008) 30 Final, Brussels: CEC.

CEC (2009a), *White Paper: Adapting to Climate Change: Towards a European Framework of Action*. COM(2009) 147 Final, SEC (2009) 386, 387, 388, Brussels: CEC.

CEC (2009b), Directive 2009/29/EC of 23 April 2009 amending Directive 2003/87/EC so as to improve and extend the greenhouse gas emission allowance trading scheme of the Community, *Official Journal*, 5 June 2009, L 140/63 (Emissions Trading Directive).

CEC (2009c), *The Copenhagen Climate Agreement: EU positions and State of Play, EC Memo/09/445*, press release, Brussels: CEC.

CEC (2009d), Directive 2009/28/EC on the promotion of the use of energy from renewable sources, *Official Journal*, 5 June 2009, L 140/17, pp. 16–62.

CEC (2009e), Directive 2009/31/EC of 23 April 2009 on the geological storage of carbon dioxide, *Official Journal*, 5 June 2009, L 140/114, pp. 114–135.

CEC (2009f), *Report from the Commission to the Council, the European Parliament, the European Economic and Social Committee and the Committee of the Regions on the Application and Effectiveness of the Directive on Strategic Environmental Assessment (Directive 2001/42/EC)*, COM(2009) 469 Final, Brussels: CEC.

CEC (2009g), *Report from the Commission to the Council, the European Parliament, the European Economic and Social Committee and the Committee of the Regions on the application and effectiveness of the EIA Directive (Directive 85/337/EEC, as amended by Directives 97/11/EC and 2003/35/EC)*, COM(2009) 378 Final, Brussels: CEC.

CEC (2009h), *A Sustainable Future for Transport: Towards an Integrated, Technology-led and User-friendly System*, COM(2009) 279/4, Brussels: CEC.

CEC (2009i), *Fourth National Report of the European Community to the Convention on Biological Diversity*. Available online at: https://www.cbd.int/doc/world/eur/eur-nr-04-en.pdf (accessed 27 May 2010).

CEC (2009j), *Message from Athens*. Available online at: http://ec.europa.eu/environment/nature/biodiversity/conference/pdf/message_final.pdf (accessed 4 July 2009).

CEC (n.d.), *A New Floods Directive*. Available online at: http://ec.europa.eu/environment/water/flood_risk/index.htm (accessed 30 July 2009).

CRED (Centre for Research in Environmental Decisions) (2008), *The Psychology of Climate Change Communication: A Guide for Scientists, Journalists, Educators, Political Aides and the Interested Public*, New York: The Trustees of Columbia University in the City of New York. Available online at: http://cred.columbia.edu/guide/guide/intro.html (accessed 15 November 2009).

CSE (Centre for Sustainable Energy) (2009), *Bristol Citywide Sustainable Energy Study: BDF Evidence Base*, Bristol: CSE.

CSE and CDE (Centre for Sustainable Energy and Community Development Exchange) (2007), *Mobilising Individual Behavioural Change Through Community Initiatives: Lessons for Climate Change*, Report for Defra, London: Defra.

CSE with Garrad Hassan & Partners Ltd., Peter Capener & Bond Pearce LLP (2009), *Delivering Community Benefits from Wind Energy Development: A Toolkit*, report for the Renewables Advisory Board, July. Available online at: http://www.decc.gov.uk/en/content/cms/what_we_do/uk_supply/energy_mix/renewable/res/res.aspx (accessed 6 August 2009).

Chatrchyan, A. M. and Doughman, P. M. (2008), Climate policy in the United States: State and regional leadership. In: H. Compston and I. Bailey (eds) *Turning Down the Heat: The Politics of Climate Policy in Affluent Democracies*, Basingstoke: Palgrave Macmillan.

Cheshire County Council (n.d.), *Ecological Network for Cheshire*. Available online at: http://maps.cheshouire.gov.uk/econet/ (accessed 1 May 2010).

CIRIA (Construction Industry Research and Information Association) (2009), Infrastructure longevity, *Evolution*, January issue: 6–7.

CIRIA (2007), *The SuDS Manual, (C697)*, London: CIRIA.

City of Rotterdam (2007), *Stadsvisie Rotterdam. Spatial Development Strategy 2030. Summary. Draft*. Available online at: http://www.roterdam.nl/Rotterdam/Internet/ Diensten/dsv/bestanden/projecten/stadsvsie/media/pdf/43212_leaflet.pdf (accessed 21 March 2008).

City of Rotterdam, Dutch Delta Water Board, Higher Water Board of Schieland and Krimpenerwaard, Higher Water Board of Delfland (2007), *Waterplan 2 Rotterdam: Working on Water for an Attractive City*, Rotterdam: Gemeente Rotterdam DsV. Available online at: http://www.gw.rotterdam.nl/Rotterdam/Openbaar/Overig/ Waterplan/PDF/Algemeen/WP-samenvattingENGA5.pdf (accessed 21 August 2008).

Clare, R. (2008), *Retrofitting Climate Change Mitigation*, unpublished MSc dissertation, Oxford: Oxford Brookes University.

Cobbold, C. and Santema, R. (2001), *Going Dutch on the Manhood Peninsula*, Chichester: West Sussex County Council.

CfIT (Commission for Integrated Transport) (2009a), *Climate Change and Transport: Meeting the Challenge of Ambitious Carbon Reduction Targets*. Available online at: http://cfit.independent.gov.uk/pubs/2009/cct/pdf/cct.pdf (accessed 5 November 2009).

CfIT (2009b), *Planning for Sustainable Travel: Key Themes: Settlement Size*. Available online at: http://www.plan4sustainabletravel.org (accessed 5 November 2009).

Compston, H. and Bailey, I. (eds) (2008), *Turning Down the Heat: The Politics of Climate Policy in Affluent Democracies*, Basingstoke: Palgrave Macmillan.

Connell, D. J. (2009), Planning and its orientation to the future, *International Planning Studies*, 14(1): 85–98.

Connelly, S. and Richardson, T. (2005), Value-driven SEA: time for an environmental justice perspective? *Environmental Impact Assessment Review*, 25(4): 391–409.

Cooper, Y. (2007), *New Eco-towns Could Help Tackle Climate Change*, press release. Available online at: http://www.communities.gov.uk/news/corporate/neweco townscould (accessed 16 June 2009).

Counsell, D., Hart, T., Jonas, A. E. G. and Kettle, J. (2007), Fragmented regionalism? Delivering integrated regional strategies in Yorkshire and Humber, *Regional Studies*, 41: 391–401.

Cowell, R. (2007), Wind power and the 'planning problem': the experience of Wales, *European Environment*, 17(5): 291–306.

Crrescendo project (2008). Available online at: http://www.crrescendo.net/cities. php?city=Almere (accessed 16 July 2009).

Crichton, D. (2001), *The Implications of Climate Change for the Insurance Industry: An Update and Outlook to 2020*, Watford: Building Research Establishment.

Cullingworth, B. and Nadin, V. (2006), *Town and Country Planning in the UK*, 14th edn, London: Routledge.

Currel, G. (2009), Ecological modernisation and climate change in Australia, *Environmental Politics* 18(2): 201–17.

Damro, C. and Mackenzie, D. (2008), The European Union and the politics of multi-level climate governance. In: H. Compston and I. Bailey (eds), *Turning Down the Heat: The Politics of Climate Policy in Affluent Democracies*, Basingstoke: Palgrave Macmillan.

Davenport, D. (2008), The international dimension of climate policy. In: H. Compston and I. Bailey (eds), *Turning Down the Heat: The Politics of Climate Policy in Affluent Democracies*, Basingstoke: Palgrave Macmillan.

Davoudi, S. (2009), Asymmetric development in spatial planning. In: S. Davoudi and I. Strange (eds), *Conceptions of Space and Place in Strategic Spatial Planning*, London: Routledge.

De Groot, R. S., Stuip, M. A. M., Finlayson, C. M. and Davidson, N. (2006), *Valuing Wetlands: Guidance for Valuing the Benefits Derived from Wetland Ecosystem Services*, Ramsar Technical Report No. 3/CBD Technical Series No. 27. Gland: Ramsar Convention Secretariat and Montreal: Secretariat of the Convention on Biological Diversity.

De La Vega-Leinert, A. C. and Nicholls, R. J. (2008), Potential implications of sea-level rise for Great Britain, *Journal of Coastal Research*, 24(2): 342–57.

de Vries, J. (2006), Climate change and spatial planning below sea-level: Water, water and more water, *Planning Theory and Practice*, 7(2): 223–27.

de Vries, J. and Wolsink, M. (2009), Making space for water: Spatial planning and water management in the Netherlands. In: S. Davoudi, J. Crawford and A. Mehmood (eds), *Planning for Climate Change: Strategies for Mitigation and Adaptation for Spatial Planners*, London: Earthscan, pp. 223–35.

Deltacommissie (2008), *Working Together with Water: A Living Land Builds for its Future. Findings of the Deltacommisie 2008*, The Hague: Deltacommissie.

Dessai, S., Lu, X. and Hulme, M. (2005), Limited sensitivity analysis of regional climate change probabilities for the 21st century, *Journal of Geophysical Research*, 110: 1–17.

DG-Regio (2009), *Panorama Inforegio: Climate Change Responses at the Regional Level*, Luxembourg: Office of Official Publications of the European Union.

Dobson, A. (ed.) (1999), *Fairness and Futurity: Essays in Environmental Sustainability and Social Justice*, Oxford: Oxford University Press.

Docherty, I. and Shaw, J. (eds) (2008), *Traffic Jam: Ten Years of 'Sustainable' Transport in the UK*, Bristol: Policy Press.

Dodd, A. M., Cleary, B. E., Dawkins, J. S., Byron, H. J., Palframan, L. J. and Williams, G. M. (2007), *The Appropriate Assessment of Spatial Plans in England: A Guide to Why, When and How to Do It*, Sandy: RSPB.

Donaghy, K. (2007), Viewpoint: climate change and planning: responding to the challenge, *Town Planning Review*, 78(4): 1–9.

Donatantonio, D. (2009), Campaigners bid to boost green policy, *Planning: The Journal of the Royal Town Planning Institute*, 1821: 1.

Douvere, F. (2008), The importance of marine spatial planning in advancing ecosystem-based sea use management, *Marine Policy*, 32(5): 762–71.

Douvere, F. and Ehler, C. N. (2007), *International Workshop on Marine Spatial Planning, UNESCO, Paris, 8–10 November 2006: A Summary*, Paris, France: UNESCO MAB/IOC Consultants, 75732.

Draaijers, G. and van der Velden, A. (2009), The NCEA's recommendations on climate change in environmental assessment. In: *NCEA, Views and Experiences from the Netherlands Commission for Environmental Assessment*, Series no. 10, Utrecht: NCEA.

Drake, F. (2009), Black gold to green gold: regional energy policy and the rehabilitation of coal in response to climate change, *Area*, 41(1): 43–54.

Dryzek, J. S. (2005), *The Politics of the Earth: Environmental Discourses*, 2nd edn, Oxford: Oxford University Press.

EA (Environmental Agency), Flood Management Division (2004), *Maintenance of Uneconomic Sea Flood Defences: A Way Forward*, London: Environment Agency. Available online at: http://www.defra.gov.uk/environment/flooding/documents/policy/guidance/seadefence.pdf (accessed 2 May 2010).

EA (2008), *Managing Water Abstraction*, Bristol: Environment Agency.

EA (2009a), *Thames Estuary 2100: Strategic Environmental Assessment. Environmental Report*, London: Environment Agency.

EA (2009b), *Response to Yorkshire and Humber Plan – 2009 Update: Spatial Options*, Wakefield: Environment Agency. Available online at: http://www.yhassembly. gov.uk/dnlds/7.%20Responses%20SO99%20-%20SO104.pdf (accessed 3 December 2009).

EA (2009c), *Flooding in England: A National Assessment of Flood Risk*, Bristol: Environment Agency.

EA (2009d), *Water for People and the Environment*, Bristol: Environment Agency.

EA (2009e), *Draft River Basin Management Plans*, Public Consultation 22 December 2008 to June 2009. Available online at: http://www.environment-agency.gov.uk/research/planning/33250.aspx (accessed December 17, 2009).

EA (2009f), *Planning Act 2008: List of Statutory Consultees for National Policy Statements. Response to Department for Communities and Local Government Consultation.* Available online at: http://www.environment-agency.gov.uk/static/documents/Research/2034_NPS_statutory_consultees.pdf (accessed 2 May 2010).

EA (2009g), *Water Cycle Study Guidance*. Available online at: http://publications. environment-agency.gov.uk (accessed 2 May 2010).

EA (2009h), *Water Neutrality: An Expanded Definition*, Environment Agency Briefing Note, September 2009, Bristol: Environment Agency.

EA (2009i), *Delivering Water Neutrality: Measures and Funding Strategies*, Resource Efficiency science programme Science report: SC080033/SR2, Bristol: Environment Agency.

EA (2009j), *High Level Target 5: Development and Flood Risk* 2007/8, report to Department for Environment, Food and Rural Affairs (Defra) and Communities and Local Government (CLG) by the Environment Agency. Available online at: http://www.environment-agency.gov.uk/static/documents/Research/HLT5_20078_.pdf (accessed 2 May 2010).

EA (2009k), *TE2100 Plan Consultation Document*, London: Environment Agency.

EA, Defra and DCLG (2007), *Towards Water Neutrality in the Thames Gateway: Summary Report.* Science report SCO60100/SR3, Bristol: Environment Agency.

EA Wales (2009), *Flooding in Wales: A National Assessment of Flood Risk*, Cardiff: Environment Agency.

Eames, M. and Skea, J. (2002), The development and use of the UK environmental futures scenarios: Perspectives from cultural theory, *Greener Management International*, 37: 53–70.

Ebrahim, A. (2009), Learning in environmental policy-making and implementation.

In: K. Ahmed and E. Sanchez-Triana (eds) *Strategic Environmental Assessment for Policies: An Instrument for Good Governance*, Washington, DC: World Bank.

Echenique, M., Hargreaves, A. and Mitchell, G. (2009a), Spatial planning, sustainability and long-run trends, *Town and Country Planning*, 78(9): 380–5.

Echenique, M., Hargreaves, A., Jin, Y., Mitchell, G. and Namdeo, A. (2009b), *SOLUTIONS: Sustainability of Land Use and Transport in Outer Neighbourhoods. Draft Final Report: Strategic Scale*. Available online at: http://www.suburbansolutions. ac.uk/DocumentManager/secure0/SOLUTIONSFinalDraftReportonStrategic ScaleResearch.pdf (accessed 10 August 2009).

EDAW, AECOM and Levett Therivel (2008), *Final Sustainability Appraisal (Integrating Strategic Environmental Assessment) of the Yorkshire and Humber RSS Revision. Prepared for Government Office for Yorkshire and Humber*. Available online at: http://www.goyh.gov.uk/497763/docs/199734/199799/689582/5_SASEA_Report.pdf (accessed 26 July 2009).

Eddington, R. (2006), *The Case for Action: Sir Rod Eddington's Advice to Government. Report to HM Treasury and DfT*, London: TSO.

EEA (European Environment Agency) (2002), *Europe's Biodiversity: Biogeographical Regions and Seas*, Copenhagen: EEA.

EEA (2004), *Impacts of Europe's Changing Climate: An Indicator-based Assessment*. EEA Report No. 2/2004, Copenhagen: EEA.

EEA (2005), *Climate Change and River Flooding in Europe, Briefing no. 1*, Copenhagen: EEA.

EEA (2006), *Urban Sprawl in Europe: The Ignored Challenge*, EEA Report No. 10/2006, Copenhagen: EEA.

EEA (2007a), *Climate Change: The Costs of Inaction and the Cost of Adaptation. Technical Report 13/2007*, Copenhagen: EEA.

EEA (2007b), *Climate Change and Water Adaptation Issues*, briefing document 2007: 01, Copenhagen: EEA.

EEA (2008a), *Energy and Environment Report 2008*, Report 6/2008, Copenhagen: EEA.

EEA (2008b), *Impacts of Europe's Changing Climate: 2008 Indicator-based Assessment*, Joint EEA-JRC-WHO report: EEA Report No. 4/2008; JRC Reference Report No. JRC47756, Copenhagen: EEA.

EEA (2008c), *Greenhouse Gas Emission Trends and Projections in Europe 2008: Tracking Progress towards Kyoto targets. EEA Report No. 5/2008, Copenhagen: EEA*.

EEA (2008d), *Beyond Transport Policy: Exploring and Managing the External Drivers of Transport Demand. Illustrative Case-studies from Europe*, EEA Report No. 12/2008, Copenhagen: EEA.

EEA (2008e), *Climate for a Transport Change: TERM 2007. Indicators Tracking Transport and Environment in the European Union*, EEA Report 1/2008, Copenhagen: EEA.

EEA (2008f), *Opinion of the EEA Scientific Committee on the environmental impacts of biofuel utilisation in the EU*, EEA press release of 10 April 2008. Available online at: http://www.eea.europa.eu/highlights (accessed 2 May 2010).

EEA (2009a), *Europe's Onshore and Offshore Wind Energy Potential: An Assessment of Environmental and Economic Constraints*, EEA Report No. 6/2009, Copenhagen: EEA.

EEA (2009b), *Ensuring Quality of Life in European Cities and Towns: Tackling the Environmental Challenges Driven by European and Global Change*, EEA Report No. 5/2009, Copenhagen: EEA.

EEA (2009c), *Transport at a Crossroads: TERM 2008: Indicators Tracking Transport and Environment in the European Union*, EEA Report No. 3/2009, Copenhagen: EEA.

EEA (2009d), *Water Resources across Europe: Confronting Water Scarcity and Drought*, EEA Report No. 2/9, Copenhagen: EEA.

EEA (2009e), *Progress Towards the European 2010 Biodiversity Target*, EEA Report 4/2009, Copenhagen: EEA.

EEA (n.d.), Sea-level rise dataset. Available online at: http://www.eea.europa.eu/data-and-maps/figures/sea-level-rise (accessed 3 June 2010).

EESDRT (East of England Sustainable Development Round Table) (2004), *Living with Climate Change in the East of England: Summary Report*, Hertford: EESDRT.

Egoh, B., Rouget, M., Revers, B., Knight, AT., Cowling, R. M., van Jaarsveld, A. S. and Welz, A. (2007), Integrating ecosystem services into conservation assessments: A review, *Ecological Economics*, 63 (4): 714–21.

Ellis, H. (2008), 'Flawed plans', *The Guardian*, 28 October 2008, G2, p. 8.

Ellis, G. E., Barry, J. and Robinson, C. (2007), Many ways to say 'no', different ways to say 'yes': Applying Q-methodology to understand public acceptance of wind farm proposals, *Journal of Environmental Planning and Management*, 50(4): 517–51.

English Heritage (2008a), *Climate Change and the Historic Environment*, London: English Heritage.

English Heritage (2008b), *Energy Conservation in Traditional Buildings*, London: English Heritage.

ERM (Environmental Resources Management) (2000), *Potential UK Adaptation Strategies for Climate Change: Technical Report*, London: DETR.

ESPACE (European Spatial Planning Adapting to Climate Events) (2006), *A Climate for Change on the Manhood Peninsula*, Chichester: West Sussex County Council.

ESPACE (European Spatial Planning Adapting to Climate Events) Partnership (2007), *ESPACE – Planning in a Changing Climate. The Strategy and Supporting Evidence*, Winchester: Hampshire County Council.

ESPACE (European Spatial Planning Adapting to Climate Events) (2008a), *Climate Change Impacts and Spatial Planning – Decision Support Guidance*, report by the Environment Agency and Halcrow for ESPACE. Available online at: http://www.espace-project.org/publications/Extension%20Outputs/EA/Espace%20Final_Guidance_Finalv5.pdf (accessed 15 December 2010).

ESPACE (European Spatial Planning Adapting to Climate Events) (2008b), *Adaptive Capacity Benchmarking: A Handbook and Toolkit*, report by Alexander Ballard Ltd. for ESPACE. Available online at: http://www.espace-project.org/part2/part2_outputs.htm (accessed 14 October 2008).

ETC/BD (2009), Distribution of Natura 2000 sites across EU-25. Available at: www.eea.europa.eu/data-and-maps/figures/distribution-of-natura-2000-sites-across-the-27-eu-member-states (accessed 1 March 2010).

Eurobarometer (2008), *Europeans' Attitudes Towards Climate Change. Special Eurobarometer 300*. Available online at: http://ec.europa.eu/public_opinion/archives/ebs/ebs_300_full_en.pdf (accessed 1 July 2009).

Eurobarometer (2009), *Europeans' Attitudes Towards Climate Change. Special Eurobarometer 313*, European Parliament and European Commission. Available online at: http://ec.europa.eu/public_opinion/archives/ebs/ebs_313_en.pdf (accessed 5 October 2009).

Eurostat (2008a), *Population in Europe 2007: First Results. Statistics in Focus 81/2008*. Available online at: http://epp. eurostat.ec.europa.eu/cache/ITY_OFFPUB/KS-SF-08–081/EN/KS-SF-08–081-EN.PDF (accessed 5 October 2009).

Evans, E., Ashley, R., Hall. J., Penning-Rowsell, E., Saul, A., Sayers, P. Thorne, C. and Watkinson, A. (2004), *Foresight: Future Flooding*, London: Office of Science and Technology.

Evans, E., Hall, J., Penning-Rowsell, E., Sayers, P., Thorne, C. and Watkinson, A. (2006), Future flood risk management in the UK, *Proceedings of the Institution of Civil Engineers: Water Management*, 159(1): 53–61.

Evans, E. P., Simm, J. D., Thorne, C. R., Arnell, N. W., Ashley, R. M., Hess, T. M., Lane, S. N., Morris, J., Nicholls, R. J., Penning-Rowsell, E. C., Reynard, N. S., Saul, A. J., Tapsell, S. M., Watkinson, A. R. and Wheater, H. S. (2008), *An Update of the Foresight Future Flooding 2004 Qualitative Risk Analysis*, London: Cabinet Office.

Every, L. E. and Styles, M. D. (2007), Sustainable water management: towards water neutral developments. In: *Proceedings of the Combined International Conference of Computing and Control for the Water Industry, CCWI2007 and Sustainable Urban Water Management, SUWM2007*, De Montfort University, Leicester, United Kingdom, pp. 585–91.

Fairburn, J., Butler, B. and Smith, G. (2009), Environmental justice in South Yorkshire: locating social deprivation and poor environments using multiple indicators, *Local Environment*, 14(2): 139–54.

Falk, N. (2008a), New communities: looking at and learning from Dutch experience, *Town and Country Planning*, 77(12): 503–8.

Falk, N. (2008b), *Making Eco-towns Work: Developing Vathorst, Amersfoort, NL*, London: URBED.

Falk, N. and Hall, P. (2009) Why not here? *Town and Country Planning*, 78(1): 27–32.

Faludi, A. (2006), From European spatial development to territorial cohesion policy, *Regional Studies*, 40(6): 667–8.

Farman, J. C., Gardiner, B. G. and Shanklin, J. D. (1985), Large losses of total ozone in Antarctica reveal seasonal ClO_x/NO_x interaction, *Nature*, (315): 207–10.

Flyvbjerg, B. (1998), *Rationality and Power: Democracy in Practice*, Chicago: The University of Chicago Press.

Foresight Land Use Futures Project (2010), *Land Use Futures: Making the Most of Land in the 21st Century. Final Project Report*, London: Government Office for Science.

Foresight SEMBE (Sustainable Energy Management and the Built Environment Project) (2008), *Final Project Report*, London: Government Office for Science.

Forester, J. (1989), *Planning in the Face of Power*, Berkeley: University of California Press.

Foster, J. (1997), *Valuing Nature? Ethics, Economics and the Environment*, London: Routledge.

Freestone, R. (2009), Planning, sustainability and airport-led urban development, *International Planning Studies*, 16(2): 161–76.

FRMRC (Flood Risk Management Research Consortium) (2008), *Flood Risk Management*. Available online at: http://www.floodrisk.org.uk (accessed 27 April 2010).

George, C. (2001), Sustainability appraisal for sustainable development: Integrating everything from jobs to climate change, *Impact Assessment and Project Appraisal*, 19(2): 95–106.

Geoscience Australia (2008), *Risk Analysis*. Available online at: http://www.ga.gov.au/image_cache/GA10820.pdf (accessed 14 September 2009).

Giddens, A. (2009), *The Politics of Climate Change*, London: Polity Press.

Gill, S. (2008), *Critical Climate Change Functions of Green Infrastructure for Sustainable Economic Development in the North West, produced as part of 'Action 4.3' of the North West Climate Change Action Plan by Community Forests Northwest*. Available online at: http://www.greeninfrastructurenw.co.uk/climatechange/ (accessed 12 January 2010).

Gill, S., Handley, J., Ennos, R. and Pauleit, S. (2007), Adapting cities for climate change: the role of the green infrastructure, *Built Environment*, 33(1): pp. 115–33.

Gilliland, P. M. and Laffoley, D. (2008), Key elements and steps in the process of developing ecosystem-based marine spatial planning, *Marine Policy*, 32(5): 787–96.

Gillman, S. (2009), Council reality checker, *Planning: The Journal of the Royal Town Planning Institute*, 1839: 13.

GLA (Greater London Authority) (2007), *Water Matters. The Mayor's Draft Water Strategy*, London: Greater London Authority.

Glasbergen, P. (1996), Learning to manage the environment. In: W. M. Lafferty and J. Meadowcroft (eds), *Democracy and the Environment: Problems and Prospects*, Cheltenham: Edward Elgar.

Glasson, J. and Marshall, T. (2007), *Regional Planning*, Abingdon: Routledge.

Glasson, J., Therivel, R. and Chadwick, A. (2005), *Introduction to Environmental Impact Assessment*, 3rd edn, London: Routledge.

Gloucestershire County Council (2008), *Strategic Flood Risk Assessment Level 1 Executive Summary*. Available online at: http://www.tewkesbury.gov.uk/media/pdf/n/4/Gloucestershire_Level_1_SFRA_Exec_Summary_FINAL.PDF (accessed 17 August 2009).

Gosden, J. and Ive, T. (2009), 'Putting 'Making Space for Water' into practice in the Lower Derwent: progress towards a "Blue Corridor"', paper presented at the CIWEM Annual Conference, 2009: Water and the Global Environment, Olympia Conference Centre, London, United Kingdom, April 2009.

GONW (Government Office for the North West) (2008), *North West of England Plan: The Regional Spatial Strategy to 2021*, Manchester: GONW.

GOSE (Government Office for the South East) (2009), *The South East Plan: Regional Spatial Strategy for the South East of England*, London: TSO.

GOYH (Government Office for Yorkshire and the Humber) (2005), *Your Climate: Yorkshire and Humber's Climate Change Action Plan*, Leeds: GOYH.

GOYH (2008), *The Yorkshire and Humber Plan: Regional Spatial Strategy to 2026*, London: TSO.

Graham, S. and Marvin, S. (2001), *Splintering Urbanism: Networked Infrastructures, Technological Mobilities and the Urban Condition*, London: Routledge.

Granberg, M. and Elander, I. (2007), Local governance and climate change: Reflections on the Swedish experience, *Local Environment*, 12(5): 537–48.

Graves, H. M. and Phillipson, M. C. (2000), *Potential Implications of Climate Change in the Built Environment, FBE Report 2*, Watford: Foundation for the Built Environment/CRC.

Grayling, T. (2009), 'More Climate Change Adaptation for Less Emissions', paper presented at the IEMA Environmental Assessment Forum, London, 30 April 2009.

Green New Deal Group (2008), *A Green New Deal: Joined-up Policies to Solve the Triple Crunch of the Credit Crisis, Climate Change and High Oil Prices*, London: New Economics Foundation.

Green, N. (2008), City-states and the spatial in-between, *Town and Country Planning*, 77(6): 222–9.

Greiving, S. Fleischhauer, M. and Lückenkötter, J. (2006a), A methodology for an integrated risk assessment of spatially relevant hazards, *Journal of Environmental Planning and Management*, 49(1): 1–19.

Greiving, S., Fleischhauer, M. and Wanczura, S. (2006b), Management of natural hazards in Europe: the role of spatial planning in selected EU member states, *Handbook of Environmental Chemistry, Water Pollution* 49(5): 739–57.

Gupta, R. (2008), Reducing carbon emission from Oxford City: plans and tools. In: P. Dreuge (ed.), *Urban Energy Transition: From Fossil Fuels to Renewable Power*, Oxford: Elsevier.

Hajer, M. (1995), *The Politics of Environmental Discourse: Ecological Modernization and the Policy Process*, Oxford: Oxford University Press.

Haines-Young, R. and Potschin, M. (2010), The links between biodiversity, eco-system services and human well-being. In: D. G. Raffaelli and C. L. J. Frid (eds), *Ecosystem Ecology: A New Synthesis*, BES Ecological Reviews Series, Cambridge: Cambridge University Press.

Halcrow (2009), *NW Bicester Eco-town. Concept Study Prepared for Cherwell District Council*, London: Halcrow. Available online at: http://www.cherwell.gov.uk/media/pdf/j/c/Bicester_Eco-Town_Concept_Study.pdf (accessed 31 July 2009).

Hall, J. W., Dawson, R. J., Walsh, C. L., Barker, T., Barr, S. L., Batty, M., Bristow, A. L., Burton, A., Carney, S., Dagoumas, A., Evans, S., Ford, A. C., Glenis, V., Goodess, C. G., Harpham, C., Harwatt, H., Kilsby, C., Kohler, J., Jones, P., Manning, L., McCarthy, M., Sanderson, M., Tight, M. R., Timms, P. M. and Zanni, A. M. (2009), *Engineering Cities: How Can Cities Grow whilst Reducing Emissions and Vulnerability?* Newcastle: Newcastle University.

Hall, P. and Pain, K. (eds) (2006), *The Polycentric Metropolis: Learning from Mega-City Regions in Europe*, London: Earthscan.

Hall, P., Thomas, R., Gracey, H. and Drewett, R. (1973), *The Containment of Urban England*, London: Allen & Unwin.

Halsnaes, K. and Shukla, P. R. (2008), Sustainable development as a framework for developing country participation in international climate change policies, *Mitigation and Adaptation Strategy for Global Change*, 13: 105–30.

Hamin, E. M. and Gurran, N. (2009), Urban form and climate change: balancing adaptation and mitigation in the US and Australia, *Habitat International*, 33(3): 238–45.

Hannah, L., Midgley, G. F. and Millar, D. (2002a), Climate change-integrated conservation strategies, *Global Ecology and Biogeography Letters*, 11(6): 485–95.

Hannah, L., Midgley, G. F., Lovejoy, T., Bond, W. J., Bush, M., Lovett, J. C., Scott, D. and Woodward, F. I. (2002b), Conservation of biodiversity in a changing climate, *Conservation Biology*, 16(1): 264–8.

Hannah, L., Midgley, G. F., Andelmand, S., Araujo, M. B., Hughes, G., Martinez-Meyer, E., Pearson, R. and Williams, P. H. (2007), Protected area needs in a changing climate, *Frontiers in Ecology and Environment*, 5: 131–8.

Hardin, G. (1968), The Tragedy of the Commons, *Science*, 162: 1243–8.

Hardy, D. (1999), *1899–1999: Tomorrow and Tomorrow: The TCPA's First 100 Years*, London: TCPA.

Haughton, G., Allmendinger, P., Counsell, D. and Vigar, G. (2010), *The New Spatial Planning: Territorial Management with Soft Spaces and Fuzzy Boundaries*, London: Routledge.

HCA (Homes and Communities Academy) (2008), *Eco-town Report: Learning from Europe on Eco-towns*. Available online at: http://showcase.hcaacademy.co.uk/files/general/eco-town-report.pdf (accessed July 2009).

HCA Academy (2009), *Practice Guidance to Support the PPS: Planning and Climate Change*. Available online at: http://www.hcaacademy.co.uk/planning-and-climate-change (accessed 1 December 2009).

Headicar, P. (2009), *Transport Policy and Planning in Great Britain*, Abingdon: Routledge.

Healey, P. (1997), *Collaborative Planning: Shaping Places in Fragmented Societies*, Basingstoke: Macmillan.

Healey, P. (2007), *Urban Complexity and Spatial Strategies: Towards a Relational Planning for our Times*, Abingdon: Routledge.

Henderson, K. (2009), GRaBS Expert Paper 1: The case for climate change adaptation, *Town and Country Planning*, 78(6): 1–8.

Herring, H. and Sorrell, S. (eds) (2009), *Energy-efficiency and Sustainable Consumption: The Rebound Effect*, Basingstoke: Palgrave Macmillan.

Hertin, J., Turnpenny, J., Jordan, A., Nilsson, M., Russel, D. and Nykvist, B. (2009) Rationalising the policy mess? Ex ante policy assessment and the utilisation of knowledge in the policy process, *Environment and Planning A*, 41(5): 1185–200.

Hetherington, P. (2009), Towards a joined-up strategy? *Town and Country Planning*, 78(7/8): 306–07.

Hickman, R. and Banister, D. (2007), Looking over the horizon: Transport and reduced CO_2 emissions in the UK by 2030, *Transport Policy*, 14: 377–87.

Hickman, R., Ashiru, O. and Banister, D. (2009), 'Backcasting' for lower transport carbon emissions, *Town and Country Planning*, 78(2): 66–70.

Hill, M. (2005), *The Public Policy Process*, 4th edn. Harlow: Pearson Longman.

Hopkins, J. J., Allison, H. M., Walmsley, C. A., Gaywood, M. and Thurgate G. (2007), *Conserving Biodiversity in a Changing Climate: Guidance on Building Capacity to Adapt*, London: Defra.

Hordijk, L., Kalden, C., Fleischhauer, M., Geluk, J. M., Haanstra, H. J., Helder, J. J., Jacob, D., Jol, A., van de Klundert, A. F., Marks, J., Nobre, C. A. and de Wit, J. C. M. (2007), Klimaat voor Ruimte (Climate *changes* Spatial Planning): Midterm Evaluation Report from the Scientific and Social Evaluation Committees. Available online at: http://www.klimaatvoorruimte.nl/pro1/general/start.asp?i=14&j=9&k=0&p=0&itemid=375 (accessed 10 June 2009).

Hough, M. (2004), *Cities and Natural Process: A Basis for Sustainability*, 2nd edn. London: Routledge.

House of Commons CLG Committee (2008), *Existing Homes and Climate Change. Seventh Report of Session 2007–08. HC 432-1*, London: TSO.

House of Commons Environmental Audit Committee (2005), *Housing: Building a Sustainable Future. First Report of Session 2004–05. HC135–1*, London: TSO.

Howard, J. (2009), Climate change mitigation and adaptation in developed nation: A critical perspective on the adaptation turn in urban climate planning. In: S. Davoudi, J. Crawford and A. Mehmood (eds), *Planning for Climate Change: Strategies for Mitigation and Adaptation for Spatial Planners*, London: Earthscan.

Huggett, D., Southgate, M. and Thompson, S. (2003), Towards spatial planning in the marine environment, *Proceedings of International Conference on Coastal Management, Coastal Management 2003*, London: Thomas Telford, pp. 256–69.

Hughes, N., Tomei, J. and Ekins, P. (2008), *Critical Review of the Application of the UKCIP Socio-economic Scenarios: Lessons Learnt and Future Directions*, London: King's College London.

Huibers, A., Kool, R. P., and Wobben, M. (2002), *Beyond HERS – the Dutch Community Energy Rating System*. Available online at http://www.reneuer.com/upload/ RENEUER-ClHouse-046.pdf (accessed 16 July 2009).

Hulme, M. (2009), *Why we Disagree about Climate Change: Understanding Controversy, Inaction and Opportunity*, Cambridge: Cambridge University Press.

Hulme, M. and Dessai, S. (2008), Negotiating future climates for public policy: A critical assessment of the development of climate scenarios for the UK, *Environmental Science and Policy*, 11(1): 54–70.

Hulme, M., Neufeldt, H. and Colyer, H. (eds) (2009), *Adaptation and Mitigation Strategies: Supporting European Climate Policy. The Final Report of the ADAM Project*, Norwich: Tyndall Centre for Climate Change Research, University of East Anglia.

Hume, D. (2007 [1739–40]), *A Treatise of Human Nature*, ed. D. F. Norton and M. J. Norton, Oxford: Oxford University Press.

IEA (International Energy Agency) (2009), *World Energy Outlook 2009*, Paris: OECD/ IEA.

IEEP (Institute for European Environmental Policy) (2009), *Positive Planning for On-shore Wind: Expanding On-shore Wind Energy Capacity while Conserving Nature, A Report by the IEEP Commissioned by the RSPB*, London: IEEP.

IEMA (Institute of Environmental Management and Assessment) (2009), *Mitigating Climate Change: A Guide for Organisations*. IEMA Practitioner Best Practice Series, Vol. 14: *Supporting Information on Climate Change Mitigation and EIA*, Lincoln: IEMA.

Inch, A. (2009), Planning at the cross-roads again: Re-evaluating street-level regulation of the contradictions in New Labour's planning reforms, *Planning Practice & Research*, 24(1): 83–101.

IME (Institution of Mechanical Engineers) (2009), *Climate Change: Adapting to the Inevitable?* London: IME.

IPCC (Intergovernmental Panel on Climate Change) (2000), *Special Report on Emissions Scenarios*, Geneva: WMO, UNEP.

IPCC (2001) *Climate Change 2001: Synthesis Report. A Contribution of Working Groups I, II, and III to the Third Assessment Report of the Integovernmental Panel on Climate Change*. Watson, R. T. and the Core Writing Team (eds). Cambridge and New York: Cambridge University Press.

IPCC (2007a), *Climate Change 2007: Synthesis Report. Contribution of Working Groups I, II and III to the Fourth Assessment Report of the Intergovernmental Panel on Climate Change*, ed. R. K. Pachauri and A. Reisinger, Geneva: IPCC.

IPCC (2007b), *Climate Change 2007: The Physical Science Basis. Contribution of Working Group I to the Fourth Assessment Report of the Intergovernmental Panel on Climate Change*, ed. S. Solomon, D. Qin, M. Manning, Z. Chen, M. Marquis, K. B. Averyt, M. Tignor and H. L. Miller, Cambridge and New York: Cambridge University Press.

IPCC (2007c), *Climate Change 2007: Impacts, Adaptation and Vulnerability. Contribution of Working Group II to the Fourth Assessment Report of the Intergovernmental Panel on Climate Change*, ed. M. L. Parry, O. F. Canziani, J. P. Palutikof, P. J. van der Linden and C. E. Hanson, Cambridge: Cambridge University Press.

IPCC (2007d), *Climate Change 2007: Mitigation. Contribution of Working Group III to the Fourth Assessment Report of the Intergovernmental Panel on Climate Change*, ed. B. Metz, O. R. Davidson, P. R. Bosch, R. Dave, L. A. Meyer, Cambridge and New York: Cambridge University Press.

IPCC (2007e), Summary for Policymakers. In: B. Metz, O. R. Davidson, P. R. Bosch, R. Dave and L. A. Meyer (eds), *Climate Change 2007: Mitigation. Contribution of Working Group III to the Fourth Assessment Report of the Intergovernmental Panel on Climate Change*, Cambridge and New York: Cambridge University Press.

IPPR (2008), *Engagement and Political Space for Policies on Climate Change: A Report for the SDC*, London: IPPR.

Isaacs, J., Falconer, R. and Blackwood, D. (2008), A unique approach to visualising sustainability in the built environment. In: *Proceedings – International Conference Visualisation, VIS 2008, Visualisation in Built and Rural Environments*, London: Computer Society Press, pp. 3–10.

Jackson, T. (2009), *Prosperity without Growth: The Transition to a Sustainable Economy*, London: Sustainable Development Commission.

Jackson, T. and Dixon, J. (2007), The New Zealand Resource Management Act: An exercise in delivering sustainable development through an ecological modernization agenda, *Environment and Planning B*, 34: 107–20.

Jacobs Engineering (2008), *Bilston Leisure Centre: Sustainability Support: Climate Change Impacts and Adaptation*. Report for Wolverhampton City Council. Available online at: http://www.bilstonurbanvillage.co.uk/ (accessed 18 August 2009).

Jacobs, M. (1991), *The Green Economy: Environment, Sustainable Development and the Politics of the Future*, London: Pluto Press.

Janssen, L., Okker, R. and Schuur, J. (2006), *Welfare, Prosperity and Quality of the Living Environment*, The Hague: MNP, CPB and RPB.

Jay, S. A. (2008), *At the Margins of Planning: Off-shore Wind Farms in the United Kingdom*, Aldershot, United Kindgom: Ashgate.

Jenkins, V. A. (2007), PPS 9 Biodiversity and Geological Conservation – strengthening nature conservation in England? *Law, Science and Policy*, 3: 89–96.

Jenks, M., Burton, E. and Williams, K. (eds) (1996), *Compact Cities: A Sustainable Urban Form?* London: E. & F.N. Spon.

JNCC (Joint Nature Conservation Committee) (2009), *Fourth National Report to the United Nations Convention on Biological Diversity: United Kingdom*. Available online at: https://www.cbd.int/doc/world/gb/gb-nr-04-en.pdf (accessed 8 November 2009).

Johnson, C., Penning-Rowsell, E. and Parker, D. (2007), Natural and imposed injustices: the challenges in implementing 'fair' flood risk management policy in England, *The Geographical Journal*, 173(4): 374–90.

Johnstone, K., Brown, A. and Goldthorpe, M. (2009), *Adapting to Climate Change: A Guide to its Management in Organisations*, IEMA Practitioner Best Practice Series Vol. 13, Lincoln: IEMA.

Jones, C., Baker, M., Carter, J., Jay, S., Short, M. and Wood, C. (eds) (2005), *Strategic Environmental Assessment and Land Use Planning: An International Evaluation*, London: Earthscan.

Jones, T. (2008), *The Role of National Cycle Network Traffic-free Paths in Creating a Cycle Culture: The Case of NCN Route 5 Stafford*, unpublished PhD thesis, Oxford: Oxford Brookes University.

Jonkman, S. N., Kok, M. and Vrijling, J. K. (2008), Flood risk assessment in the Netherlands: a case study for Dike Ring South Holland, *Risk Analysis*, 28(5): 1357–73.

Kay, J. (2009), *The Long and the Short of It: Finance and Investment for Normally Intelligent People Who are Not in the Industry*, London: The Erasmus Press.

Keeling, C. D. (1960), The concentration and isotopic abundances of carbon dioxide in the atmosphere, *Tellus*, 12(2): 200–3.

Keeling, C. D. (1998), Rewards and penalties of monitoring the earth, *Annual Review of Energy and the Environment*, 23: 25–82.

Kent CC (n.d.), *Biodiversity Opportunity Areas in Kent*. Available online at: http://www.kentbap.org.uk/resources/boas/ (accessed 2 May 2010).

Kidd, S. (2007), Towards a framework of integration in spatial planning: an exploration from a health perspective, *Planning Theory and Practice*, 8(2): 161–81.

Kidd, S. and Shaw, D. (2007), Integrated water resource management and institutional integration: realising the potential of spatial planning in England, *The Geographical Journal*, 173(4): 312–29.

Kiehl, J. T. and Trenberth, K. E. (1997), Earth's annual global mean energy budget, *Bulletin – American Meteorological Society*, 78 (2): 197–208.

Killian, J. and Pretty, D. (2008), *The Killian Pretty Review: Planning Applications: A Faster and More Responsive System – Final Report*, London: DCLG.

Kirwan, F. (2005), *A Critical Review, Investigating Awareness, Use and Users' Opinions, of the 'Strategic Environmental Assessment and Climate Change: Guidance for Practitioners' Guidance Note*, unpublished MSc dissertation, Norwich: University of East Anglia. Available online at: http://www.uea.ac.uk/env/all/teaching/eiaams/pdf_dissertations/2005/Kirwan_Frances.pdf (accessed June 2009).

Klein, R. J. T. (2006), *Climate Change Mitigation and Adaptation, GECHS Workshop on climate change and poverty*, Oslo, Norway, 6–8 January 2006.

Klein, R. J. T., Eriksen, S. E. H., Ness, L. O., Hammill, A., Tanner, T. M., Robledo, C. and O'Brien, K. (2007), Portfolio screening to support the mainstreaming of adaptation to climate change into development assistance. *Climatic Change*, 84(1): 23–44.

Klein, R. J. T., Huq, S., Denton, F., Downing, T. E., Richels, R. G., Robinson, J. B. and Toth, F. L. (2007), Inter-relationships between adaptation and mitigation. In: M. L. Parry, O. F. Canziani, J. P. Palutikof, P. J. van der Linden and C. E. Hanson (eds), *Climate Change 2007: Impacts, Adaptation and Vulnerability. Contribution of Working Group II to the Fourth Assessment Report of the IPCC*, Cambridge: Cambridge University Press.

Kolodnytska, M. (2006), *Treatment of Adaptation to Climate Change in Strategic Environmental Assessments*, unpublished MSc dissertation, Oxford: Oxford Brookes University.

Kopf, S., Ha-Duong, M. and Hallegatte, S. (2008), *Using Maps of City Analogues to Display and Interpret Climate Change Scenarios and their Uncertainty*, Nogent-sur-Marne, France: Centre International de Recherches sur l'Environnement et le Developpement. Available online at: http://www.centre-cired.fr/IMG/pdf/CIREDWP-200807.pdf (accessed 15 November 2009).

Kørnøv, L. and Thissen, W. (2000), Rationality in decision and policy-making: Implications for strategic environmental assessment, *Impact Assessment and Project Appraisal*, 18(3): 191–200.

Kortenhaus, A. (2009), Introduction – coastal flood risk, *Maritime Engineering*, 162(3): 93–6.

Kovats, S. (ed.) (2008), *Health Effects of Climate Change in the UK 2008: An Update of the DoH Report 2001/02*, London: Department of Health and Health Protection Agency.

Kumari, K., Belt, T. C. and Dos Remedios Furtado, J. I. (1997), *Mainstreaming Biodiversity for Sustainable Development: A Practical Approach*, Working Paper of the Centre for Social and Economic Research on the Global Environment, GEC 97–24, Norwich: University of East Anglia.

Lafferty, W. M. and Meadowcroft, J. (eds) (1996), *Democracy and the Environment: Problems and Prospects*, Cheltenham: Edward Elgar.

Land Use Consultants (2008), *Sustainability Appraisal (Incorporating the Requirements for Environmental Assessment and Assessment under the Habitats Regulations) of the 2009 Update of the Yorkshire and Humber Plan (The Regional Spatial Strategy). Scoping Report prepared for Yorkshire and Humber Assembly*. Available online at: http://www.yhassembly.gov.uk/dnlds/RSS%20Update%20SA%20Scoping.pdf (accessed July 2009).

Land Use Consultants and RTPI (Royal Town Planning Institute) (2008), *Issues for the Practice of Sustainability Appraisal in Spatial Planning – A Review. Final Workstream Report for the Sustainable Development Research Network*, London: LUC.

Land Use Consultants and Wilbraham (2005), *Yorkshire and Humber Regional Spatial Strategy and Climate Change Study. Summary Report*, London: LUC.

Land Use Consultants for Environment Agency, Forestry Commission, GOSE, Groundwork, Natural England, SEEDA, SEEPB and Wildlife Trusts SE (2009), *South East Green Infrastructure Framework: From Policy into Practice*, Guildford: GOSE.

Larsen, S. V. (2008), 'SEA of River Basin Management Plans: Incorporating climate change', paper presented at IAIA08, The 28th Annual Conference of IAIA – Art and Science of Impact Assessment, Perth Convention Exhibition Centre, Perth, 4–10 May 2008. Available online at: http://www.iaia.org/iaia08perth/

Larsen, K. and Gunnarsson-Östling, U. (2009), Climate change scenarios and citizen-participation: Mitigation and adaptation in constructing sustainable futures, *Habitat International*, 33(3): 260–6.

LCCP (London Climate Change Partnership) (2002), *London's Warming: The Impacts of Climate Change on London*, London: LCCP.

LCCP (2006), *Adapting to Climate Change: Lessons for London*, London: GLA.

LCCP (2009), *Economic Incentive Schemes for Retrofitting London's Existing Homes for Climate Change Impacts*, London: GLA.

LCCP, Sustainable Development Round Table for East of England (SDRTEE) and South East Climate Change Partnership (SECCP) (2005), *Adapting to Climate Change: A Checklist for Development. Guidance on Designing Developments for a Changing Climate*, London: LCCP.

LCCP, SDRTEE and SECCP (2006), *Adapting to Climate Change Impacts: A Good Practice Guide for Sustainable Communities*, London: GLA.

LCCP, SDRTEE and SECCP (2007), *Adapting to Climate Change: A Case Study Companion to the Checklist for Development*, London: Government Office for London.

Le Quéré, C., Raupach, M. R., Canadell, J. G. and Marland, G. (2009), Trends in the sources and sinks of carbon dioxide, *Nature Geoscience*, 2: 831–6.

Lenschow, A. (ed.) (2002), *Environmental Policy Integration: Greening Sectoral Policies in Europe*, London: Earthscan.

Lenton, T., Wilkinson, P., Edwards, N., Marsh, R., Price, J., Ridgewell, A., Shepherd, J. and Cox, S. J. (2006), Millennial time-scale carbon cycle and climate change in an efficient earth system model, *Climate Dynamics*, 26: 687–711.

Levett, R. (2007), Misconstrued problems, misconceived solutions, *Town and Country Planning*, 76(9): 299–302.

Levett-Therivel Sustainability Consultants, Environment Agency, Countryside Council for Wales, UKCIP, Natural England, InteREAM, CAG Consultants (2004, revised 2007), *Strategic Environmental Assessment and Climate Change: Guidance for Practitioners*, London: Environment Agency. Available online at: http://www. environment-agency.gov.uk/static/documents/Research/seaccjune07_1797458. pdf (accessed 28 May 2010).

LGA (Local Government Association) (2007), *Planning for a Sustainable Future*. Available online at: http://www.lga.gov.uk/lga/aio/103703 (accessed 14 June 2009).

LGA Climate Change Commission (2007), *A Climate of Change: Final Report of the LGA Climate Change Commission*, London: LGA.

Lindley, S., Handley, J., McEvoy, D., Peet, E. and Theuray, N. (2007), The role of spatial risk assessment in the context of planning for adaptation in UK urban areas, *Built Environment*, 33(1): 48–69.

Lindseth, G. (2004), The Cities for Climate Protection Campaign (CCPC) and the framing of local climate policy, *Local Environment*, 9(4): 325–36.

Lindseth, G. (2006), Scalar strategies in climate change politics: debating the consequences of a natural gas project, *Environment and Planning C: Governance and Policy*, 24(5): 739–54.

Linnerooth, J. and Mechler, R. (2006), Insurance for assisting adaptation to climate change in developing countries: A proposed strategy, *Climate Policy*, 6: 621–36.

Lock, D. (2009), Eco-towns: Top-down or bottom-up? *Town and Country Planning*, 78(2): 58–9.

Lomborg, B. (2007), *Cool It! The Skeptical Environmentalist's Guide to Global Warming*, London: Marshall Cavendish.

London Borough of Barking and Dagenham (LBBD) (2006), *Guide to the Barking Town Centre Energy Action Area*, London: LBBD.

Lorenzoni, I., Nicholson-Cole, S. and Whitmarsh, L. (2007), Barriers perceived to engaging with climate change among the UK public and their policy implications, *Global Environmental Change*, 17: 445–59.

Lorenzoni, I., O'Riordan, T. and Pidgeon, N. (2008) Hot air and cold feet: the UK response to climate change. In: H. Compston and I. Bailey (eds), *Turning Down the Heat: The Politics of Climate Policy in Affluent Democracies*, Basingstoke: Palgrave Macmillan.

Lovelock, J. (2006), *The Revenge of Gaia: Why the Earth is Fighting Back – and How We Can Still Save Humanity*, London: Allen Lane.

Low Carbon West Oxford (2009). Available online at: http://www.lowcarbonwest oxford.org.uk/index.php (accessed 26 September 2009).

Luisetti, T., Turner, K. and Bateman, I. (2008), *An ecosystem services approach to assess managed realignment coastal policy in England*, CSERGE Working Paper ECM 08-04. Norwich: Centre for Social and Economic Research on the Global Environment, pp. 1–25.

Lundqvist, L. L. and Biel, A. (2007), *From Kyoto to the Town Hall: Making International and National Climate Policy Work at the Local Level*, London: Earthscan.

Lynas, M. (2007), *Six Degrees: Our Future on a Hotter Planet*, London: Fourth Estate.

MACIS (Minimisation of and Adaptation to Climate Impacts on Biodiversity). Project website: http://www.macis-project.net (accessed 28 April 2010).

Mackay, D. J. C. (2009), *Sustainable Energy: Without the Hot Air*, Cambridge: UIT.

Maclean, I. M. D. and Rehfisch, M. M. (2008), *Developing Guidelines for Ornithological Cumulative Impacts Assessment Draft Discussion Document*, British Trust for Ornithology Research Report no. 513 for COWRIE, Thetford: BTO.

Maes, F. (2008), The international legal framework for marine spatial planning, *Marine Policy*, 32(5): 797–810.

Mander, S. and Randles, S. (2009), Aviation coalitions: drivers of growth and implications for carbon dioxide emissions reduction. In: S. Gössling and P. Upham (eds), *Climate Change and Aviation: Issues, Challenges and Solutions*, London: Earthscan.

Marsh, T. and Hannaford J. (2008), *The Summer 2007 Floods in England and Wales – a Hydrological Appraisal*, Wallingford: CEH.

Marshall, T. (1997), Futures, foresights and forward looks: reflections on the use of prospective thinking for transport and planning strategies, *Town Planning Review*, 68(1): 31–53.

Marshall, T. (2009a), Planning and New Labour in the UK, *Planning Practice & Research*, 24(1): 1–9.

Marshall, T. (2009b), Infrastructure planning in the Netherlands: the benefits of long-term thinking, *Town and Country Planning*, 78(10): 429–32.

Marshall, T. (2010), More ports in a storm, *Planning*, 1850: 6.

Max Lock Institute (2008), *Retrofitting Soho: Improving the Sustainability of Historic Core Areas. Executive Summary*, London: University of Westminster.

Mayor of London (2006), *London's Urban Heat Island: A Summary for Decision-makers*, London: GLA.

Mayor of London (2008a), *The London Plan: Spatial Development Strategy for Greater London. Consolidated with Alterations since 2004*, London: GLA.

Mayor of London (2008b), *Living Roofs and Walls. Technical Report: Supporting London Plan Policy*, London: GLA.

Mayor of London (2009a), *Cleaning the Air: The Mayor's Draft Air Quality Strategy for Consultation with the London Assembly and Functional Bodies*, London: GLA.

Mayor of London (2009b) *A New Plan for London: Proposals for the Mayor's London Plan. (The Spatial Development Strategy for Greater London)*. Published for initial consultation with the London Assembly and the GLA Group. London: GLA.

Mayor of London and LCCP (2005), *Climate Change and London's Transport Systems: Summary Report*, London: GLA.

MCCIP (Marine Climate Change Impacts Partnership) (2008), *Marine Climate Change Impacts: Annual Report Card 2007–2008*, Summary Report, (ed.) J. M. Baxter, P. J. Buckley, and C. J. Wallace, Lowestoft: MCCIP.

MCCIP (2009), *Marine Climate Change Impacts: Exploring Ecosystem Linkages. Report Card*. Available online at: http://www.mccip.org.uk/elr/MCCIP-ELR2009.pdf (accessed 29 June 2009).

McEvoy, D., Handley, J. F., Cavan, G., Aylen, J., Lindley, S., McMorrow, J. and Glynn, S. (2006a), *Climate Change and the Visitor Economy: The Challenges and Opportunities for England's Northwest*, Manchester: Sustainability Northwest, and Oxford: UKCIP.

McEvoy, D., Lindley, S. and Handley, J. (2006b), Adaptation and mitigation in urban areas: Synergies and conflicts, *Municipal Engineer (Proceedings of the Institution of Civil Engineers)*, 159(ME4): 185–91.

McEvoy, D., Lonsdale, K. and Matczak, P. (2008), *Adaptation and Mainstreaming of EU Climate Change Policy: An Actor-based Perspective*, CEPS Policy Brief No. 149. Available online at: http://ssm.com/abstract=1334066 (accessed 13 November 2009).

McInnes, R. J., Crane, M., Rodda, H. J. E., Danks, P. W., Hogan, D. V. and Field, A. I. (2008), *Management of the Otmoor Protected Area (Oxfordshire): (Multifunctional Wetlands in Agricultural Landscapes: An Evaluation of Values, Impacts and the Application of the Ecosystem-based Approach)*, WWT Report to Defra. Project Reference: NR0112. Slimbridge: Wildfowl & Wetlands Trust.

McKinsey Global Institute (1998), *Driving Productivity and Growth in the UK Economy*, Washington, DC: McKinsey Global Institute. Available online at: http://www.mckinsey.com/mgi/publications/uk.asp (accessed 11 August 2009).

Met Office (2008) *Climate change and the Thames Estuary*, press release. Available online at: http://www.metoffice.gov.uk/corporate/pressoffice/2008/pr20080923.html (accessed 16 August 2009).

Mickwitz, P., Aix, F., Beck, S., Carss, D., Ferrand, N., Gorg, C., Jensen, A., Kivimaa, P., Kuhlicke, C., Kuindersma, W., Manez, M., Melanen, M., Monni, S., Pedersen, A. B., Reinert, H. and van Bomel, S. (2009), *Climate Policy Integration, Coherence and Governance: PEER Report No 2*, Helsinki: Partnership for European Environmental Research.

Milligan, J. and O'Riordan, T. (2007), Governance for sustainable coastal futures. *Coastal Management*, 35(4): 499–509.

Milton Keynes Council (2007), *The Milton Keynes Urban Development Area Tariff SPD Consultation Draft*, Milton Keynes, United Kindgom: Milton Keynes Council.

Milton Keynes Partnership and English Partnerships (2007), *The Milton Keynes Tariff: An Overview of the Infrastructure Tariff and How it Works*, Milton Keynes: Milton Keynes Partnership.

Minton, A. (2006), *The Privatisation of Public Space*, London: RICS.

Minton, A. (2009), *Ground Control: Fear and Happiness in the Twenty-first Century*, London: Penguin.

Mitchell, R., Morecroft M., Acreman, M., Crick, H., Frost, M., Harley, M., Maclean, I., Mountford, O., Piper, J., Pontier, H., Rehfisch, M., Ross, L., Smithers, R., Stott, A., Walmsley, C., Watts, O. and Wilson, E. (2007), *England Biodiversity Strategy – Towards Adaptation to Climate Change*, London: Defra.

MNP (Milieu en Natuur Planbureau) (2007), *Later Netherlands: The Physical Living Environment in the Netherlands*. Available online at: http://www.rivm.nl/bibliotheek/rapporten/500127001.pdf (accessed 22 September 2009).

Morecroft, M. D., Bealey, C. E., Beaumont, D. A., Benham, S., Brooks, D. R., Burt, T. P., Critchley, C. N. R., Dick, J., Littlewood, N. A., Monteith, D. T., Scott, W. A., Smith, R. I., Walmsley, C. and Watson, H. (2009), The UK Environmental Change Network: emerging trends in the composition of plant and animal communities and the physical environment, *Biological Conservation*, 142(12): 2814–32.

Morris, P. and Therivel, R. (eds) (2009), *Methods of Environmental Impact Assessment*, 3rd edn. London: Routledge.

Moser, S. (2006), Talk of the city: engaging urbanites on climate change, *Environmental Research Letters*, 1: 1–10.

Moser, S. C. and Dilling, L. (eds) (2007), *Creating a Climate for Change: Communicating Climate Change and Facilitating Social Change*, Cambridge: Cambridge University Press.

Mostert, E. (2006), Integrated water resources management in the Netherlands: how concepts function, *Journal of Contemporary Water Research and Education*, 135: 19–27.

Mostert, E., Pahl-Wostl, C., Rees, Y., Searle, B., Tàbara, D. and Tippett, J. (2007), Social learning in European river-basin management: barriers and fostering mechanisms from 10 river basins, *Ecology and Society*, 12(1): 19. Available online at: http://www.ecologyandsociety.org/vol12/iss1/art19/ (accessed 29 April 2010).

Munro, D. and Holdgate, M. (eds) (1991), *Caring for the Earth: A Strategy for Sustainable Living*, Gland, Switzerland: IUCN, UNEP and WWF.

MVenW (Ministry of Transport, Public Works and Water Management) (2000), *A Different Approach to Water: Water Management Policy in the 21st Century*. Available online at: http://www.safecoast.org/editor/databank/File/Anders%20leven%20met%20water%20ENG.pdf (accessed 10 June 2009).

MVenW (2006), *Spatial Planning Key Decision: Room for the River. Investing in the Safety and Vitality of the Dutch River Basin Region*. Available online at: http://www.ruimtevoorderivier.nl/files/Files/brochures/EMAB%20PBK%20Engels.pdf (accessed 10 June 2009).

MVenW (2009), *National Water Plan – a Summary*. Available online at: http://www.verkeerenwaterstaat.nl/images/58392ne (accessed 18 September 2009).

Nadin, V. (2002), Visions and visioning in European spatial planning. In: Faludi, A. (ed.), *European Spatial Planning*, Cambridge, MA: Lincoln Institute of Land Policy.

Nadin, V. (2006), *The Role and Scope of Spatial Planning: Spatial Plans in Practice Literature Review Summary*, London: Communities and Local Government. Available online at: http://www.communities.gov.uk/index.asp?id=1504896 (accessed 2 May 2010).

National Trust (2005a), *Shifting Shores: Living with a Changing Coastline*, London: National Trust.

National Trust (2005b), *Forecast – Changeable*, London: National Trust.

National Trust (2007), *Shifting Shores: Living with a Changing Coastline*, Cardiff: National Trust Wales.

National Trust (2009), *The National Trust Annual Report 2008–09: Time Well Spent*, Swindon: National Trust.

National Trust, RHS and UKCIP (2002), *Gardening in the Global Greenhouse: The Impacts of Climate Change on Gardens in the UK*, Oxford: UKCIP.

Natural Economy North West (2008), *The Economic Value of Green Infrastructure*. Available online at: http://www.naturaleconomynorthwest.co.uk/resources+reports.php (accessed 2 December 2009).

Natural England (2008), *Responding to the Impacts of Climate Change on the Natural Environment: Dorset Downs and Cranborne Chase. A summary*, Peterborough: Natural England. Available online at: http://naturalengland.etrader stores.com (accessed 08 November 2009).

Natural England (2009a), 'Green growth for green communities: a selection of regional case studies', paper presented at ParkCity Conference, London, 23 March. Available online at: http://www.naturalengland.org.uk/Images/GI%20case%20studies_tcm6–10331.pdf (accessed 15 July 2009).

Natural England (2009b), *No Charge? Valuing the Natural Environment*. Peterborough: Natural England.

Natural England (2009c), Natural England's Policy on the Impacts of Climate Change on Biodiversity. NECR 004. Available online at: http://naturalengland. etraderstores.com/NaturalEnglandShop/NECR004 (accessed 3 June 2010).

Natural England (2009d), *Natural England's Response to IUSS Report on SSSIs*, press release, 29 July 2009.

Natural Resources Canada (2006), *Enhancing Resilience in a Changing Climate (ERCC) Program*, Ottawa: Dept of Natural Resources.

NCEA (Netherlands Commission for Environmental Assessment) (2009), *Views and Experiences from the Netherlands Commission for Environmental Assessment*, Series no. 10, Utrecht: NCEA.

NEAA (Netherlands Environmental Assessment Agency) (n.d.), *Environmental Data Compendium. Designation of the National Ecological Network (terrestrial)*, available online at: http://www.mnp.nl/mnc/i-en-1298.html (accessed 2 May 2010).

NECF (North East Community Forest) (2006), *Green Infrastructure Planning Guide*. Available online at: http://www.greeninfrastructure.eu/index.php?section=006. 002&page=39 (accessed 22 August 2009).

Needham, B. (2006), The new Dutch Spatial Planning Act: continuity and change in the way in which the Dutch regulate the practice of spatial planning, *Planning Practice & Research*, 20(3): 327–40.

Newman, P. and Jennings, I. (2008), *Cities as Sustainable Ecosystems: Principles and Practices*. Washington, DC: Island Press.

Next Generation (2008), *Developing Homes for a Changing Climate: Bench-marking how UK home builders are responding to climate change risks and opportunities*, London: WWF.

Nicholson-Cole, S. (2008), *The Tyndall Centre Coastal Simulator*. Available online at: http://www.tyndall.ac.uk/sites/default/files/bn18.pdf (accessed 15 November 2009).

Norman, C., DeCanio, S. and Fan, L. (2008), The Montreal Protocol at 20: Ongoing opportunities for integration with climate protection, *Global Environmental Change*, 18(2): 330–40.

Notenboom, J., van Veem, M. and Wesselink, L. G. (2006), *Halting the Loss of Biodiversity in The Netherlands*, MNP report 500094001, Utrecht: Netherlands Environmental Assessment Agency.

Nowell, R. and Bray, B. (2009), *The development of a SUDS Strategy and Planning Model for Housing Re-development*, Presentation to SUDSnet at the National SUDS conference, Coventry University. Available online at: http://sudsnet.abertay.ac.uk (accessed 28 April 2010).

Nunes, P. A. L. D. and Van den Bergh, J. C. J. M. (2001), Economic valuation of biodiversity: sense or nonsense? *Ecological Economics*, 39(2): 203–22.

O'Brien, E. (2003), Human values and their importance to the development of forestry policy in Britain: a literature review, *Forestry – An International Journal of Forest Research*, 76(1): 2–17.

O'Neill, S. and Nicholson-Cole, S. (2009), 'Fear won't do it': promoting positive engagement with climate change through visual and iconic representations, *Science Communication*, 30(3): 355–79.

Oberthür, S. and Ott, H. E. (1999), *The Kyoto Protocol: International Climate Policy for the 21st Century*, Berlin: Springer-Verlag.

Ockwell, D., Whitmarsh, L. and O'Neill, S. (2009), Reorienting climate change communication for effective mitigation: forcing people to be green or fostering grass-roots engagement? *Science Communication*, 30(3): 305–27.

OECD/DAC (Development Assistance Committee) Network on Environment and Development Co-operation (Environet) (2008), *Strategic Environmental Assessment and Adaptation to Climate Change*, Paris: OECD.

ONS (Office for National Statistics) (2008), *National Population Projections 2006-based. Series PP2 No. 26*, Basingstoke: Palgrave Macmillan.

Ofwat (The Water Services Regulation Authority) (2007), *Security of Supply: 2006–07 Report*, Birmingham: Ofwat.

Olshansky, R. B. (2006), Planning after Hurricane Katrina, *Journal of American Planning Association*, 72(2): 147–53.

Opdam P., Steingrover, E. and van Rooij, S. (2006), Ecological networks: a spatial concept for multi-actor planning of sustainable landscapes, *Landscape and Urban Planning*, 75: 322–32.

OSPAR Commission (1992), *Convention for the Protection of the Marine Environment of the North-East Atlantic*. Available online at: http://www.ospar.org (accessed 16 August 2009).

Ove Arup and Partners Ltd (2009), *Renewable Energy Capacity in Regional Spatial Strategies: Final Report*, London: DCLG.

Owen, E. (2008), Mayor drops objections to Beckton desalination plant, *New Civil Engineer*. 12 May 2008. Available online at: http://www.nce.co.uk/mayor-drops-objections-to-beckton-desalination-plant/1329856.article (accessed 25 January 2010).

Owens, S. and Cowell, R. (2001) *Land and Limits: Interpreting Sustainability in the Planning Process*, London: Routledge.

Owens, S., Rayner, T. and Bina, O. (2004), New agendas for appraisal: reflections on theory, practice and research, *Environment and Planning A*, 36: 1943–59.

Oxfam International (2008), *Viet Nam: Climate Change, Adaptation and Poor People*, Hanoi and Oxford: Oxfam International.

Oxfam International (2009), *The Right to Survive in a Changing Climate*, Oxfam Background Paper. Available online at: http://www.oxfam.org.uk/resources/policy/climate_change/downloads/right_to_survive_climate.pdf (accessed 29 June 2009).

Paavola, J., Adger, W. N. and Huq, S. (2006), Multifaceted justice in adaptation to climate change. In: W. N. Adger, J. Paavola, S. Huo and M. Mace (eds), *Fairness in Adaptation to Climate Change*, Cambridge, MA and London: MIT Press, pp. 263–77.

Page, E. (2006), *Climate Change, Justice and Future Generations*, Cheltenham: Edward Elgar.

Parry, M., Palutikof, J., Hanson, C. and Lowe, J. (2008), Squaring up to reality, *Nature Reports: Climate Change*, 2: 68–70.

Parry, M., Arnell, N., Berry, P., Dodman, D., Fankhauser, S., Hope, C., Kovats, S., Nicholls, R., Satterthwaite, D., Tiffin, R. and Wheeler, T. (2009), *Assessing the Costs of Adaptation to Climate Change: A Review of the UNFCCC and Other Recent Estimates*, London: International Institute for Environment and Development and Grantham Institute for Climate Change.

Parry, M. L., Canziani, O. F., Palutikof, J. P., van der Linden, P. J. and C. E. Hanson (eds) (2007), *Fourth Assessment Report of the IPCC*, Cambridge: Cambridge University Press.

Paterson, J. S., Araújo, M. B., Berry, P. M., Piper, J. M. and Rounsevell, M. D. A. R. (2008), Mitigation, adaptation and the threat to biodiversity, *Conservation Biology*, 22 (5): 1352–5.

PBL (Netherlands Environmental Assessment Agency) (2006) *Climate Adaptation in the Netherlands*. Available online at: http://www.pbl.nl/en/publications/2006/cli mateadaptationintthenetherlands.html (accessed 23 June 2009).

Pearce, D., Markandya, A. and Barbier, E. (1989), *Blueprint for a Green Economy*, London: Earthscan.

Peel, D. and Lloyd, M. G. (2004) The social reconstruction of the marine environment. Towards marine spatial planning? *Town Planning Review*, 75(3): 359–78.

Peel, D. and Lloyd, M. G. (2009), New Labour and the planning system in Scotland: an overview of a decade, *Planning Practice & Research*, 24(1): 103–18.

Pelling, M. and High, C. (2005), *Social Learning and Adaptation to Climate Change*, Benfield Hazard Research Centre Disaster Studies Working Paper 11, London: King's College.

Petts, J. (2007), Learning about learning: lessons from public engagement and deliberation on urban river restoration, *The Geographical Journal*, 173(4): 300–11.

Pfeifer, S. and Sullivan, R. (2008), Public policy, institutional investors and climate change: a UK case study, *Climatic Change*, 89(3–4): 245–62.

Phillips, H. (2008), In the know on adaptation? *Town and Country Planning*, 77(10): 411–15.

Pickett, S. T., Ostfeld, R. E., Shachak, M. and Likens, G. E. (1997), *The Ecological Basis of Conservation: Heterogeneity, Ecosystems and Biodiversity*, London and New York: Chapman & Hall.

Pielke, R., Jr., Prins, G., Rayner, S. and Sarewitz, D. (2007), Climate change 2007: Lifting the taboo on adaptation, *Nature*, 445: 597–8.

Piper, J. M., Wilson E., Weston J., Thompson S. and Glasson J. (2006), *Spatial Planning for Biodiversity in our Changing Climate, English Nature Report No. 677*, Peterborough: English Nature.

Pitt, M. (2008), *The Pitt Review: Learning Lessons from the 2007 Floods, an Independent Review by Sir Michael Pitt*, London: Cabinet Office.

Pizarro, R. E. (2009), The mitigation/adaptation conundrum in planning for climate change and human settlements: introduction, *Habitat International*, 33(3): 227–9.

Plasman, C. (2008), Implementing marine spatial planning: a policy perspective, *Marine Policy*, 32: 811–15.

Poole and Christchurch Bays Coastal Group (2009), *Poole and Christchurch Bays Shoreline Management Plan Review*. Available online at: http://www.twobays.net (accessed 1 May 2010).

POST (Parliamentary Office for Science and Technology) (2007), Urban flooding, *Postnote No. 289*, London: POST.

POST (2008), The transition to a low carbon economy, *Postnote*, 318. London: POST.

Power, A. (2008), Does demolition or refurbishment of old and inefficient homes help to increase our environmental, social and economic viability? *Energy Policy*, 36(12): 4487–501.

Project Group Rotterdam Climate Initiative (2007), *The World Capital of CO_2-free Energy*, Rotterdam: Rotterdam Climate Initiative.

PRP Ltd, URBED and Design for Homes (2008), *Beyond Eco-towns: Applying the Lessons from Europe. Report and Conclusions*, London: PRP Architects.

PUSH (Partnership for Urban South Hampshire) (2008), *South Hampshire: Integrated Water Management Strategy*, Consultants' report (Atkins) for PUSH. Available online at: http://www.push.gov.uk/pdf/PUSH%20Publications/PUSH%20Research%20&%20Consultancy%20Reports/081223%20-%20IWMS%20final.pdf (accessed 17 August 2009).

Rachwal, T. (2007), 30 Years of technical and organisational development in the UK water sector: Thames Water's experiences of moving from public to private sector, *Journal of Water Supply: Research and Technology – AQUA*, 56(6–7): 419–23.

Raupach, M. R., Marland, G., Ciais P., Le Quéré, C., Canadell, J. G., Klepper, G. and Field C. B. (2007), Global and regional drivers of accelerating CO_2 emissions, *Proceedings of the National Academy of Sciences of the United States of America*, 104(24): 10288–93.

Rawls, J. (1972), *A Theory of Justice*, Oxford: Clarendon Press.

RCEP (Royal Commission on Environmental Pollution) (1994), *Transport and the Environment. Eighteenth Report*, Cm2674, London: HMSO.

RCEP (2004), *Turning the Tide: Addressing the Impact of Fisheries on the Marine Environment. Twenty-fifth Report*, Cm 6392, London: RCEP.

Read, D. J., Freer-Smith, P. H., Morison, J. I. L., Hanley, N., West, C. C. and Snowdon, P. (eds) (2009), *Combating Climate Change – a Role for UK Forests. An assessment of the Potential of the UK's Trees and Woodlands to Mitigate and Adapt to Climate Change. The Synthesis Report*, Edinburgh: The Stationery Office.

Reader, M. C. and Boer, G. J. (1998), The modification of greenhouse gas warming by the direct effect of sulphate aerosols, *Climate Dynamics*, 14(7–8): 593–607.

Reeder, T., Donovan, B. and Wicks, J. (2005), 'Broad scale tidal flood risk assessment for London using MDSF and Floodranger', paper presented at 3rd Annual CIWEM Conference, Wakefield, United Kingdom, 6–8 September 2005.

Reynard, N. S., Kay, A. L. and Crooks, S. M. (2007), Flood risk in the UK: current and future. In: C. A. Brebbia, and K. L. Katsifarakis (eds), *River Basin Management IV (River Basin Management 2007)*, Southampton: WIT Press.

RIBA (Royal Institute of British Architects) Building Futures and Institution of Civil Engineers (ICE) (2010), *Facing up to Rising Sea Levels: Retreat? Defend? Attack?* Available online at: http://www.buildingfutures.org.uk/assets/downloads/Facing_Up_To_Rising_Sea_Levels.pdf (accessed 24 January 2010).

Rickwood, P., Glazebrook, G. and Searle, G. (2008), Urban structure and energy – a review, *Urban Policy and Research*, 26(1): 57–81.

Roaf, S., Crichton, D. and Nicol, F. (2009), *Adapting Buildings and Cities to Climate Change: A 21st Century Survival Guide*, 2nd edn. Oxford: Architectural Press.

Roberts, S. (2008), Effects of climate change in the built environment, *Energy Policy*, 36(12): 4552–7.

RTCCP (Round Table on Climate Change and Poverty) (2008), *Tackling Climate Change, Reducing Poverty: The First Report of the Round Table on Climate Change and Poverty in the UK*, London: New Economics Foundation.

RSPB (Royal Society for the Protection of Birds) (2007), *Strategic Environmental Assessment: Learning from Practice*, Sandy: RSPB.

RSPB (2009a), *UK Can Have Wind Power and Wildlife*, press release, 23 March (2009). Available online at: http://www.rspb.org.uk/news/details.asp?id=tcm:9–213213 (accessed 2 April 2009).

RSPB (2009b), *Severn Reef Better than a Barrage*, press release, November 2008. Available online at: http://www.rspb.org.uk/news/details.asp?id=tcm:9–203827 (accessed 2 November 2009).

Rupprecht Consult and International Ocean Institute (2006), *Evaluation of Integrated Coastal Zone Management (ICZM) in Europe*, Final Report to European Commission, Brussels: EC.

Ruth, M. (ed.) (2006), *Smart Growth and Climate Change: Regional Development, Infrastructure and Adaptation*, Cheltenham: Edward Elgar.

Rydin, Y. (2003), *Conflict, Consensus and Rationality in Environmental Planning: An Institutional Discourse Approach*, Oxford: Oxford University Press.

Rydin, Y. (2009), Thinking through the energy uncertainties, *Town and Country Planning*, 78(5): 232–35.

Rydin, Y., Amjad, U. and Whitaker, M. (2007) Environmentally sustainable construction: knowledge and learning in London planning departments, *Planning Theory and Practice*, 8(3): 363–80.

Saavedra, C. and Budd, W. W. (2009), Climate change and environmental planning: working to build community resilience and adaptive capacity in Washington State, USA, *Habitat International*, 33(3): 301–9.

Sankaran, M. and McNaughton, S. J. (1999), Determinants of biodiversity regulate compositional stability of communities, *Nature*, 401(6754): 691–3.

Schneider, S. H., Semenov, S., Patwardhan, A., Burton, I., Magadza, C. H. D., Oppenheimer, M., Pittock, A. B., Rahman, A., Smith, J. B., Suarez A. and Yamin, F. (2007), Assessing key vulnerabilities and the risk from climate change. In: IPCC (2007c), *Climate Change 2007: Impacts, Adaptation and Vulnerability. Contribution of Working Group II to the Fourth Assessment Report of the Intergovernmental Panel on Climate Change*, M. L. Parry, O. F. Canziani, J. P. Palutikof, P. J. van der Linden and C. E. Hanson (eds), Cambridge: Cambridge University Press.

Scott Wilson, Levett-Therivel Sustainability Consultants, Treweek Environmental Consultants and Land Use Consultants (2006), *Appropriate Assessment of Plans*. Available online at: http://www.sea-info.net/files/general/Appropriate_Assessment_of_Plans.pdf

Scrase, J. I. and Sheate, W. R. (2002), Integration and integrated approaches to assessment: what do they mean for the environment? *Journal of Environmental Policy and Planning*, 4(2) 75–94.

SDC (Sustainable Development Commission) (2006), *Stock Take: Delivering Improvements in Existing Housing*, London: SDC.

SDC (2007), *Turning the Tide: Tidal Power in the UK*, London: SDC.

SDC (2008), *Breaking the Holding Pattern: A New Approach to Aviation Policy Making in the UK*, London: SDC.

SDC (2009), *A Sustainable New Deal: A Stimulus Package for Economic, Social and Ecological Recovery*, London: SDC.

SEECCP (South East England Climate Change Partnership) (2004), *Meeting the Challenge of Climate Change: Summary of the South East Climate Threats and Opportunities Research Study (SECTORS): A study of climate change impacts and adaptation for key sectors*, Guildford: SEEDA.

SEEPB (South East England Partnership Board) (2009), *Climate Change within Local Development Frameworks: Incorporating the Climate Change Aspects of the South East Plan into Local Development Frameworks*, Guildford: SEEPB.

SEERA (South East England Regional Assembly) and ESPACE (2007), *Climate Change*

Mitigation and Adaptation Implementation Plan for the Draft South East Plan, prepared by Collingwood Environmental Planning and Land Use Consultants, Guildford: SEERA.

Selman, P. (2006), *Planning at the Landscape Scale*, London: Routledge.

Selman, P. and Bailey, R. (2009), Case study: engaging local communities in the sustainable planning and management of rivers. In ESRC and HCA, *Skills and Knowledge for Sustainable Communities*. Available online at: http://www.strath.ac.uk/gs/sustainablecommunities/ (accessed 28 April 2010).

Seyfang, G. and Smith, A. (2006), Community action: a neglected site of innovation for sustainable development? *CSERGE Working Paper*, EDM 06–10. Norwich: CSERGE.

Shaw, R., Colley, M. and Connell, R. (2007), *Climate Change Adaptation by Design*, London: TCPA.

Sheate, W. R., Rosario do Partidario, M., Byron, H., Bina, O. and Dagg, S. (2008), Sustainability assessment of future scenarios: methodology and application to mountain areas of Europe, *Environmental Management*, 41: 282–99.

Sheppard, S. R. J. (2005), Landscape visualisation and climate change: the potential for influencing perceptions and behaviour, *Environmental Science and Policy*, 8: 637–54.

Sheppard, S. R. J. (2008), Local climate change visioning: a new process for community planning and outreach using visualization tools, *Plan Canada*, 48(1): 36–40.

Sheppard, S. R. J. and Tatebe, K. (2009), *Citizens' Conservation Councils on Climate Action Presentations: Summary Report*, Vancouver: UBC. Available online at: http://www.calp.forestry.ubc.ca/pdfs/CALP_CCC%20Report_20090603.pdf (accessed 21 September 2009).

Shipley, R. (2002), Visioning in planning: Is it based on sound theory? *Environment and Planning A*, 34(1): 7–22.

Siebenhüner, B. and Suplie, J. (2005), Implementing the access and benefit-sharing provisions of the CBD: A case for institutional learning, *Ecological Economics*, 53(4): 507–22.

Slootweg, R. and van Beukering, P. (2008), *Valuation of Ecosystem services and Strategic Environmental Assessment: Lessons from Influential Cases*, Utrecht: Netherlands Commission for Environmental Assessment.

Smith, A. (2007), Emerging in between: the multi-level governance of renewable energy in the English regions, *Energy Policy*, 35: 6266–80.

Smith, A. and Kern, F. (2007), *The Transitions Discourse in the Ecological Modernisation of the Netherlands*, paper no. 60, SPRU Electronic Working Paper Series, Brighton: University of Sussex.

Smith, A. and Kern, F. (2009), The transitions storyline in Dutch environmental policy, *Environmental Politics*, 18(1): 78–98.

Smith, J. B., Schneider, S. H., Oppenheimer, M., Yohe, G. W., Hare, W., Mastrandrea, M. D., Patwardhan, A., Burton, I., Corfee-Morlot, J., Magadza, C. H. D., Füssel, H. M., Pittock, A. B., Atiq Rahman, A., Suarez, A. and van Ypersele, J. P. (2009), Assessing dangerous climate change through an update on the International Panel on Climate Change (IPCC) "reasons for concern", *Proceedings of the National Academy of Sciences in the United States of America*, 106: 4133–7.

Smith, P. and Pearson, J. (2008), An environmental limits approach to spatial planning, *Town and Country Planning*, 77(12): 511–14.

SNIFFER (Scotland and Northern Ireland Forum for Environmental Research) (2009), *Differential Impacts of Climate Change in the UK*, Project UKCC22, Edinburgh: SNIFFER.

Spangenberg, J. H. (2006), Biodiversity pressure and the driving forces behind, *Ecological Economics* 61(1): 146–58.

Stallworthy, M. (2006), Sustainability, coastal erosion and climate change: an environmental justice analysis, *Journal of Environmental Law* 18(3): 357–73.

Standley, S., Miller, K., Okamura, S., Wynn, D., Greenhalgh, S. and Horrocks, L. (2009), *Wild Weather Warning: A London Climate Impacts Profile*, London: GLA.

Stern, N. (2007), *The Economics of Climate Change: The Stern Review*, Cambridge: Cambridge University Press.

Stern, N. (2009), *A Blueprint for a Safer Planet. How to Manage Climate Change and Create a New Era of Progress and Prosperity*, London: The Bodley Head.

Strachan, P. A., Lal, D. and von Malmborg, F. (2006), The evolving UK wind industry: critical policy and management aspects of the emerging research agenda, *European Environment*, 16(1): 1–18.

Stratton, A. (2009), Opposing wind farms should be socially taboo, says Ed Miliband, *Guardian*, 24 March 2009. Available online at: http://www.guardian.co.uk/environment/2009/mar/24/wind-farms-opposition-ed-miliband (accessed 21 August 2009).

Sukdev, P. (2008), *The Economics of Ecosystems and Biodiversity. Interim report*, Brussels: European Commission.

Sunikka, M. (2005), *The Energy Performance of Buildings Directive (EPBD): Improving the Energy Efficiency of the Existing Housing Stock. Optimising the Impact of Article 7 on the Energy Certificate*, Delft: Delft University of Technology.

Sunstein, C. R. (2007), Of Montreal and Kyoto: a tale of two protocols, *Harvard Environmental Law Review*, 31(1): 1–65.

Swain, C. and Konvitz, E. (2009), Foresight, planning and climate change, *Town and Country Planning*, 78(6): 271–8.

Swart, R. and Raes, F. (2007), Making integration of adaptation and mitigation work: mainstreaming into sustainable development policies? *Climate Policy*, 7(4): 288–303.

Swart, R., Biesbroek, R., Binnerup, S., Carter, T. R., Cowan, C., Henrichs, T., Loquen, S., Mela, H., Morecroft, M., Reese M. and Rey, D. (2009), Europe adapts to climate change: comparing national adaptation strategies. (Partnership for European Environmental Research project.) Available at: http://peer-initiative.org/media/m256_PEER_Report1.pdf (accessed 11 October 2009).

Tamis, W. L. M., van 't Zelfde, M. and van der Meijden, R. (2005) Effects of climate change on vascular plants in the Netherlands in the 20th century, *Gorteria*, 29(4): 93–98.

Taussik, J. (2007), The opportunities of spatial planning for integrated coastal management, *Marine Policy*, 31(5): 611–18.

TCPA (Town and Country Planning Association) (2006a), *Sustainable Energy by Design: A TCPA 'By Design Guide' for Sustainable Communities*, London: TCPA.

TCPA (2006b), *Connecting England: A Framework for Regional Development. Final Report of the TCPA-appointed Hetherington Committee on the Future Development Needs and Priorities of England*, London: TCPA.

TCPA (2006c), *Using the 'Merton Rule': Report of a TCPA Survey of Local Authority Planning Departments in England*, London: TCPA.

TCPA (2007), *Best Practice in Urban Extensions and New Settlements: A Report on Emerging Good Practice*, London: TCPA.

TCPA (2008), *Design to Delivery: Eco-towns Transport Worksheet*, London: TCPA.

TCPA (2009a), Campaign gets off to a flying start as Government commits to update planning policy on climate change, press release. Available online at: http://www.tcpa.org.uk/resources.php?action=resource&id=593 (accessed 13 August 2009).

TCPA (2009b), *Towns and Countryside for a New Age of Challenge. A Manifesto from the TCPA*. Available online at: http://www.tcpa.org.uk/data/files/tcpa_manifesto.pdf (accessed 16 June 2009).

TCPA and FoE (Friends of the Earth) (2006), *Tackling Climate Change Through Planning: The Government's Objectives, PPS26*, London: TCPA.

TCPA and FoE on behalf of the Planning and Climate Change Coalition (2009), *Planning and Climate Change Coalition Position Statement*, London: TCPA.

TCPA, Natural England and DCLG (2009), *Biodiversity Positive: eco-towns biodiversity worksheet*, http://www.tcpa.org.uk/data/files/etws_biodiversity.pdf (accessed 2 May 2010).

ten Brinke, W. B. M., Saeijs, G. E. M., Helsloot, I. and van Alphen, J. (2008), Safety chain approach in flood risk management, *Municipal Engineer*, 161(2): 93–102.

Tew, T. (2009), 'Creating a new prosperity: Fresh approaches to ecosystem services and human well-being,' opening address to the *FRESH Seminar Series*, Royal Goegraphical Society, London, 4 September.

Tewdwr-Jones, M. and Allmendinger, P. (eds) (2006), *Territory, Identity and Spatial Planning: Spatial Governance in a Fragmented Nation*, London: Routledge.

TfL (Transport for London)/Mayor of London (2008), *Central London Congestion Charging Impacts Monitoring: Sixth Annual Report*, London: TFL.

Thames Water (2006), *The Upper Thames Major Resource Development: Stage 1 Needs and Alternatives Report. Summary and Overview*, Reading: RWE Group.

Thames Water (2009a), *How Climate Change Could Affect our Business*, Reading: Thames Water. Available online at: http://www.thameswater.co.uk/cps/rde/xchg/corp/hs.xsl/3778.htm (accessed 27 July 2009).

Thames Water (2009b), *Statement of Response Draft Water Resources Management Plan*. Reading: Thames Water. Available online at: http://www.nce.co.uk/Journals/3/Files/2009/3/9/statement-of-response.pdf (accessed 5 October 2009).

Thames Water (2009c), *Securing Supplies for the Future: Upper Thames Reservoir*, Reading: Thames Water. Available online at: http://www.thameswater.co.uk/cps/rde/xchg/corp/hs.xsl/2550.htm (accessed 16 January 2010).

The Wildlife Trusts (2009) *A Living Landscape – Schemes*. Available online at: http://www.wildlifetrusts.org/?section=environment:livinglandscapes:schemes (accessed 30 July 2009). River Itchen scheme details available online at: http://www.wildlifetrusts.org/?section=environment:livinglandscapes:schemes (accessed 30 July 2009).

Therivel R., Wilson, E., Thompson, S., Heaney, D. and Pritchard, D. (1992), *Strategic Environmental Assessment*, London: Earthscan.

Therivel, R. and Partidario, M. R. (eds) (1996), *The Practice of Strategic Environmental Assessment*, London: Earthscan.

Thomas, C. D., Cameron, A., Green, R. E., Bakkenes, M., Beaumont, L. J., Collingham, Y. C., Erasmus, B. F. N., Ferreira De Siqueira, M., Grainger, A., Hannah, L., Hughes, L., Huntley, B., Van Jaarsveld, A. S., Midgley, G. F., Miles, L., Ortega-Huerta, M. A.,

Peterson, A. T., Phillips, O. L. and Williams, S. E. (2004), Extinction risk from climate change, *Nature*, 427(6970): 145–8.

Thompson, D. (2008), *Carbon Management by Land and Marine Managers*, Natural England Research Report NERR 26, Peterborough: Natural England.

Thornton, A. (2009), *Public Attitudes and Behaviours towards the Environment – Tracker Survey: A Report to DEFRA, TNS*, London: Defra.

Three Regions Climate Change Group (LCCP, SDRTEE and SECCP) (2008), *Your Home in a Changing Climate: Retrofitting Existing Homes for Climate Change Impacts. Report for Policy Makers*, London: GLA.

Thuiller, W. and Lafourcade, B. (2008), Deliverable 3.5: report on the results of the run of improved modeling to Europe. Available online at: http://www. macis-project.net/MACIS-Deliverable-3.5-Oct.2008.pdf (accessed 2 May 2010).

Tillie, N. (2007), 'Climate change, city change,' in *Metrex (Network of European Regions and Areas) Conference on Climate Change*, Hamburg, Germany, 28 Nov–1 Dec. Available online at: http://www.eurometrex.org/euco2/DOCS/Hamburg/14Rotterdam.pdf (accessed 27 June 2008).

Tillie, N., van den Dobbelsteen, A., Doepel, D., de Jager, W., Joubert, M. and Mayenburg, D. (2009), *REAP: Rotterdam Energy Approach and Planning. Towards CO_2 Neutral Urban Development*, Rotterdam: Rotterdam Climate Initiative.

Tilman, D., Reich, P. B. and Knops, J. M. H. (2006), Biodiversity and ecosystem stability in a decade-long grassland experiment, *Nature*, 441(7093): 629–32.

Toke, D., Breukers, S. and Wolsink, M. (2008), Wind power deployment outcomes: how can we account for the differences? *Renewable and Sustainable Energy Reviews*, 12(4): 1129–47.

Tol, R. (2005), Adaptation and mitigation: trade-offs in substance and methods, *Environmental Science and Policy*, 8(6): 572–8.

Tollefson, J. (2008), Save the trees, *Nature*, 452: 8–9.

Tompkins, E. L., Few, R. and Brown, K. (2008), Scenario-based stakeholder engagement: incorporating stakeholders' preferences into coastal planning for climate change, *Journal of Environmental Management*, 88(4): 1580–92.

Transport Planning Society, UKCIP and Nottingham Declaration Partnership (2009), *Local Transport: Adapting to Climate Change*. Available online at: http://www.energysavingtrust.org.uk/nottingham/Nottingham-Declaration/local (accessed 3 January 2010).

Trudgill, S. T. (1990), *Barriers to a Better Environment*, London: Belhaven.

Tuininga, E-J. (2007), Going Dutch in environmental policy: a case of shared responsibility, *European Environment* 4(4): 8–15.

Tyldesley, D. (2009), *Climate Change and Biodiversity Adaptation: The Role of the Spatial Planning System*, Natural England Commissioned Report, Number 004, Peterborough, United Kindgom: Natural England.

UKBP (UK Biodiversity Partnership) (2007), *Conserving Biodiversity – the UK approach*, London: Defra.

UKCIP (UK Climate Impacts Programme) (2001), *Socio-economic Scenarios for Climate Change Impact Assessment: A Guide to their Use in the UK Climate Impacts Programme*, Oxford: UKCIP.

UKCIP (2006), *Guidance to the Water Project of Defra funded 'Climate Change Impacts and Adaptation: Cross-regional Research Programme' on pairing climate and socio-economic scenarios*, Oxford: UKCIP.

UKCIP (2008a) *The UK Adaptation Wizard* v.2.0, UKCIP: Oxford.

UKCIP (2008b), *A Local Climate Impacts Profile: LCLIP*, Oxford: UKCIP.

UK-GBC (UK Green Building Council) (2008), *Low Carbon Existing Homes*, London: UK-GBC.

UK-GBC (2009), *Making the Case for a Code for Sustainable Buildings*, London: UK-GBC.

UN (United Nations) (1988), *Protection of Global Climate for Present and Future Generations of Mankind*, General Assembly resolution A/RES/43/53. Available online at: http://www.un.org/documents/ga/res/43/a43r053.htm (accessed 24 April 2010).

UN (1992), *United Nations Framework Convention on Climate Change*. FCCC/INFORMAL/84 GE.05–62220 (E) 200705. Signed and authorized 9 May 1992, New York. Available online at: http://unfccc.int/essential_background/convention/background/items/1413.php (accessed 24 April 2010).

UN (1998), *Kyoto Protocol to the United Nations Framework Convention on Climate Change*, Bonn: UNFCCC.

UNDP (United Nations Development Programme) (2007), *Human Development Report 2007/08: Fighting climate change: Human Solidarity in a Divided World*. Available online at: http://hdr.undp.org/en/media/HDR_20072008_Summary_English.pdf (accessed 2 May 2010).

UNEP/GRID Arendal (n.d.), *Vital Water Graphics*. Available online at: http://www.grida.no/publications/vg/water2/page/3289.aspx (accessed 24 August 2009).

UNFCCC (United Nations Framework Convention on Climate Change) (2008), *Investment and Financial Flows to Address Climate Change: An Update. Technical Paper*, Bonn: UNFCCC.

UNFCCC (2009), 'Addendum to the Report of the Conference of the Parties serving as the meeting of the Parties to the Kyoto Protocol on its fourth session. Decision 1/CMP.4 Adaptation Fund', at The United Nations Climate Change Conference, Poznan, Poland, 1–2 December Available online at: http://unfccc.int/meetings/cop_14/items/4481.php (accessed 24 August 2009).

Urban Task Force (1999), *Towards an Urban Renaissance. Final Report of the Urban Task Force chaired by Lord Rogers of Riverside*, London: Urban Task Force.

Uttlesford District Council (2007), *Climate Change Strategy: A Greener Uttlesford*, Saffron Walden: Uttlesford District Council.

Van Eck, M. (2009), Strategic environmental assessment in long-term structural design planning, in NCEA, *Views and Experiences from the Netherlands Commission for Environmental Assessment 2009*, Series no. 10, Utrecht: NCEA.

Van Veen, M. P., ten Brink, B. J. E., Braat, L. C. and Melman, T. C. P. (2008), *Halting Biodiversity Loss in the Netherlands: Evaluation of Progress*, Bilthoven: Netherlands Environmental Assessment Agency.

Vigar, G. (2002), *The Politics of Mobility*, London: Spon.

Vos, C., Berry, P., Opdam, P., Baveco, H., Nijhof, B., O'Hanley, J., Bell, C. and Kuipers H. (2008), Adapting landscapes to climate change: examples of climate-proof ecosystem networks and priority adaptation zones, *Journal of Applied Ecology*, (45): 1722–31.

VROM (Ministry of Housing, Physical Planning and Environment) (1989), *Highlights of the Dutch NEPP. A Clean Environment: Choose it or Lose It*, The Hague: VROM.

VROM (2001), *Where There's a Will There's a World: Working on Sustainability. 4th National Environmental Policy Plan Summary*. Available online at: http://www.sharedspaces.nl/Docs/internationaal/NMP4wwwengels.pdf (accessed 10 June 2009).

VROM (2008a), *Randstad 2040: Summary of the Structural Vision*, The Hague: VROM.

VROM (2008b), *Fourth Netherlands National Communication Under the United Nations Framework Convention on Climate Change*, The Hague: VROM.

VROM, LNV, MVenW, and EZ (2006), *Nota Ruimte. National Spatial Strategy, Creating Space for Development, Summary*, Amsterdam: VROM LNV, VenW and EZ.

VROM, MVenW, LNV, EZ, IPO, VNG and UvW (2007a), *Make Room for the Climate! Initial Steps towards a National Adaptation Strategy. Memorandum for Policy Discussion* http://www.waterandclimateinformationcentre.org/resources/6182007_ARK_ make_room_for_climate.pdf (accessed 17 August 2009).

VROM, MVenW, EZ, LNV, IPO, VNG and UvW (2007b), *National Programme on Climate Adaptation and Spatial Planning: The National Strategy on Climate Adaptation and Spatial Planning*, The Hague: VROM.

Wade, S., Hossell, J., Hough, M. and Fenn, C. (eds) (1999), *Rising to the Challenge: Impacts of Climate Change in the South East in the 21st Century*, Kingston: Surrey County Council.

Walker, G. and Cass, N. (2007), Carbon reduction, 'the public' and renewable energy: engaging with socio-technical configurations, *Area*, 39(4): 458–69.

Walker, G., Burningham, K., Fielding, J., Smith, G., Thrush, D. and Fay, H. (2006), *Addressing Environmental Inequalities: Flood Risk*. Science Report SC0200061/SR1, Bristol: Environment Agency.

Walmsley, C. A., Smithers, R. J., Berry, P., Harley, M., Stevenson, M. J. and Catchpole, R. (eds) (2007), *MONARCH – Modelling Natural Resource Responses to Climate Change – A Synthesis for Biodiversity Conservation*, Oxford: UKCIP. Available online at: http://www.ukcip.org.uk/images/stories/Pub_pdfs/Monarch3synthesis.pdf (accessed 27 May 2010).

Walsh, C. L., Hall, J. W., Street, R. B., Blanksby, J., Cassar, M., Ekins, P., Glendinning, S., Goodess, C. M., Handley, J., Noland, R. and Watson, S. J. (2007), *Building Knowledge for a Changing Climate: Collaborative Research to Understand and Adapt to the Impacts of Climate Change on Infrastructure, the Built Environment and Utilities*, Newcastle: Newcastle University.

Ward, S. V. (2002), *Planning the Twentieth Century City: The Advanced Capitalist World*, Chichester: John Wiley & Sons.

Ward, S. V. (2004), *Planning and Urban Change*, 2nd edn. London: Sage.

Water UK (n.d.) *Water Companies and the Law*. Available online at: http://www.water. org.uk/home/policy/positions/legislation (accessed 8 November 2009).

Waterwise (2009), *Waterwise Response to Draft Planning Policy Statement: Eco Towns*. Available online at: www.waterwise.org.uk/images/site/Policy/Consultations/ waterwise%20response%20to%20eco%20town%20pps%20-%20march%202009. pdf (accessed 4 August 2009).

Watkiss, P. (2005), *Adaptation Policy (Developing Indicators for Adaptation Policies)*. Available online at: http://forum.europa.eu.int/Public/irc/env/eccp_2/library?l=/ impacts_adaptation/strategies_adaptation/presentationpdf_5/_EN_1.0_&a=d (accessed 2 May 2010).

Watkiss, P., Hunt, A. and Horrocks, L. (2009), *Final Report for the Scoping Study for a National Climate Change Risk Assessment and Adaptation Economic Analysis*, Defra Contract number GA0208. Metroeconomica, AEA Group, and Paul Watkiss Associates. London: Defra.

WCED (World Commission on Environment and Development) (1987), *Our Common Future*, Oxford: Oxford University Press.

Weale, A. (1992), *The New Politics of Pollution*, Manchester: Manchester University Press.

Weatherhead, K., (2008), 'Water – future availability, demand and management', paper presented at the Oxford Farming Conference, Oxford, United Kingdom, 10 March 2008.

Welsh Water (n.d.), *Waterfacts*. Available online at: http://www.dwrcymru.co.uk/English/waterefficiency/school/_pdf/waterfacts.pdf (accessed 17 August 2009).

West, C. and Gawith, M. (eds) (2005), *Measuring Progress: Preparing for Climate Change through the UK Climate Impacts Programme*, UKCIP Technical Report, Oxford: UKCIP.

Weston, J. (2000), EIA, decision making theory and screening and scoping in UK practice, *Journal of Environmental Planning and Management*, 43(2): 185–203.

Weston, J. (2004), EIA in a risk society, *Journal of Environmental Planning and Management*, 47(2): 313–25.

While, A. (2008), 'Carbon control and new ecological dominations', paper presented to the ESRC Seminar Towards Post Carbon Local Economies, Liverpool, United Kingdom, December 2008.

White I. and Alarcon, A. (2009), Planning policy, sustainable drainage and surface water management: a case study of Greater Manchester, *Built Environment*, 35(4): 516–30.

White, I. and Richards, J. (2007), Planning policy and flood risk: the translation of national guidance into local policy, *Planning Practice and Research*, 22(4): 513–34.

White, R. R. (2001), *Building the Ecological City*, Cambridge: Woodhead Publishing.

Wiering, M. and Immink, I. (2006), When water management meets spatial planning: a policy-arrangements perspective, *Environment and Planning C: Government and Policy*, 24(3): 423–38.

Wilby, R. (2007), A review of climate change impacts on the built environment, *Built Environment*, 33(1): 31–45.

Williams, K. (ed.) (2005), *Spatial Planning, Urban Form and Sustainable Transport*, Aldershot: Ashgate.

Willows, R. and Connell, R. (eds) (2003), *Climate Adaptation: Risk, Uncertainty and Decision-Making*. UKCIP Technical Report, Oxford: UKCIP.

Wilson, E. (2006a), Developing UK spatial planning policy to respond to climate change, *Journal of Environmental Policy and Planning*, 8(1): 9–25.

Wilson, E. (2006b), Adapting to climate change at the local level: the spatial planning response, *Local Environment*, 11(6): 609–25.

Wilson, E. (2007), Response to *Planning Theory and Practice* 2006, 7(2), Interface: is the issue of climate change too big for spatial planning? *Planning Theory and Practice*, 8(1): 125–7.

Wilson, E. (2009a), Use of scenarios for climate change adaptation in spatial planning. In: S. Davoudi, J. Crawford and A. Mehmood (eds), *Planning for Climate Change: Strategies for Mitigation and Adaptation for Spatial Planners*, London: Earthscan.

Wilson, E. (2009b), Multiple scales for environmental intervention: spatial planning and the environment under New Labour, *Planning Practice & Research*, 24(1): 119–38.

Wilson, E., Nicol, F., Nanayakkara, L. and Ueberjahn-Tritta, A. (2008), Public urban open space and human thermal comfort: the implications of alternative climate change and socio-economic scenarios, *Journal of Environmental Policy & Planning*, 10(1): 31–45.

Woking Borough Council (2008), *Climate Change Strategy 2008–2013: Think Globally, Act Locally*, Woking: Woking Borough Council.

Woltjer, J. and Al, N. (2007), Integrating water management and spatial planning: strategies based on the Dutch experience, *Journal of the American Planning Association*, 73(2): 211–22.

Wood, P., Berry, P. and Lonsdale, K. (2006), *Future Landscape Scenarios around Little Wittenham, South Oxfordshire: Technical Report*, Oxford: Northmoor Trust and Environmental Change Institute, University of Oxford. Available online at: http://www.projecttimescape.co.uk/timescape/research/climate (accessed 6 January 2009).

Woodworth, P. and Horsburgh, K. (2008), Sea level – observed, *MCCIP Annual Report Card 2007–2008 Scientific Review*, Liverpool: MCCIP.

World Bank (2009), *World Development Report 2010: Development and Climate Change*, Washington, DC: World Bank.

World Meteorological Organization (WMO) (1986), Report of the International Conference on the assessment of the role of carbon dioxide and of other greenhouse gases in climate variations and associated impacts, statement by the UNEP/WMO/ICSU International Conference on the Assessment of the Role of Carbon Dioxide and of other Greenhouse Gases in Climate Variations and Associated Impacts, Villach, Austria, 9–15 October 1986. Available online at: http://www.icsu-scope.org/downloadpubs/scope29/statement.html (accessed 2 May 2010).

WRI (World Resources Institute) (2005), *Millennium Ecosystem Assessment, 2005. Ecosystems and Human Well-being: Biodiversity Synthesis*, Washington, DC: World Resources Institute.

Wright, P. (1985), *On Living in an Old Country: The National Past in Contemporary Britain*, London: Verso.

WS Atkins, Stockholm Environment Institute and Met Office (2002), *Warming up the Region: the Impacts of Climate Change in the Yorkshire and Humber Region*, Epsom: WS Atkins.

WWF (World Wide Fund for Nature) (2008), *Weathercocks and Signposts: The Environment Movement at a Crossroads*, Godalming: WWF.

WWF (2009), *Simple and Painless? The Limitations of Spillover in Environmental Campaigning*, Godalming: WWF.

Yorkshire and Humber Regional Assembly (2008), *The Housing Challenge: The Yorkshire and Humber Plan – 2009 Update. Spatial Options*, Wakefield: YHA and Regional Strategic Partnership. Available online at: http://www.yhassembly.gov.uk/dnlds/RSS%20Update%20Spatial%20Options.pdf (accessed July 2009).

Young, R. (2009), Coastal planning – plus ça change! *Town and Country Planning*, 78(10): 418–22.

Zedan, H., Wijnstekers, W., Hepworth, R., Bridgewater, P. and Bandarin, F. (2005), *Biodiversity: Life Insurance for our Changing World*. Press release from the CBD, CITES, CMS Ramsar, and World Heritage Conventions on the Millennium Development Goals. Available online at: http://www.un-ngls.org/orf/un-summit-BIODIV.pdf (accessed 3 June 2010).

Zetter, J. (2009), It isn't broken – but we may still have to fix it, *Town and Country Planning*, 78(6): 258–63.

Zonneveld, W. (2005), Expansive spatial planning: the new European transnational spatial visions, *European Planning Studies*, 13(1): 137–56.

UK Government publications

Unless otherwise stated, these are published in London by TSO (The Stationery Office – formerly HMSO), or by the relevant Government Department. Most publications since 1997 are also available on the relevant Departmental website.

HMG (HM Government)

—— (2005), *Securing the future – The UK Government Sustainable Development Strategy*, Cm 6467.
—— (2007), *Planning for a Sustainable Future: White Paper* Cm 7120.
—— (2008a), *Climate Change Act 2008.*
—— (2008b), *Planning Act 2008.*
—— (2009a), *The UK Low Carbon Transition Plan: National Strategy for Climate and Energy. Presented to Parliament pursuant to Sections 12 and 14 of the Climate Change Act 2008.*
—— (2009b), *The UK Renewable Energy Strategy*, Cm 7686.
—— (2009c), *Building Britain's Future*, Cm 7654.
—— (2009d), *World Class Places: The Government's Strategy for Improving Quality of Place.*
—— (2010a), *Government Response to the First Annual Progress Report of the Committee on Climate Change.*
——— (2010b), *Warm Homes, Greener Homes: A Strategy for Household Energy Management.*
—— (2010c), Flood and Water Management Act.

DCLG (Department for Communities and Local Government) since 2006

—— (2006a), *Consultation Planning Policy Statement: Planning and Climate Change: Supplement to Planning Policy Statement 1.*
—— (2006b), *Code for Sustainable Homes: A Step-change in Sustainable Home-building Practice.*
—— (2006c), *Planning Policy Statement 25: Development and Flood Risk.*
—— (2006d), *Planning Policy Statement 3: Housing.*
—— (2006e), *Review of the Sustainability of Existing Buildings: The Energy Efficiency of Dwellings – Initial Analysis.*
—— (2006f), *New Growth Points Partnership for Growth with Government.*
—— (2007a), *Planning Policy Statement: Planning and Climate Change. Supplement to Planning Policy Statement 1.*
—— (2007b), *Planning White Paper Consultation: Government Response to Consultation Replies.*
—— (2007c), *Homes for the Future: More Affordable, More Sustainable*, Cm 7191.
—— (2007d), *Eco-towns Prospectus.*

———— (2008a), *Greener Homes for the Future*.

———— (2008b), *Planning Policy Statement 12: Local Spatial Planning*.

———— (2008c), *Thames Gateway Parklands Vision*.

———— (2008d), *Draft Planning Policy Statement: Eco-towns – Consultation*.

———— (2009a), *Housing Growth*.

———— (2009b), *Infrastructure Planning Commission: Implementation Route Map December 2009*.

———— (2009c), *Planning Policy Statement: Eco-towns – a Supplement to Planning Policy Statement 1*.

———— (2009d), *Eco-towns: Location Decision Statement*.

———— (2009e), *Initial Review of the Implementation of Planning Policy Statement 25 Development and Flood Risk*.

———— (2009f), *Multi-criteria Analysis: A Manual*.

———— (2009g), *Thames Gateway Eco-quarter: Consultation*.

———— (2010a), *Consultation on a Planning Policy Statement: Planning for a Low Carbon Future in a Changing Climate*, London: DCLG.

———— (2010b), *Planning Policy Statement 25 Supplement: Development and Coastal Change*, London: DCLG.

———— (2010c) *Consultation paper on a new Planning Policy Statement: Planning for a Natural and Healthy Environment*.

———— (2010d) *Planning Policy Statement 25: Development and Flood Risk* (Revision).

DCLG and DCMS (2009), *Consultation Paper on a new Planning Policy Statement 15: Planning for the Historic Environment*.

BERR (Department for Business, Enterprise and Regulatory Reform) 2007–2009

———— (2008), *Meeting the Energy Challenge: a White Paper on Nuclear Power*, Cm 7296.

DECC (Department of Energy and Climate Change) since 2008

———— (2009a), *Draft National Policy Statement for Nuclear Power Generation (EN-6)*.

———— (2009b), *A Prevailing Wind: Advancing UK Offshore Wind Deployment*.

———— (2009c), *UK Offshore Energy Strategic Environmental Assessment: Environmental Report*.

———— (2009d), *Offshore Energy SEA: Comments Received*.

———— (2009e), *Offshore Energy SEA Post Consultation Report*.

———— (2009f), *Consultation Draft Heat and Energy Saving Strategy*.

DECC, South West RDA and Welsh Assembly Government (2009), *Severn Tidal Power Phase One Consultation: Government Response*.

Defra (Department for Environment, Food and Rural Affairs) since 2001

—— (2002), *Guidelines for Environmental Risk Assessment and Management.*
—— (2004a), *Making Space for Water.*
—— (2004b), *Guidance on Water Level Management Plans for European Sites.*
—— (2005), *Making Space for Water,* Government response to the autumn 2004 *Making Space for Water* consultation exercise.
—— (2006a), *River Basin Planning Guidance.*
——— (2006b), *Local Sites: Guidance on their Identification, Selection and Management.*
—— (2007a), *Taking Forward the UK Climate Change Bill: The Government Response to Pre-Legislative Scrutiny and Public Consultation,* Cm 7225.
—— (2007b), *Biodiversity Indicators in your Pocket.*
—— (2007c), *Securing a Healthy Natural Environment: An Action Plan for Embedding an Ecosystems Approach.*
—— (2007d), *An Introductory Guide to Valuing Ecosystem Services.* [Web document only].
—— (2008a), *Future Water: The Government's Water Strategy for England,* Cm7319.
—— (2008b), *A Strategy for Promoting an Integrated Approach to the Management of Coastal Areas in England.*
—— (2008c), *The Government's Response to Sir Michael Pitt's Review of the Summer 2007 Floods.*
—— (2008d), *Defra Guidance on the Improved Local Biodiversity Indicator (NI 197).*
—— (2008e), *A Framework for Pro-environmental Behaviours: Report.*
—— (2009a), *Adapting to Climate Change: UK Climate Projections.*
—— (2009b), *UK Sustainable Development Indicators in your Pocket.*
—— (2009c), *Consultation on Coastal Change Policy.*
—— (2009d), *Improving Surface Water Drainage.*
—— (n.d.), *Securing a Healthy Natural Environment: An Action Plan for Embedding an Ecosystems Approach.*
Defra and ODPM (2004), *Creating Sustainable Communities: Greening the Gateway. A Greenspace strategy for Thames Gateway.*
Defra, Scottish Executive and Welsh Assembly (2002), *Safeguarding Our Seas: A Strategy for the Conservation and Sustainable Development of our Marine Environment.*

DETR (Department of the Environment, Transport and the Regions) 1997–2001

—— (1998), *A New Deal for Transport: Better for Everyone,* Cm 3950.
—— (2000a), *Climate Change: the UK Programme,* Cm 4913.
—— (2000b), *Our Towns and Cities: The Future. Delivering an Urban Renaissance,* Cm 4911.
—— (2000c), *Planning Policy Guidance Note 3: Housing.*
—— (2001), *Planning Policy Guidance Note 13: Transport.*

DfT (Department for Transport) since 2002

—— (2003), *The Future of Air Transport*, Cm 6046.
—— (2007a), *Towards a Sustainable Transport System: Supporting Economic Growth in a Low Carbon World*, Cm 7226.
—— (2007b), *Manual for Streets*.
—— (2008a), *Delivering a Sustainable Transport System: Main Report*.
—— (2008b), *Building Sustainable Transport into New Developments: A Menu of Options for Growth Points and Eco-towns*.
—— (2009a), *Draft National Policy Statement for Ports*.
—— (2009b), *Delivering Sustainable, Low Carbon Travel: An Essential Guide for Local Authorities*.
—— (2009c), *Low Carbon Transport: A Greener Future. A Carbon Reduction Strategy for Transport*, Cm7682.
—— (2009d), *Guidance to Regions on Delivering a Sustainable Transport System*.
DfT/National Statistics (2009a), *Transport Statistics Bulletin: National Travel Survey 2008*.
DfT/National Statistics (2009b), *Transport Trends 2008 Edition*.

ODPM (Office of the Deputy Prime Minister) 2002–06

—— (2002), *Sustainable Communities: Delivering through Planning*.
—— (2003), *Sustainable Communities: Building for the Future*.
—— (2004a), *Draft Planning Policy Statement 1: Creating Sustainable Communities*.
—— (2004b), *Planning Policy Statement 22: Renewable Energy*.
—— (2004c), *Planning Policy Statement 11: Regional Spatial Strategies*.
—— (2005a), *Planning Policy Statement 1: Delivering Sustainable Development*.
—— (2005b), *Sustainability Appraisal of Regional Spatial Strategies and Local Development Documents: Guidance for Regional Planning Bodies and Local Planning Authorities*.
—— (2005c), *Planning Policy Statement 9: Biodiversity and Geological Conservation*.
—— (2006), *Review of PPS22: Renewables Policies in Emerging Development Plans*.
ODPM, Welsh Assembly Government and Scottish Executive (2004), *The Planning Response to Climate Change: Advice on Better Practice*.
ODPM, Scottish Executive, Welsh Assembly Government and Department of the Environment, Northern Ireland (2005), *A Practical Guide to the Strategic Environmental Assessment Directive*.

Other Government departments

DoE (Department of the Environment) 1970–1997

—— (1991), *Policy Appraisal and the Environment: A Guide for Government Departments*.
—— (1993), *Environmental Appraisal of Development Plans: A Good Practice Guide*.

DoE (DoE and Welsh Office) (1992), *Planning Policy Guidance (PPG) 20: Coastal Planning*.

DTI (Department of Trade and Industry) 1983–2007

—— (2007), *Meeting the Energy Challenge: A White Paper on Energy* Cm 7124.

Scottish Executive, Scottish Government

Scottish Executive (2004a), *National Planning Framework for Scotland*, Edinburgh: Scottish Executive.
—— (2004b), *Scotland's Biodiversity: It's in Your Hands*, Edinburgh: Scottish Executive.
Scottish Executive (Natural Scotland) (2006), *Strategic Environmental Assessment Toolkit*, Edinburgh: Scottish Executive.
SEDD (Scottish Executive Development Department) (2007), *Scottish Planning Policy 6: Renewable Energy*, Edinburgh: Scottish Executive.
Scottish Government (2009), *National Planning Framework for Scotland 2*, Edinburgh: Scottish Government.
—— (2010), *Beauly to Denny Statement*.

WAG (Welsh Assembly Government)

Welsh Assembly Government (2004), *People, Places, Futures: The Wales Spatial Plan*, Cardiff: Welsh Assembly Government.
—— (2005), *Planning Policy Wales Technical Advice Note 8: Planning for Renewable Energy*, Cardiff: Welsh Assembly Government.

Index

garden cities 11, 198
gas: licensing 147, 161; offshore 12, 158–9; pipeline 104; production 106, 162; storage 159–60, 162 *see also* natural gas
GDP (Gross Domestic Product) 23, 61, 135, 137, 180, 202, 229, 300
geothermal energy 117
Germany 12, 33, 115, 173, 199, 215, 234, 242, 324, 359
Giddens, A. 13, 14, 121
GIS (Geographical Information System) 41, 221, 293, 367, 387
glaciers 301
Global Climate Model 24, 39
global credit crisis 106, 125, 134
globalization 94, 130, 136, 387
goodwill payments 114
green belts 11, 172, 184
green infrastructure 17, 26, 42, 196–7, 232–3, 240, 246–50, 327–8, 330–1; functions of 250; provision of 17, 172, 247, 375, 386
Green Paper (EU): on adaptation to climate change 53, 64; on Energy Efficiency 54; on the Urban Environment 172
green roofs *see* living roofs
greenhouse: effect 5–6; gas 5–9, 19–23, 44–6, 48–9, 51–4, 60–1, 94–5, 143–4, 148, 150–5, 153–4, 159–61, 176–8, 194–5, 201–2, 207–9
Greenland ice sheet 7
greywater 242, 275
groundwater 255, 260, 267, 279–80, 298, 318

Habitats Directive 116, 144, 256, 263, 304, 312, 321–2, 324
Habitats Regulations 261, 322
habitats 18–19, 42, 116, 147–9, 192–3, 256, 261, 263, 303–5, 312, 315–28, 332–6, 338, 340–5
Hadley Centre 57, 74
hazard 36–40, 190, 285, 293
Healey, P. 10, 14, 16, 73, 122
health 9–10, 23–25, 44–5, 50, 52–5, 122, 125–6, 137, 143, 148, 177, 188, 222, 229, 236, 247, 255, 285, 343, 345–6, 373
heat 41–2, 137–8, 140, 209, 220–1, 223, 225–31, 236, 238–41, 250, 317; mapping 221; stress 41, 236; waves 9, 18, 26, 124, 137–8, 229–30, 236–7, 239, 243
heating 54, 208, 210–11, 220; urban 233, 246

historic: buildings 217, 310; environment 216–17
Homes and Communities Academy 357, 361
horticulture 12, 172
housing 80, 82–4, 106, 155–6, 171–2, 174, 180–3, 197–9, 213–15, 219–22, 224–6, 274–5, 380–1
HRA (Habitats Regulations Assessment) 147–9, 200, 327
hydrocarbons 44, 160
hydropower 117, 210, 140, 165

IAIA (International Association for Impact Assessment) 146
ICE (Institution of Civil Engineers) 310
Iceland 48
ICLEI (International Council for Local Environmental Initiatives) 79, 96, 100
ICZM (Integrated Coastal Zone Management) 66, 103, 301–2, 312
IDB (Internal Drainage Board) 288, 293–4, 299
IEMA (Institute of Environmental Management and Assessment) 151, 153, 167
IME 231–2
impact assessment 24–6, 43, 102, 142–68, 195, 261, 352, 373
industrialized countries 11, 14–15, 48–9, 94, 206–7, 332
infrastructure 9–10, 26–9, 53–5, 103–6, 192–4, 204–7, 229–37, 239–40, 246–52, 269–72, 281–5, 289, 342–5; blue 246–7, 249–51; green 17, 26, 42, 66, 172, 193–4, 196–7, 232–4, 240, 246–50, 252, 271, 278, 298, 327, 331, 360, 373, 375, 386, 388; planning 9, 103, 164, 202; and sewage 104, 231, 240, 265, 289, 295, 307; and transport 41, 54, 106, 164, 173, 176, 205, 236; urban 127, 172, 344; and water 254, 257
inland waterways 177, 241, 260
insulation 16, 58, 154, 225
insurance 76–7, 88–9, 125, 127–8, 292
Integrated Risk Assessment 40
Integrated Water Resources Studies 265, 268, 292
integration: horizontal, vertical, cross-scale; of mitigation and adaptation 43, 104, 112, 218, 252, 376
interdependencies 231
Intergovernmental Panel on Climate Change *see* IPCC
invasive species 25–6, 320–1, 344

p91 - autt jusr → SP

- CC   ph
- public space - smart
- maslow + ph.

Spirit level . Assumpt. Measuring.